The Guinness book

BOX OFFICE

HITS

PHIL SWERN

Consultant: MIKE CHILDS

IN ASSOCIATION WITH

GUINNESS PUBLISHING

I should like to extend my thanks to the Press Officers of all the film companies who have supplied information, the British Film Institute and the staff in the library who have all been so very helpful, HMV Megastore in Oxford Street, London, and 58 Dean Street Records in London. I would also like to extend a huge thank you to all the staff at *Screen International* who helped with both the chart listings and the supply of pictures.

A special thanks to Jeremy Pascall and Simon Potter for their contributions and help which saved the day on more than one occasion, to Sharon Kent, who provided so much input and research as well as putting up with the authors, and to Jane Judd, who turned out to be a special agent.

My gratitude goes out to many of the staff, past and present, at Guinness for believing in the project, especially Mark Cohen who set the ball rolling, and Tina Persaud and Stephen Adamson for their continued support. Also to Paul Gambaccini and Fred Bronson who both understand what it's like to work on a book of this nature and whose advice in the early stages was invaluable.

Emotional support has proven to be of foremost importance on a project this size, and I'd like to thank the following who between them stopped me throwing the word processor out of the window on more than a few occasions: David Hughes, Bob Fisher, Alan Freeman, Pete Daws, Lesley McWilliams, Gareth Davies, Jackie Gill, John Craig, Tim Blackmore, Shaun Greenfield, Johnny Beerling, Jeremy Beadle, Bob Harris, Suzanne DeSimone, Tony Blackburn, Mark Robson, Alison McDowell, Iain Johnstone, Andy Aliffe, Graham Walker, Alan Jones, Lyndsey Daley, Ann Osborne, Geoff Mullin, Chris Mason, Natalie Haughton, Amanda Beel, Damian Christian, Richard Evans, Adrian Williams and Kit Buckler.

I'm sure there are dozens of other people whose names have been omitted from the acknowledgements for which I apologize in advance, but you know who you are and I thank you all.

Published in Great Britain by
Guinness Publishing Ltd
33 London Road, Enfield, Middlesex EN2 6DJ

'GUINNESS' is a registered trademark of
Guinness Publishing Ltd

First published 1995
Reprint 10 9 8 7 6 5 4 3 2 1 0

Copyright © Phil Swern and Mike Childs 1995

The right of Phil Swern and Mike Childs to be identified as
Authors of this work has been asserted in accordance with
the Copyright, Designs and Patents Act, 1988

ISBN 0–85112–670–7

A catalogue record for this book is available from the
British Library

Designed by Stonecastle Graphics Ltd and Wilderness Design
Picture Research by Tina Persaud, Image Select, Alan Jones
Typeset by Ace Filmsetting Ltd, Frome, Somerset
Printed and bound in Great Britain by
The Bath Press, Bath
Front cover photography by Geoffrey Frosh

CONTENTS

INTRODUCTION

Cinema celebrates its centenary in 1995 and this book looks at the top box office favourites from cinema's half century from 1945 to the present day. It's a book of facts, statistics, trivia, information and much much more on nearly 700 films. Until 1969 reliable box office figures were not made freely available to the cinema press of the day and therefore the first 25 years covered are necessarily based on information from a variety of sources. Distributors and exhibitors kept their receipts a closely guarded secret, but trade publication *Kinematograph Weekly* and its dedicated staff kept a very close eye on the business and were able to determine which films were the hits, and which were the misses.

At each year's end *Kinematograph Weekly* published comprehensive lists of 'Box-Office Winners' and 'Hits of the Year' based on statistics provided by exhibitors and independent cinema owners, and used their knowledge and expertise of the business to rank movies according to their own judgement. Review Editor R.H. 'Josh' Billings would then table the films by theme, i.e. Best British Film, Best Musical, Best War Documentary, etc. From these tables we've narrowed down all the hits in the given years and chosen ten in each year from 1945 until 1968 (inclusive), and five from the early months of 1969 as fully detailed charts were printed for the first time in July of that year in rival publication *Today's Cinema*. This had started life in 1912 as *The Cinema News and Property Gazette* before merging in 1957 with *The Daily Film Renter*. In July 1969 it was the first publication to guarantee hard facts and box office statistics and introduced a brand new feature called *Box Office*. It was trumpeted as 'a vital weekly thermometer of fact – presenting up-to-date 'takes' of all West End cinemas. *Today's Cinema* wants Facts. Only now have the true figures been promised. *Today's Cinema* prints the news.' And so began the first true statistical reading of a film's success or failure at the box office. *Today's Cinema* merged with *Kinematograph Weekly* (which by then was known as *Kine Weekly*) in 1971, becoming *Cinema And Television Today*. It eventually settled on the name *Screen International*, which it bears to this day.

There will undoubtedly by some argument and controversy over the choice of films given the accolade 'box office number one' in the early years, but please remember these are lists based on painstaking research and the most accurate information available, so please don't blame us if your favourite doesn't appear!

For each film in the book we've included the following details: title, year of first appearance in the UK*, distributor, director, producer, screenplay, music, cast list of main characters, synopsis, trivia and facts, Academy Awards, significant or memorable songs and video availability. (Video availability changes constantly so video availability means the film is, or has been at some time, available to rent or buy.)

From 1969 also included is the date that each film reached number one, the number of weeks it held the top-spot, and the top five films in its first week at the top. Not all the films were at number one for consecutive weeks and those with an * indicate non-consecutive weeks at number one.

The boxes of Top Ten and Top Twenty films in individual years are based on the amount grossed by each film in the UK in that year. They are the year's top-grossing films in descending order and have nothing to do with weeks at number one or in the top five.

* Films like *The Sound of Music* are only included in the year they opened even though they played for several years and were constantly featured in the year-end charts of the time. However, films which are later re-released and go back to number one are featured again.

THE 1940s

Even though Britain had been at war since September 1939, audiences still flocked to the cinema to escape from the harsh realities of life. Movies were part of the fabric of everyday existence and provided much relief in troubled times. Our first look at the box office successes begins in the year war ended, 1945, and moving pictures celebrated its 50th birthday.

From biblical epics to block-busting musicals, and from Hope and Crosby comedies to gritty thrillers, the years 1945 to 1949 produced films for everyone's taste. The British film industry was in an extremely healthy state with studios like Rank and Ealing making top-quality entertainment for home consumption, and the large American studios like MGM providing the escapist fare which was so needed in those austere postwar years. Great works of literature were regularly adapted for the big screen and there was a growth of home-grown talent for writing original stories.

Home-grown stars like Anna Neagle and Elizabeth Taylor were doing great business alongside established American screen legends like Rita Hayworth and Judy Garland, and actors like Jack Warner and John Mills were more than holding their own against American counterparts like Alan Ladd and Danny Kaye.

New American stars like Gregory Peck and Kirk Douglas were being groomed by the Hollywood studios and were given dramatic roles respectively in the films *Champion* and *Twelve O'Clock High*, while the consistently successful actresses, Bette Davis and Joan Crawford, continued to draw in the crowds with films like *Mildred Pierce* and *The Corn Is Green*.

British stars James Mason and Jean Simmons began to achieve international success with films like *The Wicked Lady* and *Hamlet*. These were the years which also saw the emergence of actors of the calibre of Dirk Bogarde and Alec Guinness who would prove to have durable careers in the movies.

Re-issues did well during the latter half of the 1940s, giving audiences a second chance to catch up on old favourites, or, for returning servicemen, a first look at some films which had become classics. Previously released films which did very well second time around included *The Maltese Falcon*, which dated back to 1941, *Gunga Din* originally from 1939, and Disney's cartoon favourite *Pinocchio* from 1940.

A diverse selection indeed, and the following pages contain just some of the popular postwar hits at the local Odeons, ABCs and Gaumonts around the country.

ANCHORS AWEIGH

1945	
Studio/Distributor:	MGM
Director:	George Sidney
Producer:	Joe Pasternak
Screenplay:	Isobel Lennart
Music:	George Stoll

CAST
Frank Sinatra . . . . *Clarence Doolittle*
Kathryn Grayson . . . . *Susan Abbott*
Gene Kelly . . . . *Joseph Brady*
José Iturbi . . . . *Himself*
Dean Stockwell . . . . *Donald Martin*
Pamela Britton . . . . . . *Girl From Brooklyn*
'Rags' Ragland . . . . *Police Sergeant*

Clarence Doolittle and Joseph Brady, a pair of sailors on leave in Hollywood, hit the town for a night of fun. Clarence is rather reserved but Joseph is determined to educate him in the art of picking up women. Thanks to Joseph's tuition, they both end up falling for the same girl. The film is probably best remembered for Kelly's live action dance routine with the cartoon characters Tom and Jerry.

Dean Stockwell, who went on to star in *Married To The Mob*, *Blue Velvet* and *Dune*, made one of his earliest screen appearances as an eight-year-old boy determined to join the navy.

Gene Kelly's assistant on the film Stanley Donen, had to teach Sharon McManus a dance routine with a skipping rope. It took him seven hours to teach her one step. By the time she'd mastered the routine, the pair were sworn enemies.

Academy Awards: Best Scoring of a Musical (George Stoll)

Music: 'Jealousy', 'The Donkey Serenade', 'If You Knew Susie', 'I Fall in Love too Easily'

Video availability

BRIEF ENCOUNTER

1945	
Studio/Distributor:	Eagle-Lion
Director:	David Lean
Producer:	Noel Coward
Screenplay:	Noel Coward, David Lean, Ronald Neame
Music:	Rachmaninov

CAST
Celia Johnson . . . . *Laura Jesson*
Trevor Howard . . . . *Alec Harvey*
Stanley Holloway . . . . *Albert Godby*
Joyce Carey . . . . *Myrtle Bagot*
Cyril Raymond . . . . *Fred Jesson*
Everley Gregg . . . . *Dolly Messiter*
Margaret Barton . . . . *Beryl Walters*
Valentine Dyall . . . . *Stephen Lynn*

Alec, a doctor, and Laura, a housewife, both married to other people, regularly travel into town by train each Thursday. They meet by chance at the fictitious Milford Junction when Alec offers to remove a piece of grit from Laura's eye, and discover they both make the same trip each week. Their conversation leads to a casual friendship to begin with, but their meetings turn into something much stronger than either had ever intended and they embark upon a short but wonderful love affair.

The film, which was based on Noel Coward's 1935 short playlet *Still Life*, was made in eight weeks on a budget of £270,000. It featured Trevor Howard in his first starring role, and was the first film for which a British director – David Lean – had been nominated for an Oscar. Still a firm favourite with the public, the film owes much of its resonance to Rachmaninov's piano concerto no. 2.

Music: Rachmaninov's piano concerto no. 2

Video availability

THE LOST WEEKEND

1945	
Studio/Distributor:	Paramount
Director:	Billy Wilder
Producer:	Charles Brackett
Screenplay:	Charles Brackett, Billy Wilder
Music:	Miklos Rozsa

As the train pulls out of Milford Junction station Laura Jesson (Celia Johnson) and Alec Harvey (Trevor Howard) find that parting is such sweet sorrow in David Lean's Brief Encounter.

CAST
Ray Milland .... *Don Birnam*
June Wyman .... *Helen St James*
Philip Terry .... *Nick Birnham*
Howard de Silva ...... *Nat, the Bartender*
Doris Dowling .... *Gloria*
Frank Faylen .... *Bim*
Mary Young .... *Mrs Deveridge*
Anita Bolster .... *Mrs Foley*
Lillian Fontaine .... *Mrs St James*

A hard-hitting story of alcoholism, it starred Ray Milland as Don Birnam, a drunk who constantly boasts to everyone that he is about to write his first novel, although it never seems to materialize. His brother, Nick, with whom he shares an apartment, goes away for the weekend, leaving Don to his own devices. Trying to search out the booze his brother has hidden, Birnam's alcoholism drags him down into an urban nightmare.

Billy Wilder had great difficulty in persuading Paramount to allow him to make this film. It was only after he added a romantic angle and changed Don Birman's obsession from homosexuality to writer's block that the project was given the green light. The liquor industry was less than impressed with the picture. Feeling it would harm sales, it allegedly offered the studio $5 million not to release the film. It finally opened to great critical acclaim and became one of Paramount's biggest hits of the year.

Academy Awards: Best Film (Producer Charles Brackett), Best Direction (Billy Wilder), Best Actor (Ray Milland), Best Screenplay (Billy Wilder and Charles Brackett)

MILDRED PIERCE

1945	
Studio/Distributor:	Warner
Director:	Michael Curtiz
Producer:	Jerry Wald
Screenplay:	Ranald MacDougall
Music:	Max Steiner

CAST
Joan Crawford .... *Mildred Pierce*
Jack Carson .... *Wally*
Zachary Scott .... *Monte Bergaron*
Eve Arden .... *Ida*
Ann Blyth .... *Veda Pierce*
Bruce Bennett .... *Bert Pierce*
Lee Patrick .... *Mrs Biederhof*

Joan Crawford plays the title role in Mildred Pierce, *the story of a discontented housewife-turned successful restaurateur who is determined to hang on to playboy Monte Bergaron (Zachary Scott).*

Mildred is obsessed with her older daughter, Veda, and will go to any lengths to protect her. When the girl's marriage breaks up, Mildred takes up waitressing in order to keep the greedy Veda in the manner to which she has become accustomed. Mildred later marries a high-class playboy who goes through her savings faster than the speed of sound, and at the same time has an affair with Veda. Mildred Pierce is, however, finally saved by true love.

Seven writers worked on the screenplay for the film, but they couldn't get any version past the censors until Ranald MacDougall hit on the idea of telling the story in flashback.

Bette Davis, Rosalind Russell and Barbara Stanwyck were interested in the lead but Joan Crawford won this plum role. However, director Michael Curtiz became so fed up with Joan Crawford's tantrums on the set during the making of the film that he tore the shoulder pads off one of the dresses she was wearing.

Academy Awards: Best Actress (Joan Crawford)

NATIONAL VELVET

1945	
Studio/Distributor:	MGM
Director:	Clarence Brown
Producer:	Pandro S Berman
Screenplay:	Theodore Reeves, Helen Deutsch
Music:	Herbert Stothart

CAST

Mickey Rooney	*Mi Taylor*
Donald Crisp	*Mr Brown*
Elizabeth Taylor	*Velvet Brown*
Ann Revere	*Mrs Brown*
Angela Lansbury	*Edwina Brown*
Jackie Jenkins	*Donald Brown*

Young Sussex girl Velvet Brown has her dreams come true when she enters a raffle and wins a horse, which she names Pie. With the help of Mi Taylor, a retired jockey who has developed a fear of horses, she begins to train the animal with the hope of entering the Grand National. Her mother parts with her life savings to pay the entrance fee for the race which turns out to be a sound investment.

At the age of 12, Elizabeth Taylor was considered too short for the part, and only after a three-month crash course in weight and height gaining (and through her own determination) was she given the part. She did all her own riding in the film, apart from the very dangerous jumps which were performed by a professional jockey. The 1978 sequel *International Velvet*, starred Tatum O'Neal, Anthony Hopkins and Christopher Plummer, but did not receive the critical acclaim of its predecessor.

Academy Awards: Best Supporting Actress (Anne Revere), Best Editing (Robert J. Kern)

THE PICTURE OF DORIAN GRAY

1945	
Studio/Distributor:	MGM
Director:	Albert Lewin
Producer:	Pandro S. Berman
Screenplay:	Albert Lewin
Music:	Herbert Stothart (director)

CAST
George Sanders . . . . . . *Lord Henry Wotton*
Hurd Hatfield . . . . *Dorian Gray*
Donna Reed . . . . *Gladys Hallward*
Angela Lansbury . . . . *Sibyl Vane*
Peter Lawford . . . . *David Stone*
Lowell Gilmore . . . . *Basil Hallward*

Richard Fraser . . . . *James Vane*

Based on the Oscar Wilde story, this melodramatic film tells the tale of the handsome Dorian Gray, a vain and selfish 19th-century gentleman. Gray's vanity leads him to have his portrait painted, which ages while Gray himself stays young. The depravity of Gray's subsequent life comes to a terrifying and violent end.

Academy Awards: Best black and white Cinematography (Harry Stradling)

Music: 'Goodbye Little Yellow Bird' (Angela Lansbury)

Video availability

THE SEVENTH VEIL

1945	
Studio/Distributor:	Theatrecraft
Director:	Compton Bennett
Producer:	Sydney Box
Screenplay:	Muriel Box, Sydney Box
Music:	Benjamin Frankel

CAST
James Mason . . . . *Nicholas*
Ann Todd . . . . *Francesca*
Herbert Lom . . . . *Dr Larsen*
Hugh McDermott . . . . *Peter Gay*
Albert Lieven . . . . *Maxwell Leyden*
Yvonne Owen . . . . *Susan Brook*
David Horne . . . . *Dr Kendall*
Manning Whiley . . . . *Dr Irving*

Francesca Cunningham is a brilliant modern concert pianist. However, persistent memories of the time when her hands were badly burnt in a car crash make her prone to bouts of deep depression at the thought of losing the use of her hands. The problem becomes so acute that she attempts to take her own life. When Francesca is subsequently put under psychiatric care, Dr Larson delves back into her early life. He discovers that she was beaten at school by a headmistress just before taking her final music exams, and as a result failed the tests. It is this experience that is the cause of her fear.

This film was one of the first to be tested on preview audiences as the producers were unsure of which ending to use.

Academy Awards: Best Original Screenplay (Muriel and Sydney Box)

Video availability

SPELLBOUND

1945	
Studio/Distributor:	David O. Selznick
Director:	Alfred Hitchcock
Producer:	David O. Selznick
Screenplay:	Ben Hecht, Angus MacPhail
Music:	Miklos Rozsa

CAST
Ingrid Bergman ... Dr Constance Peterson
Gregory Peck ...... J.B. (John Ballantine)
Jean Acker .... Matron
Donald Curtis .... Harry
Rhonda Fleming .... Miss Carmichael
John Emery .... Dr Fleurol
Leo G. Carroll .... Dr Murchison
Norman Lloyd .... Garmes

John Ballantine, the new head of a psychiatric hospital, is suffering from memory loss and believes he may have committed a murder. The prim and proper psychiatrist, Dr Constance Peterson, who believes he is innocent, tries to treat his condition but finds herself falling in love with her patient. The mystery is solved when the doctor manages to delve into Ballantine's past and analyse one of his recurring dreams.

Director Alfred Hitchcock, who made a cameo appearance in all his movies, turns up exiting an elevator carrying a violin case.

Academy Awards: Best Scoring of a Drama or Comedy (Miklos Rozsa)

Video availability

TO HAVE AND HAVE NOT

1945	
Studio/Distributor:	Warner
Director:	Howard Hawks
Producer:	Howard Hawks
Screenplay:	Jules Furthman, William Faulkner
Music:	Leo Forbstein

CAST
Humphrey Bogart .... Harry Morgan
Walter Brennan .... Eddie
Lauren Bacall .... Marie Browning
Dolores Moran .... Helene De Bursac
Hoagy Carmichael .... Crickett
Walter Molnar .... Paul De Bursac
Sheldon Leonard .... Lt. Coyo

Based on an Ernest Hemingway novel, it tells the story of Harry Morgan, a tough sea captain of the cruiser, *Queen Conch*. Morgan lives on the French Caribbean island of Martinique and will work for anyone willing to pay. He finds himself involved with the French Resistance after one of his customers is gunned down during a police raid in the hotel where he is staying. He then helps Marie Browning get off the island as well as agreeing to smuggle one of the Resistance's top men into Martinique.

To Have and Have Not was the first movie for Lauren Bacall (or Betty Bacall as she was then known). She had been spotted on the cover of *Vogue* Magazine by director Howard Hawks's wife. Warner Brothers publicity department dubbed Bacall 'The Look' because of the suggestive twinkle in her eye.

Music: 'Am I Blue', 'Hong Kong Blues', 'How Little We Know'

Video availability

THE WICKED LADY

1945	
Studio/Distributor:	Columbia
Director:	Leslie Arliss
Producer:	R. J. Minney
Screenplay:	Leslie Arliss, Gordon Glennon, Almee Stuart
Music:	Hans May

CAST
Margaret Lockwood .... Lady Skelton
James Mason .... Captain Jackson
Patricia Roc .... Caroline
Griffith Jones .... Sir Ralph Skelton
Enid Stamp-Taylor ...... Lady Kingsclere
Francis Lister .... Lord Kingsclere
Michael Rennie .... Kit Locksby
Felix Aylmer .... Hogarth
David Horne .... Martin Worth

Margaret Lockwood plays Lady Skelton, a 17th-century lady who marries for money. Her life is changed when she encounters and teams up with highwayman Captain Jackson. Helping the highwayman in his dastardly crimes, she has no compunction about shooting or poisoning anyone who might get in her way. Between her murderous crimes, she runs off with the fiancé of her best friend Caroline and ends up marrying him.

The *Manchester Guardian* review was less than flattering when it described it as 'A mixture of hot passion and cold suet pudding'. Some of the scenes had to be re-shot for American audiences because the censors thought many of the women's costumes were too revealing for the time.

The movie was remade in 1983, directed by Michael Winner and starring Faye Dunaway and Alan Bates.

Video availability

BEST YEARS OF OUR LIVES

1946	
Studio/Distributor;	Samuel Goldwyn
Director:	William Wyler
Producer:	Samuel Goldwyn
Screenplay:	Robert E. Sherwood
Music:	Hugo Friedhofer

CAST
Myrna Loy . . . . *Milly Stephenson*
Freddie March . . . . *Al Stephenson*
Dana Andrews . . . . *Fred Derry*
Teresa Wright. . . . . *Peggy Stephenson*
Virginia Mayo . . . . *Marie Derry*
Cathy O'Donnell . . . . *Wilma Cameron*
Hoagy Carmichael . . . . *Butch Engle*
Harold Russell . . . . *Homer Parrish*

At the end of World War II, three American servicemen return to their small hometown.

Suffering from wounds and memory lapses, they are also concerned about their future and find it difficult to readjust to family and civilian life.

Harold Russell, who played Homer Parrish, the seaman who returned home to glory, actually had both his hands blown off in a grenade explosion during his time as a Canadian paratrooper in World War II.

Academy Awards: Best Film (Producer Samuel Goldwyn), Best Direction (William Wyler), Best Actor (Fredric March), Best Supporting Actor (Harold Russell), Best Screenplay (Robert E. Sherwood), Best Editing (Daniel Mandell), Best Music Score of a Drama or Comedy (Hugo Friedhofer)

Video availability

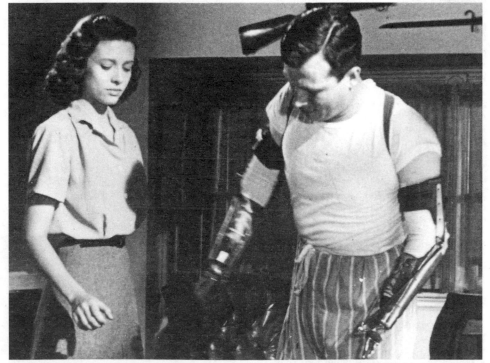

Homer (Harold Russell) and Wilma Parris (Cathy O'Donnell) learn to live with his handicap when he returns from the war in director William Wyler's classic film
The Best Years of Our Lives.

BLUE DAHLIA

1946	
Studio/Distributor:	Paramount
Director:	George Marshall
Producer:	John Houseman
Screenplay:	Raymond Chandler
Music:	Victory Young

CAST
Alan Ladd . . . . *Johnny Morrison*
Veronica Lake . . . . *Joyce Harwood*
William Bendix . . . . *Buzz Wanchek*
Howard da Silva . . . . *Eddie Harwood*
Doris Dowling . . . . *Helen Morrison*
Tom Powers . . . . *Capt. Hendrickson*

Hugh Beaumont . . . . *George Copeland*
Howard Freeman . . . . *Corelli*

Soldier Johnny Morrison, returning from military service in the Pacific, discovers that his wife has taken to drink and has been having an affair. Things take a turn for the worse when she is found murdered and Johnny becomes the prime suspect. He begins a relentless manhunt for the real killer, while avoiding a blackmailing detective.

Blue Dahlia was the only story that Raymond Chandler wrote specially for the big screen after Paramount bought it as an unfinished novel. Chandler was reported to have been unhappy with both the leading man and woman in the movie.

BLUE SKIES

1946	
Studio/Distributor:	Paramount
Director:	Stuart Heisler
Producer:	Sol C. Siegel
Screenplay:	Arthur Sheekman
Music:	Robert Emmett Dolan

CAST
Bing Crosby . . . . *Johnny Adams*
Fred Astaire . . . . *Jed Potter*
Joan Caulfield . . . . *Mary O'Hara*
Billy DeWolfe . . . . *Tony*
Olga San Juan . . . . *Nita Nova*
Mikhail Rasumny . . . . *François*
Frank Faylen . . . . *Mack*

Johnny Adams and Jed Potter are good friends and former show business partners. Johnny opens and closes night clubs and Jed is a disc jockey and dancer. However, they find themselves playing love tennis in a competition for the same girl.

There were some similarities between *Blue Skies* and the previous Crosby–Astaire collaboration, *Holiday Inn* (1942). Both had Irving Berlin scores, both featured Crosby and Astaire as song and dance partners, and both had them falling for the same girl.

The film was originally going to be produced by Mark Sandrich, who cast Paul Draper as Jed Potter. Just before shooting began, Sandrich suffered a fatal heart attack and Sol C. Siegel was brought in. He replaced Draper with Astaire, who accepted the part of Jed Potter against the wishes of his doctor, who thought the vigorous dance routines would put too much strain on the 46-year-old man. The dancer said the film would be his last but changed his mind after the success of the film.

Music: 'All By Myself', 'A Couple of Song and Dance Men', 'Puttin' on the Ritz' (the first time the song was heard), 'Blue Skies', 'A Pretty Girl is Like a Melody', 'Always', 'How Deep is the Ocean', 'White Christmas', 'Heat Wave'

CAESAR AND CLEOPATRA

1946	
Studio/Distributor:	Rank
Director:	Gabriel Pascal
Producer:	Gabriel Pascal
Screenplay:	George Bernard Shaw
Music:	Georges Auric

CAST
Vivien Leigh . . . . *Cleopatra*
Claude Rains . . . . *Caesar*
Stewart Grainger . . . . *Appollodorus*
Flora Robson . . . . *Flatateeta*
Francis L. Sullivan . . . . *Pothinus*
Basil Sydney . . . . *Ruffio*
Anthony Harvey . . . . *Ptolemy*
Raymond Harvey . . . . *Lucius Septimius*

The movie was an adaptation of George Bernard Shaw's 1898 comedy about the ageing Roman conqueror, Caesar. It told the story of Caesar's time in Alexandria and his relationship with the young Egyptian beauty, Queen Cleopatra.

The movie, which became the most expensive British production to date, brought the Rank Organization to the brink of bankruptcy. Its cast of over 100 British extras included Roger Moore and Kay Kendall.

George Bernard Shaw was so taken by Vivien Leigh that he wrote an entirely new scene just for her.

John Bryan was nominated for an Oscar for his impressive sets.

Video availability

DUEL IN THE SUN

1946	
Studio/Distributor:	Selznick International
Director:	King Vidor
Producer:	David O. Selznick
Screenplay:	David O. Selznick
Music:	Dimitri Tiomkin

CAST
Jennifer Jones . . . . *Pearl Chavez*
Joseph Cotten . . . . *Jessie McCanles*
Gregory Peck . . . . *Lewt McCanles*
Lionel Barrymore . . . . . . *Senator McCanles*
Lilian Gish . . . . *Mrs McCanles*
Walter Huston . . . . *The Sinkiller*

In this steamy Western, Pearl, a half breed, is forced to live with a Texas cattle baron and his two sons, Lewt and Jessie, after her father kills her mother and lover. The two brothers try to capture her emotions, but it's Lewt who nearly kills his brother when he discovers them together.

John Wayne considered taking the part of Lewt, but rejected the role because of the sexual connotations of the script. On release, the movie caused rows among Catholic and Protestant leaders wherever it was showing. It was censored in Memphis and banned in Connecticut, with certain scenes taken out for other states.

Producer David O. Selznick demanded that his actress protégée, Jennifer Jones, was given special attention, and he married her soon after the completion of the film. Selznick's interference in the making of the film, however, led to Director King Vidor storming off the set just days before filming ended.

Video availability

GILDA

1946	
Studio/Distributor:	Columbia
Director:	Charles Vidor
Producer:	Virginia Van Upp
Screenplay:	Marion Parsonnet
Music:	Morris Stoloff, Marlin Skiles

CAST
Rita Hayworth . . . . *Gilda*
Glenn Ford . . . . *Johnny Farrell*
George Macready . . . . . . *Ballin Mundson*
Joseph Calleia . . . . *Obregon*
Steven Geray . . . . *Uncle Pio*
Joe Sawyer . . . . *Casey*
Gerald Mohr . . . . *Captain Delgado*

Ballin Mundson, whose only real love is power, owns a plush casino in Buenos Aires. His assistant is tough guy and confirmed gambler Johnny Farrell, whom he uses to do most of his dirty work. Farrell's job includes keeping an eye on George's wife, Gilda, with whom he once had an affair and the two resume their love-hate relationship.

Studio boss Harry Cohn suspected Rita Hayworth and Glenn Ford were having an affair and had their dressing rooms bugged. When the actors discovered the microphones, they put on a special performance for Cohn's benefit.

Anita Ellis dubbed Hayworth's voice for the song 'Put the Blame on Mame', although the star does sing and play the guitar herself on the reprise. There was no stand-in for Rita Hayworth's provocative dance routines, which were modelled on a performance by a professional stripper seen by choreographer Jack Cole.

Music: 'Put the Blame on Mame'

Video availability

Rita Hayworth, in what many consider her most famous role, begins her striptease act as she sings 'Put the blame on Mame' in Gilda.

GREAT EXPECTATIONS

1946	
Studio/Distributor:	Rank
Director:	David Lean
Producer:	Ronald Neame
Screenplay:	David Lean
Music:	Walter Goehr, Ronald Neame, Anthony Havelock-Allan

CAST

John Mills . . . . *Pip*
Valerie Hobson . . . . *Estella*
Bernard Miles . . . . *Joe Gargery*
Francis L. Sullivan . . . . *Jaggers*
Finlay Currie . . . . *Magwitch*
Martita Hunt . . . . *Miss Havisham*
Alec Guinness . . . . *Herbert Pocket*

The classic Dickens tale, in its second major movie Tversion (the first was in 1934), follows the life of the orphan boy Pip, who helps Abel Magwitch, an escaped convict, stay alive before he is recaptured and transported to an Australian prison.

Later in life he receives a large inheritance that he believes to have come from an eccentric old woman, Miss Havisham, but turns out to be from the convict he helped as a child.

The British Board of Film Censors failed to give the movie a 'U' certificate on three counts. The attack on Pip by Magwitch when he grabs the boy by the throat and says 'Keep still you little devil or I'll cut your throat' was of concern. They were also disturbed by Miss Havisham burning to death and the judge wearing a black cap when pronouncing the death sentence. The film was awarded an 'A' certificate, which meant only children accompanied by an adult could see it.

The film also featured a very young Jean Simmons who played Estella as a child.

Academy Awards: Best black and white Cinematography (Guy Green), Best black and white Art Direction (John Bryan), Best Set Decoration (Wilfred Shingleton)

Video availability

Jean Simmons, who plays Estella as a child in David Lean's version of Great Expectations, *went on to play Miss Havisham in the 1989 TV serialization of the story.*

THE JOLSON STORY

1946	
Studio/Distributor:	Columbia
Director:	Alfred E. Green
Producer:	Sidney Skolsky
Screenplay:	Stephen Longstreet
Music:	M. W. Stoloff

CAST

Larry Parks	*Al Jolson*
Evelyn Keyes	*Julie Benson*
William Demarest	*Steve Martin*
Bill Goodwin	*Tom Baron*
Ludwig Donath	*Cantor Yoelson*
Tamara Shayne	*Mrs Yoelson*

The bio-pic of the early life and eventual rise to fame of Al Jolson. Jolson, the son of a cantor, meets vaudeville act Steve Martin, who encourages him with his singing and quickly becomes his mentor. With his arrogance and enormous ego, Jolson is prepared to sacrifice everything for his career, causing heartache for both his parents and his wife, Julie.

Jolson's wife in the film, Julie, is allegedly based on the character of his third of four wives, Ruby Keeler, who refused to allow her name to be used in the movie.

Jolson wanted to play himself, but film boss Harry Cohn refused, although he allowed him to coach Parks for the role, using Jolson's voice for the songs. The part of Jolson was originally offered to James Cagney, who turned it down, and to Danny Thomas, who was eventually rejected because he refused to have his nose altered for the role.

Academy Awards: Best Sound Recording (John Livadary), Best Scoring of a Musical Picture (Morris Stoloff)

Music: 'About a Quarter to Nine', 'April Showers', 'By the Light of the Silvery Moon', 'California Here I Come', 'My Mammy', 'Rock 'a' Bye your Baby with a Dixie Melody', 'She's a Latin from Manhattan', 'Swanee', 'There's a Rainbow round my Shoulder', 'You Made me Love You'

Video availability

NIGHT AND DAY

1946	
Studio/Distributor:	Warner
Director:	Michael Curtiz
Producer:	Arthur Schwartz
Screenplay:	Charles Hoffman, Leo Townsend, William Bowers
Music:	Cole Porter

CAST

Cary Grant	*Cole Porter*
Alexis Smith	*Linda Lee Porter*
Monty Woolley	*Himself*
Ginny Simms	*Carole Hill*
Jane Wyman	*Gracie Harris*
Eve Arden	*Gabrielle*
Victor Francen	*Anatole Giron*
Alan Hale	*Leon Dowling*
Dorothy Malone	*Nancy*

Night and Day was loosely based on the life and career of composer Cole Porter. Porter is born into a rich family and goes on to make even more money with his successful songwriting. He marries Linda, a nurse from an aristocratic family. The one disaster depicted in the movie is his injury from a horse-riding fall in Central Park, New York. He breaks both his legs which never mend properly, leaving him crippled for the rest of his life.

Cary Grant was very unhappy with his portrayal of Cole Porter and is understood to have told director Michael Curtiz that if he was ever caught working with him again it would be because he was either broke or mental.

Endless numbers of screen writers worked for two years to come up with an acceptable script for this project, but they all failed.

Music: 'Begin the Beguine', 'Do I Love you', 'I've Got You Under My Skin', 'Just One of Those Things', 'Miss Otis Regrets', 'My Heart Belongs to Daddy', 'Night and Day', 'What is This Thing Called Love?', 'You Do Something to Me', 'You're the Top'

Video availability

SONG OF THE SOUTH

1946	
Studio/Distributor:	Walt Disney
Director:	Harve Foster
Producer:	Walt Disney Productions
Screenplay:	Dalton Reymond, Morton Grant, Maurice Rapf
Music:	Charles Wolcott

CAST
Bobby Driscoll .... *Johnny*
Luana Patten .... *Ginny*
James Baskett .... *Uncle Remus*
Lucile Watson........... *Grandmother*
Hattie McDaniel .... *Tempy*

The film was based on the Joel Chandler Harris 19th-century stories of Uncle Remus that Walt Disney had enjoyed as a boy. The lovable Uncle lives in a humble cabin in the Old South and is a friend and storyteller to the children of the world with his many tales, including those of Brer Rabbit and Brer Fox. Disney combines live action with animated cartoon sequences.

In 1968 Bobby Driscoll, who played one of the young children in the movie (Johnny), died of a heart attack at the age of 31 after being jailed for various drug-related offences.

Academy Awards: Best Song – 'Zip-a-Dee-Doo-Dah' (Allie Wrubel, music; Ray Gilbert, lyrics)

Music: 'Zip-a-Dee-Doo-Dah', 'You'll Always be the One I Love', 'Let the Rain Pour Down'

Video availability

THE COURTNEYS OF CURZON STREET

1947	
Studio/Distributor:	Imperadio
Director:	Herbert Wilcox
Producer:	Herbert Wilcox
Screenplay:	Nicholas Phipps
Music:	Tony Collins

CAST
Anna Neagle ...... *Catherine O'Hallaron*
Michael Wilding ..... *Sir Edward Courtney*
Gladys Young........... *Lady Courtney*
Coral Browne .... *Valerie*
Michael Medwin ...... *Edward Courtney*
Daphne Slater .... *Cynthia*
Jack Watling........... *Teddy Courtney*
Helen Cherry .... *Mary Courtney*

A young Victorian baronet from a wealthy family falls in love with and marries a housemaid, much to the shock and dismay of his parents. The snobs from their social set persecute the girl by talking behind her back about her working-class origins. The twist in the tale comes when their son grows up and brings home his fiancée who is worried that her parents will be upset that she is marrying into the aristocracy.

Director Herbert Wilcox discovered Anna Neagle and directed all but two of her films. They married in 1943.

Michael Wilding and Anna Neagle worked together two years previously in *Piccadilly Incident*, but this was the movie that established them as the top British postwar screen lovers.

Music: 'Soldiers of the Queen', 'Lily Marlene'

FOREVER AMBER

1947	
Studio/Distributor:	Twentieth Century-Fox
Director:	Otto Preminger
Producer:	William Perlberg
Screenplay:	Philip Dunne, Ring Lardner Jr
Music:	David Raskin

CAST
Linda Darnell .... *Amber*
Cornel Wilde .... *Bruce Carlton*
Richard Greene .... *Lord Almsbury*
George Sanders .... *King Charles II*
Glenn Langan......... *Capt Rex Morgan*
Richard Haydn .... *Earl of Radcliffe*
Jessica Tandy .... *Nan Britton*
Anne Revere........... *Mother Red Cap*

There were more problems for the censors of the time in Forever Amber. *Amber (Linda Darnell) has a love affair with soldier Bruce Carlton (Cornel Wilde), resulting in a child, but she finds comfort with King Charles II (George Sanders).*

Based on the Kathleen Winsor novel, *Forever Amber* tells the story of the young 17th-century peasant girl, Amber. She sacrifices her honour and offers her affections and more around court to better her position in the court of King Charles II. Her tactics get her thrown into a pauper's prison, but she manages to work her way into the King's affections.

The making of *Forever Amber* was fraught with studio arguments. John Stahl was hired to direct the movie, but was sacked by studio boss Darryl F. Zanuck who replaced him with Otto Preminger, who hated the story, but was forced to work on the film due to an option in his contract. He finally agreed but fired English actress Peggy Cummins who he wanted replaced with Lana Turner. Once again Zanuck intervened and insisted the part went to Linda Darnell.

GREEN DOLPHIN STREET

1947	
Studio/Distributor:	MGM
Director:	Victor Saville
Producer:	Carey Wilson
Screenplay:	Samson Raphaelson
Music:	Bronislau Kaper

CAST
Lana Turner . . . . *Marianne Patourel*
Van Heflin . . . . *Timothy Haalam*

Donna Reed . . . . *Marguerite Patourel*
Richard Hart . . . . *William Ozanne*
Frank Morgan . . . . *Dr Edmond Ozanne*
Edmund Gwenn . . . . *Octavius Patourel*
Dame May Whitty . . . . . . *Mother Superior*
Reginald Owen . . . . *Captain O'Hara*

A deserter from the British Navy, Timothy Haalam, heads for New Zealand. He writes a love letter to Marianne Patourel, confusing her with her sister Marguerite. Marianne immediately makes her way to New Zealand to meet her alleged lover who, rather than admit his mistake, marries her, causing her spurned sister to enter a convent. The 19th-century romance ends with a violent earthquake.

The story was based on Elizabeth Goudge's novel which won the first ever MGM Novel Award and a prize of $200,000 from hundreds of entries.

Producer Carey Wilson was responsible for the long-running American TV series *Dr Kildare*, which made Richard Chamberlain a star.

Academy Awards: Best Special Effects (A. Arnold Gillsepie and Warren Newcombe (visual), Douglas Shearer and Michael Steinore (audible)

HOLIDAY CAMP

	1947
Studio/Distributor:	GFD
Director:	Ken Annakin
Producer:	Sydney Box
Screenplay:	Muriel and Sydney Box, Peter Rogers, Ted Willis, Mabel and Denis Constanduros
Music:	Bob Busby

CAST
Flora Robson . . . . *Esther Harman*
Dennis Price . . . . *Squad. Leader Hardwicke*
Jack Warner . . . . *Joe Huggett*

Kathleen Harrison . . . . *Mrs Huggett*
Hazel Court . . . . *Joan Martin*
Emrys Jones . . . . *Michael Halliday*
Yvonne Owen . . . . *Angela Kirby*

The plot of this comedy-drama, as the title suggests, revolves around the Huggett family having a whale of a time at a British holiday resort. There's love in the air and a holiday romance takes shape. But the festive atmosphere is dampened when it's discovered that there is a killer on the loose.

Two sequels followed: *Here Come the Huggetts* (1948) and *The Huggetts Abroad* in 1949. The Huggetts also became well known for their long-running BBC radio series *Meet The Huggetts*.

HUE AND CRY

	1947
Studio/Distributor:	Ealing
Director:	Charles Crichton
Producer:	Michael Balcon
Screenplay:	T.E.B. Clarke
Music:	Georges Auric

CAST
Alastair Sim . . . . *Felix Wilkinson*
Valerie White . . . . *Rhona*
Jack Warner . . . . *Nightingale*
Harry Fowler . . . . *Joe Kirby*
Frederick Piper . . . . *Mr Kirby*

Heather Delaine . . . . *Mrs Kirby*
Douglas Barr . . . . *Alec*

A gang of crooks use a story from a children's comic, *The Trump*, as the basis for passing coded messages about their crimes. Joe Kirby, an enterprising kid, spots their plan and, together with a writer of detective stories (Alastair Sim), gathers a group of his rowdy East End friends to meet at a waste disposal site to help round up the criminals. This was Ealing Studios' first postwar comedy success.

Video availability

IT ALWAYS RAINS ON SUNDAY

	1947
Studio/Distributor:	Ealing
Director:	Robert Hamer
Producer:	Michael Balcon
Screenplay:	Angus Macphail, Robert Hamer, Henry Cornelius
Music:	Georges Auric

CAST
Googie Withers . . . . *Rose Sandigate*
Edward Chapman . . . . . *George Sandigate*
Susan Shaw . . . . *Vi Sandigate*
Patricia Plunkett . . . . *Doris Sandigate*
David Lines . . . . *Alfie Sandigate*
Sydney Tafler . . . . *Morry Hyams*
Betty Ann Davies . . . . *Sadie Hyams*
John Slater . . . . *Lou Hyams*

The story of everyday folk who live in a down-trodden part of the East End of London during the 1940s. The neighbourhood has a visit from an escaped convict, seeking refuge in the home of his married girlfriend. His arrival causes total upheaval.

Googie Withers and John McCallum, who plays the convict Tommy Swan, were husband and wife in real life.

The movie featured Jack Warner in his first ever role as a policeman, playing Sgt. Fothergill. He would later fully establish his career when he played P.C. Dixon in the 1949 box office hit *The Blue Lamp*.

LIFE WITH FATHER

1947

Studio/Distributor: Warner
Director: Michael Curtiz
Producer: Robert Buckner
Screenplay: Donald Ogden Stewart
Music: Max Steiner

CAST
William Powell . . . . *Clarence Day*
Irene Dunne . . . . *Vinny Day*
Elizabeth Taylor . . . . *Mary*
Edmund Gwenn . . . . *Rev. Dr. Lloyd*
ZaSu Pitts . . . . *Cora*
James Lydon . . . . *Clarence*
Emma Dunn . . . . *Margaret*
Moroni Olsen . . . . *Dr Humphries*

Based on the autobiographical book by Clarence Day Jnr, *Life with Father* tells the story of a Victorian New York household and a lovable but eccentric father who rules his family with his authoritative manner. His wife, Vinny, although patient, shows an independent streak when she questions her authority as a woman. The film develops into a series of sketches involving the family, which include the hiring of a new maid and Vinny trying to get her husband baptised.

Both Mary Pickford and Bette Davis wanted to play the female lead and Davis even tested for the role. The film was based on the 1939 Broadway play that ran for 3224 performances, at that time the longest in history.

Video availability

ODD MAN OUT

1947

Studio/Distributor: GFD
Director: Carol Reed
Producer: Carol Reed
Screenplay: F.L. Green, R.C. Sherriff
Music: William Alwyn

CAST
James Mason . . . . *Johnny McQueen*
Robert Newton . . . . *Lukey*
Robert Beatty . . . . *Dennis*
F.J. McCormick . . . . *Shell*
Fay Compton . . . . *Rosie*
Cyril Cusack . . . . *Pat*
Dan O'Herlihy . . . . *Nolan*

Maureen Delany . . . . *Theresa*

Johnny McQueen is the leader of an IRA gang that specializes in gun-running in Northern Ireland. He has broken out of prison and is in hiding with his girlfriend, Kathleen. Short of funds, he commits a robbery where he shoots a man dead and ends up badly wounded himself, but now has to avoid the police at all costs.

Director/producer Carol Reed went on to make *The Third Man* (1949), *Trapeze* (1956), *The Agony and the Ecstasy* (1965) and *Oliver!* (1968).

Video availability

ROAD TO RIO

1947

Studio/Distributor: Paramount
Director: Norman Z. McLeod

Producer: Daniel Dare
Screenplay: Edmund Beloin, Jack Rose
Music: Robert Emmett Dolan

CAST
Bing Crosby . . . . *Scat Sweeney*
Bob Hope . . . . *Hot Lips Barton*
Dorothy Lamour . *Lucia Maria De Andrade*
Gale Sondergaard . . . . *Catherine Vail*
Frank Faylen . . . . *Trigger*
Joseph Vitale . . . . *Tony*

The fifth 'Road' film in the series finds Scat Sweeney and Hot Lips Barton down and out and broke with the added troubles of having been the cause of a circus fire. They manage to escape by hiding away on a ship bound for Rio where they meet Lucia Maria De Andrade whose schizophrenic moods are brought about by the fact that she has been hypnotized into marrying a man she doesn't love. Fun and frolics from the 'Road' regulars.

The studio originally intended to cast Fred MacMurray and Jack Oakie in the leading roles, but luckily Bob and Bing were together again for the fifth of seven 'Road' movies.

Crosby and Hope made their first 'Road' film in 1940, *The Road to Singapore*. *Road to Zanzibar* (1941), *Road to Morocco* (1942) and *Road to Utopia* (1946) followed, all starring Hope, Crosby and Lamour.

Music: 'Apalachicola Fla', 'Experience', 'You Don't Have to Know the Language', 'But Beautiful'

THE SECRET LIFE OF WALTER MITTY

1947	
Studio/Distributor:	Samuel Goldwyn
Director:	Norman Z. McLeod
Producer:	Samuel Goldwyn
Screenplay:	Ken Englund, Everett Freeman
Music:	David Raksin

CAST
Danny Kaye . . . . *Walter Mitty*
Virginia Mayo . . . . . . *Rosalind van Hoorn*
Boris Karloff . . . . *Dr Hollingshead*
Fay Bainter . . . . *Mrs Mitty*
Ann Rutherford . . . . . *Gertrude Griswold*
Thurston Hall . . . . *Bruce Pierce*
Gordon Jones . . . . *Tubby Wadsworth*

Florence Bates . . . . *Mrs Griswold*

Walter Mitty is a man who lives in two different worlds, the quiet real one and another full of fantasy created in his own mind to escape reality. He dreams that he is in a number of different situations where he is dynamic and heroic. In all his dreams, he fantasizes about Rosalind van Hoorn, who appears in his real life asking for help to escape a man who has been following her.

The film was based on the classic short story by James Thurber, who offered producer Sam Goldwyn $10,000 not to film his classic but MGM had already purchased the rights.

Music: 'Anatole of Paris'

Video availability

EASTER PARADE

1948		
Studio/Distributor:	MGM	
Director:	Charles Walters	
Producer:	Arthur Freed	
Screenplay:	Francis Goodrich, Albert Hackett, Sidney Sheldon	
Music:	Johnny Green (Musical Direction)	
	Irving Berlin (Songs)	

CAST
Judy Garland . . . . *Hannah Brown*
Fred Astaire . . . . *Don Hewes*
Peter Lawford . . . . . . *Jonathan Harrow III*
Ann Miller . . . . *Nadine Gale*
Jules Munshin . . . . *François*
Clinton Sundberg . . . *Mike, the Bartender*

Don Hewes breaks up with his dancing partner, Nadine Gale, between Easter of 1911 and 1912, when she is offered a part in a new Ziegfeld musical. Determined to get his revenge, he recruits Hannah Brown from a chorus line to take her place. He works hard with Hannah to show he can make a star out of anyone he chooses, but he doesn't find it easy, especially with the added problem that he's still in love with Nadine.

Gene Kelly was largely responsible for Fred Astaire's return to the movies. Kelly was originally supposed to play the male lead but was unable to act let alone dance after injuring his back playing volleyball, and suggested Astaire for the part.

Judy Garland's husband, Vincente Minnelli, was originally supposed to direct the movie, but because his wife had recently been released from a sanitorium doctors felt it would be a mistake for the two of them to work together as they seemed to upset each other.

Academy Awards: Best Scoring of a Musical (Johnny Green and Roger Edens)

Music: 'Easter Parade', 'A Fella with an Umbrella', 'When the Midnight Choo-Choo Leaves for Alabam', 'Steppin' out with My Baby', 'A Couple of Swells', 'I Love a Piano', 'Shakin' the Blues Away'

Video availability

HAMLET

1948

Studio/Distributor:	Rank
Director:	Laurence Olivier
Producer:	Laurence Olivier
Music:	William Walton

CAST

Laurence Olivier	Hamlet
Eileen Herlie	The Queen
Basil Sydney	The King
Norman Wooland	Horatio
Felix Aylmer	Polonius
Terence Morgan	Laertes
Jean Simmons	Ophelia
Peter Cushing	Osric

The classic Shakespeare play tells the story of tragic Danish prince, Hamlet. He promises his father's ghost that he will seek revenge for his murder by killing Claudius (his father's brother) who is now married to his mother, Gertrude. But Hamlet procrastinates with disastrous results.

The movie was originally four hours long, but some 90 minutes ended up on the cutting room floor. It was Laurence Olivier's second movie as a producer and director, his first being *Henry V* in 1944.

Jean Simmons was 18 years old when she played Ophelia. She had made her movie debut in 1944 at the age of 14 when she was chosen from a dance school to play Margaret Lockwood's sister in *Give*

Produced, directed and starring Laurence Olivier, the 1948 film version of Shakespeare's Hamlet *turned a four and a half hour play into a 155-minute movie.*

Us the Moon. Hamlet also featured Anthony Quayle in his first speaking role.

This version of *Hamlet* was actually filmed at the castle in Elsinore, Denmark.

Academy Awards: Best Film (Producer Laurence Olivier), Best Actor (Laurence Olivier), Best Black and White Art Direction (Roger K. Furse), Best Set Decoration (Carmen Dillon), Best Black and White Costume Design (Roger K. Furse)

Video availability

JOHNNY BELINDA

1948	
Studio/Distributor:	Warner
Director:	Jean Negulesco
Producer:	Jerry Wald
Screenplay:	Irmgard von Cube, Allen Vincent
Music:	Max Steiner

CAST
Jane Wyman . . . . *Belinda McDonald*
Lew Ayres . . . . *Dr Robert Richardson*
Charles Bickford . . . . *Black McDonald*
Agnes Moorehead . . . . *Aggie*
Stephen McNally . . . . *Locky*
Jan Sterling . . . . *Stella*
Rosalind Ivan . . . . *Mrs Poggety*
Dan Seymour . . . . *Pacquet*

Belinda McDonald is an unwanted deaf-mute girl who lives with her father and aunt on a remote farm in Canada. Her father blames her for the death of her mother during childbirth. She falls pregnant after being raped by a drunken village thug, but the blame is put on a local doctor who has befriended her. After the child is born, the real father tries to take the baby away from her, but Belinda kills him and is then arrested for murder.

Jane Wyman's marriage break-up from Ronald Reagan was partly blamed on her intense preparation for this difficult part, although at the time of filming she was often seen in the company of her co-star, Lew Ayres. For authenticity, Miss Wyman had her ears plugged with wax and cotton to block out all sound during filming.

Academy Awards: Best Actress (Jane Wyman)

THE NAKED CITY

1948	
Studio/Distributor:	Universal
Director:	Jules Dassin
Producer:	Mark Hellinger
Screenplay:	Albert Maltz, Malvin Wald
Music:	Miklos Rozsa, Frank Skinner, Milton Schwarzfeld (supervisor)

CAST
Barry Fitzgerald . . . . *Lt Dan Muldoon*
Howard Duff . . . . *Frank Niles*
Dorothy Hart . . . . *Ruth Morrison*
Don Taylor . . . . *Jimmy Halloran*
Ted De Corsia . . . . *Garzah*
House Jameson . . . . *Dr Stoneman*
Anne Sargent . . . . *Mrs Halloran*

Set in New York City, this drama documentary starts when a young girl is violently murdered in her apartment while taking a bath. The police organize a massive manhunt for the killer, headed by Lt Dan Muldoon and his assistant, Jimmy Halloran. With neither motive nor clues, the capture of the assassin seems more and more unlikely. However, Muldoon is a cop who doesn't give up that easily and follows up the remotest of leads.

Many of the exterior scenes were filmed through a one-way window with tinted glass from inside a parked van in order to stop passers-by realizing that a camera was rolling.

Producer Mark Hellinger, who narrates the film himself, had been a famous crime news reporter during the Prohibition era. He ends the film with the cliché 'There are eight million stories in the naked city. This has been one of them.'

Academy Awards: Best Black and White Cinematography (William Daniels), Best Editing (Paul Weatherwax)

OLIVER TWIST

1948	
Studio/Distributor:	GFD
Director:	David Lean
Producer:	Ronald Neame
Screenplay:	David Lean, Stanley Haynes
Music:	Arnold Bax

CAST

Robert Newton . . . . *Bill Sikes*
Alec Guinness . . . . *Fagin*
Kay Walsh . . . . *Nancy*
Francis L. Sullivan . . . . *Mr Bumble*
Mary Clare . . . . *Mrs Corney*
Henry Stephenson . . . . *Brownlow*
John Howard Davies . . . . *Oliver Twist*
Anthony Newley . . . . *Artful Dodger*

This version of the Dickens classic dropped some of the smaller scenes and the more minor char-acters from the story. However, the meat of the story remains intact. It tells the tale of the orphan boy who becomes involved with a pick-pocketing street gang led by Fagin, and the burgler Bill Sikes and his mistress Nancy before finding refuge with Mr Brownlow.

David Lean did not want Alec Guinness for the part of Fagin; he wanted a more sinister looking player. Eventually Guinness persuaded him to allow him to test for the part and arrived in full make-up. It impressed Lean enough to hire him, but the job required Guinness to be in make-up two and a half hours before shooting each day.

David Lean was accused by Jewish pressure groups of being anti-Semitic after the film opened. In Berlin, riots broke out between Jews and police near the Kurbel Theatre, resulting in three arrests.

Video availability

Fagin (Alec Guinness) discusses with young Oliver (John Howard Davies) how to pick a pocket or two in David lean's 1948 version of Oliver Twist.

THE PALEFACE

1948	
Studio/Distributor:	Paramount
Director:	Norman Z. McLeod
Producer:	Robert L. Welch
Screenplay:	Edmund Hartmann, Frank Tashlin, Jack Rose
Music:	Victor Young

CAST
Bob Hope . . . . *'Painless' Peter Potter*
Jane Russell . . . . *Calamity Jane*
Robert Armstrong . . . . *Terris*
Iris Adrian . . . . *Pepper*
Robert Satson . . . . *Toby Preston*
Jack Searl . . . . *Jasper Martin*
Joseph Vitale . . . . *Indian Scout*
Charles Trowbridge . . . *Governor Johnson*

In this comedy Western Bob Hope plays 'Painless' Peter Potter, a timid dentist. He is seduced into marriage by Calamity Jane who is an undercover agent hunting a gang illegally selling rifles to the Indians. When Calamity Jane takes on a feared gunman Potter becomes a hero of the West.

After leaving school, Jane Russell became a chiropodist's assistant and did some part-time modelling. Her big break came when producer Howard Hughes was sent her picture and immediately gave her the leading role in *The Outlaw* (1943). The film did not get a British release until 1946 due to censorship problems.

Academy Awards: Best Song – 'Buttons and Bows' (Jay Livingston and Ray Evans, music and lyrics)

Music: 'Buttons and Bows'

RED RIVER

1948	
Studio/Distributor:	United Artists
Director:	Howard Hawks
Producer:	Charles K. Feldman
Screenplay:	Borden Chase, Charles Schnee
Music:	Dimitri Tiomkin

CAST
John Wayne . . . . *Tom Dunson*
Montgomery Clift . . . . *Matthew Garth*
Joanne Dru . . . . *Tess Millay*
Walter Brennan . . . . *Groot Nadine*
Coleen Gray . . . . *Fen*
John Ireland . . . . *Cherry Valance*
Noah Beery Jr . . . . *Buster McGee*

Tom Dunson and his friend Groot break away from the wagon train on which they are travelling and head off on their own to Texas. They lay claim to a large piece of land and start to build it up. But Tom runs short of money and, against the advice of others, takes his workhands and a herd of cattle on a dangerous route north to Abilene in order to sell the animals and make some money.

Producer Howard Hawks had Gary Cooper in mind to play Tom Dunson but Cooper turned the part down on the grounds that he found the character too ruthless.

John Ireland, who played Cherry Valance, became very close with leading lady Joanne Dru, which annoyed director Howard Hawks who had his eye on her himself. His anger led him to cut out huge scenes which featured Ireland, who in turn had his revenge by marrying Joanne soon after filming was completed.

Video availability

THE RED SHOES

1948			
Studio/Distributor:	GFD	Producer:	Michael Powell, Emeric Pressburger
Director:	Michael Powell, Emeric Pressburger	Screenplay:	Michael Powell, Emeric Pressburger
		Music:	Brian Easdale

Talented composer Julian Craster (Marius Goring) is given the chance to collaborate on a new ballet, The Red Shoes, *with the young ballerina Victoria Page (Moira Shearer).*

CAST
Anton Walbrook . . . . *Boris Lermontov*
Marius Goring . . . . *Julian Craster*
Moira Shearer . . . . *Victoria Page*
Léonide Massine . . . . *Grischa Ljubov*
Robert Helpmann . . . . *Ivan Boleslawsky*
Albert Basserman . . . . *Ratov*
Esmond Knight . . . . *Livy*

Victoria Page is torn between two men in her life, the powerful impresario Boris Lermontov, and a young up-and-coming composer, Julian Craster who she loves. Julian has been commissioned by Boris to co-write a new ballet based on Hans Chris-

tian Andersen's *The Red Shoes*, a story about a magical pair of shoes that enables the wearer to dance magnificently, but unfortunately without the ability to stop.

Filmed in London, Paris and Monte Carlo, the movie ran more than £200,000 over budget, but met with considerable critical acclaim.

Academy Awards: Best Colour Art Direction (Heim Heckroth), Best Set Decoration (Arthur Lawson), Best Scoring of a Drama or Comedy (Brian Easdale)

Video availability

SCOTT OF THE ANTARCTIC

1948	
Studio/Distributor:	Ealing
Director:	Charles Frend
Producer:	Michael Balcon
Screenplay:	Walter Meade, Ivor Montagu, Mary Hayley Bell
Music:	Ralph Vaughan Williams

CAST
John Mills . . . . *Capt. R. Scott*
Diana Churchill . . . . *Kathleen Scott*

Harold Warrender . . . . *Dr E.A. Wilson*
Anne Firth . . . . *Oriana Wilson*
Derek Bond . . . . *Capt. L. Oates*
Reginald Beckwith . . . . *Lt. H.R. Bowers*
James Robertson Justice . . . . . *Taff Evans*
Kenneth More . . . . *Lt. Teddy Evans*

The film begins with explorer Captain Robert Scott attempting to raise money for a second expedition to the Antarctic, having failed once already. Funds are eventually granted to him by the British government and in 1911 he sets off on a quest to be the first to reach the South Pole. With their motor sledges and Siberian ponies and dogs, Scott, Capt. Oates et al befall several disasters. Five men finally make it to their destination, only to discover that they have been beaten by the Norwegians.

The British Museum lent the film-makers some of Scott's personal belongings that he actually took on the expedition, including a pocket watch and a gramophone.

Much of the movie was shot using artificial snow, which proved difficult for the cast to work in.

Video availability

THE THREE MUSKETEERS

1948	
Studio/Distributor:	MGM
Director:	George Sidney
Producer:	Pandro S. Berman
Screenplay:	Robert Ardrey
Music:	Herbert Stothart

CAST
Lana Turner .... *Lady de Winter*
Gene Kelly .... *D'Artagnan*
June Allyson............... *Constance*
Van Heflin .... *Athos*
Angela Lansbury .... *Queen Anne*
Frank Morgan........... *King Louis XIII*
Vincent Price .... *Richelieu*

Keenan Wynn............... *Planchet*

This high-spirited film, based on the Alexandre Dumas novel, has D'Artagnan heading for France to join the Musketeers and help Louis XIII fight against a plot by Cardinal Richelieu and the King's mistress, Countess de Winter, to end his reign. The Musketeers, with their motto *One for all and all for one*, and much derring-do, are not about to allow such a thing to happen.

The popular story of the three Musketeers, which was previously filmed in 1935 and 1939, was remade in 1973 with Oliver Reed, Charlton Heston, Raquel Welch, Faye Dunaway and Richard Chamberlain.

THE BLUE LAMP

Constable Dixon (Jack Warner) is shot dead by villain Tom Riley in The Blue Lamp, *only to be revived six years later for the long-running TV series,* Dixon of Dock Green.

1949	
Studio/Distributor:	Ealing
Director:	Basil Dearden
Producer:	Michael Balcon
Screenplay:	T.E.B. Clarke
Music:	Ernest Irving

CAST
Jack Warner . . . . Constable Dixon
Jimmy Hanley . . . . Constable Mitchell
Dirk Bogarde . . . . Tom Riley
Patric Doonan . . . . Spud
Robert Flemyng . . . . Sgt Roberts
Bernard Lee . . . . Inspector Cherry
Clive Morton . . . . Sgt Brooks
Peggy Evans . . . . Diana Lewis

The young Diana Lewis leaves home and becomes involved with two small-time villains who decide it's time to go for the big haul. They end up trying to avoid a murder rap after Riley, one of the gang, shoots and kills P.C. Dixon. Other underworld criminals help the police capture Riley, who is finally cornered in a busy sports stadium. This exciting police drama was shot entirely on the streets of West London.

This was the movie that introduced us to 'Police Constable 693 George Dixon – attached to Paddington Green', who went on to become the principal character in the long-running TV series *Dixon of Dock Green*, despite being killed off halfway through the film.

Video availability

CHAMPION

1949	
Studio/Distributor:	Stanley Kramer
Director:	Mark Robson
Producer:	Stanley Kramer
Screenplay:	Carl Foreman
Music:	Dimitri Tiomkin

CAST
Kirk Douglas . . . . Midge Kelly
Marilyn Maxwell . . . . Grace Diamond
Arthur Kennedy . . . . Connie Kelly
Paul Stewart . . . . Tommy Haley
Ruth Roman . . . . Emma Bryce
Lola Albright . . . . Mrs Harris ('Palmer')
Luis Van Rooten . . . . Jerome Harris
John Day . . . . Johnny Dunne

With the hope of buying his own diner, Midge Kelly travels to California with his crippled brother, Connie, but ends up working in one instead. He falls for the owner of the diner's daughter, Emma, and after they marry Midge decides to try his luck as a professional boxer. Teaming up with manager Tommy Haley, he becomes a successful and ambitious prizefighter. When he becomes involved with a crime syndicate – the fight racket – he alienates his friends and family. He sacks Haley, leaves his wife and punches out his brother. However, he later pays for his cruelty in the ring.

Kirk Douglas had no previous boxing experience and was taught for the movie by professional fighters during a month's training course.

Academy Awards: Best Editing (Harry Gerstad)

THE GREAT GATSBY

1949	
Studio/Distributor:	Paramount
Director:	Elliott Nugent
Producer:	Richard Maibaum
Screenplay:	Cyril Hume, Richard Maibaum
Music:	Robert Emmett Dolan

CAST
Alan Ladd . . . . Jay Gatsby
Betty Field . . . . Daisy Buchanan
Macdonald Carey . . . . Nick Carraway
Ruth Hussey . . . . Jordan Baker
Barry Sullivan . . . . Tom Buchanan
Howard Da Silva . . . . Wilson
Shelley Winters . . . . Myrtle Wilson
Henry Hull . . . . Dan Cody

The film was based on the F. Scott Fitzgerald novel of the same name. Jay Gatsby from Long Island is a renowned bootlegger with a mysterious past. After making a considerable amount of money, he decides to turn his energies to winning back Daisy, the girl who left him some years earlier in favour of another, far wealthier, man.

Soon after making this picture, Howard Da Silva was blacklisted by movie studios because of alleged Communist connections.

This is the first sound version of the story that was originally made as a silent movie in 1926, starring Warner Baxter in the title role. It was remade again in 1974 with Robert Redford as Jay Gatsby.

Errol Flynn was rumoured to have wanted the part of Gatsby, but the producer decided on Alan Ladd.

JOLSON SINGS AGAIN

1949

Studio/Distributor:	Columbia
Director:	Henry Levin
Producer:	Sidney Buchman
Screenplay:	Sidney Buchman
Music:	George Duning

CAST
Larry Parks . . . . *Al Jolson*
Barbara Hale . . . . *Ellen Clark*
William Demarest . . . . *Steve Martin*
Ludwig Donath . . . . *Cantor Yoelson*
Bill Goodwin . . . . *Tom Baron*
Myron McCormick . . . . *Ralph Bryant*
Tamara Shayne . . . . *Mama Yoelson*

In the sequel to the original 1946 movie (see *The Jolson Story*), Larry Parks once again slips into the successful entertainer's shoes. There's much recapping from the first film in the form of flashback, but here Al Jolson has a new wife. He finds it impossible to sit around at home for too long, and before long finds himself doing what he does best – singing.

The two Jolson pictures revived interest in the singer's career and he staged a comeback. In 1950, a year after the release of the second movie, Jolson toured Korea, entertaining the American troops. He died of a heart attack soon after his return home.

As with the first movie, many of the names of his relations and business associates were changed after they refused permission for their real names to be used.

Music: 'After You've Gone', 'I'm Just Wild about Harry', 'You Made Me Love You', 'Baby Face', 'Sonny Boy', 'My Mammy', 'For Me and My Gal', 'Give My Regards to Broadway', 'Pretty Baby'

Video availability

PASSPORT TO PIMLICO

1949

Studio/Distributor:	Ealing
Director:	Henry Cornelius
Producer:	Michael Balcon
Screenplay:	T.E.B. Clarke
Music:	Georges Auric

CAST
Stanley Holloway . . . . *Arthur Pemberton*
Betty Warren . . . . *Connie Pemberton*
Barbara Murray . . . . . . *Shirley Pemberton*
Paul Dupuis . . . . *Duke of Burgundy*
John Slater . . . . *Frank Huggins*
Jane Hylton . . . . *Molly*
Raymond Huntley . . . . *Mr Wix*
Philip Stainton . . . . *P.C. Spiller*

When an unexploded wartime bomb suddenly goes off, the inhabitants of a small community in London discover an old document that claims their territory still belongs to the Duke of Burgundy. It gives them the right to break away from British rule. Arthur Pemberton is elected head of their new government, with Mr Wix, the local bank manager, as Chancellor of the Exchequer. Ration cards are abolished and new customs established.

This comedy was the only film Henry Cornelius directed for the Ealing Studios. He previously worked as editor on the 1939 movie *The Four Feathers* and later went on to direct the hit *Genevieve* (qv).

Video availability

SAMSON AND DELILAH

1949

Studio/Distributor:	Paramount
Director:	Cecil B. DeMille
Producer:	Cecil B. DeMille
Screenplay:	Jesse L. Lasky Jnr, Frederic M. Frank
Music:	Victor Young

CAST
Hedy Lamarr	*Delilah*
Victor Mature	*Samson*
George Sanders	*The Saran of Gaza*
Angela Lansbury	*Semadar*
Henry Wilcoxon	*Ahtur*
Olive Dearing	*Miriam*
Fay Holden	*Hazelelponit*
Julia Faye	*Hisham*

This biblical epic of Samson and Delilah is probably best remembered for the scenes in which Samson, whose mighty powers are curtailed when he gets a haircut by the scheming Delilah, fights with a vicious lion that appears to be more or less in a coma. He also partakes in a savage battle in which he destroys the Philistine army and its pagan temple with the jawbone of an ass.

Samson and Delilah was Paramount's biggest profit maker to date. It cost $3 million to make but brought in an immediate return of $12 million after its initial release.

Academy Awards: Best Colour Art Direction (Hans Dreier and Walter Tyler), Best Set Decoration (Sam Comer and Ray Moyer), Best Colour Costume Design (Edith Head, Dorothy Jeakins, Eloise Jenssen, Gile Steele and Gwen Wakeling)

Video availability

SANDS OF IWO JIMA

1949	
Studio/Distributor:	Republic
Director:	Allan Dwan
Producer:	Edmund Grainger
Screenplay:	Harry Brown, James Edward Grant
Music:	Victor Young

CAST
John Wayne	*Sgt Stryker*
John Agar	*Pfc. Conway*
Adele Mara	*Allison Bromley*
Forrest Tucker	*Corp. Thomas*
Wally Cassell	*Pfc. Ragazzi*
James Brown	*Pfc. Bass*
Richard Webb	*Pfc. Shipley*
Arthur Franz	*Corp. Dunne*

In this World War II film a young marine (John Agar) finally accepts that he has to knuckle down to military discipline. John Stryker, a tough and ruthless Sergeant with a sympathetic streak, earns respect as he puts his men through their paces in preparation for the war. Stryker leads them into action at Tarawa and Iwo Jima in the Pacific Ocean where he meets his death.

This was John Wayne's first and only Oscar-nominated performance until he received the trophy for *True Grit* (1969).

Thousands of marines based in California took part as extras in the battle scenes. Three of the men who took part in the concluding scene (with the American flag being raised on Mount Suribachi) were present at the actual event.

Video availability

THE THIRD MAN

1949	
Studio/Distributor:	British Lion
Director:	Carol Reed
Producer:	Alexander Korda, David O. Selznick
Screenplay:	Graham Greene
Music:	Anton Karas

CAST
Joseph Cotten	*Holly Martins*
Alida Valli	*Anna*
Orson Welles	*Harry Lime*
Trevor Howard	*Major Calloway*
Bernard Lee	*Sgt Paine*
Paul Hoerbiger	*Porter*
Ernst Deutsch	*'Baron' Kurtz*

Holly Martins, an American novelist, arrives in Vienna to track down his old friend Harry Lime who has promised him a job. On arrival, he learns that not only is Lime dead, but that he had been accused of racketeering. Martins doesn't believe the accusations and has the uneasy feeling that his friend's death was no accident but perhaps murder. Martins decides to make his own enquiries, with the help of Harry Lime's former lover, Anna.

Anton Karas, who wrote and performed the 'Harry Lime Theme', previously played his zither in a

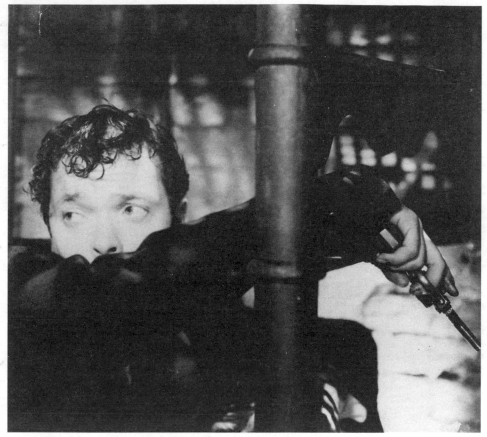

Harry Lime (Orson Welles) in The Third Man *is uncharacteristically feeling the pressure when he is forced to go on the run from both the police and his friend Holly Martins (Joseph Cotten).*

taverna in Vienna. With his royalties, he bought the taverna.

Graham Greene adapted the screenplay from his own novel.

Academy Awards: Best Black and White Cinematography (Robert Krasker)

Music: 'The Harry Lime Theme'

Video availability

12 O'CLOCK HIGH

1949	
Studio/Distributor:	Twentieth Century-Fox
Director:	Henry King
Producer:	Darryl F. Zanuck
Screenplay:	Sy Bartlett, Beirne Ley Jnr
Music:	Alfred Newman

CAST
Gregory Peck . . . . *General Savage*
Hugh Marlowe . . . . *Lt Col Ben Gately*
Millard Mitchell . . . . *General Pritchard*
Dean Jagger . . . . *Major Stovall*

Robert Arthur . . . . *Sgt McIlhenny*
Paul Stewart . . . . *Capt 'Doc' Kaiser*
John Kellogg . . . . *Major Cobb*
Bob Patten . . . . *Lt Bishop*

Told in flashback through the eyes of Major Stovall, this is a World War II story of members of an American bombing platoon based in England. Senior officer Colonel Keith Davenport is replaced by General Savage when the strain of leadership becomes too much and he becomes too involved with his men's problems. His replacement, Savage, initially lives up to his name, but eventually finds he has the same problem as his predecessor.

Years later Gregory Peck disclosed that director Henry King re-wrote entirely the final draft of the screenplay personally.

The character General Frank Savage was based on General Frank A. Armstrong who led the initial daylight attacks on the Germans.

Academy Awards: Best Supporting Actor (Dean Jagger), Best Sound Recording (Thomas T. Moulton)

Video availability

WHITE HEAT

1949	
Studio/Distributor:	Warner
Director:	Raoul Walsh
Producer:	Louis F. Edelman
Screenplay:	Ivan Goff, Ben Roberts
Music:	Max Steiner

CAST

James Cagney . . . . *Cody Jarrett*
Virginia Mayo . . . . *Verna Jarrett*
Edmond O'Brien . . . *Hank Fallon (Vic Pardo)*
Margaret Wycherly . . . . *Ma Jarrett*
Steve Cochran . . . . *'Big Ed' Somers*
John Archer . . . . *Philip Evans*
Wally Cassell . . . . *Cotton Valetti*
Mickey Knox . . . . *Het Kohler*

Unstable gangster Cody Jarrett has a fixation about his mother, who was responsible for driving him to crime. She appears to be the only person who has any influence over his behaviour and when she dies, he goes completely berserk. His psychopathic mind drives him on to ever more vicious crimes until he's caught and put in prison. The Los Angeles police introduce an undercover cop into the prison to end the reign of terror there created by Jarrett and his gang. The classic ending has Jarrett on top of an exploding gas works with his famous cry of *'Made it Ma, top of the world'*.

It was James Cagney's idea to model Cody Jarrett on the real life psychotic, Arthur 'Doc' Parker, son of the notorious Ma Parker.

Director Raoul Walsh once played John Wilkes Booth in the 1915 silent movie *'The Birth of a Nation'*.

Video availability

THE 1950s

The decade began with some of the world's finest actors and actresses giving the performances of their lives. Bette Davis gained another Oscar nomination (seven to date including two wins) for *All About Eve* and Robert Newton stamped his distinctive personality on Robert Louis Stevenson's larger-than-life Long John Silver in *Treasure Island*.

The 1950s was also the decade of the big, brash blockbuster. *The Greatest Show on Earth*, *Around the World in 80 Days*, *Ben Hur* and *The Ten Commandments* literally filled the cinema screen with colour and excitement while war films such as *The Wooden Horse*, *The Dam Busters* and *Reach for the Sky* served as reminders of the not-too-distant past for many moviegoers.

The Western went from strength to strength with directors John Ford and Fred Zinnemann leading the pack early in the decade with *Rio Grande* and *High Noon*. Western musicals were also popular with *Annie Get Your Gun* successfully combining the two genres.

On the musical front Gene Kelly was much in evidence with *An American In Paris* and *Singin' in the Rain*. Screen musicals were also brought bang up to date in the middle of the decade with the emergence of Rock 'n' Roll and the milestone movies *Rock around the Clock* with Bill Haley and *Jailhouse Rock* with Elvis Presley. Home-grown pop stars like Tommy Steele and Cliff Richard were given their first big-screen roles as producers realized the value of these 'teenage' favourites!

Alfred Hitchcock continued to shock with some of his best work, including the memorable *Dial M for Murder*, *Rear Window*, *Vertigo* and *North By Northwest*, and new stars Marlon Brando and James Dean made their mark.

Peter Cushing and Christopher Lee began a long association with Hammer Films who struck it rich with their revival of horror classics Frankenstein and Dracula.

And we can't let the 1950s pass without paying proper homage to that peculiarly British phenomenon, the *Carry On* film. The series began in 1958 with *Carry On Sergeant* and continued making cinemagoers laugh until it finally spluttered to a halt in 1992 with *Carry On Columbus*.

ALL ABOUT EVE

1950

Studio/Distributor:	Twentieth Century-Fox
Director:	Joseph L. Mankiewicz
Producer:	Darryl F. Zanuck
Screenplay:	Joseph L. Mankiewicz
Music:	Alfred Newman

CAST

Bette Davis	*Margo Channing*
Anne Baxter	*Eve*
George Sanders	*Addison De Witt*
Celeste Holm	*Karen*
Gary Merrill	*Bill Simpson*
Hugh Marlowe	*Lloyd Richards*
Thelma Ritter	*Birdie*
Marilyn Monroe	*Miss Casswell*
Gregory Ratoff	*Max Fabian*

Margo Channing is an ageing actress who befriends Eve, a young female fan who is keen to make it in the business. She takes the girl into her home, but in return Channing expects the girl to work for her. She soon finds out that Eve is slowly taking over her life and her men. The film's success was largely due to the well-crafted script, which contained lines of savage wit and one of the most quoted lines from the movies: *'Fasten your seat belts, it's going to be a bumpy night!'*

With a total of 14 Oscar nominations, *All About Eve* holds the record for being the most nominated film. *From Here to Eternity*, *Judgment at Nuremberg* and *Mary Poppins* all come a close second with 13 nominations each.

Davis fell in love with Gary Merrill during the making of the movie and they subsequently married.

Academy Awards: Best Film (Director Darryl F. Zanuck), Best Direction (Joseph L. Mankiewicz), Best Supporting Actor (George Sanders), Best Screenplay (Joseph L. Mankiewicz), Best Black and White Costume Design (Edith Head and Charles LeMaire), Best Sound Recording (W.D. Flick and Roger Heman)

Video availability

Eve (Anne Boucher) is determined not only to steal the limelight from Margo (Bette Davis), but also her man, in the somewhat risqué movie for its time, All About Eve.

ANNIE GET YOUR GUN

1950

Studio/Distributor: MGM
Director: George Sidney
Producer: Arthur Freed
Screenplay: Sidney Sheldon
Music: Irving Berlin (music and lyrics)
Adolph Deutsch (direction)

CAST
Betty Hutton .... *Annie Oakley*
Howard Keel .... *Frank Butler*
Louis Calhern .... *Buffalo Bill*
J. Carrol Naish .... *Chief Sitting Bull*
Edward Arnold .... *Pawnee Bill*
Keenan Wynn .... *Charlie Davenport*
Benay Venuta .... *Dolly Tate*
Clinton Sundberg .... *Foster Wilson*

The film version of the smash Broadway musical tells the story of Annie Oakley who falls for top marksman Frank Butler but ends up beating him in a shooting contest which drives him away. The smart Indian chief, Sitting Bull, suggests that she let Butler win the next contest. The advice seems to work as she gets her man and her gun.

The making of the film was plagued with problems. Judy Garland, who had already shot some scenes and recorded the soundtrack album, had to be replaced as Annie when she became ill. Howard Keel broke his ankle, holding up production, and Frank Morgan who had been cast as Buffalo Bill, unexpectedly died and the role was taken over by Louis Calhern. The film was a big hit, however, and its success prompted MGM to launch a programme of further high budget musicals.

Betty Hutton did not see too much more Hollywood success after *Annie Get Your Gun*. She walked out of a contract with Paramount in 1952 because they wouldn't allow her husband to direct her films. In 1967 she filed for bankruptcy after being married and divorced five times, and ended up working as a cook.

Academy Awards: Best Scoring of a Musical (Adolph Deutsch and Roger Edens)

Music: 'There's No Business Like Show Business', 'They Says it's Wonderful', 'Anything You Can Do, I Can Do Better', 'Doin' What Comes Natur'lly', 'You Do Something to Me', 'The Girl That I Marry'

CINDERELLA

1950

Studio/Distributor: Walt Disney
Director: Wilfred Jackson, Hamilton Luske, Clyde Geronimi
Producer: Ben Sharpsteen (Production Supervisor)
Screenplay: from original story by Charles Perrault
Music: Oliver Wallace, Paul Smith (Direction)
Mack David, Jerry Livingston, Al Hoffman (Songs)

CAST (Voices)
Ilene Woods .... *Cinderella*
William Phipps .... *Prince Charming*
Eleanor Audley .... *Stepmother*
Rhoda Williams .... *Anastasia*
Lucille Bliss .... *Drusilla*
Verna Felton .... *Fairy Godmother*
Luis van Rooten ...... *King, Grand Duke*
James MacDonald ..... *Jacques, Gus-Gus*

The Disneyfication of the classic tale of a poor young girl, bullied by her two ugly step-sisters. However, she ends up marrying the handsome prince with the help of a fairy godmother and a lost slipper. To expand the storyline Disney introduced extra animal cartoon characters.

The singing voice of Prince Charming was provided by Mike Douglas, a popular American TV chat show host.

Music: 'Cinderella', 'Bibbidi-Bobbidi-Boo', 'A Dream Is a Wish Your Heart Makes', 'The Work Song', 'So This is Love'

FATHER OF THE BRIDE

1950	
Studio/Distributor:	MGM
Director:	Vincente Minnelli
Producer:	Pandro S. Berman
Screenplay:	Frances Goodrich,
	Albert Hackett
Music:	Adolph Deutsch

CAST

Spencer Tracy . . . . *Stanley T. Banks*
Joan Bennett . . . . *Ellie Banks*
Elizabeth Taylor . . . . *Kay Banks*
Don Taylor . . . . *Buckley Dunstan*
Billie Burke . . . . *Doris Dunstan*
Leo G. Carroll . . . . *Mr Massoula*
Moroni Olsen . . . . *Herbert Dunstan*
Melville Cooper . . . . *Mr Tingle*

Told in flashback, Stanley T. Banks relates the cost and chaos of the wedding of his daughter Kay. The meeting with his future son-in-law, the planning, the in-laws, the decisions, the party plans, and finally the reflection when all the celebrations are over and his daughter has left for her honeymoon.

Jack Benny was tested for the role of Father at the request of the studio's Head of Production, Dore Schary. This knowledge prompted Spencer Tracy to refuse the role, but was finally talked into it by director Vincente Minnelli.

A remake of the movie, starring Steve Martin and Diane Keaton, became a number one in 1992.

Elizabeth Taylor had recently become a bride in real life, having just married Nicky Hilton. MGM capitalized on this in publicity for the film.

Video availability

One of Kay Banks's (Elizabeth Taylor) many suitors, Buckley Dunstan (Don Taylor), manages to win the hand of the woman he loves in Father of the Bride.

DESTINATION MOON

1950			
		Screenplay:	Rip Van Ronkel, R.A.
			Heinlein, James
Studio/Distributor:	Universal		O'Hanlon
Director:	Irving Pichel	Music:	Leith Stevens
Producer:	George Pal		

CAST
Warner Anderson ... *Dr Charles Cargraves*
John Archer .... *Jim Barnes*
Tom Powers .... *General Thayer*
Dick Wesson .... *Joe Sweeney*
Erin O'Brien Moore ..... *Emily Cargraves*
Ted Warde .... *Brown*

A group of American scientists ignore the familiar cries of *'Impossible!'* from their unadventurous colleagues and prepare a spaceship for a voyage that will hopefully take them to the moon before the Russians. They make it, but then face the problem of getting home when they discover that their rocket is too heavy to lift off from the moon's surface.

Woody Woodpecker makes a special guest appearance in the film to explain the workings of rocket propulsion.

It took 100 men over two months to build the film's moonscape.

Academy Awards: Best Special Effects (Lee Zavitz and George Pal)

THE HAPPIEST DAYS OF YOUR LIFE

1950	
Studio/Distributor:	British Lion
Director:	Frank Launder
Producer:	Frank Launder, Sidney Gilliat
Screenplay:	Frank Launder, John Dighton
Music:	Mischa Spoliansky

CAST
Alistair Sim........... *Wetherby Pond*
Margaret Rutherford.... *Miss Whitchurch*
John Turnbull........ *Conrad Matthews*
Richard Wattis.......... *Arnold Billings*
Guy Middleton...... *Victory Hyde-Brown*
Arthur Howard....... *Anthony Ramsden*
John Bentley .... *Richard Tassell*
Edward Rigby............. *Rainbow*

This British comedy has a girls' school being closed down due to a blunder at the Ministry of Education. All the students end up sharing the facilities in an all-boys college with the staff attempting to hide the situation from visiting parents. A rip-roaring farce with no shortage of typical English humour.

This was the movie that launched a series of St. Trinian's farces for writer, producer and director Frank Launder. Other films in the series included *The Belles of St. Trinians* (1954), *Blue Murder at St. Trinians* (1957), *The Pure Hell of St. Trinians* (1960) and *The Great St. Trinians Train Robbery* (1966).

Joyce Grenfell's mother was always unhappy about her daughter playing an overgrown schoolgirl and thought she should look more attractive to men in her movies.

Video availability

KING SOLOMON'S MINES

1950	
Studio/Distributor:	MGM
Director:	Compton Bennett, Andrew Marton
Producer:	Sam Zimbalist
Screenplay:	Helen Deutsch
Music:	Mischa Spoliansky

CAST
Deborah Kerr .... *Elizabeth Curtis*
Stewart Granger ..... *Allan Quartermain*
Richard Darlson .... *John Goode*
Hugo Haas .... *Smith*
Lowell Gilmore .... *Eric Masters*

Allan Quartermain, an African hunter, escorts Elizabeth Curtis and her brother John through dangerous parts of the jungle. They escape animal stampedes and hostile natives as they search for her missing husband who disappeared while on an expedition to find the much soughtafter treasures hidden in King Solomon's Mines.

The president of Uganda at the time, Godfrey Binaisa, was given a cameo role in the movie. He later appeared in *The African Queen*.

Stewart Granger's real name was James Stewart. He had to change it when he began his career in movies to avoid confusion.

Academy Awards: Best Colour Cinematography (Robert Surtees), Best Editing (Ralph E. Winters and Conrad A. Nervig)

PERFECT STRANGERS

1950

Studio/Distributor: MGM
Director: Bretaigne Windust
Producer: Jerry Wald
Screenplay: Edith Sommer
Music: Leigh Harline

CAST
Ginger Rogers .... Terry Scott
Dennis Morgan .... David Campbell
Thelma Ritter .... Lena Fassler
Margalo Gillmore........ Isobel Bradford
Anthony Ross............ Robert Fisher
Howard Freeman .... Timkin

Alan Reed .... Harry Patulle
Paul Ford .... Judge Byron

In this comedy-drama Ginger Rogers and Dennis Morgan play two jurors – Terry Scott and David Campbell – at a murder trial. Scott, who is married with two children, and Campbell, a divorcé, fall in love with each other. The tension of their relationship is heightened when they have to decide on the fate of a man whose deserted wife insisted on a divorce but is later found dead at the bottom of a cliff. Was she pushed or did she fall?

A film of the same name was released in 1945, starring Robert Donat and Deborah Kerr. However, the two films have nothing to do with each other.

TREASURE ISLAND

1950

Studio/Distributor: RKO/Walt Disney
Director: Byron Haskin
Producer: Perce Pearce
Screenplay: Lawrence E. Watkin
Music: Clifton Parker

CAST
Bobby Driscoll .... Jim Hawkins
Robert Newton .... Long John Silver
Basil Sydney .... Captain Smollett
Walter Fitzgerald ...... Squire Trelawney
Denis O'Dea .... Doctor Livesey
Ralph Truman............ George Merry
Finlay Currie............ Captain Bones

The Disney studio's version of the Robert Louis Stevenson tale follows the adventures and treachery experienced by a young boy on the high seas. He joins members of a ship's crew in search of treasure after being given information of its whereabouts by a dying pirate. They encounter the notorious Long John Silver and his band of buccaneers as mutiny prevails amongst the men.

Their first non-animated picture, Disney decided to change the original ending, and certain scenes were cut because of violence when the film was re-issued in 1975.

Two silent versions of the story were previously filmed in 1917 and 1920. In both instances the character Jim Hawkins was played by a female.

Video availability

THE WOODEN HORSE

1950

Studio/Distributor: British Lion
Director: Jack Lee
Producer: Ian Dalrymple
Screenplay: Eric Williams
Music: Clifton Parker

CAST
Leo Genn .... Peter
David Tomlinson .... Phil
Anthony Steel .... John

David Greene .... Bennett
Peter Burton.................... Nigel
Patrick Waddington.. Senior British Officer
Michael Goodliffe .... Robbie
Anthony Dawson............. Pomfret

In this World War II film a team of three British officers, held captive in a German high-security prison, plan their escape by building a tunnel. They cover up their laborious digging by constructing a wooden horse which they use in the yard for vaulting exercises. They build their escape path underneath the horse in which they hide just before

In The Wooden Horse *British POWs use the horse for more than exercise when they conceal themselves underneath to make good their escape from the prison.*

they slip away, complete with forged papers. They head for the sea port and board a boat bound for Copenhagen and freedom.

Leo Genn was a practising barrister before making his stage debut as an actor in 1930. After the war, he acted as assistant prosecutor, investigating crimes committed in the Belsen concentration camp.

The film features an early appearance by Peter Finch, who began his career in show business as a vaudeville stooge.

Video availability

THE AFRICAN QUEEN

1951

Studio/Distributor:	IFD
Director:	John Huston
Producer:	S.P. Eagle (Sam Spiegel)
Screenplay:	James Agee, John Huston
Music:	Allan Gray

CAST
Humphrey Bogart . . . . *Charlie Allnut*
Katharine Hepburn . . . . *Rose Sayer*
Robert Morley . . . . *Brother*
Peter Bull . . . . *Captain*
Theodore Bikel . . . . *1st Officer*
Walter Gotell . . . . *2nd Officer*
Gerald Onn . . . . *Petty Officer*
Peter Swanwick . . . . *1st Officer*
Richard Marner . . . . *2nd Officer*

At the start of World War I, Charlie Allnut, a cowardly drunk, uses his badly battered river launch to transport supplies to small East African villages. He is persuaded to take the prim Rose Sayer on a dangerous mission, using his little craft as a torpedo to sink a German boat that is halting the British invasion. They battle through the elements, the dangerous wildlife and against each other before they are captured by the Germans. A happy ending finds them getting married and successfully completing their mission.

This was Bogart's only Oscar-winning performance, and the first time movie fans were able to see him in colour.

During filming, Katharine Hepburn kept her cool in the difficult African locations, but Bogart and director John Huston would partake in long drinking sessions, telling dirty jokes. For all that, they all remained good friends.

Both John Mills and David Niven were considered for the part of Charlie Allnut, as were Deborah Kerr and Bette Davis for the role of Rose.

Academy Awards: Best Actor (Humphrey Bogart)

Video availability

ALICE IN WONDERLAND

1951

Studio/Distributor: Walt Disney
Director: Clyde Geronimi, Hamilton Luske, Wilfred Jaxon
Producer: Ben Sharpsteen (supervisor)
Screenplay: Various
Music: Oliver Wallace

CAST (Voices)
Kathryn Beaumont .... Alice
Ed Wynn .... Mad Hatter
Richard Haydn .... Caterpillar
Sterling Holloway .... Cheshire Cat
Jerry Colonna .... March Hare
Verna Felton .... Queen of Hearts
Pat O'Malley .... Walrus, Carpenter, Dee and Dum

The Disney animated interpretation of Lewis Carroll's famous story includes most of Alice's better adventures. It includes the Mad Hatter's tea party and the smoking caterpillar who writes the alphabet in the air. Some of the less important scenes and characters were omitted from this movie version but parts of *Through The Looking Glass* were added.

Disney considered making the picture as a live action movie with Mary Pickford playing the lead.

The film was five years in the making and initially cost over $1 million, but ended up making a profit.

Seven songwriters contributed to the score, including two-times Oscar winner Sammy Fain and eight-times Oscar nominee Mack David.

Music: 'I'm Late', 'The Unbirthday Song', 'Very Good Advice', 'The Walrus and the Carpenter'

Video availability

AN AMERICAN IN PARIS

1951

Studio/Distributor: MGM
Director: Vincente Minnelli
Producer: Arthur Freed
Screenplay: Alan Jay Lerner
Music: Johnny Green (Director) George and Ira Gershwin (Songs)

CAST
Gene Kelly .... Jerry Mulligan
Leslie Caron .... Lise
Oscar Levant .... Adam Cook
Georges Guetary .... Henri Baurel
Nina Foch .... Milo Roberts
Eugene Borden .... Georges Mattieu

This musical set in Paris starts when former G.I. turned art student Jerry Mulligan meets Lise, a

dancer rescued from the Nazis during the war by Jerry's friend Henry. Milo Roberts, a wealthy playgirl who helps Jerry sell his paintings to her friends, wants him as one of her many lovers. However, Jerry is already falling for Lise, who is engaged to Henry and tells him they must not see each other again. After much singing and dancing and a stunning ballet sequence at an Arts Ball, Henri leaves the way open for Lise and Jerry to get together.

Gene Kelly's 18-minute dance finale took two months to rehearse and another month to film at a cost of $450,000, using several different directors. It is, however, believed that this sequence convinced Academy voters to make it the first musical since *Broadway Melody* (1929) to win the Oscar for Best Film.

Director Vincente Minnelli originally wanted Maurice Chevalier to play the part of Henri Baurel. Some say he was unavailable at the time, while others claim he turned down the part because he didn't get the girl.

This was Leslie Caron's movie debut. She was discovered at the age of 15 by Gene Kelly when he was in Paris.

Academy Awards: Best Film (Producer Arthur Freed), Best Story and Screenplay (Alan Jay Lerner), Best Colour Cinematography (Alfred Gilks and John Alton), Best Colour Art Direction (Cedric Gibbons and Preston Ames), Best Set Decoration (Edwin B. Willis and Keogh Gleason), Best Colour Costume Design (Orry-Kelly, Walter Plunkett and Irene Sharaff), Best Scoring of a Musical (Johnny Green and Saul Chaplin)

Music: 'An American in Paris', 'Nice Work If You Can Get It', 'Embraceable You', 'Fascinating Rhythm', 'I Got Rhythm', 'S'Wonderful', 'Love Walked In', 'I've Got a Crush On You'

Video availability

Painter and art student Jerry Mulligan (Gene Kelly) meets dancer Lise (Leslie Caron) in An American in Paris.

THE GREAT CARUSO

1951	
Studio/Distributor:	MGM
Director:	Richard Thorpe
Producer:	Joe Pasternak, Jesse L. Lasky
Screenplay:	Sonya Levien, William Ludwig
Music:	Johnny Green (Supervisor)

CAST
Mario Lanza . . . . *Enrico Caruso*
Ann Blyth . . . . *Dorothy Benjamin*
Dorothy Kirsten . . . . *Louise Heggar*
Jarmila Novotna . . . . *Maria Selka*
Richard Hageman . . . . *Carlo Santi*
Carl Benton Reid . . . . *Park Benjamin*
Eduard Franz . . . . *Giulio Gatti-Casazza*

This rags to riches bio-pic, with as much fiction as fact, tells the story of Enrico Caruso. The son of poor Italian peasants, he spends his early life earning money singing in local cafés, which sets him on his road to fame. Packed with 27 well-loved operatic arias, the film also tells of his parents' disapproval of his romance and subsequent marriage.

Mario Lanza claimed in many press interviews that Caruso was the inspiration for his own career, and on the film set was often heard saying that he was Caruso. He became impossible with his rudeness and arrogance on the film set, refusing to bathe and going on constant drinking sprees after being warned about his weight problem.

Director Richard ('One-Take') Thorpe later went on to direct another great singer, Elvis Presley, in *Jailhouse Rock* (1957) and *Fun In Acapulco* (1963).

Academy Awards: Best Sound Recording (Douglas Shearer).

Music: 'Vesti la Giubba', 'Ave Maria', 'The Loveliest Night of the Year', 'Because', 'Mattinata', 'La Donna é Mobile'

Video availability

THE LADY WITH A LAMP

1951

Studio/Distributor: British Lion
Director: Herbert Wilcox
Producer: Herbert Wilcox
Screenplay: Warren Chetham-Strode
Music: Anthony Collins

CAST
Anna Neagle ...... *Florence Nightingale*
Michael Wilding ..... *Hon. Sidney Herbert*
Gladys Young .... *Mrs Braccbridge*
Felix Aylmer .... *Lord Palmerston*
Julian D'Albie .... *Mr Braccbridge*
Arthur Young .... *Rt. Hon. W.E. Gladstone*

Edwin Styles .... *Mr Nightingale*

This was the film version of the true story of Florence Nightingale. She is born into a wealthy family, but, instead of having a life of leisure, insists on pursuing a nursing career. She is commissioned to head up a team of nurses to help the wounded in Scutari during the Crimean War. Battling disease and appalling conditions, the nurses provide much needed comfort and care for the injured British soldiers.

After completion of the film, Michael Wilding was released from his contract with the production company owned by Anna Neagle and Herbert Wilcox in order to go and live in America with his new fiancée, Elizabeth Taylor.

THE LAVENDER HILL MOB

1951

Studio/Distributor: Ealing
Director: Charles Crichton
Producer: Michael Balcon, Michael Truman
Screenplay: T.E.B. Clarke
Music: Georges Auric

CAST
Alec Guinness .... *Holland*
Stanley Holloway .... *Pendlebury*
Sidney James .... *Lackery*
Alfie Bass .... *Shorty*
Marjorie Fielding .... *Mrs Chalk*
Edie Martin .... *Miss Evesham*
John Salew .... *Parkin*
Ronald Adam .... *Turner*

This Ealing comedy classic sees Henry Holland, a quiet, unassuming bank clerk, hatching a scheme

to steal a truck loaded with gold bullion. He enlists the help of two small-time villains and his old friend Pendlebury, a paperweight manufacturer. After the successful hijack, Pendlebury hides the gold by melting it down and turning it into miniature Eiffel Towers, but crime proves once again not to pay.

In the opening scene you can get a quick look at a very young Audrey Hepburn and later the young child actor James Fox, who was then billed as William.

The film contains a parody of a car chase from an earlier Ealing hit, *The Blue Lamp* (1949).

Alec Guinness was Oscar-nominated for his role of mousy Henry Holland.

Academy Awards: Best Story and Screenplay (T.E.B. Clarke)

Video availability

QUO VADIS

1951	
Studio/Distributor:	MGM
Director:	Mervyn LeRoy
Producer:	Sam Zimbalist
Screenplay:	John Lee Mahin, S.N. Behrman, Sonya Levien
Music:	Miklos Rozsa

CAST
Robert Taylor . . . . *Marcus Vinicius*
Deborah Kerr . . . . *Lygia*
Leo Genn . . . . *Petronius*
Peter Ustinov . . . . *Nero*
Patricia Laffan . . . . *Poppaea*
Finlay Currie. . . . . *Peter*
Abraham Sofaer. . . . . *Paul*
Marina Berti . . . . *Eunice*

The biblical movie hit of 1951 is set in Rome during the reign of the barbaric Emperor Nero. The heroic army commander Marcus Vinicius attempts to make Lygia, a Christian, his mistress while the persecution of six hundred other Christian hostages continues (they are released into the den of 120 lions). Spectacular sequences include chariot races, gladiatorial contests, battles, rampaging bulls and the aforementioned deadly lions.

The film took over a year to make and featured thousands of extras, including an unknown fifteen-year-old girl called Sophia Loren. Peter Ustinov was nominated for an Oscar as Best Supporting Actor for his role as the Emperor Nero, but lost out to Karl Malden who won for *A Streetcar Named Desire*.

Video availability

SHOWBOAT

1951	
Studio/Distributor:	Universal
Director:	George Sidney
Producer:	Arthur Freed
Screenplay:	John Lee Mahin
Music:	Jerome Kern Oscar Hammerstein II (song lyrics)

CAST
Kathryn Grayson . . . . *Magnolia Hawks*
Ava Gardner. . . . . *Julie Laverne*
Howard Keel . . . . *Gaylord Ravenal*
Joe E. Brown . . . . *Captain Andy Hawks*
Marge Champion . . . . *Ellie May Shipley*
Gower Champion. . . . . *Frank Schultz*
Robert Sterling . . . . *Stephen Baker*

This film version of the classic Broadway musical recounts the lives and troubles of Mississippi showboat folk. The young Magnolia runs off with hardened gambler turned showman Gaylord Ravenal. They eventually marry, but he finds that his addiction to gambling ruins their relationship. Magnolia returns to the boat to have their baby and several years later manages a reconciliation.

A special boat was constructed for this production, at a cost of over $125,000. It was over 170 feet long and almost 60 feet high.

P.G. Wodehouse wrote the new lyrics to the song 'Bill'.

Music: 'Make Believe', 'Can't Help Lovin' dat Man', 'Ol' Man River', 'You are Love', 'After the Ball', 'Why do I Love You?'

Video availability

STRANGERS ON A TRAIN

1951	
Studio/Distributor:	Warner
Director:	Alfred Hitchcock
Producer:	Alfred Hitchcock
Screenplay:	Raymond Chandler, Czenzi Ormonde
Music:	Dimitri Tiomkin

CAST
Farley Granger . . . . *Guy Haines*
Ruth Roman . . . . *Anne Morton*
Robert Walker . . . . *Bruno Antony*
Leo G. Carroll . . . . *Senator Morton*
Patricia Hitchcock . . . . . . *Barbara Morton*
Laura Elliott . . . . *Miriam*
Marion Lorne . . . . *Mrs Antony*

Murder and intrigue by the master of suspense, Alfred Hitchcock, in Strangers on a Train. *Two strangers meet by chance on a train, leading to the violent murder of a young woman.*

Jonathan Hale . . . . *Mr Antony*
Howard St John . . . . *Capt. Turley*

A gripping suspense-thriller from Alfred Hitchcock. Guy Haines and Bruno Antony are two total strangers who meet on a train journey and have a discussion about their personal problems. Guy is married but wants to divorce and re-marry a senator's daughter, only his wife is standing in his way, while Bruno is stuck with an unpleasant father. Bruno suggests a scenario in which they would be rid of their problems by each murdering the other's trouble-maker. Neither man would be suspected, with no motive and a secure alibi. Guy finds the whole idea ludicrous but Bruno goes ahead and carries out his part of the deal, murdering Guy's wife. To Guy's horror, he finds he is now expected to return the 'favour' and is suspected of murdering his wife.

Hitchcock originally wanted William Holden to play Guy, but was more than happy with Granger who was under contract to the studio.

Alfred Hitchcock's daughter, Patricia, plays Anne Morton's inquisitive sister Barbara.

Video availability

TOM BROWN'S SCHOOLDAYS

1951	
Studio/Distributor:	RKO
Director:	Gordon Parry
Producer:	George Minter
Screenplay:	Noel Langley
Music:	Richard Addinsell

CAST
John Howard Davies . . . . *Tom Brown*
Robert Newton . . . . *Doctor Arnold*
Diana Wynyard . . . . *Mrs Arnold*
Francis De Wolff . . . . *Squire Brown*
Kathleen Byron . . . . *Mrs Brown*
Hermione Baddeley . . . . . . *Sally Harrowell*

James Hayter . . . . *Old Thomas*
Rachel Gurney . . . . *Mrs Arthur*

Based on the Thomas Hughes novel, the film is an account of the hazardous life in a Victorian public boys' school. Life improves with the arrival of new pupil Tom Brown, who takes on Flashman, (played by John Forrest), the school bully. Dr Arnold then arrives, taking up the post of headmaster, and shows somewhat more humanity towards the boys than other members of staff.

The movie features a young Max Bygraves in an early film role.

Hermione Baddeley went on to great success on TV in the 1970s as Mrs Bridges, the cook, in the long-running *Upstairs Downstairs*.

Video availability

THE GREATEST SHOW ON EARTH

1952	
Studio/Distributor:	Paramount
Director:	Cecil B. DeMille
Producer:	Cecil B. DeMille
Screenplay:	Frederic M. Frank, Barre Lyndon, Theodore St John
Music:	Victor Young

CAST
Betty Hutton . . . . *Holly*
Cornel Wilde . . . . *Sebastian*
Charlton Heston . . . . *Brad*
Dorothy Lamour . . . . *Phyllis*
Gloria Grahame . . . . *Angel*
James Stewart . . . . *Buttons the Clown*
Henry Wilcoxon . . . . *FBI Man*
Lyle Bettger . . . . *Klaus*

This circus drama has the Ringling Brothers, Barnum and Bailey, with all the thrills and spills of the big top extravaganza together with the behind-the-scenes life of the performers. There's lovesick trapeze artist, Holly, who is keen on Brad, the circus manager who is also being pursued by Angel, the elephant girl, and 'Buttons' the clown, who is never seen without his make-up as he's on the run from the law.

This was Cecil B. DeMille's 69th film as a director. At the time he had just reached his 70th birthday.

The film includes uncredited cameo appearances by Bob Hope and Bing Crosby as members of the audience enjoying peanuts as they watch the show. It also featured real-life Barnum and Bailey circus acts.

Academy Awards: Best Film (Producer Cecil B. DeMille), Best Motion Picture Story (Frederick M. Frank, Theodore St John and Frank Cavett)

Video availability

HANS CHRISTIAN ANDERSEN

1952	
Studio/Distributor:	Samuel Goldwyn
Director:	Charles Vidor
Producer:	Samuel Goldwyn
Screenplay:	Moss Hart
Music:	Walter Scharf (Director) Frank Loesser (Music and Lyrics)

CAST
Danny Kaye . . . . . *Hans Christian Andersen*
Farley Granger . . . . *Niels*
Zizi Jeanmaire . . . . *Doro*
Joey Walsh . . . . *Peter*
Philip Tonge . . . . *Otto*
John Brown . . . . *Schoolmaster*
John Qualen . . . . *Burgomaster*

Jeanne Lafayette . . . . *Celine*

This fictional tale bears little resemblance to the true life story of the Danish master of fairy tales, Hans Christian Andersen. In the movie he is a cobbler who is deeply in love with Doro, a beautiful ballerina. But instead of finding happiness with her, he takes off with his faithful companion, Peter, in search of fame and fortune as a writer and teller of children's stories.

The people of Denmark slated the film even before it had opened on the grounds that the movie had turned the life story of their hero into another kind of fairy tale. When it opened, however, it was a huge success. The movie cost over $4 million to produce, with $400,000 of the budget being spent on the 17-minute ballet sequence, $175,000 to Danny Kaye,

$14,000 on shoes for the cast and thousands more on 21 completed but rejected manuscripts.

Gary Cooper was the original choice for the starring role. Moira Shearer was chosen as Doro, the ballerina, but became pregnant and was replaced by Zizi Jeanmaire.

Danny Kaye's song from the movie, 'Wonderful Copenhagen', was his only British hit.

Music: 'The King's New Clothes', 'The Ugly Duckling', 'Wonderful Copenhagen', 'Thumbelina', 'Inchworm', 'Anywhere I Wander'

Video availability

HIGH NOON

1952	
Studio/Distributor:	Stanley Kramer
Director:	Fred Zinnemann
Producer:	Stanley Kramer
Screenplay:	Carl Foreman
Music:	Dimitri Tiomkin

CAST

Gary Cooper	*Will Kane*
Thomas Mitchell	*Jonas Henderson*
Lloyd Bridges	*Harvey Pell*
Katy Jurado	*Helen Ramirez*
Grace Kelly	*Amy Kane*
Otto Kruger	*Percy Mettrick*
Lon Chaney	*Martin Howe*
Henry Morgan	*Sam Fuller*

In this tense Western drama Marshal Will Kane has to deal with a gang of outlaws who are out to kill him. The outlaws organize the attack on the day he's planning to leave town for good after marrying his bride, Amy. But Kane gets no help from the cowardly townspeople. The gang, headed by Frank Miller, who Kane had sent to prison some years earlier, are due to arrive in town at high noon. The clock ticks as the hour approaches.

During filming, Gary Cooper was suffering with a perforated ulcer as well as a hip injury. Some say the pain was reflected in his face.

Charlton Heston and Marlon Brando were both offered the lead before it went to Gary Cooper.

Academy Awards: Best Actor (Gary Cooper), Best Editing (Elmo Williams and Harry Gerstad), Best Music Score of a Drama or Comedy (Dimitri Tiomkin), Best Song – 'High Noon' ('Do Not Forsake Me, Oh My Darlin'') (Dimitri Tiomkin, music; Ned Washington, lyrics)

Music: 'High Noon' ('Do Not Forsake Me, Oh My Darlin'')

Video availability

Will Kane (Gary Cooper) has a heart to heart talk with Martin Howe (Lon Chaney Jnr) as the clock ticks towards High Noon *in Fred Zinneman's classic western.*

IVANHOE

1952	
Studio/Distributor:	MGM
Director:	Richard Thorpe
Producer:	Pandro S. Berman
Screenplay:	Noel Langley, Aeneas MacKenzie
Music:	Miklos Rozsa

CAST
Robert Taylor .... Ivanhoe
Elizabeth Taylor .... Rebecca
Joan Fontaine .... Rowena
George Sanders .... DeBois-Guilbert
Emlyn Williams .... Wamba
Robert Douglas .... Sir Hugh De Bracy
Finlay Currie................... Cedric
Felix Aylmer.................. Isaac

In an adaptation of Sir Walter Scott's work the gallant Sir Wilfred of Ivanhoe attempts to raise money in order to free King Richard from an Austrian prison where he is being held for ransom. When he rescues the rich Jew, Isaac, from the Normans, Isaac's grateful daughter, Rebecca, with more than an eye for the knight, finances him to take part in a jousting contest to raise more money for the ransom.

Ivanhoe became the most expensive movie ever produced in England at that time, due largely to the fact that MGM had accumulated so much money in British banks which they were unable to take out of the country because of Government restrictions.

Video availability

LIMELIGHT

1952	
Studio/Distributor:	United Artists
Director:	Charles Chaplin
Producer:	Charles Chaplin
Screenplay:	Charles Chaplin
Music:	Charles Chaplin

CAST
Charles Chaplin .... Calvero
Claire Bloom................... Terry
Sydney Chaplin .... Neville
André Eglevsky .... Harlequin
Melissa Hayden .... Columbine

Calvero, once a big comedy star of the British music hall, is reduced to a downtrodden alcoholic, living alone in London in 1914. He meets Terry, a ballet dancer, who suffers such severe depression over her lack of success that she attempts suicide. Calvero decides to help with her career, and as Terry's popularity rises, he too makes a short-lived comeback.

This was the first major movie appearance for Claire Bloom, although she had previously appeared in the 1948 film *Blind Goddess* starring Eric Portman. It was also Chaplin's first film since the boycotted *Monsieur Verdoux* (1947).

Charles Chaplin's son, Sydney, has a major role in the movie as Neville, a young composer. Another of Chaplin's sons, Charles Jnr, plays a clown, and three street urchins, who make a brief appearance, are played by Josephine, Geraldine and Michael Chaplin.

Academy Awards: Best Original Dramatic Score (Charles Chaplin, Raymond Rasch and Larry Russell)

Music: 'Theme from Limelight'

Video availability

MANDY

1952	
Studio/Distributor:	Ealing
Director:	Alexander Mackendrick
Producer:	Michael Balcon
Screenplay:	Nigel Balchin, Jack Whittingham
Music:	William Alwyn

CAST
Phyllis Calvert .... Christine
Jack Hawkins .... Searle
Terence Morgan .... Harry
Godfrey Tearle .... Mr Garland
Mandy Miller .... Mandy
Marjorie Fielding .... Mrs Garland
Edward Chapman .... Ackland

Mandy is the story of a deaf and dumb girl. Her parents are faced by a dilemma when they are made to choose between keeping her at home and sending her to a special school where she can be taught to lip-read. Headmaster Searle patiently helps Mandy to learn to communicate with other people.

Mandy Miller is probably best remembered for her recording of the popular children's favourite 'Nellie the Elephant'.

This was Jack Hawkins's first leading role for Ealing Studios.

MOULIN ROUGE

1952

Studio/Distributor:	Romulus
Director:	John Huston
Producer:	Jack Clayton
Screenplay:	John Huston, Anthony Veiller
Music:	Georges Auric

CAST

José Ferrer	*Toulouse-Lautrec*
Colette Marchand	*Marie Charlet*
Suzanne Flon	*Myriamme*
Zsa Zsa Gabor.	*Jane Avril*
Katherine Kath	*La Goulue*
Claude Nollier	*Countess de Toulouse-Lautrec*

This bio-pic depicts the life of the 19th-century deformed art genius Henri Toulouse-Lautrec, whose growth is stunted after he is involved in a hunting accident in his childhood. His unhappy life turns him into an alcoholic. He ends up spending a considerable amount of time in Parisian establishments of ill repute, where he is humiliated by a prostitute. When he finally meets a woman who really cares for him, he is unable to reciprocate her affection.

José Ferrer had to wear a special harness, which painfully strapped his legs back in order for him to wear his shoes on his knees.

The film features an early movie appearance by Zsa Zsa Gabor, the former Miss Hungary of 1936, as Jane Avril. Peter Cushing and Christopher Lee also have minor roles.

Academy Awards: Best Colour Art Direction (Paul Sheriff), Best Set Decoration (Marcel Vertes), Best Colour Costume Design (Marcel Vertes)

Music: 'The Moulin Rouge Theme'

Video availability

THE QUIET MAN

1952

Studio/Distributor:	Republic
Director:	John Ford
Producer:	John Ford, Merian C. Cooper
Screenplay:	Frank S. Nugent
Music:	Victor Young

CAST

John Wayne	*Sean Thornton*
Maureen O'Hara	*Mary Kate Danaher*
Barry Fitzgerald	*Michaeleen Flynn*
Ward Bond	*Father Lonergan*
Victor McLaglen	*'Red' Will Danaher*
Mildred Natwick	*Mrs Tillane*
Francis Ford	*Robin*
Eileen Crowe	*Mrs Playfair*

Wealthy farmer Sean Thornton is a quiet man, and, after retiring from boxing (where he'd killed an opponent in the ring), returns to his native Ireland to buy a plot of land and the cottage where he was born. The purchase displeases 'Red' Will Danaher, who wanted the land for himself. Thornton then falls for Danaher's sister and wants to marry her, but needs Danaher's blessing, which is not forthcoming. However, Thornton tricks Danaher and marries Mary. The two men end up brawling through the village streets and pubs, but they eventually gain respect for each other and become friends.

Director John Ford's brother, Francis Ford, appeared in the film, as did his son-in-law, Ken Curtis. Four of John Wayne's children also had parts.

Academy Awards: Best Direction (John Ford), Best Color Cinematography (Winton C. Hoch and Archie Stout)

Video availability

*Having given up his career as a boxer and returned to Ireland, Sean Thornton prepares to marry
Mary Kate Danaher (Maureen O'Hara) but is frustrated by Irish shenanigans in* The Quiet Man.

SINGIN' IN THE RAIN

1952	
Studio/Distributor:	MGM
Director:	Gene Kelly, Stanley Donen
Producer:	Arthur Freed
Screenplay:	Betty Comden, Adolph Green
Music:	Lennie Hayton (Director)

CAST

Gene Kelly	*Don Lockwood*
Donald O'Connor	*Cosmo Brown*
Debbie Reynolds	*Kathy Selden*
Jean Hagen	*Lina Lamont*
Millard Mitchell	*R.F. Simpson*
Cyd Charisse	*Guest Artist*
Rita Moreno	*Zelda Zanders*
Douglas Fowley	*Roscoe Dexter*

Singin' in the Rain is the musical story of Holly-wood's transition period from the silent movies to the talkies. It deals with the problems of performers who were fine on the big screen until they opened their mouths. Lina Lamont, the romantic on-screen partner of film star Don Lockwood, is discovered to have a squeaky voice. Her other problem is that she tries to carry the screen romance into real life, but Don has his eyes on the silky-voiced Kathy. The stunning song-and-dance routines include Donald O'Connor's terrific 'Make 'em Laugh' number.

With the exception of two songs specially written for the movie, 'Fit As A Fiddle' and 'Moses Supposes', all the numbers had been previously featured in earlier MGM musicals. Even the title song originally cropped up in the movie *Hollywood Review of 1939.*

During a dress rehearsal for the famous title song, the water was switched on but produced only a slow dribble; it was bath time and the residents of Culver City were all using the water supply at the time.

The film had its own share of difficulties with the voices of its stars. Debbie Reynolds's speaking voice was considered to have too much of a Texan drawl. Jean Hagen, who played an actress with a high squeaky voice in the movie, used her natural tones to dub Miss Reynolds's lines, who in the film was supposed to be dubbing for her. The song 'Would You', sung by Debbie, was dubbed by Betty Noyes.

Music: 'All I do is Dream of You', 'Singin' in the Rain', 'Make 'em Laugh', 'You were Meant for Me', 'Moses Supposes', 'You Are My Lucky Star', 'Broadway Melody', 'Broadway Rhythm'

Video availability

Don Lockwood (Gene Kelly) is just 'Singin' in the Rain', one of the most memorable scenes from a Hollywood movie.

SNOWS OF KILIMANJARO

1952	
Studio/Distributor:	Twentieth Century-Fox
Director:	Henry King
Producer:	Darryl F. Zanuck
Screenplay:	Casey Robinson
Music:	Bernard Herrmann

CAST

Gregory Peck	*Harry*
Susan Hayward	*Helen*
Ava Gardner	*Cynthia*
Hildegarde Neff	*Countess Liz*
Leo G. Carroll	*Uncle Bill*
Torin Thatcher	*Johnson*
Ava Norring	*Beatrice*
Helene Stanley	*Connie*

Based on Ernest Hemingway's novel, the *Snows of Kilimanjaro* has wealthy writer Harry Street on the verge of death on an African plain beneath the mountain of Kilimanjaro. Hallucinating, with his wife by his side, he relieves his youth, living in France and falling in love with Cynthia, the subject of his first novel. Other memories include brief affairs with Connie, adventures while big-game hunting and involvement in the Spanish Civil War.

Ernest Hemingway hated the film because he thought producer Darryl F. Zanuck had made too many changes. He claimed the movie should have been called 'The Snows Of Zanuck'.

Video availability

CALAMITY JANE

1953			
		Screenplay:	James O'Hanlon
		Music:	Ray Heindorf (Director)
Studio/Distributor:	Warner		Original Songs: Sammy
Director:	David Butler		Fain (music), Paul
Producer:	William Jacobs		Francis Webster (lyrics)

Doris Day in Calamity Jane *followed in the footsteps of Betty Hutton, who appeared in* Annie Get Your Gun.

CAST

Doris Day . . . . *Calamity Jane*
Howard Keel . . . . *Wild Bill Hickock*
Allyn McLerie . . . . *Katie Brown*
Philip Carey . . . . *Lt Gilmartin*
Dick Wesson . . . . *Francis Fryer*
Paul Harvey . . . . *Henry Miller*
Chubby Johnson . . . . *Rattlesnake*
Gale Robbins . . . . *Adelaide Adams*

Calamity Jane spends much of her time in this musical Western proving that she is as good as any man, which doesn't go a long way to impress Wild Bill Hickock. He only realizes that plain Jane isn't so plain when she decides to dress and behave more like a woman.

The song 'Secret Love' was a number one hit in the UK singles chart for Doris Day.

Academy Awards: Best Song – 'Secret Love' (Sammy Fain, music; Paul Francis Webster, lyrics)

Music: 'The Deadwood Stage', 'The Black Hills of Dakota', 'A Woman's Touch', 'Tis Harry I'm Plannin' to Marry', 'Secret Love'

Video availability

CALL ME MADAM

1953

Studio/Distributor: **Twentieth Century-Fox**
Director: **Walter Lang**
Producer: **Sol C. Siegel**
Screenplay: **Arthur Sheekman**
Music: **Irving Berlin**
    Alfred Newman
    (Musical Direction)

CAST

Ethel Merman . . . . *Mrs Sally Adams*
Donald O'Connor . . . . *Kenneth*
Vera-Ellen . . . . *Princess Maria*
George Sanders . . . . . . *Cosmo Constantine*
Billy De Wolfe . . . . . . *Pemberton Maxwell*
Helmut Dantine . . . . *Prince Hugo*

Loosely based on the hit Broadway musical, *Call Me Madam* is the story of Perle Mesta, 'The hostess with the mostes' from Washington DC. Sally Adams is appointed the Ambassadress to the mythical kingdom of Lichtenberg, where she loses her heart to an important general, who is the minister for foreign affairs and about to become her husband.

This was the only singing role in the movies for George Sanders. Vera-Ellen's singing voice was dubbed by Carole Richards. Ethel Merman's own voice can be heard in the movie, although Dinah Shore sang her part on early copies of the RCA soundtrack recording.

Academy Awards: Best Scoring of a Musical (Alfred Newman)

Music: 'The Hostess with the Mostes", 'It's a Lovely Day Today', 'Marrying for Love', 'Something to Dance About', 'You're Just in Love'

FROM HERE TO ETERNITY

1953

Studio/Distributor: **Columbia**
Director: **Fred Zinnemann**
Producer: **Buddy Adler**
Screenplay: **Daniel Taradash**
Music: **George Duning**

CAST

Burt Lancaster . . . . *Sgt Milton Warden*
Montgomery Clift . . *Robert E. Lee Prewitt*
Deborah Kerr . . . . *Karen Holmes*
Donna Reed . . . . *Lorene*
Frank Sinatra . . . . *Angelo Maggio*
Philip Ober . . . . *Capt. Dana Holmes*
Mickey Shaughnessy . . . . *Sgt. Leva*
Ernest Borgnine . . . . *Sgt 'Fatso' Judso*

In this tense World War II army drama Robert E. Lee Prewitt is transferred to barracks at Pearl Harbor where he finds himself under the command of the mean Captain Holmes. He has his eye on becoming a bugler, and is told the position is his if he joins the boxing team. He refuses and instead is given the worst tasks available in the company. The lives and loves of those on the base, including the steamy affair between Sgt. Warden and Karen Holmes, come to an abrupt halt on 7 December 1941 when the Japanese launch their attack on the barracks and base.

The picture picked up eight Academy Awards, the greatest amount won by a single film since *Gone With The Wind*, which won eight plus a special award.

Joan Crawford was originally set to play Karen Holmes, and although it was widely reported that she turned the part down, it is believed that she fell out with studio boss Harry Cohn over her wardrobe demands and was replaced by Deborah Kerr.

Academy Awards: Best Film (Producer Buddy Adler), Best Direction (Fred Zinnemann), Best Supporting Actor (Frank Sinatra), Best Supporting Actress (Donna Reed), Best Screenplay (Daniel Taradash), Best Black and White Cinematography (Burnett Guffey), Best Sound Recording (John P. Livadary), Best Editing (William Lyon)

Video availability

GENEVIEVE

1953	
Studio/Distributor:	GFD
Director:	Henry Cornelius
Producer:	Henry Cornelius
Screenplay:	William Rose
Music:	Larry Adler

CAST
John Gregson . . . . *Alan McKim*
Dinah Sheridan . . . . *Wendy McKim*
Kenneth More . . . . . *Ambrose Claverhouse*
Kay Kendall . . . . *Rosalind Peters*
Geoffrey Keen . . . . *First Speed Cop*
Harold Siddons . . . . . . *Second Speed Cop*

In this British comedy Alan and Wendy McKim are the owners of 'Genevieve', a 1904 Darracq vintage car. Together with Ambrose Claverhouse and girlfriend Rosalind, another pair of classic car enthusiasts, they enter their old crocks in the famous annual London to Brighton car rally. For the journey home they decide to have a friendly race against each other, which becomes rather intense and a little out of hand as they race for the finishing line at Westminster Bridge.

Kay Kendall looked set to become a major movie star after the success of *Genevieve*, but her career was cut short when she died of leukaemia six years later.

The British Film Academy voted *Genevieve* the best film of 1953.

Video availability

THE HOUSE OF WAX

1953	
Studio/Distributor:	Warner
Director:	Andre de Toth
Producer:	Bryan Foy
Screenplay:	Crane Wilbur
Music:	David Buttolph

CAST
Vincent Price . . . . *Professor Jarrod*
Frank Lovejoy . . . . *Lt Brennan*
Phyllis Kirk . . . . *Sue Allen*
Carolyn Jones . . . . *Cathy Gray*
Paul Picerni . . . . *Scott Andrews*
Roy Roberts . . . . *Matthew Burke*
Angela Clarke . . . . *Mrs Andrews*
Paul Cavanagh . . . . *Sidney Wallace*
Dabbs Greer . . . . *Sgt Shane*
Charles Buchinsky . . . . *Igor*
Reggie Rymal . . . . *Barker*

The action takes place inside a New York wax museum run by Matthew Burke and his sinister partner, Professor Henry Jarrod, obsessed by his sculptures. Because the business is losing money, Burke burns the building down in order to collect the insurance money. Jarrod is believed to have perished in the fire, but turns up badly scarred and kills his partner. He rebuilds the museum but injuries force him to hire two assistants to create new life-like models, which he achieves by pouring hot wax over human bodies.

This was the first major movie filmed in 3-D and is packed full of gimmicks, including chairs appearing to be thrown into the audience and villains popping out of the screen. Director Andre De Toth was unable to appreciate the 3-D effect, however, as he had only one eye.

Charles Buchinsky, who plays the deaf-mute Igor, is Charles Bronson. He changed his name the following year.

Video availability

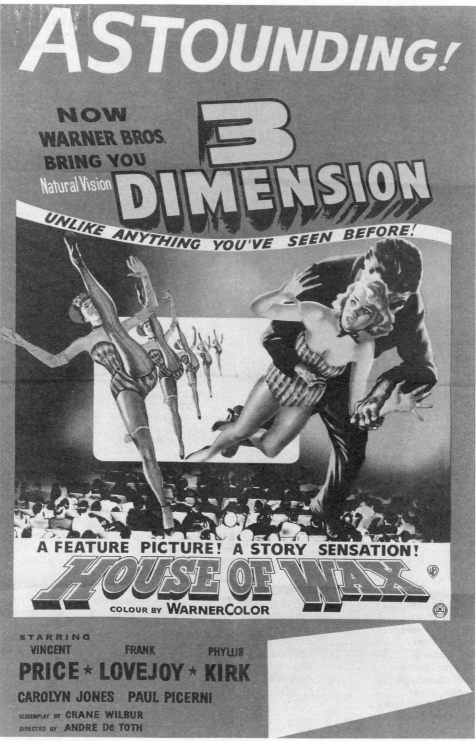

In Warner Brother's first major feature film shot in 3-D, House of Wax, Professor Henry Jarrod (Vincent Price) has his wax museum destroyed by fire after a violent row with his unscrupulous partner Matthew Burke (Roy Roberts).

HOW TO MARRY A MILLIONAIRE

1953	
Studio/Distributor:	Twentieth Century-Fox
Director:	Jean Negulesco
Producer:	Nunnally Johnson
Screenplay:	Nunnally Johnson
Music:	Cyril Mockridge

CAST

Betty Grable	*Loco*
Marilyn Monroe	*Pola*
Lauren Bacall	*Schatze Page*
David Wayne	*Freddie Denmark*
Rory Calhoun	*Eben*
Cameron Mitchell	*Tom Brookman*
Alex D'Arcy	*J. Stewart Merrill*
Fred Clark	*Waldo Brewster*

This colourful comedy has three unattached women going out on the town after setting themselves up in an expensive apartment in New York. Their intention is to find themselves wealthy husbands. They each trap an unsuspecting bachelor, none of whom meet the specifications the women had when they first started their hunt. Eventually all three come to the same conclusion that money isn't everything.

Marilyn Monroe lived in a world of her own during the making of the movie, and made little contact with the rest of the cast and crew when the camera wasn't rolling. Betty Grable at this time was Twentieth Century-Fox's biggest star, but was soon eclipsed by Marilyn Monroe.

Video availability

Schatze Page (Lauren Bacall) and Pola (Marilyn Monroe) are on the look out for unattached, wealthy men in How To Marry a Millionaire.

PETER PAN

1953			
		Director:	Hamilton Luske, Clyde Geronimi, Wilfred Jackson
Studio/Distributor:	Walt Disney		
Producer:	Walt Disney		
Screenplay:	various	Music:	Oliver Wallace

CAST (Voices)
Bobby Driscoll . . . . *Peter Pan*
Kathryn Beaumont . . . . *Wendy*
Hans Conried . . . . *Hook, Mr Darling*
Bill Thompson . . . . *Smee*
Tom Conway . . . . *Narrator*

Disney produced this charming cartoon interpretation of the James M. Barrie story of the boy who never grew up. Peter Pan takes the three Darling children, Wendy, John and Michael, on a flight across London to Never Never Land with the help of his sidekick, the fairy Tinker Bell. Here they embark on numerous adventures, including the battle with Captain Hook and his pirates. They also encounter the clock-swallowing crocodile, an In-dian tribe and The Lost Boys, before returning to the safety of their home.

One of the more popular songs, 'Never Smile at a Crocodile', has since been cut from the film and now only appears in instrumental form.

Disney originally filmed a live action version of the film in order to give his animators something on which to base their drawings.

Music: 'You Can Fly', 'The Elegant Captain Hook', 'A Pirate's Life', 'Never Smile at a Crocodile'

Video availability

ROMAN HOLIDAY

1953	
Studio/Distributor:	Paramount
Director:	William Wyler
Producer:	William Wyler
Screenplay:	Ian McLellan Hunter, John Dighton
Music:	Georges Auric

CAST
Gregory Peck . . . . *Joe Bradley*
Audrey Hepburn . . . . *Princess Anne*
Eddie Albert . . . . *Irving Radovich*
Hartley Power . . . . *Mr Hennessy*
Harcourt Williams . . . . *Ambassador*
Margaret Rawlings . . . *Countess Vereberg*

Princess Anne is tired of all her royal European engagements and when she arrives in Rome with her over-protective entourage, she slips unnoticed out of the palace where she's staying. By chance she meets Joe Bradley, a reporter who has been trying to get an interview with her. Realizing who she is, he offers to show her round the city, all the time having photographs taken for his newspaper. He ends up hiding her in his apartment from the authorities who are by now concerned about the disappearance of the princess.

Frank Capra was originally intended as director, but he was unable to find a suitable actress to play the Princess. When William Wyler took over, he wanted Elizabeth Taylor for the role, but MGM refused to release her from her contract.

When Audrey Hepburn was hired, the studio requested that she change her name so she wouldn't be confused with Katharine. She refused, but the studio finally backed down.

Ian McLellan Hunter co-scripted *Roman Holiday* with John Dighton, but the 'story' for the film was conceived by the blacklisted writer Dalton Trumbo. Hunter 'fronted' for Trumbo and ended up winning an Oscar – Best Motion Picture Story – for someone else's work. Trumbo did receive belated credit for his work, almost 40 years later, when the Writers Guild of America determined that Trumbo was responsible for the screen story. Ironically, Hunter was subsequently blacklisted.

Academy Awards: Best Actress (Audrey Hepburn), Best Motion Picture Story (Ian McLellan Hunter; see above), Best Black and White Costume Design (Edith Head)

Video availability

SHANE

1953	
Studio/Distributor:	Paramount
Director:	George Stevens
Producer:	George Stevens
Screenplay:	A.B. Guthrie Jr, Jack Sher
Music:	Victor Young

CAST
Alan Ladd . . . . *Shane*
Jean Arthur . . . . *Mrs Starrett*
Van Heflin . . . . *Mr Starrett*
Brandon De Wilde . . . . *Joey Starrett*
Jack Palance . . . . *Wilson*
Ben Johnson . . . . *Chris*
Edgar Buchanan . . . . *Lewis*
Emile Meyer . . . . *Ryker*

Shane is a mysterious retired gunslinger who rides through the town of Wyoming and meets the Starrett family. They are struggling to protect their land from the greedy cattle baron Ryker and his gang of killers. The family give Shane a job as a ranch hand, but Mrs Starrett and her son Joey both show great affection for him as he helps fight off Ryker.

The film climaxes with a showdown between Shane and hired killer Wilson.

Western star Jack Palance was Oscar nominated as Best Supporting Actor for this role, losing out to Anthony Quinn in *Viva Zapata*. Palance was actually uncomfortable with horses around him and had to do several takes of the scenes which involved him climbing on or off the animals. Many years later Palance won an Academy Award for Best Supporting Actor in the comedy *City Slickers* (1991), in which he spent a lot of time on horseback.

Academy Awards: Best Colour Cinematography (Loyal Griggs)

Video availability

THE WAR OF THE WORLDS

1953	
Studio/Distributor:	Paramount
Director:	Byron Haskin
Producer:	George Pal
Screenplay:	Barre Lyndon
Music:	Leith Stevens

CAST
Gene Barry . . . . *Clayton*
Ann Robinson . . . . *Sylvia*
Les Tremayne . . . . *Gen. Mann*
Bob Cornthwaite . . . . *Dr Pryor*
Sandro Giglio . . . . *Dr Bilderbeck*
Lewis Martin . . . . *Pastor Collins*

Strange spider-like creatures from Mars pay an unwelcome visit to Earth in
The War of the Worlds.

A major science fiction picture of the 1950s, the film was adapted from the H.G. Wells novel, but moved the action from 19th-century London to 20th-century Los Angeles. A huge object lands in a field in California from which emerges a giant spider-like creature with a long neck. The creature uses its heat ray in an orgy of destruction as it becomes apparent that Earth has been invaded by Martians.

Producer George Pal discovered that Paramount had owned the rights to this story since 1925, but had for many years lost interest in filming it. He resurrected the project and brought it to the silver screen.

The film was narrated by Sir Cedric Hardwicke.

Gordon Jennings won a posthumous Oscar for his special effects. He died soon after filming had been completed.

Academy Awards: Best Special Effects (Paramount Studios)

Video availability

THE CAINE MUTINY

1954	
Studio/Distributor:	Columbia
Director:	Edward Dmytryk
Producer:	Stanley Kramer
Screenplay:	Stanley Roberts
Music:	Max Steiner

CAST
Humphrey Bogart . . . . *Captain Queeg*
José Ferrer . . . . *Lt Barney Greenwald*
Van Johnson . . . . *Lt Steve Maryk*
Fred MacMurray . . . . *Lt Tom Keefer*
Robert Francis . . . . *Ensign Willie Keith*
May Wynn . . . . *May Wynn*
Tom Tully . . . . *Captain DeVriess*
Arthur Franz . . . . *Lt Paynter*
E.G. Marshall . . . . *Lt Cdr Challee*

A fter many years at sea, Captain Queeg is beginning to feel the toll of war. Lieutenant Keefer is aware of the captain's shortcomings, which he points out to the rest of the crew, suggesting that their leader is no longer worthy of his position. Lieutenant Steve Maryk enforces an old marine law, which allows the second in charge to take command in the event of an emergency situation. On their return to the homeland, he is court martialled for his actions, but Queeg goes to pieces in the witness box, giving credence to Maryk's actions.

Robert Francis, who played Willie Keith, was killed in a plane crash the year after the picture was released, at the age of just 25.

Look out for Lee Marvin in an early role as 'Meatball'.

Music: 'I Can't Believe that You're in Love with Me' (Jimmy McHugh, Clarence Gaskill), 'Yellowstain Blues' (Fred Karger, Herman Wouk)

Video availability

THE DAM BUSTERS

1954	
Studio/Distributor:	Associated British
Director:	Michael Anderson
Producer:	Robert Clark,
	W.A. Whitaker
Screenplay:	R.C. Sherriff
Music:	Eric Coates, Leighton
	Lucas

CAST
Michael Redgrave . . . . *Dr B.N. Wallis*
Ursula Jeans . . . . *Mrs Wallis*
Stanley Van Beers . . . . *Sir David Pye*
Raymond Huntley *Physical Laboratory Official*
Hugh Manning . *Aircraft Production Official*
Patrick Barr . . . . *Capt Joseph Summers*
Basil Sydney . . . . *Air Chief Marshal*

D uring World War II, a small fleet of British airforce planes, carrying Dr Barnes Wallis's new invention, the 'bouncing bomb', successfully complete a raid on the previously impregnable Ruhr dams. They cut off the water supply essential to German factories and cause complete havoc with the Nazi war programme. Meticulous preparation pays off for the aerial bombers who manage to hit their target with pinpoint accuracy.

Warner Brothers, the American distributors of the film, were not over-interested in the movie for the USA. When they finally released it, they made severe edits, which caused questions to be raised in the House of Commons.

Music: 'The Dam Busters March'

Video availability

In The Dam Busters, *a small brigade of British air force pilots, led by Wing Commander Guy Gibson (Richard Todd) and armed with Barnes Wallis's new bouncing bombs, successfully destroy Germany's Ruhr dams.*

DIAL M FOR MURDER

1954

Studio/Distributor:	Warner
Director:	Alfred Hitchcock
Producer:	Alfred Hitchcock
Screenplay:	Frederick Knott
Music:	Dimitri Tiomkin

CAST

Ray Milland	*Tony Wendice*
Grace Kelly	*Margot Wendice*
Robert Cummings	*Mark Halliday*
John Williams	*Inspector Hubbard*
Anthony Dawson	*Capt. Leggate*
Patrick Allen	*Pearson*
George Leigh	*Williams*

Based on Frederick Knott's stage play, *Dial M for Murder* has wealthy Margot Wendice married to retired tennis pro Tony. He believes she is about to leave him for novelist Mark Halliday. Unwilling to be parted from his wife's money, Tony blackmails an old friend, Captain Leggate, into agreeing to murder his wife while he finds himself a perfect alibi. Unfortunately the plan goes horribly wrong and Margot ends up killing Leggate. A police investigation follows, and, although Tony thinks he has covered all his tracks, the clever Chief Inspector Hubbard tricks Tony into a compromising situation, and saves Margot from the gallows.

Hitchcock has been credited with launching Grace Kelly's career with this movie. Prior to this major role, she was constantly hired out to other studios by MGM, who had shown little interest in her talent. Hitchcock looked upon the film as something for him to do while he was waiting to begin work on *Rear Window*.

All Grace Kelly movies are now banned in Monaco by order of Prince Rainier because he finds films made by his late wife too upsetting.

Video availability

DOCTOR IN THE HOUSE

1954

Studio/Distributor: Rank
Director: Ralph Thomas
Producer: Betty E. Box
Screenplay: Nicholas Phipps
Music: Bruce Montgomery

CAST

Dirk Bogarde . . . . *Simon Sparrow*
Muriel Pavlow . . . . *Joy*
Kenneth More . . . . *Grimsdyke*
Donald Sinden . . . . *Benskin*
Kay Kendall . . . . *Isobel*
James R. Justice . . . . *Sir Lancelot*
Donald Houston . . . . *'Taffy'*
Suzanne Cloutier . . . . *Stella*

*D*octor in the House was the first of a successful series of British 'Doctor' comedies. At the be-ginning of his five-year slog at medical school Simon Sparrow is taken in hand by three older students – Grimsdyke, Benskin and Taffy – who have all failed their initial exams. With many things on their minds, least of all medicine, they come under the scrutiny of the aggressive Sir Lancelot, the hospital's Head of Medicine.

Dirk Bogarde initially turned down the part as Simon Sparrow, but his agent convinced him it would be a good career move.

Sequels included *Doctor at Sea* (1955), *Doctor at Large* (1957), *Doctor in Love* (1960), *Doctor in Distress* (1963), *Doctor in Clover* (1966) and *Doctor in Trouble* (1970). Bogarde left the series after *Doctor in Distress*.

Video availability

THE GLENN MILLER STORY

1954

Studio/Distributor: Universal
Director: Anthony Mann
Producer: Aaren Rosenberg
Screenplay: Valentine Davies, Oscar Brodney
Music: Joseph Gershenson, Henry Mancini

CAST

James Stewart . . . . *Glenn Miller*
June Allyson . . . . *Helen Miller*
Charles Drake . . . . *Don Haynes*
George Tobias . . . . *Si Schribman*
Henry Morgan . . . . . . *Chummy MacGregor*
Frances Langord . . . . *Herself*
Louis Armstrong . . . . *Himself*

*J*ames Stewart led this true story of the highly successful bandleader whose plane went missing during World War II. Miller spends many years searching for a blend of instruments that will give his band an individual sound, which he finds by accident when he splits his lip and is forced to allow the clarinet player to take over the lead on 'Moonlight Serenade'. His popularity explodes when he plays for the troops overseas after enlisting in the army.

Although James Stewart didn't actually play the trombone in the movie, he was determined to look as though he was. He took lessons from Joe Yukl, who wanted to quit teaching Stewart because he claimed the noises he was making with the instrument were causing him to swear at his wife when he went home. However, Yukl agreed to continue and Stewart eventually improved.

Academy Awards: Best Sound Recording (Leslie I. Carey)

Music: 'Moonlight Serenade', 'Tuxedo Junction', 'Little Brown Jug', 'St. Louis Blues', 'In the Mood', 'String of Pearls', 'Pennsylvania 6 5000', 'American Patrol', 'Basin Street Blues', 'Otchi-tchor-hi-ya'

Video availability

ON THE WATERFRONT

1954

Studio/Distributor:	Columbia
Director:	Elia Kazan
Producer:	Sam Spiegel
Screenplay:	Budd Schulberg
Music:	Leonard Bernstein

CAST

Marlon Brando	Terry Malloy
Karl Malden	Father Barry
Lee J. Cobb	Johnny Friendly
Rod Steiger	Charley Malloy
Pat Henning	'Kayo' Dugan
Eva Marie Saint	Edie Doyle
Leif Erickson	Glover
James Westerfield	Big Mac

Failed boxer Terry Malloy gets caught up in the battle between the dock workers of New Jersey and the corrupt unions. Johnny Friendly is the dockland boss who pays Terry, the brother of his dubious lawyer, Johnny, to run errands for him. Johnny gets Terry to inadvertently set up the murder of a worker. His feelings for the dead man's sister, Edie, and his relationship with Father Barry force him to take action against Friendly.

On completion, Marlon Brando announced that he was unhappy with the picture and walked out of the first screening. After that he cut off all contact with director Elia Kazan, but his mood seemed to change after he won an Oscar for his performance. The movie, which cost just under $1 million to make, made a return of over $9 million.

Frank Sinatra really wanted to play Terry, but after being considered, the role went to Brando who was thought to be a bigger attraction at the time. Ironically the film was made on location in Sinatra's birthplace, Hoboken, New Jersey.

Academy Awards: Best Film (Producer Sam Spiegel), Best Direction (Elia Kazan), Best Actor (Marlon Brando), Best Supporting Actress (Eva Marie Saint), Best Story and Screenplay (Budd Schulberg), Best Black and White Cinematography (Boris Kaufman), Best Black and white Art Direction (Richard Day), Best Editing (Gene Milford)

Video availability

REAR WINDOW

1954

Studio/Distributor:	Paramount
Director:	Alfred Hitchcock
Producer:	Alfred Hitchcock
Screenplay:	John Michael Hayes
Music:	Franz Waxman

CAST

James Stewart	Jeff Jeffries
Grace Kelly	Lisa Fremont
Wendell Corey	Thomas J. Doyle
Thelma Ritter	Stella
Raymond Burr	Lars Thorwald
Judith Evelyn	Miss Lonely Hearts
Ross Bagdasarian	Song writer
Georgine Darcy	Miss Torso

The second Hitchcock hit of the year again featured Grace Kelly. Jeff Jeffries is a news photographer confined to his apartment with a broken leg in plaster. He finds there is nothing to do all day except look out of his rear window. His neighbours include Miss Lonely Hearts, yearning for a man in her life, a honeymoon couple and a song composer along with other interesting singles and duos. But he begins to suspect that one of his neighbours, Lars Thorwald, has murdered his wife. He calls Lisa, a young model who is in love with him, to help investigate.

Grace Kelly, who was one of Hitchcock's favourite actresses, had the part specially written for her in the film. Her character never appeared in Cornell Woolrich's original story.

The set for the apartment block was at the time one of the biggest ever constructed on Paramount's lot, containing 31 separate apartments.

Video availability

GRACE **KELLY** · WENDELL **COREY** · co-starring THELMA **RITTER**

with   Directed by   Screenplay by
RAYMOND BURR · ALFRED HITCHCOCK · JOHN MICHAEL HAYES

BASED ON THE SHORT STORY BY CORNELL WOOLRICH · A PARAMOUNT PICTURE

Most of the action in Alfred Hitchcock's Rear Window *takes place in a single courtyard apartment, in which Jeff (James Stewart) is confined with a broken leg.*

SEVEN BRIDES FOR SEVEN BROTHERS

1954

Studio/Distributor:	MGM
Director:	Stanley Donen
Producer:	Jack Cummings
Screenplay:	Albert Hackett, Frances Goodrich, Dorothy Kingsley
Music:	Adolph Deutsch (Director)

CAST

Howard Keel .... Adam
Jeff Richards .... Benjamin
Russ Tamblyn .... Gideon
Tommy Rall................... Frank
Marc Platt................... Daniel
Matt Mattox .... Caleb
Jacques d'Amboise .... Ephraim
Jane Powell .... Milly
Julie Newmeyer .... Dorcas
Nancy Kilgas .... Alice
Betty Carr.................... Sarah
Virginia Gibson .... Liza
Ruta Kilmonis................. Ruth
Norma Doggett .... Martha
Ian Wolfe .... Revd. Elcott

Howard Petrie .... Pete Perkins

In this rousing musical Adam Pontabee, the oldest of seven brothers who live in Oregon, marries a waitress named Milly and takes her back to the family ranch. The other brothers decide they too are in need of female company and each of them bring home local girls whom they've kidnapped. They are all snowed in for the winter, and by spring the parents of the girls have come up with a plan for a group wedding.

It was usual for Broadway musicals to become films, but it was the film of *Seven Brides for Seven Brothers* that spawned a Broadway musical.

Julie Newmeyer later changed her name to Newmar and went on to appear as Catwoman in the TV series *Batman*.

Academy Awards: Best Scoring of a Musical (Adolph Deutsch and Saul Chaplin)

Music: 'Bless your Beautiful Hide', 'Wonderful Wonderful Day', 'When You're in Love', 'Lonesome Polecat', 'Spring, Spring, Spring'

Video availability

20,000 LEAGUES UNDER THE SEA

1954

Studio/Distributor:	Walt Disney
Director:	Richard Fleischer
Producer:	Walt Disney
Screenplay:	Earl Fenton
Music:	Bernhard Kaun

CAST

Kirk Douglas .... Ned Land
James Mason .... Captain Nemo
Paul Lukas .... Professor Aronnax
Peter Lorre .... Conseil
Robert J. Wilke........ Mate on Nautilus
Carleton Young .... John Howard
Ted de Corsia .... Captain Farragut
Percy Helton................... Diver

Walt Disney adapted Jules Verne's classic novel set in the late 19th century for the big screen.

A scare is running through seafarers in San Francisco over reports that a giant monster is roving about the sea, destroying any ship that goes near it. The government send out a warship to investigate, which is promptly sunk by the monster. Three survivors are picked up by the *Nautilus*, a submarine commanded by Captain Nemo. *Nautilus* and the giant octopus battle it out underwater.

When he was first offered the part of Captain Nemo, James Mason turned it down on the grounds that he didn't feel the Disney studios had enough experience in making live action films and the end result would not be sufficiently adult in its concept. But he was wrong.

Academy Awards: Best Colour art Direction (John Meehan), Best Set Decoration (Emile Kuri), Best Special Effects (Disney Studios)

Video availability

WHITE CHRISTMAS

1954	
Studio/Distributor:	Paramount
Director:	Michael Curtiz
Producer:	Robert Emmett Dolan
Screenplay:	Norman Krasna, Norman Panama, Melvin Frank
Music:	Joseph J. Lilley

CAST
Bing Crosby . . . . *Bob Wallace*
Danny Kaye . . . . *Phil Davis*
Rosemary Clooney . . . . *Betty*
Vera-Ellen . . . . *Judy*
Dean Jagger . . . . *General Waverly*
Mary Wickes . . . . *Emma*
John Brascia . . . . *Joe*
Anne Whitfield . . . . *Susan*

Two army pals, Bob Wallace and Phil Davis, form a partnership after the war and become a successful song-and-dance act. Once established, and after several years of hard work, they decide to invite entertainers and sisters Betty and Judy to join them for a Christmas break at a ski resort in Vermont. On arrival, they discover the place is run by their ex-army boss, General Waverly, who is in dire financial difficulties, so they put on a show to help keep his business alive.

At the 1954 Oscars, Danny Kaye was given an honorary award for his unique talents, his services to the Academy, the motion picture industry and the American people. Nearly thirty years later, at the 1981 Oscars, Kaye was the recipient of the Jean Hersholt Humanitarian Award for 'reflecting credit on the industry', a prize only awarded in years when the Governor's Board feels there is a deserving winner.

The Song 'White Christmas' was first featured by Bing Crosby in *Holiday Inn* (1942).

Music: 'White Christmas', 'Count Your Blessings Instead of Sheep', 'Heat Wave', 'Snow', 'Blue Skies'

Video availability

COCKLESHELL HEROES

1955	
Studio/Distributor:	Columbia
Director:	José Ferrer
Producer:	Phil C. Samuel
Screenplay:	Bryan Forbes, Richard Malbaum
Music:	John Addison

CAST
José Ferrer . . . . *Major Stringer*
Trevor Howard . . . . *Captain Thompson*
Victor Maddern . . . . *Sergeant Craig*
Anthony Newley . . . . *Marine Clarke*
David Lodge . . . . *Marine Ruddock*
Peter Arne . . . . *Marine Stevens*
Percy Herbert . . . . *Marine Lomas*
Graham Stewart . . . . *Marine Booth*

A tough Sergeant-Major puts a special voluntary task force, made up of eight Royal Marines, through vigorous training during World War II in preparation for their dangerous mission, known as 'Cockleshell'. The operation involves slipping into enemy waters – by canoe – in order to destroy a fleet of Nazi battleships by planting limpet mines on the sides of the boats in the German-held French port in Bordeaux.

Actor and director José Ferrer intended to be an architect before getting a job as a stage manager. His first movie role was as Iago in the 1948 film *Joan of Arc*, starring Ingrid Bergman. *Cockleshell Heroes* was the second film he directed and starred in. *The Shrike* (also 1955) with June Allyson was the first.

Video availability

THE COURT JESTER

1955			
Studio/Distributor:	Paramount	Producer:	Norman Panama, Melvin Frank
Director:	Norman Panama, Melvin Frank	Screenplay:	Norman Panama, Melvin Frank
		Music:	Victor Shoen

CAST

Danny Kaye	*Hawkins*
Glynis Johns	*Maid Jean*
Basil Rathbone	*Sir Ravenhurst*
Angela Lansbury	*Princess Gwendolyn*
Cecil Parker	*King Roderick*
Mildred Natwick	*Griselda*
Robert Middleton	*Sir Griswold*
Michael Pate	*Sir Locksley*

In this medieval comedy Hawkins, a simple pot boy to a forest leader, manages to rise to the position of the leader of a peasant rebellion. He sets his sights on overthrowing the evil King Roderick and restoring the rightful heir as ruler of England. Hawkins gets himself hired as a court jester to gain access to the true power behind the throne and is imprisoned in the palace in order to put his plans into operation.

Sammy Cahn co-wrote the songs with Sylvia Fine who was then Danny Kaye's wife. Cahn won a total of 4 Oscars during his long song-writing career. His awards were for the songs 'Three Coins in the Fountain' from the film of the same name, 'High Hopes' from *A Hole in the Head*, 'All the Way' from *The Joker is Wild* and 'Call Me Irresponsible' from *Papa's Delicate Condition*.

Music: 'Outfox the Fox', 'Life Could Not Better Be', 'I'll Take You Dreaming', 'My Heart Knows a Love Song', 'Maladjusted Jester'

Video availability

DAVY CROCKETT, KING OF THE WILD FRONTIER

1955

Studio/Distributor:	Walt Disney
Director:	Norman Foster
Producer:	Bill Walsh
Screenplay:	Tom Blackburn
Music:	George Bruns

CAST

Fess Parker	*Davy Crockett*
Buddy Ebsen	*George Russel*
Basil Ruysdael	*Andrew Jackson*
Hans Conried	*Thimblerig*
William Bakewell	*Tobias Norton*
Kenneth Tobey	*Col. Jim Bowie*
Pat Hogan	*Chief Red Stick*
Helene Stanley	*Polly Crockett*

Tennessee hunter Davy Crockett, the man in the coonskin hat, makes peace with the Indian Chief Red Stick and rids a small town of a bunch of trouble-makers. 'The King Of The Wild Frontier' then runs for Congress and heads for Washington DC. He finally makes his way to the Alamo where he eventually dies.

The movie was originally filmed as three fifty-minute episodes for the popular Disney TV series, which made Davy Crockett famous, then assembled into a full-length feature film to capitalize on the phenomenal success of the TV series in the USA. A sequel, *Davy Crockett and the River Pirates*, was released in the same year, constructed from two further episodes of the television series.

Music: 'The Ballad of Davy Crockett'

GUYS AND DOLLS

1955

Studio/Distributor:	Samuel Goldwyn
Director:	Joseph L. Mankiewicz
Producer:	Samuel Goldwyn
Screenplay:	Joseph L. Mankiewicz
Music:	Frank Loesser

CAST

Marlon Brando	*Sky Masterson*
Jean Simmons	*Sarah Brown*
Frank Sinatra	*Nathan Detroit*
Vivian Blaine	*Miss Adelaide*
Robert Keith	*Lt Brannigan*
Stubby Kaye	*Nicely-Nicely Johnson*
B.S. Pully	*Big Jule*
Johnny Silver	*Benny Southstreet*

In this lavish musical Sarah Brown, a Salvation Army Sergeant, encounters heavy gambler and New York mobster Sky Masterson, who sweeps her off to Havana for a romantic interlude. The Damon Runyon-created characters they meet include the likeable Nathan Detroit, the harassed cop Lt. Brannigan, and Nicely-Nicely Johnson who gets the whole mission jumping with his stirring rendition of 'Sit Down, you're Rockin' the Boat'.

Producer Samuel Goldwyn paid $1 million for the rights to film Guys and Dolls *and spent a further $4 million on the making of the lavish musical which starred Marlon Brando as Sky Masterson.*

There was a certain amount of friction on the set between Frank Sinatra and Marlon Brando. Sinatra had still not completely recovered from losing the lead to Brando in *On The Waterfront*, and apparently kept objecting to Brando's laboured style of acting.

This was producer Sam Goldwyn's penultimate movie. *Porgy and Bess* (1959) was his last in a career which began with *The Squaw Man*, a silent which he co-produced in 1913.

Music: 'Guys and Dolls', 'Follow the Fold', 'The Oldest Established', 'A Woman in Love', 'If I Were a Bell', 'Luck be a Lady Tonight'

Video availability

THE LADY AND THE TRAMP

1955

Studio/Distributor: **Walt Disney**
Director: **Hamilton Luske, Clyde Geronimi, Wilfred Jackson**
Producer: **Walt Disney**
Screenplay: **Erdman Penner, Joe Rinaldi, Ralph Wright, Don DaGradi**
Music: **Oliver Wallace**

CAST (Voices)
Peggy Lee . . . . *Darling, Peg, Si and Am*
Barbara Luddy . . . . *Lady*
Larry Roberts . . . . *Tramp*
Bill Thompson . . . . *Jock, Bull, Dachsie*
Stan Freberg . . . . *Beaver*
Verna Fulton . . . . *Aunt Sarah*

Alan Reed . . . . *Boris*

In this Disney canine classic the high-class pedigreed Lady falls in love with a mutt named Tramp after he rescues her from a vicious gang of dogs from a rough part of town. Lady gets her first kiss from Tramp when they eat the same strand of spaghetti and their lips finally meet. She is less than pleased with him when they are both locked up for chicken raiding, but all ends happily as she gives birth to a litter of pups.

The original story by Ward Greene was called 'Happy Dan the Whistling Dog and Miss Patsy the Beautiful Spaniel'.

In 1988 Peggy Lee filed a huge law suit against the Disney studios claiming that they had released the video of the movie, which contained her voice and songs, without securing her consent.

Apart from *Ben-Hur* and *The Ten Commandments*, *The Lady and the Tramp* made more money than any other film in the 1950s.

Music: 'He's a Tramp', 'The Siamese Cat Song', 'Bella Notte', 'La La Lu', 'Peace on Earth'

Video availability

THE LADYKILLERS

1955	
Studio/Distributor:	Ealing
Director:	Alexander Mackendrick
Producer:	Michael Balcon
Screenplay:	William Rose
Music:	Tristram Cary

CAST

Alec Guinness	The Professor
Cecil Parker	The Major
Herbert Lom	Louis
Peter Sellers	Harry
Danny Green	One-Round
Katie Johnson	Mrs Wilberforce
Jack Warner	Police Superintendent
Frankie Howerd	Barrow Boy

In this black comedy Mrs Wilberforce, a harmless landlady with rooms to rent in London, takes in 'The Professor', a crook masquerading as a musician. His gang of villains gathers at the landlady's house not to rehearse, as she thinks, but to plot a robbery. After the heist they enlist the old lady's help, although she is completely unaware of what she is getting involved in when she agrees to fetch some luggage for them. When she accidentally discovers their crime, the gang decide they'll have to kill her, but one by one they end up dead themselves, leaving Mrs Wilberforce with their stolen cash. She attempts to put things right by informing the police but they don't believe her and tell her to keep the money.

The last of the comedies to be produced by the Ealing Studios, the film featured cameo appearances by Kenneth Connor and Stratford Johns. William Rose was Oscar nominated for the screenplay. He missed out this time, but he did win in 1967 for *Guess Who's Coming to Dinner*.

Video availability

THE MAN FROM LARAMIE

1955	
Studio/Distributor:	Columbia
Director:	Anthony Mann
Producer:	William Goetz
Screenplay:	Philip Yordan, Frank Burt
Music:	George Duning

CAST

James Stewart	Will Lockhart
Arthur Kennedy	Vic Hansbro
Donald Crisp	Alec Waggoman
Cathy O'Donnell	Barbara Waggoman
Alex Nicol	Dave Waggoman
Aline MacMahon	Kate Canaday
Wallace Ford	Charley O'Leary
Jack Elam	Chris Boldt

Army Captain Will Lockhart is home on leave and intends to begin a search for the men who have been selling rifles to the Apache Indians. The guns were used to kill a small cavalry troop, one of the members of which was his younger brother. His search leads him to a town in New Mexico which is run by Alec Waggoman, a sadistic rancher who has been making the life of Kate Canaday, a fellow rancher, a misery. Waggoman's sons are also fighting each other over who will inherit their ageing father's land. In his quest for justice, Lockhart finds himself caught up in the middle of both the ranchers' and the sons' problems.

Director Anthony Mann previously worked with James Stewart on many projects, most of them Westerns, including *Winchester '73* (1950), *Where the River bends* (1952), *The Naked Spur* (1953), *The Glenn Miller Story* (1953) and *The Far Country* (1954).

Music: 'The Man from Laramie'

Video availability

MISTER ROBERTS

1955

Studio/Distributor: Warner
Director: John Ford, Mervyn LeRoy
Producer: Leland Hayward
Screenplay: Frank Nugent, Joshua Logan
Music: Franz Waxman

CAST
Henry Fonda . . . . *Lt (J.G.) Roberts*
James Cagney . . . . *The Captain*
William Powell . . . . *Doc*
Jack Lemmon . . . . *Ensign Pulver*
Betsy Palmer . . . . *Lt Ann Girard*
Ward Bond . . . . *C.P.O. Dawdy*
Phil Carey . . . . *Mannion*
Nick Adams . . . . *Reber*

Lt. J.G. Roberts is unhappy working on board the cargo ship U.S.S *Reluctant.* under the command of an eccentric captain during World War II. The crew are doing nothing more than taking supplies to other ships while he is desperate to be serving in the middle of the Pacific, fighting the enemy. Ensign Pulver schemes against his Captain but there are laughs as well as drama on board the little cargo ship.

Henry Fonda was involved in a punch up on the set with director John Ford over changes Ford wanted to make. Having played his part hundreds of times on Broadway, Fonda wanted to keep things as they were. Ford was soon after replaced by Mervyn LeRoy, with the studio stating that Ford had bowed out through illness. It was Henry Fonda's first screen appearance for seven years as theatre acting had kept him away from the film sets.

Academy Awards: Best Supporting Actor (Jack Lemmon)

Video availability

OKLAHOMA!

1955

Studio/Distributor: Magna/Rodgers and Hammerstein
Director: Fred Zinnemann
Producer: Arthur Hornblow Jnr
Screenplay: Sonya Levien, William Ludwig
Music: Richard Rodgers Oscar Hammerstein II (Lyrics)

CAST
Gordon MacRae . . . . *Curly*
Gloria Grahame . . . . *Ado Annie*
Gene Nelson . . . . *Will Parker*
Charlotte Greenwood . . . . *Aunt Eller*
Shirley Jones . . . . *Laurey*
Eddie Albert . . . . *Ali Hakim*
James Whitmore . . . . *Carnes*
Rod Steiger . . . . *Jud Fry*
Barbara Lawrence . . . . *Gertie*

This was yet another hit Broadway musical adapted for the big screen, with plenty of exciting song and dance sequences. The dislikeable farmhand Jud Fry tries to steal land from an Indian. The good Curly helps to fight the cause while falling in love with Laurey, who is being chased by Fry. However, all ends well when Curly and Laurey drive off in their Surrey with the fringe on top!

Director Fred Zinnemann admitted several years after making the film that he didn't feel he had done a good job on his first musical, and that he was in awe of Richard Rodgers and Oscar Hammerstein. Gloria Grahame wasn't happy either. She hated her role as Ado Annie, and was so unpleasant to everyone on the set that they all ignored her at the end of filming party. Both Paul Newman and James Dean were tested for the part of Curly.

The movie introduced cinema audiences to the new wide-screen system known as Todd AO, but the film company were less than happy with the process and the picture was re-released in CinemaScope.

Academy Awards: Best Scoring of a Musical (Robert Russell Bennett, Jay Blackton and Adolph Deutsch), Best Sound Recording (Fred Hynes)

Music: 'Oklahoma', 'Oh What a Beautiful Mornin'', 'The Surrey with the Fringe on Top', 'I Cain't Say No', 'People Will Say We're in Love', 'The Farmer and the Cowman'

Video availability

THE SEVEN YEAR ITCH

1955	
Studio/Distributor:	Twentieth Century-Fox
Director:	Billy Wilder
Producer:	Billy Wilder, Charles K. Feldman
Screenplay:	George Axelrod, Billy Wilder
Music:	Alfred Newman

CAST

Marilyn Monroe . . . . *The Girl*
Tom Ewell . . . . *Richard Sherman*
Evelyn Keyes . . . . *Helen Sherman*
Sonny Tufts . . . . *Tom McKenzie*
Robert Strauss . . . . *Druhulik*
Oscar Homolka . . . . *Dr Brubaker*
Marguerite Chapman . . . . *Miss Morris*
Victor Moore . . . . *Plumber*

This comedy has middle-aged book publisher Richard Sherman all alone when his wife and child go off on holiday on their own. He tries his luck with a beautiful blonde actress living in the apartment above, and although his attempts at seducing her fall flat, in his imagination he's actually getting somewhere. He believes this so fully that he begins to develop a guilt complex about his misbehaviour.

The famous scene in which Marilyn Monroe's white dress is blown up by a gust of wind from a vent was filmed outside the Trans Lux Theater in New York. It could have been shot on a mock-up set on the studio lot, but the publicity department wisely felt that they couldn't pass up the opportunity of having over two thousand passers-by and press photographers present.

Video availability

Playboy *magazine's first centrefold pin-up, Marilyn Monroe, plays the girl in Billy Wilder's* Seven Year Itch. *She moves into the same apartment block as Richard Sherman (Tom Ewell).*

AROUND THE WORLD IN EIGHTY DAYS

1956

Studio/Distributor:	United Artists
Director:	Michael Anderson
Producer:	Michael Todd
Screenplay:	S.J. Perelman, John Farrow, James Poe
Music:	Victor Young

CAST
David Niven . . . . *Phileas Fogg*
Cantinflas . . . . *Passepartout*
Robert Newton . . . . *Mr Fix*
Shirley MacLaine . . . . *Aouda*
Charles Boyer . . . . *Mon. Gasse*
Joe E. Brown . . . . *Stationmaster*
Martine Carol . . . . *Tourist*
John Carradine . . . . *Colonel Proctor*

In the film adaptation of the Jules Verne novel the perfect English gentleman Phileas Fogg takes a bet with members of his London club that he can make it around the world in under three months even with the slower forms of transport in 1872. He sets off for Paris with his companion and valet, Passepartout. Throughout his trip he is trailed by Mr Fix, a detective who believes Fogg to be the perpetrator of a robbery at the Bank of England. Arriving back from his adventure, Fogg thinks he's lost the bet, only to discover that by travelling east he's gained a day and has thus won his wager.

Because the film was nearly three hours long, producer Michael Todd was worried that audiences might be tempted to watch the clock. As a precaution he had all clocks removed from the cinemas where the film was playing.

S.J. Perelman's Academy Award for Best Screenplay Adaptation was disputed at the time by the Writers' Guild, who claimed that James Poe had worked on the script. Both Poe and short-lived director John Farrow were later recognized for their writing contributions. Director John Farrow was replaced by Michael Anderson after just one day of filming.

The movie took in over 100 different natural locations on 140 sets and was packed with actors making cameo appearances, including Noel Coward, Buster Keaton, Marlene Dietrich, George Raft and Frank Sinatra as a pianist.

Academy Awards: Best Film (Producer Michael Todd), Best Screenplay (Adapted James Poe, John Farrow and S.J. Perelman), Best Colour Cinematography (Lionel Lindon), Best Editing (Gene Ruggiero and Paul Weatherwax), Best Music Score of a Drama or Comedy (Victor Young)

Music: 'Around the World in Eighty Days'

Video availability

GIANT

1956

Studio/Distributor:	Warner
Director:	George Stevens
Producer:	George Stevens
Screenplay:	Fred Guiol, Ivan Moffat
Music:	Dimitri Tiomkin

CAST
Elizabeth Taylor . . . . *Leslie Lynnton*
Rock Hudson . . . . *Bick Benedict*
James Dean . . . . *Jett Rink*
Carroll Baker . . . . *Luz Benedict II*
Jane Withers . . . . *Vashti Snythe*
Chill Wills . . . . *Uncle Bawley*
Mercedes McCambridge . . . . *Luz Benedict*
Sal Mineo . . . . *Angel Obregon III*

This epic movie is set during the demise of the old-style Texas as it enters into the era of the big oil tycoons. Bick Benedict and Jett Rink represent two generations of Texan rivalry. The strait-laced rancher Benedict marries Leslie and forces her to adapt to his way of life, while ranch hand Jett strikes oil and becomes rich, much to the annoyance of Bick. However, the more money Jett makes, the more disagreeable he becomes.

Director George Stevens deliberately tried to create a feeling of animosity between James Dean and Rock Hudson, for better performances on screen.

James Dean often caused chaos on the set by driving his motorbike around the sound stages, performing dangerous stunts. Two weeks after completion of the movie, Dean, at the age of 24, was killed while racing his Porsche. He never knew of his Oscar nomination.

Academy Awards: Best Direction (George Stevens)

Video availability

Star-crossed lovers Leslie Lynnton (Elizabeth Taylor), Bick Benedict (Rock Hudson) and Jett Rink (James Dean) are at the centre of the 1956 film Giant. *Despite Leslie's marriage to Bick, Jett continues to love Leslie as much as he hates Bick.*

HIGH SOCIETY

1956	
Studio/Distributor:	MGM
Director:	Charles Walters
Producer:	Sol C. Siegel
Screenplay:	John Patrick
Music:	Cole Porter

CAST

Bing Crosby	C.K. Dexter-Haven
Grace Kelly	Tracy Lord
Frank Sinatra	Mike Connor
Celeste Holm	Liz Imbrie
John Lund	George Kittredge
Louis Calhern	Uncle Willie
Sidney Blackmer	Seth Lord
Louis Armstrong	Himself

In this sparkling musical comedy socialite Tracy Lord is about to get married in Newport but is surrounded by three troublesome men. George Kittredge is her sensible but narrow-minded fiancé. C.K. Dexter-Haven is her dashing ex-husband with intentions of changing her mind about marrying George and winning her back. Mike Connor is a happy-go-lucky reporter who has been sent by his magazine to cover the event and imagines himself in love with Tracy. The eve of the wedding turns into a merry-go-round, but all is resolved the following day, with a marriage taking place although not quite as planned.

This was Grace Kelly's final film before marrying Prince Rainier of Monaco. The film company didn't want Grace Kelly to sing with Bing Crosby on 'True Love', feeling that a better voice was needed. Kelly wasn't concerned either way, but Crosby insisted the duet was performed with her. The single became a huge hit in the UK, reaching number four and staying in the charts for 27 weeks.

The only song not specially written for the film was 'Well Did You Evah?', which first appeared in Cole Porter's 1939 hit Broadway musical *Dubarry was a Lady* when it was sung by Betty Grable.

Music: 'High Society Calypso', 'True Love', 'I Love You Samantha', 'Well Did You Evah?', 'Who Wants to be a Millionaire?', 'You're Sensational'

Video availability

THE KING AND I

1956

Studio/Distributor:	Twentieth Century-Fox
Director:	Walter Lang
Producer:	Charles Brackett
Screenplay:	Ernest Lehman
Music:	Richard Rodgers
	Oscar Hammerstein II
	(Lyrics)

CAST

Deborah Kerr .... *Anna*
Yul Brynner .... *The King*
Rita Moreno .... *Tuptim*
Martin Benson .... *Kralahome*
Terry Saunders .... *Lady Thiang*
Rex Thompson .... *Louis Leonowens*
Carlos Rivas .... *Lun Tha*
Patrick Adiarte ..... *Prince Chulalongkorn*

In this faithful screen adaptation of a Broadway musical Victorian English school teacher Anna journeys with her son Louis from England to Siam, having been summoned to educate the King's many children. The arrogant King himself finds the difference between Far Eastern and Western cultures confusing and begins fighting with Anna because she won't give in to his every whim. Eventually she helps him to understand a little better and wins his respect.

There were many conflicts between director Walter Lang and Yul Brynner, who insisted on doing everything his way.

Deborah Kerr's singing voice was dubbed by the invisible queen of musical films, Marnie Nixon, who was the wife of composer Ernest Gold.

At the time of his death in 1985, Yul Brynner had played the King over 4000 times on the stage.

Academy Awards: Best Actor (Yul Brynner), Best Colour Art Direction (Lyle R. Wheeler and John DeCuir), Best Set Decoration (Walter M. Scott and Paul S. Fox), Best Colour Costume Design (Irene Sharaff), Best Sound Recording (Carl Faulkner), Best Scoring of a Musical (Alfred Newman and Ken Darby)

Music: 'Shall We Dance?', 'March of the Siamese Children', 'I Whistle a Happy Tune', 'Hello Young Lovers', 'Getting to Know You', 'Something Wonderful', 'Shall I Tell You What I Think of You?'

Video availability

MOBY DICK

1956

Studio/Distributor:	Warner
Director:	John Huston
Producer:	John Huston
Screenplay:	Ray Bradbury, John
	Huston
Music:	Philip Stainton

CAST

Gregory Peck .... *Captain Ahab*
Richard Basehart .... *Ishmael*
Leo Genn .... *1st Mate Starbuck*
Harry Andrews .... *2nd Mate Stubb*
Seamus Kelly .... *3rd Mate Flask*
Friedrich Ledebur .... *Queequeg*
Orson Welles .... *Father Mapple*
Bernard Miles .... *Manxman*

This film adaptation of Herman Melville's great tale is set in 1840 in New Bedford, a town known for its whaling. A stranger named Ishmael joins the crew of the *Pequod* to take part in the journey. After the ship sets sail, the ugly peg-legged Captain Ahab announces that there will be no whaling on this voyage but instead they would be going to search out and destroy the great white that had torn off his leg. By the time Moby Dick is sighted, both captain and crew have become obsessed with destroying him.

Producer/director John Huston had wanted to make this film some twenty years earlier with his father Walter playing the lead.

The cost of the movie soared due to delays brought about by bad weather on location in Ireland, and long production hold-ups.

Video availability

REACH FOR THE SKY

1956	
Studio/Distributor:	Rank
Director:	Lewis Gilbert
Producer:	Daniel M. Angel
Screenplay:	Lewis Gilbert
Music:	John Addison

CAST
Kenneth More .... *Douglas Bader*
Muriel Pavlow .... *Thelma Bader*
Lyndon Brook .... *Johnny Sanderson*
Lee Patterson .... *Turner*
Alexander Knox .... *Mr Joyce*
Dorothy Alison .... *Nurse Brace*
Michael Warre .... *Harry Day*
Sydney Tafler .... *Robert Desoutier*

Kenneth More played the lead role in this true-life story of the courageous British aviator, Douglas Bader. He loses both his legs in a plane crash when showing off his aerobatic stunts to other RAF officers. Fitted with artificial limbs, he takes to the air again to fight in World War II, only to be forced to bail out before being captured by the Germans. In the top-security camp the Germans confiscate his legs after three attempted escapes.

Richard Burton was originally offered the leading role as Douglas Bader but turned it down.

Kenneth More was probably not unhappy that the role fell to him as he received a flat fee of £25,000 for his part in the movie, his highest payment to date.

Producer Danny Angel, who owned the screen rights to the movie, lost the use of his legs after contracting polio while serving in the Army in India.

Video availability

ROCK AROUND THE CLOCK

1956	
Studio/Distributor:	Columbia
Director:	Fred F. Sears
Producer:	Sam Katzman
Screenplay:	Robert Kent, James B. Gordon
Music:	Fred Karger (Supervisor)

CAST
Bill Haley and the Comets .... *Themselves*
The Platters .... *Themselves*
Tony Martinez Band .... *Themselves*
Freddie Bell and the Bellboys . *Themselves*
Alan Freed .... *Himself*
Johnny Johnston .... *Steve Hollis*
Alix Talton .... *Corinne Talbot*
Lisa Gaye .... *Lisa Johns*
John Archer .... *Mike Dennis*

Steve Hollis is a manager of big bands and decides it's time to find a new sound. He dumps all his existing acts and heads for New York with his sidekick, Corny LaSalle (Henry Slate). Here they discover Bill Haley and his Comets, managed by dancer Lisa Johns, with whom Hollis falls in love. He convinces top American DJ Alan Freed to book Haley's band for his TV show, after which they take off like a comet.

The title song first appeared in the 1955 movie *The Blackboard Jungle*, starring Sidney Poitier, Glenn Ford and Ann Francis but is a reworking of an old blues number called 'My Daddy Rocks Me with a Steady Roll'. The song was Bill Haley's only UK number one hit single, spending 5 weeks at the top of the charts in 1955/56.

Music: 'Rock Around the Clock', 'Rudy's Rock', 'Rock-a-Beatin' Boogie', 'See You Later Alligator', 'Razzle Dazzle' (Bill Haley and the Comets); 'Only You', 'The Great Pretender' (The Platters); 'Giddy Up a Ding Dong' (Freddie Bell and the Bellboys)

THE SEARCHERS

1956			
Studio/Distributor:	Warner	Producer:	Merian C. Cooper, C.V. Whitney
Director:	John Ford	Screenplay:	Frank S. Nugent
		Music:	Max Steiner

John Ford's classic western, The Searchers, *stars John Wayne as Ethan Edwards. Mysteriously absent for two years after the end of the civil war, Ethan returns to his brother Aaron's (Walter Coy) home in Texas, but tragedy strikes before he can enjoy his homecoming.*

CAST

John Wayne . . . . *Ethan Edwards*
Jeffrey Hunter . . . . *Martin Pawley*
Vera Miles . . . . *Laurie Jorgensen*
Ward Bond . . . . *Capt. Revd. S. Clayton*
Natalie Wood . . . . *Debbie Edwards (No. 2)*
John Qualen . . . . *Lars Jorgensen*
Olive Carey . . . . *Mrs Jorgensen*
Henry Brandon . . . . *Chief Scar*

After fighting in the Civil War for three years, Ethan Edwards finally returns home to his brother Aaron's family. The family farm is destroyed by a tribe of Commanche Indians who also slaughter or abduct most of the family. Ethan and Martin, a young boy who was brought up by the Edwards family, survive. After finding the mangled body of the eldest of the two daughters Nathan and Ethan go in search of revenge and to find the youngest daughter, Debbie,

who was taken by the Commanche. It takes seven years before they finally track down the younger girl but Martin realizes that Ethan intends to kill her because she has become a squaw. At the last minute, however, Ethan relents and she is returned to live with a friendly family.

The Searchers is a firm favourite with modern directors like George Lucas and Martin Scorsese who allude to it in their later work.

Natalie Wood's real younger sister, Lana Wood, plays the young girl Debbie – referred to as 'No. 1' in the credits. Although Natalie went on to achieve great fame, little was heard of sister Lana until her memorable performance as Plenty O'Toole in the 1972 James Bond film *Diamonds Are For Ever*.

Video availability

THE TEN COMMANDMENTS

	1956
Studio/Distributor:	Paramount
Director:	Cecil B. DeMille
Producer:	Cecil B. DeMille
Screenplay:	Aeneas MacKenzie, Jesse L. Lasky Jr, Fredric M. Frank, Jack Gariss
Music:	Elmer Bernstein

CAST

Charlton Heston . . . . *Moses*
Yul Brynner . . . . *Rameses*
Anne Baxter . . . . *Nefretiri*
Edward G. Robinson . . . . *Dathan*
Yvonne De Carlo . . . . *Sephora*
Debra Paget . . . . *Lilia*
John Derek . . . . *Joshua*
Nina Foch . . . . *Bithiah*

Cecil B. DeMille's huge biblical epic begins when the Jewish baby boy is placed in a basket in the River Nile after the Lord of the Pharaohs orders the slaughter of all newly born Hebrew boys. The baby Moses is discovered by the Princess Bithiah and brought up as a prince, much to the annoyance of Rameses, the Pharaoh's son who inherits the throne. When Moses' true religion is eventually discovered, he is banished to the desert where God reveals to him, through the burning bush, that his destiny is to lead the Israelites out of Egypt to their promised land.

Cecil B. DeMille wanted his final movie to be the crowning moment in his career with the remake of his silent classic from 1923. One of his reasons for casting Charlton Heston as Moses was that he thought the actor bore a strong resemblance to Michelangelo's Moses in St Peter's Square in Rome.

The movie ran into costs exceeding $13 million, becoming the most expensive movie ever made at the time but it ended up grossing over $80 million.

The effect of the parting of the Red sea was created by running film of miniature waterfalls backwards and blending it with actual shots of the sea and huge amounts of water pouring into an enormous tank on the Paramount set. To create the fire from the finger of God burning the commandments on to the stone tablets, animated fire was drawn on to the film.

DeMille used around 12,000 Arabs to play the Jews on their way to the promised land. The scene also called for over 15,000 animals.

Academy Awards: Best Special Effects (John Fulton)

Video availability

TRAPEZE

1956	
Studio/Distributor:	**United Artists**
Director:	**Carol Reed**
Producer:	**James Hill**
Screenplay:	**James R. Webb**
Music:	**Malcolm Arnold**

CAST

Burt Lancaster	*Mike Ribble*
Tony Curtis	*Tino Orsini*
Gina Lollobrigida	*Lola*
Katy Jurado	*Rosa*
Thomas Gomez	*Bouglione*
John Puleo	*Max*

In Trapeze *Tino Orsini (Tony Curtis) joins a travelling circus in order to meet Mike Ribble (Burt Lancaster), who was once one of the world's finest trapeze artists. His career was cut short by an injury sustained when a fellow team member failed to catch him in a mid-air stunt.*

Minor Watson . . . . . . *John Ringling North*
Gerard Landry . . . . *Chikki*

Ex-trapeze artist Mike Ribble retires after a high-wire accident leaves him crippled and starts work as a menial helper at a French circus. He meets Tino Orsini, the son of an old friend. He meets Tino is eager for the older man to teach him the impossible 'triple' move, which was the cause of Mike's accident. After much persuasion, he reluctantly agrees to teach the youngster. Life is complicated by the fact that Mike is being seduced by Lola, a circus tumbler who is keen to get in on the new act. After her advances to Mike fall on stony ground, she attempts to seduce Tino, while Mike learns how to perform the elusive triple somersault.

Burt Lancaster had been a real circus acrobat before finding fame in the movies, and performed all his own dare devil stunts in this film.

Video availability

THE ADMIRABLE CRICHTON

1957	
Studio/Distributor:	Columbia
Director:	Lewis Gilbert
Producer:	Ian Dalrymple
Screenplay:	Vernon Harris, Lewis Gilbert
Music:	Douglas Gamley

CAST
Kenneth More . . . . *Crichton*
Diane Cilento . . . . *Tweeny*
Cecil Parker . . . . *Lord Loam*
Sally Ann Howes . . . . *Lady Mary*
Martita Hunt . . . . *Lady Brocklehurst*
Jack Watling . . . . *Treherne*
Peter Graves . . . . *Brocklehurst*
Gerald Harper . . . . *Ernest*

This comedy was adapted from J.M. Barrie's famous play about the English butler, Crichton. The butler comes to the rescue by taking control when he is shipwrecked with his employer, an English Lord, and his three daughters. Stranded on an island, Crichton takes over his master's role, organizing the other castaways, only to revert to his original status when they are rescued by a passing cruiser.

Kenneth More was really in difficulty on location in Bermuda in a scene where he is supposed to be drowning. It was only Diane Cilento's strong swimming ability that saved him.

The Admirable Crichton was the first play Kenneth More ever appeared in, when it was produced as one of his school plays. He also took the lead in the short-lived musical called *Our Man Crichton*.

THE BRIDGE ON THE RIVER KWAI

1957	
Studio/Distributor:	Columbia
Director:	David Lean
Producer:	Sam Spiegel
Screenplay:	Pierre Boulle
Music:	Malcolm Arnold

CAST
William Holden . . . . *Shears*
Alec Guinness . . . . *Colonel Nicholson*
Jack Hawkins . . . . *Major Warden*
Sessue Hayakawa . . . . *Colonel Saito*
James Donald . . . . *Major Clipton*
Geoffrey Horne . . . . *Lieutenant Joyce*
André Morell . . . . *Colonel Green*
Peter Williams . . . . *Captain Reeves*

The resourceful British Colonel Nicholson is being held prisoner along with his regiment by the Japanese in Burma during World War II. He convinces his fellow prisoners to help build a bridge over the River Kwai for the Japanese commander, Colonel Saito. Shears, another officer who recently escaped captivity, returns with plans to destroy it. Nicholson is so proud of the efforts of his men and the magnificent bridge they've built that he can't bear to see it destroyed.

Carl Foreman and Michael Wilson were co-writers of the movie but their names were deliberately omitted from the credits because they were black-listed for alleged involvement with the Communist Party. Pierre Boulle, the author of the original novel, was awarded an Oscar for Best Screenplay, although he had nothing to do with the writing of the picture. Only later, after the problem subsided, were Foreman and Wilson credited for their work on the screenplay, which David Lean always questioned. Lean took issue with the posthumous Oscar awarded to Carl Foreman for his work on the movie, claiming that not a word of Foreman's work was used in the final screenplay and that he had written most of it himself.

Academy Awards: Best Film (Producer Sam Spiegel), Best Direction (David Lean), Best Actor (Alec Guinness), Best Screenplay (Pierre Boulle; see above), Best Cinematography (Jack Hildyard), Best Editing (Peter Taylor), Best Music Scoring (Malcolm Arnold)

Video availability

THE CURSE OF FRANKENSTEIN

1957

Studio/Distributor:	Warner/Hammer
Director:	Terence Fisher
Producer:	Anthony Hinds
Screenplay:	Jimmy Sangster
Music:	Leonard Salzedo

CAST
Peter Cushing . . . *Baron Victor Frankenstein*
Christopher Lee . . . . *The Creature*
Hazel Court . . . . *Elizabeth*
Robert Urquhart . . . . *Paul Krempe*
Valerie Gaunt . . . . *Justine*
Noel Hood . . . . *Aunt Sophia*
Marjorie Hume . . . . *Mother*

Loosely based on Mary Shelley's classic novel *Frankenstein*, the film was the first of the Hammer studios' long-running series of Frankenstein horror movies. Baron Frankenstein gathers together an assortment of human organs in order to fulfil his lifelong ambition of creating a living person through a scientific process. Unfortunately the creature has been built with parts belonging to criminals, and goes on the rampage. The story is told in flashback by the Baron who is charged with the series of grisly murders committed by his creation.

The film featured Christopher Lee's one and only appearance as the Creature, although *The Curse of Frankenstein* produced six sequels. Peter Cushing, however, reprised his role as the Baron several times, notably in *The Evil of Frankenstein* (1964), *Frankenstein Created Woman* (1967), *Frankenstein Must be Destroyed* (1969) and *Frankenstein and the Monster from Hell* (1973).

The film was a remake of the 1931 movie *Frankenstein*. The film company was not allowed to copy the designs used for Boris Karloff's original monster due to copyright.

Video availability

In Hammer Studio's first Frankenstein movie, The Curse of Frankenstein, *Baron Victor Frankenstein (Peter Cushing) goes in search of human organs with which to build his monster.*

DOCTOR AT LARGE

1957	
Studio/Distributor:	Rank
Director:	Ralph Thomas
Producer:	Betty E. Box
Screenplay:	Nicholas Phipps
Music:	Bruce Montgomery

CAST

Dirk Bogarde . . . . *Simon Sparrow*
Muriel Pavlow . . . . *Joy*
Donald Sinden . . . . *Benskin*
James Robertson Justice . . . . *Sir Lancelot*
Shirley Eaton . . . . *Nan*
Derek Farr . . . . *Dr Potter-Shine*
Michael Medwin . . . . *Bingham*

Simon Sparrow is let loose again in this third 'Doctor' romp. This time the arrogant Sir Lancelot, Chief of Medicine at St Swithins Hospital, refuses him the opportunity to practise surgery. Searching for employment he finds himself in Park Lane, London, assisting a doctor in luxurious surroundings. He soon leaves his mean employer, but still needs to pay the rent. After more adventures he finds himself safely back at St Swithins.

After the success of the 'Doctor' movies, producer Betty Box admitted to using the project more as a cash cow to finance other more exciting projects, rather than for the art.

Video availability

GUNFIGHT AT THE OK CORRAL

1957	
Studio/Distributor:	Paramount
Director:	John Sturges
Producer:	Hal Wallis
Screenplay:	Leon Uris
Music:	Dimitri Tiomkin

CAST

Burt Lancaster . . . . *Wyatt Earp*
Kirk Douglas . . . . *Doc Holliday*
Rhonda Fleming . . . . *Laura Denbow*
Jo Van Fleet . . . . *Kate Fisher*
John Ireland . . . . *Ringo*
Lyle Bettger . . . . *Ike Clanton*
Frank Faylen . . . . *Cotton Wilson*
Earl Holliman . . . . *Charles Bassett*

Doc Holliday and Marshal Wyatt Earp's hostility towards each other turns into mutual respect and friendship, especially after Earp saves Doc from a beating by a gang of thugs in the Texan town of

Fort Griffin. Together they take on the mean Clanton gang at the OK Corral in Tombstone, Arizona. Earp and Holliday prove to be faster on the draw in the legendary shoot-out.

Both Burt Lancaster and Kirk Douglas originally turned down the offer to appear in the movie, but Douglas had second thoughts and convinced Lancaster to change his mind.

Once on set both Lancaster and Douglas were constantly trying to override decisions taken by John Sturges, but more often than not were beaten down by the strong-willed director.

The gunfight at the end was worked out like a dance routine, with every move carefully planned. The real life duel was all over in a matter of a few seconds, but in the movie it takes up most of the last reel.

Video availability

JAILHOUSE ROCK

1957	
Studio/Distributor:	MGM
Director:	Richard Thorpe
Producer:	Pandro S. Berman
Screenplay:	Guy Trosper
Music:	Jeff Alexander
	(Supervisor)

CAST

Elvis Presley . . . . *Vince Everett*
Judy Tyler . . . . *Peggy Van Alden*
Mickey Shaughnessy . . . . *Hunk Houghton*
Vaughn Taylor . . . . *Mr Shores*
Jennifer Holden . . . . *Sherry Wilson*
Dean Jones . . . . *Teddy Talbot*
Anne Neyland . . . . *Laury Jackson*

The good-natured country boy Vince Everett (Elvis Presley) ends up in prison after killing a man in a barroom fight. His voicebox, however, is still free to sing.

In his third outing on the big screen Elvis plays Vince Everett, who gets into a barroom fight over a lady and accidentally kills a man, resulting in a jail sentence for manslaughter. In prison he shares a cell with Hunk Houghton who is organizing a show for the inmates and convinces Vince to perform. On release, he meets Peggy Van Alden who helps him progress in his singing career. Together they form their own record label and move on to Hollywood to find fame and fortune. Hunk becomes jealous of Vince's success and injures the singer, who may never be able to perform again.

Crispy bacon and mashed potato in gravy were added to the menu of the MGM canteen during filming as it was one of Elvis's favourite meals. However, we are not sure whether it was while eating this dish that he swallowed a tooth cap, which required him to be hospitalized for a day.

Vince's prison number was 6239, but during the 'Jailhouse Rock' production number he wore the number 6240.

Former welterweight boxer Johnny Indrisano was hired as technical advisor for the fight sequences.

During the final day's filming, a fire broke out in Jennifer Holden's dressing room while she was in it. Elvis carried her out as others put out the flames.

Music: 'Jailhouse Rock', 'Young and Beautiful', 'Treat Me Nice', '(You're So Square) Baby I Don't Care', 'I Want to be Free', 'Don't Leave me Now'

Video availability

PAL JOEY

1957	

Studio/Distributor: Columbia
Director: George Sidney
Producer: Fred Kohlmar
Screenplay: Dorothy Kingsley
Music: Richard Rodgers
                      Lorenz Hart (Lyrics)

CAST
Rita Hayworth . . . . *Vera Simpson*
Frank Sinatra . . . . *Joey Evans*
Kim Novak . . . . *Linda English*
Barbara Nichols . . . . *Gladys*
Bobby Sherwood . . . . *Ned Galvin*
Hank Henry . . . . *Mike Miggins*
Elizabeth Patterson . . . . *Mrs Casey*
Robin Morse . . . . *Bartender*

In this musical Vera Simpson, an ex-stripper, now wealthy widow, offers to buy sleazy saloon singer Joey Evans the nightclub he has always dreamed of. However she refuses to part with the required money unless he agrees to let his girlfriend Linda go. Linda persuades Vera to part with the money and agrees to disappear. Rid of her rival, Vera proposes marriage to Joey in order to put an end to all his financial problems.

Aspects of the original play were changed for the film. The original stage show had Vera as a married woman, but the film company thought it too risqué for the movie, so she became a widow. Also the setting of the movie was changed from Chicago to San Francisco, and Joey's apartment became a yacht.

Rita Hayworth's singing voice was dubbed by Jo Ann Greer, and Kim Novak's by Trudy Erwin for the song 'I Could Write A Book'.

Music: 'Bewitched Bothered and Bewildered', 'I Could Write a Book', 'My Funny Valentine', 'There's a Small Hotel', 'I Didn't Know What Time It Was', 'The Lady is a Tramp'

Video availability

THE PRINCE AND THE SHOWGIRL

1957	

Studio/Distributor: Warner
Director: Laurence Olivier
Producer: Laurence Olivier
Screenplay: Terence Rattigan
Music: Richard Addinsell

CAST
Marilyn Monroe . . . . *Elsie Marina*
Laurence Olivier . . . . *The Regent*
Sybil Thorndyke . . . . *Queen Dowager*
Richard Wattis . . . . *Northbrook*
Jeremy Spenser . . . . *King Nicolas*
Esmond Knight . . . . *Col Hoffman*
Paul Hardwick . . . . *Major Domo*
Rosamund Greenwood . . . . *Maud*

In 1911 Charles, the Prince Regent of Carpathia, is in London with his deaf mother-in-law, the Queen Dowager, and his son King Nicholas for the corona-tion of George V. He meets American chorus girl Elsie Marina and invites her to dinner in his room at the embassy with the intention of seducing her. His plan fails because she falls asleep after drinking too much alcohol. The following morning he insists she leaves, but by now she has fallen for him. Later she helps resolve a feud between Charles and his son who is annoyed with his father for treating him like a child.

It was alleged that Monroe and Olivier hated each other by the time they had started filming. At the age of 30, it was Monroe's 25th movie and the first made by her independent company. It was reported she earned 75 per cent of the profits. Laurence Olivier appeared in a stage version of the story with his wife, Vivien Leigh, four years earlier and Marilyn Monroe only agreed to do the film if he repeated his stage role with her. She claimed that it might give her career some extra weight. The film was based on Terence Rattigan's play *The Sleeping Prince*.

Video availability

THE TOMMY STEELE STORY (AKA ROCK AROUND THE WORLD)

1957	
Studio/Distributor:	Insignia Films
Director:	Gerard Bryant
Producer:	Herbert Smith
Screenplay:	Norman Hudis
Music:	Tommy Steele, Lionel Bart, Michael Pratt

CAST

Tommy Steele	*Tommy Steele*
Patrick Westwood	*Brushes*
Hilda Fenemore	*Mrs Steele*
Charles Lamb	*Mr Steele*
Peter Lewiston	*John Kennedy*
John Boxer	*Paul Lincoln*
Mark Daly	*Junkshop Man*

At the height of his rock 'n' roll career and at the age of 21, it was felt that British star Tommy Steele had achieved sufficient show business status to play himself in the story of his life. Born in Bermondsey, he was hospitalized at an early age and taught himself to play guitar as therapy. He went on to join the Merchant Navy before becoming a singer in Soho's Two I's coffee bar where he was discovered. He went on to have a string of top twenty hits in the UK.

Tommy Steele was the youngest subject ever of a bio-pic.

His movie debut was a cameo role in the British thriller *Kill Me Tomorrow*, released in the same year and starring Pat O'Brien and Lois Maxwell. Other films he appeared in include *Tommy the Toreador* (1960), *The Happiest Millionaire* (1967), *Half a Sixpence* (1967) and *Finian's Rainbow* (1968). He has mainly concentrated on theatrical work since then, appearing with great success in *Singin' in the Rain* and *Some Like it Hot* on the London stage.

Music: 'Rock with the Caveman', 'A Handful of Songs', 'Singing the Blues', 'Butterfingers', 'Water Water', 'Elevator Rock', 'Take Me Back Baby', 'You Gotta Go'

WITNESS FOR THE PROSECUTION

1957	
Studio/Distributor:	United Artists
Director:	Billy Wilder
Producer:	Arthur Hornblow
Screenplay:	Billy Wilder, Harry Kurnitz
Music:	Matty Malneck

CAST

Tyrone Power	*Leonard Vole*
Marlene Dietrich	*Christine Vole*
Charles Laughton	*Sir Wilfrid Robarts*
Elsa Lanchester	*Miss Plimsoll*
John Williams	*Brogan-Moore*
Henry Daniell	*Mayhew*
Ian Wolfe	*Carter*
Una O'Connor	*Janet McKenzie*

In this screen adaptation of Agatha Christie's celebrated stage play about a sensational murder trial Leonard Vole stands accused of killing a rich widow. His only alibi is his wife, who it turns out is not legally married to him and refuses to back up his story. To add further complication, it is believed that he has inherited a tidy sum from the deceased's estate. He is defended at the Old Bailey by Sir Wilfrid Robarts who comes out of retirement for a case he can't resist.

The producers were so keen on the story that they paid a record $430,000 for the movie rights. Several male stars turned down the leading role before it was offered to and accepted by Tyrone Power as part of a two picture deal which cost the studio $600,000 and included *Solomon and Sheba*. This proved to be an expensive deal as Power died during the shooting of the latter film.

Elsa Lanchester and Charles Laughton were real life husband and wife.

Music: 'I May Never Go Home Again'

Video availability

THE BIG COUNTRY

1958	
Studio/Distributor:	United Artists
Director:	William Wyler
Producer:	William Wyler, Gregory Peck
Screenplay:	James R. Webb, Sy Bartlett, Robert Wilder
Music:	Jerome Moross

CAST

Gregory Peck . . . . *James McKay*
Jean Simmons . . . . *Julie Maragon*
Carroll Baker . . . . *Patricia Terrill*
Charlton Heston . . . . *Steve Leech*
Burl Ives . . . . *Rufus Hannassey*
Charles Bickford . . . . . *Major Henry Terrill*
Alfonso Bedoya . . . . *Ramon*
Chuck Connors . . . . *Buck Hannassey*

In this sprawling Western a major feud develops between Rufus Hannassey, a rugged and uncouth man with similar sons, and Henry Terrill, owner of a large ranch and a beautiful daughter, Patricia. Central to the feud is the argument over the rights to a watering hole for the cattle. Patricia's fiancé, James McKay, is drawn into the struggle which is only resolved with the deaths of the two patriarchs.

This was Gregory Peck's debut as a movie producer. He fell out with director William Wyler after he refused to re-shoot a scene Peck was unhappy about. The two finished the movie without exchanging another word. The feud, which lasted two years, ended at an Academy Awards ceremony when they shook hands and agreed to forgive and forget. Charlton Heston, however, had to hide his annoyance at William Wyler who meticulously insisted on re-takes of nearly every scene.

Academy Awards: Best Supporting Actor (Burl Ives)

Video availability

CARRY ON SERGEANT

1958	
Studio/Distributor:	Anglo Amalgamated
Director:	Gerald Thomas
Producer:	Peter Rogers
Screenplay:	Norman Hudis
Music:	Bruce Montgomery

CAST

William Hartnell . . . . *Sgt Grimshawe*
Bob Monkhouse . . . . *Charlie Sage*
Shirley Eaton . . . . *Mary*
Eric Barker . . . . *Captain Potts*
Dora Bryan . . . . *Nora*
Bill Owen . . . . *Corporal Copping*
Kenneth Connor . . . . *Horace Strong*
Kenneth Williams . . . . *James Bailey*
Hattie Jacques . . . . *Captain Clark*

The very first 'Carry On' movie has a loud-mouthed army Sergeant about to retire from the service. Before he leaves, he takes a bet that he can successfully train a mixed bag of new recruits, with hilarious results.

A further 28 'Carry On' movies were made over the next twenty years. They were sometimes made at a rate of two a year, becoming something of a British institution in the film world. 'Carry On' regulars included Kenneth Williams, Kenneth Connor, Charles Hawtrey and Hattie Jacques.

Video availability

CAT ON A HOT TIN ROOF

1958	
Studio/Distributor:	MGM
Director:	Richard Brooks
Producer:	Lawrence Weingarten
Screenplay:	Richard Brooks, James Poe
Music:	no credit

CAST

Elizabeth Taylor . . . . *Maggie*
Paul Newman . . . . *Brick*
Burl Ives . . . . *Big Daddy*
Jack Carson . . . . *Gooper*
Judith Anderson . . . . *Big Mama*
Madeleine Sherwood . . . . *Mae*
Larry Gates . . . . *Dr Baugh*
Vaughn Taylor . . . . *Deacon Davis*

In America's deep South multi-millionaire Big Daddy is dying of cancer. His eldest son, Gooper, has his eye on a major share in the estate. His younger son, Brick, has taken to drink since the death of his best friend for which he blames his wife, Maggie. With the help of his wife, Mae, Gooper attempts to stir up trouble for Brick and Maggie by pointing to their unhappy, childless marriage. Big Daddy forces Brick and Maggie to tell each other the truth.

The part of Maggie was originally intended for Grace Kelly, but by the time they were ready to shoot the movie, Miss Kelly was the Princess of Monaco. While Elizabeth Taylor was making the movie her husband, Mike Todd, was killed in a plane crash.

The film was an adaptation of Tennessee Williams's play. Burl Ives was the only actor who appeared in both the play and the film. Director Richard Brooks helped adapt the script from the play and cleaned it up for the movie version.

Paul Newman was Oscar nominated but lost to David Niven who won for his performance in *Separate Tables*. Elizabeth Taylor was also nominated, losing to Susan Hayward in *I Want To Live*.

Video availability

DRACULA

The blood-drinking Count Dracula (Christopher Lee), who sleeps by day, decides to go out one evening for a quick bite.

1958	
Studio/Distributor:	Rank/Hammer
Director:	Terence Fisher
Producer:	Anthony Hinds
Screenplay:	Jimmy Sangster
Music:	James Bernard

CAST
Peter Cushing . . . . *Dr Van Helsing*
Christopher Lee . . . . *Count Dracula*
Michael Gough . . . . *Arthur*
Melissa Stribling . . . . *Mina*
Carol Marsh . . . . *Lucy*
Olga Dickie . . . . *Gerda*
John Van Eyssen . . . . *Jonathan*
Valerie Gaunt . . . . *Vampire Woman*

The film tells the familiar story of Count Dracula asleep in his coffin by day and a vampire by night. He awakens to go on his evil rampages, sucking his victims' blood in order to give himself eternal life. Bram Stoker's classic tale was given the Hammer Horror treatment by the team responsible for the smash hit *Curse Of Frankenstein* (1957). Cushing and Lee reunited with director Terence Fisher for the first of a long series featuring the vampiric Count and his foe, Dr Van Helsing.

Dracula has often been acknowledged as the best movie ever to come out of the Hammer Studios.

Video availability

DUNKIRK

1958	
Studio/Distributor:	MGM/Ealing
Director:	Leslie Norman
Producer:	Michael Balcon
Screenplay:	David Divine, W.P. Lipscomb
Music:	Malcolm Arnold

CAST
John Mills . . . . *Binns*
Robert Urquhart . . . . *Mike*
Ray Jackson . . . . *Barlow*
Meredith Edwards . . . . *Dave Bellman*
Anthony Nicholls . . . . . *military spokesman*
Michael Shillo . . . . *Jouvet*
Bernard Lee . . . . *Charles*
Richard Attenborough . . . . *Holden*

This was Ealing Studios' account of the famous World War II rescue operation and the Allied retreat from the advancing Nazis in 1940. A small group of men detach themselves from their main unit and head for the beaches of Normandy without realizing the real danger they are in. With stiff upper lips the men take their tiny craft across the English Channel and rescue the forces cut off from any escape routes.

The movie, directed by the father of movie critic Barry Norman, featured cameo appearances by music hall stars Bud Flanagan and Chesney Allen from 'The Crazy Gang', who had appeared in many films of their own between 1935 and 1958.

Video availability

GIGI

1958	
Studio/Distributor:	MGM
Director:	Vincente Minnelli
Producer:	Arthur Freed
Screenplay:	Alan Jay Lerner
Music:	Frederick Loewe
	Alan Jay Lerner (Lyrics)
	André Previn (Supervision)

CAST
Leslie Caron . . . . *Gigi*
Maurice Chevalier . . . . . . *Honoré Lachaille*
Louis Jourdan . . . . *Gaston Lachaille*

Hermione Gingold . . . . *Mme Alvarez*
Eva Gabor . . . . *Liane D'Exelmans*
Jacques Bergerac . . . . *Sandomir*
Isabel Jeans . . . . *Aunt Alicia*
John Abbott . . . . *Manuel*

This charming MGM musical is set in turn-of-the-century Paris. Gigi is a young girl who is encouraged by her grandmother and great aunt to follow family tradition and become a high-class courtesan. She meets the handsome Gaston Lachaille who at first accepts Gigi as a mistress but eventually proposes marriage.

The film was an adaptation of the novel *Colette* by Pierre Laroche. The script had to be adapted somewhat by producer Arthur Freed because the censors objected to some of the immoral elements of Colette's original story.

Initially, the French authorities refused permission for filming to take place in Paris. When they finally relented, the budget went sky-high due to hold-ups on the scenes shot on location. Following dreadful reviews after initial previews, about twenty-five minutes of the movie were re-written and re-shot.

Maurice Chevalier won an honorary Oscar for his career achievement after 50 years' work in the world of entertainment.

Academy Awards: Best Film (Producer Arthur Freed), Best Direction (Vincente Minnelli), Best Screenplay (Alan Jay Lerner), Best Colour Cinematography (Joseph Ruttenberg), Best Colour Art Direction (William A. Horning and Preston Ames), Best Set Decoration (Henry Grace and Keogh Gleason), Best Colour Costume Design (Cecil Beaton), Best Editing (Adrienne Fazan), Best Scoring of a Musical Picture (André Previn), Best Song – 'Gigi' (Frederick Loewe, music; Alan Jay Lerner; lyrics)

Music: 'Gigi', 'Thank Heaven for Little Girls', 'The Night They Invented Champagne', 'I Remember it well', 'I'm Glad I'm Not Young Anymore'

Video availability

THE INN OF THE SIXTH HAPPINESS

1958	
Studio/Distributor:	Twentieth Century-Fox
Director:	Mark Robson
Producer:	Buddy Adler
Screenplay:	Isobel Lennart
Music:	Malcolm Arnold

CAST
Ingrid Bergman . . . . *Gladys Aylward*
Curt Jurgens . . . . *Capt Lin Nan*
Robert Donat . . . . *the Mandarin*
Ronald Squire . . . . *Sir Francis*
Noel Hood . . . . *Miss Thompson*
Joan Young . . . . *Cook*
Moultrie Kelsall . . . . *Dr Robinson*
Edith Sharpe . . . . *Secretary*

The film is based on the true story of the English servant Gladys Aylward who decided to make her own way to pre-World War II China to become a missionary. She is met with hostility from the natives, but works to gain their respect. She becomes involved in the Sino-Japanese war and helps guide 100 children to the safety of a northern mission by leading them on a dangerous journey through enemy territory. The inn she establishes becomes a refuge for travellers who are welcomed with hospitality and Bible readings as they cross the mountains.

This was Robert Donat's final movie as he died soon after its completion. At the age of eleven, Robert Donat started taking elocution lessons to overcome a stutter. He also suffered from asthma, which was linked to his untimely death.

In reality, Gladys Aylward was upset that she was depicted in the movie as having an affair with a Chinese army officer.

Music: 'The Children's Marching Song (This Old Man)'

Video availability

KING CREOLE

1958	
Studio/Distributor:	Paramount
Director:	Michael Curtiz
Producer:	Hal B. Wallis
Screenplay:	Michael V. Gazzo,
	Herbert Baker
Music:	Walter Scharf

CAST
Elvis Presley . . . . *Danny Fisher*
Carolyn Jones . . . . *Ronnie*
Walter Matthau . . . . *Maxie Fields*
Dolores Hart . . . . *Nellie*
Dean Jagger . . . . *Mr Fisher*
Liliane Montevecchi . . . . *Nina*
Vic Morrow . . . . *Shark*
Paul Stewart . . . . *Charlie Le Grand*

Set in New Orleans and based on Harold Robbins's novel, *A Stone For Danny Fisher*, the film features Elvis in the lead role. He plays Danny Fisher, a boy who gets involved with petty crime but then has a chance of becoming a nightclub singer at Charlie Le Grand's Vieux Carre saloon. Crime boss Maxie Fields persuades Danny to sing at his place but

Danny's girlfriend Ronnie comes between the two. Tragedy ensues before Danny can resume his career at Charlie Le Grand's night club and be reunited with his real love, Nellie.

In the Robbins book the story was set in New York and Danny was a boxer, not a singer. Two working titles for the movie were 'Danny' and 'Sing You Sinners'.

Carolyn Jones is best remembered for her part as Morticia Addams in the TV series *The Addams Family*.

Candy Candido who played a doorman in the movie was the cartoon voice of Popeye The Sailor Man in the 1930s.

Music: 'King Creole', 'Steadfast Loyal and True', 'Hard Headed Woman', 'Lover Doll', 'New Orleans'

Video availability

SOUTH PACIFIC

1958

Studio/Distributor:	Magna Theatre Corp
Director:	Joshua Logan
Producer:	Buddy Adler
Screenplay:	Paul Osborn, Richard Rodgers, Oscar Hammerstein II, Joshua Logan
Music:	Richard Rodgers

CAST
Rossano Brazzi . . . . *Emile DeBecque*
Mitzi Gaynor . . . . *Nellie Forbush*
John Kerr . . . . *Lieutenant Cable*
Ray Walston . . . . *Luther Billis*
Juanita Hall . . . . *Bloody Mary*
France Nuyen . . . . *Liat*
Russ Brown . . . . *Captain Brackett*
Jack Mullaney . . . . *Professor*

This adapted Broadway musical is set on the magical island of Bali Ha'i in the South Pacific. Widowed and left with his children, French planter Emile DeBecque falls in love with the very much younger Nellie Forbush, a Navy nurse from the midwest. With romance in the air, Luther Billis, a young marine, finds his heart pounding when he's in the company of a local native girl, Liat.

Although Juanita Hall sang the role of Bloody Mary in the Broadway production, Richard Rodgers was unhappy with the tone of her voice on the soundtrack so dubbed her vocals using Muriel Smith. Rossano Brazzi's singing voice was dubbed by Giorgio Tozzi and John Kerr's was supplied by Bill Lee.

Elizabeth Taylor auditioned for the part of Nellie Forbush, but when she sang for Richard Rodgers she was so nervous that her voice came out as little more than a croak. However, by 1978 her confidence and singing had improved considerably and she belted out Sondheim's showstopper 'Send in the Clowns' in the movie musical *A Little Night Music*.

Academy Awards: Best Sound Recording (Fred Hynes)

Music: 'I'm Gonna Wash that Man Right Outa my Hair', 'Younger Than Springtime', 'Some Enchanted Evening', 'There's Nothin' Like a Dame', 'Bali Ha'i', 'A Wonderful Guy', 'Happy Talk'

Video availability

VERTIGO

1958

Studio/Distributor:	Paramount
Director:	Alfred Hitchcock
Producer:	Alfred Hitchcock
Screenplay:	Alec Coppel, Samuel Taylor
Music:	Bernard Herrmann

CAST
James Stewart . . . . *Scottie*
Kim Novak . . . . *Madeleine and Judy*
Barbara Bel Geddes . . . . *Midge*
Tom Helmore . . . . *Gavin Elster*
Henry Jones . . . . *Official*
Raymond Bailey . . . . *Doctor*

Scottie Ferguson, a San Francisco police officer, suffers from vertigo. He believes his vertigo prevented him from saving the life of a fellow cop when they were chasing a villain across a rooftop. Still

'Scottie' Ferguson (James Stewart) becomes obsessed with the beautiful Madeleine (Kim Novak), the wife of an old friend, but his fear of heights prevents him from saving her from death in Vertigo.

recovering, Ferguson agrees to trail the wife of an old pal who fears his wife is suicidal. Before long Ferguson falls in love with his charge, Madeleine, and cracks up completely when she commits suicide. When he is released from the mental institution he sees a shop assistant, Judy, who resembles Madeleine. Still obsessed with Madeleine, Ferguson pursues Judy and tries to mould her into the woman who still haunts him. However, Judy is not all she seems and Ferguson soon realizes she is involved in a complicated murder plot. To force a confession, he takes Judy to the scene of Madeleine's death, the Mission tower, and she, like Madeleine, falls to her death.

Hitchcock wanted Vera Miles for the parts of Madeleine and Judy, but she was pregnant at the time and he couldn't delay filming. Set entirely in San Francisco, Hitchcock made great use of the city's picturesque locations, including the Golden Gate Bridge and the Mission at San Juan Batista.

Bernard Herrmann also scored Hitchcock's *Psycho*, *Marnie*, *North By Northwest*, *The Man Who Knew too Much* and *The Wrong Man*.

Video availability

BEN-HUR

1959	
Studio/Distributor:	MGM
Director:	William Wyler
Producer:	Sam Zimbalist
Screenplay:	Karl Tunberg
Music:	Miklos Rozsa

CAST

Charlton Heston	Judah Ben-Hur
Jack Hawkins	Quintus Arrius
Stephen Boyd	Messala
Haya Harareet	Esther
Hugh Griffith	Sheik Ilderim
Martha Scott	Miriam
Sam Jaffe	Simonides
Cathy O'Donnell	Tirzah

Judah (Charlton Heston) and the mean Messala (Stephen Boyd) are matched against each other in a heart-stopping chariot race in Ben Hur.

This spectacular Roman epic tells the story of Jewish-born Ben-Hur and Roman Messala, friends since childhood. Messala grows up with such a strong allegiance to the Roman Empire that it eventually turns him into a dangerous enemy. Quintus Arrius, the Roman Consul, adopts Ben-Hur after he survives a period as a galley slave, but the embittered Ben-Hur is determined to seek revenge on his one-time good friend Messala. He also searches for his missing mother and sister, who he finds in a leper colony. He is converted to Christianity after he sees Jesus restore his mother's eyesight. The film climaxes with the famous 40-minute chariot race between Ben-Hur and Messala.

The film was a remake of the 1925 silent movie version starring Ramon Novarro, on which director William Wyler worked as an assistant. The cost of making the epic practically bankrupted MGM, but the final result was worth all the pressures: it netted over $40 million profit. Producer Sam Zimbalist did not reap the rewards, however, as he died of a heart attack in Rome just before completion of the movie. It took five years of preparation and nine months to edit. There were 50,000 extras, 100,000 costumes and 300 sets.

Heston and Boyd did most of their own chariot driving, which often left them battered and bruised.

Kirk Douglas wanted to play the lead, and when director William Wyler offered him the part of Messala by way of consolation, he turned it down.

Ben-Hur holds the joint record for Oscars won, with a total of 11, all competitive. *West Side Story* (1961) also has 11, winning in 10 categories with one special Oscar for choreography.

Academy Awards: Best Film (Producer Sam Zimbalist), Best Direction (William Wyler), Best Actor (Charlton Heston), Best Supporting Actor (Hugh Griffith), Best Colour Cinematography (Robert Surtees), Best Colour Art Direction (William A. Horning and Edward Carfagno), Colour Set Decoration (Hugh Hunt), Best Colour Costume Design (Elizabeth Haffenden), Best Editing (Ralph E. Winters and John D. Dunning), Best Sound (Franklin E. Milton), Best Sound Effects (A. Arnold Gillespie), Visual Effects (Robert MacDonald), Audible Effects (Milo Lory), Best Music Score of a Drama or Comedy (Miklos Rozsa)

Video availability

CARRY ON NURSE

1959	
Studio/Distributor:	Anglo Amalgamated
Director:	Gerald Thomas
Producer:	Peter Rogers
Screenplay:	Norman Hinds
Music:	Bruce Montgomery

CAST
Kenneth Connor . . . . *Bernie Bishop*
Kenneth Williams . . . . *Oliver Reckitt*
Charles Hawtrey . . . . *Hinton*
Terence Longden . . . . *Ted York*
Bill Owen . . . . *Percy Hickson*
Leslie Phillips . . . . *Jack Bell*
Cyril Chamberlain . . . . *Bert Able*
Brian Oulton . . . . *Henry Bray*

Carry on Nurse was the second of the 'Carry On' movies and one of the several to take a humorous look at the day-to-day running of a local hospital. It involved a string of bizarre sketches with madhouse doctors and nurses making improper suggestions to one another as they attend eccentric patients in larger-than-life situations.

The first 'Carry On' sequel, much to the studio's surprise, did almost as well in America as it did in Britain.

The movie gave Kenneth Williams his first love scene with the late Jill Ireland, who later married Charles Bronson.

Video availability

EXPRESSO BONGO

1959	
Studio/Distributor:	BL/Britannia
Director:	Val Guest
Producer:	Val Guest
Screenplay:	Wolf Mankowitz
Music:	Monty Norman, Robert Farnon, Norrie Paramor, Bunny Lewis

CAST
Laurence Harvey . . . . *Johnny Jackson*
Sylvia Sims . . . . *Maisie King*
Yolande Donlan . . . . *Dixie Collins*
Cliff Richard . . . . *Bongo Herbert*
Meier Tzelniker . . . . *Mayer*
Ambrosine Philpotts . . . . . *Lady Rosemary*
Eric Pohlmann . . . . *Leon*
Gilbert Harding . . . . *Gilbert Harding*

In Cliff Richard's second venture into the movie world he plays Bongo, who sings and plays bongos in Soho's coffee bars. He is discovered by a less than reputable music promoter, Johnny Jackson, who offers him a contract that guarantees to sign his life away. With his name firmly on the dotted line, Jackson uses every trick in the book to boost his protégé to stardom. However, Bongo is underage, making the contract invalid and Bongo free to move on.

The story had already been a play in London's West end, starring Paul Scofield as the manager and James Kenny as Bongo.

The character Johnny Jackson was modelled on the real life show business manager Larry Parnes.

Marty Wilde was originally considered for the part of Bongo, but producer Val Guest finally decided the public would find it difficult to feel sorry for a boy who was six feet three inches tall. Cliff Richard's 'Expresso Bongo' E.P. which featured the songs 'Love', 'Voice in the Wilderness', 'The Shrine on the Second Floor' and 'Bongo Blues', was a top 20 hit in 1959, reaching number 14 in the charts.

Music: 'A Voice in the Wilderness', 'The Shrine on the Second Floor', 'Bongo Blues', 'Love'

Video availability

I'M ALL RIGHT JACK

1959		Producer:	Roy Boulting
		Screenplay:	Frank Harvey, John Boulting
Studio/Distributor:	British Lion		
Director:	John Boulting	Music:	Ken Hare

CAST
Ian Carmichael . . . . *Stanley Windrush*
Peter Sellers . . . . *Fred Kite*
Terry-Thomas . . . . *Major Hitchcock*
Richard Attenborough　*Sidney de Vere Cox*
Dennis Price . . . . *Bertram Tracepurcel*
Margaret Rutherford . . . . *Aunt Dolly*
Irene Handl . . . . *Mrs Kite*
Liz Fraser . . . . *Cynthia Kite*

Union shop steward Fred Kite calls for strike action when unskilled labourer Stanley Windrush comes up with plans to streamline his shop floor working habits in order to cut costs. Windrush has in fact been planted in the factory, owned by his uncle, to deliberately cause a walkout and allow his uncle to put one of his dirty financial schemes into practice. Typically British comedy poking fun at trade unions.

During the run up to the 1979 General Election, BBC Television cancelled a broadcast of *I'm All Right Jack* because they were scared the subject might influence voters.

When the Boulting brothers originally sent Peter Sellers the script, which they wrote for him, he quickly turned it down because he didn't think it was funny. He was finally convinced his character would bring home the laughs after he received a round of applause from the crew after he completed a screen test.

Peter Sellers was taken over by the character Fred Kite. Even off the set, he walked, talked, ate and generally behaved like the shop steward.

Video availability

THE MUMMY

1959	
Studio/Distributor:	Hammer
Director:	Terence Fisher
Producer:	Michael Carreras
Screenplay:	Jimmy Sangster
Music:	Frank Reizenstein

CAST
Peter Cushing . . . . *John Banning*
Christopher Lee . . . . *Kharis*
Yvonne Furneaux . . . . *Isobel and Ananka*
Eddie Byrne . . . . *Mulrooney*
Felix Aylmer . . . . *Stephen Banning*
Raymond Huntley . . . . . *Joseph Whemple*

During an archaeological dig in Egypt, a 4000-year-old mummy is discovered that comes back to life to plague John Banning and his team of scientists who have disturbed its slumber. The tomb has encased the Egyptian Princess Ananka and her lover, Kharis, who was buried alive when she died. Kharis travels back to England with the intention of killing the explorer, but is stopped in his tracks when he sets eyes on Banning's wife, Isobel, who is the spitting image of Ananka.

Christopher Lee's portrayal of the mummy completed his trilogy of classic horror parts, having already played Dracula and Frankenstein's monster.

Sequels included *Curse of the Mummy's Tomb* (1964), *The Mummy's Shroud* (1966), and *Blood from the Mummy's Tomb* (1971).

PORGY AND BESS

1959	
Studio/Distributor:	Columbia
Director:	Otto Preminger
Producer:	Samuel Goldwyn
Screenplay:	N. Richard Nash
Music:	George Gershwin

CAST
Sidney Poitier . . . . *Porgy*
Dorothy Dandridge . . . . *Bess*
Sammy Davis Jr . . . . *Sportin' Life*
Pearl Bailey . . . . *Maria*
Brock Peters . . . . *Crown*
Leslie Scott . . . . *Jake*
Diahann Carroll . . . . *Clara*
Ruth Attaway . . . . *Serena*

This musical is set in the squalor of South Carolina's Catfish Row. Porgy is a crippled beggar who loves Bess, a girl brought up in the slums and admired by several other men including 'Sportin' Life', who is her heroin supplier, and Crown, who kills a man in an argument and then has to hide from the police. When Crown returns, Bess has settled with Porgy, who in turn kills Crown. Bess then takes off for New York with Sportin' Life, but with the passing of time, Porgy sets off in his goat cart to find her again.

The part of Porgy was originally offered to Harry Belafonte who turned it down. Sidney Poitier was initially reluctant to accept the part on the grounds of its racial implications.

This was Samuel Goldwyn's final movie. He was aged 75 at the time. He fired director Robert Mamoulin, who first staged the opera, halfway through the project because of creative differences.

Sidney Poitier's singing voice was dubbed by Robert McPherrin, and Dorothy Dandridge's by Adele Addison. Diahann Carroll's voice was dubbed by Loulie Jean Norman and Ruth Attaway's by Inez Matthews.

A fire raced through the studio set in July 1958, causing thousands of dollars worth of damage to props and costumes.

Academy Awards: Best Scoring of a Musical (André Previn and Ken Darby)

Music: 'Summertime', 'I Got Plenty o' Nuthin'', 'It ain't Necessarily So', 'I Loves you Porgy', 'Bess you is my Woman Now', 'Oh I Can't Sit Down'

ROOM AT THE TOP

1959	
Studio/Distributor:	Remus
Director:	Jack Clayton
Producer:	John Woolf, James Woolf
Screenplay:	Neil Paterson
Music:	Mario Nascimbene

CAST
Laurence Harvey . . . . *Joe Lampton*
Simone Signoret . . . . *Alice Aisgill*
Heather Sears . . . . *Susan Brown*
Donald Wolfit . . . . *Mr Brown*
Ambrosine Philpotts . . . . *Mrs Brown*
Donald Houston . . . . *Charles Soames*
Raymond Huntley . . . . *Mr Hoylake*
John Westbrook . . . . *Jack Wales*

Joe Lampton is a poorly-paid accountant with very little prospects living in Bradford but he has his financial eye on Susan Brown whose father is an industrialist millionaire who owns half the town. Mr Brown rapidly sends his daughter abroad to forget about Joe, who then turns his attentions to Alice Aisgill, a performer in a local theatre group who is unhappily married to George. Joe, still obsessed with improving his financial status, begins to fall for Alice but her husband refuses her a divorce. A gritty British slice-of-life drama.

Based on John Braine's best-selling novel, the movie produced two sequels, *Life at the Top* and *Man at the Top*. The former also starred Laurence Harvey.

This was director Jack Clayton's first full-length feature film, although he only just lost out to William Wyler to work on *Ben-Hur*. He went on to make a successful version of *The Great Gatsby*, starring Robert Redford.

The film included stunning camera work from Freddie Francis, who won two Oscars for his cinematography in *Sons and Lovers* (1960) and *Glory* (1989).

Academy Awards: Best Actress (Simone Signoret), Best Screenplay (Neil Paterson)

Video availability

SLEEPING BEAUTY

1959	
Studio/Distributor:	Walt Disney
Director:	Clyde Geronimi
Producer:	Walt Disney
Screenplay:	Erdman Penner
Music:	George Bruns (adaptation)

CAST (Voices)
Mary Costa . . . . *Princess Aurora*
Bill Shirley . . . . *Prince Philip*
Eleanor Audley . . . . *Maleficent*
Verna Felton . . . . *Flora*
Barbara Jo Allen . . . . *Fauna*
Barbara Luddy . . . . *Merryweather*
Bill Thompson . . . . *King Hubert*
Taylor Holmes . . . . *King Stefan*

Princess Aurora finds herself under the spell of the bad fairy, Maleficent. The curse means that she will prick her finger on a spinning wheel and die. Fortunately, the good fairies Flora, Fauna and Merryweather manage to adapt the spell, allowing the Princess to remain alive but fall into a deep sleep to last until she is awakened by a kiss from her childhood sweetheart, Prince Philip.

Work on the film began in 1950 but didn't go into full production until 1953. There were further de-lays because it clashed with the development and opening of the Disneyland theme park in California.

Music was adapted from Tchaikovsky's 'Sleeping Beauty' ballet. .

Music: 'Once Upon a Dream'

Video availability

THE SQUARE PEG

1959	
Studio/Distributor:	Rank
Director:	John Paddy Carstairs
Producer:	Hugh Stewart
Screenplay:	Jack Davies
Music:	Philip Green

CAST
Norman Wisdom . *Norman Pitkin, General Schreiber*
Honor Blackman . . . . *Leslie Cartland*
Edward Chapman . . . . *Mr Grimsdale*
Campbell Singer . . . . *Sergeant Loder*
Hattie Jacques . . . . *Gretchen*
Brian Worth . . . . *Henri Le Blanc*
Terence Alexander . . . . . *Captain Wharton*

In this British comedy a young road repair man (Norman Wisdom) suddenly finds he is recruited into the army and moves from white lines to enemy lines with his bad-tempered boss, Mr Grimsdale. He then gets into all kinds of tangles after discovering that he looks almost identical to a German general. Somehow he ends up a war hero.

The Rank Organization plucked Norman Wisdom from under the noses of executives at ABC, but were mystified as to what to do with him. He wanted straight roles, they wanted him to play comedy. In this film, of course, he manages to combine the two by playing dual characters, the bumbling Norman Pitkin and the Nazi General Schreiber, who is played very straight. The movie provided Oliver Reed with one of his first screen appearances.

THE 39 STEPS

1959	
Studio/Distributor:	Rank
Director:	Ralph Thomas
Producer:	Betty Box, Ralph Thomas
Screenplay:	Frank Harvey
Music:	Clifton Park

CAST
Kenneth More . . . . *Richard Hannay*
Taina Elg . . . . *Fisher*
Brenda de Banzie . . . . *Nellie Lumsden*
Barry Jones . . . . *Professor Logan*
Reginald Beckwith . . . . *Lumsden*
Faith Brook . . . . *Nannie*
Michael Goodliffe . . . . *Brown*
James Hayter . . . . *Mr Memory*

A young woman tells Richard Hannay about a secret organization's plans to smuggle secret information out of the country. Unfortunately she doesn't know much about the leader apart from the fact that he has a piece of his little finger missing on his right hand. She then mentions the 39 steps. Later she is found murdered and Hannay becomes prime suspect. With 48 hours to prove his innocence, he travels to Scotland searching for answers before returning to London and finding Mr Memory, the music hall act who holds the key to the mystery.

Apart from being in colour, this was almost a scene-by-scene remake of Alfred Hitchcock's 1935 version which starred Robert Donat. The story was remade yet again in 1978, with Robert Powell playing Richard Hannay.

Video availability

THE 1960s

From biblical epic to kitchen-sink dramas, the 1960s were a time of change for the film industry. Television, which had been making inroads into our leisure time since the early 1950s, was now a common feature in every household in the land. The film business needed to fight back and one way to arrest the decline in audience was to make films bigger and better, more colourful and spectacular, and provide a true alternative to the flickering black and white tube in the corner at home.

And so the decade began with big blockbusters like *Exodus*, *Spartacus* and *The Magnificent Seven*. These huge films captured the grandeur and sheer breathtaking scope of the great outdoors which could never be rivalled by any television series. *The Guns of Navarone*, *How the West was Won* and *Lawrence of Arabia* continued the trend for huge epic pictures, but there was another saviour for the film business on the horizon. His name? Bond, James Bond.

The Ian Fleming novels had been huge best-sellers but no one was prepared for the impact that British Secret Agent 007 would have on cinema audiences throughout the world. *Dr No* kicked off the series in 1962 and Sean Connery went on to play Bond four more times during the decade before handing the mantle briefly to George Lazenby. The series set the template for many spy movies.

Big screen musicals continued to clock up huge audiences in the 1960s with *Can Can*, *Camelot*, *Half a Sixpence*, *My Fair Lady* and *Funny Girl* all posting record receipts. It certainly wasn't unusual for big hits to play at showcase cinemas in large cities for many months at a time and films like *Doctor Zhivago* were still playing at the Empire, Leicester Square more than two years after their premiere. The biggest of all the musicals in the 1960s was the phenomenally successful *The Sound of Music*.

Gritty realism was the order for the day as British film-makers developed a new domestic dramatic strand known as 'kitchen-sink'. Films like *Saturday Night and Sunday Morning*, *This Sporting Life* and *A Taste of Honey* launched the careers of actors like Richard Harris and Albert Finney and became big hits for the new wave of British directors, which included Lindsay Anderson and Tony Richardson.

Other more modest UK-made hits were musicals like *The Young Ones* and *Summer Holiday* from Cliff Richard, and two films from the pop sensation of the 1960s, *A Hard Day's Night* and *Help!*, from The Beatles. And for the fifth decade running Alfred Hitchcock managed to surpass himself with two magnificent thrillers, *Psycho* and *The Birds*.

Violence and sex in the movies became ever more graphic as the 1960s progressed. At the start of the decade nudity on screen was comparatively rare. However, times were changing, and the 'swinging' 1960s meant a re-appraisal of moral values and censorship, although as late as 1967 seemingly innocuous films like *Here We Go Round the Mulberry Bush* and *The Virgin Soldiers* from 1969 were still attracting the X certificate. Violence on screen had been gathering speed through the popularity of the 'Spaghetti Westerns', which were pouring in from Italy, and although today the 'horror' in the Hammer series of films looks laughable they still attracted X certificates. It wasn't until the early 1970s, with films like *Straw Dogs* and *A Clockwork Orange*, that the barriers were really tested.

THE ALAMO

1960	
Studio/Distributor:	United Artists
Director:	John Wayne
Producer:	John Wayne
Screenplay:	James Edward Grant
Music:	Dimitri Tiomkin

CAST
John Wayne . . . . *Col David Crockett*
Richard Widmark . . . . *Col James Bowie*
Laurence Harvey . . . . . . *Col William Travis*
Frankie Avalon . . . . *Smitty*
Patrick Wayne . *Capt James Butler Bonham*
Linda Cristal . . . . *Flaca*
Joan O'Brien . . . . *Mrs Dickinson*

John Wayne plays Davy Crockett in this successful movie, which he also produced and directed. It recounts how a handful of Americans, fighting for independence for the State of Texas in 1836, manage to hold off the deathly fire from 7000 men of the Mexican Santa Anna Army for thirteen days. The main heroes, Colonel William Travis, Jim Bowie and Davy Crockett, who falls in love with the Mexican girl Flaca, attempt to hold the fort but eventually succumb to the overwhelming manpower of the Mexican army.

The movie was produced by John Wayne's Batjac Productions, and was his debut as a director. One of John Wayne's best friends, director John Ford, acted as an uncredited second assistant on the movie. Some 26 minutes were cut from the film shortly after its initial release.

John Wayne's son Patrick makes an appearance as Captain James Butler Bonham.

The movie cost around $12 million to make, with about $1 million spent on just re-creating the fort.

Academy Awards: Best Sound (Gordon E. Sawyer and Fred Hynes)

Music: 'The Green Leaves of Summer'

Video availability

In a film that he also produced and directed, John Wayne plays Colonel David Crockett in The Alamo, *fighting for Texan independence.*

THE APARTMENT

1960	
Studio/Distributor:	United Artists
Director:	Billy Wilder
Producer:	Billy Wilder
Screenplay:	Billy Wilder, I.A.L. Diamond
Music:	Adolph Deutsch

CAST

Jack Lemmon . . . . C.C. Baxter
Shirley MacLaine . . . . Fran Kubelik
Fred MacMurray . . . . J.D. Sheldrake
Ray Walston . . . . Mr Dobisch
David Lewis . . . . Mr Kirkeby
Jack Kruschen . . . . Dr Dreyfuss
Joan Shawlee . . . . Sylvia

C.C. Baxter is an insurance clerk who works for a firm that has five senior partners. In order to keep himself in favour, and eventually earn promotion to the executive floor, Baxter lets them use his local apartment for their amorous extra-marital affairs. He finds himself playing nursemaid to Fran, the elevator girl, who tries to take her own life after she is dumped by Baxter's boss, J.D. Sheldrake. Before long the two are falling in love, and Baxter withdraws his apartment facility, finally finding peace of mind.

The Apartment was later turned into a stage musical called Promises, Promises, with music by Burt Bacharach and Hal David. It produced the hit song 'I'll Never Fall in Love Again'.

None of the stars knew the ending of the film until the final day's shooting, when director Billy Wilder handed out the last few pages of the script.

This was the last black and white Best Picture Oscar winner until Schindler's List in 1994.

Academy Awards: Best film (Producer Billy Wilder), Best Direction (Billy Wilder), Best Story and Screenplay (Billy Wilder and I.A.L. Diamond), Best Black and White Art Direction (Alexander Trauner), Black and White Set Decoration (Edward G. Boyle), Best Editing (Daniel Mandell)

Video availability

CAN-CAN

1960	
Studio/Distributor:	Twentieth Century-Fox
Director:	Walter Lang
Producer:	Jack Cummings
Screenplay:	Dorothy Kingsley, Charles Lederer
Music:	Nelson Riddle (arrangement)

CAST

Frank Sinatra . . . . François Durnais
Shirley MacLaine . . . . Simone Pistache
Maurice Chevalier . . . . Paul Berriere
Louis Jourdan . . . . Philippe Forrestier
Juliet Prowse . . . . Claudine
Marcel Dalio . . . . André, Headwaiter
Leon Belasco . . . . Orchestra Leader

In this Cole Porter musical set in 1890s Paris, cafe-owner La Mome Pistache is tangled up with two men in her life. She faces prosecution for allowing the can-can dance to be performed in her establishment, Bal du Paradis, even though she tries to pay police to allow the illegal dance to take place. She hires a lawyer (Frank Sinatra) to defend her in court and wins an acquittal.

One of two top-ten hits this year for Shirley MacLaine, the other being The Apartment. She also appears in Around the World in Eighty Days (1956) and Irma La Douce (1963).

It was reported that Russian leader Nikita Khrushchev thought Can-Can to be crude and vulgar.

Music: 'C'est Magnifique', 'It's All Right with Me', 'Let's Do It', 'You Do Something to Me', 'Just One of those Things', 'I Love Paris'

Video availability

DOCTOR IN LOVE

1960

Studio/Distributor: Rank
Director: Ralph Thomas
Producer: Betty E. Box
Screenplay: Nicholas Phipps
Music: Bruce Montgomery

CAST
Michael Craig . . . . Dr Richard Hare
Virginia Maskell . . . Dr Nicholas Barrington
Leslie Phillips . . . . Dr Tony Burge
James Robertson Justice Sir Lancelot Spratt
Carole Lesley . . . . Kitten Strudwick
Reginald Beckwith . . . . Wildewinde
Nicholas Phipps . . . . Dr Clive Cardew

Doctor in Love, based on the books by Richard Gordon, has more comedy capers from the 'Doctor' team. This time out two of the young doctors go to work in a country practice, and one falls in love with his nurse. Two doctors become volunteers trying to find a cure for the common cold, and Sir Lancelot ends up in a strip club when he should be addressing a medical conference. Just run-of-the-mill occurrences for the St Swithins Hospital.

This was the first 'Doctor' movie without Dirk Bogarde, who was replaced by Michael Craig. Only James Robertson Justice had appeared in all four 'Doctor' movies to date.

Video availability

EXODUS

1960

Studio/Distributor: United Artists
Director: Otto Preminger
Producer: Otto Preminger
Screenplay: Dalton Trumbo
Music: Ernest Gold

CAST
Paul Newman . . . . Ari Ben Canaan
Eva Marie Saint . . . . Kitty Fremont
Ralph Richardson . . . . Gen. Sutherland
Peter Lawford . . . . Major Caldwell
Lee J. Cobb . . . . Barak Ben Canaan
Sal Mineo . . . . Doy Landau
John Derek . . . . Taha
Hugh Griffith . . . . Mandria

This epic, based on the Leon Uris best-seller, depicts the struggle of Jewish refugees, who have escaped from a Cyprus detention centre, to reach Israel. It highlights the struggle by the Jewish people to gain the recognition of Palestine as a Jewish state, so heavily opposed by the Arabs, and the somewhat reluctant part played by Great Britain as the United Nations decided on the future of this new nation. Newman plays the Jewish resistance leader who falls in love with American nurse Kitty Fremont, who is caring for injured Jewish refugees in Cyprus.

Author of the book, Leon Uris, was fired from the film as producer Otto Preminger felt he didn't have the ability to turn his work into a screenplay. Preminger also fell out with Newman, the star of the movie. Newman, being a perfectionist, wanted more time for re-takes, while Preminger just wanted to get on with the job in hand.

Although parts of the script were constantly being re-written in order to please both the Arab and Jewish communities, there were still complaints and Preminger and Newman both received death threats during filming.

Academy Awards: Best Music Score of a Drama or Comedy (Ernest Gold)

Music: 'Theme from Exodus'

Video availability

THE MAGNIFICENT SEVEN

1960

Studio/Distributor: United Artists
Director: John Sturges

Producer: John Sturges
Screenplay: William Roberts
Music: Elmer Bernstein

Chris (Yul Brynner), Vin (Steve McQueen), Chico (Horst Buchholz), Harry (Brad Dexter), O'Reilly (Charles Bronson), Lee (Robert Vaughn) and Britt (James Coburn) are the Magnificent Seven, *who help save a small Mexican village from a gang of bandits.*

CAST
Yul Brynner . . . . *Chris*
Eli Wallach . . . . *Calvera*
Steve McQueen . . . . *Vin*
Horst Buchholz . . . . *Chico*
Charles Bronson . . . . *O'Reilly*
Robert Vaughn . . . . *Lee*
Brad Dexter . . . . *Harry Luck*
James Coburn . . . . *Britt*

A small Mexican village is under attack by the mean bandit Calvera and his gang, who pillage and steal from the village on a regular basis. The locals are too weak to fight back so they decide to hire a group of seven American gunfighters who hang out around the Rio Grande. The seven train the villagers to fight and then set a trap for Calvera's men. However, Calvera fights back after being am-bushed and the seven need to regroup and re-think before returning to the village and eventual victory.

Three sequels followed: *The Return of the Magnificent Seven* (1966), *Guns of the Magnificent Seven* (1969) and *The Magnificent Seven Ride!* (1972).

The movie was an American version of Akira Kurosawa's Japanese epic, *The Seven Samurai* (1954).

Elmer Bernstein's classic music score was Oscar nominated but lost to Ernest Gold's stirring score for *Exodus*.

Music: 'Theme from the Magnificent Seven'

Video availability

PSYCHO

1960

Studio/Distributor: Paramount
Director: Alfred Hitchcock
Producer: Alfred Hitchcock
Screenplay: Joseph Stefano
Music: Bernard Herrmann

CAST
Anthony Perkins . . . . *Norman Bates*
Janet Leigh . . . . *Marion Crane*
Vera Miles . . . . *Lila Crane*
John Gavin . . . . *Sam Loomis*
Martin Balsam . . . . *Milton Arbogast*
John McIntire . . . . *Sheriff Chambers*
Simon Oakland . . . . *Dr Richmond*

The somewhat disturbed Norman Bates (Anthony Perkins), who has a fixation about his ageing
mother, is the proprietor of a less than appealing motel in Psycho. *But 'Mother is not quite herself'*
on the day that Norman visits Marion Crane (Janet Leigh) in the shower.

Norman Bates is a disturbed young man who runs a badly kept motel. He lives under the influence of his ageing mother, who protects him from himself, especially where young women guests are concerned. One night Marion Crane checks into a room having stolen a large sum of money from her workplace in the hope that her lover, Sam Loomis, will leave his wife and marry her. Telling Bates of her predicament, he suggests she returns the money, but she's killed in the shower before she can leave the motel and Norman buries her, and her car, in quicksand at the back of his property.

Chocolate sauce was used for the scenes that showed blood flowing down the drain of the shower.

The music for the entire soundtrack was composed and played entirely on strings.

Alfred Hitchcock shot screenwriter Joseph Stefano's very first draft script, requesting only one scene to be changed. However, at one point, Hitchcock decided he didn't like the completed film and considered cutting it down to 60 minutes for a TV movie.

Although the movie was made for Paramount Pictures, Hitchcock financed the entire project himself and did everything he could to keep the costs down. Anthony Perkins would have been too expensive for the movie had he not owed Paramount one film from an old contract.

Actor John Gavin was embarrassed about playing a scene bare chested, despite having recently finished making *Spartacus* (also 1960), in which all his scenes were 'topless'. Hitchcock would not allow Janet Leigh to be filmed nude, even for the short flashes on screen. Instead he hired a stand-in model. Perkins also wasn't required for the shower scene, and was in fact in New York when the scene was shot in Hollywood.

Video availability

SATURDAY NIGHT AND SUNDAY MORNING

1960	
Studio/Distributor:	Bryanston
Director:	Karel Reisz
Producer:	Harry Saltzman, Tony Richardson
Screenplay:	Alan Sillitoe
Music:	Johnny Dankworth

CAST
Albert Finney . . . . Arthur
Shirley Anne Field . . . . Doreen
Rachel Roberts . . . . Brenda
Hylda Baker . . . . Aunt Ada
Norman Rossington . . . . Bert
Bryan Pringle . . . . Jack
Robert Cawdron . . . . Robboe
Edna Morris . . . . Mrs Bull
Elsie Wagstaff . . . . Mrs Seaton

In this gritty British kitchen-sink drama Arthur Seaton is a Nottingham factory worker with a job he hates, operating a lathe. But he enjoys the money he earns and gets much satisfaction by rebelling against authority. He spends his Saturday nights and Sunday mornings getting into drunken fights and seducing any woman willing to submit to his charms. He then meets Doreen Gretton with whom he falls in love, but she refuses to sleep with him unless he agrees to marry her, a commitment he seems unable to make.

Alan Sillitoe, who wrote the original novel and the screenplay that was based on it, actually worked at the Nottingham factory depicted in the film.

Albert Finney had previously worked with Shirley Anne Field in the same year when they appeared together in his first movie, *The Entertainer*, which starred Laurence Olivier.

As well as being Alan Sillitoe's first screenplay, the film was the first feature film to be directed by Karel Reisz.

Video availability

SINK THE BISMARCK!

1960	
Studio/Distributor:	Twentieth Century-Fox
Director:	Lewis Gilbert
Producer:	John Brabourne
Screenplay:	Edmund H. North
Music:	Clifton Parker

CAST
Kenneth More . *Captain Jonathan Shepard*
Dana Wynter . . . . *Anne Davis*
Carl Mohner . . . . *Captain Lindemann*
Laurence Naismith . . . . *First Sea Lord*
Geoffrey Keen . . . . *A.C.N.S.*
Karel Stepanek . . . . *Admiral Lutjens*
Michael Hordern . . . *Commander on King George*
Maurice Denham . . . *Commander Richards*
Esmond Knight . . *Captain, Prince of Wales*
Michael Goodliffe . . . . . . *Captain Banister*

In 1938 the German's most powerful warship, *The Bismarck*, is launched in Hamburg by the proud Nazi chiefs. In England Captain Jonathan Shepard plans to attack and destroy *The Bismarck*. From the war room of the British Admiralty he learns the enemy vessel has sunk *The Hood*, considered Britain's best naval fighter. It seems *The Bismarck* is indestructible until Shepard sends *The Ark Royal*, a ship on which his son is a gunner, to attack the German ship. They succeed in damaging it and more boats are sent in to finish off the job.

Producer John Brabourne's father-in-law, Earl Mountbatten of Burma, gave the production team the benefit of his experience with technical advice.

Director Lewis Gilbert was himself a child actor on the stage and in the movies. He went on to direct a series of blockbusters, including *Alfie* (1966), *You Only Live Twice* (1967), *Educating Rita* (1983) and *Shirley Valentine* (1989).

Video availability

SPARTACUS

1960	

Studio/Distributor: Universal
Director: Stanley Kubrick
Producer: Edward Lewis
Screenplay: Dalton Trumbo
Music: Alex North

CAST

Kirk Douglas .... Spartacus
Laurence Olivier............... Crassus
Jean Simmons .... Varinia
Charles Laughton .... Gracchus
Peter Ustinov .... Batiatus
John Gavin .... Caesar
Nina Foch .... Helena

The rebellious slave Spartacus is purchased in 73 BC by Lentulus Batiatus, who runs a school for gladiators, where he is trained to fight in order that he can be sold on for a profit to other Roman coliseum owners. Spartacus organizes a revolt with an army of fellow slaves. They launch an attack on the Romans, commanded by Marcus Licinius Crassus, in order to help stop the oppression, but their revolt is ultimately quashed by the Roman army after a long, bloody battle. Spartacus's lover, Varinia, has been captured by Crassus but is smuggled to safety, along with Spartacus's new-born son, by Batiatus. Spartacus and his fellow slaves are crucified, but before he dies he glimpses his son and Varinia.

The screenplay was written by Dalton Trumbo. It was the first time in many years he was allowed to use his real name as he was one of the writers jailed in 1950 for his alleged Communist involvement. He refused to declare whether he belonged to the Communist Party and served time for contempt of Congress. After his release, he was reduced to working on B movies under the pseudonym of Robert Rich.

It took $12 million and two years of hard work to bring this picture to the screen. Director Stanley Kubrick hired 8000 Spanish soldiers as extras to become Roman Legionaries for the large-scale battle scenes, which were filmed on the outskirts of Madrid.

Anthony Mann was originally hired to direct the movie, but because of differences of opinion, Kirk Douglas, the movie's star and executive producer, dismissed him after a week's filming.

Some fifteen minutes were taken out of the movie when it was first released. The scenes involved were thought lost forever until they were discovered and restored in 1991 thanks to painstaking research by the American Film Institute.

Academy Awards: Best Supporting Actor (Peter Ustinov), Best colour Cinematography (Russell Metty), Best Colour Art Direction (Alexander Golitzen and Eric Orbom), Set Decoration (Russell A. Gausman and Julia Heron), Best Colour Costume Design (Valles and Bill Thomas)

Video availability

THE ABSENT-MINDED PROFESSOR

1961	

Studio/Distributor: Walt Disney
Director: Robert Stevenson
Producer: Walt Disney
Screenplay: Bill Walsh
Music: George Bruns

CAST

Fred MacMurray .... Prof Ned Brainard
Nancy Olson .... Betsy Carlisle
Keenan Wynn............ Alonzo Hawk
Tommy Kirk .... Biff Hark
Leon Ames ...... President Rufus Daggett
Elliott Reid .... Shelby Ashton
Ed Wynn .... Fire Chief

The thieving Alonzo Hawk plans to steal the formula of Professor Ned Brainard's anti-gravity invention that he calls 'flubber'. The invention is a type of rubber which, when attached to the soles of a shoe, allows the wearer to leap vast heights into the air. When a basketball team apply it to their shoes during a game, the results are amazing. The 'flubber' also enables the professor's Model T Ford car to bounce its way to Washington where he shows the Government his invention.

Three generations of Wynns were cast in the film: Keenan, the bad guy, his father Ed, playing the fire chief, and his son Ned who had a small cameo part.

Disney hired a professional science professor to come up with a believable formula for flubber for the movie script.

A few months earlier, Fred MacMurray had started a new TV comedy series, which went on to become the longest-running situation comedy show in America – *My Three Sons*.

Video availability

BREAKFAST AT TIFFANY'S

1961	
Studio/Distributor:	Paramount
Director:	Blake Edwards
Producer:	Martin Jurow, Richard Shepherd
Screenplay:	George Axelrod
Music:	Henry Mancini

CAST

Audrey Hepburn	*Holly Golightly*
George Peppard	*Paul Varjak*
Patricia Neal	*'2-E'*
Buddy Ebsen	*Doc Golightly*
Martin Balsam	*O.J. Berman*
Mickey Rooney	*Mr Yunioshi*
Vilallonga	*Jose de Silva Perriera*
John McGiver	*Tiffany Clerk*

Holly Golightly (Audrey Hepburn) is a crazy mixed-up girl in Breakfast at Tiffany's. *Her life is further complicated by her on-off relationship with writer Paul Varjak (George Peppard).*

Holly Golightly is a highly strung Manhattan playgirl with moodswings; she has lively all-night parties one night and acts as a hermit the next. She also works nightclubs where she earns money in dubious circumstances. Paul, a young writer, is her upstairs neighbour, whose affair with a wealthy woman stops him from getting together with Holly, but ultimately they find love and she is able to come to terms with herself. The film includes one of the most memorable Hollywood scenes – Holly picking up her beloved cat from the pouring rain.

The film was based on the celebrated novel by Truman Capote.

The first day's shooting took place outside Tiffany's in New York, which caused a crowd to gather outside the store. Seeing so many people, many thought a robbery was in progress.

Henry Mancini, who scored the music for the film, worked with Blake Edwards several years earlier on the successful TV series *Peter Gunn*.

'Moon River' has become a classic song. It was a hit for Danny Williams, Henry Mancini and Greyhound in the UK.

Academy Awards: Best Music Score of a Drama or Comedy (Henry Mancini), Best Song – 'Moon River' (Henry Mancini, music; Johnny Mercer, lyrics)

Music: 'Moon River'

Video availability

EL CID

1961

Studio/Distributor:	Samuel Bronston
Director:	Anthony Mann
Producer:	Samuel Bronston
Screenplay:	Fredric M. Frank, Philip Yordan
Music:	Miklos Rozsa

CAST
Charlton Heston . . . . . *Rodrigo Diaz (El Cid)*
Sophia Loren . . . . *Chimene*
Raf Vallone . . . . *Ordonez*
Ralph Truman . . . . *King Ferdinand*
Gary Raymond . . . . *Sancho*
John Fraser . . . . *Alfonso*
Genevieve Page . . . . *Urraca*

Legendary 11th-century Spanish hero El Cid drives the Moors from his country. The father of his fiancée, Chimene, accuses him unreasonably of treason. To safeguard his honour, El Cid kills him, which causes an enormous rift between the two lovers, who are still forced to marry. However, she seeks revenge for her murdered father, but all her plans fail and she enters a convent. While there, she comes to realize that she has misjudged her husband as he proves he is prepared to die for his country. Repenting, she returns to him.

Charlton Heston originally turned down the offer to star in the film because he thought the script was too weak.

At a cost of $8 million, this was the most expensive film of the year. It required 1000 authentic costumes, $40,000 worth of jewellery and $150,000 was spent on realistic 11th-century artefacts. It was director Anthony Mann's first venture into big budget epic films. He went on to make *The Fall of the Roman Empire* (1964).

The props department had to build enormous replicas of the wooden gates for the entrance to the city of Valencia. When filming was completed, producer Samuel Bronston donated the gates to the town of Pensicola, where much of the film was shot on location.

Music: 'The Falcon and the Dove'

Video availability

THE GUNS OF NAVARONE

1961

Studio/Distributor:	Columbia
Director:	J. Lee Thompson
Producer:	Carl Foreman
Screenplay:	Carl Foreman
Music:	Dimitri Tiomkin

CAST
Gregory Peck . . . . *Mallory*
David Niven . . . . *Miller*
Anthony Quinn . . . . *Andrea*
Stanley Baker . . . . *Brown*
Anthony Quayle . . . . *Franklin*
James Darren . . . . *Pappadimos*

Irene Papas . . . . *Maria*
Gia Scala . . . . *Anna*

Adapted from Alistair MacLean's novel the film is set in 1943 during World War II. A gang of men, led by Captain Mallory, give up perfectly good jobs to sabotage huge radar-controlled guns that guard the Aegean island of Navarone. Their mission is to make it possible for a large British fleet to reach Turkey to rescue another navy force in danger of destruction by the Germans. To add to their problems, they learn there is a traitor in their midst.

Just before completion of the film, David Niven suffered a near fatal septicaemia condition. It was thought that a double would probably have to finish the film, but fortunately Niven recovered in time.

James Darren, who played Pappadimos, was having hit records as a pop singer at the time this movie became a hit.

Academy Awards: Best Special Effects (Bill Warrington, visual; Vivian C. Greenham, audible)

Video availability

ONE HUNDRED AND ONE DALMATIANS

1961

Studio/Distributor:	Walt Disney
Director:	Wolfgang Reitherman, Hamilton S. Luske, Clyde Geronimi
Producer:	Walt Disney
Screenplay:	Bill Peet
Music:	George Bruns

CAST (Voices)
Rod Taylor . . . . *Pongo*
Lisa Davis . . . . *Anita*
Cate Bauer . . . . *Perdita*
Ben Wright . . . . *Roger Radcliff*
Frederic Worlock . . . . *Horace*
J. Pat O'Malley . . *Jasper/miscellaneous dogs*
Betty Lou Gerson *Cruella de Vil/Miss Birdwell*
Martha Wentworth . . . . . *Nani/Goose/Cow*
Tom Conway . . . . *Collie*
George Pelling . . . . *Great Dane*

In this full-length Disney cartoon Roger and Anita meet, fall in love and marry. The two dogs pro-duce a litter of 15 dalmatian pups. The wealthy witch-like woman, Cruella de Vil, hires two villains to steal the pups to add to the other 84 she has already kidnapped with a view to making herself a special coat. Pongo contacts London's dog kingdom who set out to rescue the 99 pups. The dogtectives, known as Twilight Bark, are successful in their rescue attempts and put Scotland Yard profession-als to shame.

Disney statisticians report there are exactly 6,469,952 spots on the backs of the dogs and puppies in 113,760 frames of film.

This was the first Disney film to use the Xerox photography technique, allowing artists to animate one group of puppies and copy them across the film without making it look too mechanical. Even so the film cost $4 million and took three years to com-plete. It used 300 artists, which worked out at three artists per dog plus one earning a little overtime.

Video availability

A TASTE OF HONEY

1961

Studio/Distributor:	British Lion
Director:	Tony Richardson
Producer:	Tony Richardson
Screenplay:	Shelagh Delaney, Tony Richardson
Music:	John Addison

CAST
Dora Bryan . . . . *Helen*
Rita Tushingham . . . . *Jo*
Robert Stephens . . . . *Peter*
Murray Melvin . . . . *Geoffrey*

Paul Danquah . . . . *Jimmy*
David Boliver . . . . *Bert*
Moira Kaye . . . . *Doris*

In this British kitchen-sink drama, based on the hit play by Shelagh Delaney, Rita Tushingham plays Jo, a young illegitimate girl. Jo's life is made a misery by her slovenly alcoholic mother, who impulsively marries Peter, one of her many suitors. Jo takes a room on her own and learns she is pregnant after a one-night stand with black sailor Jimmy. She be-friends Geoffrey, a loving homosexual who works in the same shoe shop as Jo, and moves in with him on a platonic basis. He is thrilled about the expected

In A Taste of Honey, *illegitimate Jo (Rita Rushingham) escapes from her alcoholic and promiscuous mother, Helen (Dora Bryan), and moves in with homosexual Geoffrey (Murray Melvin) when she finds she is pregnant by her abandoned lover, Jimmy (Paul Danquah).*

baby and takes on the role of the father, even offering to marry her. In the meantime, her mother splits up with Peter and expects Jo to take her in, bringing with her heaps of trouble.

This was Rita Tushingham's movie debut for which she won the British Academy Award, The New York Film Critics' Award and the Cannes Film Festival Award for Best Newcomer.

Producer and director Tony Richardson was at one time married to actress Vanessa Redgrave. He is the late father of actresses Natasha and Joely Richardson.

Music: 'A Taste of Honey'

Video availability

VICTIM

		1961

Studio/Distributor:	Rank
Director:	Basil Dearden
Producer:	Michael Relph
Screenplay:	Janet Green, John McCormick
Music:	Philip Green

CAST

Dirk Bogarde	Melville Farr
Sylvia Syms	Laura
Dennis Price	Calloway
Anthony Nicholls	Lord Fullbrook
Peter Copley	Paul Mandrake

Norman Bird	Harold Doe
Peter McEnery	Barrett
Donald Churchill	Eddy

Melville Farr is a successful lawyer with homosexual tendencies, which his wife Laura knew about when they married, but so far they have led a comparatively normal life. Jack Barrett, a boy Farr once had a relationship with, tries to contact him not only because he's in trouble and needs a lawyer but also to warn him of a possible blackmail threat. But Farr refuses to see him. The boy kills himself, and Farr, struck by guilt, sets about nailing the blackmailers, at the same time putting his marriage and career in jeopardy.

The movie became the turning point in Dirk Bogarde's career when he finally played a substantially satisfying role after years of relatively unrewarding parts, cast mainly for his matinee idol looks rather than for his acting ability.

Video availability

Director Basil Dearden was tragically killed in a car crash in 1971. His son James Dearden followed in his footsteps, and is a successful director and writer whose credits include the screenplay for *Fatal Attraction* (1988).

WEST SIDE STORY

1961	
Studio/Distributor:	United Artists
Director:	Robert Wise, Jerome Robbins
Producer:	Robert Wise
Screenplay:	Ernest Lehman
Music:	Leonard Bernstein

CAST
Natalie Wood . . . . *Maria*
Richard Beymer . . . . *Tony*
Russ Tamblyn . . . . *Riff*
Rita Moreno . . . . *Anita*
George Chakiris . . . . *Bernardo*
Simon Oakland. . . . . . . *Lieutenant Schrank*
William Bramley. . . . . *Officer Krupke*

This modern-day musical version of Romeo and Juliet concerned the hopeless love of the American boy Bernardo for the beautiful Puerto Rican girl, Anita. Bernardo is leader of the street gang, the Sharks, who are constantly fighting with rivals the Jets, headed by Riff. Bernardo's sister, Maria, falls in love with Riff's best friend, Tony, a member of the Jets. This dynamic musical, with stunning dance routines and knockout songs, transferred all the vitality of the Broadway show to the silver screen.

Jerome Robbins, who choreographed the Broadway production, was hired to work on the film but because of his attention to detail the film company had visions of a huge overspend and fired him after the first few weeks of filming. Before his departure

he had already completed work on four numbers ('The Jet Song', 'I Feel Pretty', 'Cool' and 'America'). He still received his deserved screen credits.

The Mirisch brothers, executive producers of the movie, originally wanted Elvis Presley to play Tony. They also wanted pop singers Fabian, Paul Anka and Frankie Avalon, all of whom had previously appeared in films, to play gang members.

Natalie Wood's singing voice was dubbed by Marnie Nixon, Richard Beymer's by Jimmy Bryant and Rita Moreno's by Betty Wand.

The movie cost over $6 million to make but more than tripled that amount in profits in the US alone.

Academy Awards: Best Film (Producer Robert Wise), Best Direction (Robert Wise and Jerome Robbins), Best Supporting Actor (George Chakiris), Best Supporting Actress (Rita Moreno), Best Colour Cinematography (Daniel L. Fapp), Best Colour Art Direction (Boris Leven), Set Decoration (Victor A. Gangelin), Best Colour Costume Design (Irene Sharaff), Best Sound (Fred Hynes and Gordon E. Sawyer), Best Editing (Thomas Stanford), Best Scoring of a Musical (Saul Chaplin, Johnny Green, Sid Ramin and Irwin Kostal)

Music: 'Maria', 'Somewhere', 'America', 'Tonight', 'Gee Officer Krupke', 'I Feel Pretty', 'One Hand One Heart', 'Jet Song', 'A Boy Like That', 'I Have a Love'

Video availability

WHISTLE DOWN THE WIND

1961	
Studio/Distributor:	Rank
Director:	Bryan Forbes
Producer:	Richard Attenborough, Bryan Forbes
Screenplay:	Keith Waterhouse, Willis Hall
Music:	Malcolm Arnold

CAST
Bernard Lee . . . . *Bostock*
Alan Bates . . . . *The Man*
Norman Bird. . . . . *Eddie*
Diane Clare. . . . . *Miss Lodge*
Patricia Heneghan . . . . *Salvation Army Girl*
John Arnatt . . . . *Teesdale*
Elsie Wagstaff . . . . *Auntie Dorothy*
Ronald Hines . . . . *P.C. Thurstow*
Hayley Mills . . . . *Kathy*

This gentle British film is set in Lancashire where the three Bostock children live with their father on a farm. When they save some kittens from drowning and hide them in the barn, they find Arthur Blakey, a criminal wanted for murder. The children think he is Jesus Christ after he utters that name as an expletive when they discover him. Soon word is out that Christ is alive and well and living in the Bostock's barn, where children from all over visit him, bringing gifts of food and drink, while of course keeping their discovery a secret from their parents. Blakey is eventually discovered and arrested by the police, destroying the children's illusions.

This was Bryan Forbes' first movie as director.

Apart from Hayley Mills, none of the young children in the film were given scripts to learn. They improvised every scene, which probably accounted for its strange sense of realism.

This was only the second movie produced by Richard Attenborough and the first directed by Bryan Forbes.

Video availability

THE YOUNG ONES

1961		CAST	
		Cliff Richard	*Nicky*
Studio/Distributor:	ABP	Robert Morley	*Hamilton*
Director:	Sidney J. Furie	Carole Gray	*Toni*
Producer:	Kenneth Harper	Richard O'Sullivan	*Ernest*
Screenplay:	Peter Myers, Ronald Cass	Melvyn Hayes.	*Jimmy*
		Teddy Green.	*Chris*
Music:	Peter Myers, Stanley Black	Annette Robertson	*Barbara*
		Sonya Cordeau.	*Dorinda*
		Sean Sullivan	*Eddie*

Jet Harris, Tony Meehan, Bruce Welsh and Hank B. Marvin (The Shadows) provide instrumental backing for Nicky (Cliff Richard) as he performs a musical number in The Young Ones.

In this British musical Nicky and his girlfriend, Toni, spend much of their spare time at the local youth club, but the site is bought up for demolition by property tycoon Hamilton Black. Unbeknown to the other club members Hamilton Black is Nicky's father. The youngsters are told that they can keep the club if they can pay five years' rent in advance, so they decide to raise money by putting on a show in a dilapidated old theatre. Hamilton Black does everything in his power to stop them succeeding, but his quest fails as the kids play to a sell-out crowd after using pirate radio transmissions to publicize the show at the Finsbury Park Empire.

The US title of the film was *Wonderful to be Young*. The movie was severely edited for the American market.

Choreographer Herbert Ross suggested to producer Kenneth Harper that Barbra Streisand play the part of Toni, portrayed by Carole Gray. Harper didn't even give Streisand an audition.

The Young Ones was Cliff Richard's most successful movie, although *Expresso Bongo* (1959), *Summer Holiday* (1962) and *Wonderful Life* (1964) all feature as Top Ten films in their respective years.

The title song gave Cliff his 5th number one hit single in the UK and sold over a million copies.

Music: 'The Young Ones', 'We Say Yeah', 'When the Girl in your Arms is the Girl in your Heart', 'Got a Funny Feeling', 'Nothing's Impossible', 'Lessons in Love', 'What d'you know We've got a Show', 'The Savage', 'Peace Pipe'

Video availability

BARABBAS

1962	
Studio/Distributor:	Columbia
Director:	Richard Fleischer
Producer:	Dino De Laurentiis
Screenplay:	Christopher Fry, Diego Fabbri, Ivo Perilli, Nigel Balchin
Music:	Mario Nascimbene

CAST
Anthony Quinn . . . . *Barabbas*
Silvana Mangano . . . . *Rachel*
Arthur Kennedy . . . . *Pilate*
Katy Jurado . . . . *Sara*
Harry Andrews . . . . *St Peter*
Valentina Cortese . . . . *Julia*
Vittorio Gassman . . . . *Sahak*
Jack Palance . . . . *Torvald*

In this biblical epic Barabbas is the thief who was released from prison and replaced on the cross by Jesus Christ 2000 years ago in Jerusalem. His friend Rachel tells him Christ will survive his crucifixion but Barabbas cannot accept this and, baffled, he returns to his old life of crime. Arrested again, he's sent to work in the sulphur mines in Sicily where he meets Sahak, a Christian who tries to convert him. Barabbas escapes death when one of the mines collapses and again during his time in the Roman gladiator arenas. However, he finally embraces Christianity when he faces crucifixion for the second time.

The shot of the eclipse of the sun was real. It was filmed in Nice on February 15th, 1961.

The Roman area scenes were filmed in a well preserved amphitheatre in Verona, Italy.

Director Richard Fleischer had less than twenty minutes to commit the crucifixion sequence to film because of the discomfort of the actors.

In 1937, Anthony Quinn married Cecil B. DeMille's adopted daughter, Katherine, although they divorced in 1965.

Video availability

DR NO

1962	
Studio/Distributor:	United Artists
Director:	Terence Young
Producer:	Harry Saltzman, Albert R. Broccoli
Screenplay:	Richard Maibaum, Johanna Harwood, Berkeley Mather
Music:	Monty Norman

CAST
Sean Connery . . . . *James Bond*
Ursula Andress . . . . *Honey*
Joseph Wiseman . . . . *Dr No*
Jack Lord . . . . *Felix Leiter*
Bernard Lee . . . . *M*
Anthony Dawson . . . . *Professor Dent*
John Kitzmiller . . . . *Quarrel*
Lois Maxwell . . . . *Miss Moneypenny*

British secret service agent James Bond 007 is sent on a mission to Jamaica to investigate the murder of a fellow agent. He becomes involved with the villainous Dr No, an evil scientist who plans to disrupt the US space programme by diverting the flight paths of rockets launched at Cape Canaveral. Aided by US agent Felix Leiter and bikini-clad Honey, who emerges from the sea, he successfully concludes his mission.

Thunderball was originally planned to become the first Bond movie, but Ian Fleming was being sued by two writers who claimed that part of their screenplay had been written into his novel. The litigation made the property too hot to touch, so *Dr No* was made in its place.

Stuntman Bob Simmons claimed that the scene in which he doubled as Bond in bed with a tarantula crawling up his body was the most terrifying moment in his career.

Albert 'Cubby' Broccoli tried to purchase the rights to the Bond stories but was beaten to them by Harry Saltzman. Broccoli then tried to buy them from Saltzman, who would only make a deal on a joint venture, which brought about their Eon (Everything or nothing) production company.

Ian Fleming suggested Noel Coward for the role of Dr No, but he declined the offer. When Sean Connery was approached to play Bond, he refused to have a screen test. His arrogance impressed 'Cubby' Broccoli, who hired him without a test.

Music: 'The James Bond Theme'

Video availability

HOW THE WEST WAS WON

| 1962 |

Studio/Distributor:	MGM
Director:	Henry Hathaway, John Ford, George Marshall
Producer:	Bernard Smith
Screenplay:	James R. Webb
Music:	Alfred Newman

CAST
Spencer Tracy . . . . *Narrator*
Carroll Baker . . . . *Eve Prescott*
Lee J. Cobb . . . . *Lou Ramsey*
Henry Fonda . . . . *Jethro Stuart*
Carolyn Jones . . . . *Julie Stuart*
Karl Malden . . . . *Zebulon Prescott*
Gregory Peck . . . . *Cleve Van Valen*
George Peppard . . . . *Zeb Rawlings*
Robert Preston . . . . *Roger Morgan*
Debbie Reynolds . . . . *Lilith Prescott*
James Stewart . . . . *Linus Rawlings*
Eli Wallach . . . . *Charlie Gant*
John Wayne . . . . *General Sherman*
Richard Widmark . . . . *Mike King*
Walter Brennan . . . . *Colonel Hawkins*

This story of the evolution of the American West is told through the experiences of the Prescott family over three generations. Zebulon, a farmer from New England, heads out towards the Erie Canal with his wife and two daughters, Eve and Lilith, where they encounter Linus Rawlings, a fur trapper who immediately falls in love with Eve. Believing she has inherited a fortune, Lilith is later pursued by Cleve Van Valen, a professional gambler, after her parents are killed in a boating accident. From wagon trains to steam trains, the film encompasses the modernization of fledgling Western America.

How the West was Won was the first real feature to be filmed in Cinerama. It required three cameras to shoot every scene simultaneously, plus a three-projector system for showing the finished product. The film creates huge problems if shown on TV or transferred to video. Much of the picture is lost and the seams are visible.

The movie was divided into three segments, with a different director for each section, John Ford for 'The Civil War', George Marshall for 'The Railroad' and Henry Hathaway for 'The Rivers' and 'The Plains and the Outlaws'.

In 1978, an American TV series was made, based on the movie and starring James Arness. Due to the high cost and comparatively low viewing figures, it ran for no more than five months.

Academy Awards: Best Story and Screenplay (James R. Webb), Best Editing (Harold F. Kress), Best Sound (Franklin E. Milton)

Music: 'Raise a Ruckus', 'Home in the Meadow', 'What was your Name in the States?', 'Shenandoah',

'Poor Wayfaring Stranger', 'When Johnny comes Marching Home', 'I'm Bound for the Promised Land', 'Battle Hymn of the Republic'

Video availability

IN SEARCH OF THE CASTAWAYS

	1962
Studio/Distributor:	Walt Disney
Director:	Robert Stevenson
Producer:	Walt Disney
Screenplay:	Lowell S. Hawley
Music:	William Alwyn

CAST
Maurice Chevalier . . . . . . *Jacques Paganel*
Hayley Mills . . . . *Mary Grant*
George Sanders . . . . *Thomas Ayrton*
Wilfrid Hyde White . . . . . . *Lord Glenarvon*
Michael Anderson Jr . . . . *John Glenarvon*
Antonio Cifariello . . . . *Thalcave*
Keith Hamshere . . . . *Robert Grant*
Wilfrid Brambell . . . . *Bill Baye*

Professor Paganel, a French scientist, discovers a message in a bottle that reveals the whereabouts of sea Captain Grant who mysteriously disappeared two years previously. The captain's two children persuade a ship owner, Lord Glenarvon, and his son John to help them track down their father. Their search takes them to South America, Australia and New Zealand, where they encounter wildlife such as giant crocodiles and condors, and survive earthquakes, fires and floods.

The film was based on the novel by Jules Verne.

At the age of 16, this was Hayley Mills's third Disney film in four years, following on from *Pollyanna* and *The Parent Trap*.

The 40 Maori tribesmen performing their ancient war dance, the Maori Haka, were filmed at the Pinewood Studios in England, along with most of the interior shots.

Video availability

LAWRENCE OF ARABIA

	1962
Studio/Distributor:	Columbia
Director:	David Lean
Producer:	Sam Spiegel
Screenplay:	Robert Bolt
Music:	Maurice Jarre

CAST
Peter O'Toole . . . . *Lawrence*
Alec Guinness . . . . *Prince Feisal*
Anthony Quinn . . . . *Auda Abu Tayi*
Jack Hawkins . . . . *General Allenby*
Omar Sharif . . . . *Sherif Ali*
José Ferrer . . . . *Turkish Bey*
Anthony Quayle . . . . *Colonel Brighton*
Claude Rains . . . . *Mr Dryden*

In this epic film David Lean tells the story of the historic British officer and his achievements in Palestine during World War I. Lawrence is sent on a mission to find and observe Prince Feisal, the man leading the Arab revolt against Turkey. Lawrence undertakes the task of helping the Arabs achieve their independence from the British, but is captured by the Turks and severely tortured. He is a mere shadow of his former self when he undertakes the responsibility of leading a force to Damascus.

Producer Sam Spiegel's good friend Katharine Hepburn recommended O'Toole for the part of Lawrence.

The movie was successfully re-released in 1971 with twenty minutes edited out, and was again issued in 1989 with the film restored to its full length by the director personally. Unfortunately it was discovered that parts of the master negative were damaged and Peter O'Toole was called in to re-dub some of his lines. Although his voice had changed over the 27-year period, it was perfectly matched by modern electronics.

This was the second and last collaboration between director David Lean and producer Sam Spiegel. They first worked together on *The Bridge on the River Kwai* (1957).

In 1958, Anthony Asquith had plans to direct Dirk Bogarde in a British-made version of 'Lawrence of Arabia', with a script by Terence Rattigan. The project was cancelled largely due to the government's 30 per cent entertainment tax that was imposed at the time. The script was adapted into a

The multi-million dollar epic, Lawrence of Arabia, *turned the then unknown actor Peter O'Toole into a star for his portrayal of T.E. Lawrence, the celebrated British officer of World War I.*

stage play which was re-named *Ross* and starred Alec Guinness.

Academy Awards: Best Film (Producer Sam Spiegel), Best Direction (David Lean), Best colour Cinematography (Freddie Young), Best Colour Art Direction (John Box and John Stoll), Set Direction (Dario Simone), Best Editing (Anne Coates), Best Sound Recording (John Cox), Best Original Music Score (Maurice Jarre)

Video availability

THE LONGEST DAY

1962

Studio/Distributor: Twentieth Century-Fox
Director: Ken Annakin, Andrew Marton, Bernhard Wicki
Producer: Darryl F. Zanuck
Screenplay: Cornelius Ryan, Romain Gary, James Jones, David Pursall, Jack Seddon
Music: Maurice Jarre, Paul Anka

CAST
John Wayne . . . . *Col. Vandervoort*
Robert Mitchum . . . . *Gen. Cota*
Henry Fonda . . . . *Gen. Roosevelt*
Robert Ryan . . . . *Gen. Gavin*
Rod Steiger . . . . *Commander*
Robert Wagner . . . . *U.S. Ranger*
Richard Beviner . . . . *Schultz*
Mel Ferrer . . . . *Gen. Haines*
Paul Anka . . . . *Ranger*

The first half of the film deals largely with the events leading to June 6th 1944, D-Day, including the long wait for the weather to break and the movement of the enormous armada across the English Channel. Then follows the eventual Allied invasion of Normandy on D-Day. The big day sees the landing at Normandy, with forces from the land, sea and air converging on the beaches to begin battle with Germany's entrenched troops.

The movie saw the first big screen appearances by pop stars Paul Anka, Fabian and Tommy Sands in dramatic roles. It featured dozens of top stars in cameo roles, including George Segal, Curt Jurgens and Peter Lawford. The movie, with practically an all-male cast, had one major female role played by director Darryl F. Zanuck's girlfriend at the time, Irina Demick, who played Janine. John Wayne, who was required for just four days of filming, received a fee of $250,000.

Members of the film crew were often used in battle scenes, and in one instance, real explosives were set off by accident, causing actors to head in the wrong direction, but these scenes were kept in.

This was one of the last major epic movies to be filmed in black and white, and became the most expensive non-colour picture ever made.

The producers hired over 20 military and technical advisors, including German war hero Frau Rommel and Commando Leader Lord Lovat.

Academy Awards: Best Black and White Cinematography (Jean Bourgoin and Walter Wottitz), Best Special Effects (Robert MacDonald, visual; Jacques Maumont, audible)

Video availability

THE MUSIC MAN

1962	
Studio/Distributor:	Warner
Director:	Morton DaCosta
Producer:	Morton DaCosta
Screenplay:	Marion Hargrove
Music:	Meredith Wilson

CAST
Robert Preston . . . . *Harold Hill*
Shirley Jones . . . . *Marian Paroo*
Buddy Hackett . . . . . . *Marcellus Washburn*
Hermione Gingold . . . . *Eulalie Shinn*
Paul Ford . . . . *Mayor Shinn*
Pert Kelton . . . . *Mrs Paroo*
Timmy Everett . . . . *Tommy Djilas*
Susan Luckey . . . . *Zaneeta Shinn*

Professor Harold Hill is a travelling salesman and con man who can sell anything to anyone. He arrives in Iowa and convinces the locals that their town is about to be corrupted by the opening of a pool room. To keep the kids away from the establishment, he suggests they start a local marching band. He says he can supply the instruments at a good price and teach the youngsters how to play. His real intention is to vanish with the money before

any goods change hands. However, romance beckons him to stay as he begins to fall in love with Marian Paroo.

Cary Grant was considered for the lead role but was quoted as saying 'Not only won't I play it, but unless Robert Preston gets the part, I won't even go to see the picture'.

Child actor Ronny Howard, who played Winthrop Paroo, the little boy with the stammer, went on to star as Richie Cunningham in the long-running TV series *Happy Days* before directing films including *Cocoon* (1985), *Backdraft* (1991), *Far and Away* (1992) and *The Paper* (1994).

Although bigger stars were considered, movie boss Jack Warner took the gamble (which paid off) of using many of the cast responsible for making the show a success on Broadway.

Academy Awards: Best Score (Adaptation or Treatment) (Ray Heindorf)

Music: 'Seventy-six Trombones', 'Goodnight my Someone', 'Being in Love', 'Till there was you', 'Trouble'

Video availability

MUTINY ON THE BOUNTY

1962	
Studio/Distributor:	MGM
Director:	Frank Lloyd
Producer:	Irving G. Thalberg
Screenplay:	Talbot Jennings, Jules Furthman, Carey Wilson
Music:	Herbert Stothart

CAST
Marlon Brando . . . . *Fletcher Christian*
Trevor Howard . . . . *Captain Bligh*
Richard Harris . . . . *John Mills*
Hugh Griffith . . . . *Alexander Smith*
Richard Haydn . . . . *William Brown*
Percy Herbert . . . . *Mathew Quintal*
Chips Rafferty . . . . *Michael Byrne*
Eddie Byrne . . . . *John Fryer*

Marlon Brando, Trevor Howard and Richard Harris starred in the screen version of the navy's most famous mutiny. After the *Bounty* sets sail in 1787 from Portsmouth to Tahiti, First Mate Fletcher Christian and the crew suffer constant humiliation from the tyrannical Captain Bligh. On the homeward voyage, Bligh becomes even more of a monster, causing Christian to head the mutiny, which climaxes on Pitcairn Island as the mutineers plot the Captain's downfall.

The story was first filmed in 1935 with Clark Gable and Charles Laughton. It was re-made again in 1984 as *The Bounty* with a host of star names, including Mel Gibson, Laurence Olivier and Anthony Hopkins.

A musical version of the story was produced on the London stage in 1985. *Mutiny* starred Frank Finlay and David Essex (who wrote the music for the show).

The ship *Bounty* that was built for the movie was 118 feet long (33 feet longer than the original boat) and constructed by the Smith and Rhuland shipyard in Nova Scotia. It was launched in February 1960 and began its 7326-mile maiden voyage to the film's locations in Tahiti and Bora Bora.

Music: 'Follow Me'

Video availability

ONLY TWO CAN PLAY

1962	
Studio/Distributor:	British Lion
Director:	Sidney Gilliat
Producer:	Leslie Gilliat
Screenplay:	Bryan Forbes
Music:	Richard Rodney Bennett

CAST
Peter Sellers . . . . John Lewis
Mai Zetterling . . . . Liz
Virginia Maskell . . . . Jean
Richard Attenborough . . . . Probert
Kenneth Griffith . . . . Jenkins
Maudie Edwards . . . . Mrs Davies
Frederick Piper . . . . Mr Davies
Graham Stark . . . . Hyman

Based on the Kingsley Amis novel *That Uncertain Feeling*, the story revolves around Lewis, a disillusioned Welsh librarian. He is fed up with lack of funds, his depressing rented home and the landlady that goes with it, and bored with his wife and two badly behaved children. However, his life becomes

more interesting when a rich society woman shows more than a passing interest in him, promising him that her husband can give him a better job. They become romantically involved, but never get past first base due to her husband's unexpected return and the frequent interruption by a herd of cows! Lewis returns to his wife to discover she's been having a bit of a fling herself.

Screenplay writer Bryan Forbes was furious with the producers for taking the decision to change the original title of Kingsley Amis's novel, *That Uncertain Feeling*. He could see no reason for doing so and felt it was an insult to such an acclaimed author.

Peter Sellers was unhappy about Virginia Maskell, claiming she hadn't the right accent and was unable to act. He also believed the film was so bad it would set his career back ten years, and sold his interest in the movie back to the film company. However, the movie became one of the year's greatest successes from the British film industry, with the share Sellers sold back earning about 600 per cent profit.

Video availability

SUMMER HOLIDAY

1962	
Studio/Distributor:	MGM
Director:	Peter Yates
Producer:	Kenneth Harper
Screenplay:	Peter Myers, Ronald Cass
Music:	Stanley Black

CAST
Cliff Richard . . . . Don
Lauri Peters . . . . Barbara
Melvyn Hayes . . . . Cyril
Una Stubbs . . . . Sandy
Teddy Green . . . . Steve

Pamela Hart . . . . Angie
Jeremy Bulloch . . . . Edwin
Jacqueline Daryl . . . . Mimsi

This good-natured British musical begins when four mechanics from London Transport borrow a double decker bus and turn it into a mobile hotel. They set off on a trip around Europe, taking on board three stranded showgirls who are heading for Athens. They also pick up Barbara, a young American singer who they initially think is a boy. Barbara's mother conspires to have the bus diverted as a publicity stunt to further her daughter's career, but the plan backfires when everyone arrives safely in Athens.

The movie was choreographed by Herbert Ross who also choreographed Cliff Richard's last big smash, *The Young Ones*. He went on to become a successful director, with credits including *Goodbye Mr Chips*, *The Sunshine Boys*, *Funny Lady* (1975) and *Footloose* (1984).

Peter Yates, who was assistant director on *The Guns of Navarone* (1961) and *A Taste of Honey* (1961), went on to direct *Bullitt* (1968), *Murphy's War* (1971) and *The Deep* (1977).

During the making of the film Lauri Peters married actor Jon Voight. She had made one previous movie,

Mr Hobbs takes a Vacation (also 1962), starring James Stewart.

Watch out for Ron Moody as Orlando, a wandering entertainer who also hitches a lift with the lads.

Music: 'Summer Holiday', 'Dancing Shoes', 'Bachelor Boy', 'The Next Time', 'Seven Days to a Holiday', 'Foot Tapper', 'Let us Take you for a Ride', 'Big News', 'All at Once'

Video availability

THE BIRDS

1963	
Studio/Distributor:	Universal
Director:	Alfred Hitchcock
Producer:	Alfred Hitchcock
Screenplay:	Evan Hunter
Music:	no credit

CAST
Rod Taylor . . . . *Mitch Brenner*
Jessica Tandy . . . . *Lydia Brenner*

Tippi Hedren . . . . *Melanie Daniels*
Suzanne Pleshette . . . . . . *Annie Hayworth*
Veronica Cartwright . . . . . *Cathy Brenner*
Ethel Griffies . . . . *Mrs Bundy*
Charles McGraw . . . . *Sebastian Sholes*
Ruth McDevitt . . . . *Mrs MacGruder*

Lawyer Mitch Brenner is pursued by rich playgirl Melanie Daniels, who has recently arrived from San Francisco carrying a pair of lovebirds in a cage as a gift. Her presence creates friction between

Tippi Hedren is no match for The Birds *in Hitchcock's Freudian thriller. As in all his films, Hitchcock makes a cameo appearance. In* The Birds *he is seen in front of a pet shop with his white poodles.*

Annie Hayworth, Mitch's ex-girlfriend, and his mother. For no real reason birds begin swooping out of the sky and creating havoc and chaos among the citizens of sleepy Bodega Bay. A seagull scratches Melanie's face, crows attack the village school, terrorizing the children, and the birds attack and kill Annie. There is no escape, as even houses and cars are vulnerable to the onslaught. Are the birds about to take over the world? And if so, why?

The film was based on a short story by Daphne du Maurier.

Alfred Hitchcock discovered Tippi Hedren when he saw her on television in an advertisement for a weight-loss drink called 'Sego'. For the scene where she is attacked in a small room, real birds were tied to her body.

Video availability

CLEOPATRA

1963	
Studio/Distributor:	Twentieth Century-Fox
Director:	Joseph L. Mankiewicz
Producer:	Walter Wanger
Screenplay:	Joseph L. Mankiewicz, Ranald MacDougall, Sidney Buchman
Music:	Alex North

CAST
Elizabeth Taylor . . . . *Cleopatra*
Richard Burton . . . . *Mark Antony*
Rex Harrison . . . . *Julius Caesar*
Pamela Brown . . . . *High Priestess*
George Cole . . . . *Flavius*
Hume Cronyn . . . . *Sosigenes*
Martin Landau . . . . *Rufio*
Roddy McDowall . . . . *Octavian*

In this lavish production Elizabeth Taylor plays the beautiful Cleopatra, Queen of the Nile. After the assassination of Julius Caesar, Cleopatra turns her attentions to Mark Antony, who becomes ruler of the Roman world with Octavian. His love for her gives him strength, but his partnership with her proves his downfall. The majestic, sweeping sequences include her triumphal entry into Rome, and the monumental battle of Actium.

Allowing for inflation, *Cleopatra* still ranks as the most expensive movie ever made, costing anywhere from $37 to $43 million. The movie was plagued with disasters from the start. Elizabeth Taylor had a string of illnesses, including double pneumonia which led to a tracheotomy operation. Other problems included a union dispute over Taylor's hairdresser and the resignation of the original director, Rouben Mamoulian. Constant bad weather halted production, meaning that after 9 months of filming in London, and $5 million later, the producers had nothing to show for their efforts. Production had to be shut down and moved to Rome.

The romance between Elizabeth Taylor and Richard Burton began during the filming of Cleopatra. They were both married at the time and a visit to the location by Burton's wife gave Taylor reason to sit up crying all night, making filming impossible the following day because of her swollen eyes.

Because of Elizabeth Taylor's obsession for sunbathing, her tan darkened, forcing lighting directors to change much of the footage with the use of colour correction.

Academy Awards: Best Colour Cinematography (Leon Shamroy), Best Colour Art Direction (John DeCuir, Jack Martin Smith, Hilyard Brown, Herman Blumenthal, Elven Webb, Maurice Pelling and Boris Juraga), Best Set Decoration (Walter M. Scott, Paul S. Fox and Ray Moyer), Best Colour Costume Design (Irene Sharaff, Vittorio Nino Novarese and Renie), Best Special Effects (Emil Kosa Jnr)

Video availability

FROM RUSSIA WITH LOVE

1963	
Studio/Distributor:	United Artists
Director:	Terence Young
Producer:	Harry Saltzman, Albert R. Broccoli
Screenplay:	Richard Maibaum
Music:	John Barry

CAST
Sean Connery . . . . *James Bond*
Daniela Bianchi . . . . . . *Tatiana Romanova*
Pedro Armendariz . . . . *Kerim Bey*
Lotte Lenya . . . . *Rosa Klebb*
Robert Shaw . . . . *Red Grant*
Bernard Lee . . . . *M*
Lois Maxwell . . . . *Miss Moneypenny*

After the success of *Dr No*, Sean Connery returned with his second outing as secret agent James Bond. He is on his way to Istanbul to retrieve a top security decoding device, known as 'the Lektor', from the Russian Embassy. International crime organization SPECTRE have plans to capture Bond, recover the machine and sell it back to Russia. Bond is on the hit list as he encounters enemy agents Rosa Klebb, who hides a poisonous blade in the tip of her shoe, and Red Grant, an assassin hired to kill Bond.

Daniela Bianchi who plays the Soviet agent Tatiana, was the runner up in the 1960 Miss World contest. Her voice was dubbed for the movie.

Pedro Armendariz, who plays Kerim Bey, Turkey's Head of Secret Service, was suffering with cancer during the filming. Because of his illness scenes were shot around him. Director Terence Young actually doubled for him in some long shots. Tragically, Armendariz committed suicide soon after the completion of the film.

While checking a location for filming, director Terence Young's helicopter developed engine trouble and crashed into the sea. Young escaped from beneath ten feet of water and returned to the set an hour later as though nothing had happened.

Robert Shaw was required to go on a crash course in bodybuilding, as well as taking Greco-Turkish wrestling lessons, for his part in the movie.

Music: 'From Russia with Love' (Matt Monro)

Video availability

THE GREAT ESCAPE

1963	
Studio/Distributor:	United Artists
Director:	John Sturges
Producer:	John Sturges
Screenplay:	James Clavell, W.R. Burnett
Music:	Elmer Bernstein

CAST
Steve McQueen . . . . *Hilts*
James Garner . . . . *Hendley*
Richard Attenborough . . . . *Bartlett*
James Donald . . . . *Ramsey*
Charles Bronson . . . . *Danny Velinski*
Donald Pleasence . . . . *Blythe*
James Coburn . . . . *Sedgwick*
David McCallum . . . . *Ashley Pitt*

Allied POWs plan a mass breakout from Stalag Luft North, a large escape-proof Nazi prison camp during World War II. Although their first of three tunnels (Tom, Dick and Harry) is discovered by the Germans after months of digging, the breakout still takes place. The men try to make their way to safety, hoping that the search for them will take some of the enemy away from the front line. Seventy-six prisoners manage to escape, but some are re-captured. The film was based on a true story.

James Garner was wounded in the Korean War while in the army and was awarded the Purple Heart.

Video availability

HEAVEN'S ABOVE!

1963	
Studio/Distributor:	British Lion
Director:	John Boulting
Producer:	John Boulting, Roy Boulting
Screenplay:	Frank Harvey, John Boulting
Music:	Richard Rodney Bennett

CAST
Peter Sellers . . . . *Rev John Smallwood*
Cecil Parker . . . . *Archdeacon Aspinall*
Isabel Jeans . . . . *Lady Despard*

Eric Sykes . . . . *Harry Smith*
Bernard Miles . . . . *Simpson*
Brock Peters . . . . *Matthew*
Ian Carmichael . . . . . *The Other Smallwood*
Irene Handl . . . . *René Smith*

The Reverend John Smallwood gets transferred from his prison chaplaincy to the wealthy parish of Orbiston Parva. The neighbourhood is controlled by the Despard family, whose Tranquilax factory keeps many of the locals in employment. It emerges that Smallwood's appointment came about through a clerical error, and the way he runs the church sends shock waves through the town. His position is not strengthened when he allows a party of homeless gypsies to live in the vicarage and the townspeople conspire to get rid of him. The church and state intervene and he's sent to the moon as its new bishop.

The plot was based on an idea by Malcolm Muggeridge. The character of Reverend John Smallwood came about when Sellers was standing in front of a mirror trying to work out how the holy man should look, when suddenly staring back at him

was Brother Cornelius, who was his old school teacher before the war.

Peter Sellers' great-great-grandfather was Daniel Mendoza, an 18th-century heavyweight boxing champion of England. Sellers intended to use his figure as a logo for the production company he never got around to forming.

Video availability

IRMA LA DOUCE

1963

Studio/Distributor:	United Artists
Director:	Billy Wilder
Producer:	Billy Wilder
Screenplay:	Billy Wilder
Music:	André Previn

CAST
Jack Lemmon . . . . *Nestor*
Shirley MacLaine . . . . *Irma La Douce*
Lou Jacobi . . . . *Moustache*
Bruce Yarnell . . . . *Hippolyte*
Herschel Bernardi . . . . . *Inspector LeFevre*
Hope Holiday . . . . *Lolita*
Joan Shawlee . . . . *Amazon Annie*
Grace Lee Whitney . . . . . . *Kiki the Cossack*

French streetwalker Irma has to hand most of her hard-earned money over to Hippolyte, her good-looking pimp. Nestor is a new cop in town who disguises himself as an English Lord to become her client. He conducts his business in a magnificently

inept fashion. However, he is horrified by the number of prostitutes on his beat and organizes a raid on a café which is frequented by many of the locals. As a result the Chief of Police is arrested and subsequently dismissed from the force. Nestor himself loses his job and ends up pimping for Irma after she sends Hippolyte packing.

Irma La Douce began as a French musical in 1956 and was adapted for the American stage in 1960, before Wilder adapted it for the screen and threw out all the songs.

A young James Caan has a very small walk on part, as does Bill Bixby of *The Incredible Hulk* fame, and Yeoman Rand of *Star Trek*. Charles Laughton was going to appear in the movie but died just before filming commenced.

This was the second collaboration between Wilder, Lemmon and MacLaine; *The Apartment* was the first (1960).

Academy Awards: Best Scoring (Adaptation or Treatment) (André Previn)

IT'S A MAD, MAD, MAD, MAD WORLD

1963

Studio/Distributor:	United Artists
Director:	Stanley Kramer
Producer:	Stanley Kramer
Screenplay:	William Rose, Tania Rose
Music:	Ernest Gold

CAST
Spencer Tracy . . . . *Capt C.G. Culpepper*
Milton Berle . . . . *J. Russell Finch*
Sid Caesar . . . . *Melville Crump*
Buddy Hackett . . . . *Benjy Benjamin*
Ethel Merman . . . . *Mrs Marcus*
Mickey Rooney . . . . *Ding Bell*
Dick Shawn . . . . *Sylvester Marcus*
Phil Silvers . . . . *Otto Meyer*

Recently released from prison and on his death bed, a gangster gives a clue to the whereabouts of $350,000 of swag, knowing it will cause a mad dash to find the treasure. The greedy parties head to the vicinity of the site, unaware that the police are watching and waiting to be led to the stolen money. Soon to retire police chief Culpepper attempts to escape with the money, but in an hilarious chase sequence the money is lost. In a slapstick finale, everyone ends up in hospital with multiple injuries, but nevertheless all in stitches of laughter.

Director Stanley Kramer can take credit for giving Spencer Tracy's career a new lease of life with this movie. Although in bad health, Tracy managed to get through the filming using a double for the more strenuous sequences. The movie boasts cameo appearances by a number of stars, including Buster Keaton and Jimmy Durante.

The original movie is believed to have been nearly six hours long, although it was cut to just over three hours for release.

Academy Awards: Best Sound Effects (Walter G. Elliott)

Music: 'It's a Mad, Mad, Mad, Mad World'

Video availability

JASON AND THE ARGONAUTS

1963	
Studio/Distributor:	Columbia
Director:	Don Chaffey
Producer:	Charles H. Schneer
Screenplay:	Jan Read, Beverley Cross
Music:	Bernard Herrmann

CAST

Todd Armstrong	Jason
Nancy Kovack	Medea
Gary Raymond	Acastus
Laurence Naismith	Argus
Niall MacGinnis	Zeus
Michael Gwynn	Hermes
Douglas Wilmer	Pelias
Jack Gwillim	King Aeetes
Honor Blackman	Hera

In this Greek mythological tale the King of Thessaly is murdered by the evil Pelias, but his young son,

Jason, escapes. When Jason reaches adulthood, he sets sail in the *Argo*, with a crew of five men and the help of Goddess Hera, in search of the Golden Fleece, which will instate him as the rightful king. On the voyage he fends off a living statue and the enormous Neptune before reaching the fleece. Guarding the fleece is the seven-headed hydra whose teeth produce sword-brandishing living skeletons, which they manage to defeat in a battle to the death.

The movie became a classic among film-makers because of its brilliant use of a stop frame animation technique from legendary stop-motion special effects expert Ray Harryhausen.

Don Chaffey directed several children's speciality films as well as adult comedies and drama. His credits include *Dentist in the Chair* (1960), *One Million Years BC* (1966) and *The Magic of Lassie* (1978).

Video availability

THE PINK PANTHER

1963	
Studio/Distributor:	United Artists
Director:	Blake Edwards
Producer:	Martin Jurow
Screenplay:	Blake Edwards, Maurice Richlin
Music:	Henry Mancini

CAST

David Niven	Sir Charles
Peter Sellers	Insp Jacques Clouseau
Robert Wagner	George
Capucine	Simone Clouseau
Claudia Cardinale	Princess Dala
Brenda De Banzie	Angela Dunning
Fran Jeffries	Greek 'Cousin'

The Pink Panther is a precious stone of untold value, owned by the Indian Princess Dala. While the Princess is on a skiing holiday in Switzerland the stone is stolen by The Phantom, a legendary jewel

thief. Sir Charles is a notorious jewel thief whose nephew George pursues a similar vocation. It's up to the bungling Inspector Clouseau to catch the thief, or thieves, and against the odds he manages to do just that.

The idea of Clouseau came to Sellers from a box of 'Captain Webb' safety matches with a label showing a man with a large moustache wearing an old-fashioned striped swimsuit. Many of the gags in the movie were improvised.

Peter Ustinov was originally offered the part of Clouseau, but turned it down.

Peter Sellers disliked the section in the cartoon credits where the Pink Panther crushes Clouseau with a set of dumb-bells, because he thought it belittled the character.

Music: 'It Had Better Be Tonight'

Video availability

TOM JONES

1963

Studio/Distributor:	United Artists
Director:	Tony Richardson
Producer:	Tony Richardson
Screenplay:	John Osborne
Music:	John Addison

CAST

Albert Finney . . . . *Tom Jones*
Susannah York . . . . *Sophie Western*
Hugh Griffith . . . . *Squire Western*
Edith Evans . . . . *Miss Western*
Joan Greenwood . . . . *Lady Bellaston*
Diane Cilento . . . . *Molly Seagrim*
George Devine . . . . *Squire Allworthy*
David Tomlinson . . . . *Lord Fellamar*

Set in 18th-century England, this is the tale of a lusty young country boy and his carefree attitude to women and life in general. He is believed to be the son of an unmarried maid who loses her job because the household suspect her of being the mother. He is brought up by Squire Allworthy and constantly falls in and out of trouble, narrowly escaping the hangman's noose after being framed for a crime that he didn't commit. After a lifetime of bawdy sex and boisterous adventures, he finally settles down with sweetheart Sophie.

Albert Finney was Oscar nominated as Best Actor but lost to Sydney Poitier for his role in *Lilies Of the Field*. Sir Laurence Olivier dubbed Finney 'The best actor of his generation'.

The movie turned Henry Fielding's novel into a best-seller 200 years after it was first published.

Academy Awards: Best Film (Producer Tony Richardson), Best Direction (Tony Richardson), Best Screenplay (John Osborne), Best Music Score (John Addison)

Video availability

Tom Jones (Albert Finney) charms the beautiful Sophie Western (Susannah York) while her father (Hugh Griffith) looks on in Tom Jones.

633 SQUADRON

1964

Studio/Distributor: **United Artists**
Director: **Walter Grauman**
Producer: **Cecil F. Ford**
Screenplay: **James Clavell, Howard Koch**
Music: **Ron Goodwin**

CAST
Cliff Robertson Wing Commander Roy Grant
George Chakiris . . . . Lt. Erik Bergman
Maria Perschy . . . . Hilde Bergman
Harry Andrews . . . . Air Marshal Davis
Donald Houston . . . . . . Wing Commander
                                        Tom Barrett

Michael Goodliffe . . . . . Squadron Leader
                                        Bill Adams

In 1944 an American Wing Commander in charge of an RAF squadron of Mosquito aircraft is commissioned to bomb a German V2 rocket fuel installation factory that overhangs a cliff in Norway. Even with the help of the local resistance, the task is fraught with complications, which are somehow overcome.

At the age of 13, Cliff Robertson cleaned out aircraft at a flying school in exchange for lessons.

Video availability

BECKET

1964

Studio/Distributor: **Paramount**
Director: **Peter Glenville**
Producer: **Hal Wallis**
Screenplay: **Edward Anhalt**
Music: **Laurence Rosenthal**

CAST
Richard Burton . . . . Thomas Becket
Peter O'Toole . . . . King Henry II
John Gielgud . . . . Louis of France
Donald Wolfit . . . . Bishop of London
Martita Hunt . . . . Queen Matilda
Pamela Brown . . . . Queen Eleanor
Paolo Stoppa . . . . Pope Alexander III
Gino Cervi . . . . Cardinal Zambello

Once good friends, Henry II and Becket, his Chancellor, become enemies after the King makes him Archbishop of Canterbury. Deeply involved with the job, Becket defends the church from the royal disregard for its beliefs. The two meet on horseback in an attempt to sort out their differences, but when Henry decides that a reconciliation is out of the question, he plans to have Becket murdered by the Barons of the palace.

Richard Burton and Peter O'Toole were both Oscar nominated for Best Actor for their roles, but lost to Rex Harrison who won for his role in *My Fair Lady*. Richard Burton was selected over Laurence Olivier to play the Archbishop of Canterbury, but only accepted the part after he learned that Peter O'Toole was to be his co-star. This was the first time they worked together.

Producer Hal B. Wallis had a difficult time convincing Paramount to invest in this movie because they felt that historical stories had passed their sell-by date.

Academy Awards: Best Screenplay (Edward Anhalt)

Video availability

THE CARPETBAGGERS

1964

Studio/Distributor: **Paramount**
Director: **Edward Dmytryk**
Producer: **Joseph E. Levine**
Screenplay: **John Michael Hayes**
Music: **Elmer Bernstein**

CAST
George Peppard . . . . Jonas Cord Jr
Alan Ladd . . . . Nevada Smith
Bob Cummings . . . . Dan Pierce
Martha Hyer . . . . Jennie Denton
Elizabeth Ashley . . . . . . Monica Winthrop
Lew Ayres . . . . McAllister
Martin Balsam . . . . Bernard B. Norman

Ralph Taeger . . . . *Buzz Dalton*
Archie Moore . . . . *Jedediah*
Leif Erikson . . . . *Jonas Cord Sr*
Carroll Baker . . . . *Rina*

Millionaire aircraft manufacturer and playboy Jonas Cord Jr dabbles in the mighty world of the motion pictures when he inherits a fortune from his recently deceased father. His greedy quest for further fortune turns him into a monster. He has increasing difficulty relating to those close to him and he takes out much of his wrath on his wife Monica and best friend Nevada Smith.

This was Alan Ladd's final movie. He was found dead at his home on 29 January 1964, having taken a fatal dose of sleeping pills and alcohol.

The Carpetbaggers, based on the best-selling novel by Harold Robbins, became Paramount's biggest hit since *The Ten Commandments* (1956). A prequel, *Nevada Smith*, tracing the life of Smith, was released in 1966, starring Steve McQueen.

⌐ THE FALL OF THE ROMAN EMPIRE ¬

1964	
Studio/Distributor:	Samuel Bronston
Director:	Anthony Mann
Producer:	Samuel Bronston
Screenplay:	Ben Barzman, Basilio Franchina, Philip Yordan
Music:	Dimitri Tiomkin

CAST
Alec Guinness . . . . *Marcus Aurelius*
Sophia Loren . . . . *Lucilla*
Stephen Boyd . . . . *Livius*
James Mason . . . . *Timonides*
Christopher Plummer . . . . *Commodus*
Anthony Quayle . . . . *Verulus*
John Ireland . . . . *Ballomar*
Mel Ferrer . . . . *Oleander*

The dying Marcus Aurelius, poisoned by his crazed son Commodus, intends to disinherit his dissolute heir as Emperor of Rome but fails to carry out his threats before his death. After his demise, Commodus inherits the throne but has no judgement to rule. Despite attempts by his sister, Lucilla, and her lover Livius to guide him, Commodus's dissipation allows Rome to be ravaged by disease and Barbarian attacks.

At the time, the set for the movie was the largest ever built for a motion picture. A re-creation of the Roman Forum, standing on a 55-acre site and measuring 1312 feet by 754 feet and rising to a height of 260 feet, included 27 full-sized buildings, 601 marble columns and 350 statues. It took 1100 men seven months to build. In 1964, the cost of the movie, $20 million, took it into the bracket of one of the most expensive films made to date.

Alec Guinness didn't enjoy making the film, nor did he particularly like the script. He claimed not to have ever seen more than about twenty minutes of the completed film.

Video availability

⌐ GOLDFINGER ¬

1964	
Studio/Distributor:	United Artists
Director:	Guy Hamilton
Producer:	Harry Saltzman, Albert R. Broccoli
Screenplay:	Richard Maibaum, Paul Dehn
Music:	John Barry

CAST
Sean Connery . . . . *James Bond*
Honor Blackman . . . . *Pussy Galore*
Gert Frobe . . . . *Goldfinger*
Shirley Eaton . . . . *Jill Masterson*
Tania Mallet . . . . *Tilly Masterson*
Harold Sakata . . . . *Odd-job*

Bernard Lee . . . . *M*
Lois Maxwell . . . . *Miss Moneypenny*

Sean Connery takes on the mean Goldfinger in his third outing as James Bond. Goldfinger plans to plant an atomic device inside Fort Knox in order to contaminate the gold reserves and so increase the value of his own illegally obtained supplies. Bond also has his first encounter with the bloodthirsty mute Odd-job, whose lethal weapon is a flying bowler hat with a razor-sharp brim.

In one part of the movie Jill Masterson (Shirley Eaton) meets her end when she is covered in gold paint. Her blood pressure and body temperature were constantly monitored during the two-hour application to avoid a genuine case of skin suffocation. A small patch of her midriff was left unpainted to allow her skin to breathe.

This was the first Bond film to win an Academy Award. It was also the first of four Bond films to be directed by Guy Hamilton, although after *Goldfinger* he didn't return to the director's chair until *Diamonds are Forever* (1972). Terence Young, who directed the first two Bond movies, bowed out this time round because he couldn't agree on contract terms.

Harold Sakata, who played Odd-job, was discovered by director Guy Hamilton at a wrestling match.

Sean Connery worried that the part of Bond didn't sufficiently tax his talent as an actor.

Academy Awards: Best Sound Effects (Norman Wanstall)

Music: 'Goldfinger' (Shirley Bassey)

Video availability

A HARD DAY'S NIGHT

1964	
Studio/Distributor:	United Artists
Director:	Richard Lester
Producer:	Walter Shenson
Screenplay:	Alun Owen
Music:	John Lennon, Paul McCartney

CAST
John Lennon . . . . *John*

Paul McCartney . . . . *Paul*
George Harrison . . . . *George*
Ringo Starr . . . . *Ringo*
Wilfrid Brambell . . . . *Grandfather*
Norman Rossington . . . . *Norm*
Victor Spinetti . . . . *TV Director*
John Junkin . . . . *Shake*
Anna Quayle . . . . *Millie*

The Beatles are living as prisoners of their own success in this day-in-the-life of the Fab Four, who board a train bound for London to appear on a

With Beatlemania sweeping across Europe and America, The Beatles emerged in 1964 with their first full-length feature film, A Hard Day's Night, *packed with a stack of new Lennon-McCartney songs, many of which became Beatle classics.*

live television show. Accompanying them is Paul's grandfather who convinces Ringo that he is not appreciated by the rest of the group, causing him to disappear just before the start of the programme.

Crowds formed outside the Pavilion Cinema in London's Piccadilly Circus days before the movie opened as fans tried to get tickets in advance.

The idea for the film came from John Lennon after he was asked how he'd enjoyed a tour of Sweden and replied 'It was a room and a car and a car and a room and a room and a car . . .' The Beatles requested

Dick Lester to direct the movie, having seen his work with Peter Sellers and *The Goons* TV series. The biggest problem when making the movie was finding locations. Wherever they went to film, the area would be swarming with fans after a couple of takes.

Music: 'A Hard Day's Night', 'Can't Buy me Love', 'I'm Happy Just to Dance with You', 'If I Fell', 'And I Love You', 'I Should Have Known Better', 'Tell me Why'

Video availability

MARY POPPINS

1964

Studio/Distributor: **Walt Disney**
Director: **Robert Stevenson**
Producer: **Walt Disney, Bill Walsh**
Screenplay: **Bill Walsh, Don DaGradi**
Music: **Richard M. Sherman, Robert B. Sherman**

CAST
Julie Andrews . . . . *Mary Poppins*
Dick Van Dyke . . . . *Bert*
David Tomlinson . . . . *Mr Banks*
Glynis Johns . . . . *Mrs Banks*
Ed Wynn . . . . *Uncle Albert*
Hermione Baddeley . . . . *Ellen*
Karen Dotrice . . . . *Jane Banks*
Matthew Garber . . . . *Michael Banks*

The Edwardian Banks family, dominated by the father, find their lives are completely changed with the arrival of their new, almost perfect, nanny. With the help of chimney sweep Bert, Mary Poppins introduces the two rowdy Banks children to real-life wonders that they couldn't imagine even in their wildest dreams, while at the same time teaching them how to behave.

According to songwriter Richard Sherman, he and his brother learned the word Supercalifragilistic-expialidocious from other kids when they were at summer camp in 1937. It was a way to show off one's memory and verbal agility.

Mary Poppins was Julie Andrews's screen debut, and Robert Stevenson's 18th movie for the Disney Studios. The movie received 13 Oscar nominations, the most ever for a Disney production.

Walt Disney was introduced to the P.L. Travers story by one of his daughters, who was reading the book, in 1948.

Academy Awards: Best Actress (Julie Andrews), Best Editing (Cotton Warburton), Best Visual Effects (Peter Ellenshaw, Hamilton Luske, Eustace Lycett), Best Original Music Score (Richard M. Sherman and Robert B. Sherman), Best Song – 'Chim Chim Cher-ee' (Richard M. Sherman and Robert B. Sherman, music and lyrics)

Music: 'A Spoonful of Sugar', 'Chim Chim Cher-ee', 'Supercalifragilisticexpialidocious', 'Step in Time', 'Let's Go Fly a Kite', 'Jolly Holiday', 'I Love to Laugh'

Video availability

MY FAIR LADY

1964

Studio/Distributor: **CBS/Warner**
Director: **George Cukor**
Producer: **Jack L. Warner**
Screenplay: **Alan Jay Lerner**
Music: **Frederick Loewe**

CAST
Audrey Hepburn . . . . *Eliza Doolittle*

Rex Harrison . . . . *Professor Higgins*
Stanley Holloway . . . . . . *Alfred Doolittle*
Wilfred Hyde-White . . . . *Col. Pickering*
Caldya Cooper . . . . *Mrs Higgins*
Jeremy Brett . . . . *Freddie*
Theodore Bikel . . . . *Zoltan Karpathy*
Mona Washbourne . . . . *Mrs Pearce*

In this highly acclaimed musical Professor Henry Higgins accepts a challenge from his friend Colo-

Thanks in part to Professor Henry Higgins (Rex Harrison), Eliza Doolittle (Audrey Hepburn) looks every inch The Fair Lady. *The film was based on George Bernard Shaw's* Pygmalion.

nel Pickering and sets about transforming flower girl Eliza Doolittle into a lady so refined that she will be accepted by the uppermost classes. After countless hours perfecting her grammar and diction, Eliza is ready for the test of an official outing in the presence of royalty - one which she passes with flying colours. The problems arise once Professor Higgins has achieved his aim in creating a lady . . . what does Eliza do with herself now that Higgins has won his bet?

Jack Warner paid $5,500,000 for the screen rights to the film, which ended up costing him, after production, a total of around $23,000,000. Despite all its success, the film did not break even.

Cary Grant was originally in the plans to play Henry Higgins, as was James Cagney for the part of Alfred Doolittle. Julie Andrews was very disappointed she didn't get to star in this picture, having played Eliza Doolittle so successfully in the stage musical. However, she had her reward that year when she won the Best Actress Oscar for *Mary Poppins*.

Marnie Nixon crops up yet again as the singer who dubbed Audrey Hepburn's voice. However, newly restored prints of the movie have included some of Hepburn's original vocals.

At the start of filming, Rex Harrison was very distant with Audrey Hepburn because he had hoped Julie Andrews would get the part, but he later warmed to her and they became friends.

Academy Awards: Best Film (Producer Jack L. Warner), Best Direction (George Cukor), Best Actor (Rex Harrison), Best Colour Cinematography (Harry Stradling), Best Colour Art Direction (Gene Allen and Cecil Beaton), Best Set Decoration (George James Hopkins), Best colour Costume Design (Cecil Beaton), Best Sound (George R. Groves), Best Music Score (Adaptation or Treatment) (André Previn)

Music: 'Get Me to the Church on Time', 'Wouldn't it be Lovely', 'With a Little Bit of Luck', 'Why Can't the English?', 'The Rain in Spain', 'I Could have Danced all Night', 'On the Street Where you Live', 'I've Grown Accustomed to Her face'

Video availability

WONDERFUL LIFE

1964

Studio/Distributor:	EMI/Elstree Distributors
Director:	Sidney J. Furie
Producer:	Kenneth Harper
Screenplay:	Peter Myers, Ronald Cass
Music:	Peter Myers, Ronald Cass

CAST
Cliff Richard . . . . *Johnnie*
Walter Slezak . . . . *Lloyd Davis*
Susan Hampshire . . . . *Jenny*
Hank B. Marvin, Bruce Welsh, Brian Bennett, John Rostill . . . . *Mood Musicians*
Melvyn Hayes . . . . *Jerry*
Una Stubbs . . . . *Barbara*

A group of merchant sailors find themselves stranded in sunny parts when they stumble over the film crew of a diabolical movie called *Beau Geste*. The leading lady is having a hard time with the director and because the picture is so bad, the boys take it upon themselves to turn it into a musical.

The original plot was to have Cliff Richard playing a guardsman who is called out to Mexico after the death of his uncle. The budget didn't stretch to such an exotic location and the whole storyline had to be re-worked. The movie was plagued with problems. Weather conditions halted filming, Melvyn Hayes fell down a flight of steps and broke his leg, and Dennis Price had to be replaced by Derek Bond because of his constant desire for one drink too many.

Wonderful Life premiered in July, the same month The Beatles made their movie debut in *A Hard Day's Night*.

Music: 'Wonderful Life', 'On the Beach', 'We Love a Movie', 'All Kinds of People', 'Theme for Young Lovers', 'A Girl in every Port', 'A Matter of Moments'

Video availability

ZULU

1964

Studio/Distributor:	Paramount
Director:	Cy Endfield
Producer:	Stanley Baker, Cy Endfield
Screenplay:	John Prebble, Cy Endfield
Music:	John Barry

CAST
Stanley Baker . . . . *Lt John Chard*
Jack Hawkins . . . . *Revd Otto Witt*
Ulla Jacobsson . . . . *Margareta Witt*
James Booth . . . . *Private Henry Hook*
Michael Caine . . . . . . *Lt Gonville Bromhead*
Nigel Green . . . . . *Colour-Sergeant Bourne*
Ivor Emmanuel . . . . *Private Owen*

The film, based on a true story, revolves around a small army of British soldiers at Rorke's Drift, South Africa in 1879. Despite warnings by the Reverend Otto Witt that a British army contingent had earlier been massacred, Lieutenant John Chard orders his soldiers to stand and fight King Cetewayo's 4000 spear-bearing Zulu warriors. The British are overwhelmingly outnumbered, but with their tremendous courage and determination manage to hold their own.

Stanley Baker, who also co-produced the movie, had an impossible time trying to explain to the Zulu warriors that he wanted them to act as they'd never seen a motion picture before. In desperation, he had an old Gene Autry Western flown into Natal where they were filming, and screened it for them as an example of what was required.

The voice of Richard Burton can be heard on the soundtrack, as narrator.

Michael Caine was originally interested in playing the cockney Private, but the part had already been cast. However, director Cy Endfield was running out of time to find an actor to play Gonville Bromhead so he let Caine audition. The screen test was a disaster but Endfield still took a chance and gave Caine the job.

Video availability

THE AGONY AND THE ECSTASY

1965	
Studio/Distributor:	Twentieth Century-Fox
Director:	Carol Reed
Producer:	Carol Reed
Screenplay:	Philip Dunne
Music:	Alex North, Franco Potenza

CAST

Charlton Heston . . . . *Michelangelo*
Rex Harrison . . . . *Pope Julius II*
Diane Cilento . . . . . . *Contessina de Medici*
Harry Andrews . . . . *Bramante*
Alberto Lupo . . . . *Duke of Urbino*
Adolfo Celi . . . . *Giovanni de Medici*
Venantino Venantini . . . . . *Paris de Grassis*
John Stacy . . . . *Sangallo*

The story concentrates on the four years of personal vendettas between the difficult sponsor, Pope Julius II, and the arrogant painter and sculptor, Michelangelo, brought about by a conflict of artistic ideas during the creation of the Sistine Chapel.

Twentieth Century-Fox were so impressed with Philip Dunne's screenplay that they agreed to pour millions of dollars into the production, despite their recent financial disaster with *Cleopatra*.

In Rome, the film-makers built a complete replica of the Sistine Chapel with photographs of the original frescos printed on to the ceiling for authenticity.

Video availability

DOCTOR ZHIVAGO

1965	
Studio/Distributor:	MGM
Director:	David Lean
Producer:	Carlo Ponti
Screenplay:	Robert Bolt
Music:	Maurice Jarre

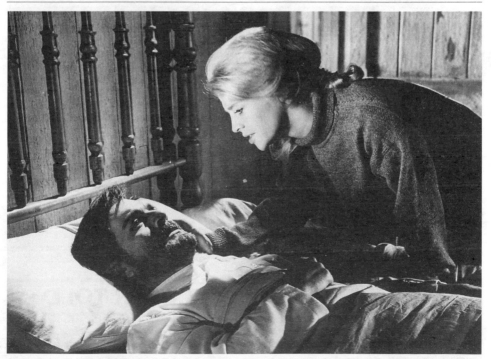

Lara (Julie Christie) tends the ailing Yuri (Omar Sharif) but their love for each other is thwarted by the upheavals of history.

CAST

Omar Sharif . . . . *Yuri Zhivago*
Geraldine Chaplin . . . . . . *Tonya Gromeko*
Julie Christie . . . . *Lara*
Tom Courtenay . . . . *Pasha/Streinikoff*
Alec Guinness . . . . *Yevgraf*
Siobhan McKenna . . . . *Anna*
Ralph Richardson . . . . *Alexander*
Rod Steiger . . . . *Komarovsky*

Omar Sharif plays Yuri Zhivago, a Moscow doctor and poet, married to Tonya. He is conscripted into the medical corps of the military service during World War I where he meets Lara, an army nurse married to the revolutionary, Pasha. The two fall hopelessly in love, but their affair is doomed by the events of the war, the Russian Revolutions, Pasha and Yuri's own guilt.

The film's budget was originally $5 million, but it ended up costing over $15 million. The movie was originally scheduled to premiere in March 1966 but they managed to finish shooting and editing down thirty-one hours of film early and the film premiered at the Capitol theatre in New York on 22 December 1965. It was re-released in 1979 when it became an official Box Office number one.

White marble dust was used for some of the snow scenes. Although filming took place in the coldest area of Spain, it was the mildest winter in history, and little real snow was available. Director David Lean wanted to make more of the movie in Finland but had to abandon the idea because it would have been impossible to hire extras; unemployment did not exist in the country.

Lean originally wanted Peter O'Toole for the lead, but the actor wasn't prepared to work with Lean after the rigours of *Lawrence of Arabia*. Producer Carlo Ponti was keen for his wife, Sophia Loren, to be cast in the movie. David Lean said he'd agree if she could prove she could convincingly play a 17-year-old virgin.

Academy Awards: Best Screenplay from another medium (Robert Bolt), Best Colour Cinematography (Freddie Young), Best Colour Art Direction (John Box and Terry Marsh), Set Decoration (Dario Simoni), Best Colour Costume Design (Phyllis Dalton), Best Music Score (Maurice Jarre)

Music: 'Lara's Theme'

Video availability

THE GREAT RACE

1965

Studio/Distributor:	Warner
Director:	Blake Edwards
Producer:	Martin Jurow
Screenplay:	Arthur Ross
Music:	Henry Mancini

CAST

Jack Lemmon . . . . *Professor Fate*
Tony Curtis . . . . *The Great Leslie*
Natalie Wood . . . . *Maggie DuBois*
Peter Falk . . . . *Mas*
Keenan Wynn . . . . *Hezekiah*
Arthur O'Connell . . . . . . *Henry Goodbody*
Vivian Vance . . . . *Hester Goodbody*
Dorothy Provine . . . . *Lily Olay*

Not unlike the plot of *Those Magnificent Men in their Flying Machines*, The Great Race, however, involved automobiles rather than aircraft. Set in 1908, the race, staged by a car manufacturer, begins in New York and ends in Paris. Entrants include two arch rival villains (Professor Fate and The Great Leslie), who will go to any length to sabotage one another's chances of winning, or anyone else's for that matter.

The film was director Blake Edwards's tribute to the great silent movies. His grandfather was silent screen director J. Gordon Edwards.

Academy Awards: Best Sound Effects (Tregoweth Brown)

Music: 'The Sweetheart Tree'

Video availability

THE GREATEST STORY EVER TOLD

1965		
	Producer:	George Stevens
	Screenplay:	George Stevens, James Lee Barrett
Studio/Distributor:	United Artists	
Director:	George Stevens	Music:	Alfred Newman

CAST

Max Von Sydow	*Jesus*
Dorothy McGuire	*Mary*
Robert Loggia	*Joseph*
Claude Rains	*Herod the Great*
José Ferrer	*Herod Antipas*
Marian Seldes	*Herodias*
John Abbott	*Aben*
Rodolfo Acosta	*Captain of Lancers*
Philip Coolidge	*Chuza*

The Greatest Story Ever Told is the story of Jesus Christ. Over nearly four hours the film covers his birth, his time as a healer (he cures Shelley Winters who plays the woman of no name) and religious leader, and finally his crucifixion and resurrection.

The film is awash with cameo appearances, including Charlton Heston, Sidney Poitier, Donald Pleasence (as the Devil), Telly Savalas, Roddy McDowall, Carroll Baker, Pat Boone and John Wayne. Wayne plays the Roman soldier who escorts Christ to the cross. His only notable words are 'Truly this man was the son of God.' Not a huge hit with the critics, Shana Alexander of *Life* magazine wrote 'As the picture ponderously unrolled, it was mainly irritation that kept me awake.'

The movie was originally 260 minutes long but was cut to 225 minutes for general release. Further cuts were made for subsequent versions, with the most brutal cut reducing it to 127 minutes.

The film-makers shot the film on location in Utah where they created a set that looked like Palestine or, as more than one critic said, a greetings card.

HELP!

1965	
Studio/Distributor:	United Artists
Director:	Richard Lester
Producer:	Walter Shenson
Screenplay:	Marc Behm, Charles Wood
Music:	Ken Thorne, John Lennon, Paul McCartney

Help!, *the second full-length film starring John, Paul, George and Ringo, finds the Fab Four heading for Salisbury Plain, but taking a short cut via the Bahamas and Austria.*

CAST

John Lennon . . . . *John*
Paul McCartney . . . . *Paul*
Ringo Starr . . . . *Ringo*
George Harrison . . . . *George*
Leo McKern . . . . *Clang*
Eleanor Bron . . . . *Ahme*
Victor Spinetti . . . . *Foot*
Roy Kinnear . . . . *Algernon*
Patrick Cargill . . . . *Superintendent*

*H*elp! was the second full-length movie vehicle for The Beatles. Set within an Eastern religious cult, Kali, a mad scientist and Eastern high priest, tries to steal a sacred ring which has been sent to Ringo by a fan. The group hire the army to protect them with tanks while they play in a field at Stonehenge.

It was the making of this film that helped the group decide it was time for them to take control of their own creative affairs. Although John Lennon enjoyed making the film, he thought it was expensive and a waste of time and money.

The original title of the movie was to be 'Eight Arms to Hold You'.

Music: 'Help!', 'The Night Before', 'Ticket to Ride', 'You've Got to Hide your Love Away', 'You're Gonna Lose that Girl'

Video availability

In the phenomenally successful 1965 movie The Sound of Music *the Von Trapp family become a singing sensation before fleeing from Nazi Austria as World War II looms.*

THE SOUND OF MUSIC

1965

Studio/Distributor: **Twentieth Century-Fox**
Director: **Robert Wise**
Producer: **Robert Wise**
Screenplay: **Ernest Lehman**
Music: **Richard Rodgers, Oscar Hammerstein II**

CAST
Julie Andrews .... Maria
Christopher Plummer ... Capt. Von Trapp
Eleanor Parker .... The Baroness
Richard Haydn .... Max Detweiler
Peggy Wood .... Mother Abbess
Charmian Carr .... Liesl
Heather Menzies .... Louisa
Nicholas Hammond .... Freidrich
Duane Chase .... Kurt

In 1938 Maria, a postulant nun, gives up her habit in Salzburg to take up the position of governess to the seven children of Austrian widower Captain Von Trapp. A former Naval Officer, Von Trapp enforces a strict regime in the home. Maria attempts to bring a little spontaneity into the household, teaching the children to sing and appreciate the beauty of the surrounding Alps. Maria wins over the children and falls in love with Von Trapp. Their happiness is soon threatened by the Nazi invasion, and Maria helps them to escape.

The Sound of Music became the industry's highest grossing picture to date.

Twentieth Century-Fox originally wanted to cast Doris Day as Maria. Marnie Nixon, the ghost singer for dozens of stars in musical films, made her first on-screen appearance in a cameo role as Sister Sophia. The real Baroness Von Trapp visited the movie set in Salzburg and ended up appearing as an extra.

In Korea, the movie industry thought the film was too long so they shortened it by editing out all the songs.

Christopher Plummer's singing voice was dubbed by Bill Lee, and Peggy Wood's by Margery McKay.

Over two thousand children turned up for auditions in New York and Los Angeles for parts in the film.

Academy Awards: Best Film (Producer Robert Wise), Best Direction (Robert Wise), Best Editing (William Reynolds), Best Sound (James P. Corcoran and Fred Hynes), Best Music Score (Adaptation) (Irwin Kostal)

Music: 'The Sound of Music', 'Do-Re-Mi', 'Edelweiss', 'Climb Ev'ry Mountain', 'Sixteen Going on Seventeen', 'My Favourite Things', 'The Lonely Goatherd', 'I have Confidence in Me'

Video availability

THOSE MAGNIFICENT MEN IN THEIR FLYING MACHINES

1965

Studio/Distributor: **Twentieth Century-Fox**
Director: **Ken Annakin**
Producer: **Stan Margulies**
Screenplay: **Jack Davies, Ken Annakin**
Music: **Ron Goodwin**

CAST
Stuart Whitman .... Orvil Newton
Sarah Miles .... Patricia Rawnsley
James Fox .... Richard Mays
Alberto Sordi ..... Count Emilio Ponticelli
Robert Morley .... Lord Rawnsley
Gert Frobe .... Col. Manfred Von Holstein
Jean-Pierre Cassel .... Pierre Dubois
Eric Sykes .... Courtney

In 1910 London newspaper proprietor Lord Rawnsley offers a prize of £10,000 to the winner of a sponsored London to Paris air race. He wants to prove that Great Britain is well ahead of the game when it comes to aviation. Pilots from all over the world take part, including the fiancé of the daughter of Lord Rawnsley. Dirty tricks and foul play take over in the rush for the finish line.

With American producer Stan Margulies in charge, the movie was one of the few British productions that became a major success in America at the time. German, French, Italian and Japanese stars were cast in order to give the movie an international appeal.

When the film was made, it was proving impossible to find airworthy vintage aircraft in Britain, so replicas had to be built.

Music: 'Those Magnificent Men in their Flying Machines'

Video availability

THUNDERBALL

1965	
Studio/Distributor:	United Artists
Director:	Terence Young
Producer:	Kevin McClory
Screenplay:	Richard Maibaum, John Hopkins
Music:	John Barry

CAST

Sean Connery	*James Bond*
Claudine Auger	*Domino Durval*
Adolfo Celi	*Emilio Largo*
Luciana Paluzzi	*Fiona*
Rik Van Nutter	*Felix Leiter*
Bernard Lee	*M*
Martine Beswick	*Paula*
Desmond Llewelyn	*Q*
Lois Maxwell	*Miss Moneypenny*

In this fourth Bond movie, 007 finds himself on the way to the Bahamas in search of an underwater aircraft containing nuclear weapons. Bond catches up with the SPECTRE agent Emilio Largo, who is holding the world to ransom, and encounters the villain's beautiful mistress, Domino Durval. After avoiding being eaten alive in a shark-infested swimming pool, 007 locates the plane, defeats the enemy scuba divers and chases Largo as he tries to escape in his super-powered yacht.

Thunderball was one of the first movies to licence its logo for the merchandizing of James Bond products such as dolls and T-shirts.

A settlement was finally reached over the plagiarism claim brought against Ian Fleming by Kevin McClory and Jack Whittingham over *Thunderball*, with the pair being named co-authors of all future editions of the novel and of the screenplay. McClory was also granted film rights. The trial adversely affected a now ailing Fleming, who died a year later.

Martine Beswick who plays Paula, a Bond helper, previously danced in the titles sequence of *Dr No* and was a gypsy girl in *From Russia with Love*.

Bonuses were offered to stuntmen who volunteered to film the scene in the shark-infested pool. Bill Cummings took the 'bait' and later Connery himself reluctantly did his scene in the pool after being convinced the creatures had been drugged.

Academy Awards: Best Special Visual Effects (John Stears)

Music: 'Thunderball' (Tom Jones), 'Mr Kiss Kiss Bang Bang'

Video availability

VON RYAN'S EXPRESS

1965	
Studio/Distributor:	Twentieth Century-Fox
Director:	Mark Robson
Producer:	Saul David
Screenplay:	Wendell Mayes, Joseph Landon
Music:	Jerry Goldsmith

CAST

Frank Sinatra	*Colonel Joseph L. Ryan*
Trevor Howard	*Major Eric Fincham*
Raffaella Carra	*Gabriella*
Brad Dexter	*Sgt Bostick*
Sergio Fantoni	*Capt Oriani*
John Leyton	*Orde*
Edward Mulhare	*Costanzo*
Wolfgang Preiss	*Major Von Klemment*

Six hundred American and British prisoners are being held captive by the Germans in a PoW camp. They stage a well-planned mass escape, led by the unpopular American Colonel Joseph Ryan, across Nazi-controlled Italy during World War II. They hijack a freight train, which is transporting more prisoners to Austria, and divert it in the hope of finding refuge in Switzerland.

Frank Sinatra refused to live in Rome during filming because some years previously he had been treated badly when he appeared in concert there and had never forgiven the locals. By way of a compromise, he took a large villa outside the city, complete with helipad.

Video availability

WHAT'S NEW PUSSYCAT?

1965

Studio/Distributor:	United Artists
Director:	Clive Donner
Producer:	Charles K. Feldman
Screenplay:	Woody Allen
Music:	Burt Bacharach

CAST
Peter Sellers . . . . *Dr Fritz Fassbender*
Peter O'Toole . . . . *Michael James*
Romy Schneider . . . . *Carol Warner*
Capucine . . . . *Renée Lefebvre*
Paula Prentiss . . . . *Liz*
Woody Allen . . . . *Victor Shakapopolis*
Ursula Andress . . . . *Rita*
Edra Gale . . . . *Anna Fassbender*

Michael James is the editor of a French fashion magazine who goes in search of psychiatric help over his growing problems with the many women in his life. He visits the eccentric Dr Fritz Fassbender who proves to be of little help, for he too has more than a passing interest in the opposite sex, which gets him into endless trouble with his jealous wife.

This was Woody Allen's debut as a screenwriter.

There is a cameo appearance by Richard Burton as a man in a bar.

Peter O'Toole's character is allegedly based on Warren Beatty.

The previous year Peter Sellers had to pull out of Billy Wilder's movie *Kiss Me Stupid* when he suffered a heart attack, but was fit enough to star in *What's New Pussycat?*

Music: 'What's New Pussycat?' (Tom Jones)

Video availability

ALFIE

1966

		Producer:	Lewis Gilbert
Studio/Distributor:	Paramount	Screenplay:	Bill Naughton
Director:	Lewis Gilbert	Music:	Sonny Rollins

Sixties swinger and playboy Alfie teaches Gilda (Julia Foster) exactly what it's all about after she becomes pregnant with his child.

CAST

Michael Caine . . . . *Alfie*
Shelley Winters . . . . *Ruby*
Millicent Martin . . . . *Siddie*
Julia Foster . . . . *Gilda*
Jane Asher . . . . *Annie*
Shirley Anne Field . . . . *Carla*
Vivien Merchant . . . . *Lily*
Eleanor Bron . . . . *The Doctor*

Alfie is an unscrupulous cocky Cockney working his way from one promiscuous female's bedroom to another. He is not too fussy about their shape, looks or size, and shows little remorse for the hurt he brings them along the way. He is finally forced to think again after he witnesses the horrific abortion that he arranges.

The story began as a radio play called 'Alfie Elkins and his Little Life', starring Bill Owen (Compo in the TV series *The Last of the Summer wine*).

Shelley Winters had trouble understanding Michael Caine's Cockney accent and ended up taking her cues from his body language. For the American market, Michael Caine had to re-voice over a hundred lines to make his accent more understandable.

Three different versions of the theme song appear in different versions of the film. The British prints all have Cilla Black singing, but the American copies vary with either Dionne Warwick or Cher.

Music: 'Alfie' (Cilla Black)

Video availability

THE BIBLE . . . IN THE BEGINNING

1966	
Studio/Distributor:	Twentieth Century-Fox
Director:	John Huston
Producer:	Dino De Laurentiis
Screenplay:	Christopher Fry
Music:	Toshiro Mayuzumi

CAST

Michael Parks . . . . *Adam*
Ulla Bergryd . . . . *Eve*
Richard Harris . . . . *Cain*
John Huston . . . . *Noah*
Stephen Boyd . . . . *Nimrod*
George C. Scott . . . . *Abraham*
Ava Gardner . . . . *Sarah*
Peter O'Toole . . . . *The Three Angels*

John Huston's epic is the first 22 chapters of the Book of Genesis transferred to the big screen, with dramatized treatments of classic stories from the Bible. The movie begins with the story of Adam and Eve in the garden of Eden. It is followed by Noah and his Ark, filled with animals boarding two by two, King Nimrod, whose monument became the Tower of Babel, and the murder of Abel by the jealous Cain. It ends with God ordering Abraham to sacrifice his son Isaac.

The original concept for the film was to retell the whole of the Old Testament, but that project seemed too daunting and was reduced to stories up to, and including, Abraham and Isaac from the Book of Genesis. Producer Dino De Laurentiis had a sign erected, which extended an entire block on Broadway in New York, claiming his film to be the most important movie of all time.

Charlie Chaplin turned down the part of Noah because he didn't want to appear in another director's film and opera star Maria Callas was producer Dino De Laurentiis's first choice for the part of Sarah.

During the making of the film, George C. Scott and Ava Gardner began a romance.

Video availability

THE BLUE MAX

1966	
Studio/Distributor:	Twentieth Century-Fox
Director:	John Guillermin
Producer:	Christian Ferry
Screenplay:	David Pursall, Jack Seddon, Gerald Hanley
Music:	Jerry Goldsmith

CAST

George Peppard . . . . *Bruno Stachel*
James Mason . . . . *Count Von Klugermann*
Ursula Andress . . . . *Countess Kaéti*
Jeremy Kemp . . . . . *Willi Von Klugermann*
Karl Michael Vogler . . . . *Heidemann*
Loni Von Friedl . . . . *Elfi Heidemann*
Anton Diffring . . . . *Holbach*

This World War I drama features an ambitious and unpleasant German pilot, Bruno Stachel, whose high-flying antics cause the deaths of other officers. He's determined to become a war hero and earn the

Blue Max, the highest award for bravery. He's also helping himself to the wife of his superior, who swears to get his revenge on the scoundrel.

This was the first movie where Ursula Andress's Swiss-German accent had worked in her favour. As a teenager, she went to Rome and appeared in several 'quickie' Italian movies.

John Guillermin went on to direct *The Towering Inferno* (1975) and *Death on the Nile* (1978).

Jeremy Kemp made his movie debut in 1963 as a minor character in *Cleopatra*.

Video availability

BORN FREE

1966	
Studio/Distributor:	Columbia
Director:	James Hill
Producer:	Sam Jaffe, Paul Radin
Screenplay:	Gerald L.C. Copley
Music:	John Barry

CAST
Virginia McKenna . . . . *Joy Adamson*
Bill Travers . . . . *George Adamson*
Geoffrey Keen . . . . *Kendall*
Peter Lukoye . . . . *Nuru*
Omar Chambati . . . . *Makkede*
Bill Godden . . . . *Sam*
Bryan Epsom . . . . *Baker*
Robert Cheetham . . . . *Ken*
Robert Young . . . . *James*

The film was adapted from Joy Adamson's book about Elsa the lion. The lion cub was brought up as a pet by Joy Adamson and her husband George during their life as game wardens in Kenya. When Elsa becomes too large to keep as a pet, and in order to avoid a government order which condemns her to a life in captivity, the couple must train her to fend for herself and release her back into the jungle.

The film was chosen for the British Royal Film Performance 1966.

A sequel followed in 1972, called *Living Free*, starring Susan Hampshire and Nigel Davenport. Geoffrey Keen made a return appearance as the Government commissioner.

Bill Travers and Virginia McKenna are married in real life and previously worked together in *The Barretts of Wimpole Street* and *The Smallest Show on Earth*, both in 1957. She was previously married to the late actor Denholm Elliott.

Academy Awards: Best Original Music Score (John Barry), Best Song – 'Born Free' (John Barry, music; Don Black, lyrics)

Music: 'Born Free' (Matt Monro)

Video availability

GEORGY GIRL

1966	
Studio/Distributor:	Columbia
Director:	Silvio Narizzano
Producer:	Robert A. Goldston, Otto Plaschkes
Screenplay:	Margaret Forster, Peter Nichols
Music:	Alexander Faris

CAST
James Mason . . . . *James Leamington*
Alan Bates . . . . *Jos*
Lynn Redgrave . . . . *Georgy Parkin*
Charlotte Rampling . . . . *Meredith*
Rachel Kempson . . . . *Ellen*
Bill Owen . . . . *Ted*

Georgy is a young unattached and unattractive dancing teacher who suffers from a degree of self pity over her loneliness. Her parents are employed by the wealthy but childless James Leamington who treats Georgy as though she was his daughter. As she grows up Leamington makes it clear he wants her as a lover. Georgy escapes life with this middle-aged man when her ungrateful flatmate, Meredith, falls pregnant by Jos (the apple of Georgy's eye) and Georgy opts to look after it.

Lynn Redgrave made her movie debut in 1963 in *Tom Jones*, starring Albert Finney and Susannah York.

The title song was co-written by Jim Dale who starred in several of the 'Carry On' movies.

Music: 'Georgy Girl' (The Seekers)

Video availability

THE GOOD, THE BAD AND THE UGLY

1966	
Studio/Distributor:	PEA
Director:	Sergio Leone
Producer:	Alberto Grimaldi
Screenplay:	Age Scarpelli, Luciano Vincenzoni, Sergio Leone
Music:	Ennio Morricone

CAST
Clint Eastwood .... Joe
Eli Wallach .... Tuco
Lee Van Cleef .... Setenza

Three drifters arrive in town during the American Civil War to lay their hands on a vast treasure buried in the unmarked grave of Bill Carson. The Good, Joe, The Bad, Setenza and The Ugly, Tuco, each have one clue as to the whereabouts of the grave but will go to any lengths to double-cross one another out of the fortune. They end up in a three-way shoot-out in a cemetery.

This was the third of a trilogy of movies, all starring Clint Eastwood, beginning with *A Fistful of Dollars* (1964) and *For a Few Dollars More* (1966). Lee Van Cleef has claimed that he was often intimidated by Clint Eastwood during their lengthy partnership in spaghetti Westerns.

Clint Eastwood made his movie debut in 1955 in *Revenge of the Creature*, which starred John Agar. Between 1959 and 1966 he was one of the leading characters in the long-running TV Western series *Rawhide*, playing the part of Rowdy Yates.

The theme music from the film was a number one hit in the music charts for Hugo Montenegro and His Orchestra.

Video availability

GRAND PRIX

1966	
Studio/Distributor:	MGM
Director:	John Frankenheimer
Producer:	Edward Lewis
Screenplay:	Robert Alan Arthur
Music:	Maurice Jarre

CAST
James Garner .... Pete Aron
Eva Marie Saint ..... Louise Frederickson
Yves Montand .... Jean-Pierre Sarti
Toshiro Mifune .... Izo Yamura
Brian Bedford .... Scott Stoddard
Jessica Walter .... Pat
Antonio Sabato .... Nino Barlini
Francoise Hardy .... Lisa

Grand Prix centres around the lives of four champion racing drivers – on and off the track. British Scott Stoddard now drives for the memory of his late brother who was killed in the sport. Frenchman Jean-Pierre Sarti is married but having an affair with an American journalist. Pete Aron from the States is single, unattached and somewhat reserved. Italian-born Romeo Nino Barlini completes the foursome, with the action following them as they battle it out in a number of European circuits.

The character of British driver Scott Stoddard was based on the real-life racing driver Stirling Moss.

Director John Frankenheimer once worked as a TV director on a live show sponsored by a cattle ranch with cows as the main stars.

Academy Awards: Best Editing (Frederic Steinkamp, Henry Berman, Stewart Linder and Frank Santillo), Best Sound (Franklin E. Milton), Best Sound Effects (Gordon Daniel)

Video availability

KHARTOUM

1966	
Studio/Distributor:	United Artists
Director:	Basil Dearden
Producer:	Julian Blaustein
Screenplay:	Robert Ardrey
Music:	Frank Cordell

The Good, The Bad and The Ugly *are three professional gunmen each in search of the unmarked grave of Bill Carson, under which lies a fortune of buried treasure.*

CAST
Charlton Heston .. *General Charles Gordon*
Laurence Olivier . . . . *the Mahdi*
Richard Johnson .. *Colonel J.D.H. Stewart*
Ralph Richardson *Prime Minister Gladstone*
Alexander Knox . . . . *Sir Evelyn Baring*
Johnny Sekka . . . . *Khaleel*
Michael Hordern . . . . *Lord Granville*

*K*hartoum chronicles the events leading up to the murder, in January 1885, of the British General, Sir Charles Gordon. The General is sent by Prime Minister Gladstone to try to make peace with a group of Arab tribesmen from Sudan and evacuate Egyptian forces from Khartoum, which is threat-ened by the Mahdi. He is killed only days before the relief of the city from a ten-month siege.

The face-to-face confrontation between Gordon and the Mahdi was a fictitious piece of drama created for the movie.

Director Basil Dearden began his movie career as an associate producer and screenwriter for Ealing Films. His other directorial credits include *The Blue Lamp* (1949) and *The Ship that Died of Shame* (1955).

Video availability

A MAN FOR ALL SEASONS

1966	
Studio/Distributor:	Columbia
Director:	Fred Zinnemann
Producer:	Fred Zinnemann
Screenplay:	Robert Bolt
Music:	Georges Delerne

CAST
Paul Scofield . . . . *Sir Thomas More*
Wendy Hiller . . . . *Alice More*
Leo McKern . . . . *Thomas Cromwell*
Robert Shaw . . . . *King Henry VIII*
Orson Welles . . . . *Cardinal Wolsey*
Susannah York . . . . *Margaret More*
Nigel Davenport . . . . *Duke of Norfolk*

King Henry VIII wants to divorce his wife, Catherine of Aragon, in order to marry Anne Boleyn. Sir Thomas More, Chancellor and Lawyer to the Crown, opposes the divorce, which creates a major conflict with the King. The crisis deepens when Sir Thomas is faced with growing pressure to publicly endorse the royal wedding of the King to Anne. Although Henry understands More's objections, he finally sentences More to death for perjury.

Vanessa Redgrave has a cameo role as Anne Boleyn and John Hurt played Richard Rich.

The film gave Paul Scofield his first major movie role although he had played the part of Sir Thomas More in the stage version both in London and on Broadway. Charlton Heston was anxious to play Sir Thomas

More in the movie and was devastated when he learned that the part had gone to Paul Scofield. Heston finally had his chance to play the part in a 1988 TV movie version, which also starred Vanessa Redgrave and Sir John Gielgud.

A Man for all Seasons became Columbia Pictures' biggest hit since *Lawrence of Arabia* in 1962.

Academy Awards: Best Film (Producer Fred Zinnemann), Best Direction (Fred Zinnemann), Best Actor (Paul Scofield), Best Screenplay (Robert Bolt), Best Colour Cinematography (Ted Moore), Best Colour Costume Design (Elizabeth Haffenden and Joan Bridge)

Video availability

WHO'S AFRAID OF VIRGINIA WOOLF?

1966

Studio/Distributor: Warner
Director: Mike Nichols
Producer: Ernest Lehman
Screenplay: Ernest Lehman
Music: Alex North

CAST
Elizabeth Taylor . . . . *Martha*
Richard Burton . . . . *George*
George Segal . . . . *Nick*
Sandy Dennis . . . . *Honey*

George is a history teacher married to the often spiteful, sometimes loving, Martha, who is the daughter of the head of the college where her husband works. Although childless, they have invented an imaginary son who seems to really exist in their minds. Their stormy marriage is tested to the full when they invite a younger couple, Nick and Honey, to their home. Martha seduces Nick while George watches but tries to ignore the situation, and Honey becomes ill through too much drink.

Who's Afraid of Virginia Woolf? was Mike Nichols's first film as director but the fourth joint movie venture for Elizabeth Taylor and Richard Burton, following *Cleopatra* (1963), *The VIPs* (1963) and *The Sandpiper* (1964).

The film, an adaptation of Edward Albee's play, was considered a milestone in cinema permissiveness. It went through major censorship problems. Anyone under the age of 18 was admitted to see the film only with an adult because it contained some of the most explicit language ever used in an American motion picture.

Academy Awards: Best Actress (Elizabeth Taylor), Best Supporting Actress (Sandy Dennis), Best Black and White Cinematography (Haskell Wexler), Best Black and White Art Direction (Richard Sylbert), Set Decoration (George James Hopkins), Best Black and White Costume Design (Irene Sharaff)

Video availability

BONNIE AND CLYDE

1967

Studio/Distributor: Warner
Director: Arthur Penn
Producer: Warren Beatty
Screenplay: David Newman, Robert Benton
Music: Charles Strouse

CAST
Warren Beatty . . . . *Clyde Barrow*
Faye Dunaway . . . . *Bonnie Parker*
Michael J. Pollard . . . . *C.W. Moss*
Gene Hackman . . . . *Buck Barrow*
Estelle Parsons . . . . *Blanche*
Denver Pyle . . . . *Frank Hamer*
Dub Taylor . . . . *Ivan Moss*
Evans Evans . . . . *Velma Davis*
Gene Wilder . . . . *Eugene Grizzard*

The favourite pastimes of Bonnie Parker (Faye Dunaway) and Clyde Barrow (Warren Beatty) are robbing banks and terrorising the local townspeople with acts of violence.

Warren Beatty and Faye Dunaway bring to life the two legendary Texas gangsters and lovers Bonnie Parker and Clyde Barrow. He is a car thief when he teams up with the daughter of one of his intended victims. Together they rob their way through Southern and Mid-West America during the depressive 1930s. With the establishment of the Barrow gang, the violence intensifies and so does the authorities' hunt for them.

Bonnie Parker was Faye Dunaway's first major screen role. The part was originally offered to both Tuesday Weld and Natalie Wood. Tuesday Weld turned it down because she was pregnant, and Natalie Wood because she didn't like Texas. The movie also brought Dunaway success on covers of leading fashion magazines as her Bonnie Parker outfits became the latest look.

Making his movie debut as a producer, Warren Beatty purchased the movie script for $75,000. He had originally wanted either François Truffaut or Jean-Luc Godard to direct the film. It did just as well under Arthur Penn, becoming Warner's second largest box office hit at the time (just after *My Fair Lady*) and grossing $23 million.

Academy Awards: Best Supporting Actress (Estelle Parsons), Best Colour Cinematography (Burnett Guffey)

Video availability

CAMELOT

1967	
Studio/Distributor:	Warner
Director:	Joshua Logan
Producer:	Jack L. Warner
Screenplay:	Alan Jay Lerner
Music:	Alfred Newman
	(Director)

CAST
Richard Harris . . . . *King Arthur*
Vanessa Redgrave . . . . *Guinevere*
Franco Nero . . . . *Lancelot*
David Hemmings . . . . *Mordred*
Lionel Jeffries . . . . *King Pellinore*
Estelle Winwood . . . . *Lady Clarinda*
Laurence Naismith . . . . *Merlin*
Pierre Olaf . . . . *Dap*

This musical tale of the Knights of the Round Table revolves around three main characters: Sir Lancelot, the ageing King Arthur, and Queen Guinevere. King Arthur loses his wife to his once trusted friend, Sir Lancelot, and is forced into war.

The movie company was keen to cast Richard Burton and Julie Andrews in the lead roles to repeat the Broadway success they had seven years previously. However, director Joshua Logan was not of the same opinion.

Vanessa Redgrave wanted to wear the same costume throughout the film, until it was pointed out to her that the story spanned 24 years.

Franco Nero's singing voice was dubbed by Gene Merlino.

Academy Awards: Best Colour Art Direction (John Truscott and Edward Carrere), Best Set Decoration (John W. Brown), Best Colour Costume Design (John Truscott), Best Music Adaptation or Treatment (Alfred Newman and Ken Darby)

Music: 'Camelot', 'If Ever I Would Leave You', 'How to Handle a Woman', 'What Do the Simple Folk Do?', 'I Wonder What the King is Doing Tonight?'. 'Follow me', 'The Lusty Month of May'

Video availability

CASINO ROYALE

1967	
Studio/Distributor:	Columbia
Director:	John Huston, Ken Hughes, Val Guest, Robert Parrish, Joe McGrath, Richard Talmadge
Producer:	Charles K. Feldman, Jerry Bresler
Screenplay:	Wolf Mankowitz, John Law, Michael Sayers
Music:	Burt Bacharach

CAST
Peter Sellers . . . . *Evelyn Tremble*
Ursula Andress . . . . *Vesper Lynd*
David Niven . . . . *Sir James Bond*
Orson Welles . . . . *Le Chiffre*
Joanna Pettet . . . . *Mata Bond*
Daliah Lavi . . . . *the Detainer*
Woody Allen . . . . *Jimmy Bond*
William Holden . . . . *Ransome*
John Huston . . . . *McTarry*

This 007 spoof stars David Niven as a retired Sir James Bond who is called back to duty when SMERSH gets up to their old tricks and are believed to have murdered M. After recruiting several other agents, all of them 007s, he discovers that the villain is none other than Jimmy Bond, his very own cousin to whom he has relinquished his position.

Despite its box office success the film was not without its problems. It had no less than six directors working on the project, cost $12 million to produce, much of that on its huge cast list, and Peter Sellers quit the movie before it was finished as his allocated time had run out and he had other things to do. The film did satisfy Ian Fleming in one way, however; he had always wanted David Niven to play his most famous character.

Music: 'The Look of Love' (Dusty Springfield)

Video availability

THE DIRTY DOZEN

1967

Studio/Distributor:	MGM
Director:	Robert Aldrich
Producer:	Kenneth Hyman
Screenplay:	Nunnally Johnson,
	Lukas Heller
Music:	Frank DeVol

CAST

Lee Marvin	*Major Reisman*
Ernest Borgnine	*General Worden*
Charles Bronson	*Joe Wladislaw*
Jim Brown	*Robert Jefferson*
John Cassavetes	*Victor Franko*
Richard Jaeckel	*Sgt Bowren*
George Kennedy	*Major Armbruster*
Trini Lopez	*Pedro Jiminez*
Telly Savalas	*Archer Maggott*
Donald Sutherland	*Vernon Pinkley*
Clint Walker	*Samson Posey*
Ben Carruthers	*Glenn Gilpin*
Al Mancini	*Tassos Bravos*
Stuart Cooper	*Roscoe Lever*
Tom Busey	*Mile Vladek*
Colin Maitland	*Seth Sawyer*

During World War II 12 hardened soldier prisoners are hand picked by the aggressive, no nonsense, Major Reisman. He offers them freedom if they survive a dangerous assignment before D-Day. Their task is to destroy a building in occupied France where top Nazi generals congregate. They undertake vigorous training in preparation for the mission. When they finally parachute into their target area they know there isn't much chance of making it back alive.

One of the Dirty Dozen, Donald Sutherland, was not considered a big enough star to include on the posters advertising the movie.

John Wayne was offered the leading role but turned it down in favour of *The Green Berets*, and Jack Palance turned down the role as the Bible-quoting fool, which was taken up by Telly Savalas.

A number of TV movies based on the film turned up in subsequent years, including *The Dirty Dozen: The Next Mission*, *The Dirty Dozen: The Deadly Mission* and *The Dirty Dozen: The Fatal Mission*.

Academy Awards: Best Sound Effects (John Poyner)

Music: 'The Bramble Bush' (Trini Lopez)

Video availability

DOCTOR DOLITTLE

1967

Studio/Distributor:	Twentieth Century-Fox
Director:	Richard Fleischer
Producer:	Arthur P. Jacobs
Screenplay:	Leslie Bricusse
Music:	Leslie Bricusse

CAST

Rex Harrison	*Doctor Dolittle*
Samantha Eggar	*Emma Fairfax*
Anthony Newley	*Matthew Mugg*
Richard Attenborough . . .	*Albert Blossom*
Peter Bull	*General Bellowes*
Muriel Landers	*Mrs Blossom*
Geoffrey Holder	*Willie Shakespeare*
Portia Nelson	*Sarah Dolittle*

The Victorian veterinary surgeon Dr Dolittle talks to animals. His neighbours think him mad and he is arrested and placed in a lunatic asylum. After escaping he makes his way, with an assortment of friends, to the South Seas in search of the Great Pink Sea Snail. On the way he meets a variety of animals. With his ability to speak 498 animal languages he is able to lovingly communicate with them, including Chee-Chee the chimp, Sophie the homesick seal and the Great Pink Sea Snail.

Alan Jay Lerner was originally going to write the screenplay and song lyrics, but after a year of trying he finally gave up, at which time Rex Harrison wanted to leave as well. He was unhappy about starring in a children's movie and only agreed when he heard that Alan Jay Lerner was involved with the project. However, Harrison was happy with the work of Lerner's replacement, Leslie Bricusse.

Two of the songs, 'Something in Your Smile' and 'Where are the Words', were cut from the British prints of the film.

Over 1500 live animals were used in the making of the movie.

Academy Awards: Best Song – 'Talk to the Animals' (Leslie Bricusse, music and lyrics)

Music: 'Doctor Dolittle', 'Talk to the Animals', 'I've Never Seen Anything Like It', 'When I Look in your Eyes', 'Fabulous Places', 'I Think I Like You', 'Something in Your Smile'

Video availability

THE GRADUATE

1967	
Studio/Distributor:	United Artists
Director:	Mike Nichols
Producer:	Lawrence Turman
Screenplay:	Calder Willingham, Buck Henry
Music:	Paul Simon, Dave Grusin

CAST
Anne Bancroft . . . . *Mrs Robinson*
Dustin Hoffman . . . . *Ben Braddock*
Katharine Ross . . . . *Elaine Robinson*
William Daniels . . . . *Mr Braddock*
Murray Hamilton . . . . *Mr Robinson*
Elizabeth Wilson . . . . *Mrs Braddock*
Brian Avery . . . . *Carl Smith*

After completing college, the shy Ben Braddock finds himself under pressure from his wealthy family and friends to get a life, a job, and a wife. Mr Robinson and his wife are close friends of the Braddock family, but Mrs Robinson takes more than a filial interest in Ben when she seduces him in a hotel room. The two embark on a sordid affair, but Ben soon falls in love with the Robinsons' daughter, Elaine. This relationship falls apart when Elaine learns of Ben's affair with her mother.

Ben Braddock was Dustin Hoffman's first major screen role, a part that was turned down by Robert Redford. Charles Grodin was in line for the role, but having auditioned for the part, it was felt that Dustin Hoffman would be better suited. Anne Bancroft's part had originally been offered to Patricia Neal who

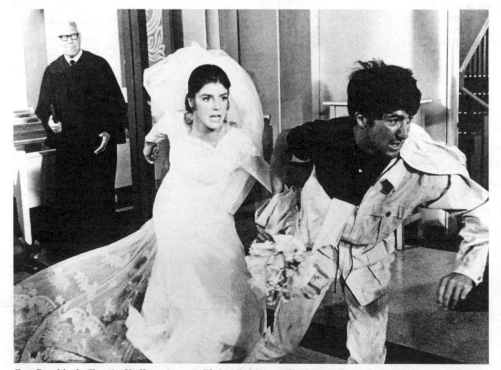

Ben Braddock (Dustin Hoffman) saves Elaine Robinson (Katherine Ross) from marrying the wrong man. He snatches her from the altar at the very last minute in The Graduate.

was just getting over a stroke and didn't feel fit enough to work. Doris Day also turned the part down as she felt the character was too promiscuous for her liking. Buck Henry, who co-wrote the screenplay, appears in the movie as a hotel clerk. There is also a cameo appearance by Richard Dreyfuss.

The Graduate ranked as the third highest grossing film of all time just behind *The Sound of Music* and *Gone with the Wind*.

Academy Awards: Best Direction (Mike Nichols)

Music: 'The Sound of Silence', 'Mrs Robinson', 'April Came She Will', 'Scarborough Fair/Canticle'

Video availability

GUESS WHO'S COMING TO DINNER

1967	
Studio/Distributor:	Columbia
Director:	Stanley Kramer
Producer:	Stanley Kramer
Screenplay:	William Rose
Music:	Frank DeVol

CAST

Spencer Tracy	*Matt Drayton*
Sidney Poitier	*John Prentice*
Katharine Hepburn	*Christina Drayton*
Katharine Houghton	*Joey Drayton*
Cecil Kellaway	*Msgr Ryan*
Beah Richards	*Mrs Prentice*
Roy E. Glenn Sr	*Mr Prentice*
Isabell Sanford	*Tilli*

Young blind Joey Drayton returns home from a holiday in Hawaii with the news that she is going to marry John Prentice, a black research scientist. When the family meets her husband-to-be they are less than thrilled with the prospect. Prentice tells them he will not go ahead with the wedding unless he has their full blessing, and the liberal Draytons are forced to overcome their prejudices.

This was the 9th and final movie that Katharine Hepburn and Spencer Tracy made together. Tracy was unwell throughout the shooting of the film, and died ten days after its completion.

The film includes the screen debut of Katharine Houghton, Katharine Hepburn's niece.

At the time the movie faced certain resistance for its patronizing view of black people.

Academy Awards: Best Actress (Katharine Hepburn), Best Story and Screenplay (William Rose)

Music: 'The Glory of Love'

Video availability

HALF A SIXPENCE

1967	
Studio/Distributor:	Paramount
Director:	George Sidney
Producer:	Charles H. Schneer, George Sidney
Screenplay:	Beverley Cross
Music:	David Heneker

CAST

Tommy Steele	*Arthur Kipps*
Julia Foster	*Ann*
Cyril Ritchard	*Chitterlow*
Penelope Horner	*Helen*
Grover Dale	*Pearce*
Elaine Taylor	*Kate*
Hilton Edwards	*Shalford*
Julia Sutton	*Flo*
Leslie Meadows	*Buggins*

This musical, based on an H.G. Wells play, stars Tommy Steele as Arthur Kipps, a young orphan lad who works as a draper's assistant. He acquires a taste for high society when he inherits a fortune. Luckily, he ends up with both feet firmly back on the ground when he realizes that wealth isn't the key to happiness, but only after he loses it all.

Tommy Steele had previously created his role as Kipps on the West End stage and on Broadway.

The movie was choreographed by Gillian Lynne, who later worked on the stage shows *The Roar of the Greasepaint - the Smell of the Crowd* and *Cats*.

Music: 'Half a Sixpence', 'I Don't Believe a Word of It', 'This is My World', 'All in the Cause of Economy', 'If the Rain's Got to Fall', 'Money to Burn', 'The Race is On', 'She's Too Far Above Me'

Video availability

The director of The Jungle Book, *Wolfgang Reitherman, was also one of the 24 credited animators on Disney's first full-length cartoon movie,* Snow White and the Seven Dwarfs, *back in 1937.*

THE JUNGLE BOOK

1967

Studio/Distributor: **Walt Disney**
Director: **Wolfgang Reitherman**
Producer: **Walt Disney**
Screenplay: **Larry Clemmons, Ralph Wright, Ken Aderson, Vance Gerry**
Music: **George Bruns**

CAST (Voices)
Phil Harris . . . . *Baloo the Bear*
Sebastian Cabot . . . . *Bagheera the Panther*
Louis Prima . . . . *King Louis of the Apes*
George Sanders . . . . *Shere Khan the Tiger*
Sterling Holloway . . . . *Kaa the Snake*
Bruce Reitherman . . *Mowgli the Man Cub*

In *Jungle Book* Walt Disney brings to life Rudyard Kipling's story of Mowgli, who is abandoned as a baby and grows up with the animals in an Indian forest. He befriends a panther who tries to assist him back to civilization, but despite all the dangers, especially from Shere Khan, the King of the apes and Kaa the snake, Mowgli wants to stay in the jungle. It is only the sight of a beautiful girl that lures him back to village life.

Jungle book appeared exactly 30 years after Disney's first full-length animated picture, *Snow White and the Seven Dwarfs*. This was the final animated film to be overseen by Walt Disney himself. It was released a few months after his death. The movie took three years to complete with 70 animators and 200 artists working full time on the project.

Music: 'I Wanna Be Like You', 'My Own Home', 'Bare Necessities', 'That's What Friends are For', 'Trust in Me'

Video availability

YOU ONLY LIVE TWICE

1967

Studio/Distributor:	United Artists
Director:	Lewis Gilbert
Producer:	Albert R. Broccoli, Harry Saltzman
Screenplay:	Roald Dahl
Music:	John Barry

CAST
Sean Connery . . . . *James Bond*
Akiko Wakabayashi . . . . *Aki*
Tetsuro Tamba . . . . *Tiger Tanaka*
Mia Hama . . . . *Kissy Suzuki*
Karin Dor . . . . *Helga Brandt*
Bernard Lee . . . . *M*
Desmond Llewelyn . . . . *Q*
Lois Maxwell . . . . *Miss Moneypenny*
Donald Pleasence . . . . *Blofeld*

In this assignment 007 investigates how an American spacecraft was swallowed up by what is believed to be a Russian capsule in the middle of an astronaut's spacewalk. His enquiries lead him to Japan where he fakes his own death and tracks one of SPECTRE's most feared villains, Blofeld. Housed in a volcano, complete with its own monorail and rocket with launch pad, Blofeld is attempting to start an all-out war.

The movie was allocated a budget of $9.5 million, roughly the combined total cost of the first four Bond films.

SPECTRE's volcano headquarters, with monorail, helicopter platform, launch pad and spaceship, cost close to $1 million and required the services of 400 workmen to build and operate.

This is the first Bond film in which the audience actually see Ernst Stavros Blofeld, who up until this point was never seen or referred to by name only.

At the end of filming *You Only Live Twice* Sean Connery announced he was resigning from the role of Bond.

Inspiration for the title of the movie came from a 17th-century Japanese poet named Bassho, who wrote 'You only live twice, once when you are born and once when you look death in the face.'

Filming in Japan was halted when some of the weapons started to damage the stonework of ancient buildings. The film company had to assure the authorities that it wouldn't happen again and that they'd make good the existing damage. At one stage, the two Japanese actresses, Akiko Wakabayashi who played Aki, and Mia Hama were going to swap parts due to Hama's problem grasping the English language. There was talk of firing her completely but it didn't come to that as she worked hard on her part and told the producers that if she was dropped she would bring dishonour to her family.

Music: 'You Only Live Twice' (Nancy Sinatra)

Video availability

2001: A SPACE ODYSSEY

1968

Studio/Distributor:	MGM
Director:	Stanley Kubrick
Producer:	Stanley Kubrick
Screenplay:	Stanley Kubrick, Arthur C. Clarke
Music:	Johann and Richard Strauss, Gyorgy Ligeti, Aram Khachaturyan

CAST
Keir Dullea . . . . *Bowman*
Gary Lockwood . . . . *Poole*
William Sylvester . . . . . *Dr Heywood Floyd*
Daniel Richter . . . . *Moonwatcher*
Douglas Rain . . . . *Hal 9000 (voice)*
Leonard Rossiter . . . . *Smyslov*
Margaret Tyzack . . . . *Elena*
Robert Beatty . . . . *Halvorsen*

Four million years ago a group of cavemen come across a large boulder which, when they touch it, converts them from peace-loving vegetarians into violent carnivores. The rock turns up again on the moon several million years later, which appears to be the cause of more strange happenings, and astronauts on the way to Jupiter discover a superior life form. The movie was said to be well ahead of its time with its forward look at scientific advances in space travel, especially the pictures of the moon well before Neil Armstrong made his walk.

The spaceship's on-board computer, HAL, got its name from a parody of IBM, taking one letter lower in the alphabet.

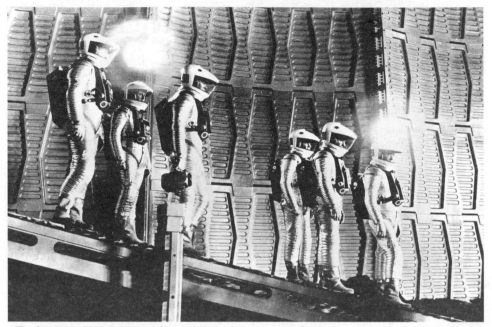

The futuristic 2001: A Space Odyssey *follows the evolution of man, by means of space travel, from early apes to the 21st century.*

The movie took three years to make at a cost of $10.5 million. It was filmed in high-security surroundings because director Stanley Kubrick didn't want leaks to the press about the plot and he refused to be interviewed about the movie's subject matter.

Video availability

Director Peter Hyams made a sequel, *2010* (1985), starring Roy Scheider and Helen Mirren.

Academy Awards: Best Special Visual Effects (Stanley Kubrick)

BULLITT

1968	
Studio/Distributor:	Warner
Director:	Peter Yates
Producer:	Philip D'Antoni
Screenplay:	Alan R. Trustman, Harry Kleiner
Music:	Lalo Schifrin

CAST

Steve McQueen	*Bullitt*
Robert Vaughn..............	*Chalmers*
Jacqueline Bisset	*Cathy*
Don Gordon	*Delgetti*
Robert Duvall..............	*Weissberg*
Simon Oakland...........	*Capt Bennet*
Norman Fell	*Baker*
George S. Brown	*Dr Willard*

Unorthodox police Lieutenant Frank Bullitt travels to San Francisco to protect a government informer who is about to stand witness against a major Mafia crime syndicate. At the request of politician Chalmers, the witness appears before a crime committee and is killed. Bullitt conceals the informer's death and plans to go after the killers himself. The movie's now famous car chase commences after Bullitt recognizes one of the murdering gang and takes off after him.

Steve McQueen insisted on doing all his own stunt car driving. During filming, a car crashed into a camera platform and blew it up. The sequence was left in the film. In order to make his role of Frank Bullitt look authentic, McQueen spent several weeks driving round in a squad car with real police officers.

Robert Duvall, who appears as a cab driver, is seen mainly through his rear view mirror.

Academy Awards: Best Editing (Frank P. Keller)

Video availability

FUNNY GIRL

1968	
Studio/Distributor:	Columbia
Director:	William Wyler
Producer:	William Wyler, Ray Stark
Screenplay:	Isobel Lennart
Music:	Walter Scharf (Supervisor)

CAST

Barbra Streisand . . . . *Fanny Brice*
Omar Sharif . . . . *Nick Arnstein*
Kay Medford . . . . *Rose Brice*
Anne Francis . . . . *Georgia James*
Walter Pidgeon . . . . *Florenz Ziegfeld*
Lee Allen . . . . *Eddie Ryan*
Mae Questel . . . . *Mrs Strakosh*

Barbra Streisand plays the less than attractive singer Fanny Brice who is determined to hit the big time. She is spotted by Nick Arnstein, a heavy, but well-connected, gambler who introduces Fanny to producer Florenz Ziegfeld who gives her a job with his new Follies show. She soon becomes the review's biggest attraction and goes on to become a national celebrity, but not before she marries Arnstein, the cause of much of her unhappiness in life.

This was Streisand's introduction to the movie world. Initially Streisand was reluctant to be in the movie because she felt self-conscious about her facial appearance, which she thought would be exaggerated on the screen.

Egyptian Omar Sharif, who plays Brice's Jewish husband, was condemned by the Arab press and considered a traitor, as the film was released at the time of the Arab–Israeli Six-Day War. There was even talk of revoking his citizenship.

The movie became the highest grossing musical since *The Sound of Music*, and spawned the sequel *Funny Lady* (1975).

Academy Awards: Best Actress (Barbra Streisand)

Music: 'Funny Girl', 'Don't Rain on My Parade', 'I'm the Greatest Star', 'People', 'You are Woman I am Man', 'His Love Makes Me Beautiful', 'Second Hand Rose'

Video availability

Barbra Streisand recreates Fanny Brice, the popular star of the 1920s in Funny Girl, *in her debut as a big-screen movie actress.*

THE LION IN WINTER

1968

Studio/Distributor: Avco Embassy
Director: Anthony Harvey
Producer: Martin H. Poll
Screenplay: James Goldman
Music: John Barry

CAST
Peter O'Toole .... *Henry II*
Katharine Hepburn . *Eleanor of Aquitaine*
Jane Merrow .... *Princess Alais*
John Castle .... *Prince Geoffrey*
Timothy Dalton .... *King Philip*
Anthony Hopkins ...... *Prince Richard the*
                          Lion-Hearted
Nigel Stock .... *William Marshall*

In the latter part of King Henry II's life, treachery within his family makes it necessary to elect a successor to the throne. The King's wife, Queen Eleanor of Aquitaine, has been imprisoned in a remote castle by the King in order to keep her from meddling in his affairs. The two spend Christmas together and immediately start arguing. The sparks fly as the King, Queen and their three sons, Geoffrey, John and Richard squabble over who should be the next ruler of England.

Director Tony Harvey contracted hepatitis during the making of the film but carried on to finish the picture.

Katharine Hepburn read every book she could find on Eleanor of Aquitaine, becoming such an expert that she was able to suggest some extra touches for her role.

Anthony Hopkins, who made his feature film debut in the film, broke several bones when he fell off a horse while shooting a scene.

Academy Awards: Best Actress (Katharine Hepburn), Best Screenplay (James Goldman), Best Original Music Score (John Barry)

Video availability

THE ODD COUPLE

1968

Studio/Distributor: Paramount
Director: Gene Saks
Producer: Howard W. Koch
Screenplay: Neal Simon
Music: Neal Hefti

CAST
Jack Lemmon .... *Felix Ungar*
Walter Matthau .... *Oscar Madison*
John Fiedler .... *Vinnie*
Herbert Edelman .... *Murray*
David Sheiner .... *Roy*
Larry Haines .... *Speed*
Monica Evans .... *Cecily*
Carole Shelley .... *Gwendolyn*

Video availability

Old friends Felix Ungar and Oscar Madison have recently separated from their respective wives and move into a New York apartment together. The two try to live as normal a life as possible but find that they get on each other's nerves. Felix tries to keep the place spotless, while Oscar is happy to live like a slob. Oscar wants to get on with life and have a good time, while Felix is happy being a hermit. The two old pals end up at each other's throat.

In 1975 *The Odd Couple* was turned into a successful TV comedy series with Tony Randall as Felix Ungar and Jack Klugman playing Oscar Madison.

In the 1980s, Neal Simon re-wrote the play with two females in the leading roles, played on stage by Rita Moreno as Olive Madison and Sally Struthers as Florence Ungar.

OLIVER!

1968

Studio/Distributor: Columbia
Director: Carol Reed

Producer: John Woolf
Screenplay: Vernon Harris
Music: Lionel Bart

CAST
Ron Moody . . . . *Fagin*
Shani Wallis . . . . *Nancy*
Oliver Reed . . . . *Bill Sikes*
Harry Secombe . . . . *Mr Bumble*
Hugh Griffith . . . . *the Magistrate*
Jack Wild . . . . *Artful Dodger*
Clive Moss . . . . *Charlie Bates*
Mark Lester . . . . *Oliver*

Mark Lester stars in this screen musical adapted from Charles Dickens's novel *Oliver Twist*. He plays the young orphan boy Oliver who gets involved in a band of thieves led by the villain, Fagin. He chooses a life on the streets in preference to living in a children's home or the bullying of his foster parents. He meets the Artful Dodger who introduces him to the art of pocket picking. The kind-hearted Nancy tries to protect him from the brutish Bill Sikes but fails, and he leaves the dangers of the street only after the arrival of his wealthy benefactor.

Originally a successful stage show, the movie picked up no less than six Oscars. It was the last British film to win an Oscar for Best Picture until 1981, when it went to *Chariots of Fire*. Carol Reed received his first and only Oscar for his direction of the film.

Mark Lester went on to star in several more successful films like *The Three Musketeers* and *The Prince and the Pauper* before retiring from the business to become an osteopath. The cast also included Leonard Rossiter and Peggy Mount.

A large portion of the film's $10 million budget went on the elaborate sets.

The stage version of the musical was revived in London in 1994.

Academy Awards: Best film (Producer John Woolf), Best Direction (Carol Reed), Best Art Direction (John Box and Terence Marsh), Set Decoration (Vernon Dixon and Ken Muggleston), Best Sound (Shepperton Studios Sound Dept), Best Musical Score Adaptation (John Green), Best Choreography (Special Award, Onna White)

Music: 'Oliver', 'Food Glorious Food', 'Consider Yourself', 'You've Got to Pick a Pocket or Two', 'I'd Do Anything', 'As Long as He Needs Me', 'Who Will Buy'

Video availability

PLANET OF THE APES

1968	
Studio/Distributor:	Twentieth Century-Fox
Director:	Franklin J. Schaffner
Producer:	Arthur P. Jacobs
Screenplay:	Michael Wilson
Music:	Jerry Goldsmith

CAST
Charlton Heston . . . . *George Taylor*
Roddy McDowall . . . . *Cornelius*
Kim Hunter . . . . *Zira*
Maurice Evans . . . . *Zaius*
James Whitmore . . . . . *Assembly President*
James Daly . . . . *Honorius*
Linda Harrison . . . . *Nova*
Robert Gunner . . . . *London*
Lou Wagner . . . . *Lucius*

An American spaceship crash lands on a mysterious and distant planet. The ship's commander, George Taylor, with the rest of the crew, have in fact been propelled on to Earth in the distant future. As they investigate the lush green land, they discover that the planet is ruled by apes, and humans have become slaves. Taylor is captured and is studied as an interesting laboratory specimen. He escapes but only with the help of a friendly ape, Cornelius.

The movie was followed by four sequels and a TV series (1974) based on the original.

Producer Arthur P. Jacobs had tried for over three years to get this project off the ground and it was only after Charlton Heston attached his name to it that studios started taking an interest. It turned out to be the first movie in which Charlton Heston appeared naked.

The movie was filmed in the national parks of Arizona and Utah.

Video availability

ROSEMARY'S BABY

1968	
Studio/Distributor:	Paramount
Director:	Roman Polanski
Producer:	William Castle
Screenplay:	Roman Polanski
Music:	Christopher Komeda

CAST

Mia Farrow . . . . *Rosemary Woodhouse*
John Cassavetes . . . . *Guy Woodhouse*
Ruth Gordon . . . . *Minnie Castevet*
Sidney Blackmer . . . . *Roman Castevet*
Maurice Evans . . . . *Hutch*
Ralph Bellamy . . . . *Dr Sapirstein*
Angela Dorian . . . . *Terry*
Patsy Kelly . . . . *Laura-Louise*

This chilling story is set in New York City where Rosemary and Guy Woodhouse are expecting their first baby. Rosemary is troubled by a dream where she is raped by a wild animal, and discovers mysterious scratches on her body. When her husband introduces her to a cult of devil worshippers she soon believes she is carrying the child of Satan.

Jane Fonda and director Roman Polanski's wife, Sharon Tate, were considered for the leading role, and Robert Redford and Warren Beatty were both at one time in line for the part of Guy Woodhouse. Tony Curtis provided the voice of Donald Baumgart, the voice that Rosemary hears, and Charles Grodin made his movie debut as the obstetrician, Dr Hill.

Producer William Castle once had cinema seats wired to give his audience slight electric shocks during the showing of his 1959 movie *Tingler*.

Rosemary's Baby was director Roman Polanski's first American-produced movie. He stopped making films after the murder of his pregnant wife, Sharon in 1969 by Charles Manson. He resumed work in 1971 with an adaptation of *Macbeth*.

Academy Awards: Best Supporting Actress (Ruth Gordon)

Video availability

Believing she is carrying Satan's child, Rosemary Woodhouse (Mia Farrow) prowls the house in the chilling Rosemary's Baby.

STAR!

1968		Producer:	Saul Chaplin
		Screenplay:	William Fairchild
Studio/Distributor:	Twentieth Century-Fox	Music:	Lenny Hayton
Director:	Robert Wise		

CAST
Julie Andrews . . . . *Gertrude Lawrence*
Richard Crenna . . . . *Richard Aldrich*
Michael Craig . . . . *Sir Anthony Spencer*
Daniel Massey . . . . *Noel Coward*
Robert Reed . . . . *Charles Fraser*
Bruce Forsyth . . . . *Arthur Lawrence*
Beryl Reid . . . . *Rose*
John Collin . . . . *Jack Roper*

This musical comedy chronicles Broadway star Gertrude Lawrence's rise to fame. Gertrude has a job in a review, but annoys the producer, André Charlot, by adding her own lines to the sketches. She marries stage manager Jack Roper, who is keen for her to give up the business, but she leaves him after giving birth to a daughter. After befriending Noel Coward, who gets her a part in a new Charlot review, she becomes an overnight star, landing major parts in many big shows. Gertrude's expensive living, however, causes serious money problems.

Daniel Massey, who played Noel Coward, was in fact Noel Coward's godson.

It has been said that Julie Andrews was cast only because she was the hottest female star around. Although her part in the film brought the audiences in when it first opened, it was not the success the movie company had hoped. They later made cuts and re-released it in America under the title *Those were the Happy Days*. Nevertheless it was not the hit that the last Julie Andrews–Robert Wise collaboration *The Sound of Music*, had been.

The movie contains an extract from Noel Coward's play, 'Private Lives'.

Music: 'Star', 'Piccadilly', 'Everything', 'Burlington Bertie from Bow', 'Limehouse Blues', 'Someone to Watch Over Me', 'I'll Find You'

Video availability

YELLOW SUBMARINE

1968	
Studio/Distributor:	King Features/Apple
Director:	George Dunning
Producer:	Al Brodax
Screenplay:	Lee Minoff, Al Brodax, Jack Mendelsohn, Erich Segal
Music:	The Beatles George Martin (Musical Director)

CAST
Paul McCartney, John Lennon, George Harrison and Ringo Starr . . . . *The Beatles (Voices)*
John Clive . . . . *John*
Geoff Hughes . . . . *Paul*
Peter Batten . . . . *George*
Paul Angelis . . . . *Ringo/Chief Blue Meanie*
Dick Emery . . . . *Lord Mayor/The Boob/Max*
Lance Percival . . . . *Old Fred*

In this full-length cartoon, based on The Beatles' hit single 'Yellow Submarine', John, Paul, George

and Ringo are featured in caricature. They embark on an incredible voyage in which they meet and help the people of Pepperland. They are under constant threat from the evil Blue Meanies who hit people over the head with apples before sucking the colour out of them.

University professor Erich Segal, who co-wrote the screenplay, went on to write *Love Story*, which became a number one hit in 1970.

The Beatles make a brief appearance in a live-action scene.

Yellow Submarine was the first full-length animated film made in Britain since *Animal Farm* in 1955. However, German artist Heinz Edelman provided the drawings and caricatures.

Music: 'Yellow Submarine', 'All Together Now', 'Hey Bulldog', 'All You Need is Love', 'Only a Northern Song', 'It's All Too Much'

Video availability

EASY RIDER

1969		Screenplay:	Peter Fonda, Dennis Hopper, Terry Southern
Studio/Distributor:	Columbia	Music:	The Byrds, The Band,
Director:	Dennis Hopper		Jimi Hendrix,
Producer:	Peter Fonda		Steppenwolf

Captain America (Peter Fonda) and Billy (Dennis Hopper) head eastward from California to New Orleans in time for the Mardi Gras in Easy Rider, *a cult 1960s movie in which bikers replaced cowboys as American heroes.*

CAST

Peter Fonda . . . . *Captain America*
Dennis Hopper . . . . *Billy*
Jack Nicholson . . . . *George Hanson*
Robert Walker Jr . . . . *Chief*
Luana Anders . . . . *Girl*

In this early road movie Captain America and Billy rebel against the establishment and become drug dealers. They motorcycle across America, selling their narcotics to hippie communes. On their way to New Orleans, to join the Mardi Gras, they are arrested and meet up with the drunken civil rights lawyer George Hanson. The lawyer experiences his first joint with the two young men and decides to join them. The three of them now journey onwards, but are beaten up by local rednecks in their continued search for a freedom they'll never find.

Many of the bit parts were played by locals who took instructions from director Dennis Hopper. Hopper's own first acting role was a small part in the 1955 James Dean movie *Rebel without a Cause*. After take 86 of a scene from the 1958 Western *From Hell to Texas*, director Henry Hathaway told Dennis Hopper that he would never work in the movies again. However. Hathaway did cast him six years later in his movie with John Wayne, *The Sons of Katie Elder*.

The scene in which a drugged Fonda talks to a statue of the Madonna in a cemetery proved difficult for the actor because it reminded him of his mother's suicide as a child.

Music: 'Ballad of Easy Rider' (Roger McGuin), 'Born To Be Wild', 'The Pusher' (Steppenwolf), 'Wasn't Born to Follow' (The Byrds), 'The Weight' (The Band), 'If Six Was Nine' (Jimi Hendrix), 'Let's Turkey Trot' (Little Eva), 'It's Alright Ma I'm Only Bleeding' (Bob Dylan)

Video availability

HELLO DOLLY!

1969	
Studio/Distributor:	Twentieth Century-Fox
Director:	Gene Kelly
Producer:	Ernest Lehman
Screenplay:	Ernest Lehman
Music:	Jerry Herman

CAST

Barbra Streisand . . . . *Dolly Levi*
Walter Matthau . . . . *Horace Vandergelder*
Michael Crawford . . . . *Cornelius Hackl*
Louis Armstrong . . . . *Orchestra leader*
Marianne McAndrew . . . . *Irene Molloy*
E.J. Parker . . . . *Minnie Fay*

Joyce Ames	*Ermengarda*
Tommy Tune	*Ambrose Kemper*

T he widowed matchmaker Dolly Levi is given the job of finding a partner for Horace Vandergelder, the pompous hay-feed merchant from Yonkers in New York. However, Dolly has her matrimonial eye on the well-known half millionaire for herself. While trying to feather her own bed, Dolly arranges for two of Horace's assistants, Barnaby and Cornelius, to spend a night on the town with dressmaker Irene Molloy and her assistant Minnie.

It was alleged that during the making of this film, Streisand slapped Matthau and he slapped her back. He complained that she was hogging the screen and she called him 'Old sewermouth'.

Because Louis Armstrong had reached number one in the American charts with the title song five years earlier, a special role was created for him in the movie, which included a duet with Streisand.

Both Julie Andrews and Elizabeth Taylor were originally considered for the lead as was Carol Channing who originated the part on the Broadway stage.

Academy Awards: Best Art Direction (John DeCuir, Jack Martin Smith and Herman Blumenthal), Set Decoration (Walter M. Scott, George Hopkins, Raphael Bretton), Best Scoring of a Musical (Lennie Hayton and Lionel Newman), Best Sound (Jack Solomon and Murray Spivak)

Music: 'Hello Dolly', 'Just Leave Everything To Me', 'It Takes a Woman', 'Put On Your Sunday Clothes', 'Before the Parade Passes by', 'It Only Takes a Moment', 'So Long Dearie'

Video availability

MIDNIGHT COWBOY

1969	
Studio/Distributor:	United Artists
Director:	John Schlesinger
Producer:	Jerome Hellman, John Schlesinger
Screenplay:	Waldo Salt
Music:	John Barry (Supervision)

CAST

Dustin Hoffman	*Enrico 'Ratso' Rizzo*
Jon Voight	*Joe Buck*
Sylvia Miles	*Cass*
John McGiver	*O'Daniel*
Brenda Vaccaro	*Shirley*
Bernard Hughes	*Towny*
Ruth White	*Sally Buck*
Jennifer Salt	*Annie*
Gil Rankin	*Woodsy Niles*

G iving up his job as a dishwasher in a small hamburger joint in Texas, Joe Buck heads north to the Big Apple. His plan is to become rich by sexually satisfying all the bored, rich women in New York City. He meets up with street hustler Enrico 'Ratso' Rizzo, who talks his way into becoming Buck's manager, and the two of them squat down in a tenement due for demolition. Buck has some success with the women but doesn't make much money. The search for cash becomes more acute as Rizzo's tuberculosis becomes worse, and, in his frustration, Buck robs and beats up a middle-aged gay man in a hotel room. He takes a Greyhound bus to Florida with Rizzo but his friend doesn't make it to the place 'where the sun keeps shining'.

At the time, *Midnight Cowboy* was the first 'X'-rated movie to win an Oscar for Best Picture. For years, most TV stations refused to show the unedited version of the movie because of the bad language.

Bob Dylan was originally asked to write a song for the movie, but he delivered 'Lay Lady Lay' too late for it to be considered. Harry Nilsson's own 'I Guess the Lord Must Be in New York City' was also passed up in favour of 'Everybody's Talkin' ', sung by Nilsson but written by Fred Neil.

Academy Awards: Best Film (Producer Jerome Hellman), Best Direction (John Schlesinger), Best Screenplay (Waldo Salt)

Music: 'Everybody's Talkin'' (Harry Nilsson)

Video availability

THE PRIME OF MISS JEAN BRODIE

1969	
Studio/Distributor:	Twentieth Century-Fox
Director:	Ronald Neame
Producer:	Robert Fryer
Screenplay:	Jay Presson Allen
Music:	Rod McKuen

CAST
Maggie Smith . . . . *Jean Brodie*
Robert Stephens . . . . *Teddy Lloyd*
Pamela Franklin . . . . *Sandy*
Gordon Jackson . . . . *Gordon Lowther*
Celia Johnson . . . . *Miss MacKay*
Jane Carr . . . . *Mary McGregor*
Diane Grayson . . . . *Jenny*
Shirley Steedman . . . . *Monica*

Jean Brodie is a teacher in an exclusive school for wealthy girls in 1930s Edinburgh. She befriends some of her students, on occasion taking them on short country trips to the home of Gordon Lowther, a fellow teacher who has more than a passing interest in her. However, Jean is involved with another school employee, Teddy Lloyd, who is married with children. She tries to play the two men off against one another in the false hope that Lloyd will leave his wife for her. Miss MacKay, the head-mistress, has suspicions about Jean's affairs and is less than happy about her behaviour, which sets a bad example for the girls.

The interior scenes were shot at Pinewood Studios, but the locations were actually filmed in Edinburgh.

British director Ronald Neame produced a number of movies for David Lean, including *Great Expectations* and *Oliver Twist*, before turning his hand to directing.

Based on the novel by Muriel Spark, the film was chosen for the British Royal Film Performance 1969.

Academy Awards: Best Actress (Maggie Smith)

Top Female Actors 1969-94

Appearances in number one movies

Maggie Smith	7
Diane Keaton	6
Talia Shire	6
Barbra Streisand	6
Meryl Streep	6
Sigourney Weaver	6
Faye Dunaway	5
Michelle Pfeiffer	5
Geena Davis	5
Anne Bancroft	4
Julie Christie	4
Mia Farrow	4
Jodie Foster	4
Barbara Hershey	4
Glenda Jackson	4
Anjelica Huston	4
Andie MacDowell	4
Kathleen Turner	4

NB Lois Maxwell hits the top spot 8 times in the Bond movies but cannot really be said to have a starring role, more of a featured cameo.

Music: 'Jean' (Rod McKuen)

Video availability

WHERE EAGLES DARE

1969

Studio/Distributor: MGM
Director: Brian G. Hutton
Producer: Jerry Gershwin, Elliot Kastner
Screenplay: Alistair MacLean
Music: Ron Goodwin

CAST
Richard Burton . . . . *John Smith*
Clint Eastwood . . . . . . *Lt. Morris Schaffer*
Mary Ure . . . . *Mary Ellison*
Michael Hordern . . . *Vice-Admiral Rolland*
Patrick Wymark . . . . *Col. Wyatt-Turner*
Robert Beatty . . . . *Cartwright-Jones*
Anton Diffring . . . . *Col. Kramer*

During World War II John Smith leads a group of seven Allied Commandos in a dangerous mission to rescue a top American General who is being held prisoner by the Nazis in an impregnable castle prison in the Bavarian Alps. Disguised in German army uniform, the men parachute into enemy territory. After infiltrating the castle and locating the General, they set about blowing the place to pieces.

Clint Eastwood would only make the film if he received equal billing with Richard Burton. At the time, Burton was a screen legend, but Eastwood was just beginning to become established, and after some arguing, Eastwood got his way.

The film was one of the many adaptations from Alistair MacLean's novels.

Video availability

THE MOST DANGEROUS MAN IN THE WORLD

11 July 1969	1 week

Distributor: Twentieth Century-Fox
Director: J. Lee Thompson
Producer: Mort Abrahams
Screenplay: Ben Maddow
Music: Jerry Goldsmith

CAST
Gregory Peck . . . . *John Hathaway*
Anne Heywood . . . . *Kay Hanna*
Arthur Hill . . . . *Shelby*
Alan Dobie . . . . *Benson*
Conrad Yama . . . . *The Chairman*
Zienia Merton . . . . *Ting Ling*
Francisca Tu . . . . *Soong Chu*

Western intelligence men implant a detonator and a transmitter into the skull of an American Nobel Prize-winning scientist, John Hathaway. They then send him on a secret mission into Red China after he has been told it would be impossible for him to visit the country. The time bomb he is carrying could be set off at any moment.

The American title for the movie is *The Chairman*.

The movie was made at Pinewood Studios in England and on location in the Far East.

Gregory Peck stars in the first Box Office Number One, as this was the first week for which reliable Box Office statistics were available. Peck appears at the top again in *The Omen* (1976). He also features in the cast of a total of nine other Box Office Hits (1945–69).

The Top Five

Week of 11 July 1969
1. The Most Dangerous Man in the World
2. Oliver!
3. Oh! What a Lovely War
4. The Italian Job
5. Gone with the Wind

OLIVER!

18 July 1969	5 weeks*

A re-release; see 1968.

The Top Five

Week of 18 July 1969
1. Oliver!
2. The Most Dangerous Man in the World
3. The Longest Day
4. Lion in Winter
5. Gone with the Wind

THREE INTO TWO WON'T GO

25 July 1969	1 week

Distributor: Universal
Director: Peter Hall
Producer: Julian Blaustein
Screenplay: Edna O'Brien
Music: Francis Lai

CAST
Rod Steiger . . . . *Steve Howard*
Claire Bloom . . . . *Frances Howard*

Judy Geeson . . . . *Ella Patterson*
Peggy Ashcroft . . . . *Belle*
Paul Rogers . . . . *Jack*
Lynn Farleigh . . . . *Janet*
Elizabeth Spriggs . . . . *Marcia*
Sheila Allen . . . . *Beth*

Based on the novel *Bouquet of Barbed Wire* by Andrea Newman, the film chronicles the rocky, childless marriage of Steve and Frances Howard. Their relationship deteriorates even further when

Steve picks up hitch-hiker Ella Patterson, who manages to move into the couple's home by convincing Frances that she had to give up her job because of Steve's sexual harassment. Ella offers her their spare room, but Steve is livid when he finds her there. Ella tells him she may be pregnant and forces him to leave his wife. She then rejects him and he goes back to his wife who also sends him packing and headlong into drink.

At the time, Rod Steiger and Claire Bloom were married in real life. They appeared together in another film in the same year, *The Illustrated Man*.

The Top Five

Week of 25 July 1969
1. Three Into Two Won't Go
2. Oliver!
3. Alfred the Great
4. Lion in Winter
5. The Most Dangerous Man in the World

THE WILD BUNCH

29 August 1969	4 weeks

Distributor:	Warner
Director:	Sam Peckinpah
Producer:	Phil Feldman
Screenplay:	Walon Green, Sam Peckinpah
Music:	Jerry Fielding

CAST
William Holden . . . . *Pike*

Ernest Borgnine . . . . *Dutch*
Robert Ryan . . . . *Deke Thornton*
Edmond O'Brien . . . . *Sykes*
Warren Oates . . . . *Lyle Gorch*
Jaime Sanchez . . . . *Angel*
Ben Johnson . . . . *Tector Gorch*
Emilio Fernandez . . . . *Mapache*

The Wild Bunch are a group of ageing outlaws in 1914, the dying days of the Wild West. They are

A gang of ageing outlaws, led by Pike (William Holden), hold up an American ammunition train on its way to Mexico in Sam Peckinpah's The Wild Bunch, *a film set in the closing days of the old west.*

being pursued by bounty hunter Deke Thornton, who was at one time a good friend of Pike Bishop, the gang leader. They decide they should retire after one more mission, but are ambushed by Thornton. They die bloodily trying to save one of the gang in a fight against a Mexican revolutionary.

The movie was originally edited down, not because of the violence but to reduce the running time. However, further cuts were made when audiences and exhibitors reacted badly to some of the more bloody scenes.

Lee Marvin was the first choice to play Pike Bishop,

but had to turn down the part because filming of *Paint your Wagon* was running well over schedule.

Video availability

BATTLE OF BRITAIN

26 September 1969	14 weeks*

Distributor:	United Artists
Director:	Guy Hamilton
Producer:	Harry Saltzman and S. Benjamin Fisz
Screenplay:	James Kennaway and Wilfred Greatorex
Music:	William Walton, Ron Goodwin

CAST
Harry Andrews . . . . *Senior Civil Servant*
Michael Caine . . . . *Sqn. Leader Canfield*
Trevor Howard   *Air Vice-Marshal Keith Park*
Curt Jurgens . . . . *Baron Von Richter*
Ian McShane . . . . *Sgt Pilot Andy*
Kenneth More . . . . . *Group Captain Baker*
Laurence Olivier . . . . *Air Chief Marshal Sir Hugh Dowding*
Nigel Patrick . . . . *Group Captain Hope*
Christopher Plummer . . *Flt Lt. Sqn. Harvey*
Michael Redgrave . . *Air Vice-Marshal Evill*
Ralph Richardson . . . . . . *British Minister in Switzerland*

This star-studded World War II epic of the Battle of Britain is packed with aviation dog fight sequences. Sir Hugh Dowding, one of the top brass of the RAF, is short on pilots and aircraft but still has to work out strategic tactics for the battles in the air as time is running out. He manages to force the Germans into making fatal mistakes while British pluck wins the day.

The movie cost the producers over $12 million to make which proved to be a less than successful investment as the picture finally lost over $10 million worldwide. However, with recent TV and video rights, things could finally be looking up. Much of the film's budget was spent on the expensive aerial shots, with Adolf Galland, one of Germany's key fliers during the war, acting as technical advisor.

The film was made to mark the 30th anniversary of the 1940 aerial attack on Great Britain.

Video availability

THE VIRGIN SOLDIERS

31 October 1969	1 week

Distributor:	Columbia
Director:	John Dexter
Producer:	Leslie Gilliat, Ned Sherrin
Screenplay:	John Hopkins
Music:	Peter Greenwell

CAST
Lynn Redgrave . . . . *Philippa Raskin*
Hywel Bennett . . . . *Brigg*
Nigel Davenport . . . . *Sgt Driscoll*
Nigel Patrick . . . . *RSM Raskin*
Rachel Kempson . . . . *Mrs Raskin*
Jack Shepherd . . . . *Sgt Wellbeloved*
Michael Gwynn . . *Lt Col Bromley-Pickering*
Tsai Chin . . . . *Juicy Lucy*

This comedy-drama covers the adventures, from the bedroom to the battlefield, of young British army recruits stationed in Singapore in 1960. The men, although unprepared for battle duty, are aware that death could be close at hand with killer terrorists stalking the streets and jungles of Malaya.

A young David Bowie had an early minor acting role, while Lynn Redgrave starred with her real-life mother, Rachel Kempson.

A less successful sequel following in 1977, entitled *Stand Up Virgin Soldiers*, starring Robin Askwith and Nigel Davenport.

The Top Five

Week of 31 October 1969
1. Virgin Soldiers
2. Battle of Britain
3. Oliver!
4. Midnight Cowboy
5. The Wild Bunch

Video availability

ON HER MAJESTY'S SECRET SERVICE

26 December 1969	6 weeks

Distributor:	United Artists
Director:	Peter Hunt
Producer:	Albert R. Broccoli, Harry Saltzman
Screenplay:	Richard Maibaum
Music:	John Barry

CAST
George Lazenby . . . . *James Bond*
Diana Rigg . . . . *Tracy*
Telly Savalas . . . . *Blofeld*
Ilse Steppat . . . . *Irma Bunt*
Gabriele Ferzetti . . . . *Draco*
Yuri Borienko . . . . *Grunther*
Bernard Horsfall . . . . *Campbell*
George Baker . . . . *Sir Hilary Bray*

In the 6th 007 movie, Bond is officially instructed to end his pursuit of Stavro Blofeld, but he surrenders his 'licence to kill' in order to continue his own personal search for Blofeld in Portugal. There he meets and marries the doomed Tracy Draco, the daughter of the boss of a crime syndicate. She helps Bond locate and penetrate Blofeld's impregnable Swiss mountain-top fortress where he is planning to sterilize the universe unless he is granted amnesty for all his past crimes.

On Her Majesty's Secret Service was the first Bond picture without Sean Connery, who was replaced by Australian male model and part-time car salesman George Lazenby. The Australian was probably best known in the UK as the Big Fry Man in a series of TV ads for confectionery!

After causing major problems for the production company, he finally resigned as Bond in the belief he was being exploited by the producers. He also believed he could establish a successful career under his own steam.

A restaurant that was still under construction was used as the fortress at the top of the mountain where Blofeld was housed. To this day, the restaurant retains its on-screen name of Piz Gloria.

Both Brigitte Bardot and Catherine Deneuve were considered for the role of Tracy Draco. Diana Rigg was cast largely because of her popularity at the time as Emma Peel in the TV series *The Avengers*.

Music: 'We have all the Time in the World' (Louis Armstrong)

Video availability

The Top Five

Week of 26 December 1969
1. On Her Majesty's Secret Service
2. Battle of Britain
3. Women in Love
4. Oliver!
5. Goodbye Mr Chips

THE 1970s

Cinemagoing in the 1970s was certainly an exciting pastime. From the thrills and spills of daredevil secret agent James Bond, who opened the decade at number one with *On Her Majesty's Secret Service*, to the warp speed of the USS *Enterprise* and her captain and crew, who boldly went into 1980 in the number one spot, the 1970s provided a real adventure for dedicated moviegoers. Big-budget disaster epics like *The Poseidon Adventure* and *The Towering Inferno* became huge blockbusters, as did *Earthquake*, which literally made the earth move if you were lucky enough to see it in a cinema equipped with the sensurround process. A young new American director called Steven Spielberg started making waves with films like *Sugarland Express* and *Duel* before really setting pulses racing with man-eating sharks in *Jaws*.

Back on dry land best-selling novels were being turned into ground-breaking movies. Mario Puzo's *Godfather* spawned two major cinematic milestones, and Eric Segal's tearjerker *Love Story* gave us the decade's first real weepie.

Historical dramas like *Anne of the Thousand Days* and *Cromwell* did well at the box office but the fashion for the past soon gave way to fascination about the future. *2001* had scored well in the late 1960s but George Lucas's *Star Wars* blew everything away in 1978. Spielberg's *Close Encounters of the Third Kind* confirmed audiences' appetite for space themes and between the two they occupied the box office top spot from January until July that year.

Superman flew into the record books and John Travolta danced his way across the screen in *Saturday Night Fever* and *Grease*. Burt Reynolds topped the popularity charts several times in the 1970s with a string of successes, including *Deliverance* and *Smokey and the Bandit*, and we were introduced to Roger Moore's debonair James Bond who scored with *Live and Let Die*, *The Man with the Golden Gun*, *The Spy Who Loved Me* and *Moonraker*.

Horrors like *The Exorcist* and *The Omen* brought the genre firmly up to date and Alfred Hitchcock signed off with *Frenzy* and his final film, *Family Plot*. Gene Hackman's Popeye Doyle proved popular in two *French Connection* movies as did Peter Sellers's inept bumbling Inspector Clouseau in three *Pink Panther* films.

So, a varied decade in which Sylvester Stallone became a superstar with *Rocky*, Jack Nicholson won his first Oscar for *One Flew over the Cuckoo's Nest*, Clint Eastwood's career continued to climb with films like *The Eiger Sanction* and the *Dirty Harry* series, and keen-eyed moviegoers first spotted a youthful Austrian bodybuilder in *Stay Hungry* and *Pumping Iron* – but more about him in the 1980s.

BUTCH CASSIDY AND THE SUNDANCE KID

20 February 1970	3 weeks*

Distributor:	Twentieth Century-Fox
Director:	George Roy Hill
Producer:	John Foreman
Screenplay:	William Goldman
Music:	Burt Bacharach

CAST
Paul Newman . . . . *Butch Cassidy*
Robert Redford . . . . *the Sundance Kid*
Katharine Ross . . . . *Etta Place*
Strother Martin . . . . *Percy Garris*
Henry Jones . . . . *Bike Salesman*
Jeff Corey . . . . *Sheriff Bledsoe*
George Furth . . . . *Woodcock*
Cloris Leachman . . . . *Agnes*

The deadly outlaw Butch Cassidy, leader of the notorious Hole in the Wall gang, hooks up with the vicious Sundance Kid to rob and plunder across the USA. Always on the run, they manage to keep one step ahead of the authorities and the railroad agents. When the heats gets too much they head for Bolivia with Sundance's girl, Etta Place, in tow. With the aid of a Spanish dictionary, the legendary outlaws strike at a series of Bolivian banks. But their luck finally runs out when they are tracked down by the law.

Butch Cassidy and the Sundance Kid saw the first pairing of Paul Newman and Robert Redford who worked together again with director George Roy Hill in *The Sting* (1973).

The 1979 prequel *Butch and Sundance: The Early Days* failed to set the Box Office alight, although it was interesting for the early appearances of Tom Berenger and Peter (Robocop) Weller.

'Raindrops Keep Fallin' on my Head' has been a hit for several artists, including Sacha Distel, Bobbie Gentry and B.J. Thomas, who sang the original on the film.

Academy Awards: Best Story and Screenplay (William Goldman), Best Cinematography (Conrad Hall), Best Original Music Score (Burt Bacharach), Best Song – 'Raindrops Keep Fallin' on my Head' (Burt Bacharach, music; Hal David, lyrics)

Music: 'Raindrops Keep Fallin' on my Head', 'On a Bicycle Built for Joy' (B.J. Thomas)

Video availability

The Top Five

Week of 20 February 1970
1. Butch Cassidy and the Sundance Kid
2. Battle of Britain
3. Paint your Wagon
4. Hello Dolly!
5. Oliver!

ANNE OF THE THOUSAND DAYS

20 March 1970	6 weeks

Distributor:	Universal
Director:	Charles Jarrott
Producer:	Hal B. Wallis
Screenplay:	Bridget Boland, John Hale
Music:	George Delerue

CAST
Richard Burton . . . . *Henry VIII*
Genevieve Bujold . . . . *Anne Boleyn*
Irene Papas . . . . *Katherine of Aragon*
Anthony Quayle . . . . *Cardinal Wolsey*
John Colicos . . . . *Cromwell*
Michael Hordern . . . . *Thomas Boleyn*
Katharine Blake . . . . *Elizabeth Boleyn*
Peter Jeffrey . . . . *Norfolk*

In this historical epic Henry VIII divorces his first wife in order to marry the young Anne Boleyn, his mistress. She bears him a daughter – the future Elizabeth I – but fails to deliver the son he desperately desires. Henry's interest in his wife cools, especially after the birth of a stillborn son. Adultery charges are trumped up by Cromwell and she is imprisoned in the Tower and finally beheaded.

The Top Five

Week of 20 March 1970
1. Anne of the Thousand Days
2. Butch Cassidy and the Sundance Kid
3. Paint your Wagon
4. Battle of Britain
5. Zabriskie Point

Paul Newman as Butch Cassidy and Robert Redford as the Sundance Kid become best of friends as well as the most charming outlaws in the west.

This was French-Canadian actress Bujold's first major film and she was Oscar nominated for her role. Her next number one was *Earthquake* in 1974. Bujold quit the cast of the *Star Trek* TV series in 1994 after only two days, saying her character lacked motivation.

The film was chosen for the British Royal Film Performance in 1970.

Academy Awards: Best Costume Design (Margaret Furse)

Video availability

AIRPORT

1 May 1970	6 weeks

Distributor: **Universal**
Director: **George Seaton**
Producer: **Ross Hunter**
Screenplay: **George Seaton**
Music: **Alfred Newman**

CAST
Burt Lancaster . . . . *Mel Bakersfeld*
Dean Martin . . . . *Vernon Demerest*
Jean Seberg . . . . *Tanya Livingston*
Jacqueline Bisset . . . . *Gwen Meighen*
George Kennedy . . . . *Patroni*
Helen Hayes . . . . *Ada Quonsett*

Based on the best-selling novel by Arthur Hailey, this all-star disaster movie begins as an assortment of passengers, with various problems, board the huge Trans Global Airlines plane. A psychopathic bomber (Van Heflin) tries to end all their problems when he blows a hole in the side of the plane. With growing hysteria on board, the airport manager (Burt Lancaster) grapples with the problem of getting the plane safely down on to a snow-filled runway. Meanwhile the pilot (Dean Martin), who is having an affair with the stewardess (Jacqueline Bisset), wrestles the controls of his damaged Boeing. Together, they land the crippled airliner safely.

George Kennedy would reprise his role of Patroni in all the subsequent Airport sequels and spin-offs, including *Airport 75*, *Airport 77* (Box Office number one in 1977) and *The Concorde - Airport 79*.

Helen Hayes, who plays the stowaway, won her first Oscar in 1931 as Best Actress in *The Sin of Madelon Claudet*, which was her first speaking role in movies.

Academy Awards: Best Supporting Actress (Helen Hayes)

Video availability

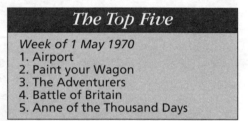

The Top Five

Week of 1 May 1970
1. Airport
2. Paint your Wagon
3. The Adventurers
4. Battle of Britain
5. Anne of the Thousand Days

PAINT YOUR WAGON

12 June 1970	1 week

Distributor: **Paramount**
Director: **Joshua Logan**
Producer: **Alan Jay Lerner**
Screenplay: **Alan Jay Lerner**
Music: **Frederick Loewe**
          André Previn (Additional music)

CAST
Lee Marvin . . . . *Ben Rumson*
Clint Eastwood . . . . *Pardner*
Jean Seberg . . . . *Elizabeth*
Ray Walston . . . . *Mad Jack Duncan*
Harve Presnell . . . . *Rotten Luck Willie*
Alan Dreeben Dexter . . . . *The Parson*
Paula Trueman . . . . *Mary Fenty*
Tom Ligon . . . . *Horton Fenty*

This big-screen treatment of Lerner and Loewe's 1951 Broadway musical is set in California during the mid-19th century goldrush. Ben Rumson and Pardner are a gold-mining team. Their living arrangements are altered when Ben decides to marry Elizabeth, the woman he bought off a passing Mormon. The three have to live together and relations become strained when Ben and Elizabeth realize that they have feelings for each other. After much soul searching, Ben and Rumson agree to share Elizabeth, who is happy with the arrangement, to avoid breaking up the partnership. Nevertheless the mining town has no other women and no fun, and Rumsen tries to remedy the situation by hijacking a passing coachload of women. Before long the town is buzzing with bars and barroom girls. Rumson and Pardner hit on the ingenious idea of digging tunnels under the town's bars to retrieve any loose gold dust which the miners and prospectors drop through the floorboards. Victims of their own success, the network of tunnels becomes so extensive that the town collapses. Rumson decides to move on, leaving Pardner and Elizabeth together.

Lee Marvin's 'Wand'rin' Star' reached number one on the British charts before the film was even released and spent 23 weeks in the top 50 with 3 weeks at the top. The flip side featured Clint Eastwood's 'I Talk to the Trees'.

For the Broadway show Lerner and Loewe had researched actual incidents from the days of the Californian goldrush to incorporate into the plot.

Jean Seberg managed two consecutive number ones by knocking herself off her top spot in *Airport* with *Paint Your Wagon*!

Music: 'Wand'rin' Star', 'I Talk to the Trees', 'I Still See Elisa', 'There's a Coach Comin' In', 'The First Thing you Know', 'They Call the Wind Maria'

Video availability

M*A*S*H

19 June 1970	4 weeks

Distributor:	**Twentieth Century-Fox**
Director:	**Robert Altman**
Producer:	**Ingo Preminger**
Screenplay:	**Ring Lardner Jr**
Music:	**Johnny Mandel**

CAST
Elliott Gould . . . . *Trapper John*

Donald Sutherland . . . . *Hawkeye*
Tom Skerritt . . . . *Duke*
Sally Kellerman . . . . *Major Hot Lips*
Jo Ann Pflug . . . . *Lt Dish*
René Auberjonois . . . . *Dago Red*
Roger Bowen . . . . *Col. Henry Blake*
Gary Burghoff . . . . *Radar O'Reilly*

In war-torn Korea a Mobile Army Surgical Hospital's (MASH) doctors and nurses tend to the injured

*In M*A*S*H a group of drunken practical joking, yet sympathetic and more than capable doctors, treat the injured during the Korean War and still find time to tease head nurse, Hot Lips Houlihan (Sally Kellerman).*

and dying soldiers with a mixture of humour and cynicism. The catalogue of characters from the mobile hospital included the cynical Trapper John and Hawkeye, sexpot Major Hot Lips and nervous Radar.

Based on a novel by Richard Hooker, the film spawned a hugely successful long-running TV series.

Ring Lardner Jr's screenplay, which won an Oscar, had apparently been turned down by several directors before Altman took on the project. The film was also nominated for Best Picture, Best Director (Robert Altman) and Best Actress (Sally Kellerman).

Academy Awards: Best Screenplay (Ring Lardner Jr)

Music: 'Suicide is Painless' (MASH)

Video availability

The Top Five

Week of 19 June 1970
1. M*A*S*H
2. Paint your Wagon
3. Anne of the Thousand Days
4. Beneath the Planet of the Apes
5. Secret of Santa Vittoria

WOODSTOCK

17 July 1970	1 week

Distributor:	Warner
Director:	Michael Wadleigh
Producer:	Bob Maurice
Music:	various (see cast)

CAST
Joan Baez, Joe Cocker, Country Joe and the Fish, Crosby, Stills and Nash, Neil Young, Arlo Guthrie, Richie Havens, Jimi Hendrix, Santana, Sha-Na-Na, Sly and the Family Stone, The Who

Woodstock is a documentary account of the 1969 pop festival held in New York State. Filmed with several crews over many weeks, the film is a superb combination of all that went on before, during and after the milestone pop music event in the 1960s. Using split-screen technology to great effect, it shows the concert from the audience's perspective, from the performer's perspective and from the perspective of the sometimes bewildered population of the small town of Bethel, New York where the festival took place.

The actual concert lasted three days and the biggest problems were sanitation, law enforcement and food supplies.

In 1994, after 25 years, the film was re-released in an extended director's cut. An anniversary festival was also organized, but ended up as a mud bath in much the same way as the original. A few of the original acts, such as Joe Cocker, performed at Woodstock '94.

Music: 'Going up the Country' (Canned Heat), 'Wooden Ships', 'Suite: Judy Blue Eyes' (Crosby, Stills and Nash, and Young), 'Dance to the Music', 'I Want to take you Higher' (Sly and the Family Stone), 'We're Gonna Take It' (The Who), 'With a Little Help from my Friends' (Joe Cocker), 'Star Spangled Banner', 'Purple Haze' (Jimi Hendrix)

Video availability

The Top Five

Week of 17 July 1970
1. Woodstock
2. M*A*S*H
3. Paint your Wagon
4. Virgin and the Gypsy
5. Anne of the Thousand Days

CROMWELL

24 July 1970	9 weeks*

Distributor:	Columbia
Director:	Ken Hughes
Producer:	Irving Allen
Screenplay:	Ken Hughes
Music:	Frank Cordell

CAST
Richard Harris .... Oliver Cromwell
Alec Guinness .... Charles I
Robert Morley .... Earl of Manchester
Dorothy Tutin .... Queen Henrietta Maria
Frank Finlay .... John Carter
Timothy Dalton .... Prince Rupert
Patrick Wymark .... Earl of Strafford

An historical drama, *Cromwell* details the feud between Britain's King Charles I and Oliver Cromwell, which led to the bloody Civil War. Cromwell is the champion of the people, who believes the court of King Charles is weak and corrupt. He also believes that the Church of England is under threat from Catholicism and is determined to overthrow the Government. The Roundheads and the Cavaliers battle at Nazeby and Edgehill and Cromwell's New Model Army emerge victorious. To put an end to royal plots to restore the monarchy, Charles I is executed.

Timothy Dalton appeared in many historical costume dramas and epics like *Cromwell* before his tenure as James Bond in the 1980s. He appears in *The Lion in Winter*, *Wuthering Heights*, *Mary Queen of Scots* and *Lady Caroline Lamb*.

The battle scenes were shot in Spain using the Spanish Army.

Academy Awards: Best Costume Design (Nino Novarese)

Video availability

The Top Five

Week of 24 July 1970
1. Cromwell
2. Woodstock
3. Paint your Wagon
4. Anne of the Thousand Days
5. Virgin and the Gypsy

LAWRENCE OF ARABIA

18 September 1970	2 weeks*

A re-release; see 1962.

The Top Five

Week of 18 September 1970
1. Lawrence of Arabia
2. Cromwell
3. Fellini Satyricon
4. Woodstock
5. A Man Called Horse

KELLY'S HEROES

25 September 1970	1 week

Distributor:	MGM
Director:	Brian G. Hutton
Producer:	Gabriel Katzka, Sidney Beckerman
Screenplay:	Troy Kennedy Martin
Music:	Lalo Schifrin

CAST
Clint Eastwood . . . . Kelly
Telly Savalas . . . . Big Joe
Don Rickles. . . . . Crapgame
Carroll O'Connor . . . . General Colt
Donald Sutherland . . . . Oddball
Gavin MacLeod . . . . Moriarty
Hal Buckley. . . . . Maitland
Stuart Margolin . . . . Little Joe

In this comedy drama set in World War II Clint Eastwood's platoon take time out from the war to steal $16 million in gold bullion from the Germans. Enlisting the help of Telly Savalas and his platoon, they are hailed as heroes by their General (O'Connor)

before splitting the proceeds with a German tank commander. Largely escapist entertainment, the film veers between comedy and drama on the battlefield.

The film was shot in Yugoslavia, with the use of the Yugoslav army.

Telly Savalas's brother George has a small role as Mulligan.

Video availability

The Top Five

Week of 25 September 1970
1. Kelly's Heroes
2. Cromwell
3. Lawrence of Arabia
4. Fellini Satyricon
5. Catch 22

TORA! TORA! TORA!

16 October 1970	3 weeks

Distributor:	Twentieth Century-Fox
Director:	Richard Fleischer, Toshio Masuda, Kinji Fukasaku
Producer:	Elmo Williams
Screenplay:	Larry Forrester, Hideo Oguni, Ryuzo Kikushima
Music:	Jerry Goldsmith

CAST

Martin Balsam	*Admiral Kimmel*
Soh Yamamura	*Admiral Yamamoto*
Joseph Cotten	*Henry Stimson*
Tatsuya Mihashi	*Commodore Genda*
E.G. Marshall	*Lt. Col. Bratton*
Takahiro Tamura	*Lt. Cdr. Fuchida*
Jason Robards	*General Short*
James Whitmore	*Admiral Halsey*

This epic, big-screen version of the Japanese attack on Pearl Harbor is told from both the Japanese and American sides. It re-creates the events leading up to the surprise attack on 7 December 1941. Intelligence officers repeatedly warn the US government that there is a possibility of an attack.

Behind-the-scenes preparations and tensions increase, and after the US ignore the Japanese ultimatum, the film concludes with the spectacularly shot attack on Pearl Harbor.

Jason Robards had actually served in the US Navy at Pearl Harbor on the day of the attack.

Richard Fleischer directed the American sequences, and Toshio Masuda and Kinji Fukasaku directed the Japanese sequences (with extensive use of subtitles).

Academy Awards: Best Special Visual Effects (A.D. Flowers and L.B. Abbott)

Video availability

The Top Five

Week of 16 October 1970
1. Tora! Tora! Tora!
2. Cromwell
3. Catch 22
4. Kelly's Heroes
5. Tropic of Cancer

At a cost of over $25 million, Tora! Tora! Tora! reconstructed the Japanese air strikes on Pearl Harbor in 1941, telling the story from both the American and Japanese point of view.

WATERLOO

6 November 1970	5 weeks

Distributor:	Columbia
Director:	Sergei Bondarchuk
Producer:	Dino De Laurentiis
Screenplay:	H.A.L. Craig, Sergei Bondarchuk, Vittorio Bonicelli
Music:	Nino Rota

CAST
Rod Steiger . . . . *Napoleon*
Christopher Plummer . . . . *Wellington*
Orson Welles . . . . *Louis XVIII*
Jack Hawkins . . . . *General Picton*
Virginia McKenna . . *Duchess of Richmond*
Dan O'Herlihy . . . . *Marshal Ney*
Rupert Davies . . . . *Gordon*
Philippa Forquet . . . . *La Bedoyere*

French Emperor Napoleon battles against the British, Russian, Austrian and Prussian armies before the battle of Waterloo. The ambitious Napoleon has been exiled to the island of Elba but returns to dominate Europe again in defiance of their King Louis XVIII. He meets his match in the British General Wellington. Enlisting the help of the Prussian army, Wellington outwits and outflanks the French. This time Napoleon is permanently exiled on St Helena.

The Russian army supplied thousands of extras for the battle scenes. They played French, Prussian and English soldiers for director Bondarchuk, himself a Russian who had made the epic *War and Peace* in 1968.

Video availability

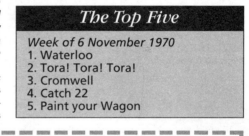

The Top Five

Week of 6 November 1970
1. Waterloo
2. Tora! Tora! Tora!
3. Cromwell
4. Catch 22
5. Paint your Wagon

SCROOGE

11 December 1970	6 weeks

Distributor:	Cinema Center
Director:	Ronald Neame
Producer:	Robert H. Solo
Screenplay:	Leslie Bricusse
Music:	Leslie Bricusse

CAST
Albert Finney . . . . *Ebeneezer Scrooge*
Alec Guinness . . . . *Marley's Ghost*
Edith Evans . . . . . *Ghost of Christmas Past*
Kenneth More . *Ghost of Christmas Present*
Paddy Stone . . . . *Ghost of Christmas Future*
Laurence Naismith . . . . *Mr Fezziwig*
Michael Medwin . . . . *Nephew*
David Collings . . . . *Bob Cratchit*
Anton Rogers . . . . *Tom Jenkins*
Suzanne Neve . . . . *Isabel*

Charles Dickens's classic 'A Christmas Carol' is brought to life for the big screen in this colourful musical. Ebeneezer Scrooge is the cold-hearted, miserly employer who thinks of nothing but saving his money. Awakened at night by the ghost of his former partner, Jacob Marley, he's told to expect visits from three ghosts. The first ghost, Christmas Past, shows him how he used to enjoy life as a boy and young man before becoming too wrapped up in his work. Christmas Present shows him his nephew's family enjoying their Christmas without him and also the plight of his employee's sickly boy, Tiny Tim. The Ghost of Christmas Future shows Scrooge unmourned and unloved when he dies. When Scrooge awakens from these hallucinations it's Christmas Day and he goes all out to make amends for his past life by treating all the kids, buying a huge turkey and dispensing oodles of goodwill and Christmas cheer.

Dickens's tale has been filmed many times, including a modern version in 1988, *Scrooged*, with Bill Murray as an unfeeling TV boss who gets the ghost treatment while preparing a seasonal special.

Albert Finney's singing career never really took off, although in the mid-1970s he released an album in the UK called 'Albert Finney's Album' on the Motown label, but with little success.

The Top Five

Week of 11 December 1970
1. Scrooge
2. Waterloo
3. Private Life of Sherlock Holmes
4. Tora! Tora! Tora!
5. Lawrence of Arabia

Music: 'Thank You Very Much', 'December Twenty-Fifth', 'I Hate People', 'I Like Life'

Video availability

MURPHY'S WAR

22 January 1971	1 week

Distributor:	Hemdale
Director:	Peter Yates
Producer:	Michael Deeley
Screenplay:	Stirling Silliphant
Music:	John Barry

CAST

Peter O'Toole	....	Murphy
Siân Phillips	....	Hayden
Philippe Noiret	....	Brezan
Horst Janson	....	Lauchs
John Hallam	....	Ellis
Ingo Mogendorf	....	Voght

Towards the end of World War II, a German U-boat fires at a navy battleship off the coast of Venezuela, killing everyone on board apart from one of the ship's mechanics, Irishman Murphy. He is rescued and taken to a local Quaker mission where he is nursed back to health. During his stay he meets another British survivor who begs Murphy to find his plane, which was shot down, before it reaches enemy hands. Murphy does find the plane, and decides to repair it in order to carry out his own private war against the Germans, determined to destroy the U-boat that sank his ship.

In the film, O'Toole is nursed back to health by his off-screen wife, Siân Phillips. The role of Murphy was his first attempt at portraying an Irishman.

Video availability

The Top Five

Week of 22 January 1971
1. Murphy's War
2. Scrooge
3. Ryan's Daughter
4. Song of Norway
5. Performance

SONG OF NORWAY

29 January 1971	5 weeks

Distributor:	ABC
Director:	Andrew L. Stone
Producer:	Andrew L. Stone, Virginia Stone
Screenplay:	Andrew L. Stone
Music:	Robert Wright and George Forrest

CAST

Toralv Maurstad	....	Edvard Grieg
Florence Henderson	....	Nina Grieg
Christina Schollin	....	Therese Berg
Frank Porretta	....	Rikard Nordraak
Harry Secombe	.....	Bjornsterne Bjornson
Robert Morley	....	Berg
Edward G. Robinson	....	Krogstad
Elizabeth Larner	....	Mrs Bjornson

This musical bio-pic is based on the life and music of Norwegian composer, Edvard Grieg. By all accounts he led a somewhat boring existence, living for his music. One of his greatest concerns in life was whether he would be able to create acceptable national music for his country. Full of impressive Norwegian scenery and well-performed musical numbers.

The film was shot entirely on location in Norway, and the music and lyrics are based on the works of Edvard Grieg, with words written by Bob Wright and Chet Forrest, the pair who borrowed Borodin to create *Kismet*.

The film was not well received by the critics, and the *New Yorker* wondered if it had been 'made by trolls'.

Music: 'Song of Norway', 'Life of a Wife of a Sailor', 'Freddy and His Fiddle', 'The Hall of the Mountain King', 'Wrong to Dream', 'Ribbons and Wrappings', 'A Rhyme and a Reason', 'Be a Boy Again'

Video availability

The Top Five

Week of 29 January 1971
1. Song of Norway
2. Ryan's Daughter
3. Murphy's War
4. Scrooge
5. There's a Girl in my Soup

THE MUSIC LOVERS

5 March 1971	1 week

Distributor:	United Artists
Director:	Ken Russell
Producer:	Ken Russell
Screenplay:	Melvyn Bragg
Music:	Peter Ilyich Tchaikovsky
	André Previn (Musical
	Director)

CAST
Richard Chamberlain .. *Peter Tchaikovsky*
Glenda Jackson .... *Nina Milukova*
Max Adrian .... *Nicholas Rubenstein*
Christopher Gable . *Count Anton Chiluvsky*
Izabella Telezynska .. *Madame Von Meck*
Kenneth Colley .... *Modeste Tchaikovsky*
Sabina Maydelle .... *Sasha*

The Music Lovers tells the story of tormented homosexual Russian composer Peter Illyich Tchaikovsky. He is loved by his patron, a middle-aged widow he never actually meets but communicates with by letter. He is forced into marriage but sends his apparently sex-crazed wife mad, and she ends up in an asylum.

After leaving school, Glenda Jackson worked in the chemists Boots in Liverpool for two years.

For *The Music Lovers*, she had her hair shaved to play the mad woman and as there was not enough time to grow it back she had to don a wig for her next role in *Sunday Bloody Sunday* (1971), which she filmed immediately afterwards.

Music: '1812 Overture', 'Russian Fair'

Video availability

The Top Five

Week of 5 March 1971
1. The Music Lovers
2. Song of Norway
3. Ryan's Daughter
4. Scrooge
5. The Owl and the Pussycat

DEATH IN VENICE

12 March 1971	1 week

Distributor:	Warner
Director:	Luchino Visconti
Producer:	Luchino Visconti
Screenplay:	Luchino Visconti and Nicola Badalucco
Music:	Gustav Mahler

The dying Gustav Von Aschenbach (Dirk Bogarde) discovers feelings he thought were lost when he sees the fair-headed boy Tadzio (Björn Andresen) in the film Death in Venice.

CAST
Dirk Bogarde . . . . *Gustav Von Aschenbach*
Björn Andresen . . . . *Tadzio*
Silvana Mangano . . . . *Tadzio's mother*
Marisa Berenson . . . *Frau Von Aschenbach*
Mark Burns . . . . *Alfried*

An ageing German composer is on the brink of a nervous breakdown, brought about by the fact that he believes that he can no longer feel any emotion. He visits disease-ridden Venice where in his hotel he sees a beautiful young boy, Tadzio, with his family. Although he makes no contact with the boy, Gustav becomes obsessed with him, constantly watching and following him. His obsession forces him to stay in the fetid city too long.

Dirk Bogarde claims that after seeing the film, a Warner Brothers executive was bowled over by the music. On being told that it was by Mahler, he replied 'Terrific, we must sign him.'

The American backers wanted to 'kill' Visconti's finished film and write it off as a tax loss, claiming it would not appeal to American audiences. However, the film had already been chosen for a royal premiere in London, and nobody wanted to upset the Queen.

Music: Mahler's Symphony no. 3 and Symphony no. 5

Video availability

The Top Five

Week of 12 March 1971
1. Death in Venice
2. Percy
3. The Music Lovers
4. Song of Norway
5. Ryan's Daughter

LOVE STORY

19 March 1971	13 weeks

Distributor:	Paramount
Director:	Arthur Hiller
Producer:	Howard G. Minsky, David Golden
Screenplay:	Erich Segal
Music:	Francis Lai

CAST
Ali MacGraw . . . . *Jenny*
Ryan O'Neal . . . . *Oliver Barrett IV*
John Marley . . . . *Phil*
Ray Milland . . . . *Oliver Barrett III*
Russell Nype . . . . *Dean*
Katherine Balfour . . . . *Mrs Barrett*

Oliver Barrett IV, a Harvard law student, meets Jenny, a music student at Radcliffe, during his final law year. They fall in love and marry, but Oliver's rich and snobbish father cuts off his allowance because he disapproves of the partnership. They both work flat out, making sacrifices along the way in order for Oliver to get his degree. Their life is shattered when Jenny is diagnosed with terminal cancer. The couple put all their energies into fighting the illness, showing the deep love they share for one another.

Michael Douglas, Jon Voight and Beau Bridges all turned down the male lead, and Ryan O'Neal was hired at the last minute, following his high-profile work on the TV series *Peyton Place*. He also starred in the 1978 sequel, *Oliver's Story*.

The movie, chosen for the British Royal Film Performance of that year, gave us the modern adage 'Love means never having to say you're sorry.'

Watch closely for an early appearance by Tommy Lee Jones (billed in the credits as Tom Lee Jones) as one of Oliver's room mates.

Coincidentally, Erich Segal and Ali MacGraw were in a college play together (Shakespeare's *All's Well that Ends Well*) some years before.

The theme from *Love Story* had lyrics added later and became 'Where Do I Begin', which was a hit for Andy Williams and Shirley Bassey.

Academy Awards: Best Original Music Score (Francis Lai)

Video availability

The Top Five

Week of 19 March 1971
1. Love Story
2. When Eight Bells Toll
3. Death in Venice
4. The Music Lovers
5. Song of Norway

VALDEZ IS COMING

18 June 1971	1 week

Distributor:	United Artists
Director:	Edwin Sherin
Producer:	Ira Steiner
Screenplay:	Roland Kibbee, David Rayfiel
Music:	Charles Gross

CAST
Burt Lancaster . . . . *Bob Valdez*
Susan Clark . . . . *Gay Erin*
John Cypher . . . . *Tanner*
Barton Heyman . . . . *El Segundo*
Richard Jordan . . . . *R.L. Davis*
Frank Silvera . . . . *Diego*
Hector Elizondo . . . . *Rider*
Phil Brown . . . . *Malson*

Burt Lancaster plays the Mexican deputy sheriff Valdez, who works part time as a guard for the rich rancher Tanner. While working for Tanner at the ranch, Valdez kills a negro in self-defence. He appeals to the powerful rancher for some compensation for the dead man's wife but is refused and is faced by prejudice and greed. Valdez takes on the job of looking after the widow who is pregnant. He is later brutally beaten up by a gang and swears revenge on those responsible.

Jon Cypher went on to play Chief Daniels in the successful TV series *Hill Street Blues* and Hector Elizondo was later seen as the hotel manager in the movie *Pretty Woman* (1990). Roberta Haynes, who had a minor part, was Gary Cooper's leading lady 18 years previously in *Return to Paradise*.

After filming *Valdez is Coming*, Burt Lancaster returned to the stage for the first time in 26 years for the Kurt Weill musical, *Knickerbocker Holiday*.

The Top Five

Week of 18 June 1971
1. Valdez is Coming
2. Love Story
3. The Music Lovers
4. Wuthering Heights
5. Ryan's Daughter

LITTLE BIG MAN

25 June 1971	2 weeks

Distributor:	Twentieth Century-Fox
Director:	Arthur Penn
Producer:	Stuart Millar, Arthur Penn
Screenplay:	Calder Willingham
Music:	John Hammond

CAST
Dustin Hoffman . . . . *Jack Crabb*
Faye Dunaway . . . . *Mrs Pendrake*
Martin Balsam . . . . *Merriweather*
Richard Mulligan . . . . *General Custer*
Chief Dan George . . . . . . *Old Lodge Skins*
Jeff Corey . . . . *Wild Bill Hickok*
Amy Eccles . . . . *Sunshine*
Kelly Jean Peters . . . . *Olga*

Jack Crabb, at the age of 121, claims to be the only survivor of the massacre at Little Big Horn. He recounts what he says is his life story in flashback. He was an orphan that was adopted and brought up by the Indians. He joins 'white' society as a con man and became friends with Wild Bill Hickok. He is with his Indian tribe when they are attacked by General Custer and his cavalry. He tries to convince them that he is white and survives the battle to tell, quite possibly a tall tale.

Little Big Man reunited director Arthur Penn with Faye Dunaway, after they worked together on the 1967 hit *Bonnie and Clyde*.

Before taking up this role, Dustin Hoffman had planned to return to the Broadway stage and fulfil his ambition of becoming a director.

Video availability

The Top Five

Week of 25 June 1971
1. Little Big Man
2. Love Story
3. Valdez is Coming
4. Ryan's Daughter
5. The Music Lovers

SUNDAY BLOODY SUNDAY

9 July 1971	2 weeks

Distributor:	United Artists
Director:	John Schlesinger
Producer:	Joseph Janni
Screenplay:	Penelope Gilliatt
Music:	Ron Geeson

CAST

Glenda Jackson	*Alex Greville*
Peter Finch	*Dr Daniel Hirsh*
Murray Head	*Bob Elkin*
Peggy Ashcroft	*Mrs Greville*
Maurice Denham	*Mr Greville*
Vivian Pickles	*Alva Hodson*
Frank Windsor	*Bill Hodson*
Thomas Baptiste	*Professor Johns*
Tony Britton	*George Harding*

At the centre of *Sunday Bloody Sunday* is the bisexual love triangle of Daniel Hirsh, Alex Greville and Bob Elkin. Daniel is a Jewish doctor and Alex a career woman on the rebound from a broken marriage. They both fall for the charms of Bob Elkin, a designer of modern sculpture with an ego almost as big as his ambitions, who divides his time between the two.

Peter Finch took over the role that was originally going to be played by Ian Bannen at very short notice.

Watch out for the brief screen debut of a 14-year-old Daniel Day-Lewis as a young vandal.

The plot called for actors Peter Finch and Murray Head to embrace in a full frontal kiss, the first in British cinema history.

Video availability

The Top Five

Week of 9 July 1971
1. Sunday Bloody Sunday
2. Love Story
3. The Music Lovers
4. Wuthering Heights
5. Ryan's Daughter

LE MANS

23 July 1971	1 week

Distributor:	Solar/Cinema Center
Director:	Lee H. Katzin
Producer:	Jack N. Reddish
Screenplay:	Harry Kleiner
Music:	Michel Legrand

CAST

Steve McQueen	*Michael Delaney*
Siegfried Rauch	*Erich Stahler*
Elga Andersen	*Lisa Belgetti*
Ronald Leigh-Hunt	*Team Manager*

Using classic-car racing footage, the movie has a documentary style. It was filmed on French location with Steve McQueen as Delaney, a driver on the Porsche team, competing in the famous race. He has just recovered from injuries sustained in an earlier race in which another driver died, but is determined to beat his main rival, Erich Stahler, driving for Ferrari, in this 24-hour marathon. Lisa Belgetti, the wife of the driver who was killed in the accident, turns up with severe emotional problems.

As in *Bullitt*, Steve McQueen did all his own driving for the movie.

Director Lee H. Katzin, who took over as director from John Sturges, gets solo screen credit. Sturges left as director due to creative disagreements. He had worked with Steve McQueen in the past on *Never So Few* (1959), *The Magnificent Seven* (1960) and *The Great Escape* (1963).

The Top Five

Week of 23 July 1971
1. Le Mans
2. Sunday Bloody Sunday
3. Love Story
4. Escape from the Planet of the Apes
5. Diary of a Mad Housewife

In Le Mans *Michael Delaney (Steve McQueen) returns to car racing after spending a year recovering from a major crash. He meets Lisa Belgetti (Elga Andersen), the widow of a driver killed in the same accident.*

THE DEVILS

30 July 1971	8 weeks

Distributor:	Warner
Director:	Ken Russell
Producer:	Robert H. Solo, Ken Russell
Screenplay:	Ken Russell
Music:	Peter Maxwell Davies

CAST

Vanessa Redgrave	*Sister Jeanne*
Oliver Reed	*Father Grandier*
Dudley Sutton	*Baron de Laubardemont*
Max Adrian	*Ibert*
Gemma Jones	*Madeleine*
Murray Melvin	*Mignon*
Michael Gothard	*Father Barre*
Georgina Hale	*Philippe*

Adapted from Aldous Huxley's novel *The Devils of Loudun*, the film begins with the erotic dreams of the humpbacked Sister Jeanne in 17th-century France. Her thoughts and desires about Father Grandier, an unethical liberated priest, begin to corrupt the other nuns in her convent. The Church summons an exorcist to go to work on the depraved women.

Vanessa Redgrave gave her entire salary from this film to a newly founded nursery school rather than the workers of a revolutionary party as was widely reported at the time. She claimed that the report hindered her future efforts to find work.

Derek Jarman was about to take up painting full time when a chance meeting with a friend of director Ken Russell led him to becoming set designer on the film. Russell had a great influence on convincing him to become a director in his own right.

Video availability

The Top Five
Week of 30 July 1971
1. The Devils
2. Le Mans
3. Sunday Bloody Sunday
4. Love Story
5. Escape from the Planet of the Apes

CARNAL KNOWLEDGE

24 September 1971	2 weeks

Distributor: Avco Embassy
Director: Mike Nichols
Producer: Mike Nichols
Screenplay: Jules Feiffer

CAST
Jack Nicholson . . . . Jonathan
Art Garfunkel . . . . Sandy
Candice Bergen . . . . Susan
Ann-Margaret . . . . Bobbie
Cynthia O'Neal . . . . Cindy
Rita Moreno . . . . Louise
Carol Kane . . . . Jennifer

The 1940s students Jonathan and Sandy embark on their sex lives while together at college. They try to match their sexual fantasies and win the heart of the same girl, Susan. She decides to give her affections to Sandy and the two marry, although they eventually separate. By middle age Jonathan is bored with life and sex, and grudgingly agrees to marry the beautiful model Bobbie, who loves him even though he is cruel to her. Not surprisingly their marriage falls apart and Jonathan resorts to hiring a prostitute to help him play out his sexual fantasies.

At the time the film was released, some exhibitors were worried that they may be prosecuted for screening such an obscene movie. One London critic advised his readers not to see it with anyone they love, and it was actually banned in the American state of Georgia. The film, and particularly Jack Nicholson's chauvinistic role, incurred the wrath of Women's Liberation groups across America.

Video availability

The Top Five

Week of 24 September 1971
1. Carnal Knowledge
2. The Devils
3. Love Story
4. Willard
5. Puppet on a Chain

THE GO-BETWEEN

8 October 1971	3 weeks

Distributor: EMI
Director: Joseph Losey
Producer: John Heyman/Norman
                Priggen
Screenplay: Harold Pinter
Music: Richard Rodney Bennett

CAST
Julie Christie . . . . Marian
Alan Bates . . . . Ted Burgess
Margaret Leighton . . . . Mrs Maudsley
Michael Redgrave . . . . Colston
Michael Gough . . . . Mr Maudsley
Edward Fox . . . . Hugh Trimingham
Dominic Guard . . . . Leo Colston
Richard Gibson . . . . Marcus

An old Leo Colston reflects on his childhood around the turn of the century and the events that probably stopped him from marrying. As a 12-year-old boy Leo meets a friend's sister, Marian Maudsley, who is engaged to be married to British aristocrat, Hugh Trimingham. When Marian falls in love with Ted Burgess, a humble farmer, she asks Leo to be the go-between, delivering love letters for herself and Ted. Leo's feelings become confused as he falls in love with Marian himself. The secret liaison is uncovered when Leo's mother insists on going with her son to where the lovers rendezvous.

This was the third time that writer Harold Pinter and director Joseph Losey collaborated. They previously worked together on *The Servant* (1963) and *Accident* (1967). The movie won the top prize at the 1971 Cannes Film Festival.

Video availability

The Top Five

Week of 8 October 1971
1. The Go-Between
2. Carnal Knowledge
3. The Devils
4. The Hunting Party
5. And Now for Something
   Completely Different

BEDKNOBS AND BROOMSTICKS

29 October 1971	4 weeks

Distributor: Walt Disney
Director: Robert Stevenson
Producer: Bill Walsh
Screenplay: Bill Walsh, Don DaGradi
Music: Richard M. Sherman and
               Robert B. Sherman

CAST
Angela Lansbury . . . . *Eglantine Price*
David Tomlinson . . . . *Emelius Browne*
Cindy O'Callaghan . . . . *Carrie*
Roy Smart . . . . *Paul*
Ian Weighall . . . . *Charlie*
Roddy McDowell . . . . *Mr Jelk*
Sam Jaffe . . . . *Bookman*
John Ericson . . . . *Colonel Heller*
Bruce Forsyth . . . . *Swinburne*

Eglantine Price looks after three children who are evacuated to her old house in an English seaside village during World War II. The children learn that she is studying witchcraft by mail in order to use it against the Germans should they invade. The youngsters teach themselves a few tricks of their own and between them they discover all kinds of magic and fly on a bedstead into many fantasy worlds.

Director Robert Stevenson began his career as a journalist and entered the movie industry as a screenwriter, with his first film in 1930, *Greek Street*. In order for American audiences to understand the Cockney characters, Stevenson ordered huge close ups so the actors' lips could be read.

The animated segments were directed by Ward Kimball. The flying bedstead and fantasy world scenes were created by mixing animation with live action.

Academy Awards: Best Special Visual Effects (Danny Lee, Eustace Lycett and Alan Maley)

Video availability

The Top Five

Week of 29 October 1971
1. Bedknobs and Broomsticks
2. The Go-Between
3. The Devils
4. Klute
5. Carnal Knowledge

© 1971 WALT DISNEY PRODUCTIONS

David Tomlinson stars as Emelius Browne in the 1971 movie Bedknobs and Broomsticks, *the live-action and cartoon film that is packed with magical special effects and delightful music.*

TRAFFIC

27 November 1971	1 week

Distributor: Corona (France)
Director: Jacques Tati
Producer: Robert Dorfman
Screenplay: Jacques Tati
Music: Charles Dumont

CAST
Jacques Tati . . . . *Hulot*
Maria Kimberly . . . . *Maria*
Marcel Fravel . . . . *Truckdriver*
Honoré Bostel . . . . *Boss*
Tony Kneppers . . . . *Mechanic*

In *Traffic* Monsieur Hulot is at the centre of a series of visual gags about modern traffic problems. He is joined by his company's public relations girl, Maria, en route from Paris to Amsterdam for a motor show. Hulot drives a truck that supports his newly invented camper and Maria rides along in her red convertible sports car. Along the way, the truck has a flat tyre and Hulot is nearly killed when changing it. After a chain of disastrous events, he decides to take the train home, leaving Maria to her own devices.

This was only Jacques Tati's 5th picture in 25 years. His fourth, *Playtime*, although made in 1967, was not released until 1973. Tati reluctantly resurrected his most famous character because of his precarious financial situation. Initially the film was to be made for TV, but the finished script became a movie screenplay and the film was well received, not least because for the first time, Hulot gets his girl.

The Top Five

Week of 27 November 1971
1. Traffic
2. Bedknobs and Broomsticks
3. Doc/The Red Baron
4. The Devils
5. Carnal Knowledge

STRAW DOGS

4 December 1971	1 week

Distributor: Talent Associates
Director: Sam Peckinpah
Producer: Daniel Melnick
Screenplay: David Zelag Goodman, Sam Peckinpah
Music: Jerry Fielding

CAST
Dustin Hoffman . . . . *David Sumner*
Susan George . . . . *Amy Sumner*
Peter Vaughan . . . . *Tom Hedden*
T.P. McKenna . . . . *Major Scott*
Del Henney . . . . *Venner*
Ken Hutchinson . . . . *Scutt*
Colin Welland . . . . *Reverend Hood*
Jim Norton . . . . *Cawsey*
Sally Thomsett . . . . *Janice*

Mathematician David Sumner and his wife Amy are looking for a quieter life when they move to a new house near Amy's birthplace in Cornwall. They find it less than easy to get along with some of the more aggressive locals. Four men, one an ex-boyfriend of Amy's, are hired to work on the couple's house and make life unpleasant. The violent assaults on both David and Amy increase after they hide Henry, a village idiot who accidentally kills a young girl, and refuse to hand him over to the aggressive locals.

The film, based on Gordon M. Williams's novel *The Siege at Trencher's Farm*, was considered very violent. A report in *Variety* magazine stated that many theatres showing *Straw Dogs* were having to schedule a five-minute break between showings, presumably to allow audiences to recover from the movie's emotional impact. Because of its violent nature, the movie was banned from British television for many years.

Susan George only landed the female lead after ten readings for director Sam Peckinpah and further tests with Dustin Hoffman. It became her first important international role.

The Top Five

Week of 4 December 1971
1. Straw Dogs
2. Traffic
3. Bedknobs and Broomsticks
4. Carnal Knowledge
5. The Devils

David (Dustin Hoffman) must face the sudden violence that lies beneath the surface in a seemingly peaceful Cornwall village in Sam Peckinpah's Straw Dogs.

NICHOLAS AND ALEXANDRA

11 December 1971	3 weeks*

Distributor:	Columbia
Director:	Franklin J. Schaffner
Producer:	Sam Spiegel
Screenplay:	James Goldman
Music:	Richard Rodney Bennett

CAST
Michael Jayston . . . . Nicholas
Janet Suzman . . . . Alexandra
Roderic Noble . . . . Alexis
Fiona Fullerton . . . . Anastasia
Ania Marson . . . . Olga
Lynne Frederick . . . . Tatiana
Candace Glendenning . . . . Marie
Harry Andrews . . . . . Grand Duke Nicholas
Irene Worth . . . . Queen Mother Marie
Feodorovna
Tom Baker . . . . Rasputin
Jack Hawkins . . . . Count Fredericks
Timothy West . . . . Dr Botkin
Katherine Schofield . . . . Tegleva
Laurence Olivier . . . . Count Witte
Michael Redgrave . . . . Sazonov

The first boy and heir to the Romanov throne is born to Nicholas II, the Emperor, and his wife Alexandra, the Empress of Russia. Their plans for the child are threatened when they discover that the child is a haemophiliac. Nicholas's concern for the boy causes him to lose sight of his people's needs, while Alexandra puts all her hopes in Rasputin, a monk who she believes has mystic powers and can cure the child. In the midst of their personal misfortune thousands of Russians continue to live in poverty. The death toll of World War I proves too much for the people and helps spark the Russian Revolution in 1917. The Tsar and his family are executed when the Bolsheviks came to power.

Top Ten Films of 1971

1 The Aristocats
2 On the Buses
3 Soldier Blue
4 There's a Girl in my Soup
5 Percy
6 The Railway Children
7 Too Late the Hero/Tales of Beatrix Potter
8 Up Pompeii/The Last Valley
9 Butch Cassidy and the Sundance Kid
10 When 8 Bells Toll/Tora! Tora! Tora!/Dad's Army/Little Big Man

The movie, based on a novel by Robert K. Massie, was shot on location in Spain and the former Yugoslavia, and never fully recouped its $11 million cost.

Laurence Olivier had been ill with pleurisy and a thrombosis, but defied doctors to work for five days on the film.

Academy Awards: Best Art Direction (John Box, Ernest Archer, Jack A. Maxsted and Gil Parrondo), Best Set Decoration (Vernon Dixon), Best Costume Design (Yvonne Blake and Antonio Castillo)

The Top Five

Week of 11 December 1971
1. Nicholas and Alexandra
2. Straw Dogs
3. Bedknobs and Broomsticks
4. Traffic
5. Carnal Knowledge

Video availability

FIDDLER ON THE ROOF

25 December 1971	1 week

Distributor:	United Artists/Mirisch
Director:	Norman Jewison
Producer:	Norman Jewison
Screenplay:	Joseph Stain
Music:	Jerry Bock
	Sheldon Harnick (Lyrics)

CAST

Chaim Topol	Tevye
Norma Crane	Golde
Leonard Frey	Motel
Molly Picon	Yante
Paul Mann	Lazar Wolf
Rosalind Harris	Tzeitel
Michele Marsh	Hodel
Michael Glaser	Perchik

The film, adapted from the stage musical, is set in the town of Anatevka in the Ukraine during 1905. Tevye lives with his wife Golde and their three daughters who in turn find husbands, all of which Tevye disapproves. Meanwhile members of his community are about to be driven out of their homes by the Tsar and his Cossacks who have destroyed Anatevka. Tevye, still holding on to his faith and traditions, prepares to take what's left of his family to America.

Before the start of rehearsals, the original title for the musical was *Tevye and His Daughters*.

When Topol was nominated for an Oscar he was in the army and had to request permission for leave from his unit, which was on active duty at the time, in order to attend the awards ceremony.

Academy Awards: Best Cinematography (Oswald Morris), Best Sound (Gordon K. McCallum and David Hildyard), Best Scoring: Adaptation and Original Song Score (John Williams)

Music: 'If I Were a Rich Man', 'Sunrise, Sunset'

Video availability

The Top Five

Week of 25 December 1971
1. Fiddler on the Roof
2. Nicholas and Alexandra
3. Bedknobs and Broomsticks
4. Traffic
5. Gumshoe

DIAMONDS ARE FOREVER

8 January 1972	12 weeks*

Distributor:	United Artists
Director:	Guy Hamilton
Producer:	Albert R. Broccoli, Harry Saltzman
Screenplay:	Richard Maibaum
Music:	John Barry

CAST

Sean Connery	James Bond
Jill St John	Tiffany Case
Charles Gray	Blofeld
Lana Wood	Plenty O'Toole
Jimmy Dean	William Whyte
Bruce Cabot	Saxby
Bruce Glover	Wint
Putter Smith	Kidd
Bernard Lee	M
Desmond Llewelyn	Q
Lois Maxwell	Miss Moneypenny

In his sixth outing as James Bond Sean Connery pits his wits against the evil Blofeld who wants to blow up the world with the nuclear technology he has at his disposal. The diamonds from the title are being smuggled by Jill St John into the USA and Bond gets to travel to Los Angeles and Las Vegas (where he drives a moon buggy through the Nevada desert) before confronting Blofeld and saving the world.

Sean Connery returned to the role of Bond after George Lazenby's one outing in *On Her Majesty's Secret Service*. He quit again after this film and Roger Moore took up the mantle, but he returned in 1983 for *Never Say Never Again*, which was a remake of the *Thunderball* story.

Lana Wood, who plays Plenty O'Toole, a Las Vegas casino showgirl, is Natalie Wood's sister.

Music: 'Diamonds are Forever' (Shirley Bassey)

Video availability

The Top Five

Week of 8 January 1972
1. Diamonds are Forever
2. Fiddler on the Roof
3. Nicholas and Alexandra
4. Bedknobs and Broomsticks
5. Gumshoe

THE FRENCH CONNECTION

18 March 1972	1 week

Distributor:	Twentieth Century-Fox
Director:	William Friedkin
Producer:	Philip D'Antoni
Screenplay:	Ernest Tidyman
Music:	Don Ellis

CAST
Gene Hackman . . . . *Jimmy Doyle*
Fernando Rey . . . . *Alain Charnier*
Roy Scheider . . . . *Buddy Russo*

Tony LoBianco . . . . *Sal Boca*
Marcel Bozzuffi . . . . *Pierre Nicoli*
Frederic De Pasquale . . . . *Devereaux*
Bill Hickman . . . . *Mulderig*
Ann Rebbot . . . . *Marie Charnier*

Two New York narcotics officers (Hackman and Scheider) track down the largest-ever drugs shipment into the United States. Almost by accident they hear of the plot to smuggle in huge amounts of heroin from Marseilles in a car and the plan nearly succeeds. In his determination to catch the drug

New York detective Jimmy Doyle (Gene Hackman) is on the trail of drug pushers from Marseilles, who are shipping their illicit cargo to the United States in The French Connection.

smugglers, Doyle undertakes a heart-stopping car chase under New York's elevated railway system, which is now a cinema classic.

Hackman won his first Oscar for his brilliant portrayal of the narcotics cop 'Popeye' Doyle, beating off the competition from Peter Finch (*Sunday Bloody Sunday*), Walter Matthau (*Kotch*), George C. Scott (*The Hospital*) and Topol (*Fiddler on the Roof*). He went on to star in another seven number ones, including *French Connection 2* (1975) and Clint Eastwood's *Unforgiven* (1992), for which he won another Oscar, this time as Best Supporting Actor.

Academy Awards: Best Film (Producer Philip D'Antoni), Best Direction (William Friedkin), Best Actor (Gene Hackman), Best Screenplay (Ernest Tidyman), Best Editing (Jerry Greenberg)

Video availability

The Top Five

Week of 18 March 1972
1. The French Connection
2. Fiddler on the Roof
3. Diamonds are Forever
4. A Clockwork Orange
5. The Boyfriend

MARY, QUEEN OF SCOTS

8 April 1972	5 weeks

Distributor:	Universal
Director:	Charles Jarrott
Producer:	Hal B. Wallis
Screenplay:	John Hale
Music:	John Barry

CAST
Vanessa Redgrave . . . . . *Mary of Scotland*
Glenda Jackson . . . . *Queen Elizabeth*
Patrick McGoohan . . . . *James Stuart*
Timothy Dalton . . . . . *Lord Henry Darnley*
Nigel Davenport . . . . *Lord Bothwell*
Trevor Howard . . . . *William Cecil*
Daniel Massey . . . . *Robert Dudley*
Ian Holm . . . . *David Riccio*

This historical drama charts the enmity between Queen Elizabeth I of England and Mary Stuart, Queen of Scots. To ensure that Mary does not take her throne, Elizabeth has Mary imprisoned and finally executed.

Mary, Queen of Scots was another number one costume drama for the young Timothy Dalton. Others include *The Lion in Winter* (1968) and *Lady Caroline Lamb* (1972). He hit the top spot again in the 1980s as James Bond in *The Living Daylights* (1987) and *Licence To Kill* (1989).

The scene in which the two queens meet face to face probably never happened in real life.

The Top Five

Week of 8 April 1972
1. Mary, Queen of Scots
2. Fiddler on the Roof
3. Dirty Harry
4. A Clockwork Orange
5. Diamonds are Forever

A CLOCKWORK ORANGE

13 May 1972	1 week

Distributor:	Warner
Director:	Stanley Kubrick
Producer:	Stanley Kubrick
Screenplay:	Stanley Kubrick
Music:	Walter Carlos

CAST
Malcolm McDowell . . . . *Alex*
Patrick Magee . . . . *Mr Alexander*
Michael Bates . . . . *Chief Guard*
Warren Clarke . . . . *Dim*
John Clive . . . . *Stage Actor*
Adrienne Corri . . . . *Mrs Alexander*

Carl Duering . . . . *Dr Brodsky*
Paul Farrell . . . . *Tramp*

Set in the violent near-future young thug Alex and his gang of Droogs fight, rob, rape, and kill anything or anyone who crosses their path. Captured after a particularly nasty rape, the authorities attempt to cure Alex and at first think they've succeeded.

This nightmarish vision of the future has been banned in the UK for many years and has never been commercially released on video. Director Kubrick won't grant permission for screenings after the initial release of the film prompted several copycat acts of violence which were attributed to the film.

In the futuristic Clockwork Orange *everyday people are terrorised by violent sadistic gangs who prowl the streets at night looking for trouble.*

Pop band Heaven 17 took their name from a fictitious band featured on a top ten list that appears in a boutique in the film.

A Clockwork Orange also won the New York Film Critics Award for Best Picture and Director, and was nominated for four Oscars.

A musical based on the film, starring Phil Daniels with music by U2, played a short season at the Barbican in the late 1980s.

The Top Five

Week of 13 May 1972
1. A Clockwork Orange
2. Fiddler on the Roof
3. Dirty Harry
4. Kidnapped
5. Never Give an Inch

THE HOSPITAL

20 May 1972	2 weeks

Distributor: United Artists
Director: Arthur Hiller
Producer: Howard Gottfried
Screenplay: Paddy Chayefsky
Music: Morris Surdin

CAST
George C. Scott . . . . *Dr Herbert Bock*
Diana Rigg . . . . *Barbara Drummond*
Barnard Hughes . . . . *Mr Drummond*
Nancy Marchand . . . . *Head Nurse*

This irreverent black comedy is set in a New York hospital with chaotic conditions, crazy patients, psychotic staff and a mysterious killer on the loose. Chief of Medicine, Dr Bock, is overworked and slowly getting suicidal while all around him chaos reigns. His marriage has broken up and he falls for Barbara Drummond who is in the hospital because her father, also a doctor, has been poorly treated by another doctor.

Paddy Chayefsky won the second of his three Oscars for this film. His first was for *Marty* in 1955 and his next came in 1976 for the equally anarchic *Network*.

George C. Scott was also Oscar nominated but did not win in the end.

Diana Rigg is one of England's greatest actresses but rarely appears on the silver screen. Her only other roles in number one films are as James Bond's (short-lived) wife in *On Her Majesty's Secret Service* (1969) and a suspect in the Agatha Christie mystery *Evil Under The Sun* (1981).

Academy Awards: Best Story and Screenplay (Paddy Chayefsky)

The Top Five

Week of 20 May 1972
1. The Hospital
2. Fiddler on the Roof
3. A Clockwork Orange
4. The Boyfriend
5. Dirty Harry

FRENZY

3 June 1972	1 week

Distributor: Universal
Director: Alfred Hitchcock
Producer: Alfred Hitchcock
Screenplay: Anthony Shaffer
Music: Ron Goodwin

CAST
Jon Finch . . . . *Richard Blaney*
Barry Foster . . . . *Robert Rusk*
Barbara Leigh-Hunt . . . . . . *Brenda Blaney*
Anna Massey . . . . *Babe Milligan*
Alec McCowen . . . . *Inspector Oxford*
Vivien Merchant . . . . *Mrs Oxford*

A series of stranglings has gripped London and down on his luck Blaney is the chief suspect. His friend Rusk, a Covent Garden vegetable salesman, is the real killer, and it's down to the police, led by Scotland Yard's finest, Inspector Oxford, to unravel the clues and eventually solve the mystery of the sadistic 'Necktie Murderer'.

Hitchcock's stylish thriller had plenty of humour to offset the gruesome subject matter, in particular the repartee between Inspector Oxford and his wife at the dinner table.

Filmed in and around London, Hitchcock made great use of the old Covent Garden fruit and vegetable market before the traders moved out to new premises. Other locations include the Coburg Hotel in Bayswater. The story itself was based on the book *Goodbye Piccadilly, Farewell Leicester Square* by Arthur La Bern.

Video availability

The Top Five

Week of 3 June 1972
1. Frenzy
2. Fiddler on the Roof
3. The Hospital
4. A Clockwork Orange
5. Dirty Harry

CABARET

10 June 1972	5 weeks

Distributor: ABC Pictures/Allied Artists
Director: Bob Fosse
Producer: Cy Feuer
Screenplay: Jay Presson Allen
Music: Ralph Burns (director)
               John Kander, Frebb Ebb
               (songs)

CAST

Liza Minnelli . . . . *Sally Bowles*
Michael York . . . . *Brian Roberts*
Helmut Griem . . . . *Max*
Marisa Berenson . . . . *Natalia*
Fritz Wepper . . . . *Fritz*
Joel Grey . . . . *M.C.*

Sally Bowles arrives in 1930s Berlin from America and takes up cabaret work in the Kit Kat Club, with Master of Ceremonies Joel Grey. She befriends travelling Englishman, Brian Roberts, and together they enjoy the decadent high life of Berlin. But the city is not only a hotbed of vice but is steeped in anti-Semitism as the Nazi movement in Germany grows. During the gathering storm of Nazi violence the club is forced to close.

The film was based on the 1966 Broadway musical, which was itself adapted from Christopher Isherwood's Berlin stories. Joel Grey created the role of the M.C. in the Broadway musical.

Cabaret was Liza Minnelli's second Oscar nomination and first win. She was previously nominated for the 1969 *Sterile Cuckoo* but it was another five years before she hit number one again with *New York, New York*. Her film work was not prolific in the intervening years, with only *Lucky Lady*, alongside Burt Reynolds, making much of a mark. *Arthur* in 1981 was her third number one.

In Cabaret *Sally Bowles (Liza Minnelli) performs one of her show stoppers at the Kit Kat Club, a sleazy cabaret spot in the heart of Berlin in Germany during the 1930s.*

Academy Awards: Best Direction (Bob Fosse), Best Actress (Liza Minnelli), Best Supporting Actor (Joel Grey), Best Cinematography (Geoffrey Unsworth), Best Arts Direction (Rolf Zehetbauer and Jurgen Kiebach), Best Set Decoration (Herbert Strabl), Best Editing (David Bretherton), Best Sound (Robert Knudson and David Hildyard), Best Scoring: Adaptation and Original Song Score (Ralph Burns)

Music: 'Two Ladies', 'Maybe This Time', 'Sitting Pretty', 'Tiller Girls'. 'Money Money', 'If You Could See Her', 'Tomorrow Belongs to Me', 'Cabaret'

The Top Five

Week of 10 June 1972
1. Cabaret
2. How to Steal a Diamond in Four Uneasy Lessons
3. Frenzy
4. A Clockwork Orange
5. Chato's Land

Video availability

WHAT'S UP DOC?

15 July 1972	2 weeks

Distributor:	Warner
Director:	Peter Bogdanovich
Producer:	Peter Bogdanovich
Screenplay:	Buck Henry, Robert Benton, David Newman
Music:	Artie Butler

CAST
Barbra Streisand . . . . *Judy Maxwell*
Ryan O'Neal . . . . *Howard Bannister*
Kenneth Mars . . . . *Hugh Simon*
Austin Pendleton . . . . . *Frederick Larrabee*
Sorrell Booke . . . . *Harry*
Stefan Gierasch . . . . *Fritz*
Mabel Albertson . . . . *Mrs Van Hoskins*
Michael Murphy . . . . *Mr Smith*

In this madcap comedy set in San Francisco four identical suitcases with wildly different contents become muddled up and fall into the wrong hands. As suitcase owners musicologist O'Neal and zany Streisand are involved in a series of highly improbable incidents and spectacular car chases.

What's Up Doc? saw the first pairing for O'Neal and Streisand. They were reunited for *The Main Event* in 1979. The film was also Bogdanovich's first number one, *Paper Moon*, the following year, was his only other one, again with Ryan O'Neal.

As the title was Bugs Bunny's famous catchphrase, the film ends with Porky Pig's equally famous 'That's All Folks!' line as the porcine character bursts through his drum.

Music: 'As Time Goes By', 'You're The Top' (Barbra Streisand)

Video availability

The Top Five

Week of 15 July 1972
1. What's Up Doc?
2. Cabaret
3. The Nightcomers
4. The Garden of the Finzi Continis
5. How to Steal a Diamond in Four Uneasy Lessons

YOUNG WINSTON

29 July 1972	5 weeks

Distributor:	Columbia
Director:	Richard Attenborough
Producer:	Carl Foreman
Screenplay:	Carl Foreman
Music:	Alfred Ralston

CAST
Simon Ward . . . . *Winston Churchill*
Robert Shaw . . . . *Lord Randolph Churchill*
Anne Bancroft . . . *Lady Randolph Churchill*
Jack Hawkins . . . . *Mr Welldon*
Ian Holm . . . . *George E. Buckle*
Anthony Hopkins . . . . *Lloyd George*

Attenborough's biopic of the early years of Britain's famous wartime prime minister, Sir Winston Churchill, begins with his lonely childhood. The son of a British politician and an American mother, he endures his school years before first experiencing battle as a war correspondent. On active service in the Boer War he becomes a war hero and returns to England to begin his first foray into the political scene as a Member of Parliament.

Young Winston was the first of Richard Attenborough's five number ones as a director; the others were *A Bridge Too Far* (1977), *Gandhi* (1982), *A Chorus Line* (1985), and *Cry Freedom* (1987). As an actor, however, he appeared in a number one movie after a 15-year absence in Spielberg's *Jurassic Park* (1993). Attenborough has used the talents of Anthony Hopkins many times. As well as appearing in Attenborough's *Young Winston* (as Lloyd George), he pops up in *A Bridge Too Far*, *Magic* (1978), *Chaplin* (1992) and *Shadowlands* (1993).

The Top Five

Week of 20 July 1972
1. Young Winston
2. Fritz the Cat
3. What's Up Doc?
4. A Clockwork Orange
5. Cabaret

Video availability

THE GODFATHER

2 September 1972	13 weeks

Distributor:	Paramount
Director:	Francis Ford Coppola
Producer:	Albert S. Ruddy
Screenplay:	Mario Puzo, Francis Ford Coppola
Music:	Nino Rota
	Carlo Savina (conductor)

CAST
Marlon Brando . . . . *Don Vito Corleone*
Al Pacino . . . . *Michael Corleone*

James Caan . . . . *Sonny Corleone*
Richard Castellano . . . . *Clemanza*
Robert Duvall . . . . *Tom Hagen*
Sterling Hayden . . . . *McCluskey*
John Marley . . . . *Jack Woltz*
Diane Keaton . . . . *Kay Adams*

Don Vito Corleone is the head of a huge Italian Mafia family who are one of the largest gangster organizations in the United States. He oversees the business with an iron hand and while his son, Sonny, and adopted son, Tom, join the family firm, Michael (Pacino) attempts to lead a straight life away from

In The Godfather, *the first in a trilogy of* Godfather *movies, the rivalry between two Mafia families, the Corleones and the Tattaglias, leads to an explosion of violence.*

the crime and carnage. But as a feud with another mafia family comes to a head Michael is sucked into the violence.

The great success of *The Godfather*, based on Mario Puzo's best-selling book, led to two sequels, *The Godfather Part II* (1974) and *The Godfather Part III* (1990), both of which were also number one movies. Francis Ford Coppola's daughter appeared as a baby in this film and in *Godfather Part III* (as Michael Corleone's daughter).

The town of Corleone in Sicily, in which Michael becomes an exile, is a real hilltop town but was not used as the location for that part of the film.

Marlon Brando parodied his Don Corleone character in *The Freshman* (1990) with Matthew Broderick.

Lyrics were added to the 'Love Theme' from *The Godfather* and became a minor hit for Andy Williams in 1972.

Academy Awards: Best Film (Producer Albert S. Ruddy), Best Actor (Marlon Brando), Best Screenplay (Mario Puzo and Francis Ford Coppola)

Video availability

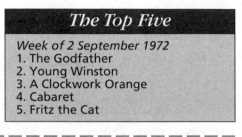

The Top Five

Week of 2 September 1972
1. The Godfather
2. Young Winston
3. A Clockwork Orange
4. Cabaret
5. Fritz the Cat

LADY CAROLINE LAMB

2 December 1972	4 weeks

Distributor:	EMI
Director:	Robert Bolt
Producer:	Fernando Ghia
Screenplay:	Robert Bolt
Music:	Richard Rodney Bennett

CAST
Sarah Miles . . . . Lady Caroline Lamb
Jon Finch . . . . William Lamb
Richard Chamberlain . . . . Lord Byron
John Mills . . . . Canning
Margaret Leighton . . . . . Lady Melbourne
Laurence Olivier . . . . . Duke of Wellington
Pamela Brown . . . . Lady Bessborough
Ralph Richardson . . . . The King

In this historical drama the wife of British politician William Lamb, loves two men, her husband, and the charismatic romantic poet Lord Byron. The very public affair causes a great scandal and almost capsizes her husband's political career before she bows out of his life.

Lady Caroline Lamb was the second number one of 1972 for both Jon Finch and John Mills. Finch's first had been *Frenzy* and Mills' *Young Winston*.

Sarah Miles was married to Robert Bolt, who died in 1995. *Lady Caroline Lamb* was his first film as a director although he had enjoyed great success as the screenwriter of *Lawrence of Arabia* (1962), *Doctor Zhivago* (1965) and *A Man for All Seasons* (1966).

Laurence Olivier played opposite Sarah Miles for the then enormous fee of £20,000 for five days' work.

Video availability

The Top Five

Week of 2 December 1972
1. Lady Caroline Lamb
2. The Mechanic
3. The Godfather
4. Young Winston
5. The Triple Echo

ALICE'S ADVENTURES IN WONDERLAND

23 December 1972	3 weeks

Distributor:	Twentieth Century-Fox
Director:	William Sterling
Producer:	Derek Horne
Screenplay:	William Sterling
Music:	John Barry

CAST
Fiona Fullerton . . . . Alice
Michael Crawford . . . . White Rabbit
Ralph Richardson . . . . Caterpillar

Flora Robson .... *Queen of Hearts*
Peter Sellers .... *March Hare*
Robert Helpmann .... *Mad Hatter*
Dudley Moore .... *Dormouse*

This 1970s British version of Lewis Carroll's classic tale features all the familiar characters. With expensive settings and high-powered effects, the film is packed with star names that also include Spike Milligan, Dennis Price and Rodney Bewes.

Alice's Adventures includes 16 tunes written by John Barry and Don Black. John Barry also provided the music for the year's first chart-topper, *Diamonds Are Forever*, and *Mary Queen of Scots*.

Michael Crawford got up at 4.30 am to film at Pinewood Studios by day, then went on to appear on the West End stage in *No Sex Please, We're British* at night. His working day ended at 11 pm. Perhaps not surprisingly, his marriage collapsed at around the same time.

Music: 'Curioser and Curioser', 'You've Gotta Know When to Stop', 'Pun Song', 'I've Never Been This Far Before', 'Me I Never Knew', 'Will You Walk a Little Faster', 'Lobster Quadrille', 'They Told Me You Have Been to Her'

Top Twenty Films of 1972

1 Diamonds are Forever
2 The Godfather
3 Fiddler on the Roof/Bedknobs and Broomsticks
4 The Devils
5 Steptoe and Son
6 The French Connection
7 Nicholas and Alexandra
8 Ryan's Daughter
9 Dirty Harry
10 Mary, Queen of Scots
11 A Clockwork Orange
12 What's Up Doc?
13 Straw Dogs
14 Shaft
15 Klute/Young Winston
16 The Go-Between
17 Mutiny on the Buses
18 Sleeping Beauty
19 Please, Sir!
20 Up The Chastity Belt

The Top Five

Week of 23 December 1972
1. Alice's Adventures In Wonderland
2. Lady Caroline Lamb
3. The Mechanic
4. The Great Waltz
5. Play It Again Sam

THE VALACHI PAPERS

20 January 1973	2 weeks

Distributor:	Columbia
Director:	Terence Young
Producer:	Dino De Laurentiis
Screenplay:	Stephen Geller
Music:	Riz Ortolani

CAST
Charles Bronson .... *Joseph Valachi*
Lino Ventura .... *Vito Genovese*
Jill Ireland .... *Maria Valachi*
Walter Chiari .... *Gap*
Joseph Wiseman .... *Marazano*
Gerald S. O'Loughlin .... *Ryan*
Amedeo Nazzari .... *Gaetano Reina*
Fausto Tozzi .... *Albert Anastasia*

The Valachi Papers was based on true stories of the mobster Joseph Valachi. While serving a life sentence for his part in organized crime, Valachi grasses on the Mafia. He divulges to a Federal Agent the inside structure of the Mafia in America. The sometimes brutal stories of three decades of crimes and well-kept secrets are told mainly in flashback.

Mrs Valachi is played by Charles Bronson's late wife, Jill Ireland.

Shanghai-born director Terence Young is probably best remembered for his work on the first two James Bond movies, *Dr No* and *From Russia with Love*.

The Top Five

Week of 20 January 1973
1. The Valachi Papers
2. Lady Caroline Lamb
3. A Clockwork Orange
4. Fellini's Roma
5. Alice's Adventures in Wonderland

THE GETAWAY

3 February 1973	5 weeks

Distributor: Solar/First Artists
Director: Sam Peckinpah
Producer: David Foster, Mitchell Brower
Screenplay: Walter Hill
Music: Quincy Jones

CAST
Steve McQueen . . . . Doc McCoy
Ali MacGraw. . . . . Carol McCoy
Ben Johnson. . . . . Jack Benyon
Sally Struthers . . . . Fran Clinton
Al Lettieri . . . . Rudy

Doc McCoy's wife, Carol, has a relationship with Jack Benyon, who has strong political connections, in order to get her husband released on parole from prison. In return, Benyon asks her to arrange a bank raid. With Doc, a band of professional thieves and Carol as the getaway driver, they successfully relieve the Southwestern Bank of $500,000, but one of the guards is killed in the raid.

Steve McQueen actually went to reform school in California as a child, where he escaped and ended up in prison. His first appearance on the big screen was as an extra in the 1956 movie *Somebody Up There Likes Me*, starring Paul Newman. McQueen was paid $19 a day.

Despite being married to producer Robert Evans, Ali MacGraw started an affair with Steve McQueen during the making of the movie. The pressure of the relationship led to a bout of nervous exhaustion, requiring her to take a two-week break from filming.

The Top Five

Week of 3 February 1973
1. The Getaway
2. Lady Caroline Lamb
3. The Valachi Papers
4. Fellini's Roma
5. The Great Waltz

Video availability

TRAVELS WITH MY AUNT

10 March 1973	2 weeks

Distributor: MGM
Director: George Cukor
Producer: Robert Fryer, James Cresson
Screenplay: Jay Presson Allen, Hugh Wheeler
Music: Tony Hatch

CAST
Maggie Smith . . . . Aunt Augusta
Alec McCowen . . . . Henry
Lou Gossett . . . . Wordsworth
Robert Stephens . . . . Visconti
Cindy Williams . . . . Tooley
Robert Flemyng . . . . Crowder

In this adaptation of a Graham Greene best-seller, Maggie Smith plays an eccentric old lady who takes her nephew all over Europe on a series of adventures, after the death of his mother. It transpires, however, that Aunt Augusta has a more dubious reason for the trip, and it has something to do with an old lover.

Maggie Smith and Robert Stephens were a real-life husband and wife team when they made this film. They also appeared together with great success on the stage, particularly in a fine Shaftesbury Avenue production of Noel Coward's *Private Lives*.

Katharine Hepburn wanted the leading role but the studio decided on Maggie Smith.

Academy Awards: Best Costume Design (Anthony Powell)

The Top Five

Week of 10 March 1973
1. Travels with my Aunt
2. Super Fly
3. The Getaway
4. Lady Caroline Lamb
5. The Poseidon Adventure

LAST TANGO IN PARIS

24 March 1973	11 weeks*

Distributor: Les Artistes Associés/PEA/ United Artists
Director: Bernardo Bertolucci
Producer: Alberto Grimaldi
Screenplay: Bernardo Bertolucci, Franco Arcalli
Music: Gato Barbieri

CAST
Marlon Brando . . . . *Paul*
Maria Schneider . . . . *Jeanne*
Jean-Pierre Léaud . . . . *Tom*
Darling Legitmus . . . . *Concierge*
Massimo Girotti . . . . *Marcel*
Laura Betti . . . . *Miss Blandish*
Veronica Lazare . . . . *Rosa*

Paul, a middle-aged American, is alone in Paris after his wife commits suicide. While looking at a new apartment he meets Jeanne with whom he has an intense sexual encounter. They decide to meet regularly at the same apartment without exchanging names or personal details. After their rendezvous, he returns to the hotel where his wife took her life, and she goes off to meet her fiancé who is a film-maker making a picture about her life. Despite their agreement, Jeanne admits to Paul that she is falling in love with him, an admission he treats with complete indifference. The doomed love affair ends in violence.

The film was first screened on 14 October 1972 at the New York Film Festival. Shocked audiences gasped at the explicit sex scenes, in particular the now infamous 'butter' scene.

Marlon Brando agreed to do the film without reading the script. Director Bernardo Bertolucci gave him a verbal outline and Brando was convinced of its merits. Following completion of the movie, Brando announced his short-lived retirement.

Video availability

The Top Five

Week of 24 March 1973
1. Last Tango in Paris
2. Travels with my Aunt
3. King Boxer
4. Pete 'n' Tillie
5. Lady Caroline Lamb

The unusual sexual behaviour of a confused middle-aged man (Marlon Brando) and a young woman (Maria Schneider) lies at the centre of Last Tango in Paris, *which includes one of the most graphic sex scenes ever to appear in a major full-length motion picture.*

HITLER – THE LAST TEN DAYS

19 May 1973	1 week

Distributor:	MGM
Director:	Ennio de Concini
Producer:	Wolfgang Reinhardt
Screenplay:	Ennio de Concini, Marie Pia
	Fusco, Wolfgang Reinhardt
Music:	Mischa Spoliansky

CAST
Alec Guinness . . . . *Adolf Hitler*
Simon Ward . . . . . . *Hauptmann Hoffmann*
Adolfo Celi . . . . *General Krebs*
Diane Cilento . . . . *Hanna Reitsch*
Gabriele Ferzetti . . . . . *Fieldmarshal Keitel*
Eric Porter . . . . *General von Greim*
Doris Kunstmann . . . . *Eva Braun*

The story, as the title suggests, offers a treatment of Hitler's final days in his bunker where he is thought to have committed suicide with his wife, Eva Braun, after learning of the defeat of his country at the end of World War II.

The cast of the movie are mainly British and Italian actors. Only Doris Kunstmann, who plays Eva Braun, is actually German, and most of the film was shot at Shepperton Studios in England. Alec Guinness claimed that in the end he was disappointed with his performance. He did ten months' research for the role of Hitler, which included an interview with German Captain Boldt, who was present in the bunker and worked as advisor on the film.

Israel banned the film because it represented Hitler in a humane light.

Video availability

The Top Five

Week of 19 May 1973
1. Hitler – The Last Ten Days
2. Last Tango in Paris
3. O Lucky Man!
4. Cabaret
5. The Thief Who Came to Dinner

A TOUCH OF CLASS

9 June 1973	1 week

Distributor:	Avco
Director:	Melvin Frank
Producer:	Melvin Frank
Screenplay:	Melvin Frank, Jack Rose
Music:	John Cameron
	George Barrie, Sammy Cahn
	(Songs)

CAST
George Segal . . . . *Steve Blackburn*
Glenda Jackson . . . . *Vicki Allessio*
Paul Sorvino . . . . *Walter Menkes*
Hildegard Neil . . . . *Gloria Blackburn*
Cec Linder . . . . *Wendell Thompson*
K. Callan . . . . *Patty Menkes*
Mary Barclay . . . . *Marsha Thompson*

In this romantic comedy Steve Blackburn, a married American executive living in London, meets Vicki Allessio, a divorcee with two children. Vicki is an independent, sharp-tongued woman and Steve does not get the sexually pliant mistress he envisaged. While in Spain together the two spark off each other, but they have a wonderful time until a huge row forces them to break up in a hotel room. They resume their affair in London, but when Vicki be-

comes the clock-watching mistress and Steve the guilty husband they realize it's time to part.

The company behind the movie was Brut Productions, part of the Brut cosmetics organization, whose boss George Barrie always wanted to be a songwriter. He co-wrote with Sammy Cahn the movie's Oscar-nominated song 'All That Love Went To Waste'.

The softball scene at the beginning of the film features several ex-patriate Americans who were living in London at the time and played the game regularly.

Academy Awards: Best Actress (Glenda Jackson)

Music: 'All That Love Went To Waste'

Video availability

The Top Five

Week of 9 June 1973
1. A Touch of Class
2. Last Tango in Paris
3. Hitler – The Last Ten Days
4. O Lucky Man!
5. Lady Sings the Blues

THE DAY OF THE JACKAL

23 June 1973	3 weeks

Distributor: Universal
Director: Fred Zinnemann
Producer: John Woolf
Screenplay: Kenneth Ross
Music: Georges Delerue

CAST
Edward Fox .... *The Jackal*
Alan Badel .... *The Minister*
Tony Britton .... *Inspector Thomas*
Cyril Cusack .... *Gunsmith*
Michel Lonsdale ..... *Commissioner Lebel*
Eric Porter .... *Rebel Leader Rodin*
Delphine Seyrig .... *Colette*

The Jackal, one of the world's deadliest killers, is hired by a secret French military organization to murder President De Gaulle. A top police investigator named Lebel finds out about the plot and the name Jackal from an informer and works out the identity of the would-be killer. The film follows the Jackal's plans for the assassination, which include a number of disguises, and Lebel's tactics for catching him.

Director Fred Zinnemann trained as a violinist and as a lawyer before turning to movie-making. He had a small acting part in the 1930 film *All Quiet on the Western Front*, starring Lew Ayres. *The Jackal* was Zinnemann's first film since his success with *A Man for all Seasons* (1966). His projected movie version of André Malraux's novel *Man's Fate* was cancelled at the last moment by MGM in 1969. The decision started a long legal battle between the studio and the director, which was finally settled out of court.

Video availability

The Top Five

Week of 23 June 1973
1. The Day of the Jackal
2. Last Tango in Paris
3. The Canterbury Tales
4. A Touch of Class
5. Jimi Hendrix

LIVE AND LET DIE

14 July 1973	10 weeks

Distributor: United Artists
Director: Guy Hamilton
Producer: Albert R. Broccoli, Harry
Saltzman
Screenplay: Tom Mankiewicz
Music: George Martin

CAST
Roger Moore .... *James Bond*
Yaphet Kotto .... *Kananga*
Jane Seymour .... *Solitaire*
Clifton James .... *Sheriff*
Bernard Lee .... *M*
Lois Maxwell .... *Miss Moneypenny*

In the eighth 007 adventure, M gives Bond the task of investigating a number of murders in the Caribbean. They appear to be linked to a heavyweight criminal, Dr Kananga, who masquerades as a top diplomat. He is planning to cultivate a large crop of cocaine and distribute it free through a Harlem drugs dealer, thus forcing all other dealers out of business and at the same time increasing the number of addicts. Then, with his monopoly, he will be able to charge top prices for the narcotics. Bond has to face Kananga's henchman Tee Hee who has a steel hook for a hand.

Roger Moore had been best known to audiences for his TV series *The Saint*, in which he played the debonair Simon Templar. George Lazenby had proved less than successful as Bond in *O.H.M.S.S.* and Sean Connery didn't want to come out of Bond retirement a second time so the hunt was on for someone to take over the mantle of the United Kingdom's best-loved Secret Serviceman. Moore got the job and stayed with the series for a further 6 outings. United Artists wanted to pursue Burt Reynolds, Paul Newman and Robert Redford for the Bond role, but Albert 'Cubby' Broccoli was keen on Roger Moore. It was doubtful that he'd be available as he was appearing in the TV series *The Persuaders* with Tony Curtis, but the new series was cancelled leaving Moore free to play 007.

Music: 'Live and Let Die' (Paul and Linda McCartney)

Video availability

The Top Five

Week of 14 July 1973
1. Live and Let Die
2. The Day of the Jackal
3. Last Tango in Paris
4. Soylent Green
5. A Touch of Class

SCORPIO

22 September 1973	4 weeks

Distributor:	United Artists
Director:	Michael Winner
Producer:	Walter Mirisch
Screenplay:	David W. Rintels, Gerald Wilson
Music:	Jerry Fielding

CAST

Burt Lancaster	....	*Cross*
Alain Delon	....	*Laurier*
Paul Scofield	....	*Sharkov*
John Colicos	....	*McLeod*
Gayle Hunnicutt	....	*Susan*
J.D. Cannon	....	*Filchock*
Joanne Linville	....	*Sarah*
Melvin Stewart	....	*Pick*

Michael Winner's spy thriller revolves around the mysterious assassination of an unidentified Arab government official. When CIA hired killer Cross tries to retire he finds himself caught up in the mystery and being chased by Delon, a hired killer that Cross had originally trained.

In 1969 Alain Delon and his wife Natalie were at the centre of a massive scandal that threatened to expose some of the best known personalities from the showbusiness world in France. Delon's bodyguard was shot dead and left on a garbage dump. Delon was later cleared of any suspicion from a series of events that could have ended his career.

Much of the location filming took place in Washington D.C., and large crowds gathered to watch the action, prompting Lancaster to comment 'This is the first time in years where I have been made so conscious of being a movie star.'

The Top Five

Week of 22 September 1973
1. Scorpio
2. Live and Let Die
3. Doctor Zhivago
4. Last Tango in Paris
5. A Touch of Class

DON'T LOOK NOW

20 October 1973	37 weeks

Distributor:	BL/Casey/Eldorado
Director:	Nicholas Roeg
Producer:	Peter Katz
Screenplay:	Allan Scott, Chris Bryant
Music:	Pino Donaggio

CAST

Julie Christie	....	*Laura Baxter*
Donald Sutherland	....	*John Baxter*
Hilary Mason	....	*Heather*
Clelia Matania	....	*Wendy*
Massimo Serato	....	*Bishop Barbarigo*
Renato Scarpa	....	*Inspector Longhi*

Laura and John Baxter travel to Venice after their daughter is killed in what is believed to be an accidental drowning in England. John begins restoration work on a church but begins to hear messages from his dead daughter. The supernatural presence of the dead child becomes more pronounced when two eerie sisters, Wendy and Heather, claim to have visions of the dead girl. John refuses to believe them until he sees a young girl dancing around in clothes worn by his daughter.

Top Twenty Films of 1973

1 Live and Let Die
2 The Godfather
3 A Clockwork Orange
4 Snow White and the Seven Dwarfs
5 The Poseidon Adventure
6 Last Tango In Paris
7 Cabaret
8 The Day of the Jackal
9 Lady Caroline Lamb
10 That'll Be the Day
11 Lady Sings the Blues
12 Lost Horizon
13 High Plains Drifter
14 Fear is the Key
15 Love Thy Neighbour
16 Alice's Adventures in Wonderland/Super Fly/King Boxer/Fuzz
17 The Great Waltz
18 Mary Poppins
19 The Mechanic
20 The Sword in the Stone/Jesus Christ Superstar

Donald Sutherland, who was bullied at school, got his first job at the age of 14 in Nova Scotia as a disc jockey for a radio station. Before moving into films, he appeared in episodes of two British TV series, *The Saint* and *The Avengers*.

Despite the film's apparent success with both the critics and the public, for reasons best known to the producers, it failed financially.

Nicholas Roeg adapted the screenplay from Daphne Du Maurier's short story, and although it was thought that she hated it, Roeg received a very complimentary note from her after she'd viewed it.

The Top Five

Week of 20 October 1973
1. Don't Look Now
2. The Adventures of Barry McKenzie
3. Jesus Christ Superstar
4. Last Tango in Paris
5. Doctor Zhivago

Video availability

PAPER MOON

8 December 1973	2 weeks

Distributor:	Paramount
Director:	Peter Bogdanovich
Producer:	Peter Bogdanovich
Screenplay:	Avin Sargent

CAST
Ryan O'Neal . . . . *Moses (Moze) Pray*
Tatum O'Neal . . . . *Addie Loggins*
Madeline Kahn . . . . *Trixie Delight*
John Hillerman . . . . *Bootlegger and Sheriff*
P.J. Johnson . . . . *Imogene*

Moses Pray, a Bible salesman and con man, finds himself lumbered with the badly behaved young orphan Addie Loggins when he promises to deliver her to relatives in Missouri. Together they become a perfect pair of con artists with Addie proving to be even more resourceful than Moses. Their adventures lead to encounters with several strange folk, including the outrageous entertainer Trixie Delight, who turns out to be a hooker, and her black teenage maid.

A short-lived TV series, based on the movie, was made in 1974, with Chris Connelly as Moses and Jodie Foster as Addie.

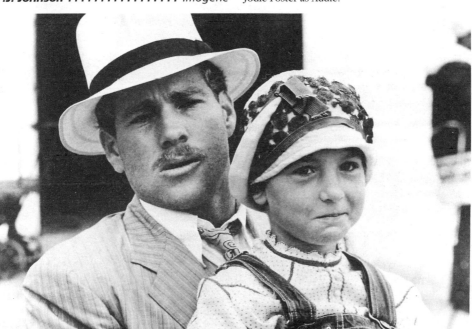

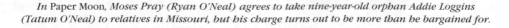

In Paper Moon, *Moses Pray (Ryan O'Neal) agrees to take nine-year-old orphan Addie Loggins (Tatum O'Neal) to relatives in Missouri, but his charge turns out to be more than he bargained for.*

Originally Paul Newman was to play Moses, and his daughter was to be played by Nell Potts.

The movie was Tatum O'Neal's screen debut, and it was Polly Platt, the wife of director Peter Bogdanovich, who suggested her. Bogdanovich agreed to use Tatum O'Neal on the condition that Ryan O'Neal (who had worked successfully with him on *What's Up Doc?* (1972)) take the part of Moses.

Academy Awards: Best Supporting Actress (Tatum O'Neal)

Music: 'A Picture of Me Without You', 'Mississippi

The Top Five

Week of 8 December 1973
1. Paper Moon
2. Don't Look Now
3. Day For Night
4. The Adventures of Barry McKenzie
5. The Belstone Fox

Mud', 'Georgia on My Mind', 'After You've Gone', 'About a Quarter to Nine'

Video availability

MAGNUM FORCE

22 December 1973	1 week

Distributor:	Warner
Director:	Ted Post
Producer:	Robert Daley
Screenplay:	John Milius
Music:	Lalo Schifrin

CAST
Clint Eastwood	Harry Callahan
Hal Holbrook	Lt Briggs
Felton Perry	Early Smith
Mitchell Ryan	Charlie McCoy
David Soul	Davis
Tim Matheson	Sweet
Robert Urich	Grimes

Detective Harry Callahan from San Francisco is back on the force after throwing in his badge at the end of the original film (*Dirty Harry*; 1971). This time he has to contend with hijackers, bombers and robbers, as well as tracking down a gang of vigilante cops who have been committing bloody murders in the city's underworld. It transpires that his boss is behind the killings, but with Harry on their trail there's no place to hide.

Clint Eastwood is re-united with director Ted Post, who directed a number of episodes of the TV series *Rawhide*. They met up again when Eastwood asked for him to work on *Hang 'em High*.

The film attracted a tremendous amount of flak for what many saw as gratuitous violence and shabby treatment of women. Clint Eastwood was moved to defend this Dirty Harry sequel by claiming that excessive violence had to be countered with a similar show of force.

Video availability

The Top Five

Week of 22 December 1973
1. Magnum Force
2. Robin Hood
3. Paper Moon
4. Don't Look Now
5. The Day of the Jackal

ROBIN HOOD

29 December 1973	2 weeks

Distributor:	Walt Disney
Director:	Wolfgang Reitherman
Producer:	Wolfgang Reitherman
Screenplay:	Larry Clemmens
Music:	George Bruns

CAST (Voices)
Brian Bedford	Robin Hood
Peter Ustinov	Prince John
Terry-Thomas	Sir Hiss
Roger Miller	Allan-a-Dale
Phil Harris	Little John
Andy Devine	Friar Tuck
Monica Evans	Maid Marion
Pat Buttram	Sheriff of Nottingham
Carole Shelley	Lady Kluck
George Lindsey	Trigger

In this cartoon feature by the Disney studio all the characters are played by animals. The evil Prince

John and the Sheriff of Nottingham go out of their way to make the people's lives a misery, but fear not, help is on the way in the shape of the fearless fox, Robin Hood. The movie features the voices of such stars as Peter Ustinov, Phil Harris, Terry-Thomas and Brian Bedford.

The film depicts Prince John as a thumb-sucking lion, Little John as a bear and Friar Tuck as a badger. There is also a chain gang of raccoons. Maid Marion, fortunately, is also a fox.

Director Wolfgang Reitherman also directed the hugely successful *The Jungle Book* (see 1967, 1975, 1983 and 1993).

The Top Five

Week of 29 December 1973
1. Robin Hood
2. The Sting
3. Magnum Force
4. Paper Moon
5. The Golden Voyage of Sinbad

Music: 'The Phony King of England', 'Love'

THE STING

12 January 1974	5 weeks*

Distributor:	Universal
Director:	George Roy Hill
Producer:	Tony Bill, Michael Phillips, Julia Phillips
Screenplay:	David S. Ward
Music:	Marvin Hamlisch

CAST
Paul Newman . . . . *Henry Gondorff*
Robert Redford . . . . *Johnny Hooker*
Robert Shaw . . . . *Doyle Lonnegan*
Charles Durning . . . . *Lt Snyder*
Ray Walston . . . . *Singleton*
Eileen Brennan . . . . *Billie*
Harold Gould . . . . *Kid Twist*
John Heffernan . . . . *Niles*

Johnny Hooker (Robert Redford) masterminds an enormous swindle on Doyle Lonnegan (Robert Shaw) to avenge the death of Luther Coleman (Robert Earl Jones), the man who taught him everything about the con business in The Sting.

Redford is a small time con artist in the 1930s who ends up on the run after his partner is killed. He teams up with Paul Newman in Chicago and the two of them plan the biggest 'sting' of their lives to stitch up Doyle Lonnegan, the gangster who had Redford's partner killed. The pair set up a fake gambling joint in order to effect the 'sting' on Shaw and relieve him of his fortune, but there are many surprises before the finale in this charming and well-acted roguish comedy.

Seven Oscars were won with this re-teaming of Newman and Redford, who had worked together so well in *Butch Cassidy and the Sundance Kid*. There was no such luck for the ill-advised sequel *The Sting II* (1983), which starred Jackie Gleason and Mac Davis in the Newman and Redford roles.

Academy Awards: Best Film (Producers Tony Bill, Michael and Julia Phillips), Best Direction (George Roy Hill), Best Story and Screenplay (David S. Ward), Best Art Direction (Henry Bumstead), Set Decoration (James Payne), Best Costume Design (Edith Head), Best Editing (William Reynolds), Best Music Score (adaptation) (Marvin Hamlisch)

Music: 'The Entertainer'

Video availability

The Top Five

Week of 12 January 1974
1. The Sting
2. Magnum Force
3. Robin Hood
4. Paper Moon
5. The Golden Voyage of Sinbad

ENTER THE DRAGON

19 January 1974	2 weeks

Distributor: Warner
Director: Robert Clouse
Producer: Fred Weintraub, Paul Heller
Screenplay: Michael Allin
Music: Lalo Schifrin

CAST
Bruce Lee .... Lee
John Saxon .... Roper
Jim Kelly .... Williams
Shih Kien .... Han
Bob Wall .... Oharra
Ahna Capri .... Tania
Angela Mao Ying .... Su-Lin
Betty Chung .... Mei Ling

In this martial arts thriller Bruce Lee is a secret agent. He enters a Kung Fu tournament on an oriental island fortress to investigate the organizer's criminal links. Bruce Lee appears in a series of battles with the best of the world's experts in the art of self-defence, including Jim Kelly, as the American representative, and John Saxon.

Bruce Lee died at the age of 33, a few weeks after finishing *Enter The Dragon*, which was his most successful western film. He was the subject of the 1993 biopic *Dragon: The Bruce Lee Story*.

Video availability

The Top Five

Week of 19 January 1974
1. Enter the Dragon
2. The Sting
3. Robin Hood
4. Magnum Force
5. Paper Moon

THE WAY WE WERE

16 February 1974	3 weeks*

Distributor: Columbia
Director: Sydney Pollack
Producer: Ray Stark
Screenplay: Arthur Laurents
Music: Marvin Hamlisch

CAST
Barbra Streisand .... Katie
Robert Redford .... Hubbell
Bradford Dillman .... J.J.
Patrick O'Neal .... George Bissinger
Viveca Lindfors .... Paula Resiner
Lois Chiles .... Carol Ann

This romantic drama follows the lives of Katie and Hubbell, two college chums in the 1930s whose lives and paths cross several times over the next decades. She is politically active while he is more concerned with writing than politics. Their romance blossoms and they marry, but after World War II they break up when she becomes involved with the McCarthy Hollywood witch-hunt. They re-meet several years later but the magic has gone.

Streisand sang the title song, which became a huge worldwide hit and her first number one in the USA, but curiously reached only number 31 in the UK.

Marvin Hamlisch appears briefly in a cameo role. Streisand and Hamlisch are great friends and he was her orchestra conductor during her much talked about world concert tour in 1994.

Academy Awards: Best Original Dramatic Score (Marvin Hamlisch), Best song – 'The Way We Were'

(Marvin Hamlisch, music; Alan and Marilyn Bergman, lyrics)

Music: 'The Way We Were'

Video availability

The Top Five

Week of 16 February 1974
1. The Way We Were
2. The Sting
3. Enter the Dragon
4. Executive Action
5. Robin Hood

THE EXORCIST

23 March 1974	11 weeks*

Distributor:	Warner
Director:	William Friedkin
Producer:	William Peter Blatty
Screenplay:	William Peter Blatty
Music:	Jack Nitzsche

CAST
Ellen Burstyn . . . . *Mrs MacNeil*
Max von Sydow . . . . *Father Merrin*
Lee J. Cobb . . . . *Lt Kinderman*
Kitty Winn . . . . *Sharon*
Jack MacGowran . . . . *Burke Dennings*
Jason Miller . . . . *Father Karras*
Linda Blair . . . . *Regan MacNeil*

In Exorcist *young clergyman Father Karras (Jason Miller) tries to release the spirit of the devil from 12-year-old Regan MacNeil (Linda Blair) only to have the demon spirit enter his own body and cause his death.*

This supernatural horror film begins when a pagan hex is uncovered during an archaeological expedition. Ellen Burstyn's young daughter, Linda Blair, becomes possessed by the Devil. She becomes more and more violent, mouthing obscenities, vomiting, and having huge fits. As the demon inside her grows more violent it is decided that she needs a religious exorcism to rid her body of the Devil.

The film was based on the William Peter Blatty best-seller, which in turn was based on true events of a documented possession in 1949.

Two sequels, *Exorcist II: The Heretic* (1977) and *The Exorcist III* (1990), both failed to make much impression.

Academy Awards: Best Screenplay (William Peter Blatty), Best Sound (Robert Knudson and Chris Newman)

Music: 'Tubular Bells' (Mike Oldfield)

The Top Five

Week of 23 March 1974
1. The Exorcist
2. Papillon
3. The Sting
4. Westworld
5. The Way We Were

THE GREAT GATSBY

25 May 1974	8 weeks

Distributor:	Paramount
Director:	Jack Clayton
Producer:	David Merrick
Screenplay:	Francis Ford Coppola
Music:	Nelson Riddle

CAST
Robert Redford . . . . *Jay Gatsby*
Mia Farrow . . . . *Daisy Buchanan*
Bruce Dern . . . . *Tom Buchanan*
Karen Black . . . . *Myrtle Wilson*
Scott Wilson . . . . *George Wilson*
Sam Waterston . . . . *Nick Carraway*
Lois Chiles . . . . *Jordan Baker*

Jay Gatsby is a retired bootlegger and gangster who dragged himself up from humble beginnings. He has all the trappings of wealth and class in his luxurious home on Long Island. He surrounds himself with the rich and beautiful set, and pursues his aristocratic ex-lover Daisy, now married to Tom. Despite his money Jay is still unhappy, and his quest for Daisy is as much about finding personal happiness as about finding a sense of belonging.

The film, based on F. Scott Fitzgerald's novel, was beautiful to look at, with scenery shots and expensive costumes. Much of the film was made at Pinewood Studios. The costumes by Theoni V. Aldredge created a sensation, and for a brief time in 1974 every fashion house strived to get out a Gatsby 'look' in their clothing lines.

The story had already been filmed in 1926 and 1942.

Academy Awards: Best Costume Design (Theoni V. Aldredge), Best Original Song Score (Nelson Riddle)

Video availability

The Top Five

Week of 25 May 1974
1. The Great Gatsby
2. The Exorcist
3. Papillon
4. Sleeper
5. The Sting

FOR PETE'S SAKE

3 August 1974	2 weeks

Distributor:	Columbia
Director:	Peter Yates
Producer:	Martin Erlichman, Stanley Shapiro
Screenplay:	Stanley Shapiro, Maurice Richlin
Music:	Artie Butler

CAST
Barbra Streisand . . . . *Henry*
Michael Sarrazin . . . . *Pete*
Estelle Parsons . . . . *Helen*
William Redfield . . . . *Fred*
Molly Picon . . . . *Mrs Cherry*
Louis Zorich . . . . *Nick*
Vivian Bonnell . . . . *Loretta*

Retired millionaire and gangster Jay Gatsby (Robert Redford) pursues his lost lover Daisy Buchanan (Mia Farrow), who is unhappily married to the sinister and mean Tom (Bruce Dern) in the remake of The Great Gatsby.

In this New York comedy Streisand is a brash Brooklyn housewife who is unable to pay back an underworld loan when her investment in Pork Belly Futures doesn't pay off. She needs the money so that her taxi-driver husband (Sarrazin) can go back to college. The laughs start after she is persuaded by Molly Picon to try and earn some money as a hooker! All's well that ends well when the price of Pork Bellies goes through the roof and they can buy themselves back out of trouble.

The film's original title was July Pork Bellies, which means nothing at all to the popcorn crowd!

Barbra's then boyfriend hairdresser, Jon Peters, worked on her hair (or rather her wig) for this film, earning his first major screen credit. Nowadays he is credited as producer, for instance on *A Star is Born* (1976), *The Witches of Eastwick* (1987) and *Batman* (1989).

Music: 'For Pete's Sake' (Barbra Streisand)

Video availability

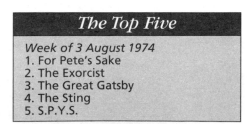

The Top Five

Week of 3 August 1974
1. For Pete's Sake
2. The Exorcist
3. The Great Gatsby
4. The Sting
5. S.P.Y.S.

CHINATOWN

17 August 1974	4 weeks

Distributor: Paramount
Director: Roman Polanski
Producer: Robert Evans
Screenplay: Robert Towne
Music: Jerry Goldsmith

CAST

Jack Nicholson . . . . *J.J. Gittes*
Faye Dunaway . . . . *Evelyn Mulwray*
John Huston . . . . *Noah Cross*
Perry Lopez . . . . *Escobar*
John Hillerman . . . . *Yelburton*
Darrell Zwerlind . . . . *Hollis Mulwray*
Diane Ladd . . . . *Ida Sessions*
Roy Jenson . . . . *Mulvihill*

In Los Angeles 1937, J.J. Gittes is a private detective who specializes in gathering evidence for divorce cases. Out of favour with the local police, he takes on a case involving a prominent city official's wife. The investigation leads to an intrigue of public scandal and murder. Gittes becomes personally involved when he falls for the central femme fatale, Faye Dunaway. But all in Chinatown is not what it seems and Gittes is not prepared for the final revelations.

Roman Polanski described *Chinatown* as a 'traditional detective story with a new, modern shape', and indeed the film was one of the first modern *film noir* pictures. Polanski has a small part in the film as a nasty knife-wielding thug. His credit in the film reads 'Man with Knife'.

Nicholson directed the belated 1990 sequel *The Two Jakes*, reprising his role as investigator Gittes with the voice of Faye Dunaway also making a contribution. However, the film was not a success.

Academy Awards: Best Original Screenplay (Robert Towne)

Music: 'Love is Just Around the Corner' (Leo Robin and Lewis E. Gensler), 'Easy Living' (Leo Robin and Ralph Rainger), 'The Way You Look Tonight' (Jerome Kern and Dorothy Fields), 'Some Day', 'The Vagabond King Waltz' (Brian Hooker and Rudolph Friml)

Video availability

The Top Five

Week of 17 August 1974
1. Chinatown
2. Caravan to Vaccares
3. The Exorcist
4. For Pete's Sake
5. The Sting

GOLD

14 September 1974	3 weeks*

Distributor: Hemdale
Director: Peter Hunt
Producer: Michael Klinger
Screenplay: Wilbur Smith, Stanley Price
Music: Elmer Bernstein

CAST

Roger Moore . . . . *Rod Slater*
Susannah York . . . . *Terry Steyner*
Ray Milland . . . . *Harry Hirschfeld*
Bradford Dillman . . . . *Manfred Steyner*
John Gielgud . . . . *Farrell*
Simon Sabela . . . . *Bing King*

Rod Slater is a tough South African working in a goldmine. An unscrupulous gang tries to deliberately flood the goldmine, owned by Harry Hirschfeld, in order to hike up the price of gold on the world market. Intrigue abounds as mine operator Steyner is in on the plot, but he reckons without the resources of his wife Terry and her grumpy old grandfather Hirschfeld as they discover what's going on.

The film, adapted from Wilbur Smith's novel *Goldmine*, was filmed entirely on location in South Africa, and included several stunning shots of the region and spectacular special effects when the water floods the mines.

Elmer Bernstein, who wrote the stirring score, also had success with the music from *Airplane!* (1980),

The Top Five

Week of 14 September 1974
1. Gold
2. Chinatown
3. The Tamarind Seed
4. The Exorcist
5. The Sting

Trading Places (1983), *Airplane II: The Sequel* (1983) and *Ghostbusters* (1984).

Music: 'Wherever Loves Takes Me' (Maureen McGovern), 'Gold' (Jimmy Helms), 'Where Have You Been All My Life' (Trevor Chance)

Video availability

THUNDERBOLT AND LIGHTFOOT

28 September 1974	1 week

Distributor:	United Artists
Director:	Michael Cimino
Producer:	Robert Daley
Screenplay:	Michael Cimino
Music:	Dee Barton

CAST
Clint Eastwood . . . . *Thunderbolt*
Jeff Bridges . . . . *Lightfoot*
George Kennedy . . . . *Red Leary*
Geoffrey Lewis . . . . *Goody*
Gary Busey . . . . *Curly*

Bank robber John 'Thunderbolt' Doherty is being hunted by his former partners who think he's stolen the entire half million dollars from their last bank job. He goes on the run disguised as a preacher and is rescued by Lightfoot. They travel to Montana to pick up the cash, which has been hidden in an old schoolhouse. The schoolhouse has disappeared so they team up with Red Leary and Eddie Goody from Thunderbolt's old gang to plan another robbery. The heist is successful but the police are soon on their trail and the gang fall out again. Thunderbolt and Lightfoot then discover that the old schoolhouse with the loot from the first robbery has only been moved and not destroyed so they collect the money. Their luck does not last and Lightfoot is caught by Red and beaten to death.

Thunderbolt and Lightfoot was Michael Cimino's first film as director. Eastwood had used him to write the screenplay for *Magnum Force* and signed him to direct this for Malpaso, his own production company.

Video availability

The Top Five

Week of 28 September 1974
1. Thunderbolt and Lightfoot
2. Gold
3. Chinatown
4. The Exorcist
5. Ash Wednesday

The first film to be directed by Michael Cimino, who later went on to make The Deer Hunter *and* Heaven's Gate, Thunderbolt and Lightfoot *finds drifter Lightfoot (Jeff Bridges) team up with ex-con John 'Thunderbolt' Doherty (Clint Eastwood).*

EMMANUELLE

12 October 1974	3 weeks*

Distributor: Trinacra/Orphée
Director: Just Jaeckin
Producer: Yves Rousset-Rouard
Screenplay: Jean-Louis Richard
Music: Pierre Bachelet

CAST
Sylvia Kristel . . . . *Emmanuelle*
Alain Cuny . . . . *Marco*
Daniel Sarky . . . . *Jean*
Jeanne Colletin . . . . *Marie Louise*
Marika Green . . . . *Bee*

In this soft-core, soft-focus French sex film newly wed Emmanuelle flies off to join her husband at the French Embassy in Bangkok where he works. A wealthy diplomat, he has a lavish lifestyle, which includes a sumptuous house, servants and all the other trappings of diplomatic life. Emmanuelle, however, is more interested in the pleasures of the flesh and embarks on a journey of sexual discovery that involves a series of sensuous encounters.

The movie was much talked about and hyped on its release and spawned seven sequels and various spin-offs, such as *Emmanuelle Goes to Cannes* and *Emmanuelle's Silver Tongue*, which bear little relation to the original film.

Sylvia Kristel appears only in *Emmanuelle 2* and *Emmanuelle 7*.

Video availability

The Top Five

Week of 12 October 1974
1. Emmanuelle
2. That's Entertainment
3. Thunderbolt and Lightfoot
4. Gold
5. Chinatown

Top Twenty Films of 1974

1 The Sting
2 The Exorcist
3 Enter The Dragon
4 The Three Musketeers
5 Papillon
6 Herbie Rides Again
7 Robin Hood
8 The Great Gatsby
9 Mary Poppins
10 The Way We Were
11 Golden Voyage of Sinbad
12 Don't Look Now
13 Chinatown
14 The Way of the Dragon
15 Blazing Saddles
16 Confessions of a Window Cleaner
17 Stardust
18 Gold
19 Last Tango in Paris
20 American Graffiti

THE ODESSA FILE

26 October 1974	4 weeks

Distributor: Columbia
Director: Ronald Neame
Producer: John Woolf
Screenplay: Kenneth Ross, George Markstein
Music: Andrew Lloyd Webber Tim Rice (song lyric)

CAST
Jon Voight . . . . *Peter Miller*
Maximilian Schell . . . . *Eduard Roschmann*
Maria Schell . . . . *Mrs Miller*
Mary Tamm . . . . *Sigi*
Derek Jacobi . . . . *Klaus Wenzer*
Samuel Rodensky . . . . . *Simon Weisenthal*

Martin Brandt . . . . *Marx*

In 1963 the diary of a Jewish prison camp survivor falls into the hands of a young German reporter (Voight). The diary leads him to a group of former Nazi officers still living in Germany. One in particular, Roschmann, is high up in industry. In a classic

The Top Five

Week of 26 October 1974
1. The Odessa File
2. Emmanuelle
3. Juggernaut
4. That's Entertainment
5. Chinatown

story of investigative journalism, he sets out to uncover their covert plan to bomb Israel.

The Odessa File was one of Andrew Lloyd Webber's few excursions to date into the world of film music. His only other big screen credit was for the music score for the 1971 Albert Finney film *Gumshoe*, although plans have been announced to turn some of his stage musicals like *Cats* and *Phantom of the Opera* into motion pictures.

Video availability

MURDER ON THE ORIENT EXPRESS

30 November 1974	1 week

Distributor:	EMI
Director:	Sidney Lumet
Producer:	John Brabourne, Richard Goodwin
Screenplay:	Paul Dehn
Music:	Richard Rodney Bennett

CAST
Albert Finney . . . . *Hercule Poirot*
Lauren Bacall . . . . *Mrs Hubbard*
Martin Balsam . . . . *Bianchi*
Ingrid Bergman . . . . *Greta*
Jacqueline Bisset . . . . . *Countess Andrenyi*
Jean Pierre Cassel . . . . *Pierre*
Sean Connery . . . . *Colonel Arbuthnott*
John Gielgud . . . . *Beddoes*

This sumptuous murder mystery, with its all-star cast, is set on board the legendary Orient Express train on a three-day journey across Europe. The usual bunch of wealthy foreign passengers endure the probings of Agatha Christie's celebrated Belgian detective while snow-bound in a carriage that has become detached from the rest of the train.

First published in 1934, *Murder on the Orient Express* has become one of Agatha Christie's best-selling mysteries.

Original pieces of an old Orient Express train were meticulously reassembled like a giant jigsaw at Elstree studios for use in the film.

Academy Awards: Best Supporting Actress (Ingrid Bergman)

Video availability

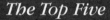

The Top Five
Week of 30 November 1974
1. Murder on the Orient Express
2. Emmanuelle
3. That's Entertainment
4. The Odessa File
5. Juggernaut

EARTHQUAKE

7 December 1974	3 weeks

Distributor:	Universal
Director:	Mark Robson
Producer:	Mark Robson
Screenplay:	George Fox, Mario Puzo
Music:	John Williams

CAST
Charlton Heston . . . . *Graff*
Ava Gardner . . . . *Remy Graff*
George Kennedy . . . . *Patrolman Slade*
Lorne Greene . . . . *Royce*
Genevieve Bujold . . . . *Denise*
Richard Roundtree . . . . *Miles*
Marjoe Gortner . . . . *Jody*
Barry Sullivan . . . . *Dr Stockle*

This spectacular disaster movie is set in Los Angeles. When the earthquake hits town buildings collapse, hundreds of people are buried, bridges buckle, dams burst, freeways twist, vehicles tumble and heroes and villains emerge from the chaos.

Walter Matthau was billed in the credits under his real name, Walter Matuschanskayasky.

The publicity boards outside cinemas showing *Earthquake* warned: 'Attention! This motion picture will be shown in the startling new multi-dimension of SENSURROUND. Please be aware that you will feel as well as see and hear realistic effects such as might

The Top Five
Week of 7 December 1974
1. Earthquake
2. Murder on the Orient Express
3. Emmanuelle
4. The Odessa File
5. That's Entertainment

be experienced in an actual earthquake. The management assume no responsibility for the physical or emotional reactions of the individual viewer.'

Academy Awards: Best Sound (Ronald Pierce and Melvin Metcalfe Snr), Best Visual Effects (Frank Brendel, Albert Whitlock and Glen Robinson), (Special Achievement Oscar 'for the realistic depiction of the devastation of Los Angeles by an earthquake')

Video availability

THE MAN WITH THE GOLDEN GUN

28 December 1974	6 weeks

Distributor:	United Artists
Director:	Guy Hamilton
Producer:	Albert R. Broccoli, Harry Saltzman
Screenplay:	Richard Maibaum, Tom Mankiewicz
Music:	John Barry Don Black (song lyric)

CAST
Roger Moore .... *James Bond*
Christopher Lee .... *Scaramanga*
Britt Ekland .... *Mary Goodnight*
Maud Adams .... *Andrea*
Herve Villechaize .... *Nick Nack*
Clifton James .... *Sheriff Pepper*
Bernard Lee .... *M*
Lois Maxwell .... *Miss Moneypenny*

Arch villain Scaramanga uses solid gold bullets to despatch his enemies, and Bond is charged with the mission of finding this dastardly international assassin who is holed up in a far eastern island hideaway. Caught up in the action are *Live And Let Die*'s Sheriff Pepper, special agent and romance interest Mary Goodnight, and Scaramanga's short sidekick Nick Nack.

All the regulars are here, including Bernard Lee, Lois Maxwell and Desmond Llewellyn.

John Barry again wielded the baton for the music, having only missed the first Bond, *Dr No*, in 1962.

Music: 'The Man with the Golden Gun' (Lulu)

Video availability

The Top Five

Week of 28 December 1974
1. The Man with the Golden Gun
2. Airport
3. Earthquake
4. Murder on the Orient Express
5. The Island at the Top of the World

THE TOWERING INFERNO

8 February 1975	7 weeks

Distributor:	Twentieth Century-Fox
Director:	John Guillermin, Irwin Allen
Producer:	Irwin Allen
Screenplay:	Stirling Silliphant
Music:	John Williams

CAST
Steve McQueen ... *Fire Chief O'Hallorhan*
Paul Newman .... *Doug Roberts*
William Holden .... *Jim Duncan*
Faye Dunaway .... *Susan*
Fred Astaire .... *Harlee Claiborne*
Susan Blakely .... *Patty Simmons*
Richard Chamberlain .... *Simmons*
O.J. Simpson ...... *Security Chief Jernigan*
Robert Wagner .... *Bigelow*
Jennifer Jones .... *Lisolette*
Robert Vaughn .... *Senator Parker*

It is the opening night party of the world's tallest building. The rich and famous of San Francisco congregate in the tower to toast the success of its owner, Jim Duncan. But disaster looms. The supervisor of construction, Richard Chamberlain, cut corners during construction to save money and the wiring is faulty. When fire breaks out panic sets in and it's a race against time to save the guests. Steve McQueen, O.J. Simpson and the architect Paul Newman put their brains and brawn together to find an all-or-nothing solution.

Because both Fox and Warners bought the rights to similar novels, Richard Stern's *The Tower* and Thomas Scortia's *The Glass Inferno*, the two studios decided to join forces and make one picture derived from combining the two stories.

Faye Dunaway earnt a reputation for holding up filming while she altered her make-up or adjusted her hair. Her timekeeping was abysmal until William Holden expressed his disapproval in no uncertain terms.

Some 57 sets were built for the movie, a record for a single film. By completion of filming, only 8 were left standing.

Fred Astaire thought long and hard before making a guest appearance as a confidence trickster, this being a very difficult part for him. After some gentle persuasion from his family he took the role, which won him Golden Globe and BAFTA awards.

Academy Awards: Best Cinematography (Fred Koenekamp and Joseph Biroc), Best Editing (Harold F. Kress and Carl Kress), Best Song – 'We May Never Love Like This Again' (Al Kasha and Joel Hirschhorn, music and lyrics)

Music: 'We May Never Love Like This Again'

Video availability

The Top Five

Week of 8 February 1975
1. The Towering Inferno
2. Earthquake
3. The Man with the Golden Gun
4. Emmanuelle
5. Murder on the Orient Express

FUNNY LADY

29 March 1975	1 week

Distributor:	Columbia
Director:	Herbert Ross
Producer:	Ray Stark
Screenplay:	Jay Presson Allen, Arnold Schulman
Music:	John Kander, Fred Ebb (Original songs) Peter Matz (Music arrangement)

CAST
Barbra Streisand . . . . *Fanny Brice*
James Caan . . . . *Billy Rose*
Omar Sharif . . . . *Nick Arnstein*
Roddy McDowall . . . . *Bobby*
Ben Vereen . . . . *Bert Robbins*
Carole Wells . . . . *Norma Butler*
Larry Gates . . . . *Bernard Baruch*

This sequel to the 1968 smash *Funny Girl* sees Streisand once again in the role of Fanny Brice, with more triumphs on stage but endless problems in her personal life. She divorces gambler Nick Arnstein and on the rebound meets and marries showman Billy Rose during the Depression years. The marriage is unfortunately destined for failure, with Billy's infidelities and Fanny's professional commitments keeping them apart.

Director Herbert Ross was once a dancer and chore-ographer who came into the movie business as dance director on the 1954 movie *Carmen Jones*. He choreographed *Funny Girl* and moved up to direct this sequel. He previously directed Barbra Streisand in the 1970 film *The Owl and the Pussycat*.

Streisand made the film in response to Liza Minnelli's award-winning performance in *Cabaret* and her TV show, *Liza With a Z*. Streisand was painfully aware that Minnelli was moving in on her musical territory and wanted to make the strongest possible stand.

Music: 'How Lucky Can You Get', 'I Found a Million Dollar baby (In a Five and Ten Cent Store)'. 'Me and my Shadow', 'It's Only a Paper Moon', 'Clap Hands Here Comes Charley', 'Am I Blue'

Video availability

The Top Five

Week of 29 March 1975
1. Funny Lady
2. The Towering Inferno
3. Earthquake
4. Emmanuelle
5. The Land that Time Forgot

TOMMY

5 April 1975	14 weeks*

Distributor:	Hemdale
Director:	Ken Russell
Producer:	Robert Stigwood
Screenplay:	Ken Russell
Music:	Pete Townshend, John Entwistle, Keith Moon

CAST

Ann-Margret	Nora Walker
Oliver Reed	Frank Hobbs
Roger Daltrey	Tommy
Elton John	Pinball Wizard
Keith Moon	Uncle Ernie
Jack Nicholson	Specialist
Pete Townshend, Roger Daltrey, John Entwistle, Keith Moon	The Who

The story of Tommy, a deaf, dumb and blind kid is told entirely in song. Tommy shuts out the rest of the world after seeing his real father killed in a fight with his stepfather. His mother takes him to a doctor, but no treatment seems to help until he discovers how to play the pinball machine, using his sense of smell, which changes his life. He even manages to beat the pinball wizard.

The Who's rock opera had an all-star cast, including Eric Clapton, Robert Powell, Paul Nicholas and Tina Turner. Ann-Margret, who plays Tommy's mother, was Oscar nominated for Best Actress but was beaten by Louise Fletcher for her performance in One Flew Over the Cuckoo's Nest.

The Who originally recorded the album 'Tommy' in 1969 when it reached number two in the UK album chart. The single from the album, 'Pinball Wizard', was a top-five hit for the band, staying in the charts for 13 weeks.

The heavy-handed South African censors cut much of the film in the belief that it was 'pagan' and thus a threat to the country's spiritual well-being, much to director Ken Russell's disgust.

Music: 'Tommy Can You Hear Me', 'Pinball Wizard', 'See Me Feel Me', 'I'm Free', 'The Acid Queen', 'Cousin Kevin', 'Do You Think It's Alright?', 'It's a Boy'

Video availability

The Top Five

Week of 5 April 1975
1. Tommy
2. Funny Lady
3. Earthquake
4. The Towering Inferno
5. The Four Musketeers

THE GODFATHER PART II

24 May 1975	5 weeks

Distributor:	Paramount
Director:	Francis Ford Coppola
Producer:	Francis Ford Coppola
Screenplay:	Francis Ford Coppola, Mario Puzo
Music:	Nino Rota (Composer) Carmine Coppola (Conductor)

CAST

Al Pacino	Michael Corleone
Robert Duvall	Tom Hagen
Diane Keaton	Kay
Robert De Niro	Vito Corleone
John Cazale	Fredo Corleone
Talia Shire	Connie Corleone
Lee Strasberg	Hyman Roth
James Caan	Sonny

Both a sequel and a prequel to the original God-father movie, Godfather Part II moves backwards and forwards in time. Director Francis Ford Coppola intercuts the reign of Don Michael Corleone as family leader, with stories of the earlier life of his father, Vito, in New York and Sicily in 1901, when he was the only survivor of a family vendetta. The later years find Michael Corleone pronounced as the unchallenged don, feared by other families but estranged from the wife he still loves.

Paramount wanted Marlon Brando to return to his previous role but he wanted too much money and was also having a major dispute with the studio head. His replacement, Robert De Niro, watched the original movie dozens of times, trying to pick up some of Brando's mannerisms for his own part.

Al Pacino, after seeing an early draft of the script, insisted his character was toned down.

In critical, Oscar and Box Office terms, this was the most successful sequel ever made. Coupled with the success of French Connection 2 in the same year, the sequel, previously considered a cheap rip-off, became respectable.

The Top Five

Week of 24 May 1975
1. The Godfather Part II
2. Tommy
3. Shampoo
4. Paper Tiger
5. Earthquake

Academy Awards: Best film (Producer Francis Ford Coppola), Best Direction (Francis Ford Coppola), Best Supporting Actor (Robert De Niro), Best Screenplay Adaptation (Francis Ford Coppola and Mario Puzo), Best Art Direction (Dean Tavoularis and Angelo Graham), Set Decoration (George R. Nelson), Best Original Dramatic Score (Nino Rota and Carmine Coppola)

Video availability

FRENCH CONNECTION II

2 August 1975	1 week

Distributor:	Twentieth Century-Fox
Director:	John Frankenheimer
Producer:	Robert L. Rosen
Screenplay:	Robert and Laurie Dillon, Alexander Jacobs
Music:	Don Ellis

CAST
Gene Hackman . . . . *Popeye Doyle*
Fernando Rey . . . . *Charnier*
Bernard Fresson . . . . *Inspector Barthelemy*
Jean-Pierre Castaldi, Charles Millot
Barthelemy Aides
Cathleen Nesbitt . . . . *Mrs Charnier*

New York cop Popeye Doyle is back with an assignment that takes him again to Marseilles in the search for drugs baron Charnier. His new partners Barthelemy, Raoul and Miletto have been the victims of an elaborate Underworld set-up and Doyle is less than pleased. Captured and pumped full of drugs, Doyle has to undergo an unpleasant withdrawal and rehabilitation programme before he can again take up the chase. Once recovered, he is back on the trail of his Private Enemy Number One, and finally catches his prey after a long and exciting chase through the teeming streets of Marseilles.

The film was the sequel to the hugely successful *French Connection* (1971), which won Hackman his first Oscar.

Video availability

The Top Five

Week of 2 August 1975
1. French Connection II
2. Tommy
3. Hennessy
4. Emmanuelle
5. Lady and the Tramp

THE DROWNING POOL

23 August 1975	1 week

Distributor:	Warner
Director:	Stuart Rosenberg
Producer:	Lawrence Turman, David Foster
Screenplay:	Tracy Keenan Wynn, Lorenzo Semple Jr, Walter Hill
Music:	Michael Small, Charles Fox

CAST
Paul Newman . . . . *Lew Harper*
Joanne Woodward . . . . *Iris Devereaux*
Tony Franciosa . . . . . . *Detective Broussard*
Murray Hamilton . . . . *Kilbourne*
Gail Strickland . . . . *Mavis Kilbourne*
Melanie Griffith . . . . . *Schuyler Devereaux*
Linda Hayes . . . . *Gretchen*

Paul Newman returns to the part of Private Detective Lew Harper. He is investigating a blackmail letter sent to the husband of his former New Orleans lover, claiming that she has been unfaithful. He has to battle through a sea of hookers, gangsters and the murdered mother of the victim before discovering the source of the letters.

Paul Newman first played the part of Lew Harper in the 1966 film *Harper*. The detective's name in the Ross MacDonald novel, from which both films were adapted, was Archer. The reason for the name change was Newman's superstition. His two most successful movies had titles beginning with 'H' – *The Hustler* and *Hud* – and he felt the letter might still be lucky. It was. Both *Harper* and the following year's *Hombre* did well for him.

The Top Five

Week of 23 August 1975
1. The Drowning Pool
2. Tommy
3. Shampoo
4. French Connection II
5. Emmanuelle

Melanie Griffith, who is the daughter of Tippi Hedren and the partner of Don Johnson (of *Miami Vice* fame), made her film debut in *Night Moves* (1973), appearing topless 33 minutes into the picture. She appeared in her first TV commercial when she was nine months old.

THE EIGER SANCTION

30 August 1975	2 weeks*

Distributor:	Universal
Director:	Clint Eastwood
Producer:	Robert Daley
Screenplay:	Hal Dresner, Warren B. Murphy, Rod Whitaker
Music:	John Williams

CAST

Clint Eastwood	*Jonathan Hemlock*
George Kennedy	*Ben Bowman*
Vonetta McGee	*Jemima Brown*
Jack Cassidy	*Miles Mellough*
Heidi Bruhl	*Mrs Montaigne*
Thayer David	*Dragon*
Reiner Schoene	*Freytag*
Michael Grimm	*Meyer*

Clint Eastwood is Jonathan Hemlock, a retired assassin now employed as an art teacher in a small college. He is called back to work for the CII, a secret intelligence organization, in order to head an assignment in Switzerland. Tempted by the offer of a valuable painting to add to his collection, he agrees to the sanction (a euphemism for assassination) but finds he has to climb up the treacherous north face of the Eiger mountain in order to get his man. To prepare himself for the ordeal, he travels to Arizona to visit his old friend Ben who is an expert climber, seeking advice and training. Arriving in Switzerland the two meet up with the rest of the climbing team, which both Ben and Jonathan are to join. As the ascent begins Hemlock still does not know who his victim is.

To some it's a mystery why Clint Eastwood made the *Eiger Sanction*. The original story's main character is a mild-mannered art teacher, so the screenplay had to be drastically changed to fit Eastwood's qualities.

The climbing sequences, and in particular the ascent up the north face of the Eiger, meant a director with climbing experience was needed. As there was none available Eastwood took on the task himself. He is also credited with performing all his own climbing stunts without doubles.

Video availability

The Top Five

Week of 30 August 1975
1. The Eiger Sanction
2. Tommy
3. The Drowning Pool
4. Shampoo
5. French Connection II

ROLLERBALL

13 September 1975	3 weeks

Distributor:	United Artists
Director:	Norman Jewison
Producer:	Norman Jewison
Screenplay:	William Harrison
Music:	André Previn

CAST

James Caan	*Jonathan E.*
John Houseman	*Bartholomew*
Maud Adams	*Ella*
John Beck	*Moonpie*
Moses Gunn	*Cletus*
Pamela Hensley	*Mackie*
Barbara Trentham	*Daphne*
Ralph Richardson	*Librarian*

This action-packed movie features the fast and furious rollerball game of life and death. Played by two teams, each consisting of seven roller-skaters and three motor cyclists, the object of the game is to throw a large steel ball into your own magnetic goal. Caan's Houston team have won through to the

The Top Five

Week of 13 September 1975
1. Rollerball
2. The Eiger Sanction
3. Tommy
4. Emmanuelle
5. Shampoo

quarter finals of the World Championship but the all-powerful Corporation want him to retire from the game. His team win their way to the Tokyo semi-finals and the Corporation change the game's rules and the game then becomes much more violent and deadly.

The movie, based on a short story, 'Rollerball Murder', by Paul Schrader, ran an advertising campaign 'In the not too distant future, wars will no longer exist. But there will be Rollerball.'

Video availability

In the year 2018, James Caan takes part in the world sport of Rollerball, *in which death is a major part of the game's enjoyment.*

THREE DAYS OF THE CONDOR

4 October 1975		4 weeks

Distributor:	Paramount
Director:	Sydney Pollack
Producer:	Stanley Schneider
Screenplay:	Lorenzo Semple Jr, David Rayfiel
Music:	David Grusin

CAST
Robert Redford .... *Turner*
Faye Dunaway .... *Kathy*
Cliff Robertson .... *Higgins*
Max Von Sydow .... *Joubert*
John Houseman .... *Wabash*
Addison Powell .... *Atwood*
Michael Kane .... *Wicks*

In this gripping political thriller Robert Redford is Joe Turner, a special agent working as a reader for the Literary Historical Society which is a front for the CIA. One morning he leaves his Manhattan offices to buy lunch and returns to find all his associates have been murdered. He learns it's an inside plot by an agency member who has been planning the massacre for some time and has to go on the run to escape with his own life. Turner manages to expose the whole affair by kidnapping an innocent press photographer, Kathy Hale, and forcing her to help him get newspaper coverage for his revelations.

The film was based on James Grady's book, *Six Days of the Condor* but underwent a time compression to speed up the action. The movie gained extra momentum due to publicity surrounding the inside workings of the CIA at the time of release.

Video availability

THE JUNGLE BOOK

1 November 1975	11 weeks*

Distributor:	Walt Disney
Director:	Wolfgang Reitherman
Producer:	Walt Disney
Screenplay:	Larry Clemmons, Ralph Wright, Ken Anderson, Vance Gerry
Music:	George Bruns

CAST (Voices)
Phil Harris . . . . *Baloo the Bear*
Sebastian Cabot . . . *Bagheera the Panther*
Louis Prima . . . . *King Louis of the Apes*
Sterling Holloway . . . . *Kaa the Snake*

George Sanders . . . . *Shere Khan the Tiger*
Bruce Reitherman . . *Mowgli the Man Cub*
J. Pat O'Malley *Colonel Hathi the Elephant*

(A re-release; see 1967)

LISZTOMANIA

22 November 1975	2 weeks

Distributor:	Warner
Director:	Ken Russell
Producer:	Roy Baird, David Puttnam
Screenplay:	Ken Russell
Music:	Rick Wakeman, Jonathan Benson, Franz Liszt, Richard Wagner

CAST
Roger Daltrey . . . . *Franz Liszt*
Sara Kestelman . . . . *Princess Carolyn*
Paul Nicholas . . . . *Richard Wagner*
Fiona Lewis . . . . *Countess Marie*
Veronica Quilligan . . . . *Cosima*
Nell Campbell . . . . *Olga*
Andrew Reilly . . . . *Hans von Bulow*

Franz Liszt is portrayed in Ken Russell's film as one of music's first teen idols. Scenes of audience hysteria at his concerts with screaming girls drowning out the music are plentiful. Backstage many of Liszt's contemporaries on the music scene are introduced, including Chopin, Mendelssohn, Rossini and Strauss. We also meet Liszt's close friend, the revolutionary Richard Wagner, who, after having his career launched by Liszt, proceeds to infuriate everyone from the Pope (Ringo Starr) down.

The music by Liszt and Wagner was adapted for the film by Rick Wakeman who has a brief cameo as a beer-drinking monster. The music featured in the film includes 'Chopsticks', 'Fantasia', 'Love's Dream' and 'Rape, Pillage and Burn'.

Lisztomania was the first mainstream movie to use the new Dolby optical stereo sound system, now used by most major film-makers.

Music: 'Love's Dream', 'Peace at Last', 'Orpheus Song' (Roger Daltrey), 'Hell' (Linda Lewis), 'Excelsior Song' (Paul Nicholas)

Video availability

LENNY

6 December 1975	2 weeks

Distributor: United Artists
Director: Bob Fosse
Producer: Marvin Worth
Screenplay: Julian Barry
Music: Ralph Burns

CAST
Dustin Hoffman . . . . *Lenny Bruce*
Valerie Perrine . . . . *Honey Bruce*
Jan Miner . . . . *Sally Marr*
Stanley Beck . . . . *Artie Silver*
Gary Morton . . . . *Sherman Hart*
Rashel Novikoff . . . . *Aunt Mema*

Dustin Hoffman plays the central character in this biographical film about the life of comedian Lenny Bruce. The story picks up in 1951 when Lenny is working as a second-rate stand-up comic who seems destined for obscurity. He falls in love with and marries stripper Honey Harlow and together they set up a double act. The act goes nowhere but when she's dropped from the act, and Bruce's jokes get a little near the knuckle people start flocking to see him in the expectation of being outraged. Busted by the police for using the 'c' word, his fame starts to spread until he hits the skids in the early 1960s and dies broke and broken in 1966.

Cliff Gorman, who played Lenny on Broadway, was considered for the role, as were Al Pacino and Ron Liebman. Despite his Oscar nomination, Hoffman was deeply dissatisfied with elements of his performance and didn't attend the Academy Awards ceremony, which the Hollywood establishment took as a great insult. Tuesday Weld and Ann-Margret were candidates for the part of Lenny's wife.

Top Twenty Films of 1975

1 The Towering Inferno
2 The Exorcist
3 The Man with the Golden Gun
4 Emmanuelle
5 Earthquake
6 Airport '75
7 Murder on the Orient Express
8 Papillon
9 Stardust
10 Island at the Top of the World
11 Confessions of a Window Cleaner
12 Tommy
13 Blazing Saddles
14 The Land that Time Forgot
15 Death Wish
16 The Four Musketeers
17 Freebie and the Bean
18 The Lady and the Tramp
19 Monty Python and the Holy Grail
20 Rollerball

The film was shot in black and white by director Bob Fosse who had also made *Sweet Charity* and *Cabaret*.

Video availability

The Top Five

Week of 6 December 1975
1. Lenny
2. Jungle Book
3. Three Days of the Condor
4. Tommy
5. Lisztomania

BARRY LYNDON

20 December 1975	2 weeks

Distributor: Warner
Director: Stanley Kubrick
Producer: Stanley Kubrick
Screenplay: Stanley Kubrick
Music: Leonard Rosenman

CAST
Ryan O'Neal . *Redmond Barry/Barry Lyndon*
Marisa Berenson . . . . *Lady Lyndon*
Patrick Magee . . . . *The Chevalier*

Hardy Kruger . . . . *Capt. Polzdorf*
Gay Hamilton . . . . *Nora*
Leonard Rossiter . . . . *Capt. Quin*
Godfrey Quigley . . . . *Capt. Grogan*
Arthur O'Sullivan . . . . *Highwayman*

Ryan O'Neal plays the central character in this story of the 18th-century Irish social climber with a hunger for success. After leaving home he teams up with a highwayman, Captain Polzdorf, and a spy, who teach him about the less agreeable side of life. He uses his charm to join European high society and marries a wealthy widow, Lady Lyndon, who Barry sees as a meal ticket to a better life.

The film was an adaptation of a William Thackeray novel.

Academy Awards: Best Cinematography (John Alcott), Best Art Direction (Ken Adam and Roy Walker), Set Decoration (Vernon Dixon), Best Costume Design (Ulla-Britt Soderlund and Milena Canonero), Best Music Scoring – Adaptation (Leonard Rosenman)

The Top Five

Week of 20 December 1975
1. Barry Lyndon
2. Lenny
3. The Streetfighter
4. Jungle Book
5. Emmanuelle

Video availability

JAWS

3 January 1976	9 weeks

Distributor: Universal
Director: Steven Spielberg
Producer: Richard D. Zanuck, David Brown
Screenplay: Peter Benchley, Carl Gottlieb
Music: John Williams

CAST
Roy Scheider . . . . Chief Martin Brody
Robert Shaw . . . . Quint
Richard Dreyfuss . . . . Matt Hooper
Lorraine Gary . . . . Mrs Brody
Murray Hamilton . . . . Mayor Vaughn
Carl Gottlieb . . . . Editor Meadows
Jeffrey Kramer . . . . . . Policeman Hendricks
Susan Backlinie . . . . Chrissie

The small East Coast beach resort of Amity is paralysed with fear after discovering that they are playing host to a Great White Shark with an appetite for bathers. Police chief Brody's job of protecting the town's inhabitants is made difficult by an obstructive Mayor Vaughn who is more worried about losing seasonal trade. Local fisherman Quint is hired to catch the shark that has been terrorising the swimmers and he is accompanied by scientist Matt Hooper and Brody. The struggle to capture and kill the malevolent shark takes the men to the edge of death.

This truly gripping film, based on Peter Benchley's best-seller, became Steven Spielberg's first big hit after *Sugarland Express*, and his first number one. It made great use of John Williams's music with its strident theme which has now been parodied many times. Watch out for author Benchley in a small cameo as a TV newsman.

The film spawned three sequels: *Jaws 2* (1978), *Jaws 3-D* (1983) and *Jaws 4 – The Revenge* starring Michael Caine. The location shooting of the shark movie prevented Caine from picking up his Oscar for *Hannah and Her Sisters* in person.

Academy Awards: Best Editing (Verna Fields), Best Sound (Robert Hoyt, Roger Heman, Earl Madery and John Carter), Best Original Score (John Williams)

Video availability

The Top Five

Week of 3 January 1976
1. Jaws
2. Barry Lyndon
3. Dog Day Afternoon
4. The Man Who Would Be King
5. Once is Not Enough

ONE FLEW OVER THE CUCKOO'S NEST

6 March 1976	8 weeks*

Distributor: United Artists
Director: Milos Forman
Producer: Saul Zaentz, Michael Douglas
Screenplay: Lawrence Hauben, Bo Goldman
Music: Jack Nitzsche

CAST
Jack Nicholson . . . . . . Randel P. McMurphy
Louise Fletcher . . . . Nurse Ratched
William Redfield . . . . Harding
Dean Brooks . . . . Dr Spivey
Scatman Crothers . . . . Orderly Turkle
Danny De Vito . . . . Martini
William Duell . . . . Sefelt
Brad Dourif . . . . Billy Bibbit

Brody (Roy Scheider) and Quint (Robert Shaw) help the people of Amity Island hunt down the shark that has been attacking holiday makers taking a dip in the ocean in Jaws.

Jack Nicholson stars as a convict who opts to enter a mental hospital rather than stay in prison. Once inside, however, he wreaks havoc and confusion by questioning the authority of the hospital's supervisors and attempts to shatter the inmates' apathy towards their situation by introducing them to the joys of basketball. Eventually they side with him against the tyrannical ward supervisor, Nurse Ratched, when he decides they should watch the World Series on TV instead of working. Matters come to a head when he leads several patients away from the hospital on a fishing trip. The authorities decide he is seriously disturbed and dangerous and should stay in the institution for the rest of his life. The suicide of a young patient is blamed on Nicholson and before he can realize his plan to escape, undergoes a lobotomy.

Nicholson and De Vito worked together many years later on *Hoffa*, and they both starred as the villains in two batman movies: Nicholson as the Joker in *Batman* and De Vito as the Penguin in *Batman Returns*.

One Flew Over the Cuckoo's Nest was one of only two films that have won all of the top five Oscars

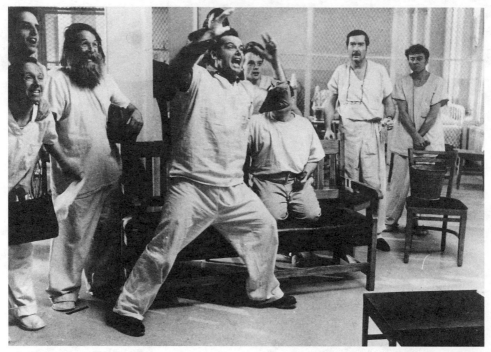

In order to avoid working on a prison farm, convict Randel P. McMurphy (Jack Nicholson) fakes madness in order to gain entrance to a mental institution, where he brings new life to the community in One Flew Over the Cuckoo's Nest.

(Picture, Director, Screenplay, Actor, Actress). The other was *It Happened One Night* (1934).

Academy Awards: Best Film (Producers Mike Douglas and Saul Zaentz), Best Direction (Milos Forman), Best Actor (Jack Nicholson), Best Actress (Louise Fletcher), Best Screenplay (Lawrence Hauben and Bo Goldman)

Video availability

The Top Five

Week of 6 March 1976
1. One Flew Over the Cuckoo's Nest
2. Jaws
3. The Return of the Pink Panther
4. Farewell My Lovely
5. Hustle

SHOUT AT THE DEVIL

24 April 1976	1 week

Distributor:	Tonav/Hemdale
Director:	Peter Hunt
Producer:	Michael Klinger
Screenplay:	Wilbur Smith, Stanley Price, Alistair Reid
Music:	Maurice Jarre

CAST
Lee Marvin . . . . Flynn
Roger Moore . . . . Sebastian
Barbara Parkins . . . . Rosa
Ian Holm . . . . Mohammed
Rene Kolldehoff . . . . Fleischer
Horst Janson . . . . Kyller

Karl Michael Vogler . . . . Von Kleine

Moore and Marvin star as two ivory hunters in East Africa in the years before World War I. Marvin is the gin-swigging Irish-American who hires suave Englishman Moore to help him in his poach-

The Top Five

Week of 24 April 1976
1. Shout at the Devil
2. One Flew Over the Cuckoo's Nest
3. The Slipper and the Rose
4. Mahogany
5. Jaws

ing business. The area's German commissioner vows to hunt them down while at the same time preparing for the oncoming war. When war breaks out, Moore falls in love with Marvin's daughter but his domestic life is interrupted when the British Army hire Moore and Marvin to hunt out the Germans from their inland hiding places.

Shout at the Devil was Roger Moore's second number one film for director Peter Hunt, the first had been *Gold* (1974). Peter Hunt had also been responsible for a previous number one, the Bond hit from 1969 *On Her Majesty's Secret Service*.

Video availability

ALL THE PRESIDENT'S MEN

8 May 1976	10 weeks

Distributor:	Warner
Director:	Alan J. Pakula
Producer:	Walter Coblenz
Screenplay:	William Goldman
Music:	David Shire

CAST
Dustin Hoffman . . . . *Carl Bernstein*
Robert Redford . . . . *Bob Woodward*
Jack Warden . . . . *Harry Rosenfeld*
Martin Balsam . . . . *Howard Simons*
Hal Holbrook . . . . *Deep Throat*
Jason Robards . . . . *Ben Bradlee*
Jane Alexander . . . . *Bookkeeper*

In this big screen adaptation of the Watergate exposé Hoffman and Redford play the two *Washington Post* reporters Carl Bernstein and Bob Woodward. Once they make the connection with Deep Throat who has inside information, Bernstein and Woodward follow the murky trail that links President Nixon to the Watergate break in. Their investigative journalism gets bogged down when

the world and their own superiors on the paper suggest the allegations are figments of their imaginations.

The film features the great pairing of two of Hollywood's biggest stars, Redford and Hoffman, both with a great long list of number one smash movies to their credit. Interestingly Redford is said to have turned down Hoffman's part in *The Graduate*!

Academy Awards: Best Supporting Actor (Jason Robards), Best Screenplay (William Goldman), Best Art Direction (George Jenkins), Best Set Decoration (George Gaines), Best Sound (Arthur Piantadosi, Les Fresholtz, Dick Alexander and Jim Webb)

Video availability

The Top Five
Week of 8 May 1976
1. All the President's Men
2. One Flew Over the Cuckoo's Nest
3. Shout at the Devil
4. The Man Who Fell to Earth
5. Mahogany

THE MISSOURI BREAKS

17 July 1976	2 weeks

Distributor:	United Artists
Director:	Arthur Penn
Producer:	Elliott Kastner, Robert M. Sherman
Screenplay:	Thomas McGuane
Music:	John Williams

CAST
Marlon Brando . . . . *Lee Clayton*
Jack Nicholson . . . . *Tom Logan*
Kathleen Lloyd . . . . *Jane Braxton*
Randy Quaid . . . . *Little Tod*
Frederick Forrest . . . . *Cary*
Harry Dean Stanton . . . . *Calvin*
John McLiam . . . . *David Braxton*

Set in the lush Montana countryside, *The Missouri Breaks* tells the tale of horse thief Tom Logan and his gang who buy a ranch for their stolen horses. Lee Clayton is a vicious gunman hired by the local sheriff to shoot Logan's gang. Romance beckons briefly between Logan and ranch boss Braxton's daughter, Jane, but the manly struggle continues against the backdrop of the Missouri river and mountains.

The Top Five
Week of 17 July 1976
1. The Missouri Breaks
2. Lipstick
3. All The President's Men
4. One Flew Over the Cuckoo's Nest
5. Emmanuelle

Brando's character of Lee Clayton is both comic and menacing. At one point he stalks his prey in a dress and bonnet, and in another he dedicates a love song and a kiss to his horse.

The film's success came hot on the heels of

Nicholson's other hit that year, *One Flew Over the Cuckoo's Nest*. It was also the second successful film score of the year for John Williams. He had just completed the much-emulated music for *Jaws*.

Video availability

Horse thief Tom Logan (Jack Nicholson) lies wounded after a shoot-out with the mercurial gunslinger Lee Clayton (Marlon Brando) in The Missouri Breaks.

BUGSY MALONE

31 July 1976	1 week

Distributor: Rank
Director: Alan Parker
Producer: Alan Marshall
Screenplay: Alan Parker
Music: Paul Williams

CAST
Scott Baio . . . . *Bugsy Malone*
Jodie Foster . . . . *Tallulah*
Florrie Dugger . . . . *L. Blousey*
John Cassisi . . . . *Fat Sam*
Martin Lev . . . . *Dandy Dan*

Paul Murphy . . . . *Leroy*

In this tongue-in-cheek gangster musical all the characters are played by children. In 1929 Fat Sam fights with Dandy Dan for the hand of Tallulah using splatter guns, which fire ice cream instead of bullets! All the old gangster movie clichés are here but this is a charming and good-natured film which marries the two genres, gangster and musical, with novel effect.

Bugsy Malone was Jodie Foster's first number one, which was made when she was 14. Among her other hit movies are *Silence of the Lambs* (1991), *Sommersby* (1992) and *Maverick* (1994). She's one of a handful of actresses to win two Oscars; the first for *The Accused* in 1988 and the second for *The Silence of the Lambs*. She is also an accomplished director, debuting with *Little Man Tate* (1991).

Music: 'Bad Guys', 'Bugsy Malone', 'Ordinary Fool', 'You Give a Little Love', 'I'm Feeling Fine', 'My Name is Tallulah', 'Tomorrow'

Video availability

THE MESSAGE (Mohammad, Messenger of God)

7 August 1976	1 week

Distributor:	Filmco International
Director:	Moustapha Akkad
Producer:	Moustapha Akkad
Screenplay:	H.A.L. Craig
Music:	Maurice Jarre

CAST
Anthony Quinn	Hamza
Irene Papas	Hind
Michael Ansara	Bu-Sofyan
Johnny Sekka	Bilal
Michael Forest	Khalid
Damien Thomas	Zaid
Garrick Hagon	Ammar

This epic historical drama takes on the weighty subject of the birth of Islam. The Prophet Mohammad is never seen on screen but his followers, including Hamza, go into battle against the old order. After several bloody battles the disciples overturn the old rulers and make a triumphal entry into the holy city of Mecca. There is plenty of action amongst the storytelling in this true account of the beginnings of Islam.

Anthony Quinn, who was born in Mexico, has made a long career playing other nationalities. He was a Greek in *Zorba the Greek* (1964), a Mexican in *Viva Zapata* (1952), a Russian in *Shoes of the Fisherman* (1968), an Italian in *The Secret of Santa Vittoria* (1969) and French in *The Hunchback of Notre Dame* (1956).

Video availability

THE OUTLAW JOSEY WALES

14 August 1976	2 weeks

Distributor:	Warner
Director:	Clint Eastwood
Producer:	Robert Daley
Screenplay:	Phil Kaufman, Sonia Chernus
Music:	Jerry Fielding

CAST
Clint Eastwood	Josey Wales
Chief Dan George	Lone Watie
Sondra Locke	Laura Lee
Bill McKinney	Terrill
John Vernon	Fletcher
Paula Trueman	Grandma Sarah
Sam Bottoms	Jamie

Set in the American Civil War, Eastwood plays a farmer whose family has been murdered by bandits. Taking the law into his own hands he tracks down the murderers and kills them one by one. He enlists the help of an old Indian chief (Chief Dan George) to help him hunt the killers. In his search for the killers he meets a number of waifs and strays, including Sondra Locke, whom he helps out. These encounters help to heal his emotional wounds, but the violence continues until his quest is done.

The Outlaw Josey Wales was the second of Clint Eastwood's directed films to hit the number one spot. *The Eiger Sanction* (1975) was the first and his third, fourth and fifth came with *Sudden Impact* (1983), *Pale Rider* (1985), and *Unforgiven* (1992).

Sondra Locke worked with Eastwood for the first time on the *Outlaw Josey Wales*, and, after they became lovers, the two worked on a series of films together: *The Gauntlet* (1977), *Every Which Way But Loose* (1978), *Bronco Billy* (1980), *Any Which way You Can* (1980) and *Sudden Impact* (1983) after which they split up.

Video availability

The Top Five

Week of 14 August 1976
1. The Outlaw Josey Wales
2. The Message
3. Bugsy Malone
4. All the President's Men
5. Lipstick

FAMILY PLOT

28 August 1976	1 week

Distributor:	Universal
Director:	Alfred Hitchcock
Producer:	Alfred Hitchcock
Screenplay:	Ernest Lehman
Music:	John Williams

CAST
Karen Black . . . . *Fran*
Bruce Dern . . . . *Lumley*
Barbara Harris . . . . *Blanche*
William Devane . . . . *Adamson*
Ed Lauter . . . . *Maloney*
Cathleen Nesbitt . . . . *Julia Rainbird*
Katherine Helmond . . . . *Mrs Maloney*
Warren J. Kemmerling . . . . *Grandison*

*F*amily Plot, Alfred Hitchcock's final film, is a comedy-thriller based on the novel *The Rainbird Pattern* by Victor Canning. A phoney psychic (Harris) and her partner (Dern) try to find a missing heir to the vast Rainbird family fortune. They become involved with two sinister criminals (Devane and Black) and soon realize they are out of their depth. However, after a series of mishaps, adventures, and high-speed car chases the suspense never lets up until the final moments.

This was Alfred Hitchcock's 53rd and final film after a career which had begun in 1925. Most of his films reached the top spot and his last number one had been in 1972 with *Frenzy*. Among the other classic films he directed were *The Thirty-Nine Steps*, *The Lady Vanishes*, *Spellbound*, *Strangers on a Train*, *Vertigo*, *Dial M for Murder* and, of course, *Psycho*.

Video availability

The Top Five

Week of 28 August 1976
1. Family Plot
2. The Message
3. The Outlaw Josey Wales
4. Taxi Driver
5. Bugsy Malone

MURDER BY DEATH

4 September 1976	2 weeks

Distributor:	Columbia
Director:	Robert Moore
Producer:	Ray Stark
Screenplay:	Neil Simon
Music:	Dave Grusin

CAST
Eileen Brennan . . . . *Tess Skeffington*
Truman Capote . . . . *Lionel Twain*
James Coco . . . . *Milo Perrier*
Elsa Lanchester . . . . *Jessica Marbles*
Peter Falk . . . . *Sam Diamond*
Alec Guinness . . . . *Butler Bensonmum*
David Niven . . . . *Dick Charleston*
Peter Sellers . . . . *Sidney Wang*
Maggie Smith . . . . *Dora Charleston*

*I*n this star-studded comedy the world's finest detectives are invited to the home of Sheridan Whiteside, a wealthy whodunnit fan who sets them the task of solving a series of mysteries. Recognizable screen detectives are parodied by the cast. David Niven and Maggie Smith are Dick and Dora Charleston, a take-off of the *Thin Man* characters Nick and Nora Charles, Peter Falk is Sam Diamond, taking off Bogart's Sam Spade from *The Maltese Falcon*, and Elsa Lanchester is Jessica Marbles, based loosely around Agatha Christie's fictional detective, Miss Marple. This great ensemble piece includes Truman Capote as one of the detectives.

Author Truman Capote had previously written *Breakfast at Tiffany's* and *In Cold Blood*, but *Murder By Death* saw his first film appearance as an actor.

Neil Simon's prolific output has ensured a steady stream of Broadway stage successes and movie hits including *Barefoot in the Park* (1967) with Jane Fonda and Robert Redford, *The Sunshine Boys* (1975) with George Burns and Walter Matthau and *The Goodbye Girl* (1978) with Marsh Mason and Richard Dreyfuss.

Video availability

The Top Five

Week of 4 September 1976
1. Murder By Death
2. The Message
3. The Outlaw Josey Wales
4. Family Plot
5. Taxi Driver

DRUM

18 September 1976	1 week

Distributor:	Dino De Laurentiis Corp
Director:	Steve Carver
Producer:	Ralph Serpe
Screenplay:	Norman Wexler
Music:	Charlie Smalls

CAST
Warren Oates . . . . *Hammond Maxwell*
Isela Vega . . . . *Marianna*
Ken Norton . . . . *Drum*
Pamela Grier . . . . *Regine*
Yaphet Kotto . . . . *Blaise*
John Colicos . . . . *DeMarigny*
Fiona Lewis . . . . *Augusta Chauvet*
Paula Kelly . . . . *Rachel*

This historical tale is set among the 19th-century Louisiana slave traders in and around New Orleans. Hammond Maxwell breeds slaves for money and he buys Drum and Blaise from a brothel owner.

When the slaves revolt against their cruel conditions on the plantations blood is shed as the cruel slave owners get their just rewards.

Drum was the sequel to *Mandingo* (1975), which again starred world heavyweight boxing champ Ken Norton as the slave Drum. *Mandingo* had starred James Mason and Susan George but only Norton and Brenda Sykes made it through to this film, which was based on a novel by Kyle Onstott.

Video availability

The Top Five

Week of 18 September 1976
1. Drum
2. Taxi Driver
3. Murder By Death
4. The Outlaw Josey Wales
5. The Message

THE OMEN

25 September 1976	6 weeks

Distributor:	Twentieth Century-Fox
Director:	Richard Donner
Producer:	Harvey Bernhard
Screenplay:	David Seltzer
Music:	Jerry Goldsmith

CAST
Gregory Peck . . . . *Robert Thorn*
Lee Remick . . . . *Katherine Thorn*
David Warner . . . . *Jennings*
Billie Whitelaw . . . . *Mrs Baylock*
Leo McKern . . . . *Archaeologist*
Harvey Stevens . . . . *Damien*
Patrick Troughton . . . . . . *Father Brennan*
Martin Benson . . . . *Father Spiletto*

American Ambassador in London Robert Thorn is persuaded to accept another baby when his wife Katherine loses theirs in childbirth. The child is far from innocent and as he grows his presence wreaks havoc and destruction. Their nanny hangs herself during a children's party and the evil Mrs Baylock arrives to look after the satanic child. Various priests and experts try to warn Thorn about his son Damien's demonic behaviour and recommend that he kills the child to prevent a diabolical Armageddon. Thorn will not believe his son is the Anti-Christ until he sees the 666 on the scalp of the sleeping boy's head. His realization, however, comes too late.

The film featured particularly innovative death scenes, using David Warner's photographic special effects, including a decapitation and a stake through Patrick Troughton. The death scenes became the hallmarks of its sequels: *Damien: Omen 2* (1978), *The Final Conflict* (1981) and *Damien IV: The Awakening*.

Robert Thorn (Gregory Peck) learns that his adopted son Damien (Harvey Stevens) is the child of the Devil, intent on taking over the world in Omen.

Jerry Goldsmith's stirring music 'Ave Satani' won an Oscar, although the use of Carl Orff's 'Carmina Burana' also helped create an atmosphere.

Gregory Peck was second choice for the role of the Ambassador, it had previously been earmarked for Charlton Heston.

Academy Awards: Best Original Music Score (Jerry Goldsmith)

Music: 'Ave Satani' (Jerry Goldsmith)

Video availability

The Top Five

Week of 25 September 1976
1. The Omen
2. Murder By Death
3. Taxi Driver
4. Drum
5. The Message

Top Twenty Films of 1976

1 Jaws
2 One Flew Over the Cuckoo's Nest
3 Jungle Book
4 The Return of the Pink Panther
5 Emmanuelle
6 Rollerball
7 The Omen
8 It Shouldn't Happen to a Vet
9 The Outlaw Josey Wales
10 All the President's Men
11 The Slipper and the Rose
12 Death Race 2000
13 Bambi
14 Shout at the Devil
15 Tommy
16 Gone with the Wind
17 The Sound of Music
18 At the Earth's Core
19 Adventures of a Taxi Driver
20 Barry Lyndon/Confessions of a Driving Instructor/The Streetfighter

THE RETURN OF A MAN CALLED HORSE

6 November 1976	1 week

Distributor: United Artists
Director: Irvin Kershner
Producer: Terry Morse Jr.
Screenplay: Jack De Witt
Music: Laurence Rosenthal

CAST
Richard Harris . . . . John Morgan
Gale Sondergaard . . . . Elk Woman
Geoffrey Lewis . . . . Zenas Morro
Bill Lucking . . . . Tom Gryce
Jorge Luke . . . . Running Bull
Claudio Brook . . . . Chemin D'Fer
Enrique Lucero . . . . Raven

This number one was the sequel to the 1970 movie *A Man Called Horse*, which had starred Richard Harris as John Morgan, an aristocratic Englishman who was adopted by the Sioux tribe after undergoing some gruesome torture rituals. This time around he returns to find his Indian friends have become slaves and sets about freeing them from their new masters. Yet again he is subjected to some agonizing torture rituals before leading the tribe back to their sacred hunting grounds.

This sequel inspired another, *Triumphs of a Man Called Horse* (1982), again with Richard Harris, but this proved to be the end of the line for the man called Horse.

Richard Harris has appeared in three other number ones since 1969: *Cromwell* (1970), *Golden Rendezvous* (1977) and *Unforgiven* (1992). His only Oscar nomination came in 1990 for his portrayal of the belligerent Irish farmer in *The Field*.

Video availability

The Top Five

Week of 6 November 1976
1. The Return of a Man Called Horse
2. One Hundred and one Dalmatians
3. Picnic at Hanging Rock
4. Murder By Death
5. Taxi Driver

EMMANUELLE 2

13 November 1976	6 weeks

Distributor: Trinacra/Orphée
Director: Francis Giacobetti
Producer: Yves Rousset-Rouard
Screenplay: Francis Giacobetti
Music: Francis Lai

CAST
Sylvia Kristel . . . . Emmanuelle
Umberto Orsini . . . . Jean
Catherine Rivet . . . . Anna-Maria
Frederic Lagache . . . . Christopher
Caroline Laurence . . . . Ingrid

Following on from the success of *Emmanuelle* (1974), *Emmanuelle 2* is set in the Far East. The slight story about smuggling never gets in the way of the soft-core sex romps with any number of nubile boys and girls. The Oriental locations are good to look at but the plotting and characterization are minimal.

Sylvia Kristel reprises her role as the eponymous heroine.

Video availability

The Top Five

Week of 13 November 1976
1. Emmanuelle 2
2. The Song Remains the Same
3. The Return of a Man Called Horse
4. The Big Bus
5. Picnic at Hanging Rock

THE PINK PANTHER STRIKES AGAIN

25 December 1976	10 weeks*

Distributor: United Artists
Director: Blake Edwards

Producer: Blake Edwards
Screenplay: Frank Waldman
Music: Henry Mancini

CAST
Peter Sellers . . . *Inspector Jacques Clouseau*
Herbert Lom . . . . *Dreyfus*
Colin Blakely . . . . *Alec Drummond*
Leonard Rossiter . . . . *Quinlan*
Lesley-Anne Down . . . . *Olga*
Burt Kwouk . . . . *Cato*
André Maranne . . . . *François*

The fifth movie in the successful series of Pink Panther comedies has bumbling French detective Inspector Clouseau assuming the responsibilities of his boss, Dreyfus, who is recovering from a nervous breakdown, brought about by Clouseau's incompetence. However, Dreyfus escapes and becomes a dangerous criminal. He plans to destroy the world, and Clouseau, with a ray gun he's stolen from the crazy scientist Dr Fassbender.

Peter Sellers second number one this year. First had been *Murder By Death*.

Sellers first played Clouseau in *The Pink Panther* (1963) and visited the role a total of seven times finishing with *Revenge of the Pink Panther* (number one 1978), although after his death *The Trail of the Pink Panther* (1982) was released as Edwards attempted to keep the franchise alive.

Music: 'Come To Me'

Video availability

The Top Five

Week of 25 December 1976
1. The Pink Panther Strikes Again
2. King Kong
3. Marathon Man
4. The Enforcer
5. Victory at Entebbe

SILENT MOVIE

5 February 1977	1 week

Distributor:	Twentieth Century-Fox
Director:	Mel Brooks
Producer:	Michael Hertzberg
Screenplay:	Mel Brooks, Ron Clark, Rudy DeLuca, Barry Levinson
Music:	John Morris

CAST
Mel Brooks . . . . *Mel Funn*
Marty Feldman . . . . *Marty Eggs*
Dom DeLuise . . . . *Dom Bell*
Marcel Marceau . . . . *Marcel Marceau*
Bernadette Peters . . . . *Vilma Kaplan*
Sid Caesar . . . . *Studio Chief*
Harold Gould . . . . *Engulf*
Ron Carey . . . . *Devour*

The only word uttered throughout this movie is 'Yes' by French mime artist Marcel Marceau. Film director Mel Funn's career is on the wane, largely due to his drinking habits. Along with two of his colleagues, he attempts to convince major stars to appear in his latest film, which is to be a contemporary silent movie complete with sound effects and visual explanatory titles. Having conned a studio chief into financing the picture (and so save his studio from a takeover) the project is a huge success.

The film features several cameo appearances by such stars as Burt Reynolds, James Caan, Liza Minnelli, Anne Bancroft and Henny Youngman.

Mel Brooks began his career as a stand-up comic, co-writing his first movie, *New Faces*, in 1954, starring Harry Horner. He went on to write, direct, produce and star in *History of the World Part 1* (1981).

Video availability

The Top Five

Week of 5 February 1977
1. Silent Movie
2. The Pink Panther Strikes Again
3. Sweeney!
4. Carrie
5. Vanessa

CROSS OF IRON

19 February 1977	1 week

Distributor:	EMI
Director:	Sam Peckinpah

Producer:	Wolf C. Hartwig
Screenplay:	Julius J. Epstein, Herbert Asmodi
Music:	Ernest Gold

CAST

James Coburn	*Sgt Steiner*
Maximilian Schell	*Capt Stransky*
James Mason	*Colonel Brandt*
David Warner	*Capt Keisel*
Klaus Lowitsch	*Druger*
Roger Fritz	*Lt Triebig*
Vadim Glowna	*Kern*

Based on the novel by Willi Heinrich, *Cross of Iron* is a World War II story told from the German point of view. A German battalion is almost destroyed while retreating from the Russian front in 1943, but a cowardly officer is determined to win the Iron Cross at any cost. The men are forced to fight amongst themselves for survival, and always suppressing any emotion.

Although a specialist in violent pictures, this was the only war film that Sam Peckinpah directed. He wrote and directed many of the episodes in the TV western series *Gunsmoke*, as well as creating *The Westerner* and *The Rifleman* for television. Previous Box Office Number Ones for Peckinpah are *The Wild Bunch* (1969), *Straw Dogs* (1971) and *The Getaway* (1973).

Video availability

The Top Five

Week of 19 February 1977
1. Cross of Iron
2. The Pink Panther Strikes Again
3. Carrie
4. Silent Movie
5. When the North Wind Blows

NETWORK

26 February 1977	1 week

Distributor:	MGM
Director:	Sidney Lumet
Producer:	Howard Gottfried
Screenplay:	Paddy Chayefsky
Music:	Elliot Lawrence

CAST

Faye Dunaway	*Diana Christensen*
William Holden	*Max Schumacher*
Peter Finch	*Howard Beale*
Robert Duvall	*Frank Hackett*
Wesley Addy	*Nelson Chaney*
Ned Beatty	*Arthur Jensen*

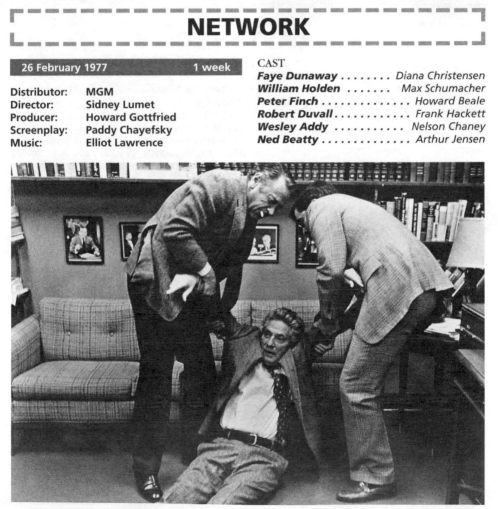

Network *newscaster Howard Beale (Peter Finch) faints and is helped to the couch by Max Schumacher (William Holden).*

Howard Beale is the reporter and anchorman for news network United Broadcasting Systems. He goes to pieces when he is told he is about to be made redundant after 25 years with the company. He finds religion and begins to spout his own views on the world live on air. Although an embarrassment to the company, the viewers love him. The TV station are forced to keep Beale and his evangelical ranting to maintain their ratings.

British actor Peter Finch died of a heart attack in January 1977, just before winning an Oscar for his part in the movie. It was accepted by his widow, Eletha. He was the first actor to be awarded an Oscar posthumously. Finch's role was originally offered to and turned down by Henry Fonda.

Car stickers were produced to promote the film which read 'I'm as mad as hell and I'm not going to take it any more', a line used in the movie when Beale invited viewers to lean out of their windows and shout the slogan.

Academy Awards: Best Actor (Peter Finch), Best Actress (Faye Dunaway), Best Supporting Actress (Beatrice Straight), Best Original Screenplay (Paddy Chayefsky)

Video availability

The Top Five

Week of 26 February 1977
1. Network
2. The Pink Panther Strikes Again
3. Cross of Iron
4. Carrie
5. When the North Wind Blows

THE LAST TYCOON

5 March 1977	1 week

Distributor: Paramount
Director: Elia Kazan
Producer: Sam Spiegel
Screenplay: Harold Pinter
Music: Maurice Jarre

CAST
Robert De Niro . . . . *Monroe Stahr*
Tony Curtis . . . . *Rodriguez*
Robert Mitchum . . . . *Pat Brady*
Jeanne Moreau . . . . *Didi*
Jack Nicholson . . . . *Brimmer*
Donald Pleasence . . . . *Boxley*
Ingrid Boulting . . . . *Kathleen*

In The Last Tycoon, *Robert De Niro plays Monroe Stahr, the whizz-kid film producer who seems unable to put a foot wrong.*

Monroe Stahr is the talented head of a 1930s Hollywood film studio who appears to be working himself to death. He spots and falls in love with a girl who reminds him of his late wife. Through human frailty he loses both his position of power and the love of his life.

The Last Tycoon was adapted from F. Scott Fitzgerald's unfinished novel, and the central character was based on the legendary 'boy wonder' of 1930s MGM, Irving Thalberg, who died at the age of 37 in 1936.

Neither the director nor the central actor was the first choice for Paramount. Mike Nichols was the studio's original choice as director but he turned it down, and the part of Monroe Stahr was first offered to Al Pacino then to Dustin Hoffman. Pacino turned it down, and Hoffman, who liked the script, took too long to make a decision. When De Niro took the part, he agreed to lose more than forty pounds in weight to play the fragile studio boss.

Ingrid Boulting is the daughter of Roy Boulting, the British film producer and director.

Video availability

The Top Five

Week of 5 March 1977
1. The Last Tycoon
2. Network
3. The Pink Panther Strikes Again
4. Cross of Iron
5. The Squeeze

A STAR IS BORN

2 April 1977	7 weeks*

Distributor:	Warner
Director:	Frank Pierson
Producer:	Jon Peters
Screenplay:	John Gregory Dunne, Joan Didion, Frank Pierson
Music:	Paul Williams, Kenny Ascher, Rupert Holms, Kenny Loggins, Alan and Marilyn Bergman, Leon Russell, Barbra Streisand

CAST
Barbra Streisand . . . . *Esther Hoffman*
Kris Kristofferson . . *John Norman Howard*
Paul Mazursky . . . . *Brian*
Gary Busey . . . . *Bobby Ritchie*
Oliver Clark . . . . *Danziger*
Vanetta Fields, Clydie King . . . . *The Oreos*
Marta Heflin . . . . *Quentin*
M.G. Kelly . . . . *Bebe Jesus*

A Star is Born is the fourth version of the story of a Hollywood love affair that is doomed to failure. Young actress Esther Hoffman hits the heights of movie success, while her once successful rock star husband (Kris Kristofferson) has developed a bad attitude, which helped to bring his days of superstardom to an end. He finds it impossible to accept his career is over and hers is just beginning, and his only consolation is the demon drink.

Top Composers 1969–94

Number of scores to appear in number one movies

John Williams	26
John Barry	17
Jerry Goldsmith	15
Maurice Jarre	11
Alan Silvestri	11
Michael Kamen	9
Marvin Hamlisch	8
James Horner	7
Lalo Schifrin	7
Richard Rodney Bennett	6
James Newton Howard	6
Trevor Jones	6
Ennio Morricone	6
Elmer Bernstein	5
Bill Conti	5
George Fenton	5
Jerry Fielding	5
Henry Mancini	5
Jack Nitzsche	5
Marc Shaiman	5
Howard Shore	5
Hans Zimmer	5

The Top Five

Week of 2 April 1977
1. A Star is Born
2. Network
3. The Pink Panther Strikes Again
4. The Last Tycoon
5. Ben Hur

Director Sam Peckinpah brought Kris Kristofferson into the forefront as a movie actor when he cast him as Billy The Kid in his 1973 movie *Pat Garrett and Billy The Kid*, although he had smaller roles in three previous pictures; his debut *The Last Movie*, followed by *Cisco Pike* and *Blume In Love*. When Kris Kristofferson was asked what it was like working with Barbra Streisand he was reported to have said that it caused him to think about giving up his acting career.

Academy Awards: Best Song – 'Evergreen' (Barbra Streisand, music; Paul Williams, lyrics)

Music: 'Evergreen', 'Watch Closely Now', 'Queen Bee', 'Lost Inside You', 'The Woman in the Moon', 'I Believe in Love', 'Everything', 'Love theme from A Star is Born' (Evergreen), 'Hellacious Acres', 'Crippled Crow', 'With One More Look At You/Watch Closely Now'

Video availability

THE EAGLE HAS LANDED

9 April 1977	1 week

Distributor: ITC
Director: John Sturges
Producer: Jack Winer, David Niven Jr
Screenplay: Tom Mankiewicz
Music: Lalo Schifrin

CAST
Michael Caine . . . . *Colonel Kurt Steiner*
Donald Sutherland . . . . *Liam Devlin*
Robert Duvall . . . . *Colonel Max Radl*
Jenny Agutter . . . . *Molly Prior*
Donald Pleasence . . . . . *Heinrich Himmler*
Anthony Quayle . *Admiral Wilhelm Canaris*
Jean Marsh . . . . *Joanna Grey*
Judy Geeson . . . . *Pamela Verecker*

Heinrich Himmler is under strict orders from Hitler to have Winston Churchill kidnapped. In November 1943 a troop of German commandos, disguised as Polish soldiers and led by Kurt Steiner, parachute into England in an attempt to kidnap the Prime Minister while he is spending a weekend at a country house in Norfolk. A fifth-columnist within the small community helps the Germans.

Much of the filming for *The Eagle Has Landed* was done just outside Berkshire, ten minutes from Michael Caine's home.

Video availability

The Top Five

Week of 9 April 1977
1. The Eagle has Landed
2. A Star is Born
3. Silver Streak
4. The Pink Panther Strikes Again
5. Network

AIRPORT '77

16 April 1977	2 weeks

Distributor: Universal
Director: Jerry Jameson
Producer: William Frye
Screenplay: Michael Scheff, David Spector
Music: John Cacavas

CAST
Jack Lemmon . . . . *Don Gallagher*
Lee Grant . . . . *Karen Wallace*
Brenda Vaccaro . . . . *Eve Clayton*
Joseph Cotten . . . . . . *Nicholas St Downs III*
Olivia de Havilland . . . . . *Emily Livingston*
Darren McGavin . . . . *Buchek*
Christopher Lee . . . . *Martin Wallace*
Robert Foxworth . . . . *Chambers*

In the third 'Airport' movie, a private jet full of VIPs and priceless paintings is hijacked by a gang and helped by the co-pilot, who redirects the plane and turns off the radar. The plane crashes into the sea off the coast of Florida and sinks to the ocean bed. The airport can't locate them, the air is running out inside the plane and it's only a matter of time before the water leaking in engulfs them all. Jack Lemmon keeps his head and finds a way of communicating

The Top Five

Week of 16 April 1977
1. Airport '77
2. The Eagle has Landed
3. A Star is Born
4. Silver Streak
5. The Pink Panther Strikes Again

with the outside world. Against the clock, the authorities mount a daring rescue attempt.

A fourth 'Airport' movie was released in 1979, *The Concorde – Airport '79*, starring Alain Delon, Robert Wagner and Sylvia Kristel. The following year saw the release of a successful parody of these films, *Airplane!* (1980).

Video availability

ROCKY

30 April 1977	3 weeks

Distributor:	United Artists
Director:	John G. Avildsen
Producer:	Irwin Winkler, Robert Chartoff
Screenplay:	Sylvester Stallone
Music:	Bill Conti

CAST
Sylvester Stallone	*Rocky*
Talia Shire	*Adrian*
Burt Young	*Paulie*
Carl Weathers	*Apollo*
Burgess Meredith	*Mickey*
Thayer David	*Jergens*
Joe Spinell	*Gazzo*
Joe Frazier	*Himself*
Judi Letizia	*Marie*

The original Rocky movie introduces us to the less than bright local Philadelphia boxer Rocky Balboa. He is picked from the boxing register by the reigning heavyweight champ, Apollo Creed, to fight in a championship match. The chance for success encourages him to give up his job as a heavy for a local hood. He trains hard for the match, with the support of his girlfriend, Adrian, and his manager, Mickey.

Rocky was Sylvester Stallone's third attempt at scriptwriting. He completed it in less than three weeks.

Burt Reynolds and James Caan were considered for the lead by the film company but Stallone held out for the part for himself. Sylvester Stallone had some empathy for his character, having attended 14 different high schools and 5 colleges before working as a zoo attendant and a pizza chef. He made his film debut in Woody Allen's 1971 movie *Bananas*.

Stallone's father, Frank, makes a cameo appearance as a timekeeper and his brother, Frank Jnr, turns up as a street singer.

Academy Awards: Best Film (Producers Irwin Winkler and Robert Chartoff), Best Direction (John G. Avildsen), Best Editing (Richard Halsey and Scott Conrad)

Music: 'Gonna Fly Now'

Video availability

The Top Five

Week of 30 April 1977
1. Rocky
2. Airport '77
3. A Star is Born
4. The Eagle has Landed
5. Silver Streak

A BRIDGE TOO FAR

2 July 1977	2 weeks

Distributor:	United Artists
Director:	Richard Attenborough
Producer:	Joseph E. Levine, Richard P. Levine
Screenplay:	William Goldman
Music:	John Addison

CAST
Dirk Bogarde	*Lt General Browning*
James Caan	*Staff Sgt Eddie Dohun*
Michael Caine	*Lt Colonel Joe Vandeleur*
Sean Connery	*Major General Robert Urquhart*
Edward Fox	*Lt General Brian Horrocks*
Elliott Gould	*Colonel Bobby Stout*
Gene Hackman	*Major General Sosabowski*

In 1944 Field Marshal Montgomery and General Eisenhower launch Operation Market Garden.

The Top Five

Week of 2 July 1977
1. A Bridge Too Far
2. A Star is Born
3. The Streetwalker
4. The Cassandra Crossing
5. Car Wash

The mission, aimed at ending the war, is carried out by 35,000 Allied troops. The plan is to secure six bridges that lead into Germany, but the operation starts to go wrong during an airdrop in Arnhem, Holland.

Often dubbed 'A Star Too Many', the film featured a list of big names, including Anthony Hopkins, Laurence Olivier, Ryan O'Neal, Robert Redford, Liv Ullman and Maximilian Schell.

The film, based on a book by Cornelius Ryan, was the second war film to be directed by Richard Attenborough. He had made his directorial debut with *Oh! What a Lovely War* in 1969.

Video availability

THE SPY WHO LOVED ME

16 July 1977	14 weeks*

Distributor:	United Artists
Director:	Lewis Gilbert
Producer:	Albert R. Broccoli
Screenplay:	Christopher Wood, Richard Maibaum
Music:	Marvin Hamlisch

CAST
Roger Moore .... James Bond
Barbara Bach ...... Major Anya Amasova
Curt Jurgens .... Stromberg
Richard Kiel .... Jaws
Caroline Munro .... Naomi
Walter Gotell .... General Gogol
Bernard Lee .... M
Lois Maxwell .... Miss Moneypenny

In this adventure James Bond teams up with one of Russia's most beautiful agents, Anya Amasova. Between amorous encounters they investigate the mysterious disappearance of nuclear submarines belonging to the British and Russian governments. The evil shipping magnate, Stromberg, is behind the plan to precipitate World War III and is swallowing the submarines in the world's largest tanker. In his efforts to save the world yet again, James Bond comes face to face with Stromberg's psychopathic henchman, Jaws.

The film was the first Bond movie not to be based on an Ian Fleming novel, although it did use the name of one of Ian Fleming's stories. The original screenplay had Bond reunited with arch enemy Blofeld and his SPECTRE organization. However, *Thunderball* director Kevin McClory claimed he had exclusive use of the SPECTRE name. He was in fact preparing his own 007 revival, 'Warhead', co-written by and starring Sean Connery. The project never got off the ground, however. Other screenplays for the film were rejected from John Landis, Anthony Burgess and Stirling Silliphant.

It was also the first time the theme song for a Bond movie had a different title. Carly Simon's 'Nobody Does It Better' (music Marvin Hamlisch, lyrics Carole Bayer Sager) did contain the lyrics 'The spy who loved me', however, and, like most other Bond songs, was a top ten hit in the UK charts.

Music: 'Nobody Does It Better' (Carly Simon)

Video availability

The Top Five

Week of 16 July 1977
1. The Spy Who Loved Me
2. A Bridge Too Far
3. A Star is Born
4. The Streetwalker
5. Fun with Dick and Jane

EXORCIST II: THE HERETIC

24 September 1977	1 week

Distributor:	Warner
Director:	John Boorman
Producer:	John Boorman, Richard Lederer
Screenplay:	William Goodhart
Music:	Ennio Morricone

CAST
Linda Blair .... Regan

Richard Burton .... Father Lamont
Louise Fletcher .... Dr Gene Tuskin
Max Von Sydow .... Father Merrin
Kitty Winn .... Sharon
Paul Henreid .... Cardinal
James Earl Jones .... Kokumo
Ned Beatty .... Edwards

The sequel to the original *Exorcist* (1974) has Linda Blair returning to her role as Regan, now under psychiatric care after her brush with the devil

Father Lamont (Richard Burton) tries to protect Gene Tuskin (Louise fletcher) from the powers of the devil still within the child Regan (Linda Blair) in Exorcist II: The Heretic.

that still lives within her. A friendly priest (Burton) turns up on the scene to try to discover the mystery surrounding the death of an old servant and help sort out the demons that Regan still carries with her.

Director John Boorman was forced to re-edit the movie after it was badly received by audiences at previews in New York.

Like *Exorcist*, the film was based on William Peter Blatty's novel. In the original movie, Blatty made a cameo appearance as a producer.

The Top Five

Week of 24 September 1977
1. The Exorcist II: The Heretic
2. New York, New York
3. The Spy Who Loved Me
4. The Other Side of Midnight
5. A Bridge Too Far

Video availability

NEW YORK, NEW YORK

1 October 1977	2 weeks

Distributor:	United Artists
Director:	Martin Scorsese
Producer:	Irwin Winkler, Robert Chartoff
Screenplay:	Earl Mac Rauch, Mardik Martin
Music:	Ralph Burns (Supervision) John Kander, Fred Ebb (Songs)

CAST
Liza Minnelli . . . . *Francine Evans*
Robert De Niro . . . . *Jimmy Doyle*
Lionel Stander . . . . *Tony Harwell*
Barry Primus . . . . *Paul Wilson*
Mary Kay Place . . . . *Bernice*

Georgie Auld . . . . *Frankie Hartel*
George Memmoli . . . . *Nicky*

In postwar New York a struggling female singer (Minnelli) meets Jimmy, an out of work saxophonist. The two fall in love and marry and begin the steady climb to the great heights of fame in the entertainment business. But for all his charm, Jimmy is irresponsible and he leaves Francine after the birth of their first child.

The opening scene filmed at Radio City Music Hall in New York involved 550 costumed extras. Stage 29 at MGM's studios in Culver City, where the film was shot, was also the set used by Liza Minnelli's father, Vincente, when he directed *The Pirate* in

At a VJ Day ball in New York, 1945, saxophone player Jimmy Doyle (Robert De Niro) joins an all-night jam session with a Harlem group in New York, New York, but he has his sights on bigger and better things.

1948, starring Liza's mother, Judy Garland. Liza was given her mother's old dressing room.

Music: 'Blue Moon', 'Honeysuckle Rose', 'The Man I Love', 'Theme From *New York, New York*', 'You Are My Lucky Star', 'You Brought a New Kind of Love to Me'

Video availability

The Top Five

Week of 1 October 1977
1. New York, New York
2. The Spy Who Loved Me
3. A Bridge Too Far
4. The Other Side of Midnight
5. The Exorcist II: The Heretic

VALENTINO

15 October 1977	2 weeks

Distributor:	Columbia
Director:	Ken Russell
Producer:	Robert Chartoff, Irwin Winkler
Screenplay:	Ken Russell, John Byram
Music:	Ferde Grofé, Stanley Black

CAST
Rudolf Nureyev	....	*Valentino*
Leslie Caron	....	*Nazimova*
Michelle Phillips	....	*Rambova*
Carol Kane	....	*Starlet*
Felicity Kendal	....	*Mathis*
Seymour Cassel	....	*Ullman*
Huntz Hall	....	*Jesse Lasky*
Alfred Marks	....	*Rowland*
David De Keyser	....	*Joe Schenck*

In yet another Ken Russell half-fact, half-fiction bio-pic, Rudolf Nureyev plays the eccentric yet tragic silent screen heart-throb, Rudolph Valentino, whose looks were said to drive women crazy. The movie consists of a series of flashbacks beginning with his funeral and moving to his early days in New York and Hollywood.

This was Rudolf Nureyev's movie debut. The story

had been filmed before, in 1951, with Anthony Dexter in the leading role. He was chosen from 2000 hopeful actors who auditioned for the part.

Michelle Phillips, who plays Valentino's wife Rambova, was once a member of the successful 1960s pop group The Mamas and the Papas.

Video availability

SALON KITTY (Madam Kitty)

19 November 1977	2 weeks

Distributor:	Twentieth Century-Fox
Director:	Giovanni Tinto Brass
Producer:	Giulio Sbarigia, Ermanno Donati
Screenplay:	Ennio de Concini, Maria Pia Fusco, Giovanni Tinto Brass
Music:	Fiorenzo Carpi

CAST
Helmut Berger . . . . *Wallenberg*
Ingrid Thulin . . . . *Kitty*
Therese Ann Savoy . . . . *Margherita*
Bekim Fehmiu . . . . *Hans*
John Steiner . . . . *Biondo*
Stefano Satta Flores . . . . *Dino*
Dan Van Husen . . . . *Rauss*
John Ireland . . . . *Clift*

Although perhaps not the best remembered movie of the 1970s, it still made number one. It's a story of Fascism and plenty of Nazis having sex. The Germans spend much of their spare time in a brothel that has been bugged by the Secret Service. Helmut Berger plays a soldier who is seen dressing up as the Snow Queen in a showpiece, but is finally gunned down in the shower wearing nothing more than Swastika wristbands.

Director Giovanni Tinto Brass also worked on *Caligula* (1980) but was fired before completion of the film and his name did not appear in the screen credits.

GOLDEN RENDEZVOUS

10 December 1977	2 weeks

Distributor:	Film Trust
Director:	Ashley Lazarus
Producer:	André Pieters
Screenplay:	Stanley Price
Music:	Jeff Wayne

CAST
Richard Harris . . . . *John Carter*
Ann Turkel . . . . *Susan Beresford*
David Janssen . . . . *Charles Conway*
Burgess Meredith . . . . *Van Heurden*
John Vernon . . . . *Luis Carreras*
Gordon Jackson . . . . *Dr Marston*
Keith Baxter . . . . *Preston*

In this adaptation of an Alistair MacLean novel, mercenary Luis Carreras organizes the hijack of a floating cargo ship and casino, the *Caribbean Star*, which is carrying a whole host of wealthy gamblers. Plenty of blood, guts and casualties as the terrorists machine gun the gaming room, but what they hadn't bargained for is the courageous first officer, Carter.

The film was re named *Nuclear Terror* for television.

Video availability

THE DEEP

24 December 1977	2 weeks*

Distributor: Columbia
Director: Peter Yates
Producer: Peter Guber
Screenplay: Peter Benchley, Tracy Keenan Wynn
Music: John Barry

CAST
Robert Shaw . . . . *Romer Treece*
Jacqueline Bisset . . . . *Gail Burke*
Nick Nolte . . . . *David Sanders*
Louis Gossett . . . . *Henri Cloche*
Eli Wallach . . . . *Adam Coffin*
Robert Tessier . . . . *Kevin*
Earl Maynard . . . . *Ronald*

Following the huge success of *Jaws*, the movie makers decided to take Peter Benchley's next novel and adapt it for the big screen. It's the story of a perilous search by two men for lost treasure in the waters of Bermuda. Their search leads to a cache of drugs hidden underwater. Before they know it they are caught up with a drug-smuggling ring, sea monsters and voodoo.

Peter Yates directed his first film some fifteen years earlier, *The Young Ones*, which was a box office smash, starring Cliff Richard. Yates went on to make *Bullitt* (1968), *Murphy's War* (1971) and *For Pete's Sake* (1974). He began his career in the movies as a dubbing assistant in a London sound studio.

Before becoming an actor, Nick Nolte had a career as a con artist. During his college days in the 1960s, he sold fake draft cards to young men but was caught by police and given a 75-year prison stretch which was later reduced to a 5-year probation.

Peter Benchley, on whose novel the film is based, is the grandson of humorist Robert Benchley, who wrote and appeared in a long series of amusing 'shorts' in the 1930s and 40s. One of them, 'How To Sleep', won an Oscar in 1935.

Video availability

Top Twenty Films of 1977

1 The Spy Who Loved Me
2 A Star Is Born
3 When the North Wind Blows
4 The Pink Panther Strikes Again
5 A Bridge Too Far
6 Sinbad and the Eye of the Tiger
7 The Omen
8 King Kong
9 Airport '77
10 The Adventures of the Wilderness Family
11 One Hundred and One Dalmatians
12 The Enforcer
13 Jaws
14 Sweeney!
15 The Eagle Has Landed
16 Emmanuelle 2
17 Bugsy Malone
18 Exorcist II: The Heretic
19 Carrie
20 Rocky

The Top Five

Week of 24 December 1977
1. The Deep
2. Golden Rendezvous
3. Valentino
4. Goodbye Emmanuelle
5. The Rescuers

STAR WARS

7 January 1978	11 weeks

Distributor: Twentieth Century-Fox
Director: George Lucas
Producer: Gary Kurtz
Screenplay: George Lucas
Music: John Williams

CAST
Mark Hamill . . . . *Luke Skywalker*
Harrison Ford . . . . *Han Solo*
Carrie Fisher . . . . *Princess Leia*
Peter Cushing . . . . *Grand Moff Tarkin*
Alec Guinness . . . . *Ben Kenobi*
Anthony Daniels *C3PO*
Kenny Baker *R2D2*
Peter Mayhew . . . . *Chewbacca*
David Prowse (James Earl Jones, voice)
Lord Darth Vader

Princess Leia (Carrie Fisher) places a message for help to Ben Kenobi in R2D2 before being captured by the Empire's evil rulers, Grand Moff Tarkin (Peter Cushing) and Lord Darth Vader (David Prowse), in Star Wars.

Princess Leia has been kidnapped by the evil Grand Moff Tarkin and Darth Vader who control the Death Star, an enormous space craft capable of destroying any planet that gets in its way. The Princess has stolen the plans for the craft and hidden them in the android, R2D2. Luke Skywalker, an orphan living on a remote farm with his relations, finds the robot wandering around the farm and learns of the abduction. With the help of the wise old Ben Kenobi, Han Solo and the hairy Chewbacca he sets out on a rescue mission, taking R2D2 and his colleague C3PO along with him.

The original *Star Wars* project was turned down by both United Artists and Universal. When Twentieth Century-Fox took it on they planned a nine-movie project, although there have been only three to date. The film was a huge financial success, the novelization of the script alone sold in excess of 3 million copies. Alec Guinness worked for a low salary and a share of the movie's profits: the film made him a millionaire.

Harrison Ford shot to screen fame with his performance as Han Solo. He had made his big screen debut in a 1966 film starring James Coburn, *Dead Heat on a Merry-Go-Round*, after which he was told that he would be well advised to give up the movie business. His co-star, Carrie Fisher, the daughter of singers Debbie Reynolds and Eddie Fisher, had her breasts taped down during filming because she said 'According to George Lucas, there are no bras in space.'

Academy Awards: Best Art Direction (John Barry, Norman Reynolds and Leslie Dilley), Best Set Decoration (Roger Christian), Best Costume Design (John Mollo), Best Sound (Don MacDougall, Ray West, Bob Minkler and Derek Ball), Best Editing (Paul Hirsch, Marcia Lucas and Richard Chew), Best Music Score (John Williams), Best Visual Effects (John Stears, John Dykstra, Richard Edlund, Grant McCune and Robert Blalack), Best Sound Effects Creations (Special Achievement Award; Benjamin Burtt, Jr)

Video availability

The Top Five

Week of 7 January 1978
1. Star Wars
2. The Gauntlet
3. The Deep
4. Rollercoaster
5. The Last Remake of Beau Geste

CLOSE ENCOUNTERS OF THE THIRD KIND

25 March 1978	16 weeks*

Distributor: Columbia
Director: Steven Spielberg
Producer: Julia and Michael Phillips
Screenplay: Steven Spielberg
Music: John Williams

CAST
Richard Dreyfuss . . . . *Roy Neary*
François Truffaut . . . . *Claude Lacombe*
Teri Garr . . . . *Ronnie Neary*
Melinda Dillon . . . . *Jillian Guiler*
Cary Guffey . . . . *Barry Guiler*
Bob Balaban . . . . *Interpreter Laughlin*
J. Patrick McNamara . . . . . *Project Leader*
Warren Kemmerling . . . . *Wild Bill*

Strange and scary things are happening in the once sleepy town of Muncie in Indiana. When Roy Neary, the local electrician, is called out to investigate a problem with the town's power his van breaks down and he is suddenly engulfed in a brilliant bright light. He becomes obsessed with the five musical notes he heard during the experience. From then on the Neary family witness a series of Unidentified Flying Objects. Another local, Jillian Guiler, and her young son Barry find their electrical appliances have gone crazy and the child's toys take on a life of their own. As scientists attempt to decipher the musical signals from the UFOs, a huge spacecraft appears with a new lifeform.

The film was originally entitled 'Watch the Skies', a phrase taken from the 1951 film *The Thing*. At the end of *The Thing* Douglas Spencer, who plays reporter Ned Scott, warns the audience to beware of alien invaders and to 'Watch the skies everywhere. Keep Looking! Keep watching the skies.'

In 1980, a shortened version of the movie was released under the title *The Special Edition*. It contained a view of the interior of the spacecraft with the song 'When You Wish Upon a Star' from *Pinocchio* playing over the soundtrack. The song was cut from the original film due to disappointing reaction at early previews.

Academy Awards: Best cinematography (Vilmos Zsigmond), Best Sound Effects Editing (Frank Warner; Special Achievement Award)

Video availability

The Top Five

Week of 25 March 1978
1. Close Encounters of the Third Kind
2. Star Wars
3. Julia
4. Looking for Mr Goodbar
5. Annie Hall

GAME OF DEATH

8 July 1978	1 week

Distributor: Columbia
Director: Robert Clouse
Producer: Raymond Chow
Screenplay: Jan Spears
Music: John Barry

CAST
Bruce Lee . . . . *Billy Lo*
Gig Young . . . . *Jim Marshall*
Dean Jagger . . . . *Dr Land*
Hugh O'Brian . . . . *Steiner*
Colleen Camp . . . . *Ann Morris*
Robert Wall . . . . *Carl Miller*
Mel Novak . . . . *Stick*

A successful Kung Fu movie star is threatened by the mob who want a piece of his action. But Billy

Lo has a very different idea of the kind of action they will get. He then fakes his own death in a plan to gain his revenge.

Bruce Lee died, in mysterious circumstances, during the making of this film. Six years later, director Clouse got the rest of the cast together and finished the movie, using Kim Tai Jong as a double for Lee

The Top Five

Week of 8 July 1978
1. Game of Death
2. Close Encounters of the Third Kind
3. 2001: A Space Odyssey
4. Saturday Night Fever
5. Bilitis

and extracts from Lee's 1973 movie, *Enter the Dragon*.

REVENGE OF THE PINK PANTHER

22 July 1978	8 weeks

Distributor: United Artists
Director: Blake Edwards
Producer: Blake Edwards
Screenplay: Frank Waldman, Ron Clark, Blake Edwards
Music: Henry Mancini

CAST
Peter Sellers . . . . *Clouseau*
Herbert Lom . . . . *Dreyfus*
Dyan Cannon . . . . *Simone Legree*
Robert Webber . . . . *Douvier*
Burt Kwouk . . . . *Cato*
Paul Stewart . . . . *Scallini*
Robert Loggia . . . . *Marchione*
Graham Stark . . . . *Auguste Balls*
Sue Lloyd . . . . *Claude Russo*

The *Revenge of the Pink Panther* was Sellers' fifth and final movie as Inspector Jacques Clouseau. In this outing he is believed to be dead. The news reaches his one-time superior, Chief Inspector Dreyfus, who is in a mental institute after years of working with Clouseau. He discharges himself and returns to work only to find the bumbling policeman miraculously alive and well and mixed up with the French Connection. Clouseau goes on the trail of a dangerous ring of drug smugglers in Hong Kong, and using a variety of disguises, he poses as a mafia Godfather to flush out the bad guys.

Burt Kwouk's martial arts expert is called Cato, a tribute perhaps to the greatest Kung Fu movie star, Bruce Lee, who played Kato in TV's *The Green Hornet*.

Peter Sellers was paid $750,000 to star in this picture, plus a 10 per cent bonus of the gross takings. Although unhappy with the first draft script, a further Pink Panther film with Sellers was being planned ('The Romance of the Pink Panther') but it was scrapped after his death in 1980.

Video availability

The Top Five

Week of 22 July 1978
1. Revenge of the Pink Panther
2. The Wild Geese
3. Saturday Night Fever
4. 2001: A Space Odyssey
5. Close Encounters of the Third Kind

HEAVEN CAN WAIT

16 September 1978	1 week

Distributor: Paramount
Director: Warren Beatty, Buck Henry
Producer: Warren Beatty
Screenplay: Warren Beatty, Elaine May
Music: Dave Grusin

CAST
Warren Beatty . . . . *Joe Pendleton*
Julie Christie . . . . *Betty Logan*
James Mason . . . . *Mr Jordan*
Jack Warden . . . . *Max Corkle*
Charles Grodin . . . . *Tony Abbott*
Dyan Cannon . . . . *Julia Farnsworth*

Joe Pendleton, a quarterback for the Los Angeles Rams, is mistakenly called to Heaven following a road accident. To make amends, he is restored back to Earth in the body of Julia Farnsworth's rich husband, who she murdered just minutes earlier. With this new found wealth and his desire to play in the super bowl, he decides to buy The Rams and hires his old coach, Max, to help them train.

Despite having the same title, this movie has nothing to do with the 1943 film that starred Don

The Top Five

Week of 16 September 1978
1. Heaven Can Wait
2. Revenge of the Pink Panther
3. The Wild Geese
4. An Unmarried Woman
5. Convoy

Ameche. It is, in fact, a remake of the 1941 picture *Here Comes Mr Jordan*, which starred Robert Montgomery and Claude Rains.

Warren Beatty, who is Shirley MacLaine's little brother, actually played in the ball game in the Superbowl sequence which was filmed in front of 60,000 fans at the Los Angeles Coliseum.

Academy Awards: Best Art Direction (Paul Sylbert and Edwin O'Donovan), Set Decoration (George Gaines)

Video availability

GREASE

23 September 1978	6 weeks

Distributor: Paramount
Director: Randal Kleiser
Producer: Robert Stigwood, Allan Carr
Screenplay: Bronte Woodard
Music: Bill Oakes (Supervision)
Jim Jacobs, Warren Casey
(Original music)

CAST
John Travolta . . . . Danny
Olivia Newton-John . . . . Sandy
Stockard Channing . . . . Rizzo
Jeff Conaway . . . . Kenickie
Didi Conn . . . . Frenchy
Jamie Donnelly . . . . Jan
Dinah Manoff . . . . Marty
Barry Pearl . . . . Doody

Sandy is the new girl at Rydell High School and Danny is the cool leader of a gang of tough rockers. They had met in the summer holidays and fallen in love but once at school Danny's behaviour towards Sandy becomes cavalier as he is at pains to play it cool in front of his friends. Sandy, on the other hand, finds it difficult to be anything but a Doris Day clone. While Danny hangs out with the gang, Sandy receives a different kind of education from Rizzo and Frenchy.

Don't they make the perfect couple. Sandy (Olivia Newton-John), a high school junior, is determined not to let go of Danny (John Travolta), the hot stud of Rydell High in Grease.

Grease features cameo appearances by Frankie Avalon, Eddie 'Kookie' Byrnes, Sid Caesar, Eve Arden and others. One of the film's stars, John Travolta, appeared in the Broadway musical version of *Grease* long before starring in the movie, although the role of Danny in the original London stage production was played by Richard Gere. Stockard Channing went on to star in her own American TV series and Jeff Conaway was cast as the struggling actor Bobby Wheeler in the successful comedy TV series *Taxi*.

A sequel, *Grease 2*, was released in 1982, starring Michelle Pfeiffer and Maxwell Caulfield.

Music: 'Grease', 'Summer Nights', 'Hopelessly Devoted To You', 'Sandy', 'Look at Me I'm Sandra Dee',

'You're the One That I Want', 'Greased Lightning', 'Blue Moon', 'Hound Dog', 'Rock 'n' Roll Is Here To Stay', 'Tears on My Pillow'

Video availability

The Top Five

Week of 23 September 1978
1. Grease
2. Heaven Can Wait
3. The Wild Geese
4. Midnight Express
5. The Cheap Detective

DEATH ON THE NILE

4 November 1978	6 weeks

Distributor:	EMI
Director:	John Guillermin
Producer:	John Brabourne, Richard Goodwin
Screenplay:	Anthony Shaffer
Music:	Nino Rota

CAST
Peter Ustinov . . . . *Hercule Poirot*
Jane Birkin . . . . *Louise Bourget*
Lois Chiles . . . . *Linnet Ridgeway*
Bette Davis . . . . *Mrs Van Schuyler*
Mia Farrow . . . . *Jacqueline De Bellefort*
Jon Finch . . . . *Mr Ferguson*
Olivia Hussey . . . . *Rosalie Otterbourne*
George Kennedy . . . . *Andrew Pennington*

Hercule Poirot is taking a well-deserved holiday and is enjoying his Egyptian cruise. His respite from crime-solving is suddenly interrupted by the murder of an arrogant young heiress who recently walked off with her best friend's fiancé. None of the passengers have a good word for the victim so there are plenty of suspects when Poirot and his sidekick, Colonel Race, finally disclose the identity of the killer in the closing scenes in the drawing room.

Peter Ustinov is the fourth actor to play Hercule Poirot on the big screen. He took over from Albert Finney who played the part in the previous Agatha Christie hit, *Murder on the Orient Express* (1974). He reprised his role as Poirot in 1988 when he starred in *Appointment With Death*. Other notable actors in *Death on the Nile* included Angela Lansbury, David Niven, Maggie Smith and Jack Warden.

Academy Awards: Best Costume Design (Anthony Howell)

The Top Five

Week of 4 November 1978
1. Death on the Nile
2. Watership Down
3. Grease
4. The Greek Tycoon
5. Eyes of Laura Mars

Video availability

Top Twenty Films of 1978

1 Star Wars
2 Grease
3 Close Encounters of the Third Kind
4 Saturday Night Fever
5 Revenge of the Pink Panther
6 The Rescuers
7 Abba – The Movie
8 The Gauntlet/Herbie Goes to Monte Carlo
9 The Stud
10 The Deep
11 Annie Hall
12 Convoy
13 The Wild Geese
14 Warlords of Atlantis
15 Candleshoe
16 The Goodbye Girl
17 Spiderman
18 Heaven Can Wait
19 Julia
20 International Velvet

FORCE 10 FROM NAVARONE

16 December 1978	1 week

Distributor: Columbia
Director: Guy Hamilton
Producer: Oliver A. Unger
Screenplay: Robin Chapman
Music: Ron Goodwin

CAST

Robert Shaw	Mallory
Harrison Ford	Barnsby
Edward Fox	Miller
Barbara Bach	Maritza
Franco Nero	Lescovar
Carl Weathers	Weaver
Richard Kiel	Drazac

Demolition expert Miller and British Major Mallory embark upon a mission to blow up a seemingly indestructible bridge in Yugoslavia, essential to the Germans' war effort. They are survivors of the last attack on Navarone (*The Guns of Navarone*) and are determined to deal with the spy who betrayed them before. The team they lead include Barnsby (Harrison Ford) and traitor Lescovar.

Robert Shaw was the father of ten children from three marriages. This was his penultimate movie, his final being *Avalanche Express* which also saw the movie swansong for director Mark Robson. Shaw features in the cast of several box office number ones, including *Jaws* (1976), which stayed at the top for 9 weeks, and *The Sting* (1994), which managed 5 weeks.

Video availability

SUPERMAN

23 December 1978	11 weeks

Distributor: Warner
Director: Richard Donner
Producer: Pierre Spengler
Screenplay: Mario Puzo, David Newman, Leslie Newman, Robert Benton
Music: John Williams

CAST

Marlon Brando	Jor-El
Gene Hackman	Lex Luthor
Christopher Reeve ..	Superman/Clark Kent
Ned Beatty	Otis
Jackie Cooper	Perry White
Glenn Ford	Pa Kent
Trevor Howard	First Elder
Margot Kidder	Lois Lane
Jack O'Halloran	Non

A young baby from the planet Krypton is sent down to Earth because his father, Jor-El, believes that Krypton is about to be destroyed. The child, who has hidden super powers, grows up with a farming family in America and assumes the name of Clark Kent. He becomes a newspaper reporter for the *Daily Planet*, where he meets and falls in love with fellow reporter Lois Lane. Clark's nervous exterior fails to inspire Lois, but once he removes his glasses and dons his tights and cape he becomes the dynamic Superman. His mission is to fight all crime, rescue those in need and deal with Lex Luthor, the greatest criminal mind of the century. He must, however, keep his true identity a secret, even from Lois.

Several uncredited writers contributed to the screenplay, including Tom Mankiewicz.

Leslie Ann Warren was considered for the part of Lois Lane and Peter Boyle was originally planned to play Otis. There were also many candidates for the part of Superman, including Robert Redford, Sylvester Stallone, Clint Eastwood, Nick Nolte and Ryan O'Neal. Christopher Reeve, who landed the part, had a small part in only one previous movie,

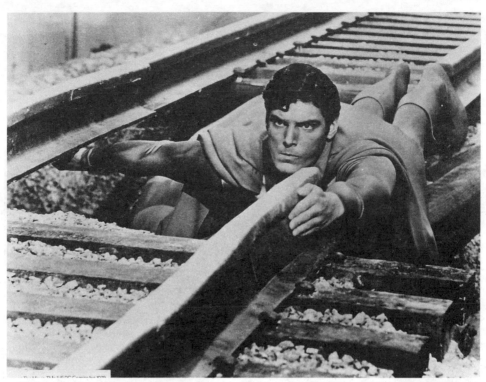

Christopher Reeve stars as Superman, *who, under the assumed identity of journalist Clark Kent, leads the continuing fight against crime and the protection of the innocent.*

Gray Lady Down, in the same year. To prepare for the role of Superman meant non-stop working out in the gym for Reeve, to build up his physique.

Academy Awards: Best Visual Effects (Special Achievement Award; Les Bowie, Colin Chilvers, Denys Coop, Roy Field, Derek Meddings and Zoran Perisic)

Video availability

THE DEER HUNTER

10 March 1979	4 weeks*

Distributor:	Universal
Director:	Michael Cimino
Producer:	Barry Spikings, Michael Deeley, Michael Cimino and John Peverall
Screenplay:	Deric Washburn
Music:	Stanley Myers

CAST

Robert De Niro	Michael
John Cazale	Stan
John Savage	Steven
Christopher Walken	Nick
Meryl Streep	Linda
George Dzundza	John
Chuck Aspegren	Axel

Michael and Nick are part of a group of young men, which includes Axel, Stan, John and Steven, who have grown up together in a Pennsylvanian steel town. They work, play pool, go deer hunting and hang out together. Soon after Steven's marriage to Angela they are called to serve in Vietnam. In the middle of battle Michael and Nick are both captured by the Vietcong and taken prisoner. They are forced to play Russian Roulette with their captors who take bets on the outcome of the loaded revolver. They escape but are separated when they reach safety. When they finally return home, the young men all find it difficult to adjust to the old life. Michael's attempt to find solace with Meryl Streep founders and he feels compelled to go back to Vietnam to find Nick.

The Deer Hunter was Meryl Streep's second movie and her first major big screen role.

Nick (Christopher Walken) is forced to play Russian roulette when he is captured by the Vietnamese enemy in The Deer Hunter. *His ordeal proves too much for him and leads to a spiral of masochism, from which even his best friend Michael (Robert De Niro) cannot save him.*

Chuck Aspegren, who played Axel, was in fact a real-life steel worker in a plant in Indiana.

Director Michael Cimino worked as co-screenwriter on *Silent Running* in 1971, and *Magnum Force* (1973) where he met Clint Eastwood. This led to his first work as a director the following year with *Thunderbolt and Lightfoot* (1974).

Two versions of the 'Theme from The Deer Hunter' (Cavatina) made the British top twenty in the charts. The Shadows reached number nine, and UK guitarist John Williams took his recording to number 13. A vocal version by Iris Williams, called 'He Was Beautiful', also made the top twenty in 1979.

Academy Awards: Best Film (Producers Barry Spikings, Michael Deeley, Michael Cimino and John Peverall), Best Direction (Michael Cimino), Best Supporting Actor (Christopher Walken), Best Editing (Peter Zinner), Best Sound (Richard Portman, William McCaughey, Aaron Rochin and Darrin Knight)

Music: 'Theme from The Deer Hunter' (Cavatina)

Video availability

The Top Five

Week of 10 March 1979
1. The Deer Hunter
2. National Lampoon's Animal House
3. The Passage
4. Superman
5. Every Which Way But Loose

CALIFORNIA SUITE

31 March 1979	5 weeks*

Distributor:	Columbia
Director:	Herbert Ross
Producer:	Ray Stark
Screenplay:	Neil Simon
Music:	Claude Bolling

CAST
Alan Alda . . . . *Bill Warren*
Michael Caine . . . . *Sidney Cochran*
Bill Cosby . . . . *Dr Willis Panama*
Jane Fonda . . . . *Hannah Warren*
Walter Matthau . . . . *Marvin Michaels*
Elaine May . . . . *Mrs Michaels*
Richard Pryor . . . . *Dr Chauncy Gump*
Maggie Smith . . . . *Diana Barrie*

Neil Simon's screenplay consists of four short films revolving around four groups of visitors to the same suite in the Beverly Hills Hotel. The British couple, Sidney Cochran, an antiques dealer, and Diana Barrie, an actress, arrive in town to attend the Academy Awards ceremony but never seem to stop fighting. Marvin Michaels has to explain to his wife Millie his infidelity, while Bill and Hannah Warren are a divorced couple fighting over custody of their child. Dr Chauncy Gump and Dr Willis Panama and their respective wives, Lola and Bettina, turn their holiday break into a series of disasters.

Maggie Smith won her first Oscar for *The Prime of Miss Jean Brodie* and became a member of a very elite club of actresses who have won both Best Actress and Best Supporting Actress Oscars, the others being Helen Hayes, Ingrid Bergman and Meryl Streep.

Director Herbert Ross has collaborated with producer Ray Stark on a number of films, including *The Owl and the Pussycat* and *Funny Lady* (1975). Their work with writer Neil Simon includes *The Goodbye Girl*, *The Sunshine Boys* and *I Ought To Be In Pictures*.

Academy Awards: Best Supporting Actress (Maggie Smith)

Video availability

The Top Five

Week of 31 March 1979
1. California Suite
2. The Deer Hunter
3. The Boys from Brazil
4. Invasion of the Body Snatchers
5. National Lampoon's Animal House

BATTLESTAR GALACTICA

21 April 1979	1 week

Distributor:	Universal
Director:	Richard A. Colla
Producer:	John Dykstra
Screenplay:	Glen A. Larson
Music:	Stu Phillips

CAST
Lorne Greene . . . . *Commander Adama*
Richard L. Hatch . . . . *Captain Apollo*
Dirk Benedict . . . . *Lt Starbuck*
Maren Jensen . . . . *Athena*
Herb Jefferson Jr . . . . *Lt Boomer*
Terry Carter . . . . *Colonel Tigh*
Jane Seymour . . . . *Serina*
John Colicos . . . . *Count Baltar*
Lew Ayres . . . . *President Adar*

The commander of a large spacecraft takes on board survivors from an attack by the Cylons, a mechanical race of beings out to destroy all human life. They are rescued from the doomed planet of Galactica in the hope of finding new homes on earth.

Battlestar Galactica was produced from the first and fifth episodes of a short-lived American TV series.

Producer John Dykstra was part of the team responsible for the special effects in the movie *Star Wars* (1978) for which he won an Oscar.

Actor Dirk Benedict went on to play Templeton 'Face' Peck in *The A Team* and Ed Begley Jr, who played Ensign Greenbean, starred as Dr Victor Ehrlich in the TV series *St Elsewhere*. The patched together film also featured veteran actor Ray Milland.

Video availability

The Top Five

Week of 21 April 1979
1. Battlestar Galactica
2. California Suite
3. The Deer Hunter
4. Fantasia
5. The Wiz

THE WARRIORS

19 May 1979	2 weeks

Distributor:	Paramount
Director:	Walter Hill
Producer:	Lawrence Gordon
Screenplay:	David Shaber, Walter Hill
Music:	Barry DeVorzon

With every rival gang out to get them and the police unable to help, The Warriors *have to fight their way home to Coney Island.*

CAST

Michael Beck	Swan
James Remar	Ajax
Thomas Waites	Fox
Dorsey Wright	Cleon
Brian Tyler	Snow
David Harris	Cochise
Tom McKitterick	Cowboy
Marcelino Sanchez	Rembrandt

A Coney Island gang called the Warriors are blamed for the killing of low-life gangster Roger Hill, leader of another gang called the Riffs. The word on the street goes out that members of the Warriors are to be eliminated. All-out gang warfare breaks out.

Director Walter Hill's other credits include *Hard Times*, his debut in 1975, *The Driver* (1978), *48 Hrs* (1982), *Red Heat* (1989) and *Another 48 Hrs* (1990). Hill, who wanted to be an illustrator of comic books, escaped the Vietnam War because he suffered from asthma. He made good use of the time, working as an assistant on *The Thomas Crown Affair* in 1968 and *Take the Money and Run* in 1969.

Music: 'Last of the Ancient Breed', 'Nowhere To Run', 'Echoes of My Mind', 'In the City'

Video availability

The Top Five

Week of 19 May 1979
1. The Warriors
2. The Lady Vanishes
3. The Deer Hunter
4. Kentucky Fried Movie
5. Battlestar Galactica

ESCAPE TO ATHENA

2 June 1979	1 week

Distributor:	ITC
Director:	George Pan Cosmatos
Producer:	Jack Wiener, David Niven Jr
Screenplay:	Richard S. Lochte, Edward Anhalt
Music:	Lalo Schifrin

CAST

Roger Moore	Major Otto Hecht
Telly Savalas	Zeno
David Niven	Professor Blake
Claudia Cardinale	Eleana
Richard Roundtree	Nat
Stefanie Powers	Dottie
Sonny Bono	Rotelli
Elliot Gould	Charlie

A group of Anglo-American POWs are being held by the Germans on a Greek island. They plan their escape with the help of Resistance leader Zeno, but decide to make their task more difficult by taking a priceless art collection along for the ride. Roger Moore is the German camp commander who tries to thwart any escape plans.

Roger Moore has it written into his movie contracts that the film company must keep him supplied with hand-rolled Monte Cristo cigars from Cuba. On one of his Bond movies, his bill for smokes totalled £3176.50.

Telly Savalas last appeared in a number one film when he starred with Clint Eastwood in *Kelly's*

Heroes (1970). He also featured in *On Her Majesty's Secret Service* (1969).

Video availability

The Top Five

Week of 2 June 1979
1. Escape to Athena
2. The Warriors
3. Battlestar Galactica
4. The Deer Hunter
5. The Lady Vanishes

THE LADY VANISHES

9 June 1979	1 week

Distributor:	Rank
Director:	Anthony Page
Producer:	Tom Sachs
Screenplay:	George Axelrod
Music:	Richard Hartley

CAST
Elliott Gould	*Robert Condon*
Cybill Shepherd	*Amanda Kelly*
Angela Lansbury	*Miss Froy*
Herbert Lom	*Dr Hartz*
Arthur Lowe	*Charters*
Ian Carmichael	*Caldicott*
Gerald Harper	*Mr Todhunter*
Jean Anderson	*Baroness Kisling*

E lliott Gould is a photographer working for *Life Magazine* and Cybill Shepherd a crazy American heiress. They are thrown together on board a German train heading for England in 1939. When a sweet British nanny mysteriously disappears and

none of the passengers remember seeing her, Gould and Shepherd discover a political conspiracy.

The Lady Vanishes is a remake of the 1938 Alfred Hitchcock classic which starred Margaret Lockwood and Michael Redgrave.

Elliott Gould hit the number one spot with both *The Lady Vanishes* and *Escape to Athena*, Other number ones featuring Gould are *A Bridge Too Far* (1977) and *M*A*S*H* (1970).

Video availability

The Top Five

Week of 9 June 1979
1. The Lady Vanishes
2. Escape to Athena
3. The World is Full of Married Men
4. The Muppet Movie
5. The Deer Hunter

THE WORLD IS FULL OF MARRIED MEN

16 June 1979	1 week

Distributor:	New Realm
Director:	Robert Young
Producer:	Malcolm Fancey
Screenplay:	Jackie Collins
Music:	Frank Musker, Dominic Bugatti

CAST
Anthony Franciosa	*David Cooper*
Carroll Baker	*Linda Cooper*
Sherrie Cronn	*Claudia Parker*
Paul Nicholas	*Gem Gemini*
Gareth Hunt	*Jay Grossman*
Georgina Hale	*Lori Grossman*
Anthony Steel	*Conrad Lee*
John Nolan	*Joe*
Jean Gilpin	*Miss Field*

D avid Cooper is a 40-year-old director of TV commercials who has more than his fair share of carnal knowledge. His latest conquest is a young model, Claudia Parker, with ambitions to make it to the top of her profession. He is found out by his wife (Carroll Baker) who decides to have her own fling with a teenage rock singer, Gem Gemini, 15 years her junior.

The story is adapted from Jackie Collins' first novel of the same name.

Paul Nicholas began his career as a pianist with Screaming Lord Sutch's band, The Savages. He sings in the film, which features music by Hot Gossip, Mick Jackson and Bonnie Tyler, and various disco tracks.

The Top Five

Week of 16 June 1979
1. The World is Full of Married Men
2. Escape to Athena
3. The Lady Vanishes
4. The Muppet Movie
5. The Deer Hunter

Video availability

In The World is Full of Married Men, *scripted by Jackie Collins from her own novel, betrayed wife Linda Cooper (Carroll Baker) decides to get her own back on her adulterous husband by having her own fling with young rock star Gem Gemini (Paul Nicholas).*

DOCTOR ZHIVAGO

23 June 1979	1 week

A re-release; see 1965

The Top Five

Week of 23 June 1979
1. Doctor Zhivago
2. Oliver's Story
3. The Buddy Holly Story
4. The Lady Vanishes
5. Escape to Athena

PLAYERS

30 June 1979	1 week

Distributor:	Paramount
Director:	Anthony Harvey
Producer:	Robert Evans
Screenplay:	Arnold Schulman
Music:	Jerry Goldsmith

CAST
Ali MacGraw . . . . *Nicole*
Dean-Paul Martin . . . . *Chris*
Maximilian Schell . . . . *Marco*
Pancho González . . . . *Himself*
Steven Guttenberg . . . . *Rusty*
Melissa Prophet . . . . *Ann*

Top tennis player Chris has fought his way to the Men's Singles final at Wimbledon. As the match is about to start Chris has flashbacks to the heartaches leading up to the final. Chris had rescued and later fallen in love with a beautiful designer, Nicole, a victim of a car accident. While he is torn between his love for her and tennis, Nicole plays her own game, jetting between Chris and her Italian yacht-owning millionaire boyfriend, Marco, who in turn is having a pretty good time with his attractive secretary. The film climaxes with the on-court battle.

Ali MacGraw once worked as an editorial assistant for the magazine *Harper's Bazaar*.

Dean-Paul Martin was singer Dean Martin's son and this was his first feature film.

Many real life tennis players are featured playing themselves, including Guillermo Vilas and Pancho González.

Video availability

The Top Five

Week of 30 June 1979
1. Players
2. Dr Zhivago
3. Oliver's Story
4. Escape to Athena
5. The Buddy Holly Story

MOONRAKER

7 July 1979	10 weeks

Distributor:	United Artists
Director:	Lewis Gilbert
Producer:	Albert R. Broccoli
Screenplay:	Christopher Wood
Music:	John Barry
	Hal David (Lyrics)

CAST
Roger Moore . . . . *James Bond*
Lois Chiles . . . . *Holly Goodhead*
Michael Lonsdale . . . . *Drax*
Richard Kiel . . . . *Jaws*
Corinne Clery . . . . *Corinne Dufour*
Bernard Lee . . . . *M*
Desmond Llewelyn . . . . *Q*
Lois Maxwell . . . . *Miss Moneypenny*

Bond is on a space-age assignment to search out a missing space shuttle on loan to the British government. The trail leads to billionaire madman Hugo Drax, who has plans to use the shuttle to transport his team of people made up of beautiful and corrupt individuals from all races to a massive city he has built in space. He intends to release satellites equipped with a lethal nerve gas to destroy the Earth. True to form, Bond manages to foil his mighty plan by destroying his city with the help of the American armed forces and his arch enemy, Jaws, from *The Spy Who Loved Me*, who switches allegiance at the last minute.

It has been claimed that *Moonraker* cost more than all of the first eight bond movies put together. On a budget of $30 million, it caused director Lewis Gilbert to comment that he could make several features just with the cost of *Moonraker*'s phone bill. Fortunately for all concerned, *Moonraker* became, at the time, the highest grossing Bond movie to date.

Bond fans were informed on the credits of the previous Bond picture, *The Spy Who Loved Me*

The Top Five

Week of 7 July 1979
1. Moonraker
2. Blazing Saddles
3. Players
4. Dr Zhivago
5. The Europeans

(1977), that 'For Your eyes Only' was to be the next adventure. However, producer Albert Broccoli decided that with all the success of the space-age movies, it was time for Bond to explore that frontier.

Lois Chiles, who plays Dr Holly Goodhead, turned down the part of Anya in *The Spy Who Loved Me*

because she had temporarily retired from acting. She met director Lewis Gilbert on an airplane and he suggested she should play Holly.

Music: 'Moonraker' (Shirley Bassey)

Video availability

ALIEN

15 September 1979	8 weeks

Distributor:	Twentieth Century-Fox
Director:	Ridley Scott
Producer:	Gordon Carroll, David Giler and Walter Hill
Screenplay:	Dan O'Bannon
Music:	Jerry Goldsmith

CAST
Tom Skerritt . . . . *Dallas*
Sigourney Weaver . . . . *Ripley*
Veronica Cartwright . . . . *Lambert*
Harry Dean Stanton . . . . *Brett*
John Hurt . . . . *Kane*
Ian Holm . . . . *Ash*
Yaphet Kotto . . . . *Parker*

A small commercial spaceship is on its way back to Earth. During the journey an alien is inadvertently brought on board the craft. The crew only become aware of the danger when an alien hatches through the stomach of John Hurt in an explosion of blood. The crew is hunted and killed by the alien one by one until the only one left is Ripley. She survives the ordeal by the skin of her teeth.

Alien marked the movie debut for Sigourney (real name Susan) Weaver, although she did have a minor non-speaking part in Woody Allen's 1976 film *Annie Hall*. Weaver's mother was actress Elizabeth Inglis, who as a child appeared in Hitchcock's *The 39 Steps* (1959). Her father, Pat Weaver, was once the president of NBC and her uncle, Doodles Weaver, was a long-time vocalist with the Spike Jones Orchestra. Sigourney appeared in the equally successful sequels *Aliens* (1986) and *Alien 3* (1992).

Academy Awards: Best Visual Effects (H.R. Gieger, Carlo Rambaldi, Brian Johnson, Nick Allder and Denys Aling)

Video availability

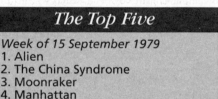

The Top Five

Week of 15 September 1979
1. Alien
2. The China Syndrome
3. Moonraker
4. Manhattan
5. Dracula

YANKS

10 November 1979	1 week

Distributor:	United Artists
Director:	John Schlesinger
Producer:	Joseph Janni, Lester Persky
Screenplay:	Colin Welland, Walter Bernstein
Music:	Richard Rodney Bennett

CAST
Richard Gere . . . . *Matt*
Lisa Eichhorn . . . . *Jean*
Vanessa Redgrave . . . . *Helen*
William Devane . . . . *John*
Chick Vennera . . . . *Danny*
Wendy Morgan . . . . *Mollie*
Rachel Roberts . . . . *Mrs Moreton*
Tony Melody . . . . *Mr Moreton*

A local English village in Lancashire is thrown into chaos during World War II when a large group of American troops appears on the scene. The GIs, including Richard Gere, immediately begin to make out with the women. While Matt falls for Jean, who is still pining for her absent boyfriend, Danny finds a willing bedfellow in Mollie. Although John and Helen are both married to other people, the frustra-

The Top Five

Week of 10 November 1979
1. Yanks
2. Prophecy
3. Alien
4. Zulu Dawn
5. Moonraker

tions of war push the two into more than a platonic relationship.

It was Gere's third film, *Looking for Mr Goodbar* (1978) in which he played Tony Lopanto, that really

brought him to the public's attention. In the early 1970s he had neglected his acting career in favour of his musical career with a rock band.

Video availability

MONTY PYTHON'S LIFE OF BRIAN

17 November 1979	8 weeks*

Distributor:	Hand Made Films
Director:	Terry Jones
Producer:	John Goldstone
Screenplay:	Graham Chapman, John Cleese, Terry Gilliam, Eric Idle, Terry Jones, Michael Palin
Music:	Geoffrey Burgeon

CAST
Terry Jones
The Virgin Mandy/Mother of Brian, a Ratbag/Colin/Simon the Holy Man/ Saintly Passer-by
Graham Chapman
1st Wise Man/Brian Called Brian/Biggus Dickus
Michael Palin
2nd Wise Man/Mr Big Nose/Francis a Revolutionary/Mrs A. Who Casts the Second Stone/ Ex-leper/Ben, an Ancient Prisoner/Pontius Pilate, Roman Governor/A Boring Prophet/Eddie/Nisus Wettus
John Cleese
3rd Wise Man/Reg, Leader of the Judean People's Front/Jewish Official at the Stoning/ Centurion of the Yard/Deadly Dick/Arthur
Kenneth Colley
Jesus the Christ
Gwen Taylor
Mrs Big Nose/Woman with Sick Donkey/Young Girl
Eric Idle
Mr Cheeky/Stan Called Loretta, a Confused Revolutionary/Harry The Haggler, Beard and Stone Salesman/Culprit Woman, Who Casts the First Stone/Intensely Dull Youth/Otto, the Nazarene Jailer's Assistant/Mr Frisbee III
Terence Bailer
Gregory/Revolutionaries and Masked Commandos/Dennis

Brian Cohen is born in a manger next to the Messiah, and is mistakenly visited by the three wise men bearing gifts. In later days, Brian's life parallels that of Jesus, earning a huge following through his disciples, and becomes involved in the terrorist People's Front of Judea. Ultimately he is condemned to the cross by Pontius Pilate, where he sings, with Eric Idle, the memorable 'Always Look on the Bright Side of Life'.

Top Twenty Films of 1979

1 Moonraker/Superman
2 Jaws 2
3 Every Which Way But Loose
4 Alien
5 Watership Down
6 The Deer Hunter
7 Grease
8 Quadrophenia
9 Pete's Dragon
10 Midnight Express
11 National Lampoon's Animal House
12 Death on the Nile
13 Porridge
14 The Cat from Outer Space
15 Battlestar Galactica
16 The 39 Steps/The Bitch/Lord of the Rings
17 The Warriors
18 Hooper
19 Piranha
20 Kentucky Fried Movie/Blazing Saddles/Monty Python and the Holy Grail

Life of Brian also featured Spike Milligan, George Harrison and Terry Gilliam.

When the film was first released, it caused much offence among certain religious groups. In fact Norway even went as far as banning the movie completely. Director Terry Jones went on to more comedy success with the number one movie *Personal Services* (1987).

Music: 'Always Look on the Bright Side of Life'

Video availability

The Top Five
Week of 17 November 1979
1. Monty Python's Life of Brian
2. Yanks
3. Mad Max
4. Zulu Dawn
5. Manhattan

STAR TREK: THE MOTION PICTURE

29 December 1979	2 weeks

Distributor: Paramount
Director: Robert Wise
Producer: Gene Roddenberry
Screenplay: Harold Livingston
Music: Jerry Goldsmith

CAST
William Shatner Captain (later Admiral) Kirk
Leonard Nimoy .... Spock
DeForest Kelley .... Dr McCoy
James Doohan .... Scotty
George Takei .... Sulu
Majel Barrett .... Dr Chapel
Walter Koenig .... Chekov
Nichelle Nichols .... Uhura

Somewhere in the 23rd century, an alien missile attack is sent to destroy the Earth. It has to be intercepted by the Starship U.S.S. *Enterprise* and its crew, led by Admiral Kirk. The starship interrupts its 2-year overhaul to embark on the mission. Along with his regular crew, Dr McCoy, Scotty, Sulu, Chekov and Uhura, Kirk picks up their Vulcan friend Spock 'to boldly go where no man has gone before'.

The movie was a spin-off from the successful TV series, which had been scrapped ten years previously, and cost in excess of $49 million to produce. To date there have been five sequels but only *Star Trek VI: The Undiscovered Country* (1991) and *Star Trek IV: The Voyage Home* (1987) made it to the top of the box office chart. The others in the series all made the top five. *Star Trek Generations* was released early in 1995.

Video availability

The Top Five

Week of 29 December 1979
1. Star Trek: The Motion Picture
2. Apocalypse Now
3. The Black Hole
4. Monty Python's Life of Brian
5. Meteor

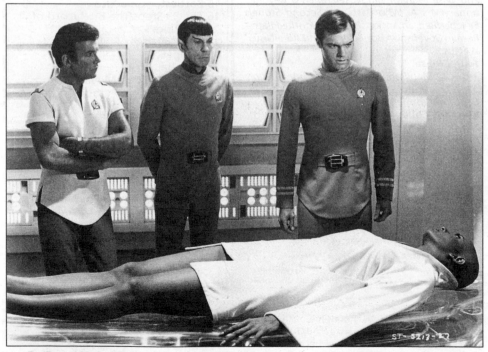

Dr 'Bones' McCoy (DeForest Kelley), Admiral James T. Kirk (William Shatner) and Mr Spock (Leonard Nimoy) go back to work in Star Trek: The Motion Picture, *with the beautiful Ilia (Persis Khambatta) on board the U.S.S.* Enterprise *to act as advisor.*

THE 1980s

The 1980s was the decade which made stars of such diverse actors as Dudley Moore and Tom Cruise, and where actresses as different as Meryl Streep and Madonna were hitting the top of the box office charts. Old favourites from the 1970s like the *Star Wars* team returned with *The Empire Strikes Back* and *Return of the Jedi* to complete the original trilogy, and James Bond and Superman both made several more trips to the top. Dustin Hoffman put on women's clothes to make us laugh in *Tootsie* and closed out the decade in Oscar-winning style as the idiot sauvant in *Rain Man*.

In 1982 scriptwriter Colin Welland won an Oscar for *Chariots of Fire* and told the watching millions 'The British Are Coming!' and, sure enough, the very next year Richard Attenborough and his team scooped eight of the statuettes for the critical and commercial success *Gandhi*.

Not content with hitting the top spot as Han Solo in the *Star Wars* series, Harrison Ford created another popular cinematic hero, Indiana Jones, who soared to number one on three occasions during the decade – and we still haven't counted *Bladerunner* and *Working Girl*. Other action-adventure heroes who became popular were Paul Hogan's *Crocodile Dundee* and Mel Gibson's *Mad Max*. And not to be outdone Sean Connery returned one more time as secret agent 007 in *Never Say Never Again*.

48 Hours made Eddie Murphy a star and *Beverly Hills Cop* consolidated his status as a top box office attraction. Michael J. Fox hit a quick hat-trick with the *Back To The Future* trilogy, and Michael Douglas found success with, among others, *Fatal Attraction* and *Wall Street*. Michael Keaton's caped crusader kept the streets of Gotham City crime-free in *Batman*, and our very own Michael, Caine that is, won a Best Supporting Actor Oscar for Woody Allen's *Hannah and Her Sisters*.

Robin Williams began to create a name for himself as an extremely versatile actor with contrasting performances in *Good Morning Vietnam* and *Dead Poets Society*, and Bob Hoskins, who first shot to fame as the gangster in *The Long Good Friday*, hit number one with *Pink Floyd: The Wall*, *Mona Lisa* and *The Cotton Club* before really testing his skills against the animated form of Roger Rabbit!

How could we let the decade go without acknowledging *E.T.?* Steven Spielberg's lovable extra-terrestrial became everybody's favourite alien in 1982, and, although the film was the decade's biggest box office blockbuster, it's refreshing that as yet there's no sign of a sequel.

But perhaps the biggest star of the 1980s was Arnold Schwarzenegger. Larger than life, the bodybuilding champion from Austria swept all before him in a series of action adventure movies including the two *Conan* films (*Barbarian* and *Destroyer*) plus *Commando*, *Predator* and *Red Heat*. He also travelled through time and space with *The Running Man*, *Terminator* and *Total Recall*, and still found time to appear in the top-grossing comedy *Twins* with Danny De Vito. What a star!

Lt Colonel Kilgore (Robert Duvall), The Chief (Albert Hall) and Captain Willard (Martin Sheen) enjoy a bit of a singalong in the crazy world of the Vietnam War in Apocalypse Now.

APOCALYPSE NOW

12 January 1980   **1 week**

Distributor:	Omni Zoetrope
Director:	Francis Coppola
Producer:	Francis Coppola
Screenplay:	John Milius, Francis Coppola
Music:	Carmine Coppola

CAST

Marlon Brando	*Colonel Kurtz*
Martin Sheen	*Captain Willard*
Robert Duvall	*Lt. Colonel Kilgore*
Fred Forrest	*Chef*
Sam Bottoms	*Lance*
Albert Hall	*Chief*
Larry Fishburne	*Clean*
Dennis Hopper	*Photo-journalist*

In 1968 Captain Willard, a special agent of the American Army, undertakes a mission to go into the Cambodian jungle during the Vietnam War. His orders are to track down and kill Colonel Kurtz, a breakaway green beret gone raving mad. Kurtz has set himself up as a dictator on a Cambodian island with a tribe of warriors to fight his own private war. Willard finds himself caught in the middle of the nightmarish battles as he continues his search for the colonel. He discovers an unspeakable horror when he finds him.

The film took five years to complete, with an original budget of $12 million finally coming to over $40 million. This included an $18 million overspend which came out of director Francis Ford Coppola's own pocket in return for the entire rights to the picture in perpetuity. One expensive decision was to use no models in the war scenes; all the tanks, aircraft and helicopters were real.

During the filming in the Philippines Martin Sheen suffered a minor heart attack and a number of doubles were used while he recovered. Sheen's character, Benjamin Willard, was named after Harrison Ford's sons, Benjamin and Willard. Ford had a cameo role in the film as George Lucas.

The Top Five

Week of 12 January 1980
1. Apocalypse Now
2. Monty Python's Life of Brian
3. Star Trek: The Motion Picture
4. The Black Hole
5. Yanks

Coppola makes a brief appearance in the film as a combat director.

Academy Awards: Best Cinematography (Vittorio Storaro), Best Sound (Walter Murch, Mark Berger, Richard Beggs and Nat Boxer)

Video availability

ESCAPE FROM ALCATRAZ

2 February 1980	2 weeks

Distributor:	Paramount
Director:	Donald Siegel
Producer:	Donald Siegel
Screenplay:	Richard Tuggle
Music:	Jerry Fielding

CAST

Clint Eastwood	....	*Frank Morris*
Patrick McGoohan	....	*Warden*
Roberts Blossom	....	*Doc*
Jack Thibeau	....	*Clarence Anglin*
Fred Ward	....	*John Anglin*
Paul Benjamin	....	*English*
Larry Hankin	....	*Charley Butts*
Bruce M. Fischer	....	*Wolf*
Frank Ronzio	....	*Litmus*

*E*scape from Alcatraz is the true story of Frank Morris' break-out from what was considered an escape-proof island penitentiary. After being sentenced to life imprisonment, Morris becomes obsessed with the idea of finding a way out of Alcatraz. He begins to dig an escape route using a pair of nail clippers. The tedium of prison life, and the unpleasant and aggressive behaviour of the wardens and fellow prisoners spur Morris on in his quest for freedom.

It was the real breakout of Frank Morris with two other prisoners in 1962 that was instrumental in the closure of the prison. The three men were never heard of again.

Escape from Alcatraz was the fifth movie that combined Don Siegel and actor Clint Eastwood.

Video availability

The Top Five

Week of 2 February 1980
1. Escape from Alcatraz
2. Monty Python's Life of Brian
3. Apocalypse Now
4. The Amityville Horror
5. The Black Hole

10

16 February 1980	5 weeks

Distributor:	Warner/Orion
Director:	Blake Edwards
Producer:	Blake Edwards, Tony Adams
Screenplay:	Blake Edwards
Music:	Henry Mancini

CAST

Dudley Moore	....	*George*
Julie Andrews	....	*Sam*
Bo Derek	....	*Jenny*
Robert Webber	....	*Hugh*
Dee Wallace	....	*Mary Lewis*
Sam Jones	....	*David*
Brian Dennehy	....	*Bartender*
Max Showalter	....	*The Reverend*

*G*eorge is a successful songwriter but is becoming frustrated with work, his girlfriend Sam and, above all, sex. He creates a ranking system from one to ten for females' sexual performances and has a dream about finding an eleven. He thinks he has found an eleven in Jenny, who, with her new husband David, is on her way to a honeymoon in Mexico. George follows them there and ends up saving David in a boating accident. While her husband is recovering in hospital, Jenny shows her appreciation to George in the bedroom.

The part of George was originally given to George Segal who quit the movie in its early stages over creative differences. Although Bo Derek found fame through this movie she failed to make any further

The Top Five

Week of 16 February 1980
1. 10
2. The Rose
3. Escape from Alcatraz
4. Monty Python's Life of Brian
5. Apocalypse Now

successful pictures. Dudley Moore played piano with the band featured on the musical soundtrack.

The film company in the US was so convinced that *10* was going to be a box office flop that they cancelled two other projects planned by director Blake Edwards.

Music: 'It's Easy To Say', 'He Pleases Me', 'Don't Call It Love', 'I Have An Ear For Love'

THE ELECTRIC HORSEMAN

22 March 1980	1 week

Distributor:	Columbia
Director:	Sydney Pollack
Producer:	Ray Stark
Screenplay:	Robert Garland
Music:	Dave Grusin

CAST
Robert Redford . . . . *Sonny Steele*
Jane Fonda . . . . *Hallie*
Valerie Perrine . . . . *Charlotta*
Willie Nelson . . . . *Wendell*
John Saxon . . . . *Hunt Sears*
Nicolas Coster . . . . *Fitzgerald*
Allan Arbus . . . . *Danny*
Wilford Brimley . . . . *Farmer*
Will Hare . . . . *Gus*

Sonny Steele was once a big rodeo star but his career is on the wane, so much so that, when he's not drunk, he turns his hand to plugging breakfast cereals on television. He is also booked to appear riding a horse valued at $12 million in a Las Vegas revue. Disgusted that the animal has been drugged, he steals it and takes off for the hills in protest, hotly pursued by TV reporter Hallie Martin, who thinks she may get an exclusive story.

This is the third time Redford and Fonda appeared together, following *The Chase* and *Barefoot in the Park*. Fonda also worked with Pollack on the 1969 film *They Shoot Horses Don't They*. Robert Redford and director Sydney Pollack first worked on a movie together in 1966 on the adaptation of the Tennessee Williams story 'This Property is Condemned'. They found even greater success with *The Way We Were* (1974) and *Three Days of the Condor* (1975).

Music: 'Mamas', 'Don't Let Your Babies Grow Up To Be Cowboys'

Video availability

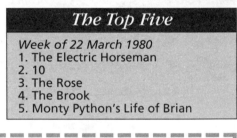

The Top Five

Week of 22 March 1980
1. The Electric Horseman
2. 10
3. The Rose
4. The Brook
5. Monty Python's Life of Brian

KRAMER VS KRAMER

29 March 1980	7 weeks

Distributor:	Columbia
Director:	Robert Benton
Producer:	Stanley R. Jaffe
Screenplay:	Robert Benton
Music:	Henry Purcell (adapted by John Kander) Antonio Vivaldi (adapted by Herb Harris)

CAST
Dustin Hoffman . . . . *Ted Kramer*
Meryl Streep . . . . *Joanna Kramer*
Jane Alexander . . . . *Margaret Phelps*
Justin Henry . . . . *Billy Kramer*
Howard Duff . . . . *John Shaunessy*
George Coe . . . . *Jim O'Connor*
Jobeth Williams . . . . *Phyllis Bernard*

Joanna Kramer walks out on her husband and child simply because she feels she needs to find herself. Ted, who has a successful career in advertising, is left to look after their six-year-old son, Billy. The strain takes its toll; Ted becomes careless at work and eventually loses his job. Joanna then decides to sue for custody of the boy, claiming that she is in a better financial position to care for him.

Producer Stanley R. Jaffe wanted François Truffaut to direct the movie, but screenwriter Robert Benton, who adapted Avery Corman's novel, insisted that the only way he would part with his property was if he was allowed to make his debut in the director's chair.

Over 200 children auditioned for the part of Billy. Justin Henry, who won the part, became, at the time, the youngest actor ever nominated for an Oscar at the age of 6. Dustin Hoffman was on the

Ted Kramer (Dustin Hoffman) is left holding the baby, well, his six-year-old son Billy (Justin Henry), when his wife Joanna (Meryl Streep) suddenly ups and leaves.

final selection committee that decided on Justin for the part and spent days with the boy teaching him how to act.

Academy Awards: Best Film (Producer Stanley R. Jaffe), Best Direction (Robert Benton), Best Actor (Dustin Hoffman), Best Supporting Actress (Meryl Streep), Best Screenplay (Robert Benton)

Video availability

The Top Five

Week of 29 March 1980
1. Kramer vs Kramer
2. The Electric Horseman
3. 10
4. Murder By Decree
5. And Justice for All

AMERICAN GIGOLO

17 May 1980	2 weeks

Distributor:	Paramount
Director:	Paul Schrader
Producer:	Jerry Bruckheimer
Screenplay:	Paul Schrader
Music:	Giorgio Moroder

CAST
Richard Gere .... Julian
Lauren Hutton .... Michelle
Hector Elizondo .... Sunday
Nina Van Pallandt .... Anne
Bill Duke .... Leon Jaimes
Brian Davies .... Charles Stratton
K Callan .... Lisa Williams
Tom Stewart .... Mr Rheiman
Patti Carr .... Judy Rheiman

Michelle is the dissatisfied wife of a leading American Senator. She hires expensive gigolo Richard Gere, who makes his living out of pleasing rich women. All is well until they fall in love. While Gere is trying to get in touch with his feelings, he finds himself a suspect in the kinky murder of an old client.

In 1973 Richard Gere played the lead role in the London production of *Grease*. The following year he was signed for his first movie, a small part in

Report to the Commissioner in which he played a pimp named Billy and appeared in just three scenes.

After *In Search of Mr Goodbar* he became a much-sought after actor, and features in five other box office number ones, the most successful being *Pretty Woman* (1990).

Music: 'Call Me' (Blondie)

Video availability

THE EMPIRE STRIKES BACK

31 May 1980	11 weeks

Distributor:	Twentieth Century-Fox
Director:	Irvin Kershner
Producer:	Gary Kurtz
Screenplay:	Leigh Brackett, Lawrence Kasdan
Music:	John Williams

CAST

Mark Hamill	*Luke Skywalker*
Harrison Ford	*Han Solo*
Carrie Fisher	*Princess Leia*
David Prowse (James Earl Jones, voice)	*Darth Vader*
Anthony Daniels	*C3PO*
Peter Mayhew	*Chewbacca*
Kenny Baker	*R2D2*
Frank Oz	*Yoda*
Alec Guinness	*Ben Kenobi*

In the sequel to *Star Wars*, the romance between Princess Leia and Han Solo goes from strength to strength in Cloud City. But the evil Darth Vader in his Galactic Empire still has his sights set on destroying the Rebel Alliance complete with the Princess, Solo and Luke Skywalker. Darth Vader follows Luke, who is searching for Yoda, a little creature who teaches him much about the Force.

Bigger and better than the original Star Wars, *the sequel* The Empire Strikes Back *has the evil Darth Vader confessing that he is in fact the father of the do-goody Luke Skywalker.*

The scene of Han Solo's starship flying into a meteorite field to escape enemy craft took two hundred pieces of film and over a week to complete, just to keep re-running the various shots into one.

The swamp scene, in which a monster shoots out of the slime and tries to grab R2D2, was filmed in George Lucas's unfinished swimming pool, which he was having built at his house in San Rafael.

Academy Awards: Best Sound (Bill Varney, Steve Maslow, Gregg Landaker and Peter Sutton), Best Visual Effects (Brian Johnson, Richard Edlund, Dennis Muren and Bruce Nicholson)

Video availability

AIRPLANE!

16 August 1980	4 weeks

Distributor:	Paramount
Director:	Jim Abrahams, David Zucker, Jerry Zucker
Producer:	Jon Davison
Screenplay:	Jim Abrahams, David Zucker, Jerry Zucker
Music:	Elmer Bernstein

CAST
Robert Hays . . . . *Ted Striker*
Julie Hagerty . . . . *Elaine*
Kareem Abdul-Jabbar . . . . *Murdock*
Lloyd Bridges . . . . *McCroskey*
Peter Graves . . . . *Captain Oveur*
Leslie Nielsen . . . . *Dr Rumack*
Lorna Patterson . . . . *Randy*
Robert Stack . . . . *Kramer*
Stephen Stucker . . . . *Johnny*

Wartime pilot Ted Striker, who now has a fear of flying, boards a commercial plane bound for Chicago. On board is his ex-girlfriend, Elaine, a stewardess on the flight. When the entire crew of the flight deck go down with food poisoning, Striker is forced to land the plane, but only manages to succeed with Elaine's encouragement, and help on the ground from Captain Kramer, an expert in aiding pilots in distress.

The film, which never missed a cliché, was a spoof of all the disaster movies, in particular the *Airport* series. Writers/directors Jim Abrahams and Jerry and David Zucker have cameo roles in the movie, Abrahams as a religious nut and the Zucker brothers as ground controllers. Another cameo appearance was Ethel Merman playing a man.

Video availability

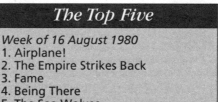

The Top Five

Week of 16 August 1980
1. Airplane!
2. The Empire Strikes Back
3. Fame
4. Being There
5. The Sea Wolves

McVICAR

13 September 1980	1 week

Distributor:	The Who Films/Brent-Walker
Director:	Tom Clegg
Producer:	Roy Baird, Bill Curbishley, Roger Daltrey
Screenplay:	John McVicar, Tom Clegg
Music:	Jeff Wayne

CAST
Roger Daltrey . . . . *McVicar*
Adam Faith . . . . *Probyn*
Cheryl Campbell . . . . *Sheila*
Steven Berkoff . . . . *Harrison*
Brian Hall . . . . *Stokes*
Jeremy Blake . . . . *Johnson*
Leonard Gregory . . . . *Collins*
Peter Jonfield . . . . *Harris*

The film was adapted from McVicar's own book on his life as a villain and eventual rehabilitation. At one time a dangerous criminal, John McVicar managed to escape from a high security prison in Durham, England, where he was serving an eight-year sentence for robbery with violence. After his recapture, he decides it's time to reform.

The Top Five

Week of 13 September 1980
1. McVicar
2. Airplane!
3. The Fiendish Plot of Dr Fu Manchu
4. The Empire Strikes Back
5. Being There

Adam Faith made his movie debut in 1960 when he appeared with Shirley Ann Field in the X-rated *Beat Girl*, followed by *Never Let Go* in the same year, *What a Whopper* in 1961 and *Mix Me a Person* in 1962.

Roger Daltrey set a trend for rock stars to play gangsters. Phil Collins played Buster Edwards in *Buster* (1988) and the Kemp brothers, Gary and Martin, played *The Krays* (1990).

Music: 'Free Me', 'Bitter and Twisted', 'Escape', 'Just a Dream Away', 'McVicar', 'My Time is Gonna Come', 'White City Lights', 'Without Your Love'

Video availability

CRUISING

20 September 1980	2 weeks

Distributor:	Lorimar
Director:	William Friedkin
Producer:	Jerry Weintraub
Screenplay:	William Friedkin
Music:	Jack Nitzsche

CAST
Al Pacino	Steve Burns
Paul Sorvino	Capt. Edelson
Karen Allen	Nancy
Richard Cox	Stuart Richards
Don Scardino	Ted Bailey
Joe Spinell	Patrolman DiSimone
Jay Acovone	Skip Lee
Randy Jurgensen	Detective Lefransky

A young New York cop (Al Pacino), just out of the police academy, is sent undercover to flush out a sadistic serial killer who is terrorizing the gay community. Managing to infiltrate the bizarre world of gay S & M, and witnessing some pretty unpleasant scenes, he picks up the trail of the killer only to find he's after the wrong guy. Eventually he's back on track but as the net closes in on the real killer it looks as though the cop is heading for a nervous breakdown after all the degradation he's seen while on the case.

Al Pacino made his movie debut in the 1969 film *Me, Natalie*, which starred Patty Duke and James Farentino. Pacino appears in the cast of a total of nine box office number ones, including *The Godfather* parts I, II, III. Director Friedkin's previous numbers ones were *French Connection* in 1972 and *The Exorcist* in 1974.

Video availability

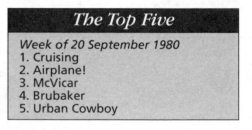

The Top Five

Week of 20 September 1980
1. Cruising
2. Airplane!
3. McVicar
4. Brubaker
5. Urban Cowboy

DRESSED TO KILL

4 October 1980	1 week

Distributor:	Filmways
Director:	Brian DePalma
Producer:	George Litto
Screenplay:	Brian DePalma
Music:	Pino Donaggio (Composer)
	Natalie Massara (Conductor)

CAST
Michael Caine	Dr Robert Elliott
Angie Dickinson	Kate Miller
Nancy Allen	Liz Blake
Keith Gordon	Peter Miller
Dennis Franz	Detective Marino
David Margulies	Dr Levy
Ken Baker	Warren Lockman
Brandon Maggart	Cleveland Sam
Susanna Clemm	Bobbi

In this murder mystery Angie Dickinson plays a sexually frustrated housewife, advised by her psychiatrist to have an extra-marital affair. She picks up a complete stranger in a museum who whisks her into the back of a New York cab for a steamy sex session. Having found that he's stolen her ring she gets into the museum elevator to try to retrieve it but she's killed by a knife-wielding woman. Liz, a high-class hooker, discovers the body, and is found with the knife in her hand and is immediately suspected of the murder. With the help of Kate's son, Liz sets out to solve the mystery of the 'woman' who always dresses to kill.

Born Maurice Micklewhite, Michael Caine took his surname from a billboard advertising 'The Caine

Mutiny'. Caine's first appearance in a number one movie is *Zulu* in 1964. He features in a total of 11 titles, the most recent being *The Fourth Protocol* (1987).

Sean Connery was the original thought for Michael Caine's part, as was Liv Ullman for the role of Kate. The European version of the movie was slightly longer and some of the more explicit scenes were left in.

A stand-in was used for some of Angie Dickinson's nude scenes.

The Top Five

Week of 4 October 1980
1. Dressed to Kill
2. Brubaker
3. Airplane!
4. Special Edition of Close Encounters of the Third Kind
5. Cruising

Video availability

THE SHINING

11 October 1980	2 weeks

Distributor:	Warner
Director:	Stanley Kubrick
Producer:	Stanley Kubrick
Screenplay:	Stanley Kubrick, Diane Johnson
Music:	Béla Bartók

CAST
Jack Nicholson . . . . *Jack Torrance*
Shelley Duvall . . . . *Wendy Torrance*
Danny Lloyd . . . . *Danny Torrance*

Scatman Crothers . . . . *Halloran*
Barry Nelson . . . . *Ullman*
Philip Stone . . . . *Grady*
Joe Turkel . . . . *Lloyd*
Anne Jackson . . . . *Doctor*
Tony Burton . . . . *Durkin*

Writer Jack Torrance moves his wife and son, Danny, to Colorado to take up a job as caretaker at the isolated Overlook hotel. The boy discovers he has the ability to see events from the past and the future and project them into other people's minds. Danny gets a bad feeling about the hotel and has

In The Shining *Wendy Torrance (Shelley Duvall) is driven to despair by her husband Jack (Jack Nicholson) when he becomes possessed by supernatural forces in the hotel where he has taken a job as caretaker.*

visions of a previous caretaker murdering his family. The hotel's supernatural forces manage to possess his father who appears to go mad and wages war on the boy and his mother.

At the age of 17, Jack Nicholson left New York and headed for California to stay with his sister. After her death he discovered that she was actually his mother. He got his first job at a film studio as an office boy for MGM, where he replied to fan mail sent to cartoon characters. He claims that he wrote the scene in *The Shining* in which he goes crazy with his wife who interrupts his work at his typewriter. It was based on a real-life incident when he was married to actress Sandra Knight.

Director Stanley Kubrick cut four minutes from the film, which is based on Stephen King's best seller, just days after the film premièred.

In the 1991 number one movie *Misery*, also based on a Stephen King novel, there is a throwaway remark about 'that guy who went mad in a nearby hotel'.

Video availability

The Top Five
Week of 11 October 1980
1. The Shining
2. Dressed to Kill
3. Brubaker
4. Being There
5. Airplane!

THE ELEPHANT MAN

25 October 1980	2 weeks

Distributor:	EMI
Director:	David Lynch
Producer:	Jonathan Sanger
Screenplay:	Christopher DeVore, Eric Bergren, David Lynch
Music:	John Morris

CAST

Anthony Hopkins	*Frederick Treves*
John Hurt	*John Merrick*
Anne Bancroft	*Mrs Kendal*
John Gielgud	*Carr Gomm*
Wendy Hiller	*Mothershead*
Freddie Jones	*Bytes*
Michael Elphick	*Night Porter*
Hannah Gordon	*Mrs Treves*
Helen Ryan	*Princess Alexandra*

John Hurt plays the lead role in this true story of John Merrick, so badly deformed that he is called the Elephant Man. He is rescued from a carnival, where he is displayed as a freak, by Dr Frederick Treves, a top surgeon, who gives him shelter in a hospital. After studying his case Treves helps him improve his speech and gain enough confidence to enter into society. However, Treves' motives are questioned by some who believe that he helped

Merrick to promote his own profile and not out of altruism or medical interest.

Several actors, including Philip Anglim, David Bowie and Mark Hamill, played John Merrick on Broadway in a 1979 New York stage play *The Elephant Man* at the Booth Theatre. It played 916 performances and won the Tony Award and the New York Drama Critics' Circle Award for Best Play that year. A legal battle raged between the producers of the Broadway show and the movie company over the title of the film. The matter was settled privately out of court.

A TV movie, based on the Bernard Pomerance's Broadway Show, was made in 1982, starring Philip Anglim and Glenn Close.

Video availability

The Top Five
Week of 25 October 1980
1. The Elephant Man
2. Dressed to Kill
3. The Blue Lagoon
4. The Shining
5. The Hunter

CALIGULA

8 November 1980	6 weeks

Distributor:	GTO	Producer:	Bob Guccione, Franco Rossellini
Director:	Giovanni Tinto Brass	Screenplay:	Uncredited
		Music:	Paul Celmente

The Elephant Man is the true story of John Merrick (John Hurt), who was so disfigured that he was treated as a funfair freak until he found understanding from Mrs Kendall (Anne Bancroft) and Frederick Treves (Anthony Hopkins).

CAST
Malcolm McDowell . . . . Caligula
Teresa Ann Savoy . . . . Drusilla
Helen Mirren . . . . Cesonia
Peter O'Toole . . . . Tiberius
John Steiner . . . . Longino
Guido Mannari . . . . Macrone
Paulo Bonacellie . . . . Cherea
Giancarlo Badessi . . . . Claudio
John Gielgud . . . . Nerva

In this costume epic the sadistic Emperor Caligula rules the ancient city of Rome. The city is rife with disease, and life is cheap and sex is rampant. The 25-year-old epileptic Emperor has no moral qualms about executing his enemies, or in fact anyone who upsets his plans, including his wife, Cesonia and Emperor Tiberius. Within the film almost all Caligula's interactions with other people include scenes of graphic sex and violence.

The film was discredited and disowned no sooner than it was finished. Gore Vidal, who wrote the original screenplay, succeeded in having his name removed from the film. The actors tried to disassociate themselves from the production, and director Tinto Brass was fired because of artistic differences with the producer. His dismissal resulted in litigation that prevented the release of the film for two years. Some of the more lascivious scenes may have been down to producer, Bob Guccione, head of *Penthouse* magazine.

Video availability

The Top Five

Week of 8 November 1980
1. Caligula
2. The Blues Brothers
3. The Elephant Man
4. Dressed to Kill
5. Snow White and the Seven Dwarfs

FLASH GORDON

20 December 1980	6 weeks

Distributor:	EMI
Director:	Mike Hodges
Producer:	Dino De Laurentiis

Screenplay:	Lorenzo Semple Jr
Music:	Howard Blake, Queen

CAST
Sam J. Jones . . . . Flash Gordon

Melody Anderson . . . . *Dale Arden*
Topol . . . . *Dr Hans Zarkov*
Max Von Sydow . . . . . . *The Emperor Ming*
Ornella Muti . . . . *Princess Aura*
Timothy Dalton . . . . *Prince Barin*
Brian Blessed . . . . *Prince Vultan*
Peter Wyngarde . . . . *Klytus*

In this modern version of the classic comic strip, Flash Gordon, with his girlfriend Dale and his associate Dr Zarkov, heads for the planet Mongo in an attempt to stop it colliding with Earth. On his journey he meets up with, amongst others, the evil Ming the Merciless, who is plotting world domination. Ming's sexy daughter takes a strong fancy to our hero and goes to some lengths to keep him.

Sam J. Jones was once a well-known American footballer and appeared in the centre page spread of *Playgirl* magazine. His only other real claim to fame was as Bo Derek's husband in the movie *10* (1980). Flash was originally played by Buster Crabbe in the vintage thirteen-part TV series based on Alex Raymond's 1930s King Features comic strip.

Some of the music and sets were borrowed from the 1935 movie *The Bride of Frankenstein*.

The Top Five

Week of 20 December 1980
1. Flash Gordon
2. Caligula
3. Raise the Titanic
4. Being There
5. Snow White and the Seven Dwarfs

The film had many cameo appearances, including one by future James Bond Timothy Dalton, and Robbie Coltrane.

The Queen single 'Flash' reached number 10 in the UK charts and the album 'Flash Gordon' reached number 10 in the UK, spending 15 weeks on the charts.

Music: 'Flash' (Queen)

Video availability

Top Twenty Films of 1980

1 The Empire Strikes Back
2 Kramer vs Kramer
3 Star Trek – The Motion Picture
4 Monty Python's Life of Brian
5 Airplane!
6 10
7 Escape from Alcatraz
8 The Black Hole
9 The Shining
10 Apocalypse Now
11 The Amityville Horror
12 McVicar
13 Last Feelings
14 Yanks
15 Friday the 13th
16 One Flew Over the Cuckoo's Nest
17 The Aristocats
18 The Bermuda Triangle
19 The Wanderers
20 Breaking Glass

THE EXTERMINATOR

31 January 1981	1 week

Distributor:	Interstar
Director:	James Glickenhaus
Producer:	Mark Buntzman
Screenplay:	James Glickenhaus
Music:	Joe Renzetti

CAST
Christopher George *Detective James Dalton*
Samantha Eggar . . . . . *Dr Megan Stewart*
Robert Ginty . . . . *John Eastland*
Steve James . . . . *Michael Jefferson*

Robert Ginty, a Vietnam vet, returns to New York where one of his wartime friends was savagely attacked and left paralysed by a street gang. He becomes a vigilante, set on gaining revenge. After dealing with the gang, Ginty then decides to clean up the rest of the city.

There was some disquiet in America about the film when the method of one murder appeared to have been copied in real life.

A sequel was released in 1984, *Exterminator II*, directed by Mark Buntzman and with a completely different cast.

Video availability

The Top Five

Week of 31 January 1981
1. The Exterminator
2. The Dogs of War
3. Flash Gordon
4. Caligula
5. Tribute

This 1980s remake of the story of Flash Gordon cost the movie company somewhere in the region of $20 million to make. Sam J. Jones plays Flash and Max Von Sydow the Emperor Ming the Merciless.

THE JAZZ SINGER

7 February 1981	3 weeks

Distributor:	EMI
Director:	Richard Fleischer
Producer:	Jerry Leider
Screenplay:	Herbert Baker
Music:	Neil Diamond/Leonard Rosenman

CAST
Neil Diamond . . . . *Jess Robin*
Laurence Olivier . . . . . . *Cantor Rabinovitch*
Lucie Arnaz . . . . *Molly Bell*
Catlin Adams . . . . *Rivka Rabinovitch*
Franklyn Ajaye . . . . *Bubba*
Paul Nicholas . . . . *Keith Lennox*
Sully Boyar . . . . *Eddie Gibbs*

In this musical remake of the 1927 Al Jolson classic, Neil Diamond plays New York cantor's son, Jess Rabinovitch. He changes his name to Robin and is disowned by his family when he decides to break away from his Jewish roots. Following his ambition to become a pop star in Los Angeles, he hooks up with agent Molly Bell, does the rounds of the record companies and music publishers and remarkably quickly makes his ascent to the top of the record charts. Fame and fortune follow before Jess be-comes reunited with his father and family and reaffirms his loyalty to his faith.

This was the third remake of Al Jolson's first 'talkie', but nowhere near as memorable. Some dislocation was caused when director Richard Fleischer took over midway through shooting from Sidney J. Furie. The film was also Neil Diamond's debut and only appearance to date on the big screen. Diamond had a hit with the film's song 'Love on the Rocks' in 1980, before the film's release in this country. It reached number 17 in the UK charts.

Music: 'Love on the Rocks', 'America', 'Hello Again', 'Jerusalem', 'On the Robert E. Lee', 'Songs of Life', 'You Baby', 'Kol Nidre'

Video availability

The Top Five

Week of 7 February 1981
1. The Jazz Singer
2. The Exterminator
3. Caligula
4. The Dogs of War
5. The Bermuda Triangle

Based on the true life story of boxing champion Jake la Motta (Robert De Niro), Raging Bull *tells the story of the boxer's rise through the ranks and his downward spiral.*

RAGING BULL

28 February 1981	1 week

Distributor:	United Artists
Director:	Martin Scorsese
Producer:	Irwin Winkler, Robert Chartoff, Peter Savage
Screenplay:	Paul Schrader
Music:	Prerecorded classical and pop music

CAST

Robert De Niro . . . . *Jake La Motta*
Cathy Moriarty . . . . *Vickie La Motta*
Joe Pesci . . . . *Joey La Motta*
Frank Vincent . . . . *Salvy*
Nicholas Colosanto . . . . *Tommy Como*
Theresa Saldana . . . . *Lenore*
Frank Adonis . . . . *Patsy*

This critically acclaimed boxing bio-pic chronicles the rise and fall of middleweight champion Jake 'Raging Bull' La Motta. He and his brother and manager, Joey, are hassled by the mafia who want to control the fighter's career. The film follows Jake's progress from a trim and slim title contender in the 1940s, through his many brutal fights both inside the ring and out, including those with his wife Vickie. When his boxing days come to an end Jake winds up an overweight night-club host, introducing strip acts.

Raging Bull saw the first pairing of De Niro and Pesci who were reunited in *Once Upon a Time In America* (1984) and memorably in director Scorsese's *GoodFellas* (1990).

To look convincing in the movie, Robert De Niro actually worked out with the real Jake La Motta for several months in a New York gym. He also dined out at all the best restaurants, eating pasta and puddings to gain around fifty pounds for the final sequences of the movie depicting La Motta at the end of his career. The movie is based on La Motta's autobiography, *Raging Bull*, which he co-wrote with Joseph Carter and Peter Savage.

Academy Awards: Best Actor (Robert De Niro), Best Editing (Thelma Schoonmaker)

Music: 'Drum Boogie'

Video availability

The Top Five

Week of 28 February 1981
1. Raging Bull
2. The Jazz Singer
3. Battle Beyond the Stars
4. Nine to Five
5. Caligula

PRIVATE BENJAMIN

7 March 1981	2 weeks

Distributor: Warner
Director: Howard Zeiff
Producer: Nancy Meyers, Charles Shyer,
               Harvey Miller
Screenplay: Nancy Meyers, Charles Shyer,
               Harvey Miller
Music: Bill Conti

CAST
Goldie Hawn . . . . *Judy Benjamin*
Eileen Brennan . . . . *Captain Doreen Lewis*
Armand Assante . . . . *Henri Tremont*
Robert Webber . . . *Colonel Clay Thornbush*
Sam Wanamaker . . . . *Teddy Benjamin*
Barbara Barrie . . . . *Harriet Benjamin*

Upper middle-class divorcée Judy Benjamin is widowed on her second wedding night. Distraught and unable to think clearly what to do with the rest of her life, she enlists in the American Army against her parents' wishes. Although she initially finds life difficult and the harshly enforced discipline hard to take, Judy eventually realizes that her previously empty life is now being fulfilled. When the third love of her life appears she has to choose between him and the army.

Goldie Hawn enjoyed considerable success with the movie in the capacity of both executive producer and actress (she was Oscar-nominated for her performance). Her big break came when she was hired as a dancer for the American TV series *The Rowan and Martin's Laugh-In*. She was later given a few lines to read which she always fluffed, but that helped develop her character. She made her film debut in the 1969 movie *Cactus Flower*.

Video availability

The Top Five

Week of 7 March 1981
1. Private Benjamin
2. The Mirror Crack'd
3. The Long Good Friday
4. Raging Bull
5. The Jazz Singer

ORDINARY PEOPLE

21 March 1981	2 weeks*

Distributor: Paramount
Director: Robert Redford
Producer: Ronald L. Schwary
Screenplay: Alvin Sargent
Music: Marvin Hamlisch

CAST
Donald Sutherland . . . . *Calvin*
Mary Tyler Moore . . . . *Beth*
Judd Hirsch . . . . *Berger*
Timothy Hutton . . . . *Conrad*
M. Emmet Walsh . . . . *Swim Coach*
Elizabeth McGovern . . . . *Jeannine*

The rich Jarrett family go to pieces after the drowning of their eldest son. The younger brother, Conrad, is full of guilt, and becomes emotionally disturbed, believing his mother hates him. He feels he is to blame for the death and even attempts suicide himself before the compassionate psychiatrist Berger helps restore some emotional calm.

Ann-Margret was originally considered for the role of Beth, but was rejected on the grounds that she would have a problem playing an unsympathetic woman. Judd Hirsch's scenes were shot out of sequence because he was starring in the TV series *Taxi* at the time and didn't want to leave the show.

The film was Robert Redford's impressive debut as a director, and was the top Oscar winner in the USA in 1980.

Academy Awards: Best Film (Producer Ronald L. Schwary), Best Direction (Robert Redford), Best Supporting Actor (Timothy Hutton), Best Screenplay (Alvin Sargent)

Video availability

The Top Five

Week of 21 March 1981
1. Ordinary People
2. The Long Good Friday
3. Private Benjamin
4. The Mirror Crack'd
5. Coalminer's Daughter

STIR CRAZY

4 April 1981	2 weeks

Distributor: Columbia
Director: Sidney Poitier
Producer: Hannah Weinstein
Screenplay: Bruce Jay Friedman
Music: Tom Scott

CAST
Gene Wilder . . . . *Skip Donahue*
Richard Pryor . . . . *Harry Monroe*
Georg Stanford Brown *Rory Schultebrand*
Jobeth Williams . . . . *Meredith*
Miguelangel Suarez . . . . *Jesus Ramirez*
Craig T. Nelson . . . . *Deputy Warden Wilson*
Barry Corbin . . . . . . *Warden Walter Beatty*
Charles Weldon . . . . *Blade*

In this comedy two New Yorkers, Skip and Harry, decide to head for California where they think their luck will improve. To make some money, they take jobs in a small-town bank, dressing as wood-peckers. When their costumes are used by a couple of bank robbers, Skip and Harry are blamed for the crime, ending up in jail. Behind bars, their friendship is put to the test as they plan their escape.

A short-lived TV series, based on the movie, was screened in America in 1985, starring Joe Guzaldo and Larry Riley as Skip and Harry.

Gene Wilder and Richard Pryor also appeared together in *Silver Streak* (1976) and *See No Evil, Hear No Evil* (1989).

Director Sidney Poitier won an Oscar in 1963 for his acting in *Lilies of the Field*, and began directing in the early 1970s with films like *Buck and the Preacher* and *Uptown Saturday Night*.

Video availability

The Top Five

Week of 4 April 1981
1. Stir Crazy
2. Ordinary People
3. The Long Good Friday
4. Coalminer's Daughter
5. Private Benjamin

SUPERMAN II

18 April 1981	4 weeks

Distributor: Warner
Director: Richard Lester
Producer: Pierre Spengler
Screenplay: Mario Puzo, David Newman, Leslie Newman
Music: Ken Thorne

CAST
Gene Hackman . . . . *Lex Luthor*
Christopher Reeve . . *Superman/Clark Kent*
Ned Beatty . . . . *Otis*
Jackie Cooper . . . . *Perry White*
Sarah Douglas . . . . *Ursa*
Margot Kidder . . . . *Lois Lane*
Jack O'Halloran . . . . *Non*
Valerie Perrine . . . . *Eve Teschmacher*
Terence Stamp . . . . *General Zod*
Susannah York . . . . *Lara*

To avoid mass destruction, Superman hurls a nuclear bomb from the Eiffel Tower into space, but the resulting cosmic explosion frees three supervillains, General Zod, Non and Ursa, from their Kryptonian prison. While the dastardly trio are making mischief on Earth, Lois Lane discovers that her mild-mannered reporter colleague on the *Daily Planet*, Clark Kent, is really Superman. He retreats to his arctic hideaway, the Fortress of Solitude, to renounce his superpowers, enabling him to build a life with Lois. However, he still needs to save the world and decides to regain his powers in order to bring peace to a world which still needs a Superhero. Lois's memory of their love affair melts away during a long, lingering superkiss.

This sequel to the immensely successful 1978 *Superman* had no Marlon Brando as Superman's pop this time around, although the original mom, Lara, returns, as do all our favourites from the Metropolis newspaper and the villainous Lex Luthor.

The Top Five

Week of 18 April 1981
1. Superman II
2. Tess
3. Ordinary People
4. Popeye
5. Chariots of Fire

Although *Superman* and *Superman II* were apparently shot simultaneously, most of this sequel is brand new material as the project took much longer to complete than anticipated.

Video availability

THE POSTMAN ALWAYS RINGS TWICE

16 May 1981	4 weeks*

Distributor:	MGM
Director:	Bob Rafelson
Producer:	Charles Mulvehill, Bob Rafelson
Screenplay:	David Mamet
Music:	Michael Small

CAST
Jack Nicholson . . . . Frank Chambers
Jessica Lange . . . . Cora Papadakis
John Colicos . . . . Nick Papadakis
Michael Lerner . . . . Katz
John P. Ryan . . . . Kennedy
Anjelica Huston . . . . Madge
William Traylor . . . . Sackett

Drifter Frank Chambers enters a roadside café and is offered a job by the owner, Nick Papadakis. After taking the position, he makes a play for Nick's younger wife, Cora, who succumbs to his rough charms. He learns of their loveless marriage and between them they hatch a plan to murder the husband only to live in fear of being found out.

This was Hollywood's second version of the notorious James M. Cain novel of 1934, in which the character Frank Chambers is executed, although in this version he escapes death. MGM were unable to touch the novel until 1946 due to the self-imposed censorship restrictions Hollywood placed on itself through the production code of Will H. Hays ('The Hays Office').

The Postman Always Rings Twice gave Jessica Lange her first appearance at number one. She went on to win an Oscar for *Tootsie* (1982). and was nominated three more times for *Country* (1984), *Sweet Dreams* (1985) and *Music Box* (1989). But none of these performances come close to her debut appearance nestled in the great ape's paw in the 1976 remake of *King Kong*.

Video availability

The Top Five

Week of 16 May 1981
1. The Postman Always Rings Twice
2. Tess
3. Superman II
4. Chariots of Fire
5. The Funhouse/My Bloody Valentine

British star Terence Stamp makes his first appearance at number one since being Oscar-nominated in 1962 for his very first film, *Billy Budd*. He makes number one again in 1988's *Wall Street*.

TESS

30 May 1981	2 weeks

Distributor:	Renn-Burrill
Director:	Roman Polanski
Producer:	Claude Berri
Screenplay:	Roman Polanski
Music:	Philippe Sarde

CAST
Nastassja Kinski . . . . Tess Durbeyfield
Leigh Lawson . . . . Alec d'Urberville
Peter Firth . . . . Angel Clare
John Collin . . . . John Durbeyfield
David Markham . . . . . . Reverend Mr Clare
Rosemary Martin . . . . Mrs Durbeyfield
Richard Pearson . . . . Vicar of Marlott
Carolyn Pickles . . . . Marian

In this Thomas Hardy story the beautiful peasant girl, Tess Durbeyfield, is sent by her destitute feckless parents to the home of the rich D'Urbervilles after they learn that the two families are related. When she arrives, Tess learns that the rich D'Urbervilles merely bought the name and claim no kinship with the Durbeyfields. However, Alec D'Urberville takes a strong fancy to Tess and offers her a job at the manor. Tess, in need of money to help her family, accepts. While at the house, Alec takes advantage of her and she falls pregnant. She returns home to have the child but it dies soon after birth. She leaves the family home to work on a dairy farm where she meets and falls in love with Angel Clare. Tess can hardly believe her good fortune when they marry but on their wedding night Tess confesses to her past. Clare finds himself unable to forgive her and makes plans to go abroad. Alone and with her family once gain in need, Tess is forced to go back to Alec with disastrous results.

Although *Tess* opened in Paris, France, in 1979, it took 18 months before it arrived in London, England. Director Roman Polanski's previous number one, *Chinatown* (1974), earned him an Oscar nomination for Best Director and he was similarly nom-inated for *Tess*. In exile in France since 1979, his feature films have been few and far between, with only *Pirates* (1985) starring Walter Matthau, *Frantic* (1988), starring Harrison Ford, and *Bitter Moon* (1992), starring Hugh Grant to date. Polanski had fled America following charges of unlawful sexual intercourse with a 13-year-old girl.

Nastassja Kinski and Roman Polanski became lovers in the mid-1970s with Polanski some 25 years older than the Polish actress. He became her mentor and gave her the starring role in *Tess*.

Academy Awards: Best Cinematography (Geoffrey Unsworth and Ghislain Cloquet), Best Art Direction (Pierre Guffroy and Jack Stevens), Best Costume Design (Anthony Powell)

Video availability

The Top Five

Week of 30 May 1981
1. Tess
2. The Postman Always Rings Twice
3. Chariots of Fire
4. Superman II
5. Green Ice

FRIDAY THE 13TH PART 2

27 June 1981	1 week

Distributor:	CIC/Georgetown
Director:	Steven Miner
Producer:	Steve Miner
Screenplay:	Ron Kurz
Music:	Harry Manfredini

CAST
Amy Steel	. . . .	*Ginny*
John Furey	. . . .	*Paul*
Adrienne King	. . . .	*Alice*
Kirsten Baker	. . . .	*Terry*
Stu Charno	. . . .	*Ted*
Warrington Gillette	. . . .	*Jason*
Walt Gorney	. . . .	*Crazy Ralph*
Marta Kober	. . . .	*Sandra*

The sequel to *Friday the 13th* (1980) begins with a recap of the events from the first movie. The only remaining survivor of the original film, Alice, is finally killed by Jason, the dead son of the woman who appeared in the first movie. The story then leaps five years to another group of sex-crazed campers who, though aware of the last massacre, undergo the same violence in true 'Friday' style.

Video availability

The Top Five

Week of 27 June 1981
1. Friday the 13th Part 2
2. The Postman Always Rings Twice
3. Chariots of Fire
4. Tess
5. The Last Metro

FOR YOUR EYES ONLY

4 July 1981	10 weeks

Distributor:	United Artists
Director:	John Glen
Producer:	Albert R. Broccoli
Screenplay:	Richard Maibaum, Michael G. Wilson
Music:	Bill Conti

CAST
Roger Moore	. . . .	*James Bond*
Carole Bouquet	. . . .	*Melina*
Chaim Topol	. . . .	*Clumbo*
Lynn-Holly Johnson	. . . .	*Bibi*
Julian Glover	. . . .	*Kristatos*
Cassandra Harris	. . . .	*Lisi*
Jill Bennett	. . . .	*Brink*
Lois Maxwell	. . . .	*Miss Moneypenny*
Desmond Llewelyn	. . . .	*Q*

In the twelfth in the series of Bond movies James is in a race against Russian agents. Both Russia and Britain are after a device known as the ATAC that can transmit the order to fire to British submarines equipped with missiles. Unfortunately marine biologist Timothy Havelock and his wife, both working for the Secret Service, are murdered before informing headquarters of the ATAC's whereabouts. Their daughter Melina, who wants to avenge her parents' death, helps lead Bond to the evil Kristatos, who intends to sell the device to the Russians.

This was the first Bond film without M, due to the death of Bernard Lee. The part was not re-cast by way of a tribute to Lee. It was also the first Bond movie that did not credit Ian Fleming, the author of the original Bond novels.

The ski resort of Cortina, where much of the movie was shot, suffered from an unusually mild winter so snow had to be imported by trucks that made 45 trips by road. Stuntman Paolo Rigon was killed in an accident when filming the dangerous ski chase.

When filming began in Greece, monks from nearby monasteries, who disliked Bond's reputation, tried to jeopardize filming with protest banners that got in the way of shots.

Music: 'For Your Eyes Only' (Sheena Easton)

Video availability

The Top Five

Week of 4 July 1981
1. For Your Eyes Only
2. Chariots of fire
3. Tess
4. Friday the 13th Part 2
5. The Last Metro

RAIDERS OF THE LOST ARK

12 September 1981	4 weeks*

Distributor:	Paramount
Director:	Steven Spielberg
Producer:	Frank Marshall
Screenplay:	Lawrence Kasdan
Music:	John Williams

CAST
Harrison Ford .... Indy

Karen Allen .... Marion
Wolf Kahler .... Dietrich
Paul Freeman .... Belloq
Ronald Lacey .... Toht
John Rhys-Davies .... Sallah
Denholm Elliott .... Brody
Anthony Higgins .... Gobler

Archaeologist and university professor Indiana Jones is approached by American intelligence

Archaeology professor Indiana Jones (Harrison Ford) swaps his blackboard and books for a bullwhip and hat as he sets off on an amazing adventure to find the lost Ark of the Covenent in Raiders of the Lost Ark.

agents who inform him of a plan by the Nazis to unearth the Lost Ark of the Covenant. He is sent on a mission to locate the Covenant before the Germans. Marion Ravenwood, the daughter of a famous archaeologist, persuades Indiana to take her along on the expedition. Together they escape the attempts on their lives from Nazis who use snakes, poisonous darts and bombs.

The cost of the movie was in excess of $22 million, taking cast and crew to Hawaii, France, Tunisia and England, where they worked at the Elstree Studios. The entire movie was completed, however, in a mere 73 days. It became the largest grossing movie of 1981 and profits now exceed $200 million. It was based on a story by George Lucas, who started thinking about the project as early as 1970. Although old friends, this was the first time that Lucas and Steven Spielberg worked together on a movie.

Harrison Ford was selected for the role after Tom Selleck had to turn the part down because he couldn't get a release from his contract for his TV series *Magnum*. Ford ignored the 'never act with animals' rule in this film (20,000 snakes) and in the third of the trilogy, *Indiana Jones and the Last Crusade*, which had him surrounded by 8000 rats. He insisted 'snakes and rats don't bother me'.

Academy Awards: Best Editing (Michael Kahn), Best Art Direction (Norman Reynolds and Leslie Dilley), Best Set Decoration (Michael Ford), Best Sound (Bill Varney, Steve Maslow, Gregg Landaker and Roy Charman), Best Visual Effects (Richard Edlund, Kit West, Bruce Nicholson and Joe Johnston), Best Sound Effects Editing (Special Achievement Award; Ben Burtt and Richard L. Anderson)

Video availability

The Top Five

Week of 12 September 1981
1. Raiders of the Lost Ark
2. For Your Eyes Only
3. Outland
4. Escape to Victory
5. The Four Seasons

THE FINAL CONFLICT

26 September 1981	1 week

Distributor:	Twentieth Century-Fox
Director:	Graham Baker

Producer:	Harvey Bernhard
Screenplay:	Andrew Birkin
Music:	Jerry Goldsmith

Sam Neill stars as Damien Thorn, the Antichrist, who grows up to become the advisor to the President of the USA. Barnaby Holm is the child who comes under Damien's evil influence in The Final Conflict, *the last chapter in the* Omen *trilogy.*

CAST
Sam Neill . . . . *Damien*
Rossano Brazzi . . . . *De Carlo*
Don Gordon . . . . *Harvey Dean*
Lisa Harrow . . . . *Kate*
Leueen Willoughby . . . . *Barbara*
Barnaby Holm . . . . *Peter*
Mason Adams. . . . . *President*
Robert Arden . . . . *Ambassador*

Damien, the son of the devil, is an adult in the third and final part of the *Omen* trilogy. Now the head of multinational conglomerate, Thorn Industries, he is about to become the American ambassador to Britain, the previous incumbent having blown his brains out. The only obstacle to his plans for world domination is the second coming of Christ, who is due to be born on a certain day in England. The Italian monks in De Carlo's monastery set about trying to kill Damien with six special daggers before he and his associate Harvey Dean can murder all newborn babies in England.

Sam Neill, who took over the part of Damien in *The Final Conflict*, went on to appear in four more number one movies: *The Hunt for Red October* (1990), *Jurassic Park* (1993), *The Piano* (1993) and *Sirens* (1994).

This was director Graham Baker's debut feature film. Like many others, including Ridley Scott, he cut his teeth making television commercials.

Video availability

The Top Five
Week of 26 September 1981
1. The Final Conflict
2. Raiders of the Lost Ark
3. For Your Eyes Only
4. Violent Streets
5. Escape to Victory

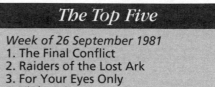

HISTORY OF THE WORLD PART 1

17 October 1981	2 weeks

Distributor:	**Brooksfilms**
Director:	**Mel Brooks**
Producer:	**Mel Brooks**
Screenplay:	**Mel Brooks**
Music:	**John Morris**

CAST
Mel Brooks . . *Moses/Comicus/Torquemada/*
Jacques/King Louis XVI
Dom DeLuise . . . . *Emperor Nero*
Madeline Kahn . . . . *Empress Nympho*
Harvey Korman . . . . *Count de Monet*
Cloris Leachman . . . . *Madame de Farge*
Ron Carey . . . . *Swiftus*
Pamela Stephenson . . . . *Mlle Rimbaud*

Mel Brooks attempts to tell the comic history of the world in several different sections: Dawn of Man; the Stone Age; Old Testament; the Roman Empire; the Spanish Inquisition; the French Revolution; and finally Coming Attractions. His regular gang are all on hand to poke fun during the musical sketches. As Moses Brooks drops one of the three stones containing the Fifteen Commandments, which instantly become the Ten Commandments. Dom DeLuise, as the Emperor Nero, gets to play Caesar's Palace in Las Vegas and Madeline Kahn as an Empress indulges her taste for young centurions.

The film includes cameo performances by Bea Arthur, Nigel Hawthorne, Hugh 'Playboy' Hefner, John Hurt, Jackie Mason, Spike Milligan, Andrew Sachs, and Orson Welles as narrator.

Video availability

The Top Five
Week of 17 October 1981
1. History of the World Part 1
2. Raiders of the Lost Ark
3. For Your Eyes Only
4. The Four Seasons
5. Escape From New York

THE FRENCH LIEUTENANT'S WOMAN

31 October 1981	7 weeks

Distributor:	**United Artists**
Director:	**Karel Reisz**
Producer:	**Leon Clore**
Screenplay:	**Harold Pinter**
Music:	**Carl Davis**

CAST
Meryl Streep . . . . *Sarah and Anna*
Jeremy Irons . . . . *Charles and Mike*
Hilton McRae . . . . *Sam*
Emily Morgan . . . . *Mary*
Charlotte Mitchell . . . . *Mrs Tranter*
Lynsey Baxter . . . . *Ernestina*

Jean Faulds . . . . *Cook*
Peter Vaughan . . . . *Mr Freeman*

Karel Reisz's cinematic adaptation of John Fowles' novel traces the love affairs of Sarah and Charles in 1867 and Anna and Mike in 1969. The upstanding 19th-century gentleman Charles is about to marry his fiancée when he meets the mysterious Sarah, ex-mistress of the French lieutenant. As the two fall in love the film includes snatches of the modern romance of sophisticated film-makers Anna and Mike.

Previous attempts to bring Fowles' story to the screen had been abandoned by several other directors, including Richard Lester, Fred Zinnemann and Mike Nichols.

This was the first leading role for Jeremy Irons although Meryl Streep had already made a name for herself in the *Deer Hunter*. She made her movie debut in the 1977 film *Julia*, directed by Fred Zinnemann. It starred Jane Fonda, Vanessa Redgrave and Jason Robards. Meryl is reported to have broken

out in hives because of the presence of such stars, even though she didn't appear in any scenes with the latter two. She played the part of Anne Marie Travers and appeared in just two scenes, for a total of 52 seconds.

Video availability

The Top Five

Week of 31 October 1981
1. The French Lieutenant's Woman
2. History of the World Part 1
3. Endless Love
4. The Fox and the Hound
5. Blow Out

Top Twenty Films of 1981

1 Superman II
2 For Your Eyes Only
3 Flash Gordon
4 Snow White and the Seven Dwarfs
5 Any Which Way You Can
6 Clash of the Titans
7 Private Benjamin
8 Raiders of the Lost Ark
9 The Elephant Man
10 Tess
11 The Jazz Singer
12 Chariots of Fire
13 Airplane!
14 Caligula
15 The Blue Lagoon
16 Excalibur
17 History of the World – Part 1
18 The Cannonball Run
19 The Postman Always Rings Twice
20 Popeye

GALLIPOLI

19 December 1981	1 week

Distributor:	Roadshow/Associated R & R Films
Director:	Peter Weir
Producer:	Robert Stigwood
Screenplay:	David Williamson
Music:	Brian May

CAST
Mark Lee . . . . *Archy*
Bill Kerr . . . . *Jack*
Ron Graham . . . . *Wallace Hamilton*
Harold Hopkins . . . . *Les McCann*
Charles Yunupingu . . . . *Zac*
Heath Harris . . . . *Stockman*
Gerda Nicolson . . . . *Rose Hamilton*
Mel Gibson . . . . *Frank Dunne*

Archy and Frank are two young Australian idealists from different backgrounds. They became firm friends when they enlist in the army at the outbreak of World War I. Their regiment is involved in the campaign to gain control of the Dardanelles waterway, by capturing Istanbul from the Turks.

Poor leadership and a lack of communication leads to their senseless deaths on the beaches of Gallipoli.

Australian director Peter Weir's first major feature was *The Cars that Ate Paris* (1974) although he is probably best remembered for the following year's film *Picnic at Hanging Rock*. He went on to direct *Dead Poets Society* (1989) and *Green Card* (1991) among others.

South African-born Bill Kerr, who played Jack, first made a name for himself in Britain in the 1950s as a leading character in the long-running radio series *Hancock's Half Hour*.

Video availability

The Top Five

Week of 19 December 1981
1. Gallipoli
2. The French Lieutenant's Woman
3. An American Werewolf in London
4. Mommie Dearest
5. Montenegro

ARTHUR

26 December 1981	8 weeks

Distributor: **Warner/Orion**
Director: **Steve Gordon**
Producer: **Robert Greenhut**
Screenplay: **Steve Gordon**
Music: **Burt Bacharach**

CAST
Dudley Moore . . . . Arthur Bach
Liza Minnelli . . . . Linda Marolla
John Gielgud . . . . Hobson
Geraldine Fitzgerald . . . . Martha Bach
Jill Eikenberry . . . . Susan Johnson
Stephen Elliott . . . . Burt Johnson
Ted Ross . . . . Bitterman
Barney Martin . . . . Ralph Marolla

Alcoholic millionaire Arthur Bach has to decide between money and the love of his life. He has to agree to an arranged marriage to the very rich Susan Johnson, or have his father and plain-speaking grandmother cut off his allowance. His relations insist he give up his true love, Linda Marolla, a working-class waitress whom he met when she was caught shoplifting. His loyal valet, Hobson, is never far away to help him through his ordeals.

Sir John Gielgud made his film debut in 1924 in the silent movie *Who is the Man?* but won his only Oscar (for *Arthur*) at the ripe old age of 77. (The statue is kept on a shelf in the bathroom.) Minnelli had made her first screen appearance as a baby in her mother, Judy Garland's, 1949 film *In the Good Old Summertime*. Moore's debut was in the 1966 British comedy *The Wrong Box* alongside his satirical partner Peter Cook.

The sequel, *Arthur 2: On the Rocks* (1988) was not a hit although Moore, Minnelli and John Gielgud (this time as a ghost) reprised their roles. Bud Yorkin directed the sequel as Steve Gordon had died a year after the success of *Arthur* at the age of 42.

In Arthur, *playboy Arthur Bach drinks to his own health when he learns that he is to inherit $750 million from his grandmother on condition that he marries Society girl Susan Johnson (Jill Eikenberry).*

Jill Eikenberry, who plays the unwanted Susan Johnson, later became one of the regular cast (Ann Kelsey) of the popular American TV series *L.A. Law*.

Academy Awards: Best Supporting Actor (John Gielgud), Best song – 'Arthur's Theme (Best That You Can Do)' (Burt Bacharach, Carole Bayer Sager, Christopher Cross and Peter Allen – music and lyrics)

Music: 'Arthur's Theme (The Best that You Can Do)' (Christopher Cross)

The Top Five

Week of 26 December 1981
1. Arthur
2. Lady Chatterley's Lover
3. The French Lieutenant's Woman
4. Gallipoli
5. Eye of the Needle

Video availability

DEATH WISH 2

20 February 1982	2 weeks

Distributor:	Cannon
Director:	Michael Winner
Producer:	Menahem Golam, Yoram Globus
Screenplay:	David Engelbach
Music:	Jimmy Page

CAST
Charles Bronson . . . . *Paul Kersey*
Jill Ireland . . . . *Geri Nichols*
Vincent Gardenia . . . . *Frank Ochoa*
J.D. Cannon . . . *New York District Attorney*
Anthony Franciosa *L.A. Police Commissioner*
Ben Frank . . . . *Lt. Mankiewicz*
Robin Sherwood . . . . *Carol Kersey*
Silvana Gillardo . . . . *Rosario*

Vigilante architect Paul Kersey is on the loose again. This time he is hunting the thugs and villains on the streets of Los Angeles after his Spanish housekeeper is raped and killed. His daughter, Carol, who has still not recovered from her ordeal in the original film, is raped again before being spiked on an iron fence while trying to escape. The police are seemingly powerless as Kersey blasts his way through the gang one by one in his quest for vengeance.

This was the second of three *Death Wish* movies directed by Michael Winner before he handed over the reins to J. Lee Thompson, for number four in 1987, and to Allan A. Goldstein, for number five in 1994.

Charles Bronson and Jill Ireland were real-life husband and wife.

Video availability

The Top Five

Week of 20 February 1982
1. Death Wish 2
2. Arthur
3. Body Heat
4. Dragonslayer
5. Gallipoli

REDS

6 March 1982	3 weeks*

Distributor:	Paramount
Director:	Warren Beatty
Producer:	Warren Beatty
Screenplay:	Warren Beatty and Trevor Griffiths
Music:	Stephen Sondheim

CAST
Warren Beatty . . . . *John Reed*
Diane Keaton . . . . *Louise Bryant*
Edward Herrmann . . . . *Max Eastman*
Jerzy Kosinski . . . . *Grigory Zinovliev*
Jack Nicholson . . . . *Eugene O'Neill*
Paul Sorvino . . . . *Louis Fraina*
Maureen Stapleton . . . . . *Emma Goldman*
Nicholas Coster . . . . *Paul Trullinger*

This three-hour epic chronicles the romance of American journalist John Reed and Louise Bryant in Russia in the years before and after the Russian Revolution. The two are bonded by love and their involvement with Communism and the Russian underground movement. Louise travels through freezing conditions in search of John after he is forced to flee from the Bolsheviks.

The original screenplay by Warren Beatty and Trevor Griffiths was rejected by the film studio who hired

Robert Towne and Elaine May to work it up to an acceptable form. Although they made considerable changes in the re-write, they were not given a screen credit.

A Russian version of the story was filmed in the same year by Soviet director Sergei Bondarchuk.

Academy Awards: Best Direction (Warren Beatty), Best Supporting Actress (Maureen Stapleton), Best Cinematography (Vittorio Storaro)

The Top Five

Week of 6 March 1982
1. Reds
2. Absence of Malice
3. Death Wish 2
4. Halloween II
5. Arthur

Video availability

MAD MAX 2

13 March 1982	1 week

Distributor:	Warner
Director:	George Miller
Producer:	Byron Kennedy
Screenplay:	George Miller, Terry Hayes, Brian Hannant
Music:	Brian May

CAST

Mel Gibson . . . . *Max*
Bruce Spence . . . . *Gyro Captain*
Vernon Wells . . . . *Wez*
Emil Minty . . . . *Feral Kid*
Mike Preston . . . . *Pappagallo*
Kjell Nilsson . . . . *Humungus*
Virginia Hey . . . . *Warrior Woman*
Syd Heylen . . . . *Curmudgeon*

In this sequel to the *Mad Max* movie of 1979 road warrior Max spends much of his time helping a small oil-producing community with their basic refinery situated in the desert. He helps fight off Humungus and his bandits who are intent on getting their hands on the fuel. When it finally all gets too much for him, Max decides to go it alone when his comrade, the Gyro Captain, takes him back to their compound.

Mel Gibson was born in Peekskill, New York, and lived in the USA until he was 12 years old. He attended the National Institute of Modern Art in Sydney, and early in his acting career played Romeo to Judy Davis' Juliet. The first two *Mad Max* films were dubbed in America because of his 'incomprehensible' Australian accent.

The original *Mad Max* film was kept off the number one spot in 1979 because of *Monty Python's Life of Brian*.

Video availability

The Top Five

Week of 13 March 1982
1. Mad Max 2
2. Reds
3. Absence of Malice
4. On Golden Pond
5. Death Wish 2

EVIL UNDER THE SUN

3 April 1982	2 weeks

Distributor:	EMI
Director:	Guy Hamilton
Producer:	John Brabourne, Richard Goodwin
Screenplay:	Anthony Shaffer
Music:	Cole Porter Jack Larchbury (Arrangement)

CAST

Peter Ustinov . . . . *Hercule Poirot*
Jane Birkin . . . . *Christine Redfern*
Colin Blakely . . . . *Sir Horace Blatt*
Nicholas Clay . . . . *Patrick Redfern*
James Mason . . . . *Odell Gardener*
Roddy McDowall . . . . *Rex Brewster*
Denis Quilley . . . . *Kenneth Marshall*
Diana Rigg . . . . *Arlena Marshall*
Maggie Smith . . . . *Daphne Castle*

Inspector Hercule Poirot heads off for an old-fashioned hotel in Majorca to try to discover which of the many suspects, all with rock solid alibis, murdered a famous bitchy actress who was getting on everyone's nerves.

Director Guy Hamilton has often admitted his dislike of Agatha Christie's style of writing because of the over-crowding of characters. With screenwriter Anthony Shaffer, he removed several of the players featured in the original book and switched the setting from an English coastal town to the Adriatic.

Music: 'You're the Top'

Video availability

QUEST FOR FIRE

17 April 1982	2 weeks

Distributor:	ICC
Director:	Jean-Jacques Annaud
Producer:	Denis Heroux, John Kemeny
Screenplay:	Gerard Brach
Music:	Philippe Sarde

CAST
Everett McGill .... Noah
Rae Dawn Chong .... Ika
Ron Perlman .... Amoukar
Nameer El Kadi .... Gaw
Gary Schwartz .... Rouka (Ulam tribe)
Kurt Schiegel .... Faum (Ulam tribe)
Naseer El Kadi .... Nam (Ulam tribe)
Franck-Olivier Bonnet . Aghoo (Ulam tribe)
Jean-Michel Kindt ..... Lakar (Ulam tribe)
Brian Gill .... Modoc (Ulam tribe)

Three warriors of the prehistoric Ulam tribe go in search of a source of fire after their essential flame is cut off following an attack by a group of Neanderthals. After rescuing Ika, a young native girl, from cannibals, they discover a community of advanced humans who teach them how to create fire with the use of a flint.

Dr Desmond Morris, who wrote *The Naked Ape*, created a special body language for the movie based on actual ape gestures, while novelist and technical

Everett McGill stars as Noah, a courageous warrior of the Ulam tribe who searches for the life-sustaining element of fire at the dawning of civilization in Quest for Fire.

adviser Anthony Burgess developed a primitive sounding language.

The movie took over four years to complete at a cost of $12 million, with on-location filming in Kenya, Canada, Scotland and Iceland.

Rae Dawn Chong, who plays the tribe member Ika Avaka, is the daughter of Tommy Chong, one half of the American comedy duo Cheech and Chong.

Academy Awards: Best Makeup (Sarah Monzani and Michele Burke)

The Top Five

Week of 17 April 1982
1. Quest for Fire
2. Evil under the Sun
3. Chariots of Fire/Gregory's Girl
4. Reds
5. Sharky's Machine

Video availability

THE BORDER

1 May 1982	1 week

Distributor:	Universal
Director:	Tony Richardson
Producer:	Edgar Bronfman Jr
Screenplay:	Deric Washburn, Walon Green, David Freeman
Music:	Ry Cooder

CAST
Jack Nicholson . . . . *Charlie*
Harvey Keitel . . . . *Cat*
Valerie Perrine . . . . *Marcy*
Warren Oates . . . . *Red*
Elpidia Carrillo . . . . *Maria*
Shannon Wilcox . . . . *Savannah*
Manuel Viescas . . . . *Juan*
Jeff Morris . . . . *J.J.*
Mike Gomez . . . . *Manuel*

Hen-pecked border control guard Charlie is having problems with his wife who wants to get hold of some extra money. He gets caught up in a scheme, arranged by his superiors, taking payoffs from illegal Mexican immigrants for allowing them to cross the American border into Texas. But he shows some decency when he comes to the rescue of a kidnapped Mexican girl on her way to be sold on the black market.

British director Tony Richardson was responsible for several hit movies in the 1950s and 60s, including *Look Back in Anger, Tom Jones, The Charge of the Light Brigade* and *The Loneliness of the Long Distance Runner*.

Video availability

The Top Five

Week of 1 May 1982
1. The Border
2. Chariots of Fire/Gregory's Girl
3. Quest for Fire
4. Evil under the Sun
5. Reds

PRIVATE LESSONS

8 May 1982	2 weeks

Distributor:	Sunn Classic
Director:	Alan Myerson
Producer:	R. Ben Efraim
Screenplay:	Dan Greenburg
Music:	Robert Fawcett (Editor)

CAST
Sylvia Kristel . . . . *Nicole*
Howard Hesseman . . . . *Lester*
Eric Brown . . . . *Philly*
Patrick Piccininni . . . . *Sherman*
Ed Begley Jr . . . . *Jack Travis*
Pamela Bryant . . . . *Joyce*
Meredith Baer . . . . *Miss Phipps*

The head of the wealthy Fillmore family from Arizona is about to go away on business. Before he goes he gives instructions to the household maid, Nicole, to teach his 15-year-old son, Philly, all about sex while he's away. Philly falls for his first love but Nicole is too busy making plans to

The Top Five

Week of 8 May 1982
1. Private Lessons
2. Chariots of Fire/Gregory's Girl
3. The Border
4. Quest for Fire
5. On Golden Pond

blackmail the family with the help of her boyfriend.

The soundtrack of *Private Lessons* includes songs performed by Rod Stewart, Air Supply, Eric Clapton, Earth Wind and Fire, and John Cougar.

Sylvia Kristel has a stunt double, Judy Helden, who is used in several of the nude scenes.

Video availability

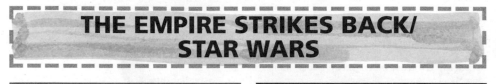

THE EMPIRE STRIKES BACK/ STAR WARS

22 May 1982	3 weeks

Two of the biggest sci-fi movies, re-released and packaged as a double bill, once again packed in the cinema crowd. For full details see *The Empire Strikes Back* (1980) and *Star Wars* (1978).

Video availability

The Top Five

Week of 22 May 1982
1. The Empire Strikes Back/Star Wars
2. I, the Jury
3. Private Lessons
4. Chariots of Fire/Gregory's Girl
5. Quest for Fire

MISSING

12 June 1982	5 weeks

Distributor:	Universal
Director:	Constantine Costa-Gavras
Producer:	Edward Lewis, Mildred Lewis
Screenplay:	Constantine Costa-Gavras, Donald Stewart
Music:	Vangelis

In Missing *Beth (Sissy Spacek) and Charles (John Shea) have enjoyed their life in South America until a coup threatens everything, including their lives.*

CAST
Jack Lemmon . . . . *Ed Horman*
Sissy Spacek . . . . *Beth Horman*
Melanie Mayron . . . . *Terry Simon*
John Shea . . . . *Charles Horman*
Charles Cioffi . . . . *Captain Ray Tower*
David Clennon . . . . *Consul Phil Putnam*
Richard Venture . . . . *US Ambassador*
Jerry Hardin . . . . *Colonel Sean Patrick*

Beth Horman is getting nowhere fast in her attempt to track down her journalist husband, Charles, who went missing in an un-named Latin American country during a military coup. Whenever she contacts the authorities for information, she is given the runaround. Desperate with worry, she asks Ed, her father-in-law, for help. Together they find themselves deeply involved in a political wrangle with the authorities who insist they have no knowledge of Charles' whereabouts. Their persistence leads to a major rebuttal from the US State department.

The film was Greek director Constantine Costa-Gavras's first American-funded movie. Despite the location never being named, it was based on real events during the 1973 Chilean coup. Jack Lemmon refused to meet the real Ed Horman until filming was completed so that he could play the part without any bias.

Academy Awards: Best Screenplay (Costa-Gavras and Donald Stewart)

Video availability

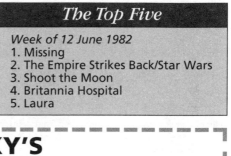

The Top Five

Week of 12 June 1982
1. Missing
2. The Empire Strikes Back/Star Wars
3. Shoot the Moon
4. Britannia Hospital
5. Laura

PORKY'S

17 July 1982	1 week

Distributor:	Melvin Simon
Director:	Bob Clark
Producer:	Don Carmody, Bob Clark
Screenplay:	Bob Clark
Music:	Carl Zittrer

CAST
Dan Monahan . . . . *Pee Wee*
Mark Herrier . . . . *Billy*
Wyatt Knight . . . . *Tommy*
Roger Wilson . . . . *Mickey*
Cyril O'Reilly . . . . *Tim*
Tony Ganios . . . . *Meat*
Kaki Hunter . . . . *Wendy*
Kim Cattrall . . . . *Honeywell*

A group of high school friends from Florida spend every free moment trying to get into Porky's, a local club of ill-repute where the women are said to be readily available. The boys, all underage, come up with every trick in the book to fool the club's doormen, to no avail. Giving up hope of ever realizing their dreams of scoring with the opposite sex,

they end up wrecking the joint as revenge. Mindless teenage mayhem.

Two sequels followed: *Porky's II – the Next Day* (1983) and *Porky's Revenge* (1985). Director Bob Clark's other credits include the musical *Rhinestone* (1984), featuring an ill-advised pairing of Sylvester Stallone and Dolly Parton, and *Murder By Decree* (1980), in which Sherlock Holmes investigates the Jack the Ripper murders.

Music: 'Blue Suede Shoes' (Carl Perkins)

Video availability

The Top Five

Week of 17 July 1982
1. Porky's
2. Annie
3. Missing
4. Fame/Coalminer's Daughter
5. The Empire Strikes Back/Star Wars

PINK FLOYD – THE WALL

24 July 1982	5 weeks*

Distributor:	MGM
Director:	Alan Parker
Producer:	Alan Marshall
Screenplay:	Roger Waters
Music:	Roger Waters, David Gilmour, Nick Mason, Richard Wright

CAST
Bob Geldof . . . . *Pink*
Christine Hargreaves . . . . . . *Pink's mother*
James Laurenson . . . . *Pink's father*
Eleanor David . . . . *Pink's wife*
Kevin McKeon . . . . *Young Pink*
Bob Hoskins . . . . *Band manager*
David Bingham . . . . *Little Pink*
Jenny Wright . . . . *American groupie*

The Wall is a visual version of Pink Floyd's multi-million-selling album, which tells the story of Pink, a rock star on the verge of a nervous breakdown. He contemplates suicide after being on the road so much that his wife has left him for another man. Trying to take stock of his life, Pink recalls his early childhood during World War II, his unhappy schooldays and the effect of his fatherless family life. He realizes that he has built a wall around himself to cut out the pain, and attempts to tear it down in order to live again.

The film makes great use of animation from political cartoonist Gerald Scarfe.

Pink Floyd's 1979 album 'The Wall', on which the film was based, spent a total of 51 weeks in the UK album charts, but only ever reached number three. However, the single 'Another Brick in the Wall' became their first and only number one in December 1979, spending 5 weeks at the top.

Music: 'Another Brick in the Wall', 'Empty Spaces', 'Is There Anybody Out There?', 'Goodbye Blue Sky'

Video availability

The Top Five

Week of 24 July 1982
1. Pink Floyd – The Wall
2. Firefox
3. Annie
4. Porky's
5. Fame/Coalminer's Daughter

ROCKY III

31 July 1982	1 week

Distributor:	United Artists
Director:	Sylvester Stallone
Producer:	Irwin Winkler, Robert Chartoff
Screenplay:	Sylvester Stallone
Music:	Bill Conti

CAST
Sylvester Stallone . . . . *Rocky Balboa*
Carl Weathers . . . . *Apollo Creed*
Mr T . . . . *Clubber Lang*
Talia Shire . . . . *Adrian*
Burt Young . . . . *Paulie*
Burgess Meredith . . . . *Mickey*
Ian Fried . . . . *Rocky Jr*
Hulk Hogan . . . . *Thunderlips*

After his tenth big win, Rocky is living a life of luxury with his wife and son. However, tough black boxer Clubber Lang is desperate to have a shot at the champ's title. Despite the good advice to give up the game, Rocky insists on meeting this big hulk in the ring and the champ goes down for the count. After his defeat he employs Apollo Creed, one of his earlier opponents, as his new trainer, in an effort to regain his title.

Stallone directs himself again, having taken on the chore for *Rocky II*, the only film in the series which didn't make the top spot.

The film features an early appearance for wrestler Hulk Hogan, who goes on to appear in several commercially successful movies, including *Suburban Commando* (1991) and *Mr Nanny* (1993). It was also the big break for Mr T, who was born Laurence Tureaud but changed his name before breaking into show business. He had previously appeared in a short-lived American comedy series, *Mr T and Tina*, before making his film debut in *Rocky III* and then enormous fame in the hit TV series *The A Team*.

Music: 'Eye of the Tiger' (Survivor)

Video availability

The Top Five

Week of 31 July 1982
1. Rocky III
2. Pink Floyd – The Wall
3. Star Trek II: The Wrath of Khan
4. Firefox
5. Annie

CONAN THE BARBARIAN

4 September 1982	1 week

Distributor:	Dino De Laurentiis Corp
Director:	John Milius
Producer:	Buzz Feitshans, Raffaella De Laurentiis
Screenplay:	John Milius, Oliver Stone
Music:	Basil Poledouris

CAST

Arnold Schwarzenegger . . . . *Conan*
James Earl Jones . . . . *Thulsa Doom*
Max Von Sydow . . . . *King Osric*
Sandahl Bergman . . . . *Valeria*
Ben Davidson . . . . *Rexor*
Cassandra Gaviola . . . . *the Witch*
Gerry Lopez . . . . *Subotai*
Mako . . . . *the Wizard*
Valerie Quennessen . . . . *the Princess*

Plenty of blood, guts and gore as the young Conan witnesses the brutal murder of his parents and other villagers at the hands of Thulsa Doom. Conan grows up as a slave but never loses sight of his aim to gain revenge on the evil cult leader. He infiltrates the cult and witnesses the hypnotic power of Thulsa Doom, who can transform into a snake, before being forced to fight to the death in the arena competition.

The story is based on, but does not draw directly from, the novels of Robert E. Howard. A sequel followed in 1984, *Conan the Destroyer*, but it was not as successful.

Conan was the first of nine number one movies for Austrian bodybuilder Arnold Schwarzenegger whose name translates as 'black ploughman'.

Video availability

The Top Five

Week of 4 September 1982
1. Conan the Barbarian
2. Who Dares Wins
3. Pink Floyd – The Wall
4. The Thing
5. The Last American Virgin

Conan (Arnold Schwarzenegger) swears revenge on Thulsa Doom (James Earl Jones), the leader of a cult and the head of a gang that murdered his parents in Conan the Barbarian.

WHO DARES WINS

11 September 1982	1 week

Distributor: Rank
Director: Ian Sharp
Producer: Euan Lloyd
Screenplay: Reginald Rose
Music: Roy Budd, Jerry and Mark
  Donohue

CAST
Lewis Collins . . . . Capt Skellen
Judy Davis . . . . Frankie Leith
Richard Widmark . . . . . . Secretary of State
Edward Woodward . . Commander Powell
Robert Webber. . . . . General Potter
Tony Doyle . . . . Colonel Hadley
John Duttine . . . . Rod
Kenneth Griffith . . . . Bishop Crick
Rosalind Lloyd . . . . Jenny Skellen

A lone officer from the British SAS, Captain Skellen, goes undercover to flush out a terrorist gang who plan to take over an American diplomatic base in England in an armed attack. The terrorists' plan is to hold top officials hostage until their demands, including the nuclear destruction of a US submarine base in Scotland, are met.

The title for American release was *The Final Option* as audiences in the USA didn't know that 'Who Dares Wins' is the motto of the Special Air Services (SAS). The story was inspired by real events involving the Iranian Embassy in London, which was taken over by terrorists on 30 April 1980. Five days later, after the shooting of two hostages, SAS commandos stormed the Embassy, releasing the remaining hostages and killing all but one of the gunmen.

Lewis Collins was already known as an action man from his role as Bodie in the TV series *The Professionals*, which ran for 57 episodes from 1977 to 1983.

Video availability

The Top Five

Week of 11 September 1982
1. Who Dares Wins
2. Conan the Barbarian
3. Pink Floyd – The Wall
4. The Thing
5. The Last American Virgin

BLADE RUNNER

18 September 1982	1 week

Distributor: Warner
Director: Ridley Scott
Producer: Michael Deeley
Screenplay: Hampton Fancher, David
  Webb Peoples
Music: Vangelis

CAST
Harrison Ford . . . . Rich Deckard
Rutger Hauer . . . . Batty
Sean Young . . . . Rachael
Edward James Olmos. . . . . Gaff
M. Emmet Walsh . . . . Bryant
Daryl Hannah . . . . Pris
William Sanderson. . . . . Sebastian
Brion James . . . . Leon
Joe Turkel . . . . Tyrell

S et in November 2019, ex-cop Rich Deckard is given the assignment, much against his will, to track down and destroy a group of androids. Known as replicants, these androids have a short life span and are designed to supply slave labour, but a group of them have mutinied on a planet in space and travelled to earth to prolong their lives. While on the mission to kill the androids, Deckard falls for the beautiful Rachael, a technically advanced replicant. She is so advanced that she doesn't realize she's not human until Deckard puts her to the test.

In 1992 *The Director's Cut* version was released which did not have the voice over by Harrison Ford, together with an altered ending.

Video availability

The Top Five

Week of 18 September 1982
1. Blade Runner
2. Who Dares Wins
3. Brimstone and Treacle
4. Pink Floyd – The Wall
5. Conan the Barbarian

POLTERGEIST

25 September 1982	2 weeks

Distributor:	MGM
Director:	Tobe Hooper
Producer:	Steven Spielberg, Frank Marshall
Screenplay:	Steven Spielberg, Michael Grais
Music:	Jerry Goldsmith

CAST

Craig T. Nelson .... Steve
Jobeth Williams .... Diane
Beatrice Straight .... Dr Lesh
Dominique Dunne .... Dana
Oliver Robins .... Robbie
Heather O'Rourke .... Carol Anne
Zelda Rubinstein .... Tangina
Martin Casella .... Marty
Richard Lawson .... Ryan

Steve, Diane and their daughter, Carol Anne, are the perfect family, living happily in their suburban home. One evening, while 5-year-old Carol Anne is watching television, pieces of furniture start to move about by their own free will and the child is suddenly sucked into the screen by unfriendly spirits. They learn from a clairvoyant that their house was built on sacred ground owned by the Indians and the gods are annoyed.

There has been much speculation about how much direction was down to producer Steven Spielberg. Although not credited for any work as a director, it is believed he did much of the preparation for the more complicated shots before handing over to Tobe Hooper, who directed the classic 1974 horror movie *The Texas Chainsaw Massacre*. The amazing visual effects were rewarded with an Oscar nomination.

Two sequels followed – *Poltergeist II* (1986) and *Poltergeist III* (1988) – although neither Spielberg nor Hooper worked on them.

Video availability

The Top Five

Week of 25 September 1982
1. Poltergeist
2. Blade Runner
3. Who Dares Wins
4. Brimstone and Treacle
5. Pink Floyd – The Wall

CAT PEOPLE

9 October 1982	1 week

Distributor:	Universal
Director:	Paul Schrader
Producer:	Charles Fries
Screenplay:	Alan Ormsby
Music:	Giorgio Moroder

CAST

Nastassja Kinski .... Irena Gallier
Malcolm McDowell .... Paul Gallier
John Heard .... Oliver Yates
Annette O'Toole .... Alice Perrin
Ruby Dee .... Female
Ed Begley Jr .... Joe Creigh
Scott Paulin .... Bill Searle

Irena moves into an apartment with her brother in New Orleans and lands a job in a nearby zoo where she meets and falls in love with the curator, Oliver. Their attraction for each other proves dangerous as Irena metamorphoses into a panther when aroused. Her incestuous relationship with her brother does not provoke the same reaction. But while she sees Oliver a large black panther is seen terrorizing the people of New Orleans. Irena fears the ancient tale of the cat people which warns that if she consummates her relationship with Oliver she will turn into a panther and be unable to become human again unless she kills.

Paul Schrader's film was a remake of the 1942 horror movie starring Simone Simon and Kent Smith. A sequel, *The Curse of the Cat People*, was made in 1944, but there has been no modern sequel to date. Schrader wrote *Taxi Driver* (1975) and *Raging Bull* (1981) for director Martin Scorsese and also directed *American Gigolo* (1980).

The Top Five

Week of 9 October 1982
1. Cat People
2. Poltergeist
3. The Entity
4. Blade Runner
5. A Midsummer Night's Sex Comedy

David Bowie's theme song 'Cat People (Putting Out Fire)' was a UK hit in 1982 but only reached number 26 in the singles charts.

Music: 'Cat People (Putting Out Fire)' (David Bowie)

Video availability

THE ENTITY

16 October 1982	2 weeks

Distributor:	Twentieth Century-Fox
Director:	Sidney J. Furie
Producer:	Harold Schneider
Screenplay:	Frank DeFelitta
Music:	Charles Bernstein

CAST
Barbara Hershey .... *Carla Moran*
Ron Silver .... *Phil Schneidermann*
David Labiosa .... *Billy*
George Coe .... *Dr Weber*
Margaret Blye .... *Cindy Nash*
Jacqueline Brookes .... *Dr Cooley*
Richard Brestoff .... *Gene Kraft*

Californian Carla Moran claims that she is being repeatedly raped by an invisible demon. Doctors and psychiatrists queue up to study what they believe is a completely mad woman until a university graduate manages to freeze the thing.

The story is claimed to be loosely based on true experiences of a Californian woman. However, it earned the wrath of women's groups and a feminist picket line, protesting about the subject matter, formed outside the cinema when the movie premiered in London.

Video availability

The Top Five

Week of 16 October 1982
1. The Entity
2. Cat People
3. Blade Runner
4. Poltergeist
5. A Midsummer Night's Sex Comedy

TRON

30 October 1982	6 weeks

Distributor:	Walt Disney
Director:	Steven Lisberger
Producer:	Donald Kushner
Screenplay:	Steven Lisberger
Music:	Wendy Carlos

CAST
Jeff Bridges .... *Kevin Flynn/Clu*
Bruce Boxleitner ...... *Alan Bradley/Tron*
David Warner .... *Ed Dillinger/Sark*
Cindy Morgan .... *Lora/Yori*
Barnard Hughes . *Dr Walter Gibbs/Dumont*
Dan Shor .... *Ram*
Peter Jurasik .... *Crom*
Tony Stephano .... *Peter/Sark's Lieutenant*

Kevin Flynn, an electronic games creator, believes that some of his best programmes have been stolen by Ed Dillinger, an ambitious employee of the company. While trying to extract information out of a giant computer he gets sucked inside the machine. He is forced to pit his wits against the computer in a life-or-death virtual reality game.

Top Twenty Films of 1982

1 Arthur
2 Chariots of Fire/Gregory's Girl
3 Porky's
4 The Fox and the Hound
5 Condorman
6 Annie
7 Rocky III
8 Herbie Goes Bananas
9 Firefox
10 Who Dares Wins
11 Mad Max 2
12 The Empire Strikes Back/Star Wars
13 Poltergeist
14 Private Lessons
15 Death Wish 2
16 The French Lieutenant's Woman
17 Star Trek II: The Wrath of Khan
18 Monty Python's Life of Brian/Airplane!
19 An American Werewolf In London
20 Pink Floyd – The Wall

The Top Five

Week of 30 October 1982
1. Tron
2. Blade Runner
3. The Entity
4. Deathtrap
5. A Midsummer Night's Sex Comedy

Jeff Bridges is the son of actor Lloyd Bridges and began his acting career when he appeared as a child in a couple of episodes of his father's TV series *Sea Hunt*, which ran from 1957 to 1961.

Video availability

GANDHI

11 December 1982	11 weeks*

Distributor:	Columbia
Director:	Richard Attenborough
Producer:	Richard Attenborough
Screenplay:	John Briley
Music:	Ravi Shankar

Attenborough's bio-pic traces the life of India's famous son, Mahatma Gandhi. The Indian spiritual leader wanted dignity, peace and independence for every man, woman and child, no matter what their race or colour. His many years of crusading against the British occupation and the Indian caste system forms the bulk of the film.

CAST
Ben Kingsley .... *Mahatma Gandhi*
Candice Bergen .. *Margaret Bourke-White*
Edward Fox .... *General Dyer*
John Gielgud .... *Lord Irwin*
Trevor Howard .... *Judge Broomfield*
John Mills .... *The Viceroy*
Martin Sheen .... *Walker*

The Top Five

Week of 11 December 1982
1. Gandhi
2. The Draughtsman's Contract
3. Dead Men Don't Wear Plaid
4. Tron
5. Porky's/Puberty Blues

Richard Attenborough's biopic, Gandhi, *traced the Indian lawyer's transformation into one of the world's great men of peace, with Ben Kingsley in the title role.*

It took Sir Richard Attenborough 20 years to convince a film studio to allow him to make the movie, one of the finest British films of the 1980s.

Academy Awards: Best Film (Producer Richard Attenborough), Best Direction (Richard Attenborough), Best Actor (Ben Kingsley), Best Original Screenplay (John Briley), Best Cinematography (Billy Williams and Ronnie Taylor), Best Art Direction (Stuart Crai and Bob Laing), Set Decoration (Michael Seirton), Best Costume Design (John Mollo and Ehanu Athaiya), Best Editing (John Bloom)

Video availability

E.T. THE EXTRA-TERRESTRIAL

18 December 1982	6 weeks

Distributor:	Universal
Director:	Steven Spielberg
Producer:	Steven Spielberg, Kathleen Kennedy
Screenplay:	Melissa Mathison
Music:	John Williams

CAST

Dee Wallace	*Mary*
Henry Thomas	*Elliott*
Peter Coyote	*Keys*
Robert MacNaughton	*Michael*
Drew Barrymore	*Gertie*
K.D. Martel	*Greg*
Sean Frye	*Steve*
Tom Howell	*Tyler*

The lonely 10-year-old Elliott, who lives with his brother, sister and divorced mother, discovers a strange-looking creature roaming about in the back yard. He takes it in and hides it from the rest of the family. But when the other children find him they all want to play with him. They realize that the creature is an extra-terrestrial from another planet with an amazing ability to heal, but they manage to teach it to talk whereupon he tells them he wants to go home. All the local kids that befriend E.T. agree to help him return to his own planet when the officials arrive to capture him for their studies.

E.T. is amongst the highest grossing movies in film history. It made over $228 million.

Three models of E.T. were built by special-effects man Carlo Rambaldi. An electronic version was used for the close-up facial movements, another mechanical one was operated by cables, and a

Elliott (Henry Thomas) takes his friend from another planet for a bike ride that takes to the air in E.T., one of the most popular movies of the 1980s.

freestanding model was operated by two dwarfs. There were also actors who played the character in certain scenes. Tamara de Treaux, a very short 2 feet 7 inches and weighing 40 pounds, was the one that walked up the ramp onto the spacecraft. E.T.'s voice is allegedly supplied by Debra Winger, and the scream when E.T. sees Elliott for the first time is the recording of an otter's shriek when electronically processed.

Neil Diamond wrote and recorded the song 'Heartlight', which was a hit in America and refers to E.T.'s glowing red heart.

Academy Awards: Best Sound (Robert Knudson, Robert Glass, Don Digirolamo and Gene Cantamessa), Best Visual Effects (Carlo Rambaldi, Dennis Muren and Kenneth F. Smith), Best Original Score (John Williams), Best Sound Effects Editing (Charles L. Campbell and Ben Burtt)

Music: 'Heartlight' (Neil Diamond)

Video availability

The Top Five

Week of 18 December 1982
1. E.T.
2. Gandhi
3. The Draughtsman's Contract
4. Tron
5. Dead Men Don't Wear Plaid

AIRPLANE II: THE SEQUEL

29 January 1983	1 week

Distributor:	Paramount
Director:	Ken Finkleman
Producer:	Howard W. Koch
Screenplay:	Ken Finkleman
Music:	Elmer Bernstein

CAST
Robert Hays . . . . Ted Striker
Julie Hagerty . . . . Elaine
Lloyd Bridges . . . . McCroskey
Peter Graves . . . . Capt. Oveur
William Shatner . . . . Murdock
Chad Everett . . . . Simon
Stephen Stucker . . . . Jacobs
Oliver Robins . . . . Jimmy
Sonny Bono . . . . Bomber

This was the comedy sequel to the immensely successful spoof airport disaster movie *Airplane!* (1980). Captain Oveur is again at the controls, but now it's a space shuttle that is in trouble instead of a regular airplane. Ted Striker and his loopy girlfriend, Elaine, are both on hand to provide help and laughs on the shuttle's maiden voyage to the moon, and McCroskey is still firmly in control in his control tower. But will the doomed shuttle make it back to earth safely?

The movie also features cameo appearances from Raymond Burr, Chuck Connors, Sonny Bono and Rip Torn.

The film produced nowhere near as many laughs as *Airplane!* probably because the creative team of Abrahams and the Zucker brothers had left the directing chores to first-time director Ken Finkleman who has yet to make another appearance at number one. However, together and separately the Zuckers and Abrahams are responsible for 6 other number one movies: *The Naked Gun, Naked Gun 2½, Ruthless People, Ghost, Big Business* and *Hot Shots*.

Video availability

The Top Five

Week of 29 January 1983
1. Airplane II: The Sequel
2. Gandhi
3. E.T.
4. The Return of the Soldier
5. Still of the Night

AN OFFICER AND A GENTLEMAN

19 February 1983	1 week

Distributor:	Paramount
Director:	Taylor Hackford
Producer:	Martin Elfand
Screenplay:	Douglas Day Stewart
Music:	Jack Nitzsche

CAST
Richard Gere . . . . Zack Mayo
Debra Winger . . . . Paula Pokrifki
Louis Gossett Jr . . . . Sgt Foley
David Keith . . . . Sid Worley
Lisa Blount . . . . Lynette Pomeroy
Lisa Ellbacher . . . . Casey Seeger
Robert Loggia . . . . Byron Mayo

Military recruits Zack and Sid are put through their paces at a naval base by a sadistic drill sergeant. During their 13-week course, they endure the discipline and training needed before they can become officers. Between drills and sit-ups they meet a few of the factory girls who work near the academy. Zack falls for Paula and Sid for Casey. Zack has nowhere else to go and puts his all into becoming an officer and gentleman, but Sid's world collapses when he fails to graduate and Casey dumps him. He commits suicide and Zack turns to Paula, sweeping her off her factory floor.

TV favourite Louis Gossett Jr won an Oscar for his performance in this film, beating off competition from Charles Durning, John Lithgow, James Mason and Robert Preston. He became the first black actor to win an Oscar since Sidney Poitier won his for *Lilies of the Field* in 1963.

Academy Awards: Best Supporting Actor (Louis Gossett Jr), Best Song – 'Up Where We Belong' (Jack Nitzsche and Buffy Sainte-Marie, music; Will Jennings, lyrics)

Music: 'Up Where We Belong' (Joe Cocker and Jennifer Warnes), 'Hungry For Your Love' (Van Morrison), 'Tush' (ZZ Top), 'Tunnel of Love' (Dire Straits), 'Treat Me Right' (Pat Benatar), 'Be Real' (Sir Douglas Quintet)

Video availability

The Top Five

Week of 19 February 1983
1. An Officer and a Gentleman
2. Gandhi
3. E.T.
4. Heat and Dust
5. Monsignor

SOPHIE'S CHOICE

23 April 1983	2 weeks

Distributor:	Universal
Director:	Alan J. Pakula
Producer:	Alan J. Pakula
Screenplay:	Alan J. Pakula
Music:	Marvin Hamlisch

CAST
Meryl Streep . . . . Sophie Zawistowska
Kevin Kline . . . . Nathan Landau
Peter MacNicol . . . . Stingo
Rita Karin . . . . Yetta Zimmerman
Stephen D. Newman . . . . Larry
Greta Turken . . . . Leslie Lapidus
Josh Mostel . . . . Morris Fink
Gunther Maria Halmer . . . . . . Rudolf Hess

Sophie is a Polish woman who survives the concentration camps of World War II. She rents a room in a house with her lover Nathan. But their relationship remains volatile while Nathan suffers from mental instability and Sophie is plagued by the terrible memories of her ordeal in Auschwitz. She meets and befriends the young writer Stingo who lives in the same house. He listens to her as she recounts the choice she made over the fate of her children.

This is Alan J. Pakula's first movie as a screenwriter, although he has a strong track record as a director with such movies as *Klute* and *All the President's Men* (1976).

He directed the Auschwitz scenes at the Jadran Studios in Zagreb in the former Yugoslavia.

Academy Awards: Best Actress (Meryl Streep)

Video availability

The Top Five

Week of 23 April 1983
1. Sophie's Choice
2. Gandhi
3. Local Hero
4. An Officer and a Gentleman
5. Table for Five

TOOTSIE

7 May 1983	5 weeks

Distributor:	Columbia
Director:	Sydney Pollack
Producer:	Sydney Pollack, Dick Richards
Screenplay:	Larry Gelbart, Murray Schisgal
Music:	Dave Grusin

CAST
Dustin Hoffman . . . . *Dorothy Michaels*
Jessica Lange . . . . *Julie*
Teri Garr . . . . *Sandy*
Dabney Coleman . . . . *Ron*
Charles Durning . . . . *Les*
Bill Murray . . . . *Jeff*
Sydney Pollack . . . . *George Fields*
George Gaynes . . . . *John Van Horn*
Geena Davis . . . . *April*

New York actor Michael Dorsey is finding it impossible to get work. He decides to dress up as a woman and audition for the female lead in a television soap opera. As Dorothy Michaels, he lands the job, and becomes the star of a top-rating show. He manages to keep his real sex a secret but his personal life is thrown into chaos when he becomes a popular personality and begins to fall in love with his TV co-star, Julie. There are more hilarious complications when Julie's father, Les, tries to seduce Dorothy during a weekend in the country.

This was the first film appearance for Geena Davis. As the TV starlet April, who shares a dressing room with Dorothy Michaels, she gives her room-mate the shock of his life when she starts undressing. Davis went on to star in *The Fly* (1987), *Thelma and*

Louise (1991) and *Accidental Hero* (1993) among others. Geena also co-stars with Bill Murray (strangely uncredited in *Tootsie* as Dustin Hoffman's room-mate) in the 1990 bank robbery comedy *Quick Change*. Director/producer Sydney Pollack plays the part of George Fields, Michael Dorsey's agent.

Hoffman claims that the title came from the name his mother used when she tossed him in the air as a child: tootsie-wootsie.

Academy Awards: Best Supporting Actress (Jessica Lange)

Music: 'Tootsie', 'It Might be You' (Stephen Bishop), 'Mary's A Grand Old Name'

Video availability

The Top Five

Week of 7 May 1983
1. Tootsie
2. Sophie's Choice
3. Gandhi
4. The Wicked Lady
5. Local Hero

RETURN OF THE JEDI

11 June 1983	6 weeks*

Distributor:	Twentieth Century-Fox
Director:	Richard Marquand
Producer:	Howard Kazanjian
Screenplay:	Lawrence Kasdan
Music:	John Williams

CAST
Mark Hamill . . . . *Luke Skywalker*
Harrison Ford . . . . *Han Solo*
Carrie Fisher . . . . *Princess Leia*
Billy Dee Williams . . . . . . *Lando Calrissian*
Anthony Daniels *C3PO*
Peter Mayhew . . . . *Chewbacca*
Ian McDiarmid . . . . *Emperor*
David Prowse (James Earl Jones, voice)
Darth Vader
Alec Guinness . . . . *Ben Kenobi*

The concluding part of the *Star Wars* trilogy finds Luke Skywalker, now a Jedi knight, trying to discover the true identity of Darth Vader who is busy building an indestructible Death Star as the space battles continue. Luke, C3PO, R2D2 and Princess Leia set about freeing Han Solo from the clutches of the evil Jabba the Hutt who is holding him prisoner in carbonite on the planet Tatooine.

The movie introduced audiences to new creatures, including benevolent cuddly bears known as Ewoks that subsequently found their way into two made-for-TV movies, *Caravan of Courage: An Ewok Adventure* (1984) and *Ewoks: The Battle for Endor* (1986).

The film was directed by Englishman Richard Marquand who began his career in television commercials and later directed the thriller *Jagged Edge* (1985). He sadly died two years later at the age of 49.

Academy Awards: Best Visual Effects (Special Achievement Award; Richard Edlund, Dennis Muren, Ken Ralston and Phil Tippett)

Video availability

The Top Five

Week of 11 June 1983
1. Return of the Jedi
2. Tootsie
3. The Hunger
4. Local Hero
5. Sophie's Choice

OCTOPUSSY

16 July 1983	4 weeks*

Distributor: Eon
Director: John Glen
Producer: Albert R. Broccoli
Screenplay: George MacDonald Fraser, Richard Malbaum and Michael G. Wilson
Music: John Barry
Tim Rice (theme song lyrics)

CAST

Roger Moore . . . . *James Bond*
Maud Adams . . . . *Octopussy*
Louis Jourdan . . . . *Kamal*
Kristina Wayborn . . . . *Magda*
Kabir Bedi . . . . *Gobinda*
Steven Berkoff . . . . *Orlov*
Desmond Llewelyn . . . . *Q*
Robert Brown . . . . *M*
Lois Maxwell . . . . *Miss Moneypenny*

In the 13th Bond movie the beautiful Octopussy runs a ring of female jewel smugglers. She helps the Russian General Orlov in his attempt to launch a nuclear strike against the American forces in West Germany. Unfortunately for them, James Bond is on their trail, which takes him as far as India in another race against time to save the world.

Maud Adams, who plays Octopussy, is the first actress to have had two major roles in two different Bond movies. She also played Scaramanga's mistress in *The Man with the Golden Gun* (1974). Swedish actress Kristina Wayborn, who plays Magda, Octopussy's assistant, was spotted by Albert Broccoli's wife, Barbara, in a TV movie.

The knife-throwing scene, which features two real-life twins, David and Tony Meyer, was originally written for *Moonraker*.

Music: 'All Time High' (Rita Coolidge)

Video availability

The Top Five

Week of 16 July 1983
1. Octopussy
2. Return of the Jedi
3. Flashdance
4. Monty Python's the Meaning of Life
5. Tootsie

Despite rumours that he was to quit his role as the secret agent, Roger Moore, as James Bond, found himself in the middle of a ring of female jewel smugglers in his sixth outing as 007 in Octopussy.

SUPERMAN III

30 July 1983	1 week

Distributor:	Dovemead/Cantharus
Director:	Richard Lester
Producer:	Pierre Spengler
Screenplay:	David and Leslie Newman
Music:	Ken Thorne
	John Williams (original
	Superman theme)
	Giorgio Moroder (songs)

CAST
Christopher Reeve .. *Superman/Clark Kent*
Richard Pryor . . . . *Gus Gorman*
Jackie Cooper . . . . *Perry White*
Marc McClure . . . . *Jimmy Olsen*
Annette O'Toole . . . . *Lana Lang*
Annie Ross . . . . *Vera Webster*
Pamela Stephenson . . . . *Lorelei Ambrosia*
Robert Vaughn . . . . *Ross Webster*
Margot Kidder . . . . *Lois Lane*

Clark Kent returns to his childhood hometown of Smallville for his school reunion, and rekindles his friendship with former sweetheart Lana Lang. Meanwhile in Metropolis, computer wiz Gus Gorman is caught embezzling the payroll of Ross Webster's huge corporation. When he appears in Smallville he engineers international chaos and develops synthetic kryptonite. Superman's powers are affected and he turns into a mischief-making anti-hero.

This was the third outing for Christopher Reeve as the man of steel. Director Richard Lester previously helmed the number one *Superman II* (1981), but made his directing debut in 1961 with the British musical *It's Trad Dad* (known in the USA as *Ring-a-Ding Rhythm*), starring Helen Shapiro, Craig Douglas, John Leyton, Chubby Checker and Del Shannon. He later made the two Beatles features, *A Hard Day's Night* (1964) and *Help!* (1965).

Video availability

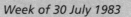

The Top Five

Week of 30 July 1983
1. Superman III
2. Octopussy
3. Return of the Jedi
4. Monty Python's the Meaning of Life
5. Flashdance

WAR GAMES

27 August 1983	5 weeks

Distributor:	MGM–United Artists
Director:	John Badham
Producer:	Harold Schneider
Screenplay:	Lawrence Lasker, Walter F.
	Parkes
Music:	Arthur B. Rubinstein

CAST
Matthew Broderick . . . . *David*
Dabney Coleman . . . . *McKittrick*
John Wood . . . . *Falken*
Ally Sheedy . . . . *Jennifer*
Barry Corbin . . . . *General Beringer*
Juanin Clay . . . . *Pat Healy*
Kent Williams . . . . *Cabot*
Dennis Lipscomb . . . . *Watson*

Computer-crazy David spends his time hacking into computer systems. He wins over his girlfriend when he taps into the school computer system and improves her grades. When he hacks into America's nuclear defence system he thinks he's playing a new game, but it's not long before he realizes it's the most realistic game he's ever played and almost starts another world war.

Director John Badham's first major success n the UK came in 1978 with the musical *Saturday Night Fever*, which made the Top 5 in July that year but remarkably did not become a number one. This was primarily due to the 18 certificate the film carried on its initial release.

Matthew Broderick's other appearances at number one are in the very diverse films *Family Business* (1990), in which he starred alongside Sean Connery

The Top Five

Week of 27 August 1983
1. War Games
2. Octopussy
3. Return of the Jedi
4. Superman III
5. Monty Python's the Meaning of Life

and Dustin Hoffman, and the 1994 blockbuster *The Lion King*, in which he is the voice of Simba.

STAYING ALIVE

1 October 1983	2 weeks

Distributor:	Paramount
Director:	Sylvester Stallone
Producer:	Robert Stigwood, Sylvester Stallone
Screenplay:	Sylvester Stallone
Music:	Bee Gees
	Robin Garb (Co-ordination)

CAST
John Travolta . . . . *Tony Manero*
Cynthia Rhodes . . . . *Jackie*
Finola Hughes . . . . *Laura*
Steve Inwood . . . . *Jesse*
Julie Bovasso . . . . *Mrs Manero*

This sequel to *Saturday Night Fever* picks up the story of Brooklyn boy Tony Manero. He moves to Manhattan and begins work as a dance instructor, hoping to make it big on Broadway. His relationship with girlfriend Jackie hits the skids when he wins a role in the chorus of British dancer Laura's new show, 'Satan's Alley'. In true showbiz tradition he is catapulted to stardom when he steps into the lead's dancing shoes on opening night.

The film title is derived from the song 'Stayin' Alive', which featured on the original soundtrack album of *Saturday Night Fever* and became a hit for the Bee Gees in 1978. Stallone's brother Frank also contributed some songs and music to this film.

Blink and you'll miss director Sylvester Stallone as a passerby in a busy street scene.

Music: 'The Woman In You', 'I Love You Too Much', 'Life Goes On', 'Far From Over'. 'Moody Girls', 'Look Out for Number One'

Video availability

The Top Five

Week of 1 October 1983
1. Staying Alive
2. War Games
3. Breathless
4. Merry Christmas Mr Lawrence
5. Octopussy

ZELIG

15 October 1983	2 weeks

Distributor:	Orion
Director:	Woody Allen
Producer:	Robert Greenhut
Screenplay:	Woody Allen
Music:	Dick Hyman

CAST
Woody Allen . . . . *Leonard Zelig*
Mia Farrow . . . . *Dr Eudora Fletcher*
Garrett Brown . . . . *Actor Zelig*
Stephanie Farrow . . . . *Sister Meryl*
Will Holt . . . . *Rally Chancellor*

In this spoof documentary set in the 1920s Leonard Zelig is neurotic. He is obsessed about being liked by others and will go to any lengths to become accepted by the people who matter, even to the point of changing his physical appearance to be like the person he's with. His strange behaviour be-

comes of great interest to psychiatrist Dr Eudora Fletcher, who ends up falling in love with him.

Mia Farrow, who has been married to André Previn and Frank Sinatra and lived with Woody Allen, is the daughter of movie director John Farrow by his marriage to actress Maureen O'Sullivan. At the age of 14 Mia had a small role in her father's 1959 film *John Paul Jones*.

Video availability

The Top Five

Week of 15 October 1983
1. Zelig
2. War Games
3. Staying Alive
4. Breathless
5. Octopussy

JUNGLE BOOK/MICKEY'S CHRISTMAS CAROL

29 October 1983	11 weeks*

Distributor: Walt Disney
Director: Burney Mattinson
Producer: Walt Disney Productions

*M*ickey's Christmas Carol is a short animated version of the well-known Dickens' *A Christmas Carol*, screened with *The Jungle Book* on its second re-release. (It was released in 1967 and 1975). *Christmas Carol* features all of Disney's favourite characters, such as Mickey Mouse as Bob Cratchit, Donald Duck as Scrooge McDuck and Jiminy Cricket playing the Ghost of Christmas Past, among others.

For details of Jungle Book see 1967.

Video availability

The Top Five

Week of 29 October 1983
1. Jungle Book/Mickey's Christmas Carol
2. National Lampoon's Vacation
3. Zelig
4. Class
5. La Traviata

TRADING PLACES

17 December 1983	2 weeks*

Distributor: Paramount
Director: John Landis
Producer: Aaron Russo
Screenplay: Timothy Harris
Music: Elmer Bernstein

CAST
Dan Aykroyd .... *Louis Winthorpe III*
Eddie Murphy .... *Billy Ray Valentine*
Ralph Bellamy .... *Randolph Duke*
Don Ameche .... *Mortimer Duke*
Denholm Elliott .... *Coleman*
Jamie Lee Curtis .... *Ophelia*

In Trading Places street bum Billy Ray (Eddie Murphy) changes places with business tycoon Louis Winthrope III following the manipulations of two wealthy brothers, Randolph and Mortimer Duke (Ralph Bellamy and Don Ameche). Jamie Lee Curtis is the hooker that comes to Winthrope's aid.

Paul Gleason	*Beeks*
Kristin Holby	*Penelope*
Robert Curtis-Brown	*Todd*

Two wealthy brothers, Mortimer and Randolph Duke, organize a social experiment when they make Billy Ray Valentine, a down-and-out street hustler, exchange places with the rich and pompous yuppy Louis Winthorpe III. One of the brother's bets the other that the two men couldn't cut it in each others' shoes. They frame Winthorpe and force him onto the street, while welcoming Valentine into their business. Winthorpe is helped by the prostitute with a heart, Jamie Lee Curtis, while Valentine has a surprise for the brothers.

The film was number one on 17 December 1983 for a week. It was replaced by *Never Say Never Again* for 4 weeks before regaining the top spot for a further week from 21 January 1984.

Alfred Drake, star of the Broadway musical stage, makes an appearance as the President of the Stock Exchange. It was also Don Ameche's first film appearance in 13 years. He was last seen on the silver screen in the 1970 movie *The Boatniks*.

Video availability

> ## The Top Five
>
> *Week of 17 December 1983*
> 1. Trading Places
> 2. The Jungle Book/Mickey's Christmas Carol
> 3. Rear Window
> 4. La Traviata
> 5. Octopussy

NEVER SAY NEVER AGAIN

24 December 1983	4 weeks

Distributor:	Warner
Director:	Irvin Kershner
Producer:	Jack Schwartzman
Screenplay:	Lorenzo Semple Jr
Music:	Michel Legrand

CAST

Sean Connery	*James Bond*
Klaus Maria Brandauer	*Largo*
Max Von Sydow	*Blofeld*
Barbara Carrera	*Fatima Blush*
Kim Basinger	*Domino*
Bernie Casey	*Felix Leiter*
Alec McCowen	*Q*
Edward Fox	*M*
Pamela Salem	*Miss Moneypenny*

Sean Connery returns as James bond to chase SPECTRE madman Largo, who has hijacked two American cruise missiles. It's the beautiful but deadly agent Fatima Blush out to do damage to our hero this time. But Bond eventually tracks Largo and his attractive assistant Domino to his luxury yacht.

After completing *Diamonds Are Forever* in 1971, Sean Connery commented that he would never play James Bond again. Twelve years on, he returned with a plan to compete with Roger Moore's *Octopussy*, released in the same year. The press were ready to report on the battle of the Bonds, but Connery's film hit production problems and the release had to be postponed. In the end *Never Say*

> ## Top Twenty Films of 1983
>
> 1 E.T.
> 2 Return of the Jedi
> 3 Octopussy
> 4 Gandhi
> 5 Tootsie
> 6 Superman III
> 7 An Officer and a Gentleman
> 8 Staying Alive
> 9 Airplane II: The Sequel
> 10 Monty Python's the Meaning of Life
> 11 Flashdance
> 12 The Dark Crystal
> 13 Tron
> 14 Educating Rita
> 15 WarGames
> 16 Local Hero
> 17 First Blood
> 18 Porky's II: The Next Day
> 19 Sophie's Choice
> 20 Friday the 13th Part III

> ## The Top Five
>
> *Week of 24 December 1983*
> 1. Never Say Never Again
> 2. Trading Places
> 3. The Jungle Book/Mickey's Christmas Carol
> 4. Jaws III D
> 5. Rear Window

Never Again was basically a remake of the 1965 Bond movie *Thunderball*.

This was director Ivan Kershner's first movie since his blockbuster hit *The Empire Strikes Back* (1980). His other credits include *Raid on Entebbe* (1976) and *Robocop II* (1990).

The film also features Rowan Atkinson as a character called Small-Fawcett.

Music: 'Never Say Never Again' (Lani Hall)

Video availability

GORKY PARK

28 January 1984	1 week

Distributor:	Orion
Director:	Michael Apted
Producer:	Gene Kirkwood, Howard W. Koch Jr
Screenplay:	Dennis Potter
Music:	James Horner

CAST
William Hurt . . . . *Arkady Renko*
Lee Marvin . . . . *Jack Osborne*
Brian Dennehy . . . . *William Kirwill*
Ian Bannen . . . . *Iamskoy*
Joanna Pacula . . . . *Irina*
Michael Elphick . . . . *Pasha*
Richard Griffiths . . . . *Anton*
Rikki Fulton . . . . *Pribluda*
Alexei Sayle . . . . *Golodkin*

Three faceless bodies, with their fingertips removed to avoid identification, are discovered in Moscow's Gorky Park. Russian police Inspector Renko is brought in to investigate the case. He initially believes it to be the work of the KGB but later finds himself on the trail of Jack Osborne, an American fur trader.

The movie, based on the novel by Martin Cruz Smith, was shot in Helsinki because the Russians refused the director permission to film in Russia. In 1989 *Red Heat* (1989) became the first American-made film to be shot in the USSR.

Video availability

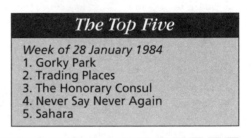

> ### *The Top Five*
>
> *Week of 28 January 1984*
> 1. Gorky Park
> 2. Trading Places
> 3. The Honorary Consul
> 4. Never Say Never Again
> 5. Sahara

SUDDEN IMPACT

4 February 1984	1 week

Distributor:	Warner
Director:	Clint Eastwood
Producer:	Clint Eastwood
Screenplay:	Joseph C. Stinson
Music:	Lalo Schifrin

CAST
Clint Eastwood . . . . *Harry Callahan*
Sondra Locke . . . . *Jennifer Spencer*
Pat Hingle . . . . *Chief Jennings*
Bradford Dillman . . . . *Captain Briggs*
Paul Drake . . . . *Mick*
Audrie J. Neenan . . . . *Ray Parkins*
Jack Thibeau . . . . *Kruger*
Michael Currie . . . . *Lt Donnelly*

In Clint Eastwood's fourth outing as Harry Callahan, or 'Dirty Harry', the detective is sent to the coastal town of San Paulo to track down a vicious killer.

Here he meets a young woman, Jennifer Spencer, who is out for revenge on a gang of thugs who raped her and her sister some time ago. The local police chief attempts to curb Harry's hot-headed methods on his territory but to no avail.

Clint Eastwood first got into the movies when he was working as a delivery boy, dropping off goods at Universal Studios. An employee managed to arrange a screen test and Eastwood was offered $75 a week for an 18-month contract, during which he

> ### *The Top Five*
>
> *Week of 4 February 1984*
> 1. Sudden Impact
> 2. Gorky Park
> 3. Trading Places
> 4. The Honorary Consul
> 5. Never Say Never Again

had several small roles in films, including *Revenge of the Creature* (1955) and *Tarantula* (1956).

SCARFACE

11 February 1984	3 weeks

Distributor: Universal
Director: Brian DePalma
Producer: Martin Bregman
Screenplay: Oliver Stone
Music: Giorgio Moroder

CAST
Al Pacino .... *Tony Montana*
Steven Bauer .... *Manny Ray*
Michelle Pfeiffer .... *Elvira*
Mary Elizabeth Mastrantonio ...... *Gina*
Robert Loggia .... *Frank Lopez*
Miriam Colon .... *Mama Montana*
F. Murray Abraham .... *Omar*

Tony Montana rises to the top of the gangland ladder. He goes to work for drug dealer Frank Lopez and gets involved with Lopez's wife. Through a bad deal, Lopez tries to kill Tony but is himself killed. On the rocks with an addiction for cocaine, Tony backs out of murdering an anti-drug campaigner for the mob, putting his own life at risk.

Video availability

The film was based on the 1932 movie of the same name, starring George Raft and Paul Muni, produced by millionaire Howard Hughes.

In 1977 Michelle Pfeiffer entered and won the Miss Orange County beauty contest. The following year she had a small part in the TV series *Fantasy Island* – so small in fact that her only line was 'Who is he, Naomi?'

Video availability

The Top Five

Week of 11 February 1984
1. Scarface
2. Sudden Impact
3. Gorky Park
4. Trading Places
5. The Honorary Consul

TO BE OR NOT TO BE

3 March 1984	3 weeks

Distributor: Alexander Korda
Director: Alan Johnson
Producer: Mel Brooks
Screenplay: Thomas Meehan, Ronny Graham
Music: John Morris

CAST
Mel Brooks .... *Frederick Bronski*
Anne Bancroft .... *Anna Bronski*
Tim Matheson .... *Lt Sobinski*
Charles Durning .... *Colonel Erhardt*
Jose Ferrer .... *Professor Siletski*
James Haake .... *Sasha*
Christopher Lloyd .... *Capt. Schultz*
George Gaynes .... *Ravitch*

Mel Brooks is in charge of a Polish theatrical group during World War II. He is forced to cancel an anti-Nazi play in favour of a production of *Hamlet* when his team of actors get involved with invading Germans during the Nazi occupation of their country. They help the Polish resistance by

impersonating German officials, including Hitler, with sometimes hilarious results.

The film was based on the original 1942 movie starring Jack Benny and Carole Lombard. At the time the film was considered to have been in bad taste. Mel Brooks and Anne Bancroft, who played husband and wife Frederick and Anna Bronski, are in fact married in real life. They'd previously appeared together in *Silent Movie* (1976), which Brooks also directed.

Music: 'Sweet Georgia Brown'

Video availability

The Top Five

Week of 3 March 1984
1. To Be or Not To Be
2. Under Fire
3. Scarface
4. Trading Places
5. Two of a Kind

Aurora (Shirley MacLaine) shares a love-hate relationship with ex-astronaut neighbour Garrett (Jack Nicholson) in Terms of Endearment.

TERMS OF ENDEARMENT

24 March 1984	4 weeks

Distributor:	Paramount
Director:	James L. Brooks
Producer:	James L. Brooks
Screenplay:	James L. Brooks
Music:	Michael Gore

CAST

Debra Winger	*Emma Greenway*
Shirley MacLaine	*Aurora Greenway*
Jack Nicholson	*Garrett Breedlove*
Jeff Daniels	*Flap Horton*
John Lithgow	*Sam*
Huckleberry Fox	*Teddy*
Troy Bishop	*Tommy*
Danny De Vito	*Vernon*

James L. Brooks' weepie spans the 30-year relationship of mother and daughter, Aurora Greenway and Emma. The family ties begin to disintegrate when Emma decides to marry her school teacher boyfriend, Flap Horton, and they move out of town to raise a family. With her daughter away, Aurora is pestered by her neighbour, a retired drunken astronaut, Garrett Breedlove, who has unsavoury manners but eventually manages to woo her. Tragedy, however, brings mother and daughter back together again.

This was the big screen debut for writer and director James L. Brooks, who had previously worked on successful TV comedies, including *The Mary Tyler Moore Show* and *Taxi*.

The fights between Shirley MacLaine and Debra Winger appeared to have continued off screen as well as in the script.

Jack Nicholson was paid $1 million for his part.

Academy Awards: Best Film (Producer James L. Brooks), Best Direction (James L. Brooks), Best Actress (Shirley MacLaine), Best Supporting Actor (Jack Nicholson), Best Screenplay (James L. Brooks)

Music: 'Anything Goes' (Ethel Merman), 'Gee Officer Krupke' (Eddie Roll, Grover Dale and The Jets), 'Rock-A-Bye Your Baby With A Dixie Melody' (Judy Garland)

Video availability

The Top Five

Week of 24 March 1984
1. Terms of Endearment
2. To Be or Not To Be
3. Champions
4. Risky Business
5. Vertigo

GREYSTOKE: THE LEGEND OF TARZAN, LORD OF THE APES

21 April 1984	4 weeks

Distributor:	Warner
Director:	Hugh Hudson
Producer:	Hugh Hudson
Screenplay:	P.H. Vazak, Michael Austin
Music:	John Scott

CAST
Ralph Richardson *The Sixth Earl of Greystoke*
Ian Holm . . . . . *Capitaine Phillippe D'Arnot*
James Fox . . . . *Lord Esker*
Christopher Lambert . . . . . . *John Clayton,*
Tarzan, Lord of the Apes
Andie MacDowell . . . . . . *Miss Jane Porter*
Cheryl Campbell . . . . . *Lady Alice Clayton*

Lord Clayton and his wife Alice become shipwrecked off the coast of Africa where they both die soon after she gives birth. The child, John, heir to the family fortune, survives and is brought up by a group of apes. He is later returned to civilization and to his ancestral estate by a Belgian explorer who teaches him English. Despite the love of Miss Jane Porter, Tarzan returns to his real home in the jungle.

Greystoke was one of Ralph Richardson's final movie appearances, along with *Give My Regards to Broad Street* later in the same year. But it was Andie MacDowell's debut. Her voice was dubbed by Glenn Close, which apparently upset MacDowell greatly. Peter Elliot, who plays John's ape father, also choreographed the ape sequences and is billed as Elliot W. Cane.

Video availability

The Top Five

Week of 21 April 1984
1. Greystoke: The Legend of Tarzan, Lord of the Apes
2. Terms of Endearment
3. Yentl
4. Silkwood
5. Footloose

AGAINST ALL ODDS

19 May 1984	3 weeks

Distributor:	Columbia
Director:	Taylor Hackford
Producer:	Taylor Hackford, William S. Gilmore
Screenplay:	Eric Hughes
Music:	Michel Colombier, Larry Carlton

CAST
Rachel Ward . . . . *Jessie*
Jeff Bridges . . . . *Terry*
James Woods . . . . *Jake*
Alex Karras . . . . *Hank*
Jane Greer . . . . *Mrs Wyler*
Richard Widmark . . . . *Caxton*
Dorian Harewood . . . . *Tommy*
Swoosie Kurtz . . . . *Edie*
Saul Rubinek . . . . *Steve*

Jake is a small-time LA villain, involved with gambling. He is stabbed by his girlfriend Jessie before she runs off to Mexico. Jake meets up with ex-team-mate and fading football star Terry, whose club is owned by the girl's mother. Jake employs him to help bring Jessie back home. After tracking her down, there is the small problem of the murder she has committed, not to mention the two of them falling in love.

The film is loosely based on the 1947 film *Build my Gallows High*, which starred Robert Mitchum and Kirk Douglas. Jane Greer played the Rachel Ward character in the 1947 film and the character's mother in *Against All Odds*.

The title song by Phil Collins reached number two in the UK singles chart.

Music: 'Take A Look At Me Now' (Phil Collins), 'Violet and Blue' (Stevie Nicks), 'Walk Through the Fire' (Peter Gabriel), 'Balcony' (Big Country), 'Mak-

The Top Five

Week of 19 May 1984
1. Against All Odds
2. Terms of Endearment
3. Greystoke: The Legend of Tarzan, Lord of the Apes
4. Silkwood
5. The Dead Zone

ing A Big Mistake' (Mike Rutherford), 'My Male Curiosity' (Kid Creole and the Coconuts)

Video availability

BREAKDANCE

9 June 1984	1 week

Distributor: **MGM–United Artists**
Director: **Joel Silberg**
Producer: **Allen DeBevoise, David Zito**
Screenplay: **Charles Parker, Allen DeBevoise, Gerald Scaife**
Music: **Gary Remal, Michael Boyd**

CAST
Lucinda Dickey . . . . *Kelly*
Adolfo (Shabba-Doo) Quinones . . *Ozone*
Michael (Bongaloo Shrimp)
   Chambers . . . . *Turbo*
Ben Lokey . . . . *Franco*
Christopher McDonald . . . . *James*
Phineas Newborn III . . . . *Adam*

A crowd of talented breakdancing youngsters from the streets are trying to get accepted by the unimaginative dance schools who think nothing of their craft. After so many displays of their art the schools come round to the kids' way of thinking.

This was the first full-length movie completely devoted to the breakdance craze. Although breakdancing is almost the exclusive property of the black and Latino communities, the movie builds much of the action around an average young white girl.

The film went under the title of *Breakin'* in the USA.

Music: 'Breakin' . . . There's No Stoppin' Us', 'When I.C.U.' (Ollie and Jerry), 'Radiotron', 'Stylin' Profilin'' (Firefox), 'Dinn Daa Daa' (George Kranz), 'Gotta Have Money' (Steve Donn), 'Believe in the Beat' (Carol Lynn Townes)

Video availability

The Top Five

Week of 9 June 1984
1. Breakdance
2. The Evil That Men Do
3. The Naked Face
4. Greystoke: The Legend of Tarzan, Lord of the Apes
5. Against All Odds

ANOTHER COUNTRY

16 June 1984	1 week

Distributor: **Twentieth Century-Fox**
Director: **Marek Kanievska**
Producer: **Alan Marshall**
Screenplay: **Julian Mitchell**
Music: **Michael Storey**

CAST
Rupert Everett . . . . *Guy Bennett*
Colin Firth . . . . *Tommy Judd*
Michael Jenn . . . . *Barclay*
Robert Addie . . . . *Delahay*
Rupert Wainwright . . . . *Devenish*
Tristan Oliver . . . . *Fowler*
Cary Elwes . . . . *Harcourt*
Frederick Alexander . . . . *Menzies*

B ased on Julian Mitchell's hit West End play, the film depicts life in a British boarding school for boys in the 1930s. The young homosexual Guy Bennett was an outsider within the oppressive public school system and embraced Marxism as an escape from the claustrophobic atmosphere. The film offers the causes of Bennett's disaffection with the establishment in Britain with not so subtle parallels with the life of Guy Burgess.

This was Rupert Everett's year with number ones with this and *Dance With a Stranger*.

Producer Alan Marshall clocked up his first number one in 1976 with *Bugsy Malone* and his second in 1982 with *Pink Floyd - The Wall*. He went on to score again with *Basic Instinct* (1992) and *Cliffhanger* (1993).

The Top Five

Week of 16 June 1984
1. Another Country
2. Breakdance
3. The Evil That Men Do
4. Greystoke: The Legend of Tarzan, Lord of the Apes
5. The Naked Face

Director of Photography Peter Biziou won the Best Artistic Contribution Award at the Cannes film Festival.

INDIANA JONES AND THE TEMPLE OF DOOM

23 June 1984	9 weeks

Distributor: Paramount
Director: Steven Spielberg
Producer: Robert Watts
Screenplay: Willard Huyck, Gloria Katz
Music: John Williams

CAST
Harrison Ford . . . . *Indiana Jones*
Kate Capshaw . . . . *Willie Scott*
Ke Huy Quan . . . . *Short Round*
Amrish Puri . . . . *Mola Ram*
Roshan Seth . . . . *Chattar Lal*
Philip Stone . . . . *Capt. Blumburtt*
Roy Chiao . . . . *Lao Che*
David Yip . . . . *Wu Han*
Ric Young . . . . *Kao Kan*

The second Jones movie is in fact a prequel to *Raiders of the Lost Ark*. Indiana has to make a fast retreat from a Shanghai nightclub with singer Willie Scott when the baddies turn up. They head, by plane, for a small Indian village in the company of a young boy named Short Round who they picked up along the way. The local village elders tell Indiana of the loss of their precious and valuable stone which brings prosperity to the community. Indiana, Willie and Short Round go in search of the evil men who have stolen it.

Video availability

When it reached number one, *Indiana Jones and the Temple of Doom* was the eighth highest grossing movie of all time, just behind *Raiders of the Lost Ark*. In 1989, the third and final sequel was released, *Indiana Jones and the Last Crusade* (1989). Both Tom Selleck and Burt Lancaster were originally offered the part of Indiana.

The nightclub in the film is called 'Obi-Wan' after Sir Alec Guinness's character in *Star Wars*, Obi Wan Kenobi.

Academy Awards: Best Visual Effects (Dennis Muren, Michael McAlister, Lorne Peterson and George Gibbs)

Video availability

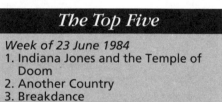

The Top Five

Week of 23 June 1984
1. Indiana Jones and the Temple of Doom
2. Another Country
3. Breakdance
4. The Evil That Men Do
5. Friday the 13th – The Final Chapter

ROMANCING THE STONE

25 August 1984	4 weeks

Distributor: Twentieth Century-Fox
Director: Robert Zemeckis
Producer: Michael Douglas
Screenplay: Diane Thomas
Music: Alan Silvestri

CAST
Michael Douglas . . . . *Jack Colton*
Kathleen Turner . . . . *Joan Wilder*
Danny DeVito . . . . *Ralph*
Zack Norman . . . . *Ira*
Alfonso Arau . . . . *Juan*
Manuel Ojeda . . . . *Zolo*

Holland Taylor . . . . *Gloria*
Mary Ellen Trainor . . . . *Elaine*

Successful romantic novelist Joan Wilder receives a package from South America containing a map that shows where a precious green jewel is hidden. This is followed by a phone call from her sister who says it was her husband who sent the map before disappearing in Colombia, and that she's been kidnapped by an art dealer and his cousin who are threatening her with death unless they get the contents of the package. Needless to say, Joan sets off for the jungle on a rescue mission, teaming up with American soldier Jack Colton along the way.

Michael Douglas backed this project when he was approached by little-known director Robert

Zemeckis, who only had two films of any note to his credit: *I Wanna Hold Your Hand* (1978) and *Used Cars* (1980) starring Kurt Russell. The success of the film spawned a sequel, *The Jewel of the Nile*, which became a box office hit of 1986.

Music: 'Romancing the Stone' (Eddy Grant)

Video availability

PARIS, TEXAS

22 September 1984	1 week

Distributor:	Road Movies
Director:	Wim Wenders
Producer:	Don Guest
Screenplay:	Sam Shepard
Music:	Ry Cooder

CAST
Harry Dean Stanton . . . . *Travis*
Nastassja Kinski . . . . *Jane*
Dean Stockwell . . . . *Walt*
Aurore Clement . . . . *Anne*
Hunter Carson . . . . *Hunter*

Bernhard Wicki . . . . *Doctor Ulmer*

Travis Clay Henderson wanders into a bar on the Texas–Mexican border and collapses. He is revived by a doctor who calls a phone number in the man's wallet and makes contact with Henderson's brother, who, it turns out, has adopted Travis' seven-year-old son. When they are re-united, father and son set off to find the missing mother of four years who is believed to be working in a strip club.

Harry Dean Stanton's role as Travis is considered to be his first truly successful lead in the movies. He was aged 58 at the time.

Travis Clay Henderson's (Harry Dean Stanton) quest for his estranged wife Jane (Nastassja Kinski) is accompanied by the haunting music of Ry Cooder in Paris, Texas.

Dean Stockwell, who plays Walt Henderson, was a child movie actor at the age of nine when he appeared in *Anchors Aweigh* (1945), starring Frank Sinatra and Gene Kelly.

Music: 'Paris Texas', 'Brothers', 'No Safety Zone', 'Dark was The Night', 'Nothing Out There'

Video availability

The Top Five

Week of 22 September 1984
1. Paris, Texas
2. Romancing the Stone
3. Indiana Jones and the Temple of Doom
4. The Hit
5. Bachelor Party

THE COMPANY OF WOLVES

29 September 1984	3 weeks

Distributor:	ITC
Director:	Neil Jordan
Producer:	Chris Brown, Stephen Woolley
Screenplay:	Angela Carter, Neil Jordan
Music:	George Fenton

CAST

Angela Lansbury	*Granny*
David Warner	*Father*
Stephen Rea	*Young Groom*
Tusse Silberg	*Mother*
Sarah Patterson	*Rosaleen*
Graham Crowden	*Priest*
Kathryn Pogson	*Bride*

Thirteen-year-old Rosaleen, who lives with her parents in a cottage on the edge of a forest, is troubled by lurid dreams caused by her grandmother's tales of men turning into wolves. When a neighbour reports a carcass of an animal that is

The Top Five

Week of 29 September 1984
1. The Company of Wolves
2. Paris, Texas
3. Lassiter
4. Streets of Fire
5. Indiana Jones and the Temple of Doom

The visual extravaganza of The Company of Wolves *was the result of filling a child's head with too many stories about men turning into wolves.*

believed to have been savaged by wolves, Rosaleen's nightmare world is revived.

Director Neil Jordan began his career in movies when he worked with John Boorman as script assistant on his 1981 film *Excalibur*.

Angela Lansbury is the granddaughter of George Lansbury who was leader of the Labour Party in Britain from 1931 to 1935.

Video availability

THE WOMAN IN RED

20 October 1984	5 weeks

Distributor:	Orion
Director:	Gene Wilder
Producer:	Victor Drai
Screenplay:	Gene Wilder
Music:	John Morris

CAST
Gene Wilder . . . . *Theodore Pierce*
Charles Grodin . . . . *Buddy*
Joseph Bologna . . . . *Joe*
Judith Ivey . . . . *Didi*
Michael Huddleston . . . . *Michael*
Kelly Le Brock . . . . *Charlotte*
Gilda Radner . . . . *Ms Milner*

In this romantic comedy happy family man Theodore Pierce meets Charlotte when she is hired as a model by the advertising agency where he works. Spotting her red dress swirling up as she walks over a hot air grate on the way to her car, his head is turned and he attempts, with hilarious non-results, to embark on an illicit affair.

The film was a remake of the 1976 French film *Un Elephant ca Trompe Enormement*, known in the USA as *Pardon Mon Affaire*. Gifted comedienne

Gilda Radner, until her untimely death in 1989, was the real wife of director and star Gene Wilder.

Stevie Wonder's Academy Award-winning song from the film, 'I Just Called To Say I Love You', became his first UK solo number one single, staying at the top of the charts for six weeks after a career which began in 1966.

Academy Awards: Best song – 'I Just Called To Say I Love You' (Stevie Wonder, music and lyrics)

Music: 'The Woman In Red', 'I Just Called To Say I Love You', 'Love Light In Flight' (Stevie Wonder), 'It's You', 'Weakness' (Stevie Wonder and Dionne Warwick), 'Moments Aren't Moments' (Dionne Warwick)

Video availability

The Top Five

Week of 20 October 1984
1. The Woman In Red
2. The Company of Wolves
3. 1984
4. Top Secret
5. Paris, Texas

1984

24 November 1984	2 weeks

Distributor:	Umbrella
Director:	Michael Radford
Producer:	Simon Perry
Screenplay:	Michael Radford
Music:	Dominic Muldowney

CAST
John Hurt . . . . *Winston Smith*
Richard Burton . . . . *O'Brien*
Suzanna Hamilton . . . . *Julia*
Cyril Cusack . . . . *Charrington*
Gregor Fisher . . . . *Parsons*
James Walker . . . . *Syme*
Andrew Wilde . . . . *Tillotson*

In George Orwell's vision of the future Winston Smith is brainwashed by Big Brother in an inhuman society where free thinking is not allowed and history is constantly being re-written. Smith falls in love with Julia, who works for the Ministry of Truth, but their illegal affair is discovered by Government official O'Brien. Disappointed by Smith's thought

The Top Five

Week of 24 November 1984
1. 1984
2. The Woman In Red
3. The Company of Wolves
4. The Natural
5. Tightrope

crimes, O'Brien punishes him with nightmarish torture until he is deemed fit to re-enter this very bleak world.

1984 saw Richard Burton's final film appearance; he died before the film was released. An earlier movie version of *1984* was made in 1956, starring Michael Redgrave and Edmond O'Brien.

John Hurt has had a history of playing tortured characters, appearing in *10 Rillington Place* (1971),

Midnight Express (1978), *Alien* (1979), *The Elephant Man* (1980) and *Spaceballs* (1987).

Eurythmics provided the song 'Sex Crime (Nineteen Eighty Four)', which reached number four in the singles charts.

Music: 'Sex Crime (Nineteen Eighty Four)' (Eurythmics)

Video availability

GIVE MY REGARDS TO BROAD STREET

8 December 1984	1 week

Distributor:	Twentieth Century-Fox
Director:	Peter Webb
Producer:	Andros Epaminondas
Screenplay:	Paul McCartney
Music:	Paul McCartney

CAST
Paul McCartney	. . . .	Paul
Bryan Brown	. . . .	Steve
Ringo Starr	. . . .	Ringo
Barbara Bach	. . . .	Journalist
Linda McCartney	. . . .	Linda
Tracey Ullman	. . . .	Sandra
Ralph Richardson	. . . .	Jim
Ian Hastings	. . . .	Harry

Paul is a performer and the boss of a massive music empire. He manages to mislay a valuable tape from a recording session which contains the only copies of a batch of new songs for his album. His future depends on the recovery of the property.

The film is filled with cameo appearances from the likes of Linda McCartney, Ringo Starr and his other half, Barbara Bach. It was intended as a double bill with a full-length animated movie of the adventures of 'Rupert The Bear'. Although this is a long-cherished project of McCartney's, so far only 'The Frog's Chorus' sequence has been completed and shown.

The musical soundtrack reached number one on the album charts in Britain just three weeks before Paul McCartney was awarded the Freedom of Liverpool in a ceremony held in his home town.

Music: 'No More Lonely Nights', 'Good Day Sunshine', 'Here There and Everywhere', 'The Long and Winding Road', 'Yesterday', 'Silly Love Songs', 'Good Night Princess'

Top Twenty Films of 1984

1 Indiana Jones and the Temple of Doom
2 Never Say Never Again
3 The Jungle Book
4 Police Academy
5 Sudden Impact
6 Terms of Endearment
7 Educating Rita
8 Trading Places
9 Greystoke: The Legend of Tarzan, Lord of the Apes
10 Jaws 3-D
11 Footloose
12 Splash
13 The Woman in Red
14 The Company of Wolves
15 Scarface
16 One Hundred and One Dalmatians
17 Yentl
18 Romancing the Stone
19 The Sword in the Stone
20 Lady and the Tramp

The Top Five

Week of 8 December 1984
1. Give My Regards to Broad Street
2. 1984
3. A Private Function
4. The Woman in Red
5. The Killing Fields

*Dr Peter Venkman (Bill Murray), Dr Raymond Stantz (Dan Ackroyd) and Dr Egon Spengler
(Harold Ramis) become company spooksmen when they set up in business to rid buildings of
ghostly spirits.*

GHOSTBUSTERS

15 December 1984	6 weeks

Distributor:	Columbia
Director:	Ivan Reitman
Producer:	Ivan Reitman
Screenplay:	Dan Aykroyd, Harold Ramis
Music:	Elmer Bernstein

CAST

Bill Murray	. . . .	*Dr Peter Venkman*
Dan Aykroyd	. . . .	*Dr Raymond Stantz*
Sigourney Weaver	. . . .	*Dana Barrett*
Harold Ramis	. . . .	*Dr Egon Spengler*
Rick Moranis	. . . .	*Louis Tully*
Annie Potts	. . . .	*Janine Melnitz*

William Atherton . . . . *Walter Peck*
Ernie Hudson . . . . *Winston Zeddmore*

Having been expelled from college, doctors Venkman and Stantz set up a business with secretary Janine Melnitz, that claims to rid buildings of demons. Their first client is the lovely cellist, Dana Barrett, whose New York home is overrun with spirits. The Ghostbusters trap several strange beings and believe the apartment is the main doorway to the spirit kingdom.

The film was originally planned as a project for John Belushi and Dan Aykroyd before Belushi's untimely death in 1982; the film was to be called 'Ghostmashers'. John Candy was also the first choice to play Rick Moranis's role of Louis Tully.

A sequel, *Ghostbusters II*, was released in 1989,

followed by a series of animated cartoons for television.

Music: 'Ghostbusters' (Ray Parker Jr), 'Cleanin' Up the Town' (Bus Boys), 'Savin' the Day' (Alessi), 'In the Name of Love' (The Thompson Twins), 'I Can't Wait Forever' (Air Supply), 'Hot Night' (Laura Branigan)

Video availability

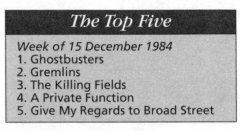

The Top Five

Week of 15 December 1984
1. Ghostbusters
2. Gremlins
3. The Killing Fields
4. A Private Function
5. Give My Regards to Broad Street

WATER

26 January 1985	1 week

Distributor:	**HandMade**
Director:	**Dick Clement**
Producer:	**Ian La Frenais**
Screenplay:	**Dick Clement, Ian La Frenais, Bill Persky**
Music:	**Mike Moran**

CAST
Michael Caine . . . . *Baxter*
Valerie Perrine . . . . *Pamela*
Brenda Vaccaro . . . . *Bianca*
Billy Connolly . . . . *Delgado*
Leonard Rossiter . . . . *Sir Malcolm*
Maureen Lipman . . . . *Prime Minister*
Dennis Dugan . . . . *Rob*
Fulton Mackay . . . . *Eric*
Chris Tummings . . . . *Garfield*

The American industrialist Baxter discovers a neglected oil well on the fictional Caribbean island of Cascara. To his surprise it contains an underground reserve of delicious mineral water. Unfortunately Cascara is a British colony and becomes the subject of an international dispute with

oilmen, newspaper reporters and diplomats all turning up on the scene for a piece of the action.

The Executive Producer of the film is ex-Beatle George Harrison and the final scenes of the movie find Ringo Starr and Eric Clapton performing a rock number at the UN in New York.

Most of the sequences were filmed on the West Indies island of St Lucia.

Music: 'Focus of Attention' (Ringo Starr and Eric Clapton)

Video availability

The Top Five

Week of 26 January 1985
1. Water
2. The Terminator
3. Ghostbusters
4. A Private Function
5. Dune

BEVERLY HILLS COP

2 February 1985	5 weeks

Distributor:	**Paramount**
Director:	**Martin Brest**
Producer:	**Don Simpson, Jerry Bruckheimer**
Screenplay:	**Daniel Petrie Jr**
Music:	**Harold Faltermeyer**

CAST
Eddie Murphy . . . . *Axel Foley*
Judge Reinhold . *Detective Billy Rosewood*

Lisa Eilbacher . . . . *Jenny Summers*
John Ashton . . . . *Sgt Taggart*
Ronny Cox . . . . *Lt Bogomil*
Steven Berkoff . . . . *Victor Maitland*
James Russo . . . . *Mickey Tandino*
Jonathan Banks . . . . *Zack*

In this action comedy Axel Foley, a streetwise Detroit cop, leaves his investigations into stolen cigarettes and goes on an unofficial search for the killers of his best friend. Enquiries lead him to Beverly Hills in California, where he is initially overwhelmed by the larger-than-life wealth and glamour of the town. He uncovers a major drug-smuggling ring, headed up by the sinister art gallery owner Victor Maitland. The local police, including the gormless Detective Billy Rosewood, don't take too kindly to this stranger on their patch, but soon assist him in events which lead to a bullet-ridden climax.

Beverly Hills Cop was Eddie Murphy's third film. He appeared previously in *48 Hrs* (1982) and *Trading Places* (1983). Both Sylvester Stallone and Mickey Rourke were considered for the role of Axel Foley.

Murphy, however, made the part his own, ad-libbing many of the lines in the film. He starred in the two sequels, *Beverly Hills Cop II* (1987) and *Beverly Hills Cop III* (1994), which failed to reach the top spot.

Harold Faltermeyer's 'Axel F' theme music single reached number two in the UK charts.

Music: 'The Heat Is On' (Glenn Frey), 'Neutron Dance' (The Pointer Sisters), 'Don't Get Stopped In Beverly Hills' (Shalamar), 'New Attitude', 'Stir It Up' (Patti LaBelle), 'Axel F' (Harold Faltermeyer), 'Tutti Frutti' (Little Richard)

Video availability

The Top Five

Week of 2 February 1985
1. Beverly Hills Cop
2. Ghostbusters
3. Water
4. A Private Function
5. The Terminator

DANCE WITH A STRANGER

9 March 1985	1 week

Distributor:	Goldcrest
Director:	Mike Newell
Producer:	Roger Randall-Cutler
Screenplay:	Shelagh Delaney
Music:	Richard Hartley

CAST
Miranda Richardson . . . . *Ruth Ellis*
Rupert Everett . . . . *David Blakeley*
Ian Holm . . . . *Desmond Cussen*
Matthew Carroll . . . . *Andy*
Tom Chadbon . . . . *Anthony Findlater*
Jane Bertish . . . . *Carole Findlater*
David Troughton . . . . *Cliff Davis*
Paul Mooney . . . . *Clive Gunnell*

Mike Newell's film is the story of Ruth Ellis, a one-time prostitute turned night-club hostess. Although living with Desmond Cussen, she falls in love with upper-class cad and bounder David

Blakeley. She persists with the relationship despite Cussen's offer of love and Blakeley's shabby treatment. When she discovers Blakeley with another woman she is driven to murder. In 1955 Ruth Ellis became the last woman to be hanged in England.

The actual case of Ruth Ellis rolled on for months, and years later Ellis's son committed suicide. She was portrayed in the movies 28 years earlier by Diana Dors in the film *Yield To The Night*.

Video availability

The Top Five

Week of 3 March 1985
1. Dance With a Stranger
2. Brazil
3. City Heat
4. Beverly Hills Cop
5. Amadeus

2010

16 March 1985	4 weeks

Distributor:	MGM–United Artists
Director:	Peter Hyams
Producer:	Peter Hyams

Screenplay:	Peter Hyams
Music:	David Shire

CAST
Roy Scheider . . . . *Heywood Floyd*

John Lithgow	*Walter Curnow*
Helen Mirren	*Tanya Kirbuk*
Bob Balaban	*R. Chandra*
Keir Dullea	*Dave Bowman*
Douglas Rain	*HAL 9000 (Voice)*
Madolyn Smith	*Caroline Floyd*
Dana Elcar	*Dimitri Moisevitch*

In this sequel to *2001: A Space Odyssey* Heywood Floyd is nine years older and Russia and the USA are on the verge of war. Heywood is one of the American team who join the Russians to investigate what went wrong with the Jupiter voyage of *Discovery* from *2001* and its surviving crew member. They embark on a return journey to try to find some answers and investigate the large orbiting monolith around the planet.

Producer and director Peter Hyams began his career as a newscaster with CBS in America. His most noted movie prior to *2010* was probably *Capricorn One*, about a bogus space mission to Mars.

Video availability

The Top Five
Week of 16 March 1985
1. 2010
2. Dance With a Stranger
3. Beverly Hills Cop
4. Brazil
5. The Killing Fields

A PASSAGE TO INDIA

13 April 1985	5 weeks

Distributor:	EMI
Director:	David Lean
Producer:	John Brabourne, Richard Goodwin
Screenplay:	David Lean
Music:	Maurice Jarre

CAST

Judy Davis	*Adela Quested*
Victor Banerjee	*Doctor Aziz*
Peggy Ashcroft	*Mrs Moore*
James Fox	*Richard Fielding*
Alec Guinness	*Godbole*
Nigel Havers	*Ronny Heaslop*
Richard Wilson	*Turton*
Antonia Pemberton	*Mrs Turton*
Michael Culver	*McBryde*

David Lean's screen adaptation of E.M. Forster's novel deals with the racial problems between the British and the Indians in the fictional town of Chandrapore. Adela is brought to live in India in order to marry Ronny, a local magistrate. A village doctor, Dr Aziz, invites Adela and some other women to visit some nearby caves, but on her return she accuses the man of attempted rape.

David Lean had tried to buy the movie rights to the book some years earlier but was turned down by author E.M. Forster, who died at the age of 91 in 1970. Lean then obtained the rights from King's College in Cambridge, to whom Forster had assigned the work. After a 14-year gap, and at the age of 75, this was Lean's first movie since *Ryan's Daughter*. It was also his last, but up to the time of his death he was struggling to bring Joseph Conrad's *The Heart of Darkness* to the screen.

Sandra Hotz, who played the wife of Richard Fielding, is in fact Mrs David Lean.

Designer John Box re-created the fictitious Chandrapore in the grounds of a Maharajah's palace in Bangalore where three water tanks had to be constructed just to keep the elephants refreshed.

Academy Awards: Best Supporting Actress (Peggy Ashcroft), Best Original Score (Maurice Jarre)

Video availability

The Top Five
Week of 13 April 1985
1. A Passage to India
2. 2010
3. Beverly Hills Cop
4. Dance With a Stranger
5. Micki and Maude

THE COTTON CLUB

18 May 1985	2 weeks

Distributor:	Zoetrope
Director:	Francis Coppola
Producer:	Robert Evans
Screenplay:	William Kennedy, Francis Coppola
Music:	John Barry

Dixie Dwyer (Richard Gere) plays the trumpet at the Cotton Club, the venue that gave the first break to many top black musicians in America despite its gangster connections.

CAST

Richard Gere . . . . *Dixie Dwyer*
Gregory Hines . . . . *Sandman Williams*
Diane Lane . . . . *Vera Cicero*
Lonette McKee . . . . *Lila Rose Oliver*
Bob Hoskins . . . . *Owney Madden*
James Remar . . . . *Dutch Schultz*
Nicolas Cage . . . . *Vincent Dwyer*
Allen Garfield . . . . . . *Abbadabba Berman*

In the 1920s the Cotton Club was the top jazz nightclub and a regular haunt for Harlem gangsters. Many top black entertainers began their careers here. Wealthy white folk came to watch them play in the club owned by white gangsters who refused admission to blacks. Coppola's film tells the story of two pairs of brothers who all have their sights set on making it big time in different ways. Sandman and Clay Williams are dancers (played by real-life brothers Gregory and Maurice Hines) who break up when Sandman decides to pursue a solo career. Dixie and Vincent Dwyer are small-time crooks who are given a chance to join the mob when Dixie saves the life of an influential mob member, Dutch Schultz. Dixie sees sense and heads for Hollywood but Vincent becomes a trigger-happy gunman.

Director Coppola reportedly spent $47 million on this film. His last trip to the top had been in 1980 with *Apocalypse Now*. His first two *Godfather*

movies both made the top spot and he also reached the summit in 1990 with *The Godfather Part III* and again in 1993 with Bram Stoker's *Dracula*. He's also had more than his fair share of flops with films like *One from the Heart* (1982) and *Rumblefish* (1983).

Nicolas Cage is Francis Ford Coppola's nephew and has appeared in several of his uncle's films, including *Rumblefish* (1983) and *Peggy Sue Got Married* (1986).

Music: 'Cotton Club Stomp', 'Mood Indigo' (Duke Ellington), 'Minnie the Moocher', 'Jumpin' Jive' (Cab Calloway), 'I Can't Give You Anything But Love', (Ethel Waters with Duke Ellington and His Orchestra), 'It Don't Mean a Thing (If It Ain't Got That Swing)' (Ivy Anderson with Duke Ellington and His Orchestra), 'Some of These Days' (Louis Armstrong), 'Undecided, Mr Paganini' (Ella Fitzgerald with Chick Webb and His Orchestra)

Video availability

The Top Five

Week of 18 May 1985
1. The Cotton Club
2. Falling In Love
3. Starman
4. A Passage to India
5. Amadeus

WITNESS

1 June 1985	3 weeks

Distributor: Paramount
Director: Peter Weir
Producer: Edward S. Feldman
Screenplay: Earl W. Wallace
Music: Maurice Jarre

CAST

Harrison Ford . . . . *John Book*
Kelly McGillis . . . . *Rachel*
Josef Sommer . . . . *Schaeffer*
Lukas Haas . . . . *Samuel*
Jan Rubes . . . . *Eli*
Alexander Godunov . . . . *Daniel*
Danny Glover . . . . *McFee*
Brent Jennings . . . . *Carter*
Patti LuPone . . . . *Elaine*

A young Amish boy visits the restroom of a train station in Philadelphia and witnesses a brutal murder. Detective John Book is assigned to the case and later the boy identifies the killer from police photographs, which puts his safety at risk, along with his mother's and Book's. Book is forced to hole up within the peaceful Amish community when he is wounded by the group that are after them. His physical and emotional wounds are healed by Rachel before the killers track them down.

The Amish people refused the production team permission to film on their farms so they had to go elsewhere.

Alexander Godunov, who plays Daniel Hochleitner, rivalling John Book for Rachel's attentions, was once a well-established Russian ballet dancer before becoming a citizen of the USA. Harrison Ford was Oscar nominated for his role, but the award was won by William Hurt for his part in *Kiss of the Spider Woman*. Ford's character name, John Book, was used ten years earlier by John Wayne in his last movie, *The Shootist*.

Academy Awards: Best Original Screenplay (Earl W. Wallace, William Kelley and Pamela Wallace), Best Editing (Thom Noble)

Video availability

The Top Five

Week of 1 June 1985
1. Witness
2. The Cotton Club
3. Starman
4. Falling In Love
5. A Passage to India

A young Amish boy, Samuel (Lukas Haas), enters a men's room at a train station and witnesses a brutal murder thus putting both his and his mother's life in danger.

A VIEW TO A KILL

22 June 1985	11 weeks

Distributor: **MGM–United Artists**
Director: **John Glen**
Producer: **Albert R. Broccoli, Michael G. Wilson**
Screenplay: **Richard Maibaum, Michael G. Wilson**
Music: **John Barry**

CAST
Roger Moore .... James Bond
Christopher Walken .... Max Zorin
Tanya Roberts .... Stacey Sutton
Grace Jones .... May Day
Patrick Macnee .... Tibbett
Fiona Fullerton .... Pola Ivanova
Desmond Llewelyn .... Q
Robert Brown .... M
Lois Maxwell .... Miss Moneypenny

In the final Bond film to star Roger Moore, 007 is hot on the heels of psychopath Max Zorin, who discovers a way to implant microchips into race horses to guarantee their victory. He becomes intent on gaining world monopoly on the microchip and in the process destroying California's Silicon valley.

Just before production began, the Bond sound stage at Pinewood Studios was burned to the ground. Because of the huge space required, no other studio could accommodate the team so production had to be postponed. In order to stop the cast and crew moving on to other projects, 'Cubby' Broccoli gave his personal assurance that the entire stage would be rebuilt within four months. To honour a well-kept word, Pinewood renamed the area 'The Albert R. Broccoli 007 Sound Stage'.

Music: 'A View to a Kill' (Duran Duran)

Video availability

The Top Five

Week of 22 June 1985
1. A View to a Kill
2. Witness
3. Birdy
4. The Cotton Club
5. Amadeus

RAMBO: FIRST BLOOD PART II

7 September 1985	1 week

Distributor: **TriStar**
Director: **George Pan Cosmatos**
Producer: **Buzz Feitshans**
Screenplay: **Sylvester Stallone, James Cameron**
Music: **Jerry Goldsmith**

CAST
Sylvester Stallone .... Rambo
Richard Crenna .... Trautman
Charles Napier .... Murdock
Julia Nickson .... Co Bao
Steven Berkoff .... Podovsky
Martin Kove .... Ericson
George Kee Sheung .... Tay
Andy Wood .... POW Banks

In the sequel to *First Blood*, Rambo returns to prove that brawn is sometimes better than brains in the jungles of Vietnam. Here he is extracted from prison and sent on a mission that his government wants to see fail. In his rescue of POWs he kills endless numbers of Vietcong and Red Army soldiers, as they escape into Thailand in a Russian helicopter that has seen better days.

The summer of 1985 saw Rambomania in the USA. Even President Reagan announced, after the release of 39 American hostages by Lebanese terrorists, 'Boy, I saw Rambo last night and I know what to do next time this happens'. A further sequel, *Rambo III*, was close behind, released in 1988.

Video availability

The Top Five

Week of 7 September 1985
1. Rambo: First Blood Part II
2. A Nightmare on Elm Street
3. A View to a Kill
4. Brewster's Millions
5. The Purple Rose of Cairo

DESPERATELY SEEKING SUSAN

| 14 September 1985 | 3 weeks |

Distributor: Orion
Director: Susan Seidelman
Producer: Sarah Pillsbury, Midge Sanford
Screenplay: Leora Barish
Music: Thomas Newman

CAST

Rosanna Arquette . . . . *Roberta*
Madonna . . . . *Susan*
Aidan Quinn . . . . *Dez*
Mark Blum . . . . *Gary*
Robert Joy . . . . *Jim*
Laurie Metcalf . . . . *Leslie*
Anne Levine . . . . *Crystal*
Will Patton . . . . *Nolan*
Peter Maloney . . . . *Ian*
John Turturro . . . . *Ray*

Roberta is a bored New Jersey housewife with a rich husband. To put some zing into her life she follows up a small ad, which reads 'Desperately Seeking Susan' in the personal column of a newspaper. Intrigued, she finds Susan and watches her enter a second hand store, selling her jacket, which contains a pair of stolen Egyptian earrings. Roberta buys the jacket and is mistaken for the real Susan. She gets more than she bargains for when the mob become involved in a bizarre chase.

'Into the Groove', which was featured in the movie, was the song that gave Madonna her first British number one hit single. Madonna's only other movie box office number one is *Dick Tracy* (1990), although she has had a prolific film career, appearing in *Shanghai Surprise* (1986), *Who's That Girl?* (1987), in which she co-starred alongside Sir John Mills, *In Bed With Madonna* (1991), *A League of their Own* (1992), Woody Allen's *Shadows and Fog* (1992) and *Body of Evidence* (1993).

Music: 'Into the Groove' (Madonna)

Video availability

The Top Five

Week of 14 September 1985
1. Desperately Seeking Susan
2. Rambo: First Blood Part II
3. Subway
4. A Nightmare on Elm Street
5. A View to a Kill

FLETCH

| 5 October 1985 | 1 week |

Distributor: Universal
Director: Michael Ritchie
Producer: Alan Greisman, Peter Douglas
Screenplay: Andrew Bergman
Music: Harold Faltermeyer

CAST

Chevy Chase . . . . *Fletch*
Dana Wheeler-Nicholson . . . *Gail Stanwyk*
Tim Matheson . . . . *Alan Stanwyk*
Joe Don Baker . . . . *Chief Karlin*
Richard Libertini . . . . *Walker*
Geena Davis . . . . *Larry*
M. Emmet Walsh . . . . *Dr Dolan*
George Wendt . . . . *Fat Sam*
Kenneth Mars . . . . *Stanton Boyd*

In this comedy mystery Chevy Chase is Fletch, a cocky newspaper reporter with a flair for disguises. He goes undercover as a down-and-out and is approached by a top business executive who claims he has an incurable disease and offers Fletch $50,000 to kill him in order that his wife can claim on the insurance. Not believing a word of it, he digs deeper and discovers a major drug ring controlled by corrupt police and businessmen.

This was American television favourite Chevy Chase's first and only appearance to date in a box office number one. His other credits include a sequel, *Fletch Lives* (1989), but he's probably best known for appearing in some of the National Lampoon series of movies, including *National Lampoon's Vacation* (1983), *National Lampoon's European Vacation* (1985) and *National Lampoon's Christmas Vacation* (1989).

The Top Five

Week of 5 October 1985
1. Fletch
2. Desperately Seeking Susan
3. A Nightmare on Elm Street
4. Cocoon
5. Rambo: First Blood Part II

Music: 'Bit by Bit' (Stephanie Mills), 'Fletch, Get Out of Town', 'Name of the Game' (Dan Hartman), 'Running for Love' (John Farnham), 'A Letter to Both Sides' (Fixx), 'Is It Over' (Kim Wilde), 'Fletch theme', 'Diggin' In', 'Running for Love' (Harold Faltermeyer)

PALE RIDER

12 October 1985	1 week

Distributor:	Warner
Director:	Clint Eastwood
Producer:	Clint Eastwood
Screenplay:	Michael Butler, Dennis Shryack
Music:	Lennie Niehaus

CAST
Clint Eastwood .... *Preacher*
Michael Moriarty .... *Hull*
Carrie Snodgress .... *Sarah Wheeler*
Christopher Penn .... *Josh LaHood*
Richard Dysart .... *Coy LaHood*
Sydney Penny .... *Megan Wheeler*
Richard Kiel .... *Club*
Doug McGrath .... *Spider Conway*
John Russell .... *Stockburn*

In this Western Clint Eastwood plays a drifter known only as the 'Preacher' after he's first seen wearing a clerical collar. He helps a group of gold prospectors who are fighting a large organization, controlled by Coy LaHood who is trying to steal away their land. LaHood's hired thugs constantly attempt to take over the land by force, but one day Preacher, the mysterious loner, is waiting for them with guns at the ready.

Pale Rider was Clint Eastwood's first Western since *The Outlaw Josey Wales* (1976).

Richard Kiel, who plays Club, appeared in other number one movies, for example as the character 'Jaws' in the two Bond movies *The Spy Who Loved Me* (1977) and *Moonraker* (1979). His other week at the top was in *Force 10 from Navarone* (1978).

Video availability

The Top Five

Week of 12 October 1985
1. Pale Rider
2. Lifeforce
3. Fletch
4. Desperately Seeking Susan
5. Cocoon

LIFEFORCE

19 October 1985	1 week

Distributor:	Cannon
Director:	Tobe Hooper
Producer:	Menahem Golan, Yoram Globus
Screenplay:	Dan O'Bannon
Music:	Henry Mancini

CAST
Steve Railsback .... *Carlsen*
Peter Firth .... *Caine*
Frank Finlay .... *Fallada*
Mathilda May .... *Space Girl*
Patrick Stewart .... *Dr Armstrong*
Michael Gothard .... *Bukovsky*
Nicholas Ball .... *Derebridge*

A British and American space expedition discovers what appears to be human remains around Halley's Comet. They return with the three preserved bodies, but also a beautiful nude female space vampire encountered on their journey home. She drains her victims of all energy and eventually manages to turn half the population of London into zombie vampires who end up crumbling into piles of dust.

The movie, adapted from the novel *The Space Vampires* by Colin Wilson, had an allocated budget of $22.5 million, and was directed by the same director as *Poltergeist* (1982), Tobe Hooper.

Video availability

The Top Five

Week of 19 October 1985
1. Lifeforce
2. Pale Rider
3. Desperately Seeking Susan
4. Fletch
5. The Black Cauldron

MAD MAX BEYOND THUNDERDOME

26 October 1985	2 weeks

Distributor: Warner
Director: George Miller, George Ogilvie
Producer: George Miller
Screenplay: Terry Hayes, George Miller
Music: Maurice Jarre

CAST

Mel Gibson . . . . *Mad Max*
Tina Turner . . . . *Aunty Entity*
Angelo Rossitto . . . . *The Master*
Helen Buday . . . . *Savannah Nix*
Rod Zuanic . . . . *Scrooloose*
Frank Thring . . . . *The Collector*
Angry Anderson . . . . *Ironbar*
Paul Larsson . . . . *The Blaster*

M ad Max, the Aussie desert warrior, enters the
evil Bartertown controlled by Aunty Entity.
She forces him to take part in a gladiatorial fight to
the death with a giant called 'The Blaster'. Max
manages to defeat him, but then finds himself banished into the desert, where he is rescued by a gang
of wild children.

Mel Gibson is one of eleven children and his mother
was an opera singer.

George Miller, who directed all three *Mad Max*
movies, qualified as a doctor before joining the
movie business.

Music: 'We Don't Need Another Hero
(Thunderdome)', 'One of the Living' (Tina Turner)

Video availability

The Top Five

Week of 26 October 1985
1. Mad Max Beyond Thunderdome
2. The Black Cauldron
3. Fletch
4. Desperately Seeking Susan
5. Lifeforce

Tina Turner stars as the charismatic and deadly Aunty Entity, ruler of Bartertown, in the all-action adventure film, Mad Max Beyond Thunderdome, *also starring Mel Gibson.*

THE EMERALD FOREST

9 November 1985	2 weeks

Distributor:	Embassy
Director:	John Boorman
Producer:	John Boorman
Screenplay:	Rospo Pallenberg
Music:	Junior Homrich

CAST
Powers Boothe . . . . *Bill Markham*
Meg Foster . . . . *Jean Markham*
Charley Boorman . . . . *Tomme*
Dira Pass . . . . *Kachiri*
Rui Polonah . . . . *Wanadi*
Claudio Moreno . . . . *Jacareh*
Tetchie Agbayani . . . . *Caya*
Paulo Vinicius . . . . *Mapi*

Bill Markham, an American building engineer, has an assignment to build a huge dam in Brazil. While on the job, Bill's son, Tomme, mysteriously disappears into the wilderness and doesn't return. Bill spends the next ten years searching for the boy, eventually discovering him still alive, having been raised by a primitive Amazon tribe. Bill's quest and discovery of the tribe brings home to him the repercussions of the destruction of the rainforest.

John Boorman's first project as a director was in 1965, when he was in charge of *Catch Us If You Can*, a vehicle for the Dave Clark Five. He is probably best remembered for his work on the 1972 movie *Deliverance*, and in 1977, *Exorcist II: The Heretic* (1977). He cast his own son, Charley, in the starring role of *The Emerald Forest*.

Video availability

The Top Five

Week of 9 November 1985
1. The Emerald Forest
2. Mad Max Beyond Thunderdome
3. Prizzi's Honour
4. Weird Science
5. Desperately Seeking Susan

PRIZZI'S HONOUR

23 November 1985	2 weeks

Distributor:	ABC
Director:	John Huston
Producer:	John Foreman
Screenplay:	Richard Condon, Janet Roach
Music:	Alex North

CAST
Jack Nicholson . . . . *Charley Partanna*
Kathleen Turner . . . . *Irene Walker*
Robert Loggia . . . . *Eduardo Prizzi*
William Hickey . . . . *Don Corrado Prizzi*
John Randolph . . . . *Angelo 'Pop' Prizzi*
Lee Richardson . . . . *Dominic Prizzi*
Anjelica Huston . . . . *Maerose Prizzi*

When Mafia killer Charley Partanna falls in love with beautiful blonde Irene Walker, he ignores his suspicions about her and asks for her hand in marriage. Unfortunately she turns out to be his female equivalent in hired killings. To fulfil one of her contracts she shoots two victims in cold blood in the hallway of an apartment. Charley's discovery of her profession has unforeseen consequences.

This was ailing director John Huston's penultimate movie, for which he was Oscar nominated, his final work being *The Dead* (1987). His daughter, Anjelica Huston, won the Best Supporting Actress Oscar for this film and became the third generation of the family to take home a statuette. Grandfather Walter won an acting Oscar and dad John the direction and screenplay Oscars for *The Treasure of the Sierra Madre* (1948).

Academy Awards: Best Supporting Actress (Anjelica Huston)

Video availability

The Top Five

Week of 23 November 1985
1. Prizzi's Honour
2. The Emerald Forest
3. Letter to Brezhnev
4. My Beautiful Laundrette
5. The Supergrass

SANTA CLAUS

7 December 1985	1 week

Distributor: Alexander Salkind
Director: Jeannot Szwarc
Producer: Ilya Salkind, Pierre Spengler
Screenplay: David Newman
Music: Henry Mancini

CAST
David Huddleston .... Santa Claus
Dudley Moore .... Patch
John Lithgow .... B.Z.
Judy Cornwell .... Anya Claus
Christian Fitzpatrick .... Joe
Carrie Kei Heim .... Cornelia
Jeffrey Kramer .... Towzer
John Barrard .... Dooley
Anthony O'Donnell .... Puffy

Santa Claus' helper and leader of the Elves and toy maker, Patch, works in the North Pole factory. Patch's resentment for the bearded one grows after he is given the heave-ho for producing a bad batch of goods. He then goes off to New York City to try and sell Santa's trade secrets to another toy manufacturer, the mean B.Z.

The songs were by Henry Mancini and Leslie Bricusse, Bill House and John Hobbs, Nick Beggs, Stuart Croxford, Neal and Steve Askew. They could not prevent the film making a box office loss of $37 million.

Music: 'Santa Claus' (Aled Jones), 'Making Toys', 'It's Christmas Again', 'Thank You Santa' (Ambrosian Children's Choir), 'It's Christmas All Over the World' (Sheena Easton), 'Shouldn't Do That' (Kajagoogoo)

Video availability

Top Twenty Films of 1985

1 Ghostbusters
2 A View to a Kill
3 Gremlins
4 Rambo: First Blood Part II
5 Beverly Hills Cop
6 Police Academy 2: Their First Assignment
7 Santa Claus – The Movie
8 A Passage to India
9 One Hundred and One Dalmatians
10 Desperately Seeking Susan
11 Mad Max Beyond Thunderdome
12 The Killing Fields
13 Witness
14 Return to Oz
15 Amadeus
16 The Care Bears Movie
17 Peter Pan
18 The Never Ending Story
19 Morons from Outer Space
20 A Private Function

The Top Five

Week of 7 December 1985
1. Santa Claus
2. Prizzi's Honour
3. My Beautiful Laundrette
4. The Emerald Forest
5. Letter to Brezhnev

BACK TO THE FUTURE

14 December 1985	5 weeks

Distributor: Universal
Director: Robert Zemeckis
Producer: Bob Gale, Neil Canton
Screenplay: Robert Zemeckis, Bob Gale
Music: Alan Silvestri

CAST
Michael J. Fox .... Marty McFly
Christopher Lloyd ..... Dr Emmett Brown
Crispin Glover .... George McFly
Lea Thompson .... Lorraine Baines
Claudia Wells .... Jennifer Parker
Thomas F. Wilson .... Biff Tannen
James Tolkan .... Mr Strickland
Marc McClure .... Dave McFly

Young college boy Marty McFly visits his friend, the crazy Dr Emmett Brown, who has spent his life working on a time-travelling machine built from an old DeLorean car. Marty activates the machine and ends up in 1955, where he meets his own parents in their youth. Unfortunately Marty's mother falls for him and he will try anything to find a way back to the future and ensure that his parents fall in love and marry in order for him to exist.

Canadian Michael J. Fox made his movie debut in the little-seen Disney picture *Midnight Madness*

Marty McFly (Michael J. Fox) and Dr Emmett Brown (Christopher Lloyd) experiment with the good doctor's time-travelling machine in Back to the Future.

(1980). Before *Back to the Future* he became one of television's most popular stars in the long-running sitcom *Family Ties*. He adopted the initial 'J' in his name because he was a big fan of the actor Michael J. Pollard who was Oscar nominated for his role in *Bonnie and Clyde* (1967). He starred in the two sequels, *Back to the Future: Part II* (1989) and *Back to the Future: Part III* (1990).

Back to the Future was the highest-grossing movie of 1986 in the UK.

Academy Awards: Best Sound Effects Editing (Charles L. Campbell and Robert Rutledge)

Music: 'The Power of Love', 'Back In Time' (Huey Lewis and The News), 'Time Bomb Town' (Lindsey Buckingham), 'Heaven Is One Step Away' (Eric Clapton), 'Johnny B. Goode' (Marty McFly With The Starlighters)

Video availability

The Top Five

Week of 14 December 1985
1. Back to the Future
2. Legend
3. Santa Claus
4. My Beautiful Laundrette
5. Letter to Brezhnev

A CHORUS LINE

18 January 1986	2 weeks

Distributor:	Embassy/Polygram
Director:	Richard Attenborough
Producer:	Cy Feuer, Ernest Martin
Screenplay:	Arnold Schulman
Music:	Marvin Hamlisch

CAST
Michael Douglas .... Zach
Terrence Mann .... Larry
Alyson Reed .... Cassie
Cameron English .... Paul
Vicki Frederick .... Sheila
Audrey Landers .... Val
Michael Blevins .... Mark
Yamil Borges .... Morales
Sharon Brown .... Kim

The movie, adapted from Michael Bennett's successful 1975 Broadway musical, follows the hardships encountered by a group of dancers trying to find work in the musical theatre. Show director Zach puts a cast of hopefuls through exacting dance

Zach (Michael Douglas) has a bitter argument with ex-girlfriend Cassie (Alyson Reed) over her decision to audition for a part in the show he is directing in Chorus Line.

routines and attempts to discover the real personalities behind the performers. The film features some great individual dancing and a spectacular end sequence when the chorus line, fully costumed, gives a stunning finale to the show.

When the movie was made, *A Chorus Line* held the record for being the longest-running show in the history of Broadway. Richard Attenborough was the last in a long line of hopefuls who had planned to make the film version of this huge Broadway success. The film rights had been bought in 1976 and the project had a rocky road from stage to screen. Mike Nichols and Sidney Lumet were just two of the directors linked at one time or another to the film.

Music: 'What I did For Love', 'I Can Do That', 'Hello Twelve Hello Thirteen Hello Love', 'The Music and the Mirror', 'I Hope I Get It', 'One'

Video availability

The Top Five

Week of 18 January 1986
1. A Chorus Line
2. Back to the Future
3. Year of the Dragon
4. Defence of the Realm
5. Silverado

ROCKY IV

1 February 1986	5 weeks

Distributor:	MGM–United Artists
Director:	Sylvester Stallone
Producer:	Robert Chartoff, Irwin Winkler
Screenplay:	Sylvester Stallone
Music:	Vince DiCola
	Bill Conti (themes from *Rocky*)

CAST

Sylvester Stallone	Rocky Balboa
Talia Shire	Adrian
Burt Young	Paulie
Carl Weathers	Apollo Creed
Brigitte Nielsen	Ludmilla
Tony Burton	Duke
Michael Pataki	Nicoli Koloff
Dolph Lundgren	Drago

American boxer Apollo Creed is badly beaten in the ring by Russia's giant champion, Ivan Drago, who has been trained more by scientists than fitness experts. Rocky feels it's not only his duty to fight for America but also to avenge his friend's beating, so he takes on the big man himself. Relinquishing his title in order to take part in an unauthorized bout in the Soviet Union, he transports himself to Russia where he trains in the freezing climate for his moment of glory.

Talia Shire is the sister of film director Francis Ford Coppola and appeared in all three *Godfather* movies. She was Oscar nominated for *Godfather II* (1974), losing to Ingrid Bergman who won Best Supporting Actress for *Murder on the Orient Express*, and nominated for the Best Actress Award for *Rocky* (1976), losing to Faye Dunaway who won for *Network*.

Swedish actor Dolph Lundgren has a college degree in mathematics, physics and chemistry. He first met Stallone when he auditioned for the role of the Russian in *Rambo: First Blood Part II* (1985). He didn't get the part (it went to Steven Berkoff) but Stallone was impressed enough to keep him in mind for *Rocky IV*.

Music: 'Burning Heart', 'Eye of the Tiger' (Survivor), 'Living In America' (James Brown), 'Double or Nothing' (Kenny Loggins and Gladys Knight), 'One Way Street' (Go West), 'Heart's on Fire' (John Cafferty), 'No Easy Way Out' (Robert Tepper)

Video availability

The Top Five

Week of 1 February 1986
1. Rocky IV
2. A Chorus Line
3. Kiss of the Spiderwoman
4. Back to the Future
5. A Chorus Line

COMMANDO

1 March 1986	2 weeks

Distributor:	Twentieth Century-Fox
Director:	Mark L. Lester
Producer:	Joel Silver
Screenplay:	Steven de Souza
Music:	James Horner

CAST
Arnold Schwarzenegger . . . . Matrix
Rae Dawn Chong . . . . Cindy
Dan Hedaya . . . . Arius
Vernon Wells . . . . Bennett
David Patrick Kelly . . . . Sully
Alyssa Milano . . . . Jenny
James Olson . . . . General Kirby
Bill Duke . . . . Cooke

Schwarzenegger takes the lead in this story of Colonel John Matrix, a secret agent who is forced out of retirement when an evil Latin dictator kidnaps his daughter Jenny. He engages the help of a stewardess (Rae Dawn Chong) to save his daughter and punish her kidnappers.

Rae Dawn Chong also reached number one in *Quest for Fire* (1982). She is the daughter of Thomas Chong, who, with his partner Cheech Marin, forms the anarchic comedy duo Cheech and Chong.

Video availability

The Top Five

Week of 1 March 1986
1. Commando
2. Spies Like Us
3. Rocky IV
4. Back to the Future
5. A Chorus Line

OUT OF AFRICA

15 March 1986	6 weeks*

Distributor:	Mirage
Director:	Sydney Pollack
Producer:	Sydney Pollack
Screenplay:	Kurt Luedtke
Music:	John Barry

CAST
Meryl Streep . . . . Karen Blixen
Robert Redford . . . . Denys
Klaus Maria Brandauer . . . . . . Bror Blixen
Michael Kitchen . . . . Berkeley
Malick Bowens . . . . Farah
Joseph Thiaka . . . . Kamante
Stephen Kinyanjui . . . . Kinanjui
Michael Gough . . . . Delamere
Suzanna Hamilton . . . . Felicity

This sumptuous costume drama begins in 1914 when young Danish woman Karen Blixen arrives in Nairobi, Kenya. She enters a marriage of convenience to the Baron Bror Blixen who runs a coffee plantation. The marriage is less than happy as

Bror has a wandering eye and a dose of the pox, and Karen is left to manage the estate single-handedly. British hunters Denys and Berkeley start visiting and when she and the Baron separate, Denys falls in love with her although he is unwilling to commit himself to marriage. He remains, along with the Africa she writes about, the love of Karen's life.

The film was based on the real life of the famous writer on Africa, Karen Blixen, who wrote under the name Isak Dinesen.

Both Orson Welles and David Lean had separately considered the project years before the making of *Out of Africa*. A movie with Julie Christie as Karen had also been considered years earlier by director Nicolas Roeg.

Academy Awards: Best Film (Producer Sydney Pollack), Best Direction (Sydney Pollack), Best Screenplay (Kurt Luedtke), Best Cinematography (David Watkin), Best Art Direction (Stephen Grimes), Set Decoration (Josie MacAvin), Best Sound (Chris Jenkins, Gary Alexander, Larry Stensvold, Peter Handford), Best Musical Score (John Barry)

Music: 'The Music of Goodbye' (Love Theme from *Out of Africa*) (Melissa Manchester and Al Jarreau)

Video availability

The Top Five

Week of 15 March 1986
1. Out of Africa
2. Ran
3. A Chorus Line
4. Commando
5. Spies Like Us

ABSOLUTE BEGINNERS

19 April 1986	2 weeks

Distributor:	Virgin/Goldcrest/Palace
Director:	Julien Temple
Producer:	Stephen Woolley, Chris Brown
Screenplay:	Richard Burridge, Christopher Wicking, Don MacPherson
Music:	David Bowie, Ray Davies, Gil Evans, Paul Weller, Patsy Kensit, Sade, Tenpole Tudor, Jerry Dammers, Nick Lowe, Ekow Abban, Working Week

CAST
Eddie O'Connell . . . . *Colin*
Patsy Kensit . . . . *Suzette*
David Bowie . . . . *Vendice Partners*
James Fox . . . . *Henley*
Ray Davies . . . . *Arthur*
Eve Ferret . . . . *Big Jill*
Anita Morris . . . . *Dido Lament*
Lionel Blair . . . . *Harry Charms*
Steven Berkoff . . . . *The Fanatic*

The film, adapted from Colin MacInnes' book, is set during the long hot summer of 1958. It is the beginning of the teenage era of coffee bars, jazz clubs and rock and roll in and around the Notting Hill Gate and Soho areas of London. Colin and Suzette are the two young lovers who are swept along by the tide of music and madness that takes hold of the streets. But they also witness the beginnings of the race problems that afflict the capital.

Director Julien Temple cut his teeth on pop videos and worked with Bowie previously on his 'Jazzin' for Blue Jean' video in 1984. The film has a tenuous link with *The Player* (1992) when *Absolute Beginners'* lengthy opening scene is referred to in *The Player*'s own lengthy opening scene!

The film gave Patsy Kensit her first appearance at number one (although she had appeared as a four-year-old in *The Great Gatsby* (1974). She crops up again in *Lethal Weapon 2* (1989) with Mel Gibson.

David Bowie's title song reached number two in the UK singles charts.

Music: 'Absolute Beginners', 'That's Motivation', 'Volare' (David Bowie), 'Quiet Life' (Ray Davies), 'Killer Blow' (Sade), 'Having It All' (Eighth Wonder featuring Patsy Kensit), 'Have You Ever Had It Blue?' (The Style Council)

Video availability

The Top Five

Week of 19 April 1986
1. Absolute Beginners
2. Out of Africa
3. Jagged Edge
4. Fright Night
5. A Room with a View

THE JEWEL OF THE NILE

10 May 1986	3 weeks

Distributor:	Twentieth Century-Fox
Director:	Lewis Teague
Producer:	Michael Douglas
Screenplay:	Mark Rosenthal, Lawrence Konner
Music:	Jack Nitzsche

CAST

Michael Douglas	Jack
Kathleen Turner	Joan
Danny DeVito	Ralph
Spiros Focas	Omar
Avner Eisenberg	Holy Man
Paul David Magid	Tarak
Howard Jay Patterson	Barak
Randall Edwin Nelson	Karak
Samuel Ross Williams	Arak

Six months after the happy ending of *Romancing the Stone*, Joan and Jack are successfully getting on each other's nerves. Joan is approached by an Arab sheik to write his autobiography and when she hesitates she is kidnapped by his band of cut throats and taken to his desert kingdom. Jack is soon in hot pursuit and on the way encounters Ralph, who is searching out another precious gem, the Jewel of the Nile.

Danny DeVito's first number one movie was *One Flew over the Cuckoo's Nest* (1975) which was produced by his co-star in *Jewel of the Nile*, Michael Douglas. He went on to direct Michael (and his other co-star here, Kathleen Turner) in *The War of the Roses* (1990).

Billy Ocean's single 'When the Going Gets Tough' was a huge worldwide hit, reaching number one in the UK and number two in the USA.

Music: 'The Jewel of the Nile' (Precious Wilson), 'When The Going Gets Tough, The Tough Get Going' (Billy Ocean), 'I'm In Love' (Ruby Turner)

Video availability

The Top Five

Week of 10 May 1986
1. The Jewel of the Nile
2. A Room with a View
3. Out of Africa
4. Jagged Edge
5. Caravaggio

DOWN AND OUT IN BEVERLY HILLS

31 May 1986	1 week

Distributor:	Touchstone
Director:	Paul Mazursky
Producer:	Paul Mazursky
Screenplay:	Paul Mazursky, Leon Capetanos
Music:	Andy Summers

CAST

Nick Nolte	Jerry Baskin
Richard Dreyfuss	Dave Whiteman
Bette Midler	Barbara Whiteman
Little Richard	Orvis Goodnight
Tracy Nelson	Jenny Whiteman
Elizabeth Pena	Carmen
Evan Richards	Max Whiteman

Jerry Baskin is an untidy and ragged street bum. He is found floating in a Beverly Hills pool belonging to the wealthy Whiteman family. Dave Whiteman, a millionaire coathanger manufacturer, thwarts Baskin's attempt to drown himself by reviving him and invites him into their home, where he ends up taking residence, living like a king and having a fling with Mrs Whiteman.

The film was inspired by the 1932 French movie *Boudu Sauve des Eaux* (*Boudu Saved from Drowning*). The original title of this movie was going to be 'Jerry Saved from Drowning'. Jack Nicholson was considered for the part of Jerry but was busy on another project. Producer and director Paul Mazursky has a cameo role as an accountant.

Music: 'Great Gosh A'Mighty! (It's a Matter of Time)', 'Tutti Frutti' (Little Richard), 'California Girls' (David Lee Roth), 'I Love L.A.' (Randy Newman)

Video availability

The Top Five

Week of 31 May 1986
1. Down and Out in Beverly Hills
2. The Jewel of the Nile
3. 9½ weeks
4. A Room with a View
5. Jagged Edge

AFTER HOURS

7 June 1986	1 week

Distributor: Warner
Director: Martin Scorsese
Producer: Amy Robinson, Griffin Dunne, Robert F. Colesberry
Screenplay: Joseph Minion
Music: Howard Shore

CAST
Griffin Dunne . . . . *Paul Hackett*
Rosanna Arquette . . . . *Marcy*
Verna Bloom . . . . *June*
Thomas Chong . . . . *Pepe*
Linda Fiorentino . . . . *Kiki*
Teri Garr . . . . *Julie*
John Heard . . . . *Tom the Bartender*
Cheech Marin . . . . *Neil*
Catherine O'Hara . . . . *Gail*

Computer programmer Paul Hackett goes in search of female company in downtown New York and meets Marcy. He ends up going to her apartment that she shares with weird sculptress Kiki. Finding the whole experience too much, he heads for home but finds he doesn't have enough money for the train ride as the fares had gone up that very night. This unfortunate problem leads him from one disaster to another, including being mistaken for a neighbourhood thief.

Screenwriter Joseph Minion wrote the story as an assignment when he was a student at a university movie school. Director Martin Scorsese insisted that Griffin Dunne give up sex and take as little sleep as possible during the making of the film in order for his level of frustration to be increased and show during filming.

Comedians Richard 'Cheech' Marin and Tommy Chong have cameo roles playing two thieves. Bronson Pinchot, who plays Balki in the TV series *Perfect Strangers*, also appears as a friend of Hackett's.

Video availability

The Top Five

Week of 7 June 1986
1. After Hours
2. Down and Out in Beverly Hills
3. 9½ Weeks
4. A Room with a View
5. Jagged Edge

A ROOM WITH A VIEW

14 June 1986	5 weeks

Distributor: Merchant Ivory–Goldcrest
Director: James Ivory
Producer: Ismail Merchant
Screenplay: Ruth Prawer Jhabvala
Music: Richard Robbins

CAST
Maggie Smith . . . . *Charlotte Bartlett*
Helena Bonham Carter . *Lucy Honeychurch*
Denholm Elliott . . . . *Mr Emerson*
Julian Sands . . . . *George Emerson*
Daniel Day-Lewis . . . . *Cecil Byse*
Simon Callow . . . . *Reverend Beebe*
Judi Dench . . . . *Miss Lavish*
Rosemary Leach . . . . *Mrs Honeychurch*

In this period romance set in 1907 Lucy Honeychurch embarks on a trip to Florence, Italy, with her prim and proper Aunt Charlotte. They take up residence in a small apartment and meet Mr Emerson and his son George. When Charlotte spots George kissing Lucy she immediately whisks her back to England where she soon becomes engaged to the rich and tiresome Cecil Byse, a friend of the family. By coincidence George moves into their village and Charlotte realizes that he is her true love, not Cecil.

The team of Director James Ivory, Producer Ismail Merchant and writer Ruth Prawer Jhabvala have been responsible for some of the classiest movies of recent years. *Heat and Dust* (1983), *Howard's End* (1992) and *The Remains of the Day* (1993) are just three of the trio's critical successes.

The film gave Daniel Day-Lewis his first appearance at number one. He hits the top spot again with *Last of the Mohicans* in 1992.

Academy Awards: Best Screenplay (Ruth Prawer

The Top Five

Week of 14 June 1986
1. A Room with a View
2. After Hours
3. Down and Out in Beverly Hills
4. 9½ Weeks
5. Jagged Edge

What started out for Lucy Honeychurch (Helena Bonham Carter) as a tour of Italy with her aunt (Maggie Smith) turns into romance in A Room with a View. *She falls for the charms of the young George Emerson (Julian Sands).*

Jhabvala), Best Art Direction (Gianni Quaranta and Brian Ackland-Snow), Set Decoration (Brian Savegar and Elio Altramura), Best Costume Design (Jenny

Beavan and John Bright)

Video availability

POLICE ACADEMY III: BACK IN TRAINING

19 July 1986	1 week

Distributor:	Warner
Director:	Jerry Paris
Producer:	Paul Maslansky
Screenplay:	Gene Quintano
Music:	Robert Folk

CAST
Steve Guttenberg . . . . *Sgt Mahoney*
Bubba Smith . . . . *Sgt Hightower*
David Graf . . . . *Sgt Tackleberry*
Michael Winslow . . . . *Sgt Jones*
Marion Ramsey . . . . *Sgt Hooks*
Leslie Easterbrook . . . . *Lt Callahan*
Art Metrano . . . . *Commandant Mauser*
Tim Kazurinsky . . . . *Cadet Sweetchuck*

O wing to lack of funds, the tight-fisted police governor decides to close down one of two rival police academies. He sets up a competition to decide which one should get the chop, leading to more knock-about comedy with another bunch of trainee police cadets.

This was the third in a series of 7 *Police Academy* movies (to date), the latest being *Police Academy 7: Mission to Moscow*, released in 1994. Steve Guttenberg appeared in the first two *Police Academy* movies, went on to star in number four but left the series after that. His other two number ones are *Three Men and a Baby* (1988) and *Three Men and a Little Lady* (1991). His other big-screen hits include *Cocoon* (1985), *Short Circuit* (1986) and *Cocoon: The Return* (1988).

Video availability

The Top Five

Week of 19 July 1986
1. Police Academy III: Back in Training
2. The Color Purple
3. A Room with a View
4. Down and Out in Beverly Hills
5. Enemy Mine

HANNAH AND HER SISTERS

26 July 1986 — **5 weeks***

Distributor:	Orion
Director:	Woody Allen
Producer:	Robert Greenhut
Screenplay:	Woody Allen
Music:	no credit

CAST

Woody Allen	Mickey
Michael Caine	Elliot
Mia Farrow	Hannah
Dianne Wiest	Holly
Carrie Fisher	April
Barbara Hershey	Lee
Max von Sydow	Frederick
Lloyd Nolan	Hannah's father
Maureen O'Sullivan	Hannah's Mother
Daniel Stern	Dusty

In this, a kind of musical chairs of relationships, a group of three sisters, their friends and their spouses, are gathered for a Thanksgiving feast. Lee is the youngest and lives with an intellectual recluse (Max von Sydow), Holly, the middle sister, is neurotic and looking for love, and Hannah is the eldest, wife of Elliot and mother to a brood of children. The family set begins to break down when Elliot begins an affair with his sister-in-law, Lee. It doesn't end there, however, and on Thanksgiving two years later most have swapped partners and Woody Allen has joined the family.

The film was at number one for two weeks from 26 July. It was knocked off by *Cobra* for a week then came back to the top for a further three weeks.

Woody Allen has always been unhappy with the film's ending, because his leading characters were too content with life, which he believes is never that straightforward.

Academy Awards: Best Supporting Actor (Michael Caine), Best Supporting Actress (Dianne Wiest), Best Original Screenplay (Woody Allen)

Video availability

The Top Five

Week of 26 July 1986
1. Hannah and Her Sisters
2. Police Academy III: Back in Training
3. The Color Purple
4. A Room with a View
5. E.T.

COBRA

9 August 1986 — **1 week**

Distributor:	Warner
Director:	George Pan Cosmatos
Producer:	Menahem Golan, Yoram Globus
Screenplay:	Sylvester Stallone
Music:	Sylvester Levay

CAST

Sylvester Stallone	Marion Cobretti
Brigitte Nielsen	Ingrid
Reni Santoni	Gonzales
Andrew Robinson	Detective Monte
Lee Garlington	Nancy Stalk
John Herzfeld	Cho
Art La Fleur	Captain Sears

Marion Cobretti, the match-chewing cop known as the Cobra, and his partner Gonzales are singled out by high-ranking American officials. They are told to work with a special LA police squad to protect a model (Brigitte Nielsen) who was witness to a murder by a serial killer whose gang has claimed 16 victims in less than a month.

Andrew Robinson, who plays a wimpy police officer, appeared as Scorpio, an evil killer in the 1971 Clint Eastwood movie *Dirty Harry*.

Stallone and director George Pan Cosmatos previously worked together on *Rambo: First Blood Part II* (1985). Cosmatos' other number one was in 1979 with *Escape To Athena*.

Stallone and co-star Brigitte Nielsen were real-life husband and wife when this film was made.

The Top Five

Week of 9 August 1986
1. Cobra
2. Hannah and Her Sisters
3. A Room with a View
4. The Karate Kid Part II
5. The Color Purple

Music: 'Loving on Borrowed Time' (Gladys Knight and Bill Medley), 'Hold On To Your Vision' (Gary Wright), 'Suave' (Miami Sound Machine), 'Cobra' (Sylvester Levay)

Video availability

ALIENS

6 September 1986	5 weeks

Distributor:	Twentieth Century-Fox
Director:	James Cameron
Producer:	Gale Anne Hurd
Screenplay:	James Cameron
Music:	James Horner

CAST
Sigourney Weaver . . . . *Ripley*
Carrie Henn . . . . *Newt*
Michael Biehn . . . . *Corporal Hicks*
Paul Reiser . . . . *Burke*
Lance Henriksen . . . . *Bishop*
Bill Paxton . . . . *Private Hudson*
William Hope . . . . *Lieutenant Gorman*
Jenette Goldstein . . . . . . *Private Vasquez*
Al Matthews . . . . *Sergeant Apone*

Ripley, the only remaining survivor from the original *Alien* voyage, learns that she has been unconscious for 57 years and that the planet where the creatures were found has become a colonial outpost. She is requested to return, with a team of marines, to investigate why all contact with the planet has been cut off. She finds only one survivor on the planet, a young girl called Newt. But before Ripley can return Newt to safety she has to destroy the breeding queen of the aliens.

In this sequel to 1979's *Alien* Weaver refused to appear in scenes involving blood and guts and would not allow a cast of her body to be made for a series of planned dream sequences. Sigourney (real name Susan Alexandra) Weaver has been Oscar nominated three times, for *Gorillas In the Mist* (1988), *Working Girl* (1989) and this film but has yet to win.

The film was director James Cameron's first number one. His others are *Terminator 2: Judgment Day*

The Top Five
Week of 6 September 1986
1. Aliens
2. Highlander
3. Hannah and Her Sisters
4. A Room with a View
5. Target

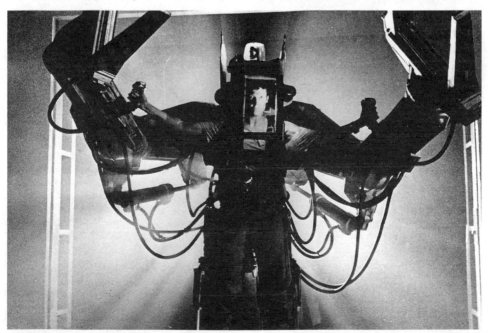

Ripley (Sigourney Weaver) comes face to face with more horrific creatures in the second Alien *movie (Aliens) when she returns to the planet where she first encountered the beasts.*

(1991) and *True Lies* (1994). He was formerly married to producer Gale Anne Hurd.

Academy Awards: Best Sound Effects Editing (Don

Sharpe), Best Visual Effects (Robert Skotak, Stan Winston, John Richardson and Suzanne Benson)

Video availability

TOP GUN

11 October 1986	3 weeks*

Distributor:	Paramount
Director:	Tony Scott
Producer:	Don Simpson, Jerry Bruckheimer
Screenplay:	Jim Cash, Jack Epps Jr
Music:	Harold Faltermeyer

CAST
Tom Cruise . . . . . . *Pete Mitchell (Maverick)*
Kelly McGillis . . . . *Charlie*
Val Kilmer . . . . *Tony Kasanzky (Ice)*
Anthony Edwards . . . . *Goose*
Tom Skerritt . . . . *Viper*
Michael Ironside . . . . *Jester*
John Stockwell . . . . *Cougar*
Barry Tubb . . . . *Wolfman*
Tim Robbins . . . . *Merlin*

L ieutenant Pete Mitchell is a hot-headed fighter pilot nicknamed Maverick for his style of flying. He is assigned to a training school for advanced lessons where the top students are awarded the coveted 'Top Gun' prize. His main rival is Tom Kasanzky, known as 'Ice'. When Maverick is not busy chasing after Charlotte Blackwood, an expert on the workings of high-speed jets, he pits his wits against Ice.

A significant proportion of *Top Gun* was shot at the

Miramar Naval Air Base in California where the movie is set. The American Navy gave their full co-operation in the making of the movie after several agreed changes were made to the plot.

Berlin's song 'Take My Breath Away (Love theme from Top Gun)' became a number one hit in the UK in November 1986, spending four weeks at the top of the charts.

Academy Awards: Best Song – 'Take My Breath Away' (Giorgio Moroder, music; Tom Whitlock, lyrics)

Music: 'Take My Breath Away (Love Theme from Top Gun)' (Berlin), 'Danger Zone', 'Playing with the Boys' (Kenny Loggins), 'Mighty Wings' (Cheap Trick), 'Lead Me On' (Teena Marie), 'Hot Summer Nights' (Miami Sound Machine), 'Heaven In Your Eyes' (Loverboy)

Video availability

The Top Five

Week of 11 October 1986
1. Top Gun
2. Aliens
3. Mona Lisa
4. About Last Night
5. A Room with a View

MONA LISA

25 October 1986	1 week

Distributor:	Handmade/Palace
Director:	Neil Jordan
Producer:	Stephen Woolley, Patrick Cassavetti
Screenplay:	Neil Jordan
Music:	Michael Kamen

CAST
Bob Hoskins . . . . *George*
Cathy Tyson . . . . *Simone*
Michael Caine . . . . *Mortwell*
Robbie Coltrane . . . . *Thomas*

G eorge has just been released from prison where he ended up after taking the rap for his gangster

boss, who now offers him a job driving a high-class call girl to her various appointments. At first he dislikes his passenger (Cathy Tyson), but that gradually changes and he ends up in love with her. They spend much of their time looking for her young friend who is mixed up with the drug trade. But

The Top Five

Week of 25 October 1986
1. Mona Lisa
2. Top Gun
3. A Nightmare on Elm Street 2 – Freddy's Revenge
4. Basil, The Great Mouse Detective
5. About Last Night

when they do find her, George realizes his love is doomed.

Neil Jordan made great use of Brighton Pier as the location for the end of the film. The pier had been used many times before, particularly to great effect in Richard Attenborough's *Oh! What a Lovely War* (1969).

Music: 'Mona Lisa', 'When I Fall In Love' (Nat King Cole)

Video availability

THE MISSION

1 November 1986	3 weeks*

Distributor:	Goldcrest
Director:	Roland Joffe
Producer:	Fernando Ghia, David Puttnam
Screenplay:	Robert Bolt
Music:	Ennio Morricone

CAST
Robert De Niro . . . . *Mendoza*
Jeremy Irons . . . . *Gabriel*
Ray McAnally . . . . *Altamirano*
Liam Neeson . . . . *Fielding*
Aidan Quinn . . . . *Felipe*
Ronald Pickup . . . . *Hontar*
Charles Low . . . . *Cabeza*
Monirak Sisowath . . . . *Ibaye*
Asuncion Ontiveros . . . . *Indian Chief*

In 1750 Gabriel, a Jesuit priest, is sent to the jungles of Brazil to build a mission for the Guarani Indians. The Indians have been under severe threat from the dangerous Mendoza, who not only murders his brother but has killed many of the tribe and captured others for slave-trading in the town. Although opponents to begin with, Gabriel and Mendoza soon establish a rapport and Mendoza joins Gabriel's mission. Together they work for the benefit of the local Indians and struggle to keep the Indians and the mission safe from the politics of the Church.

The Mission was an incredibly difficult picture to film as it was all made under difficult circumstances in the rain forests of Colombia. Rainstorms, floods and illness among the crew all but halted the production and there were many disagreements and arguments with the locals hired to help the filmmaking team. However, the finished film makes brilliant use of locations and spectacular jungle scenery, all of which helped it win the acclaimed Palme D'Or Award at the 1986 Cannes Film Festival.

Academy Awards: Best Cinematography (Chris Menges)

Video availability

The Top Five

Week of 1 November 1986
1. The Mission
2. Mona Lisa
3. Legal Eagles
4. Top Gun
5. A Nightmare on Elm Street 2 – Freddy's Revenge

RUTHLESS PEOPLE

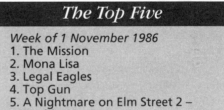

15 November 1986	2 weeks

Distributor:	Touchstone
Director:	Jim Abrahams, David Zucker, Jerry Zucker
Producer:	Michael Peyser
Screenplay:	Dale Launer
Music:	Michel Colombier

CAST
Danny DeVito . . . . *Sam Stone*
Bette Midler . . . . *Barbara Stone*
Judge Reinhold . . . . *Ken Kessler*
Helen Slater . . . . *Sandy Kessler*
Anita Morris . . . . *Carol*
Bill Pullman . . . . *Earl*
William G. Schilling . . *Police Commissioner*
Art Evans . . . . *Lt Bender*
Clarence Felder . . . . *Lt Walters*

Clothes manufacturer Sam Stone is having an affair with Carol. He is planning to murder his frightful wife Barbara, unaware that she too is having

The Top Five

Week of 15 November 1986
1. Ruthless People
2. The Mission
3. Mona Lisa
4. Top Gun
5. A Nightmare on Elm Street 2 – Freddy's Revenge

an extra-marital relationship. Before Sam is able to bump her off, another couple, Ken and Sandy, kidnap Barbara, claiming revenge for the Spandex mini-skirt, one of their designs he stole. Sam thinks his troubles are over but they've only just begun.

Madonna was considered for the role of Barbara but it was thought it would be too unbelievable that Sam would want to kill her.

Music: 'Ruthless People' (Mick Jagger), 'Give Me the Reason' (Luther Vandross), 'Modern Woman' (Billy Joel), 'Dance Champion' (Kool and the Gang), 'Stand On It' (Bruce Springsteen), 'Wherever I Lay My Hat' (Paul Young), 'Waiting To See You' (Dan Hartman)

Video availability

LABYRINTH

13 December 1986	1 week

Distributor:	Tri-Star
Director:	Jim Henson
Producer:	Eric Rattray
Screenplay:	Terry Jones
Music:	Trevor Jones
	David Bowie (songs)

CAST
David Bowie . . . . *Jareth*
Jennifer Connelly . . . . *Sarah*
Toby Froud . . . . *Toby*
Shelley Thompson . . . . *Stepmother*
Christopher Malcolm . . . . *Father*
Natalie Finland . . . . *Fairy*

In this mixture of Jim Henson puppets and live action, David Bowie is the Goblin King who takes young Sarah's baby brother to his kingdom. Sarah takes off in pursuit of the child, but to find him she must navigate the dreaded labyrinth. Along the way she encounters various creatures who advise her of the route; while some advice is good some will land Sarah in danger.

Mick Jagger, Sting and Michael Jackson were among the pop stars considered for the leading role in the movie, the inspiration for which is credited to the works of Lewis Carroll and Maurice Sendak.

Music: 'Underground', 'Magic Dance', 'Chilly Down', 'As the World Falls Down', 'Within You' (David Bowie)

Video availability

Top Twenty Films of 1986*

1 Back to the Future
2 Rocky IV
3 Out of Africa
4 Top Gun
5 Santa Claus – The Movie
6 Aliens
7 Police Academy III: Back in Training
8 Clockwise
9 Teen Wolf
10 The Jewel of the Nile
11 Mona Lisa
12 Peter Pan
13 Bambi
14 The Karate Kid Part II
15 A Room with a View
16 Hannah and Her Sisters
17 The Black Cauldron
18 Spies Like Us
19 Cobra
20 Jagged Edge

* The Top Twenty chart covers 12 months from 1 Dec 1985 to 30 Nov 1986.

The Top Five

Week of 13 December 1986
1. Labyrinth
2. The Mission
3. Top Gun
4. Round Midnight
5. Mona Lisa

CROCODILE DUNDEE

20 December 1986	9 weeks

Distributor:	Paramount	Producer:	John Cornell
Director:	Peter Faiman	Screenplay:	Paul Hogan, Ken Shadie
		Music:	Peter Best

Mike 'Crocodile' Dundee (Paul Hogan) points out to a New York mugger the dangers of playing with knives.

CAST
Paul Hogan . .   *Michael J. 'Crocodile' Dundee*
Linda Kozlowski . . . . *Sue Charlton*
John Meillon . . . . *Wally Reily*
Mark Blum . . . . *Richard Mason*
Michael Lombard . . . . *Sam Charlton*
David Gulpilil . . . . *Neville Bell*

American newspaper reporter Sue Charlton is saved by Mick 'Crocodile' Dundee from the jaws of a giant crocodile in the wilds of Australia. She convinces him to travel back to New York to help her finish her research on the Australian way of life. His rugged Aussie existence in the bush, however, is nothing compared with the dangers of the muggers and weirdos that roam the Big Apple.

Some changes in the vocabulary were made for the American market, as it was thought they wouldn't understand the Australian colloquialisms. In fact, some scenes were cut completely. The movie be-

came an instant success and Paramount immediately commissioned a sequel.

According to Paul Hogan, when he decided to raise the money for the film, so many investors were eager to put their money forward that Hogan had to send $3.5 million back.

Music: 'Live It Up' (Mental As Anything)

Video availability

The Top Five

Week of 20 December 1986
1. Crocodile Dundee
2. Labyrinth
3. The Mission
4. Top Gun
5. Round Midnight

THE FLY

21 February 1987	3 weeks

Distributor:	Twentieth Century-Fox
Director:	David Cronenberg
Producer:	Stuart Cornfeld
Screenplay:	Charles Edward Pogue,

	David Cronenberg
Music:	Howard Shore

CAST
Jeff Goldblum . . . . *Seth Brundle*
Geena Davis . . . . *Veronica Quaife*

John Getz . . . . *Stathis Borans*
Joy Boushel . . . . *Tawny*
Les Carlson . . . . *Dr Cheevers*

In this remake of the 1958 film Jeff Goldblum is the lunatic scientist Seth Brundle. Alone in his home he has invented a machine that enables man to travel anywhere in the world at the speed of light by disintegrating and then re-forming human atoms. In an experiment, a common housefly is trapped in the works, causing Brundle to re-form as half-man, half-insect.

This remake was followed in 1989 by a sequel *The Fly II*. Without any of the main original cast, it traces the misfortunes of Seth Brundle's son Martin.

Jeff Goldblum married his co-star, Geena Davis, soon after the completion of the movie.

Academy Awards: Best Makeup (Chris Walas and Stephan Dupuis)

Video availability

The Top Five

Week of 21 February 1987
1. The Fly
2. Crocodile Dundee
3. The Golden Child
4. A Room with a View
5. The Mosquito Coast

THE COLOR OF MONEY

14 March 1987	3 weeks

Distributor:	Touchstone
Director:	Martin Scorsese
Producer:	Irving Axelrad, Barbara De Fina
Screenplay:	Richard Price
Music:	Robbie Robertson

CAST
Paul Newman . . . . *Eddie*
Tom Cruise . . . . *Vincent*
Mary Elizabeth Mastrantonio . . . *Carmen*
Helen Shaver . . . . *Janelle*
John Turturro . . . . *Julian*
Bill Cobbs . . . . *Orvis*
Robert Agins . . . . *Earl*
Keith McCready . . . . *Grady Seasons*

Paul Newman re-creates his role as Fast Eddie, the hot-shot pool player from 25 years ago in *The Hustler*. No longer playing the tables after being banned from the game, Eddie finds good young players and sponsors them for a percentage of the take. Discovering Vince, a skilful player with an arrogant girlfriend, Carmen, Eddie takes them around the country, teaching Vince all the tricks of the trade.

The original screenplay was intended as an actual sequel to *The Hustler*, but director Martin Scorsese hired writer Richard Price to rework the script with his own ideas.

The film gave Paul Newman his seventh Oscar nomination, and featured John Turturro in a supporting role.

Academy Awards: Best Actor (Paul Newman)

Music: 'Who Owns this Place' (Den Henley), 'Let Yourself In For It', 'My Baby's In Love With Another Guy' (Robert Palmer), 'Werewolves of London' (Warren Zeron), 'Standing On The Edge of Love' (B.B. King), 'Don't Tell Me Nothin'' (Willie Dixon)

Video availability

The Top Five

Week of 14 March 1987
1. The Color of Money
2. The Fly
3. Children of a Lesser God
4. Crocodile Dundee
5. The Name of the Rose

THE FOURTH PROTOCOL

4 April 1987	1 week

Distributor:	Rank
Director:	John Mackenzie
Producer:	Timothy Burrill
Screenplay:	Frederick Forsyth
Music:	Lalo Schifrin

CAST
Michael Caine . . . . *John Preston*
Pierce Brosnan . . . . *Major Petrofsky*
Joanna Cassidy . . . . *Irina Vassilieva*
Ned Beatty . . . . *General Borisov*
Betsy Brantley . . . . *Eileen MacWhirter*
Peter Cartright . . . . *Jan Marais*

Although not licenced to kill, Major Petrofsky (Pierce Brosnan) receives orders to kill Irina Vassilieva (Joanna Cassidy), a task that he fulfils to the satisfaction of his superiors in The Fourth Protocol.

David Conville . . . . *Burnam*
Matt Frewer . . . . *Tom MacWhirter*

Michael Caine is a British spy catcher, engaged to foil a plan by the head of the KGB (Pierce Brosnan) to set off a nuclear bomb near a US airbase in England. The explosion would cause the British government to blame the Americans, leading to the collapse of the NATO alliance. The parts to assemble the bomb are smuggled through British customs by a Soviet undercover agent.

Pierce Brosnan was first considered as a potential James Bond in 1986. His then recently cancelled TV series, *Remington Steele*, was re-commissioned on the strength of the offer, but when it was learnt that he didn't land the part it was soon cancelled again. However, in 1994 it was announced that he will in fact play Bond in the forthcoming 007 film, *Goldeneye*.

Video availability

The Top Five

Week of 4 April 1987
1. The Fourth Protocol
2. The Color of Money
3. Crocodile Dundee
4. Children of a Lesser God
5. Little Shop of Horrors

PERSONAL SERVICES

11 April 1987		1 week

Distributor:	Zenith
Director:	Terry Jones
Producer:	Tim Bevan
Screenplay:	David Leland
Music:	John du Prez

CAST
Julie Walters . . . . *Christine Painter*

Alec McCowen . *Wing Commander Morton*
Shirley Stelfox . . . . *Shirley*
Danny Schiller . . . . *Dolly*
Victoria Hardcastle . . . . *Rose*
Tim Woodward . . . . *Timms*
Dave Atkins . . . . *Sydney*
Leon Lissek . . . . *Mr Popozogolou*

Personal Services is based on the true story of Cynthia Payne. She is portrayed in the movie as

Christine Painter, who gives up her job as a waitress and transforms into Cynthia Payne, the madam of one of England's most established brothels where most elaborate perversions are provided. At a court hearing, the judge turns out to be one of her clients.

Although Cynthia Payne was technical advisor to the film, the credits state that the story is entirely fictitious and is not about, but inspired by, her. The 1987 film *Wish You Were Here* was a kind of prequel to this film in that Emily Lloyd plays a character based on the young Cynthia Payne.

Video availability

The Top Five

Week of 11 April 1987
1. Personal Services
2. The Fourth Protocol
3. Children of a Lesser God
4. Crocodile Dundee
5. Little Shop of Horrors

THE VOYAGE HOME: STAR TREK IV

18 April 1987	2 weeks

Distributor:	Paramount
Director:	Leonard Nimoy
Producer:	Harve Bennett
Screenplay:	Harve Bennett, Steve Meerson, Peter Krikes, Nicholas Meyer
Music:	Leonard Rosenman

CAST
William Shatner . . . . *Kirk*
Leonard Nimoy . . . . *Spock*
DeForest Kelley . . . . *McCoy*
James Doohan . . . . *Scotty*
George Takei . . . . *Sulu*
Walter Koenig . . . . *Chekov*
Nichelle Nichols . . . . *Uhura*
Jane Wyatt . . . . *Amanda*
Catherine Hicks . . . . *Gillian*

In yet another time travel story our trusty heroes are heading towards Earth and present-day San Francisco to face a court martial. They are having trouble understanding the messages they receive as they move around the dark galaxy. They eventually realize they are listening to an unidentified space probe duplicating the sound of a whale, and discover that the probe will destroy the earth unless it makes verbal contact with a real whale.

This was not the first time modern-day San Francisco had been used in a time-travel movie. It featured in *Time After Time* (1979), starring Malcolm McDowell and directed by Nicholas Meyer who had, of course, directed *Star Trek II* and the sixth film in the series *Star Trek VI: The Undiscovered Country*.

The Voyage Home gave director and star Leonard Nimoy his first number one as a director. He made the top spot again the next year with *Three Men and a Baby*.

Video availability

The Top Five

Week of 18 April 1987
1. The Voyage Home: Star Trek IV
2. Blue Velvet
3. Personal Services
4. The Fourth Protocol
5. Little Shop of Horrors

PLATOON

2 May 1987	6 weeks

Distributor:	Hemdale
Director:	Oliver Stone
Producer:	Arnold Kopelson
Screenplay:	Oliver Stone
Music:	Georges Delerue

CAST
Tom Berenger . . . . *Sgt Barnes*
Willem Dafoe . . . . *Sgt Elias*
Charlie Sheen . . . . *Chris Taylor*
Forest Whitaker . . . . *Big Harold*
Francesco Quinn . . . . *Rhah*
John C. McGinley . . . . *Sgt O'Neill*
Richard Edson . . . . *Sal*
Kevin Dillon . . . . *Bunny*
Reggie Johnson . . . . *Junior*

Based on the experiences of the film's writer/director, Oliver Stone, *Platoon* gives a personal account of the nightmare life of a young American soldier behind the lines of the Cambodian border during the Vietnam War. The movie follows the exploits of Chris Taylor, a newly arrived member of the Bravo Company, and his hellish visions of his eventual sudden death while being caught up in close combat. The company are not only caught up in a war against the Vietcong but also the struggle between Barnes and Elias.

This was the first part in director Oliver Stone's intended Vietnam War trilogy of movies. The second was *Born on the Fourth of July* (1990), and the third was *Heaven and Earth* (1993). Stone, who was twice decorated for his part in the real conflict, put his cast through intense training for the film at the hands of a retired Army Sergeant. He made the film in 54 days in the Philippines, with two different endings.

Academy Awards: Best Film (Producer Arnold Kopelson), Best Direction (Oliver Stone), Best Editing (Claire Simpson), Best Sound (John K. Wilkinson, Richard Rogers, Charles 'Bud' Grenzbach and Simon Kaye)

Music: 'Tracks of My Tears' (Smokey Robinson and The Miracles), 'Hello I Love You' (The Doors), 'White Rabbit' (Jefferson Airplane), 'Respect' (Aretha Franklin), 'When a Man Loves a Woman' (Percy Sledge), 'Groovin'' (Young Rascals), '(Sittin' On) the Dock of the Bay' (Otis Redding), 'Okie from Muskogee' (Merle Haggard)

Video availability

The Top Five

Week of 2 May 1987
1. Platoon
2. The Voyage Home: Star Trek IV
3. Blue Velvet
4. Personal Services
5. Tough Guys

THE MORNING AFTER

13 June 1987	3 weeks

Distributor:	Twentieth Century-Fox
Director:	Sidney Lumet
Producer:	Bruce Gilbert
Screenplay:	James Hicks
Music:	Paul Chihara

CAST
Jane Fonda . . . . *Alex Sternbergen*
Jeff Bridges . . . . *Turner Kendall*
Raul Julia . . . . *Joaquin Manero*
Diane Salinger . . . . *Isabel Harding*
Richard Foronjy . . . . *Sgt Greenbaum*
Geoffrey Scott . . . . *Bobby Korshack*
James (Gypsy) Haake . . . . *Frankie*
Kathleen Wilhoite . . . . *Red*
Don Hood . . . . *Hurle*

Jane Fonda is an out-of-work alcoholic actress living in California. She wakes up one morning in a strange man's apartment to discover him lying next to her in bed with a knife through his heart. With an assault conviction already to her name and a history of blackouts, she removes any evidence that might suggest her involvement and heads for the airport. On the way she meets an ex-cop who agrees to help her solve the mystery and her drinking problem.

In 1963 Jane Fonda was voted the year's worst actress by the Harvard Lampoon. She had previously played an out-of-work actress in the 1981 movie *Rollover*, which also starred Kris Kristofferson.

Video availability

The Top Five

Week of 13 June 1987
1. The Morning After
2. Platoon
3. Three Amigos!
4. Prick Up Your Ears
5. The Whistle Blower

THE SECRET OF MY SUCCESS

4 July 1987	1 week

Distributor:	MGM
Director:	Herbert Ross
Producer:	Herbert Ross
Screenplay:	Jim Cash, Jack Epps, A.J. Carothers
Music:	David Foster

CAST
Michael J. Fox . . . . *Brantley Foster*
Helen Slater . . . . *Christy Wills*
Richard Jordan . . . . *Howard Prescott*
Margaret Whitton . . . . *Vera Prescott*
John Pankow . . . . *Fred Melrose*
Christopher Murney . . . . *Barney Rattigan*
Gerry Bamman . . . . *Art Thomas*
Fred Gwynne . . . . *Donald Davenport*

With dreams of becoming a millionaire, Brantley Foster leaves his home in Kansas and heads for New York. He rents the worst apartment in town and is shocked by the crime and grime of the city. He lands employment as a runner for a corporate company. Finding an abandoned office on the executive floor, he poses as one of the company's big shots, while still carrying out his mundane job. At stake is not only business success but the heart of Christy Wills.

Richard Jordan plays Howard Prescott, Foster's uncle, who set his nephew up in the menial job in the first place, and Christy's lover. He made his second appearance at number one with this movie. His first was 16 years previously in *Valdez Is Coming* (1971), which starred Burt Lancaster.

Screenwriters Jim Cash and Jack Epps also collaborated successfully on *Top Gun* (1986) and *Dick Tracy* (1990).

Video availability

The Top Five

Week of 4 July 1987
1. The Secret of My Success
2. Evil Dead II
3. Radio Days
4. The Morning After
5. Chronicle of a Death Foretold

THE LIVING DAYLIGHTS

11 July 1987	9 weeks*

Distributor:	MGM–United Artists
Director:	John Glen
Producer:	Albert R. Broccoli, Michael G. Wilson
Screenplay:	Richard Maibaum, Michael G. Wilson
Music:	John Barry

CAST
Timothy Dalton . . . . *James Bond*
Maryam d'Abo . . . . *Kara Milovy*
Jeroen Krabbe . . . . *General Georgi Koskov*
Joe Don Baker . . . . *Brad Whitaker*
John Rhys-Davies . . . . *General Pushkin*
Art Malik . . . . *Kamran Shah*
Desmond Llewelyn . . . . *Q*
Robert Brown . . . . *M*
Caroline Bliss . . . . *Miss Moneypenny*

Albert Broccoli launched his fifteenth 007 movie with his fourth leading man, Timothy Dalton. Bond is sent to Czechoslovakia to investigate a KGB defector, General Georgi Koskov. The Russian is involved in the sales of arms, murder, and the evil madman Brad Whitaker, who has an obsession for military history. Bond also encounters the lovely Kara, a Czech cellist who poses as a KGB assassin, and the menacing Necros (Andreas Wisniewski), a cold-blooded killer with a collection of unique murder weapons.

Timothy Dalton had been considered for the part of Bond on three previous occasions. He was joined by another Bond newcomer, Caroline Bliss, who became the new Miss Moneypenny.

Maryam d'Abo, who plays Kara, actually took cello lessons in order to look convincing.

Music: 'The Living Daylights' (A-Ha), 'If There Was A Man', 'Where Has Every Body Gone' (The Pretenders)

Video availability

The Top Five

Week of 11 July 1987
1. The Living Daylights
2. The Secret of My Success
3. Something Wild
4. Radio Days
5. Evil Dead II

LETHAL WEAPON

5 September 1987	1 week

Distributor:	Warner
Director:	Richard Donner
Producer:	Richard Donner, Joel Silver
Screenplay:	Shane Black
Music:	Michael Kamen, Eric Clapton

CAST
Mel Gibson . . . . *Martin Riggs*
Danny Glover . . . . *Roger Murtaugh*
Gary Busey . . . . *Joshua*
Mitchell Ryan . . . . *The General*
Tom Atkins . . . . *Michael Hunsaker*
Darlene Love . . . . *Trish Murtaugh*

Traci Wolfe . . . . *Rianne Murtaugh*
Jackie Swanson . . . . . . *Amanda Hunsaker*

Detective Roger Murtaugh inherits as his new partner the semi-psycho Martin Riggs, who still suffers, twenty years on, the effects of Vietnam. The initial hostility towards each other turns into friendship as they investigate a drug-related murder of a prostitute and uncover a narcotics smuggling operation headed by 'The General'.

Richard Donner directed two sequels, *Lethal Weapon 2* (1989) and *Lethal Weapon 3* (1992), both with Mel Gibson and Danny Glover. Donner's other credits include *The Omen* (1976), the original *Superman* blockbuster (1978), and *Maverick* (1994), again with Mel Gibson.

The 1960s pop singer, Darlene Love, who sang on hits by the Crystals and Bob B. Soxx and The Blue Jeans, makes an appearance as Danny Glover's wife, Trish.

Video availability

The Top Five

Week of 5 September 1987
1. Lethal Weapon
2. The Living Daylights
3. Blind Date
4. Radio Days
5. Jaws – The Revenge

FULL METAL JACKET

19 September 1987	1 week

Distributor:	Warner
Director:	Stanley Kubrick
Producer:	Stanley Kubrick
Screenplay:	Stanley Kubrick, Michael Herr, Gustav Hasford
Music:	Abigail Mead

CAST
Matthew Modine . . . . *Private Joker*
Adam Baldwin . . . . *Animal Mother*
Vincent D'Onofrio . . . . *Private Pyle*
Lee Ermey . . . . *Gunnery Sergeant Hartman*
Dorian Harewood . . . . *Eightball*
Arliss Howard . . . . *Cowboy*
Kevyn Major Howard . . . . *Rafterman*
Ed O'Ross . . . . *Lt Touchdown*

Based on Gustav Hasford's novel, The Short Times, Full Metal Jacket *chronicles some of the devastating horrors of the Vietnam War.*

Private Joker is one of the young marines faced with appalling conditions as he prepares for the Vietnam War. He undergoes humiliating training under the evil Gunnery Sergeant Hartman on Parris Island. The stress of the process ends up turning happy young men into hardened and terrifying killers.

A devastated gasworks in London's East End, bombed during World War II, was used as a setting in the movie but only after the crew caused further destruction for an even better effect. Military barracks on the outskirts of London were used to depict Parris Island.

Lee Ermey who plays Sgt Hartman was a real Drill Instructor in the Marines.

Music: 'Full Metal Jacket (I Wanna Be Your Drill Instructor)' (Abigail Mead and Nigel Goulding), 'Chapel of Love' (The Dixie Cups), 'Woolly Bully' (Sam the Sham and the Pharaohs), 'These Boots Are Made for Walkin'' (Nancy Sinatra), 'Surfin' Bird' (The Trashmen), 'I Feel It Like That' (Chris Kenner)

Video availability

The Top Five

Week of 19 September 1987
1. Full Metal Jacket
2. Outrageous Fortune
3. The Living Daylights
4. Lethal Weapon
5. Hellraiser

THE UNTOUCHABLES

26 September 1987	4 weeks

Distributor:	Paramount
Director:	Brian DePalma
Producer:	Art Linson
Screenplay:	David Mamet
Music:	Ennio Morricone

CAST
Kevin Costner .... Eliot Ness
Sean Connery .... Jim Malone
Charles Martin Smith ...... Oscar Wallace
Andy Garcia .... George Stone
Robert De Niro .... Al Capone
Richard Bradford .... Mike
Jack Kehoe .... Payne
Brad Sullivan .... George
Billy Drago .... Nitti

The Untouchables was a successful TV series that found its way onto the big screen with some adaptations. Kevin Costner plays the part of Eliot Ness, who pits his wits against Chicago Mafia boss Al Capone and his mob in an all-out attempt to break his bootleg trading. Ness recruits ageing cop Jim Malone who is streetwise to the workings of the underworld.

Both Harrison Ford and Mel Gibson were considered for the part of Eliot Ness, but it was Steven Spielberg who suggested Kevin Costner. Bob Hoskins had already been signed to play Al Capone but was paid his fee in full by director Brian DePalma when Robert De Niro became available for the film. Robert De Niro was required to gain 30 pounds in weight for his part of Al Capone. He achieved this by stuffing himself full of starchy foods on a ten-week trip to Italy.

Academy Awards: Best Supporting Actor (Sean Connery)

Video availability

The Top Five

Week of 26 September 1987
1. The Untouchables
2. Full Metal Jacket
3. Outrageous Fortune
4. The Living Daylights
5. Lethal Weapon

BEVERLY HILLS COP II

24 October 1987	1 week

Distributor:	Paramount
Director:	Tony Scott
Producer:	Don Simpson, Jerry Bruckheimer
Screenplay:	Larry Ferguson,

	Warren Skaaren
Music:	Harold Faltermeyer

CAST
Eddie Murphy............... Axel Foley
Judge Reinhold .... Billy Rosewood
Jurgen Prochnow .... Maxwell Dent

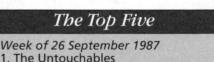

Bad-mouthed cop Axel Foley (Eddie Murphy) fights his way out of another tricky situation in
Beverly Hills Cop II.

Ronny Cox . . . . *Andrew Bogomil*
John Ashton . . . . *John Taggart*
Brigitte Nielsen . . . . *Karla Fry*
Allen Garfield . . . . *Harold Lutz*
Dean Stockwell . . . . *Chip Cain*

A xel Foley, the loud-mouthed cop from Detroit, is
taken off a case involving credit card fraud. He
makes tracks to California to help search out a
Beverly Hills gang that are responsible for the fatal
shooting of a police captain. Foley finds himself
investigating the 'Alphabet Crimes', a series of violent robberies at well-guarded properties, which in
turn leads him to the pursuit of a dangerous arms
dealer (Jurgen Prochnow) and his female sidekick
(Brigitte Nielsen), who instigates all her boss's hits.

In 1987 Eddie Murphy was rated the top male box
office draw in the annual Quigley Publications poll,
and number two for the whole of the 1980s, topped
only by Clint Eastwood.

The film was Brigitte Nielsen's third number one.
She was previously on top with *Rocky IV* and *Cobra*

both with Sylvester Stallone in 1986. Judge Reinhold
had previously hit number one with *Beverly Hills
Cop* (1984) and *Ruthless People* (1986). A third film
in the series directed by John Landis failed to make
the top spot in 1994.

Music: 'Shakedown' (Bob Seger), 'Be There' (The
Pointer Sisters), 'In Deep' (Charlie Sexton), 'I Want
Your Sex' (George Michael), 'Cross My Broken
Heart' (The Jets), 'All Revved Up' (Jermaine Jackson),
'36 Lovers' (Ready for the World)

Video availability

The Top Five

Week of 24 October 1987
1. Beverly Hills Cop II
2. The Untouchables
3. Angel Heart
4. Hope and Glory
5. Full Metal Jacket

THE WITCHES OF EASTWICK

31 October 1987	5 weeks

Distributor:	Warner	**Producer:**	Neil Canton, Peter Guber, Jon Peters
Director:	George Miller	**Screenplay:**	Michael Cristofer
		Music:	John Williams

CAST

Jack Nicholson	*Daryl Van Horne*
Cher	*Alexandra Medford*
Susan Sarandon	*Jane Spofford*
Michelle Pfeiffer	*Suki Ridgemont*
Veronica Cartwright	*Felicia Alden*
Richard Jenkins	*Clyde Alden*
Keith Jochim	*Walter Neff*
Carel Struycken	*Fidel*

George Miller's film, loosely based on a John Updike novel, tells the story of three women from New England in search of the perfect man. Alexandra, Jane and Suki, however, all unknowingly possess the powers of a witch and through their fantasies conjure up Daryl Van Horne, the man of all their dreams. He turns out to be the devil himself and seduces each of them in turn. When they learn of their own abilities and discover who he really is, they devise a way to divest him of his power.

Just days before filming began Cher and Susan Sarandon swapped roles, at Cher's request, and they both had to learn each other's lines.

Cher has twice played herself in films, first in 1967 in *Good Times*, her first movie role with George Sanders, and again in the 1992 film *The Player*, starring Tim Robbins and Whoopi Goldberg.

Video availability

The Top Five

Week of 31 October 1987
1. The Witches of Eastwick
2. Beverly Hills Cop II
3. The Untouchables
4. Angel Heart
5. Snow White and the Seven Dwarfs

CRY FREEDOM

5 December 1987	5 weeks

Distributor:	Universal
Director:	Richard Attenborough
Producer:	Richard Attenborough
Screenplay:	John Briley
Music:	George Fenton, Jonas Gwangwa

In Richard Attenborough's Cry Freedom *Denzel Washington plays Black South African activist Steve Biko who pays the ultimate price in his fight against Apartheid.*

CAST
Kevin Kline . . . . *Donald Woods*
Penelope Wilton . . . . *Wendy Woods*
Denzel Washington . . . . *Steve Biko*
Kevin McNally . . . . *Ken*
John Thaw . . . . *Kruger*
Timothy West . . . . *Capt Devett*

*C*ry Freedom is based on the true story of South African activist Steve Biko, who crusaded with his people in the fight against apartheid. Biko befriends the journalist Donald Woods, who is the editor of a liberal white newspaper, *The Daily Dispatch*, and pledges his support for the cause. After Biko is brutally murdered by the South African police, Woods refuses to accept the official cause of death, said to have been brought about by a hunger strike, and sets out to find the truth.

This was the movie that established Denzel Washington as a film actor. He was previously known for his regular part as Dr Philip Chandler in the American TV hospital drama *St Elsewhere*. He went on to

appear in two other number one movies, *Malcolm X* (1993) and *Philadelphia* (1994), and won an Oscar as Best Supporting Actor for his performance in *Glory* (1989).

Video availability

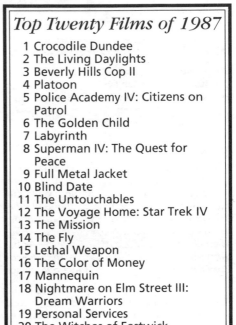

Top Twenty Films of 1987

1 Crocodile Dundee
2 The Living Daylights
3 Beverly Hills Cop II
4 Platoon
5 Police Academy IV: Citizens on Patrol
6 The Golden Child
7 Labyrinth
8 Superman IV: The Quest for Peace
9 Full Metal Jacket
10 Blind Date
11 The Untouchables
12 The Voyage Home: Star Trek IV
13 The Mission
14 The Fly
15 Lethal Weapon
16 The Color of Money
17 Mannequin
18 Nightmare on Elm Street III: Dream Warriors
19 Personal Services
20 The Witches of Eastwick

The Top Five

Week of 5 December 1987
1. Cry Freedom
2. Inner Space
3. The Witches of Eastwick
4. Roxanne
5. Best Seller

PREDATOR

9 January 1988	2 weeks

Distributor:	Twentieth Century-Fox
Director:	John McTiernan
Producer:	Lawrence Gordon, Joel Silver, John Davis
Screenplay:	Jim Thomas, John Thoma
Music:	Alan Silvestri

CAST
Arnold Schwarzenegger . . . . *'Dutch'*
Carl Weathers . . . . *Dillon*
Elpidia Carrillo . . . . *Anna*
Bill Duke . . . . *Mac*
Jesse Ventura . . . . *Blain*
Sonny Landham . . . . *Billy*
Richard Chaves . . . . *Poncho*
R.G. Armstrong . . . . *General Phillips*
Shane Black . . . . *Hawkins*

*M*ajor Alan 'Dutch' Shaefer and his military team, which includes an old CIA friend, Dillon, are

hired by the US Government to rescue a group of soldiers and a cabinet minister held prisoner in the South American jungle. They soon discover their predators are not human but aliens from outer space. With laser guns and the ability to make themselves invisible, the creatures set about methodically killing the team one by one.

A sequel, *Predator 2*, was released in 1990, starring Danny Glover and Gary Busey but without Arnold Schwarzenegger. Carl Weathers had hit the top spot four times before with *Rocky* (1977), *Force 10 from*

The Top Five

Week of 9 January 1988
1. Predator
2. Cry Freedom
3. Wish You Were Here
4. Little Dorrit
5. The Witches of Eastwick

Navarone (1978), *Rocky III* (1982) and *Rocky IV* (1986). He appeared in *Close Encounters of the Third Kind* (1978).

Director John McTiernan also directed *Die Hard*

(1989), *The Hunt for Red October* (1990) and *Last Action Hero* with Arnold Schwarzenegger (1993), the last of which did not make number one.

Video availability

FATAL ATTRACTION

23 January 1988	4 weeks*

Distributor:	Paramount
Director:	Adrian Lyne
Producer:	Stanley R. Jaffe, Sherry Lansing
Screenplay:	James Dearden
Music:	Maurice Jarre

CAST
Michael Douglas . . . . *Dan Gallagher*
Glenn Close . . . . *Alex Forrest*
Anne Archer . . . . *Beth Gallagher*
Ellen Hamilton Latzen . . . . *Ellen Gallagher*
Stuart Pankin . . . . *Jimmy*
Ellen Foley . . . . *Hildy*
Fred Gwynne . . . . *Arthur*
Meg Mundy . . . . *Joan Rogerson*
Tom Brennan . . . . *Howard Rogerson*

Lawyer Dan Gallagher is happily married with a young daughter, until he meets Alex Forrest. While Dan's wife Beth is out of town he has a two-

day fling with Alex in her apartment. She becomes besotted with him and refuses to accept that the affair is over. She proceeds to turn both his and his family's life into a nightmare.

Glenn Close was not the first choice for the part of Alex Forrest but she requested a screen test for the role. The original ending of the movie had Alex committing suicide, but the public preview reaction convinced the company to re-think the final scenes.

Video availability

The Top Five
Week of 23 January 1988
1. Fatal Attraction
2. No Way Out
3. Predator
4. Cry Freedom
5. Wish You Were Here

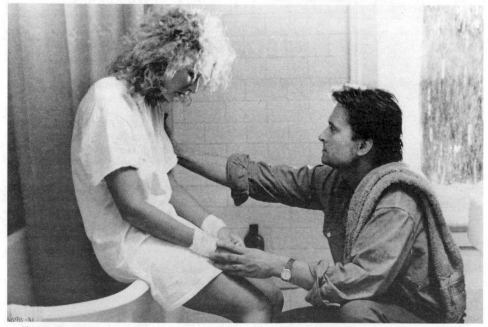

Alex Forrest (Glenn Close) is unable to forget the few nights of passion she shared with married man Dan Gallagher (Michael Douglas), and her passion soon turns into an obsession that threatens Gallagher and his family.

ROBOCOP

13 February 1988	2 weeks

Distributor: Rank–Orion
Director: Paul Verhoeven
Producer: Arne Schmidt
Screenplay: Edward Jeumeier, Michael Miner
Music: Basil Poledouris

CAST
Peter Weller . . . . . . *Robocop/Alex Murphy*
Nancy Allen . . . . *Lewis*
Ronny Cox . . . . *Jones*
Kurtwood Smith . . . . *Clarence*
Miguel Ferrer . . . . *Morton*
Robert DoQui . . . . *Sgt Reed*
Daniel O'Herlihy . . . . *the old man*

During a rising wave of crime in futuristic Detroit street cop Alex Murphy is killed by a gang of thugs. His body is transformed into a cyborg by scientists at Omni-Consumer Products who now run the police department. The now perfect cop keeps getting memory bursts of his previous life and seeks out, for different reasons, his widow and the gang who killed him.

Robocop spawned two sequels, *Robocop 2* (1990), also starring Peter Weller and Nancy Allen, and *Robocop 3* (1993 but made in 1991) with Nancy Allen and Robert John Burke as the cop.

Academy Awards: Best Sound Effects (Special Achievement Award; Stephen Flick and John Pospisil)

Video availability

The Top Five

Week of 13 February 1988
1. Robocop
2. Fatal Attraction
3. No Way Out
4. White Mischief
5. Cry Freedom

THE LAST EMPEROR

5 March 1988	5 weeks

Distributor: Columbia
Director: Bernardo Bertolucci
Producer: Jeremy Thomas
Screenplay: Mark Peploe, Bernardo Bertolucci
Music: Ryuichi Sakamoto

CAST
John Lone . . . . *Pu Yi*
Joan Chen . . . . *Wan Jung*
Peter O'Toole . . . . . *Reginald Johnson (R.J.)*
Ying Ruocheng . . . . *The Governor*
Victor Wong . . . . *Chen Pao Shen*
Dennis Dun . . . . *Big Li*
Ryuichi Sakamoto . . . . *Amakasu*
Maggie Han . . . . *Eastern Jewel*

Bertolucci's epic film was inspired by the true story of Pu Yi, the last emperor of China, who is crowned in 1908 at the age of three. Pu Yi's reign, which spans the early years of the 20th century, ends when he is forced to abdicate during the Chinese revolution (1911–12). The Japanese make him dictator of Manzhuguo in 1932 and Pu Yi is imprisoned as a war criminal after World War II. After his pardon in 1959 he writes his memoirs and ends his life as a gardener back in China.

After a six-year absence from movie-making, Italian director Bernardo Bertolucci returned to work on this highly acclaimed biography. The musical score was by Ryuichi Sakamoto, who was responsible for the music in *Merry Christmas Mr Lawrence*, and David Byrne, a member of the group Talking Heads. *The Last Emperor* is one of only two films to win the Oscar in every category for which they were nominated. The other is *Gigi* (1958).

Academy Awards: Best Film (Producer Jeremy Thomas), Best Direction (Bernardo Bertolucci), Best Screenplay (Mark Peploe and Bernardo Bertolucci), Best Cinematography (Vittorio Storaro), Best Art

The Top Five

Week of 5 March 1988
1. The Last Emperor
2. Fatal Attraction
3. Stakeout
4. Robocop
5. White Mischief

Pu Yi, crowned the emperor of China at the age of three, ends his days working as a gardener at the Botanical Gardens in Peking in Bertolucci's lavish The Last Emperor.

Direction (Ferdinando Scarfiotti), Set Decoration (Bruno Cesari and Osvaldo Desideri), Best Costume Design (James Acheson), Best Editing (Gabriella Cristiani), Best Sound (Bill Rowe and Ivan Sharrock), Best Original Score (Ryuichi Sakamoto, David Byrne and Cong Su)

Video availability

THREE MEN AND A BABY

9 April 1988	4 weeks

Distributor:	Touchstone
Director:	Leonard Nimoy
Producer:	Ted Field, Robert W. Cort
Screenplay:	James Orr, Jim Cruickshank
Music:	Marvin Hamlisch

CAST

Tom Selleck	....	Peter
Steve Guttenberg	....	Michael
Ted Danson	....	Jack
Nancy Travis	....	Sylvia
Margaret Colin	....	Rebecca
Philip Bosco	.... Detective Melkowitz
Lisa Blair, Michelle Blair	.... Baby (Mary)

Peter, Michael and Jack are three confirmed bachelors who spend most of their social time together with few responsibilities. Their routine is turned upside down when a baby is left on the doorstep of their apartment. All three men try to do what a mum should do with an infant with varying degrees of ineptitude.

The film was an American remake of an earlier 1985 French movie, *Trois Hommes et un Couffin* (Three Men and a Cradle), using an almost identical storyline. The sequel *Three Men and a Little Lady* (1991) also stars Tom Selleck, Steve Guttenberg, Ted Danson and Nancy Travis.

Music: 'The Minute I Saw You' (John Parr), 'Goodnight Sweetheart, Goodnight' (The Spaniels), 'Conga', 'Bad Boy' (Miami Sound Machine), 'Good Lovin'' (The Young Rascals), 'Daddy's Girl' (Peter Cetera), 'The Right Thing' (Simply Red)

Video availability

The Top Five

Week of 9 April 1988
1. Three Men and a Baby
2. Empire of the Sun
3. Moonstruck
4. The Last Emperor
5. Someone to Watch Over Me

WALL STREET

7 May 1988	8 weeks

Distributor:	Edward R. Pressman/American Entertainment
Director:	Oliver Stone
Producer:	Edward R. Pressman
Screenplay:	Oliver Stone, Stanley Weiser
Music:	Stewart Copeland

CAST

Charlie Sheen	*Bud Fox*
Michael Douglas	*Gordon Gekko*
Martin Sheen	*Carl Fox*
Terence Stamp	*Sir Larry Wildman*
Sean Young	*Kate Gekko*
Daryl Hannah	*Darien Taylor*
Sylvia Miles	*Realtor*
James Spader	*Roger Barnes*

Bud Fox is an ambitious and ruthless stockbroker who lands himself a plum job with the firm run by his hero, Gordon Gekko. He acquires a big car, a huge salary, the penthouse of his dreams and the perfect girlfriend (Daryl Hannah). The more money he makes the more hungry he becomes for success, which tempts him to participate in some insider dealing, passing on information on the airline company where his father works.

Oliver Stone is in fact the son of a successful stockbroker and he approached several Wall Street traders, as well as a confirmed inside trader, for technical advice on the movie. He makes a brief cameo appearance in the film.

Academy Awards: Best Actor (Michael Douglas)

Video availability

The Top Five

Week of 7 May 1988
1. Wall Street
2. Three Men and a Baby
3. Broadcast News
4. The Last Emperor
5. The Unbearable Lightness of Being

CROCODILE DUNDEE II

2 July 1988	5 weeks

Distributor:	Paramount
Director:	John Cornell
Producer:	John Cornell, Jane Scott
Screenplay:	Paul Hogan, Brett Hogan
Music:	Peter Best

CAST

Paul Hogan	*Mick 'Crocodile' Dundee*
Linda Kozlowski	*Sue Charlton*
Charles Dutton	*LeRoy Brown*
Hechter Ubarry	*Rico*
Juan Fernandez	*Miguel*
John Meillon	*Walter*

Crocodile Dundee returns for a further adventure, this time looking for employment in New York. His plans are interrupted when the ex-lover of his girlfriend, Sue Charlton, is murdered. When Dundee realizes the young man was killed for taking photos of a drug dealer's hideout he is hot on the heels of Rico, the man responsible.

The character is known as Mick 'Crocodile' Dundee because of his well-documented fight with one of the gigantic reptiles. Linda Kozlowski, who plays the helpless Sue Charlton, is Paul Hogan's real wife. Hogan has sworn he will never play Dundee again . . .

Video availability

The Top Five

Week of 2 July 1988
1. Crocodile Dundee II
2. Throw Momma from the Train
3. Wings of Desire
4. A Handful of Dust
5. Wall Street

COMING TO AMERICA

6 August 1988	5 weeks*

Distributor:	Paramount

Director:	John Landis
Producer:	George Folsey Jr, Robert D. Wachs

Screenplay:	David Sheffield, Barry W. Blaustein
Music:	Nile Rodgers

CAST

Eddie Murphy	*Prince Akeem, others*
Arsenio Hall	*Semmi, others*
John Amos	*Cleo McDowell*
James Earl Jones	*King Jaffe Joffer*
Shari Headley	*Lisa McDowell*
Madge Sinclair	*Queen Aoleon*
Erip LaSalle	*Darryl*
Allison Dean	*Patrice McDowell*

His Royal Highness Akeem, the Prince of Zamunda, is being forced by the palace into a royal marriage. He decides he wants to 'get a life' and find a bride of his own choosing. He runs away to New York with his friend Semmi, and the two take on work as cleaners in a hamburger bar. The Prince goes in search of the woman who will love him for himself and she turns up in the shape of one Lisa McDowell, the daughter of the hamburger bar owner.

Both Eddie Murphy and Arsenio Hall play a number of minor comic characters in the film, such as the pair of bickering barbers and the religious revivalist.

The make-up artist supplying the disguises used in the movie was Rick Baker, who had previously worked with director John Landis on *An American Werewolf in London*, for which he won an Oscar. Landis also worked with Michael Jackson on the Thriller video.

Music: 'Coming to America' (System), 'Better Late Than Never' (The Cover Girls), 'All Dressed Up' (Chico Debarge), 'I Like It Like That' (Michael Rodgers), 'That's the Way it Is' (Mel and Kim), 'Living the Good Life' (Sister Sledge), 'Come Into My Life' (Laura Branigan and Joe Esposito), 'Addicted to You' (Levert), 'Transparent' (Nona Hendryx)

Video availability

The Top Five

Week of 6 August 1988
1. Coming to America
2. Crocodile Dundee II
3. The Jungle Book
4. Vice Versa
5. The Couch Trip

RAMBO III

3 September 1988	1 week

Distributor:	Carolco
Director:	Peter Macdonald
Producer:	Buzz Feitshans
Screenplay:	Sylvester Stallone, Sheldon Lettich
Music:	Jerry Goldsmith

CAST

Sylvester Stallone	*Rambo*
Richard Crenna	*Trautman*
Mark de Jonge	*Zaysen*
Kurtwood Smith	*Griggs*
Spiros Focas	*Masoud*
Sasson Gabai	*Moussa*
Doudi Shoua	*Hamid*
Randy Raney	*Kurov*

In his third outing, John Rambo is taking a course in Buddhist meditation in Thailand, where he now lives. But ever loyal, he breaks off from his meditations to go behind Russian occupied lines in Afghanistan to rescue his former boss and friend, Trautman. He is being held in a remote top-security prison by a Soviet General.

Stallone's rugged action films have always fared better than his excursions outside the genre. Neither his non-macho musical *Rhinestone* (1984), with Dolly Parton, nor his comedy *Oscar* (1991) appear in this book, while muscle-bound *Cliffhanger* (1993) and *Demolition Man* (1993) both reached number one. However, despite its box office success, *Rambo III* lost nearly $30 million of its $60 million cost.

Music: 'It's Our Destiny' (Bill Medley), 'He Ain't Heavy . . . He's My Brother' (Bill Medley)

Video availability

The Top Five

Week of 3 September 1988
1. Rambo III
2. Coming to America
3. Beetlejuice
4. Big Business
5. A World Apart

BIG BUSINESS

17 September 1988	1 week

Distributor: Buena Vista
Director: Jim Abrahams
Producer: Steve Tisch, Michael Peyser
Screenplay: Dori Pierson, Marc Rubel
Music: Lee Holdridge

CAST
Bette Midler . . . . Sadie and Sadie
Lily Tomlin . . . . Rose and Rose
Fred Ward . . . . Roone Dimmick
Edward Herrmann . . . . Graham Serbourne
Michele Placido . . . . Fabio Alberici
Daniel Gerroll . . . . Chuck
Barry Primus . . . . Michael
Michael Gross . . . . Dr Marshall

Two sets of twins are mixed up at birth in a small rural hospital. Several years later, the four meet up in New York. The Ratcliff twins have arrived for a showdown with a big organization only to find it is run by the other twins, the Sheltons, who are threatening closure of their office branch in Jupiter Hollow where they were born and where many of the town's inhabitants work.

Big Business was Bette Midler's third number one movie. She previously starred in *Down and Out in Beverly Hills* and *Ruthless People*, both number ones in 1986. She went on to appear in the equally successful *Beaches* (1989).

Video availability

The Top Five

Week of 17 September 1988
1. Big Business
2. The Last Temptation of Christ
3. Beetlejuice
4. Coming To America
5. Rambo III

BUSTER

24 September 1988	2 weeks

Distributor: Vestron
Director: David Green
Producer: Norma Heyman
Screenplay: David Shindler
Music: Anne Dudley

CAST
Phil Collins . . . . Buster
Julie Walters . . . . June
Larry Lamb . . . . Bruce
Stephanie Lawrence . . . . Franny
Ellen Beaven . . . . Nicky
Michael Attwell . . . . Harry
Ralph Brown . . . . Ronnie
Christopher Ellison . . . . George
Sheila Hancock . . . . Mrs Kothery

David Green's film is based on the true story of Buster Edwards, one of the Great Train Robbery gang. Buster is a working-class petty thief, but he has dreams of greater things for himself and his family, particularly his wife June. He becomes involved with the gang who pull off Britain's greatest train robbery in August 1963, getting away with an estimated £2.5 million. With police pressure mounting, the family are forced to go into hiding in Switzerland and later in Mexico. His relationship with his wife becomes fraught when she insists they return home.

Although not depicted in the film, the train driver during the actual robbery was violently beaten by members of the gang and later died.

Phil Collins played another thief over 20 years earlier when he appeared as the Artful Dodger in a 1964 London stage version of the musical *Oliver*. He also appeared as an extra in the Beatles' first full-length movie *A Hard Day's Night* (1964).

Buster Edwards himself could be found selling flowers at London's Waterloo Station until late 1994 when he died.

Music: 'Two Hearts', 'A Groovy Kind of Love', 'Big Noise' (Phil Collins), 'Sweets For My Sweet' (The Searchers), 'I Got You Babe' (Sonny and Cher), 'Loco In Acapulco' (The Four Tops), 'How Do You Do It?' (Gerry and The Pacemakers), 'Just One Look' (The Hollies)

Video availability

The Top Five

Week of 24 September 1988
1. Buster
2. Frantic
3. The Last Temptation of Christ
4. Coming To America
5. Big Business

Through his radio show, an outrageous raucous mixture of humour and rock 'n' roll, DJ Cronauer (Robin Williams) becomes a favourite with the Vietnam War troops in Good Morning Vietnam.

GOOD MORNING VIETNAM

8 October 1988	2 weeks

Distributor: Touchstone
Director: Barry Levinson
Producer: Mark Johnson, Larry Brezner
Screenplay: Mitch Markowitz
Music: Alex North

CAST
Robin Williams . . . . *Adrian Cronauer*
Forest Whitaker . . . . *Edward Garlick*
Tung Thanh Tran . . . . *Tuan*
Chintara Sukapatana . . . . *Trinh*
Bruno Kirby . . . . *Lt Steve Hauk*
Robert Wuhl . . . . *Marty Lee Dreiwitz*
J.T. Walsh . . . . *Sgt Major Dickerson*
Noble Willingham . . . . *General Taylor*

Barry Levinson's film stars Robin Williams as Adrian Cronauer, an Armed Forces Radio disc jockey. The DJ's manic programme presentation plays havoc with the top brass when he's brought to Saigon in 1965 to entertain the troops over the airwaves. He is unable to take the war seriously and makes up his own mind about what the troops want to hear on air. He is proved right, much to the dismay of the top brass. His time in Asia, however, is not all fun, and as he gets to know some of the locals he realizes the misery US forces are bringing to the country.

When Robin Williams was filming the scenes broadcasting in the radio studio the cameras just kept on rolling and he did something different with each take. The real Adrian Cronauer was nothing like the character portrayed by Williams. He was a very quiet and shy man who was surprised that he was made to appear so funny in the film.

Music: 'Nowhere To Run' (Martha and The Vandellas), 'What a Wonderful World' (Louis Armstrong), 'Game of Love' (Wayne Fontana and The Mindbenders), 'I Get Around', 'The Warmth of the Sun' (The Beach Boys), 'I Got You (I Feel Good)' (James Brown), 'Five O'Clock World' (The Vogues), 'Sugar and Spice' (The Searchers)

Video availability

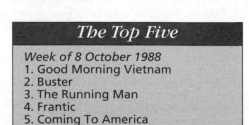

The Top Five

Week of 8 October 1988
1. Good Morning Vietnam
2. Buster
3. The Running Man
4. Frantic
5. Coming To America

A FISH CALLED WANDA

22 October 1988	7 weeks

Distributor:	MGM
Director:	Charles Crichton
Producer:	Michael Shamberg
Screenplay:	John Cleese
Music:	John Du Prez

CAST
John Cleese .... Archie Leach
Jamie Lee Curtis............... Wanda
Kevin Kline..................... Otto
Michael Palin .... Ken
Maria Aitken .... Wendy
Tom Georgeson .... George
Patricia Hayes .... Mrs Coady

Archie Leach is a successful lawyer whose world is thrown into turmoil when he meets Wanda. She's a con artist and the girlfriend of George, the criminal Archie is defending. She gives Archie the come on in the hope of finding out where George has hidden jewels from a recent robbery. Archie seems quite happy to put everything at risk for a romp with the sexy Wanda, but Wanda's other lover, Otto, is at pains to stop them.

Director Charles Crichton made a return to the movie business after several years absence. He is probably best remembered for his work on the Ealing comedies *The Lavender Hill Mob* (1951) and *The Titfield Thunderbolt*.

Sophie Johnstone, who plays one of the children in the film, is the daughter of film critic and broadcaster Iain Johnstone, who is currently writing a sequel with John Cleese.

Academy Awards: Best Supporting Actor (Kevin Kline)

Video availability

The Top Five

Week of 29 October 1988
1. A Fish Called Wanda
2. Good Morning Vietnam
3. Midnight Run
4. Buster
5. Au Revoir les Enfants

WHO FRAMED ROGER RABBIT

10 December 1988	6 weeks

Distributor:	Warner
Director:	Robert Zemeckis
Producer:	Robert Watts, Frank Marshall
Screenplay:	Jeffrey Price, Peter S. Seaman
Music:	Alan Silvestri

CAST
Bob Hoskins .... Eddie Valiant
Christopher Lloyd .... Judge Doom
Joanna Cassidy .... Dolores
Stubby Kaye.............. Marvin Acme
Alan Tilvern .... R.K. Maroon
Richard Le Parmentier........ Lt Santino
Joel Silver................. Raoul Raoul
Betsy Brantley . Jessica performance model

Magically mixing live action with animation, cartoon character Roger Rabbit, one of the leading stars of Maroon Studios, is having a hard time with his career ever since breaking up with his wife Jessica. He becomes chief suspect in a murder case and can only prove his innocence with the help of private detective Eddie Valiant. Valiant finds himself

Top Twenty Films of 1988

1 Fatal Attraction
2 Crocodile Dundee II
3 Three Men and a Baby
4 A Fish Called Wanda
5 Coming to America
6 Good Morning Vietnam
7 The Last Emperor
8 The Jungle Book
9 Buster
10 Beetlejuice
11 Cry Freedom
12 Snow White and the Seven Dwarfs
13 Big
14 Wish You Were Here
15 Police Academy 5: Assignment Miami Beach
16 Robocop
17 Wall Street
18 Predator
19 Innerspace
20 The Running Man

In Who Framed Roger Rabbit, *a cartoon film for grown-ups, Roger Rabbit hires down-and-out detective Eddie Valiant (Bob Hoskins) to help clear his name when he is accused of murdering the head of a movie studio.*

caught up in a conspiracy after being hired by studio boss Marvin Acme.

Kathleen Turner's voice was used for Jessica, the sultry nightclub singer, but her singing voice was Amy Irving.

Many other cartoon characters appeared in the film, including Mickey Mouse, Donald Duck and Tweetie Pie. Animator Richard Williams won an honorary Oscar for his work in animation.

Most of the time Bob Hoskins had to play Eddie Valiant in an empty space, but occasionally Charles Fleischer, the voice of Roger, would turn up on the set in a full rabbit suit.

Academy Awards: Best Editing (Arthur Schmidt), Best Sound Effects Editing (Charles L. Campbell and Louis L. Edemann), Best Visual Effects (Ken Ralston, Richard Williams, Edward Jones and George Gibbs)

Music: 'Why Don't You Do Right?' (Amy Irving)

Video availability

The Top Five

Week of 10 December 1988
1. Who Framed Roger Rabbit
2. A Fish Called Wanda
3. Scrooged
4. Bird
5. Colors

RED HEAT

21 January 1989	1 week

Distributor:	Columbia Tri-Star
Director:	Walter Hill
Producer:	Walter Hill, Gordon Carroll
Screenplay:	Harry Kleiner, Walter Hill, Troy Kennedy Martin
Music:	James Horner

CAST
Arnold Schwarzenegger . . . . . *Ivan Danko*

James Belushi . . . . *Art Ridzik*
Peter Boyle . . . . *Lou Donnelly*
Ed O'Ross . . . . *Viktor Rostavili*
Larry Fishburne . . . . *Lt Stobbs*
Gina Gershon . . . . *Cat Manzetti*
Richard Bright . . . . *Sgt Gallagher*
Brent Jennings . . . . *Abdul Elijah*

Danko, an unorthodox member of the Soviet police, witnesses the death of a colleague while chasing a drug dealer. He decides to tail Viktor, the despicable Russian drug dealer who was responsible for his friend's death, to Chicago. Danko teams up with the vulgar Chicago cop Art Ridzik to bust the international drug ring.

This was the first American-made film that was granted permission to be shot in the USSR.

Video availability

The Top Five

Week of 21 January 1989
1. Red Heat
2. Who Framed Roger Rabbit
3. Dead Ringers
4. Pascali's Island
5. A Fish Called Wanda

COCKTAIL

28 January 1989	2 weeks

Distributor:	Warner/Touchstone
Director:	Roger Donaldson
Producer:	Ted Field, Robert W. Cort
Screenplay:	Heywood Gould
Music:	J. Peter Robinson

CAST

Tom Cruise	*Brian Flanagan*
Bryan Brown	*Doug Coughlin*
Elisabeth Shue	*Jordan Mooney*
Lisa Banes.	*Bonnie*
Laurence Luckinbill	*Mr Mooney*
Kelly Lynch	*Kerry Coughlin*
Gina Gershon	*Coral*
Ron Dean	*Uncle Pat*
Ellen Foley	*Eleanor*

Another young hotshot, Brian Flanagan, recently demobbed from the army, quits business school to make his fortune in New York. He finds himself a sensation with the girls when he takes a job as a bartender in a cocktail lounge and learns all the tricks of the trade from cocktail veteran Doug Coughlin. There he meets his true love, Jordan, a wealthy woman who is devoted to him and soon becomes pregnant.

Tom Cruise accepted the part in *Cocktail* while waiting for the script for *Rain Man* to be completed after one of many rewrites was ordered by the studio. Cruise made his film debut in the 1981 movie *Endless Love*, which starred Brooke Shields and was also the debut movie for James Spader.

This is the third number one film which features the song 'Tutti Frutti' by Little Richard in the soundtrack. It also comes up in *Beverly Hills Cop* (1985) and *Down and Out in Beverly Hills* (1986).

Music: 'Kokomo' (The Beach Boys), 'Wild Again' (Starship), 'Don't Worry, Be Happy' (Bobby McFerrin), 'Hippy Hippy Shake' (The Georgia Satellites), 'All Shook Up' (Ry Cooder), 'Rave On' (John Cougar Mellencamp), 'Tutti Frutti' (Little Richard)

Video availability

The Top Five

Week of 28 January 1989
1. Cocktail
2. Red Heat
3. Dead Ringers
4. Who Framed Roger Rabbit
5. Pascali's Island

DIE HARD

11 February 1989	1 week

Distributor:	Fox/Gordon Company
Director:	John McTiernan
Producer:	Lawrence Gordon, Joel Silver
Screenplay:	Jeb Stuart, Steven E. de Souza
Music:	Michael Kamen

CAST

Bruce Willis	*John McClane*
Alan Rickman	*Hans Gruber*
Bonnie Bedelia . . .	*Holly Gennaro McClane*
Alexander Godunov	*Karl*
Reginald Veljohnson	*Sgt Al Powell*
Paul Gleason	*Dwayne T. Robinson*

On Christmas Eve, New York policeman John McClane visits his estranged wife in Los Angeles. While he is in the washroom the highrise office building is taken over by a group of terrorists, led by the sadistic Hans Gruber. Hiding from the gunmen, John becomes a one-man army with little help from the local police.

Much of the action was filmed around a 34-storey building in Century City, California where several models of the skyscraper were constructed and substituted in some of the movie's more difficult shots.

Bonnie Bedelia, who plays Holly in both this film and the sequel, *Die Hard 2: Die Harder* (1990), is the aunt of *Home Alone* star Macaulay Culkin.

Video availability

The Top Five
Week of 11 February 1989
1. Die Hard
2. Cocktail
3. Gorillas In the Mist
4. Salaam Bombay
5. A Fish Called Wanda

Bruce Willis as New York cop John McClane in Diehard *single-handedly takes on a group of terrorists that have taken over the office building where his wife works.*

NAKED GUN: FROM THE FILES OF POLICE SQUAD!

18 February 1989	3 weeks

Distributor:	UIP
Director:	David Zucker
Producer:	Robert K. Weiss
Screenplay:	Jerry Zucker, Jim Abrahams, David Zucker, Pat Proft
Music:	Ira Newborn

CAST
Leslie Nielsen . . . . *Frank Drebin*
George Kennedy . . . . *Ed Hocken*
Priscilla Presley . . . . *Jane Spencer*
Ricardo Montalban . . . . . *Vincent Ludwig*
O.J. Simpson . . . . *Nordberg*
Nancy Marchand . . . . *Mayor*

At the centre of this zany comedy, based on the short-lived TV series *Police Squad*, is the idiot police officer Frank Drebin. He manages to get caught up in a case involving the shooting of a fellow cop and heroin smuggling. This leads him to shipping tycoon Vincent Ludwig and his beautiful but clumsy assistant, Jane Spencer, with whom Drebin falls in love. Drebin's boss, Captain Ed Hocken, also learns of a plan to assassinate Queen Elizabeth during a Royal visit to a Los Angeles baseball game and Drebin is again on the case.

There have been two sequels: *Naked Gun 2½ - The Smell of Fear* (1991) and *Naked Gun 33⅓ - The Final Insult* (1994).

Priscilla Presley had appeared in the long-running TV series *Dallas* before creating the role of Jane Spencer in the *Naked Gun* films.

Video availability

SCANDAL

11 March 1989	1 week

Distributor:	Palace
Director:	Michael Caton-Jones
Producer:	Stephen Woolley
Screenplay:	Michael Thomas
Music:	Carl Davis

CAST

John Hurt	*Stephen Ward*
Joanne Whalley-Kilmer	*Christine Keeler*
Bridget Fonda	*Mandy Rice-Davies*
Ian McKellen	*John Profumo*
Leslie Phillips	*Lord Astor*
Britt Ekland	*Mariella Novotny*
Roland Gift	*Johnnie Edgecombe*
Jeroen Krabbe	*Eugene Ivanov*

In the swinging 1960s Secretary of State for War John Profumo is introduced to a high-class call girl, Christine Keeler, by Dr Stephen Ward, an osteopath. Ward had also introduced Christine to Eugene Ivanov, a Soviet attaché believed to be a spy. Christine and her friend Mandy are just out to have fun and don't realize the significance of the situation, and Christine allows her affair with Profumo to continue. Her life is shattered when the scandal breaks and Profumo is eventually forced to resign from the Government and Ward is arrested and charged with living off the immoral earnings of prostitutes.

The Profumo Affair is alleged to have helped bring down the Conservative Party in the early 1960s. The script was assembled from a variety of books written on the subject.

Music: 'Nothing Has Been Proved' (Dusty Springfield), 'Johnny Remember Me' (John Leyton), 'What Do You Want' (Adam Faith), 'Only Sixteen' (Craig Douglas), 'Three Steps To Heaven' (Eddie Cochran), 'I Remember You' (Frank Ifield)

Video availability

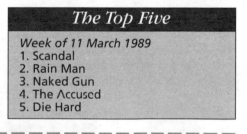

RAIN MAN

18 March 1989	4 weeks

Distributor:	United Artists
Director:	Barry Levinson
Producer:	Mark Johnson
Screenplay:	Ronald Bass, Barry Morrow
Music:	Hans Zimmer

CAST

Dustin Hoffman	*Raymond Babbitt*
Tom Cruise	*Charlie Babbitt*
Valeria Golino	*Susanna*
Jerry Molen	*Dr Bruner*
Jack Murdock	*John Mooney*
Michael D. Roberts	*Vern*
Ralph Seymour	*Lenny*
Lucinda Jenney	*Iris*

Charlie Babbitt returns home for the funeral of his father, who he hasn't seen in years, to learn that not only has he been cut out of the will but he also has an autistic brother, Raymond. It is Raymond who receives the estate and $3 million. Believing he can convince his brother to turn half the family fortune over to him, Charlie decides to take Raymond under his wing. The two of them make a journey across America that profoundly changes both their lives.

Director Barry Levinson originally turned down the project but later accepted it after insisting on several changes to the screenplay. Directors Steven Spielberg and Sydney Pollack both expressed interest in work-

Autistic Raymond Babbitt (Dustin Hoffman) inherits an estate worth over $3 million from his late father. His brother Charlie (Tom Cruise) is intent on getting half the money for himself and ends up taking Raymond on a trip across America that changes both their lives.

ing on the movie. Levinson makes a cameo appearance at the end of the movie as a psychiatrist.

Academy Awards: Best Film (Producer Mark Johnson), Best Direction (Barry Levinson), Best Actor (Dustin Hoffman), Best Original Screenplay (Ronald Base and Barry Morrow (story by Morrow))

Music: 'Iko Iko' (The Belle Stars), 'Scatterings of Africa' (Johnny Clegg and Savuka), 'Dry Bones' (The Delta Rhythm Boys), 'Nathan Jones' (Bananarama)

Video availability

The Top Five

Week of 18 March 1989
1. Rain Man
2. Scandal
3. Dangerous Liaisons
4. Naked Gun
5. The Accused

WORKING GIRL

15 April 1989	3 weeks

Distributor: Twentieth Century-Fox
Director: Mike Nichols
Producer: Douglas Wick
Screenplay: Kevin Wade
Music: Carly Simon

CAST
Melanie Griffith . . . . *Tess McGill*
Harrison Ford . . . . *Jack Trainer*
Sigourney Weaver . . . . . *Katherine Parker*
Joan Cusack . . . . *Cyn*
Alec Baldwin . . . . *Mick Dugan*
Philip Bosco . . . . *Oren Trask*
Nora Dunn . . . . *Ginny*
Oliver Platt . . . . *Lutz*
James Lally . . . . *Turkel*

Secretary Tess McGill travels every day to her Manhattan office where she works for a firm of brokers in the Wall Street district. Her new boss, Katherine Parker, steals one of Tess's ideas and attempts to pass it off as her own. A skiing accident leaves Katherine out of town and Tess takes over her office and sets up a major deal with broker Jack Trainer. But what Tess doesn't know is that Jack is Katherine's boyfriend. Matters become really complicated when Katherine returns home and discovers that her secretary has not only come up with some brilliant new ideas, but has also fallen in love with her man. She fires Tess but is herself given the push after businessman Oren Trask discovers that all the clever ideas had been Tess's and not Katherine's.

Melanie Griffith was Oscar nominated as Best Actress for her role but lost to Jodie Foster who won for *The Accused*. Both Joan Cusack and Sigourney Weaver were nominated in the Supporting Actress category but the award went to Geena Davis for *The Accidental Tourist*. The film itself lost Best Film honours to *Rain Man*, but they didn't go away totally empty handed as Carly Simon won for the Best Song, 'Let The River Run'.

Academy Awards: Best Song – 'Let The River Run' (Carly Simon, music and lyrics)

Music: 'Let The River Run', 'Carlotta's Heart' (Carly Simon), 'I'm So Excited' (Pointer Sisters), 'Lady In Red' (Chris De Burgh)

Video availability

The Top Five

Week of 15 April 1989
1. Working Girl
2. Rain Man
3. Dangerous Liaisons
4. Twins
5. Alien Nation

MY STEPMOTHER IS AN ALIEN

6 May 1989	1 week

Distributor: Columbia Tri-Star
Director: Richard Benjamin
Producer: Ronald Parker, Franklin R. Levy
Screenplay: Jerico Weingrod, Herschel Weingrod, Timothy Harris, Jonathan Reynolds
Music: Alan Sylvestri

CAST
Dan Aykroyd . . . . *Dr Steve Mills*
Kim Basinger . . . . *Celeste*
Jon Lovitz . . . . *Ron Mills*
Alyson Hannigan . . . . *Jessie Mills*
Joseph Maher . . . . *Dr Lucas Gudlong*
Ann Prentiss . . . . *Voice of Purse*

Dr Steve Mills is a widowed, unkempt and overweight scientist. He attracts a spacecraft through a high-powered satellite dish signal, causing it to land in California. One of the aliens, Celeste, is a beautiful woman who knows nothing about sex. She marries the scientist who thinks she is human, but her only intentions are to save her planet.

Kim Basinger's first appearance in a number one movie was as a Bond girl in the 1983 film *Never Say Never Again*. She went on to hit the top again in 1989 with *Batman*. Dan Aykroyd's other number

The Top Five

Week of 6 May 1989
1. My Stepmother Is an Alien
2. Rain Man
3. Dangerous Liaisons
4. Working Girl
5. The Tall Guy

ones are *Trading Places* (1983) and *Ghostbusters* (1984). He had made his name on the popular American TV show *Saturday Night Live* before graduating to films like Spielberg's *1941* (1979) and *The Blues Brothers* (1980), both of which co-starred John Belushi.

Music: 'Room To Move' (Animotion), 'I Like The World' (Cameo), 'Pump Up The Volume' (M.A.R.R.S.), 'Not Just Another Girl' (Ivan Neville), 'Hot Wives' (Dan Aykroyd)

Video availability

NIGHTMARE ON ELM STREET PART FOUR: THE DREAM MASTER

13 May 1989	1 week

Distributor:	Palace
Director:	Renny Harlin
Producer:	Robert Shaye, Rachel Talalay
Screenplay:	Brian Helgeland, Scott Pierce
Music:	Craig Safan

CAST
Robert Englund . . . . *Freddy Krueger*
Lisa Wilcox . . . . *Alice*
Rodney Eastman . . . . *Joey*
Danny Hassel . . . . *Danny*
Andras Jones . . . . *Rick*
Tuesday Knight . . . . *Kristen Parker*
Toy Newkirk . . . . *Sheila*
Ken Sagoes . . . . *Kincaid*

Freddy returns to gain revenge on those kids whose parents killed him for merely murdering a few children. Freddy concentrates his efforts on

the friends of his earlier victims and manages to keep turning up in their dreams.

Although the fourth in the series, it was the first *Nightmare on Elm Street* movie to give Robert Englund star billing. It was also director Renny Harlin's first appearance at number one. He went on to direct *Die Hard 2: Die Harder* (1990) and *Cliffhanger* (1993).

Video availability

The Top Five

Week of 13 May 1989
1. Nightmare on Elm Street Part Four: The Dream Master
2. My Stepmother Is an Alien
3. Mississippi Burning
4. Dangerous Liaisons
5. Working Girl

MISSISSIPPI BURNING

20 May 1989	4 weeks

Distributor:	Rank/Orion
Director:	Alan Parker
Producer:	Frederick Zollo, Robert F. Colesberry
Screenplay:	Chris Gerolmo
Music:	Trevor Jones

CAST
Gene Hackman . . . . *Agent Anderson*
Willem Dafoe . . . . *Agent Ward*
Frances McDormand . . . . *Mrs Pell*
Brad Dourif . . . . *Deputy Pell*
R. Lee Ermey . . . . *Mayor Tilman*
Gailard Sartain . . . . *Sheriff Stuckey*
Stephen Tobolowsky . . . . *Townley*
Michael Rooker . . . . *Frank Bailey*

In the summer of 1964 one black and two white Jewish civil rights workers mysteriously disappear in a small Mississippi town. Two FBI agents, Anderson and Ward, are sent to investigate. Anderson

is an ex-Southerner with some knowledge of the local people while the young Ward is frustrated by the inhabitants of the town. They discover the men have been murdered by the Ku Klux Klan. Both men are sickened by the racist violence they witness before bringing the perpetrators to book.

The film was based on true events and the film company was sued by a former sheriff of Mississippi who claimed that the character was based on him, causing him substantial harm.

The Top Five

Week of 20 May 1989
1. Mississippi Burning
2. Nightmare On Elm Street Part Four: The Dream Master
3. My Stepmother Is an Alien
4. Rain Man
5. Dangerous Liaisons

Two FBI agents, Anderson and Ward (Gene Hackman and William Dafoe), are sent to investigate the murder of civil rights workers in a small bigoted Southern town in Mississippi Burning.

For the fire sequences, derelict buildings in and around the Mississippi river were bought by the film company and set ablaze.

Academy Awards: Best Cinematography (Peter Biziou)

Music: 'Take My Hand Precious Lord' (Mahalia Jackson), 'Try Jesus' (Vesta Williams), 'Walk By Faith' (Lannie McBride)

Video availability

BEACHES

17 June 1989	1 week

Distributor:	Warner
Director:	Garry Marshall
Producer:	Bonnie Bruckheimer-Martell, Bette Midler, Margaret Jennings South
Screenplay:	Mary Agnes Donoghue
Music:	Georges Delerue

CAST
Bette Midler . . . . *CC Bloom*
Barbara Hershey . . . *Hillary Whitney Essex*
John Heard . . . . *John Pierce*
Spalding Gray . . . . *Dr Richard Milstein*
Lainie Kazan . . . . *Leona Bloom*
James Read . . . . *Michael Essex*
Grace Johnston . . . . *Victoria Essex*

*B*eaches tells the story of a 30-year friendship between two young girls CC Bloom and Hillary Whitney Essex. The girls are from very different backgrounds who meet on the beach of Atlantic City. CC Bloom, from the Bronx, lives and breathes showbusiness and has her sights firmly set on be-coming a successful singing star. Hillary, who has an extremely wealthy family, intends to become a top lawyer but is very unhappy with her life.

This was the first film to be produced by Bette Midler's company, All Girl Productions.

The song from the movie, 'The Wind Beneath My Wings', became Midler's first and only number one hit in America.

Music: 'Wind Beneath My Wings', 'Under The Boardwalk', 'I Think It's Going To Rain Today', 'The Glory of Love' (Bette Midler)

Video availability

The Top Five

Week of 17 June 1989
1. Beaches
2. Lawrence of Arabia
3. Mississippi Burning
4. Torch Song Trilogy
5. Paris By Night

LICENCE TO KILL

24 June 1989	4 weeks*

Distributor:	UIP
Director:	John Glen
Producer:	Albert R. Broccoli, Michael G. Wilson
Screenplay:	Richard Maibaum, Michael G. Wilson
Music:	Michael Kamen

CAST

Timothy Dalton	James Bond
Carey Lowell	Pam Bouvier
Robert Davi	Franz Sanchez
Talisa Soto	Lupe Lamora
Anthony Zerbe	Milton Krest
Frank McRae	Sharkey
Desmond Llewelyn	Q
Robert Brown	M
Caroline Bliss	Miss Moneypenny

New villains, new effects and the most spectacular action is offered up in this sixteenth Broccoli-produced Bond film. 007 attends the wedding of his CIA friend Felix Leiter in Florida and drags him away to help capture Colombian drugs dealer Franz Sanchez. The drug dealer later escapes and mounts a vicious attack on Leiter. Bond's intended revenge gets his licence to kill revoked.

The movie was originally planned to deal with a drug lord in China but the idea was shelved owing to the release of *The Last Emperor*, which was filmed in the Orient. Richard Maibaum, who worked on the revised script, had to withdraw from the project due to a writers' strike. He was still credited as co-author.

Timothy Dalton insisted on doing most of his own stunt work, although he is reluctant to talk about it.

This was only the second Bond movie not to be shot at Pinewood (*Moonraker* was the first). It was filmed on location and at Churubusco Studios in Mexico.

Music: 'Licence to Kill' (Gladys Knight)

Video availability

The Top Five

Week of 24 June 1989
1. Licence to Kill
2. Women on the Verge of a Nervous Breakdown
3. Beaches
4. Hellbound: Hellraiser II
5. Mississippi Burning

INDIANA JONES AND THE LAST CRUSADE

8 July 1989	4 weeks

Distributor:	UIP/Paramount
Director:	Steven Spielberg
Producer:	Robert Satts
Screenplay:	Jeffrey Boam
Music:	John Williams

CAST

Harrison Ford	Indiana Jones
Sean Connery	Professor Henry Jones
Denholm Elliott	Marcus Brody
Alison Doody	Elsa
John Rhys-Davies	Sallah
Julian Glover	Walter Donovan
River Phoenix	Young Indy
Michael Byrne	Vogel

Indiana Jones goes on his third and final adventure, set this time in 1938. Jones leaves his teaching post to rescue his father, Professor Henry Jones, who set out to find the obsession of his life, the Holy Grail, which offers eternal life. Jones Senior is kidnapped by the evil art collector Walter Donovan and the Nazis who hope to use him to find the Grail. Once rescued, however, Jones Junior and Senior become an unbeatable team.

This was the second *Indiana* film to pick up an Oscar. *Indiana Jones and the Temple of Doom* had won a Best Visual Effects statuette in 1984. Although

The Top Five

Week of 8 July 1989
1. Indiana Jones and the Last Crusade
2. Licence to Kill
3. Dirty Rotten Scoundrels
4. Do the Right Thing
5. Women on the Verge of a Nervous Breakdown

the last film in the series, Harrison Ford has not ruled out playing the character again 'if the script is right'.

The late River Phoenix plays the young Indiana in a sequence set in 1915.

Academy Awards: Best Sound Effects Editing (Ben Burtt and Richard Hymns)

Video availability

BATMAN

19 August 1989	5 weeks

Distributor:	Warner
Director:	Tim Burton
Producer:	Jon Peters, Peter Guber
Screenplay:	Sam Hamm, Warren Skaaren
Music:	Danny Elfman

CAST
Michael Keaton .... *Batman/Bruce Wayne*
Jack Nicholson .... *Joker/Jack Napier*
Kim Basinger .... *Vicki Vale*
Robert Wuhl .... *Alexander Knox*
Pat Hingle .... *Commissioner Gordon*
Billy Dee Williams .... *Harvey Dent*
Michael Gough .... *Alfred*
Jack Palance .... *Carl Grissom*

Batman is without Robin in his fight with the bad guys of Gotham City, in particular the badly disfigured Joker. The villain is intent on taking over the world by poisoning the population with toxic chemicals. Crime boss Carl Grissom is also doing his bit to make the people's life in the city a misery,

while the beautiful journalist Vicki Vale is determined to reveal once and for all that Bruce Wayne is really Batman.

This year's most successful film, shot entirely in a studio in London, made Jack Nicholson a cool $50 million from his percentage of the gross income and merchandising takings. Bob Kane, the creator of *Batman*, makes a cameo appearance.

Academy Awards: Best Art Direction (Anton Furst), Best Set Decoration (Peter Young)

Video availability

The Top Five

Week of 19 August 1989
1. Batman
2. Indiana Jones and the Last Crusade
3. Licence To Kill
4. The Return of the Musketeers
5. Dirty Rotten Scoundrels

LETHAL WEAPON 2

23 September 1989	2 weeks

Distributor:	Warner
Director:	Richard Donner
Producer:	Richard Donner, Joel Silver
Screenplay:	Jeffrey Boam
Music:	Michael Kamen

CAST
Mel Gibson .... *Martin Riggs*
Danny Glover .... *Roger Murtaugh*
Joe Pesci .... *Leo Getz*
Joss Ackland .... *Arjen Rudd*
Derrick O'Connor .... *Pieter Vorstedt*
Patsy Kensit .... *Rika van den Haas*
Darlene Love .... *Trish Murtaugh*
Traci Wolfe .... *Rianne Murtaugh*

Odd couple detectives Martin Riggs and Roger Murtaugh head for Southern California after chasing and retrieving a red BMW. Although the driver escapes, they discover a fortune in gold coins

stacked in the trunk. To keep them out of further trouble they are assigned the task of looking after a witness (Joe Pesci) in a drug-smuggling case. But never taking the easy option, they set off in pursuit of the particularly unsavoury gang of South African drug dealers and diplomats, where they come face to face with 'The General' (Mitchell Ryan), the head of the operation. Our two heroes once again make sure that justice rules.

Lethal Weapon 2 gave Danny Glover his third appearance in a major role in a number one movie.

The Top Five

Week of 23 September 1989
1. Lethal Weapon 2
2. Sex, Lies and Videotape
3. Batman
4. Indiana Jones and the Last Crusade
5. The Fly

He first made it in *Witness* (1985), followed by the first of the *Lethal Weapon* movies (1987). He, of course, lived to score again with *Lethal Weapon 3*. Patsy Kensit's first movie appearance at number one was in *The Great Gatsby* (1974) when she was just four years old!

Music: 'Cheer Down' (George Harrison), 'Still Cruisin' (After All These Years)' (The Beach Boys), 'Knockin' On Heaven's Door' (Randy Crawford with Eric Clapton and David Sanborn)

Video availability

DEAD POETS SOCIETY

7 October 1989	3 weeks

Distributor:	Warner/Touchstone
Director:	Peter Weir
Producer:	Steven Haft, Paul Junger Witt, Tony Thomas
Screenplay:	Tom Schulman
Music:	Maurice Jarre

CAST
Robin Williams . . . . *John Keating*
Robert Sean Leonard . . . . *Neil Perry*
Ethan Hawke . . . . *Todd Anderson*
Josh Charles . . . . *Knox Overstreet*
Gale Hansen . . . . *Charlie Dalton*
Dylan Kussman . . . . *Richard Cameron*
Allelon Ruggiero . . . . *Steven Meeks*
James Waterson . . . . *Gerard Pitts*

English teacher John Keating has a passion for poetry, which he teaches at a private boys school in 1959. He tries to encourage the same passion in his teaching and impresses upon his pupils the importance of getting the most out of life, to 'seize the day'. One of his students, Neil Perry, learns about the Dead Poets Society, a secret club run by Keating during his school days, and tries to revive it. Parental objections to these artistic pursuits leads to tragedy.

Robin Williams originally turned down the role of John Keating but accepted it after Peter Weir was hired as director and the screenplay was revised. The original screenplay had Keating suffering from, and eventually dying of, leukaemia.

Academy Awards: Best Original Screenplay (Tom Schulman)

Top Twenty Films of 1989

1 Indiana Jones and the Last Crusade
2 Who Framed Roger Rabbit
3 Batman
4 Rain Man
5 The Naked Gun
6 Licence to Kill
7 Lethal Weapon 2
8 Twins
9 Dead Poets Society
10 Cocktail
11 Shirley Valentine
12 A Fish Called Wanda
13 See No Evil Hear No Evil
14 The Accused
15 Moonwalker
16 Scandal
17 The Karate Kid Part III
18 Back to the Future Part II
19 Working Girl
20 Die Hard

The Top Five

Week of 7 October 1989
1. Dead Poets Society
2. Lethal Weapon 2
3. Sex, Lies and Videotape
4. The Bear
5. Batman

Video availability

SHIRLEY VALENTINE

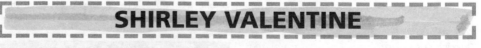

28 October 1989	5 weeks

Distributor:	UIP
Director:	Lewis Gilbert
Producer:	Lewis Gilbert
Screenplay:	Willy Russell
Music:	George Hadjinassios, Willy Russell

CAST
Pauline Collins . *Shirley Valentine/Bradshaw*
Bernard Hill . . . . *Joe Bradshaw*
Tom Conti . . . . *Costas Caldes*
Alison Steadman . . . . *Jane*
Julia McKenzie . . . . *Gillian*
Joanna Lumley . . . . *Marjorie*
Sylvia Syms . . . . *Headmistress*

Shirley Valentine is a 42-year-old Liverpudlian housewife, so bored with middle-aged life that she finds herself talking to her kitchen wall. Her friend Jane books a holiday for two and invites Shirley along. After much agonizing she decides to leave her husband Joe at home while she enjoys the sunny charms of Mykonos in Greece. Once there Shirley falls for the charms of Costas Caldes, an attractive local taverna owner, and finds herself wanting to stay on instead of returning to her dismal existence in Liverpool. Meanwhile Shirley's husband, who can't believe she actually left, is trying to figure out how to get her to come home.

The film was based on Willy Russell's hugely successful one-woman stage play.

Joanna Lumley, who plays one of Shirley's old school friends and a high-class prostitute, went on to star with Jennifer Saunders in the immensely popular TV comedy series *Absolutely Fabulous*.

Music: 'The Girl Who Used to be Me' (Patti Austin)

Video availability

The Top Five

Week of 28 October 1989
1. Shirley Valentine
2. Dead Poets Society
3. Star Trek V: The Final Frontier
4. The Cook, The Thief, His Wife and Her Lover
5. Henry V

BACK TO THE FUTURE PART II

2 December 1989	3 weeks

Distributor:	Universal
Director:	Robert Zemeckis
Producer:	Bob Gale, Neil Canton
Screenplay:	Bob Gale
Music:	Alan Silvestri

CAST
Michael J. Fox . *Marty McFly/Marty McFly Jr/ Marlene McFly*
Christopher Lloyd . . . . . *Dr Emmett Brown*
Lea Thompson . . . . *Lorraine*
Thomas F. Wilson . . . . . . *Biff Tannen/Griff*
Harry Waters Jr . . . . *Marvin Berry*
Charles Fleischer . . . . *Terry*

Marty McFly picks up where the original *Back to the Future* left off. McFly and Dr Brown take off in their time machine to visit the year 2015, where Marty's children could face an awful fate, which could land them in prison. They also have to deal with Biff Tannen who borrows the DeLorean (time machine) and heads back to the 1950s armed with future sports results in order to win a fortune by betting.

Christopher Lloyd is probably best remembered as the strange Reverend Jim in the highly successful American comedy series *Taxi*. His first movie appearance was in *One Flew Over The Cuckoo's Nest* (1975) as one of the inmates.

Back to the Future Part III was filmed at the same time as Part II, but not released until the following year.

Video availability

The Top Five

Week of 2 December 1989
1. Back to the Future Part II
2. Wilt
3. Shirley Valentine
4. Field of Dreams
5. Dead Poets Society

WHEN HARRY MET SALLY

23 December 1989	6 weeks

Distributor:	Palace
Director:	Rob Reiner
Screenplay:	Nora Ephron
Music:	Marc Shaiman (adaptation and arrangement) Harry Connick Jr (special musical performances and arrangements)
Producer:	Rob Reiner, Andrew Scheinman

CAST
Billy Crystal . . . . *Harry Burns*
Meg Ryan . . . . *Sally Albright*
Carrie Fisher . . . . *Marie*
Bruno Kirby . . . . *Jess*
Steven Ford . . . . *Joe*
Lisa Jane Persky . . . . *Alice*

Sex gets in the way of friendship for Harry Burns (Billy Crystal) and Sally Albright (Meg Ryan) despite all their best intentions in When Harry Met Sally.

Michelle Nicastro . . . . *Amanda*

When Harry first meets Sally they are both fresh out of college and she rejects his flippant advances. They meet again some years later after both have emerged from broken relationships. Harry, who always thought it was impossible for a 'man and a woman to have a successful relationship without sex getting in the way' attempts to keep Sally as a close friend and not become involved romantically. But as the friendship deepens sex gets in the way.

One of the most memorable scenes in the movie takes place in Katz's New York Deli where Meg Ryan fakes an orgasm over a sandwich. Estelle, the mother of director Rob Reiner, plays the Deli customer who asks for whatever Meg Ryan is having.

The film was Reiner's first number one movie. His other successful movies are: *This is Spinal Tap* (1985), *Stand By Me* (1986), *Postcards from the Edge* (1991), *Regarding Henry* (1991) and *Sleepless in Seattle* (1993).

Music: 'It Had To Be You', 'But Not for Me', 'Let's Call the Whole Thing Off', 'I Could Write a Book', 'Where or When', 'Don't Get Around Much Anymore' (Harry Connick Jr)

Video availability

The Top Five

Week of 12 December 1989
1. When Harry Met Sally
2. Back to the Future Part II
3. Ghostbusters II
4. Shirley Valentine
5. The Dream Team

THE 1990s

So far it's been the decade of film stars and phenomena like Macaulay Culkin, Julia Roberts, Kevin Costner and Tom Hanks. Old favourite Sylvester Stallone came back from a comparatively barren patch with *Cliffhanger*, *Demolition Man* and *The Specialist*, and his restaurant-owning partner Arnold Schwarzenegger survived the critical and popular mauling of *Last Action Hero* to bounce back in 1994 with the spectacular blockbuster *True Lies*.

Kenneth Branagh kept the British flag flying with *Dead Again*, *Peter's Friends* and *Much Ado About Nothing*, while his wife Emma Thompson scooped a Best Actress Oscar for her performance in *Howards End* before rounding out 1994 by co-starring with Schwarzenegger and Danny De Vito in the Hollywood comedy, *Junior*.

Steven Spielberg began the decade with another number one, *Hook*, his reworking of the J.M. Barrie classic tale about the boy who didn't grow up, Peter Pan. But after the monster success of the dinosaur movie, *Jurassic Park*, in 1993, he directed his most powerful picture to date: *Schindler's List*.

Both of Quentin Tarantino's first two films hit the top spot. *Reservoir Dogs* was not to everyone's taste, but *Pulp Fiction* showed that this original and creative director was not just a flash in the pan. And he was responsible for putting John Travolta back at the top of the charts!

The decade began with a love story – *When Harry Met Sally* – and films like *Ghost*, *Pretty Woman* and *Frankie and Johnny* showed that the cinema audience still had a huge appetite for a good romantic tale. *Four Weddings and a Funeral* was a truly original slant on the old boy-meets-girl theme and in 1994 became the most successful British film ever, making a star of Hugh Grant.

Walt Disney redefined the art of the animated film, earning mega-millions and hitting the top spot with *Beauty and the Beast*, *Aladdin* and *The Lion King*, and utilizing such British talents as Sir Tim Rice and Elton John for some memorable movie songs.

Action adventure films like *Speed* and *Backdraft* showed that there's no substitute for a big screen and a great sound system to really appreciate the thrills and spills which only the movies can provide.

Cartoon favourites *The Addams Family* and *Dick Tracy* were given the live-action treatment, as was *The Mask*, which consolidated Jim Carrey's meteoric rise to stardom after many years as a TV favourite. His first film, *Ace Ventura: Pet Detective*, shot straight to number one.

So as we approach the millennium what do the movies have in store? More surprises, more excitement, more romance, more action, more comedy, more variety and many more number one box office hits!

BLACK RAIN

3 February 1990	2 weeks

Distributor:	Paramount
Director:	Ridley Scott
Producer:	Stanley R. Jaffe, Sherry Lansing
Screenplay:	Craig Bolotin, Warren Lewis
Music:	Hans Zimmer

CAST

Michael Douglas	Nick
Andy Garcia	Charlie
Ken Takakura	Masahiro
Kate Capshaw	Joyce
Yusaku Matsuda	Sato
Shigeru Koyama	Ohashi
John Spencer	Oliver
Guts Ishimatsu	Katayama

Nick, a dishonoured New York cop, and his partner Charlie are given the job of dispatching the ruthless Sato from New York back to Osaka. Sato is wanted for counterfeiting and drug trafficking, and, with his oriental gang, he has been trying to avenge the Hiroshima horror by spreading counterfeit money across the USA to cause chaos with the country's economy. En route to Osaka the criminal is snatched from under the noses of Nick and Charlie, forcing them to go in pursuit of the escapee with the help of the Japanese police.

Michael Douglas began his film career as assistant editor on his father's (Kirk Douglas) 1962 picture *Lonely Are the Brave*. His first on-screen appearance was in the 1969 movie *Hail, Hero*, which also introduced us to another young actor, Peter Strauss. He co-starred with Karl Malden in the American TV series *The Streets of San Francisco* (1972–77), several episodes of which he directed.

Andy Garcia fled from the Castro regime in Havana with his family at the age of five, living in Miami where his father set up a successful cosmetics company.

Ridley Scott began his career in directing with BBC Television, working on the successful 1960s cop series *Z Cars*.

Music: 'I'll Be Holding On' (Greg Allman), 'Living on the Edge of the Night' (Iggy Pop)

Video availability

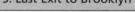

The Top Five

Week of 3 February 1990
1. Black Rain
2. When Harry Met Sally
3. Parenthood
4. Turner and Hooch
5. Last Exit to Brooklyn

New York detectives Nick Conklin (Michael Douglas) and Charlie Vincent (Andy Garcia) are given the job of delivering a brutal killer to the Japanese police in Osaka. But the assignment leads them into the exotic Osaka underworld in Black Rain.

FAMILY BUSINESS

17 February 1990	1 week

Distributor:	Palace/TriStar
Director:	Sidney Lumet
Producer:	Lawrence Gordon
Screenplay:	Vincent Patrick
Music:	Cy Coleman

CAST
Sean Connery . . . . *Jessie*
Dustin Hoffman . . . . *Vito*
Matthew Broderick . . . . *Adam*
Rosana DeSoto . . . . *Elaine*
Janet Carroll . . . . *Margie*
Victoria Jackson . . . . *Christine*

Veteran thief Jessie is released from prison on bail having recently beaten up an off-duty policeman. He joins forces with his grandson, Adam, in an attempt to pull off a huge robbery. The young Adam has masterminded the plan and believes he has devised the perfect crime, stealing plasma worth millions from a lab with very little security. Adam's father and Jessie's son, Vito, has put his criminal life behind him and foresees trouble for his father and son on the latest heist. He agrees to take part in order to protect Adam and sure enough the robbery goes wrong.

Sean Connery plays Dustin Hoffman's father, although he is only seven years older. In *Indiana Jones and the Last Crusade* (1989), Connery plays Harrison Ford's father, which means he conceived Indy at the rather more feasible age of 13.

This was director Sidney Lumet's 35th film in a career which began with *Twelve Angry Men* in 1957, the film that gave Henry Fonda's career a new lease of life. He made his one and only on-screen appearance at the age of 15 in the 1939 film *One Third of a Nation*, which starred Sylvia Sidney.

Video availability

The Top Five

Week of 17 February 1990
1. Family Business
2. Honey, I Shrunk The Kids
3. Black Rain
4. Steel Magnolias
5. When Harry Met Sally

SEA OF LOVE

24 February 1990	2 weeks

Distributor:	Universal
Director:	Harold Becker
Producer:	Martin Bregman
Screenplay:	Richard Price
Music:	Trevor Jones

CAST
Al Pacino . . . . *Frank Keller*
Ellen Barkin . . . . *Helen*
John Goodman . . . . *Sherman*
Michael Rooker . . . . *Terry*
William Hickey . . . . *Frank Keller Sr*
Richard Jenkins . . . . *Gruber*
Christine Estabrook . . . . . . *Gina Gallagher*
Barbara Baxley . . . . *Miss Allen*

Frank Keller is a middle-aged veteran New York cop prone to bouts of heavy drinking. He and his partner, Sherman, a happy family man, investigate the murders of several men found dead in their beds after responding to personal ads. Keller places his own ad in the hope of identifying the killer but falls in love with Helen, the prime suspect.

John Goodman has appeared in many movies and *Sea of Love* was the first of three number one movies, the others being *Arachnophobia* (1991) and *The Flintstones* (1994). However, he is probably still best known for his role in the hit American comedy *Roseanne*, in which he plays Roseanne's husband Dan.

Al Pacino returned to the silver screen after an absence of nearly four years, following his less than successful 1986 film *Revolution*.

Music: 'Sea of Love' (Phil Phillips and The Twilights), 'Sea of Love' (Tom Waits)

Video availability

The Top Five

Week of 24 February 1990
1. Sea of Love
2. Honey, I Shrunk The Kids
3. Family Business
4. Black Rain
5. Steel Magnolias

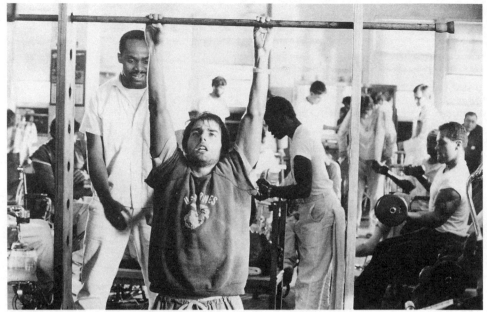

Marine Ron Kovic (Tom Cruise) becomes paralysed from the chest down during the Vietnam War, but struggles to make sense of his life by campaigning against war in Born on the Fourth of July.

BORN ON THE FOURTH OF JULY

10 March 1990	1 week

Distributor:	UIP
Director:	Oliver Stone
Producer:	A. Kitman Ho, Oliver Stone
Screenplay:	Oliver Stone, Ron Kovic
Music:	John Williams

CAST

Tom Cruise	*Ron Kovic*
Raymond J. Barry	*Mr Kovic*
Caroline Kava	*Mrs Kovic*
Kyra Sedgwick	*Donna*
Willem Dafoe	*Charlie*
Bryan Larkin	*Young Ron*
Jerry Levine	*Steve Boyer*
Josh Evans	*Tommy Kovic*
Jamie Talisman	*Jimmy Kovic*

Ron Kovic sets very high standards for himself when he joins the Marines at the height of the Vietnam War. In 1963 he is plunged into the middle of hellish combat, returning home paralysed from the chest down. His rehabilitation programme is a long and hard process, after which he dedicates his life to running an anti-war campaign, which turns out to be as much an ordeal as the jungles of Vietnam.

Born on the Fourth of July was the second in Oliver Stone's trilogy of Vietnam films, which began with *Platoon*. Stone is himself a decorated Vietnam Vet. He won an Oscar for the screenplay of *Platoon* and also for *Midnight Express*.

Both the director and the real Ron Kovic, on whom the story was based, make short appearances in the film. Stone as a television reporter and Kovic as an extra in the opening parade scene.

Academy Awards: Best Direction (Oliver Stone), Best Editing (David Brenner and Joe Hutshing)

Music: 'A Hard Rain's A Gonna Fall' (Edie Brickell and New Bohemians), 'Brown Eyed Girl' (Van Morrison), 'American Pie' (Don McLean), 'My Girl' (The Temptations), 'Soldier Boy' (The Shirelles), 'Venus' (Frankie Avalon)

Video availability

The Top Five

Week of 10 March 1990
1. Born on the Fourth of July
2. Sea of Love
3. Family Business
4. Trop Belle pour Troi
5. Honey, I Shrunk The Kids

THE WAR OF THE ROSES

17 March 1990	4 weeks

Distributor: Fox
Director: Danny DeVito
Producer: James L. Brooks, Arnon Milchan
Screenplay: Michael Leeson
Music: David Newman

CAST
Michael Douglas . . . . *Oliver Rose*
Kathleen Turner . . . . *Barbara Rose*
Danny DeVito . . . . *Gavin D'Amato*
Marianne Sagebrecht . . . . *Susan*
Sean Astin . . . . *Josh at 17*
Heather Fairfield . . . . *Carolyn at 17*
G.D. Spradlin . . . . *Harry Thurmont*
Peter Donat . . . . *Larrabee*

Divorce lawyer Gavin D'Amato tells the story of Oliver and Barbara Rose to a potential client. The Roses are the perfect couple, have a perfect wedding, find a perfect house and have a perfect life – until the bubble bursts. Gradually their love for each other turns to dislike, then outright hatred when divorce proceedings begin and they have to decide who will get what in the split. The sadistic atrocities the couple plot against each other make a very black comedy.

Danny DeVito, Michael Douglas and Kathleen Turner previously starred together in *Romancing the Stone* (1984) and *The Jewel of the Nile* (1984). *The War of the Roses* was Danny DeVito's second movie as director, following his debut in 1987, *Throw Momma from the Train*, in which he also starred alongside Billy Crystal.

Kathleen Turner made her movie debut in the 1981 film *Body Heat*, which starred William Hurt.

Video availability

The Top Five

Week of 17 March 1990
1. The War of the Roses
2. Born on the Fourth of July
3. Sea of Love
4. Trop Belle pour Troi
5. Driving Miss Daisy

LOOK WHO'S TALKING

14 April 1990	2 weeks

Distributor: Columbia Tri-Star
Director: Amy Heckerling
Producer: Jonathan D. Krane
Screenplay: Amy Heckerling
Music: David Kitay

CAST
John Travolta . . . . *James*
Kirstie Alley . . . . *Molly*
Olympia Dukakis . . . . *Rosie*
George Segal . . . . *Albert*
Abe Vigoda . . . . *Grandpa*
Bruce Willis . . . . *Voice of Mikey*

When Molly becomes pregnant she believes her married boyfriend will leave his wife in order to bring up baby. This is not to be so Molly turns her attentions on kindly taxi driver James, who helps her through her pregnancy. Bruce Willis provides the voice of the child, who shares its thoughts with the audience from sperm to toddler.

Four different babies played the leading role although none of them looked much alike. The baby's comical remarks were all written by uncredited Joan Rivers. Two sequels followed, *Look Who's Talking Too* (1990) and *Look Who's Talking Now* (1993), both with Travolta and Kirstie Alley again. The movie also inspired an American TV series called *Baby Talk*.

Music: 'Walking on Sunshine', 'Sun Street' (Katrina and the Waves)

Video availability

The Top Five

Week of 14 April 1990
1. Look Who's Talking
2. The War of the Roses
3. Driving Miss Daisy
4. Born on the Fourth of July
5. Tango and Cash

THE HUNT FOR RED OCTOBER

28 April 1990	1 week

Distributor: Paramount
Director: John McTiernan
Producer: Mace Neufeld
Screenplay: Larry Ferguson, Donald
                Stewart
Music: Basil Poledouris

CAST
Sean Connery . . . . *Capt. Marko Ramius*
Alec Baldwin . . . . *Jack Ryan*
Scott Glenn . . . . *Capt. Bart Mancuso*
Sam Neill . . . . *Capt. Borodin*
James Earl Jones . . . . *Admiral Greer*
Joss Ackland . . . . *Andrei Lysenko*
Richard Jordan . . . . *Jeffrey Pelt*
Peter Firth . . . . *Ivan Putin*
Tim Curry . . . . *Dr Petrov*

Russian submarine Captain Marko Ramius is charged with the new undetectable nuclear vessel *Red October* on its maiden voyage. He murders a high-ranking officer on board and destroys his orders to demonstrate the ability of the craft and instead plans what is believed to be an attack on the American coast. The film was based on a Tom Clancy thriller novel.

Alec Baldwin got his acting break when he appeared in the American TV soap *The Doctors*, playing Billy Allison Aldrich. Baldwin did not appear in the sequel to *The Hunt for Red October*. Instead, Harrison Ford played the part of Jack Ryan in *Patriot Games* (1992). In *The Hunt for Red October* Jack Ryan is a CIA analyst whose services are called upon by the Americans because of his expert knowledge of Ramius.

Academy Awards: Best Sound Effects Editing (Cecilia Hall and George Watters II)

Video availability

The Top Five

Week of 28 April 1990
1. The Hunt for Red October
2. Look Who's Talking
3. Driving Miss Daisy
4. Cinema Paradiso
5. Uncle Buck

THE KRAYS

5 May 1990	2 weeks

Distributor: Rank
Director: Peter Medak
Producer: Dominic Andiano, Ray Burdis
Screenplay: Philip Ridley
Music: Michael Kamen

CAST
Billie Whitelaw . . . . *Violet Kray*
Gary Kemp . . . . *Ronald Kray*
Martin Kemp . . . . *Reginald Kray*
Susan Fleetwood . . . . *Rose*
Charlotte Cornwell . . . . *May*
Jimmy Jewel . . . . *Canonnball Lee*
Avis Bunnage . . . . *Helen*
Kate Hardie . . . . *Frances*
Alfred Lynch . . . . *Charlie Kray Sr*

The Krays is based on the true story of the rise and fall of two of the most violent East End villains who terrorized London's underworld in the 1950s and 60s. Ron and Reggie Kray's psychopathic attacks on rival thugs and their hunger for power in the clubs and on the streets leads to their inevitable downfall.

Gary Kemp was formerly the guitarist with the successful pop group 'Spandau Ballet'. He was given his first guitar at the age of nine, and the following year took some lessons at Anna Scher's Children's Theatre for acting. He appears in another number one film in 1993, *The Bodyguard*. Gary's brother Martin, who played bass with Spandau Ballet, was an excellent soccer player, and in his teens trained with Arsenal Football Club.

Veteran comedian Jimmy Jewel makes an appearance as the Kray brothers' inebriated uncle and actor Steven Berkoff makes a cameo appearance as George Cornell, one of the twins' victims.

Director Peter Medak actually knew the Krays in his younger days as an art director.

Video availability

The Top Five

Week of 5 May 1990
1. The Krays
2. The Hunt for Red October
3. Look Who's Talking
4. Driving Miss Daisy
5. Cinema Paradiso

Rich businessman Edward Lewis (Richard Gere) employs the services of high-class call girl Vivian Ward (Julia Roberts) as his companion for a week in Pretty Woman, *a* Cinderella *story of the 1990s.*

PRETTY WOMAN

19 May 1990	8 weeks

Distributor:	Buena Vista
Director:	Garry Marshall
Producer:	Arnon Milchan, Steven Reuther
Screenplay:	J.F. Lawton
Music:	James Newton Howard

CAST
Richard Gere . . . . *Edward Lewis*
Julia Roberts . . . . *Vivian Ward*
Ralph Bellamy . . . . *James Morse*
Jason Alexander . . . . *Philip Stuckey*
Laura San Giacomo . . . . *Kit De Luca*
Hector Elizondo . . . . *Hotel Manager*
Alex Hyde-White . . . . *David Morse*

Millionaire business tycoon Edward Lewis meets LA hooker Vivian Ward quite by chance. He offers her luxury and money to become his companion for a week, having just broken up with his girlfriend. Vivian manages to mellow the hard-bitten businessman while he transforms her into a stylish young woman who looks quite the part amongst his friends. In time Cinderella style they fall in love.

Julia Roberts' first big film was *Mystic Pizza* (1988), but her breakthrough movie came the following year with *Steel Magnolias*, in which she co-starred alongside Shirley MacLaine, Sally Field, Dolly Parton and Olympia Dukakis. She was rewarded with an Oscar nomination for Best Supporting Actress, but the award went to Brenda Fricker for her role in *My Left Foot*. Roberts is the sister of actor Eric Roberts, who was nominated for an Oscar in 1985 as Best Supporting Actor for his role in *Runaway Train*. He was beaten by Don Ameche in *Cocoon*.

Director Garry Marshall was responsible for a string of successful TV comedy shows before turning his hand to the movies. His hits include *The Odd Couple*, *Mork and Mindy* and *Happy Days*.

Music: 'Oh Pretty Woman' (Roy Orbison), 'Wild Women Do' (Natalie Cole), 'Fame '90' (David Bowie), 'Wishful Thinking' (Go West), 'It Must Have Been Love' (Roxette), 'Life In Detail' (Robert Palmer)

Video availability

The Top Five

Week of 19 May 1990
1. Pretty Woman
2. The Krays
3. The Hunt for Red October
4. Internal Affairs
5. Look Who's Talking

DICK TRACY

14 July 1990	2 weeks*

Distributor: Touchstone/Silver Screen
Director: Warren Beatty
Producer: Warren Beatty
Screenplay: Jim Cash, Jack Epps Jr
Music: Danny Elfman
Stephen Sondheim (songs)

CAST
Warren Beatty . . . . Dick Tracy
Charlie Dorsmo . . . . Kid
Glenne Headly . . . . Tess Trueheart
Madonna . . . . Breathless Mahoney
Al Pacino . . . . Big Boy Caprice
Dustin Hoffman . . . . Mumbles
William Forsythe . . . . Flattop
Charles Durning . . . . Chief Brandon
Mandy Patinkin . . . . 88 Keys

Based on the famous comic strip, police detective Dick Tracy, sporting a black suit, red tie and yellow raincoat, encounters amongst others Mumbles, Lips and Pruneface in his pursuit of underworld chief Big Boy Caprice. The arch villain has decided he wants to unite gangland and place himself in the boss's chair.

Dick Tracy began life as a comic strip in the *Detroit Mirror* in 1931. Ralph Byrd first played the character Dick Tracy in the movies in a series of Saturday matinee specials during the 1930s. John Landis was originally earmarked to direct the movie but decided to pursue other projects when Clint Eastwood turned down the leading role. The entire process, from acquiring the screen rights to film completion, took ten years.

Madonna scooped an Oscar with the brilliant Stephen Sondheim song 'Sooner or Later (I Always Get My Man)'.

Academy Awards: Best song – 'Sooner or Later (I Always Get My Man)' (Stephen Sondheim, music and lyrics), Best Art Direction (Richard Sylbert), Set Decoration (Rick Simpson), Best Make-up (John Caglione Jr and Doug Drexler)

Music: 'Ridin' The Rails' (kd lang and Take 6), 'It Was The Whisky Talkin' (Not Me)' (Jerry Lee Lewis), 'You're In the Doghouse Now' (Brenda Lee), 'Looking Glass Sea' (Erasure), 'Rompin' and Stompin'' (Al Jarreau), 'Sooner or Later (I Always Get My Man)' (Madonna), 'What Can You Lose' (Mandy Patinkin and Madonna), 'Live Alone and Like It' (Mel Torme), 'Back In Business' (Janis Siegel, Cheryl Bentyne, Lorraine Feather)

Video availability

The Top Five

Week of 14 July 1990
1. Dick Tracy
2. Pretty Woman
3. Tie Me Up! Tie Me Down!
4. Joe Versus The Volcano
5. Music Box

BACK TO THE FUTURE PART III

21 July 1990	1 week

Distributor: Universal
Director: Robert Zemeckis
Producer: Bob Gale, Neil Canton
Screenplay: Bob Gale
Music: Alan Silvestri

CAST
Michael J. Fox . . . . Marty/Seamus McFly
Christopher Lloyd . . . . . Dr Emmett Brown
Mary Steenburgen . . . . Clara Clayton
Thomas F. Wilson . . . . . Buford (Mad Dog) Tannen/Biff Tannen
Lea Thompson . . . . Maggie/Lorraine McFly
Elisabeth Shue . . . . Jennifer

In the final part of the trilogy, Marty McFly is transported back to the Wild West with the help of Dr Emmett Brown's time-travelling machine, the DeLorean. Adopting the name Clint Eastwood, his mission is to save the good doctor from being murdered by the evil Mad Dog Tannen in the gold rush town of Hill Valley.

Although there was room for yet another sequel, director Robert Zemeckis decided to call it a day by using the words 'The End' for the closing credits.

Actress Mary Steenburgen, who plays Clara Clayton,

The Top Five

Week of 21 July 1990
1. Back to the Future Part III
2. Dick Tracy
3. Pretty Woman
4. Tie Me Up! Tie Me Down!
5. Music Box

was discovered by Jack Nicholson. He requested her as his leading lady in his 1978 movie *Goin' South*.

Video availability

TOTAL RECALL

4 August 1990	3 weeks

Distributor:	Guild
Director:	Paul Verhoeven
Producer:	Buzz Feitshans, Ronald Shusett
Screenplay:	Ronald Shusett, Dan O'Bannon, Gary Goldman
Music:	Jerry Goldsmith

CAST
Arnold Schwarzenegger . . . *Quaid/Hauser*
Rachel Ticotin . . . . *Melina*
Sharon Stone . . . . *Lori*
Ronny Cox . . . . *Cohaagen*
Michael Ironside . . . . *Richter*
Marshall Bell . . . . *George/Kuato*
Mel Johnson Jr . . . . *Benny*
Michael Champion . . . . *Helm*

In 2084 construction worker Doug Quaid wants to visit the now earth-owned colony of Mars. As a cheaper option he decides to have a memory implant of a Mars holiday, complete with 'ego' trip. However, the implant operation goes wrong and the holiday firm Rekall tell him he has in fact actually been to Mars as a secret agent. Smelling a rat, he goes in search of the truth and his real identity.

At a cost of $65 million, *Total Recall* became the second most expensive movie of the year, topped only by *Die Hard II: Die Harder*. Over $7 million was wasted on ditched footage and over fifty rejected scripts. The original story ('We Can Remember It For You Wholesale') was by Philip K. Dick, who also wrote the 1982 blockbuster *Blade Runner*. The Disney studios had first option on the project but turned it down.

Both Richard Dreyfuss and Patrick Swayze were considered for the part of Doug Quaid.

Academy Awards: Best Visual Effects (Special Achievement Award; Eric Brevig, Rob Bottin, Tim McGovern, Alex Funke)

Video availability

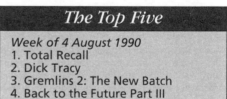

The Top Five

Week of 4 August 1990
1. Total Recall
2. Dick Tracy
3. Gremlins 2: The New Batch
4. Back to the Future Part III
5. Pretty Woman

Employees of a unique travel service struggle to subdue Quaid (Arnold Schwarzenegger) when a memory implant procedure accidentally unlocks a completely separate personality suppressed in Quaid's mind in Total Recall.

DIE HARD 2: DIE HARDER

25 August 1990	3 weeks

Distributor:	Fox/Gordon Company
Director:	Renny Harlin
Producer:	Lawrence Gordon, Joel Silver, Charles Gordon
Screenplay:	Steven E. de Souza, Doug Richardson
Music:	Michael Kamen

CAST

Bruce Willis	. . . .	John McClane
Bonnie Bedelia	. . . .	Holly McClane
William Atherton	. . . .	Thornberg
Reginald VelJohnson	. . . .	Al Powell
Franco Nero	. . . .	Esperanza
William Sadler	. . . .	Stuart
John Amos	. . . .	Grant
Dennis Franz	. . . .	Carmine Lorenzo
Art Evans	. . . .	Barnes

New York cop John McClane has been reconciled with his wife Holly and has joined the LAPD. While McClane waits to pick her up at Washington DC airport before spending Christmas with their family terrorists gain control of the airport. They want to free the foreign dictator Esperanza, who is accused of drug smuggling and is about to land at the airport. With only bungling security police for help, John has to save the day on his own.

At the time of release, this film was said to have the highest body count of any movie to date – 264. It also became the most expensive film of the year, at a cost of $70 million.

Director Renny Harlin, who took over from John McTiernan who worked on the original movie, is married to actress Geena Davis. His first major success was also a sequel, the 1988 *Nightmare on Elm Street Part Four: The Dream Master*.

Franco Nero, who plays General Ramon Esperanza, is the father of Vanessa Redgrave's son Carlos.

Video availability

The Top Five

Week of 25 August 1990
1. Die Hard 2: Die Harder
2. Total Recall
3. Dick Tracy
4. Pretty Woman
5. Days of Thunder

MEMPHIS BELLE

15 September 1990	2 weeks

Distributor:	Warner
Director:	Michael Caton-Jones
Producer:	David Puttnam, Catherine Wyler
Screenplay:	Monte Merrick
Music:	George Fenton

CAST

Matthew Modine	. . . .	Dennis
Eric Stoltz	. . . .	Danny
Tate Donovan	. . . .	Luke
D.B. Sweeney	. . . .	Phil
Billy Zane	. . . .	Val
Sean Astin	. . . .	Rasca
Harry Connick Jr.	. . . .	Clay
Reed Diamond	. . . .	Virge
Courtney Gains	. . . .	Eugene

The *Memphis Belle*, a cramped flying fortress and probably the best known of all the British-based American Air Force B-17 bombers, is sent over to Germany for the plane's final bombing raid during World War II. The hopes, fears, loves and hates of the young crew make up the story.

Producer Catherine Wyler's father, director William Wyler, made a documentary film about the *Memphis Belle* in 1944, extracts from which were used in this movie.

Memphis Belle saw the acting debut of singer Harry Connick Jr, who previously worked on the soundtrack album of the 1989 film *When Harry Met Sally*.

Video availability

The Top Five

Week of 15 September 1990
1. Memphis Belle
2. Die Hard 2: Die Harder
3. Wild at Heart
4. Total Recall
5. Crimes and Misdemeanors

ANOTHER 48 HRS

29 September 1990	1 week

Distributor: Paramount
Director: Walter Hill
Producer: Lawrence Gordon, Robert D. Wachs
Screenplay: John Fasano, Jeb Stuart, Larry Gross
Music: James Horner

CAST
Eddie Murphy . . . . *Reggie Hammond*
Nick Nolte . . . . *Jack Cates*
Brion James . . . . *Ben Kehoe*
Kevin Tighe . . . . *Blake Wilson*
Ed O'Ross . . . . *Frank Cruise*
David Anthony Marshall . . . . *Willy Hickok*
Andrew Divoff . . . . *Cherry Ganz*
Bernie Casey . . . . *Kirkland Smith*

Hard-nosed cop Jack Cates again teams up with the wise-cracking ex-con Reggie Hammond. When their car blows up they head off in pursuit of a drug baron known only as 'The Iceman'. They also have to avoid getting in the line of fire of two hit men (one the brother of a villain killed in the original film) who are sent to kill Reggie.

In this sequel and in the original *48 Hrs*, Nick Nolte and Eddie Murphy added much to the script with their on-screen improvisation, which many felt should have been acknowledged in the credits.

Nolte's first major break as an actor was as co-star to Peter Strauss in the 1976 TV series *Rich Man, Poor Man*. *Another 48 Hrs* was the third of 5 number one movies for Nolte. His first was *The Deep* (1977), followed by *Down and Out in Beverly Hills* (1986). In 1990 he scored two in a row with *The Prince of Tides* and *Cape Fear*.

Music: '(The Boys Are) Back In Town' (Brian O'Neal), 'I Just Can't Let It End', 'I've Got My Eye On You' (Lamont Dozier)

Video availability

The Top Five
Week of 29 September 1990
1. Another 48 Hrs
2. Memphis Belle
3. Wild At Heart
4. Total Recall
5. Crimes and Misdemeanors

PRESUMED INNOCENT

6 October 1990	1 week

Distributor: Warner
Director: Alan J. Pakula
Producer: Sydney Pollack
Screenplay: Frank Pierson, Alan J. Pakula
Music: John Williams

CAST
Harrison Ford . . . . *Rusty Sabich*
Brian Dennehy . . . . *Raymond Horgan*
Raul Julia . . . . *Alejandro (Sandy) Stern*
Bonnie Bedelia . . . . *Barbara Sabich*
Paul Winfield . . . . *Judge Larren Lyttle*
Greta Scacchi . . . . *Carolyn Polhemus*
John Spencer . . . . *Detective Llpranzer*

Towards the end of his term in office, District Attorney Raymond Horgan launches his campaign for re-election, but his campaign is thrown into turmoil when Carolyn Polhemus, a prosecutor of sex crimes, is brutally murdered. The long list of suspects is narrowed down to one single name, that of Rusty Sabich, a prosecuting lawyer who was having an affair with the dead woman and whose

fingerprints are found on a glass near the victim's body. Only Sabich's wife seems sure he didn't do it.

Before making it into the movies, producer Sydney Pollack directed many episodes of various hit TV series, including *The Defenders*, *The Fugitive*, *Naked City* and *Dr Kildare*.

Harrison Ford appeared in several 1960s TV series, including *Gunsmoke* and *Ironside*. After a few minor film roles, he gave up acting and went to work as a carpenter until he was offered a part in the 1973 film *American Graffiti*.

Video availability

The Top Five
Week of 6 October 1990
1. Presumed Innocent
2. Another 48 Hrs
3. Memphis Belle
4. Wild At Heart
5. Mo' Better Blues

The ghost of Sam Wheat (Patrick Swayze) manages to speak to his girlfriend Molly Jensen (Demi Moore) through psychic Oda Mae Brown (Whoopi Goldberg) in the high-spirited Ghost.

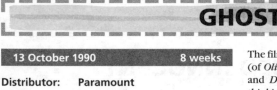

GHOST

13 October 1990	8 weeks

Distributor: Paramount
Director: Jerry Zucker
Producer: Lisa Weinstein
Screenplay: Bruce Joel Rubin
Music: Maurice Jarre

CAST

Patrick Swayze . . . . *Sam Wheat*
Demi Moore . . . . *Molly Jensen*
Whoopi Goldberg . . . . . . *Oda Mae Brown*
Tony Goldwyn . . . . *Carl Brunner*
Rick Aviles . . . . *Willie Lopez*
Gail Boggs . . . . *Louise*
Amelia McQueen . . . . *Clara*

Sam, a successful stockbroker, and Molly, the woman he loves, are a happy New York couple having just moved into their new loft. Coming home one night they are held up by a mugger and Sam is shot dead in the street. Molly's life is in danger after she witnessed the killing and Sam comes back as a ghost to warn her. He's unable to communicate directly with her so uses a charlatan spirit medium, Oda Mae, who discovers she really does have psychic powers. Molly is sceptical when Oda Mae first attempts to pass Sam's warnings on but eventually she is convinced, and is forewarned of the dangers ahead.

The film company originally wanted Swoozie Kurtz (of *Oliver's Story* (1978), *Against All Odds* (1984) and *Dangerous Liaisons* (1988)) to play Molly, thinking they could get some mileage out of promoting Swoozie and Swayze together. However, Whoopi Goldberg eventually talked them out of the idea. The eventual Molly, Demi Moore, once posed naked on the cover of *Oui* magazine, before finding work in later editions of the American television soap series *General Hospital*, in which she played reporter Jackie Templeton. She appeared naked again twice for the magazine *Vanity Fair*.

Academy Awards: Best Supporting Actress (Whoopi Goldberg), Best Original Screenplay (Bruce Joel Rubin)

Music: 'Unchained Melody' (Righteous Brothers)

Video availability

The Top Five

Week of 13 October 1990
1. Ghost
2. Presumed Innocent
3. Hardware
4. Wild At Heart
5. Memphis Belle

TEENAGE MUTANT NINJA TURTLES

8 December 1990	1 week

Distributor: **Virgin**
Director: **Steve Barron**
Producer: **Kim Dawson, Simon Fields, David Chan**
Screenplay: **Todd W. Langen, Bobby Herbeck**
Music: **John Du Prez**

CAST
Judith Hoag .... *April O'Neil*
Elias Koteas .... *Casey Jones*
Joch Paid .... *Raphael*
Michelan Sisti............ *Michelangelo*
Leif Tilden .... *Donatello*
David Forman............... *Leonardo*
Michael Turney ...... *Danny Pennington*
Jay Patterson .... *Charles Pennington*

Four baby turtles, Raphael, Michelangelo, Leonardo and Donatello, accidentally fall into a New York sewer and become mutated through toxic nuclear waste. They grow to human size and develop the power of speech. Living in the sewers, they eat pizza (mostly with banana and sausage topping), which they share with their leader, Splinter, a rat from Japan who teaches them the ancient art of ninjitsu. Crusading TV reporter April O'Neil makes friends with this unusual group and between them they become a self-styled vigilante force and try to stop a gang called 'The Foot Clan' from terrorizing the streets of New York.

Although the film ended up costing in excess of $14 million, more than twice its original budget, its first week's takings were around $25 million. The Ninja Turtles originated in a comic strip by Peter Laird and Kevin Eastman in the early 1980s. To date, two sequels have appeared, *Teenage Mutant Ninja Turtles II – The Secret of the Ooze* (1991) and *Teenage Mutant Ninja Turtles III – The Turtles are Back . . . In Time* (1993).

Top Twenty Films of 1990

1 Ghost
2 Pretty Woman
3 Look Who's Talking
4 Honey, I Shrunk the Kids
5 Total Recall
6 Ghostbusters II
7 Back to the Future Part III
8 Gremlins 2: The New Batch
9 Back to the Future Part II
10 When Harry Met Sally
11 Shirley Valentine
12 Parenthood
13 The War of the Roses
14 Dick Tracy
15 Die Hard 2: Die Harder
16 Presumed Innocent
17 Memphis Belle
18 The Little Mermaid
19 Turner and Hooch
20 Bird on a Wire

Director Steve Barron came from the world of music video where he'd worked with Michael Jackson and Dire Straits.

Music: 'This Is What We Do' (M.C. Hammer), 'Spin That Wheel' (Hi Tek 3), 'Turtle Power' (Partners In Kryme), 'Let The Walls Come Down' (Johnny Kemp)

Video availability

The Top Five

Week of 8 December 1990
1. Teenage Mutant Ninja Turtles
2. The Sheltering sky
3. Ghost
4. Metropolitan
5. Henry and June

HOME ALONE

15 December 1990	4 weeks

Distributor: **Twentieth Century-Fox**
Director: **Chris Columbus**
Producer: **John Hughes**
Screenplay: **John Hughes**
Music: **John Williams**

CAST
Macaulay Culkin ...... *Kevin McCallister*
Joe Pesci....................... *Harry*
Daniel Stern .... *Marv*
Catherine O'Hara .... *Kate McCallister*
John Heard .... *Peter McCallister*
Roberts Blossom .... *Marley*
John Candy............... *Gus Polinski*

Eight-year-old Kevin McCallister is accidentally left at home when his family flies to Paris for a vacation. His free run of the house, and the refrigerator, is brought to an end by the unwelcome attention of two inept burglars, Harry and Marv. However, they don't bargain for the ingenious set of booby traps Kevin sets to defend his home.

Macaulay's father, Kit, was also a child actor, but, after a small part in the movie *West Side Story*, failed to make the transition into adult roles. Both father and son danced the Prince in stage productions of *The Nutcracker*, a role taken by Macaulay in the 1994 movie version. Macaulay is named after the English 19th-century historian and critic Lord (Thomas Babbington) Macaulay.

Video availability

The Top Five

Week of 15 December 1990
1. Home Alone
2. The Sheltering Sky
3. Ghost
4. Teenage Mutant Ninja Turtles
5. Metropolitan

ARACHNOPHOBIA

11 January 1991	1 week

Distributor:	Hollywood Pictures
Director:	Frank Marshall
Producer:	Kathleen Kennedy, Richard Vane
Screenplay:	Don Jakoby, Wesley Strick
Music:	Trevor Jones

CAST
Jeff Daniels . . . . *Dr Ross Jennings*
Harley Jane Kozak . . . . . . *Molly Jennings*
John Goodman . . . . . . *Delbert McClintock*
Julian Sands . . . . *Dr James Atherton*
Stuart Pankin . . . . *Sheriff Parsons*
Brian McNamara . . . . *Chris Collins*
Mark L. Taylor . . . . *Jerry Manley*
Henry Jones . . . . *Dr Sam Metcalf*

Dr Ross Jennings and his wife Molly return from an expedition in the Venezuelan jungle and set up home in a small town in California with their two children. A giant killer spider has stowed away among their equipment, which has been transported from the jungle. Settling into the Jennings' barn, it soon reproduces and before long the town is infested with its offspring, which terrorizes the community. Dr Jennings must overcome his arachnophobia (fear of spiders) to rid the town of the horrific creatures.

Real South American tarantulas were used in the making of the film, along with many mechanical versions, which were built by special-effects expert Chris Walas.

The movie was Frank Marshall's debut as a director, although he produced or co-produced dozens of successful movies, including *Raiders of the Lost Ark* (1981), *Poltergeist* (1982), *Who Framed Roger Rabbit* (1988) and *Hook* (1992).

Music: 'Arachnophobia' (Brent Hutchins), 'Don't Bug Me' (Jimmy Buffet), 'To The Light' (Sara Hickman)

Video availability

The Top Five

Week of 11 January 1991
1. Arachnophobia
2. Home Alone
3. Air America
4. The Sheltering Sky
5. Ghost

CYRANO DE BERGERAC

18 January 1991	2 weeks

Distributor:	Hachette Premiere/Camera One
Director:	Jean-Paul Rappeneau
Producer:	René Cleitman, Michel Seydoux
Screenplay:	Jean-Paul Rappeneau, Jean-Claude Carriere
Music:	Jean-Claude Petit

CAST
Gérard Depardieu . . . *Cyrano de Bergerac*
Anne Brochet . . . . *Roxane*
Vincent Perez . . . . *Christian de Neuvillette*
Jacques Weber . . . . *Count de Guiche*
Roland Bertin . . . . *Rageuneau*
Philippe Morier-Genoud . . . . *Le Bret*
Philippe Volter . . . . *Viscount of Valvert*

Cyrano de Bergerac is a fearless 17th-century Gascon swordsman, wit and poet. Despite his way with words, he is unable to confess his love for his beautiful cousin Roxane because of his huge and ugly nose. When his friend and fellow soldier, Christian de Neuvillette, falls in love with Roxane and she with him, Cyrano agrees to pen Christian's love letters and supply him with the words of love.

Gérard Depardieu's nose in the movie is his own in shape, but made somewhat longer. It was decided not to make it look grotesque, just long.

Cyrano de Bergerac, based on the classic story by Edmond Rostand, became France's most expensive movie to date, costing $20 million to make. This was even after cutting costs by filming in Hungary. The movie won Depardieu the Best Actor Award at the 1990 Cannes Film Festival, but failed to do likewise at the Oscars.

The play was first seen on the French stage in 1898 and is still performed all over the world today. The story was also filmed in 1950, when José Ferrar won an Oscar for his portrayal of Cyrano. A parody version, *Roxanne*, starring Steve Martin, was a top five hit in 1987.

Academy Awards: Best Costume Design (Franca Squarciapino)

The Top Five

Week of 18 January 1991
1. Cyrano de Bergerac
2. Arachnophobia
3. Air America
4. The Sheltering Sky
5. Home Alone

ROCKY V

1 February 1991	1 week

Distributor:	UIP
Director:	John G. Avildsen
Producer:	Irwin Winkler, Robert Chartoff
Screenplay:	Sylvester Stallone
Music:	Bill Conti

CAST
Sylvester Stallone . . . . *Rocky*
Talia Shire . . . . *Adrian*
Burt Young . . . . *Paulie*
Sage Stallone . . . . *Rocky Jr*
Burgess Meredith . . . . *Mickey*
Tommy Morrison . . . . *Tommy*
Richard Gant . . . . *George W. Duke*
Tony Burton . . . . *Tony*
James Gambina . . . . *Jimmy*

Broke and brain damaged, Rocky is told it's too dangerous for him to ever fight again. He sells his expensive home and moves back to Philadelphia where he is talked into training a young potential for a fight. The kid becomes too big time for his own

good, so Rocky returns to the fray just one more time to show the punk who's boss.

Sylvester Stallone's son in the movie is in fact Stallone's real son, Sage.

John G. Avildsen, who directed the original *Rocky* movie, returned to work on this fourth sequel. *Rocky II*, *III* and *IV* were directed by Stallone himself.

Music: 'That's What I Said', 'Feel My Power' (M.C. Hammer), 'The Measure of a Man' (Elton John), 'Keep It Up' (Snap)

Video availability

The Top Five

Week of 1 February 1991
1. Rocky V
2. Postcards from the Edge
3. Cyrano de Bergerac
4. Reversal of Fortune
5. Havana

KINDERGARTEN COP

8 February 1991	1 week

Distributor:	Universal
Director:	Ivan Reitman
Producer:	Ivan Reitman, Brian Grazer
Screenplay:	Murray Salem, Herschel Weingrod, Timothy Harris
Music:	Randy Edelman

CAST
Arnold Schwarzenegger . . . . *John Kimble*
Penelope Ann Miller . . . . *Joyce*
Pamela Reed . . . . *Phoebe*
Linda Hunt . . . . *Miss Schlowski*
Richard Tyson . . . . *Cullen Crisp*
Carroll Baker . . . . *Mrs Crisp*
Joseph Cousins, Christian Cousins *Dominic*

Detective John Kimble is a serious Los Angeles cop on the trail of violent drug dealer, Cullen Crisp. To get to Crisp the LAPD decide they should find Crisp's lover, Joyce. Joyce is keeping her identity hidden, scared that Crisp will come after her for the money she stole from him when she fled with their child, Dominic. The plan is for Kimble's assistant, Phoebe, to pose as a teacher at a kindergarten and find out which kid is Crisp's son in the hope that he'll lead them to Joyce. The fun starts when Phoebe falls ill and Kimble's only option is to take on the role himself. The mean machine cop can cope with the violent criminals on the streets of LA but not with a class full of screaming five-year-olds.

In 1970, director Ivan Reitman was fined and sentenced to a year's probation for the contents of his first movie, *Columbus of Sex*. Among his later successes were *Ghostbusters* (1984), *Legal Eagles* (1986) and *Twins* (1989). He teamed up again with Arnold Schwarzenegger for *Junior*, also a number one in 1994.

This was the first number one movie for Pamela Reed, who made her debut in *The Long Riders* (1980), and appeared in *Rachel River* (1987), which was directed by her husband, Sandy Smolar.

Music: 'The Party Starts Now!' (Manitoba's Wild Kingdom), 'La Manito' (Pochi Y Su Cocoband)

Video availability

The Top Five

Week of 8 February 1991
1. Kindergarten Cop
2. Postcards from the Edge
3. Cyrano de Bergerac
4. The Grifters
5. Rocky V

THREE MEN AND A LITTLE LADY

15 February 1991	3 weeks

Distributor:	Touchstone
Director:	Emile Ardolino
Producer:	Ted Field, Robert W. Cort
Screenplay:	Charlie Peters
Music:	James Newton Howard

CAST
Tom Selleck .... Peter
Steve Guttenberg .... Michael
Ted Danson .... Jack
Nancy Travis .... Sylvia
Robin Weisman .... Mary
Christopher Cazenove .... Edward
Sheila Hancock .... Vera
Fiona Shaw .... Miss Lomax

In this sequel to *Three Men and a Baby*, baby Mary is five years old and attending school. Her mother, Sylvia, decides it's time Mary had a proper father and accepts a marriage offer from a British movie mogul. This, of course, means moving to England, much to the dismay of the three bachelor dads, especially Peter, who has fallen in love with Sylvia himself but has been afraid to admit it.

Director Emile Ardolino, whose first full-length feature film was *Dirty Dancing* (1987), took over from actor/director Leonard Nimoy for this sequel to *Three Men and a Baby*, which was also a number one (1988).

Steve Guttenberg made his name when he appeared in several of the *Police Academy* movies. Prior to those he featured in *Rollercoaster* (1977), *The Boys from Brazil* (1978) and *Diner* (1982).

Music: 'Waiting for a Star to Fall' (Boy Meets Girl), 'The Three Men Rap' (Tom Selleck, Steve Guttenberg and Ted Danson), 'Dance' (David Baerwald), 'Always Thinking of You' (Donna DeLory)

Video availability

The Top Five

Week of 15 February 1991
1. Three Men and a Little Lady
2. Dances with Wolves
3. Postcards from the Edge
4. Cyrano de Bergerac
5. Kindergarten Cop

GREEN CARD

8 March 1991	2 weeks*

Distributor:	Touchstone
Director:	Peter Weir
Producer:	Peter Weir

Screenplay:	Peter Weir
Music:	Hans Zimmer

CAST
Gérard Depardieu .... George Faure

It was not love at first sight for George Faure (Gérard Depardieu) and Brontë Parrish (Andie MacDowell) in Green Card. *He was looking for an American wife to stay in the country and she just wanted a husband to secure her dream apartment.*

Andie MacDowell . . . . *Brontë Parrish*
Bebe Neuwirth . . . . *Lauren*
Gregg Edelman . . . . *Phil*
Robert Prosky . . . . *Brontë's lawyer*
Jessie Keosian . . . . *Mrs Bird*
Ethan Philips . . . . *Gorsky*
Mary Louise Wilson . . . . *Mrs Sheehan*

Frenchman George needs an American wife so he can stay in the USA. American Brontë needs a husband to secure an apartment with the greenhouse she's always wanted. After a brief meeting, the two marry then go their separate ways. When the authorities begin to ask questions, George and Brontë find they must get to know each other very well, very quickly, in order to pass their marriage off as the real thing.

Australian director Peter Weir first made his name in 1975 with *Picnic at Hanging Rock*. His successes since then include *Gallipoli* (1981), *Witness* (1985) and *Dead Poets Society* (1989).

Gérard Depardieu has appeared in over 70 films in his native France. *Green Card* was the first major film in which he spoke English, and his first American movie.

Music: 'Storms In Africa' (Enya)

Video availability

The Top Five

Week of 8 March 1991
1. Green Card
2. Dances With Wolves
3. Three Men and a Little Lady
4. The Russia House
5. Pacific Heights

THE GODFATHER PART III

15 March 1991	1 week

Distributor: Paramount
Director: Francis Ford Coppola
Producer: Francis Ford Coppola
Screenplay: Mario Puzo, Francis Ford Coppola

Music: Carmine Coppola

CAST
Al Pacino . . . . *Michael Corleone*
Diane Keaton . . . . *Kay Adams*
Sofia Coppola . . . . *Mary Corleone*
Talia Shire . . . . *Connie Corleone Rizzi*

Andy Garcia . . . . *Vincent Mancini*
Eli Wallach . . . . *Don Altobello*
Joe Mantegna . . . . *Joey Zasa*
George Hamilton . . . . *B.J. Harrison*
Bridget Fonda . . . . *Grace Hamilton*

Godfather Michael Corleone is a lonely, grey-haired man who misses his wife, Kay, and wants to spend more time with his daughter, Mary. He decides to abandon crime and make his business concerns legitimate. He takes on Vincent Mancini but the young man remains attached to the old violent ways of the Mafia and has taken up with Corleone's daughter against the Godfather's wishes. As Corleone tries to break away from the Mafia he is forced back into the criminal world through his links with money laundering in the Catholic Church.

Francis Ford Coppola was reluctant to make another *Godfather* sequel. Paramount started looking around for another director and Robert Benton and James Bridges were considered, by which time Coppola had changed his mind as he needed to raise some cash.

When Al Pacino demanded a ridiculous fee for the movie, it was decided to kill him off at the start. When he found out about the plans, he immediately dropped his price. Robert Duvall turned down his original role as Tom Hagen, the Corleone lawyer, after he was refused equal billing and the same fees

as Al Pacino. Winona Ryder, who was to play Michael's daughter, Mary, claimed she was suffering from exhaustion just as filming was about to commence. Director Francis Ford Coppola replaced her with his own daughter, Sofia.

The original budget for the movie was $44 million, but the film ended up costing more than $65 million due to production delays.

At an early screening at a cinema in Long Island, a real shoot-out took place, leaving a 15-year-old boy dead and another seriously injured.

Music: 'Promise Me You'll Remember' (Love Theme from *The Godfather Part III*; Harry Connick Jr), 'To Each His Own' (Al Martino)

Video availability

The Top Five

Week of 15 March 1991
1. The Godfather: Part III
2. Green Card
3. Dances With Wolves
4. Three Men and a Little Lady
5. The Russia House

DANCES WITH WOLVES

29 March 1991	3 weeks

Distributor: Guild
Director: Kevin Costner
Producer: Jim Wilson, Kevin Costner
Screenplay: Michael Blake
Music: John Barry

CAST
Kevin Costner . . . . *Lt John Dunbar*
Mary McDonnell . . . . *Stands with a Fist*
Graham Greene . . . . *Kicking Bird*
Rodney A Grant . . . . *Wind in his Hair*
Floyd Red Crow Westerman . . . *Ten Bears*
Tantoo Cardinal . . . . *Black Shawl*
Robert Pastorelli . . . . *Timmons*
Charles Rocket . . . . *Lt Elgin*

During the American Civil War, Lt John Dunbar makes his way to a distant outpost on the frontier where he is completely alone apart from his horse. His only visitor is a lone wolf until an Indian discovers him. After a difficult start, Dunbar slowly befriends the whole tribe of Indians and eventually decides to become one of them, calling himself

Dances with Wolves. Speaking none of the Sioux's Lakota language, he manages to communicate with the Indians with the help of Stands with a Fist, a white woman who was adopted by the tribe. When the American soldiers eventually remember Dunbar's existence and come looking for him, they consider him a traitor and the Indians their enemy.

Kevin Costner found it impossible to get a movie studio to back him on the project because of the length of the film (183 minutes) and the amount of Sioux Lakota language with subtitles, which he insisted remained rather than have them speak English. The project finally got off the ground thanks to foreign backing. It was Costner's debut as a director. He made his acting debut in a movie called *Sizzle Beach, U.S.A.* (made in 1978 but released in the early 1980s), which was re-released after his success in *Dances with Wolves* with the credit reading 'Special Guest Star Kevin Costner'. Costner also had a part in *The Big Chill* (1983), in which he spoke just one line, and appeared as a corpse in the opening credits sequence. After completing *Dances with Wolves*, the tribe of Sioux Indians admitted Costner as a full tribal member.

Lt John Dunbar (Kevin Costner) carries the injured Stands with a Fist (Mary McDonnell) back to her Indian tribe. She has been adopted by the Sioux and helped Dunbar communicate and befriend the local Indians.

Academy Awards: Best Film (Producers Jim Wilson and Kevin Costner), Best Direction (Kevin Costner), Best Screenplay (Michael Blake), Best Cinematography (Dean Semler), Best Editing (Neil Travis), Best Original Score (John Barry), Best Sound (Russell Williams II, Jeffrey Perkins, Bill W. Benton and Greg Watkins)

Video availability

The Top Five

Week of 29 March 1991
1. Dances with Wolves
2. Green Card
3. Look Who's Talking Too
4. The Godfather: Part III
5. Awakenings

HIGHLANDER II: THE QUICKENING

19 April 1991	1 week

Distributor:	Entertainment
Director:	Russell Mulcahy
Producer:	Peter S. Davis, William Panzer
Screenplay:	Peter Bellwood
Music:	Stewart Copeland

The Highlander Connor MacLeod from the planet Zeist has given up his immortality for life on earth and is joined by his sidekick Ramirez. MacLeod helps scientists from an unethical organization to create a shield, projected into space, that acts as the ozone layer. The evil dictator on Zeist is wreaking havoc on earth, forcing MacLeod out of retirement.

CAST
Christopher Lambert . . . *Connor MacLeod*
Sean Connery . . . . *Ramirez*
Virginia Madsen . . . . *Louise Marcus*
Michael Ironside . . . . *Katana*
John C. McGinley . . . . *David Blake*
Allan Rich . . . . *Alan Neyman*
Steven Grives . . . . *Hamlet*

The Top Five

Week of 19 April 1991
1. Highlander II: The Quickening
2. Sleeping with the Enemy
3. Dances with Wolves
4. Awakenings
5. Green Card

The original *Highlander* did not make it to number one, but went close, reaching number two in 1986. It was kept off the top spot by the sequel *Aliens*.

The music was written by Stewart Copeland, once a member of the successful pop group Police. Among his other credits is the incidental music and theme to the successful TV series *The Equalizer*, starring Edward Woodward.

Music: 'Trust' (Heeren Stevens), 'As Time Goes By' (Brenda Russell), 'Who's That Man' (The Magnetic AKA), 'Haunted' (Glenn Hughes)

Video availability

SLEEPING WITH THE ENEMY

26 April 1991	3 weeks

Distributor:	Twentieth Century-Fox
Director:	Joseph Ruben
Producer:	Leonard Goldberg
Screenplay:	Ronald Bass
Music:	Jerry Goldsmith

CAST
Julia Roberts .... *Sara/Laura*
Patrick Bergin .... *Martin*
Kevin Anderson .... *Ben*
Elizabeth Lawrence .... *Chloe*

The beautiful young Laura is married to Martin, a possessive, pedantic and violent man. In order to escape from her wealthy but hellish life, Laura fakes her own death and establishes herself with a new identity in a distant state. She starts to build a new life with the help of her neighbour, Ben. However, her well-thought-out plan had one flaw, which gives the now very angry Martin enough clues to track her down and threaten her life.

The movie was shot in North and South Carolina and the seaside resort of Wilmington, where the couple's five-room beach house was purpose built as no suitable property could be found.

Julia Roberts made her movie debut as a musician in a pop group in *Satisfaction* (1987). Roberts took percussion lessons in order to qualify for an audition for the part.

Music: 'Brown Eyed Girl' (Van Morrison)

Video availability

The Top Five

Week of 26 April 1991
1. Sleeping with the Enemy
2. Highlander II: The Quickening
3. Dances with Wolves
4. Green Card
5. Awakenings

MISERY

17 May 1991	3 weeks

Distributor:	Columbia
Director:	Rob Reiner
Producer:	Andrew Scheinman, Rob Reiner
Screenplay:	William Goldman
Music:	Marc Shaiman

CAST
James Caan.............. *Paul Sheldon*
Kathy Bates .... *Annie Wilkes*
Frances Sternhagen........... *Virginia*
Richard Farnsworth............ *Buster*
Lauren Bacall .... *Marcia Sindell*
Graham Jarvis .... *Libby*
J.T. Walsh .... *Chief Sherman Douglas*

Paul Sheldon is a well-known author of romance novels featuring a character named Misery Chastaine. Driving through thick snow in Colorado, he is involved in a car crash and is rescued by ex-nurse

Annie Wilkes. At first Annie appears only concerned with nursing Sheldon back to health, but as he begins to recover and thinks about going home she turns ugly and reveals that she's obsessed with Sheldon's writing, particularly with Misery who is to be killed off in his next book. The psychotic woman holds Sheldon prisoner in her remote house and forces him to write the character back into the plot or else.

Much of the exteriors were shot in Nevada, after which the house was reconstructed in California where filming was completed.

The Top Five

Week of 17 May 1991
1. Misery
2. The Doors
3. Sleeping with the Enemy
4. Dances with Wolves
5. The Hard Way

Bette Midler was considered for the role of Annie Wilkes, but she turned it down believing it was the wrong part for her image.

William Goldman has written screenplays for four other number one movies: *Butch Cassidy and the Sundance Kid* (1970), *All The President's Men* (1976) *A Bridge Too Far* (1977) and *Maverick* (1994).

Academy Awards: Best Actress (Kathy Bates)

Video availability

THE SILENCE OF THE LAMBS

7 June 1991	4 weeks

Distributor:	Orion
Director:	Jonathan Demme
Producer:	Edward Saxon, Kenneth Utt, Ron Bozman
Screenplay:	Ted Tally
Music:	Howard Shore

CAST

Jodie Foster	. . . .	*Clarice Starling*
Anthony Hopkins	. . . . .	*Dr Hannibal Lecter*
Scott Glenn	. . . .	*Jack Crawford*
Ted Livine	. . . .	*James Gumb*
Anthony Heald	. . . . . .	*Dr Frederick Chilton*
Brooke Smith	. . . .	*Catherine Martin*
Diane Baker	. . . .	*Senator Ruth Martin*
Kasi Lemmons	. . . .	*Ardelia Mapp*

Clarice Starling, a trainee FBI agent, is recruited to win the confidence of psychopathic killer Hannibal Lecter, a former psychiatrist who developed an urge to eat his victims. He is believed to hold key information on the identity and whereabouts of a crazed serial killer dubbed 'Buffalo Bill' who is terrorizing the country. With a young girl missing, believed to be Buffalo Bill's next victim, Starling is racing against time to fathom Lecter's clues and track down the maniac.

The film was based on the novel by Thomas Harris, who had another of his stories, *Red Dragon*, filmed in 1986, which also featured the character Hannibal Lecter, then played by Brian Cox.

At the age of four, Jodie Foster appeared in a Coppertone Sun Oil advertisement in 1966. She also appeared in several Disney films as a child, and turned up in episodes of the TV series *The Partridge Family* and *My Three Sons*. Her role of Clarice

FBI trainee Clarice Starling (Jodie Foster) is sent to meet the psychopath Dr Hannibal Lecter (Anthony Hopkins) in his cell in Baltimore Asylum. He plays games with Starling as she tries to get information on a serial killer on the loose.

Starling was originally offered to and turned down by Michelle Pfeiffer.

Academy Awards: Best film (Producers Edward Saxon, Kenneth Utt and Ron Bozman), Best Direction (Jonathan Demme), Best Actor (Anthony Hopkins), Best Actress (Jodie Foster), Best Screenplay (Ted Tally)

Video availability

> ### *The Top Five*
>
> *Week of 7 June 1991*
> 1. The Silence of the Lambs
> 2. Mermaids
> 3. Misery
> 4. LA Story
> 5. Sleeping with the Enemy

NAKED GUN 2½: THE SMELL OF FEAR

5 July 1991	2 weeks

Distributor:	UIP
Director:	David Zucker
Producer:	Robert K. Weiss
Screenplay:	David Zucker, Pat Proft
Music:	Ira Newborn

CAST
Leslie Nielsen . . . . *Lt Frank Drebin*
Priscilla Presley . . . . *Jane Spencer*
George Kennedy . . . . *Capt. Ed Hocken*
O.J. Simpson . . . . *Nordberg*
Robert Goulet . . . . *Quentin Hapsburg*
Richard Griffiths *Dr Meinheimer/Earl Hacker*
Jacqueline Brookes *Commissioner Brumford*

Lieutenant Frank Drebin is back on the scene in hot pursuit of bad man Quentin Hapsburg who kidnaps a wheelchair-bound oil baron and replaces him with a lookalike in an attempt to change the country's energy policies. Drebin also tries to rekin-

dle the flame with Jane Spencer, who lost interest in him two years ago.

Although Robert Goulet has made a habit of appearing in screen comedies, often sending up his own smooth character, his real forté is the musical stage. He was a Broadway star, appearing in shows like *Camelot*, with Richard Burton and Julie Andrews, long before he sought silver screen success. The film features cameo appearances by other veteran stars, including Zsa Zsa Gabor and Mel Torme.

Video availability

> ### *The Top Five*
>
> *Week of 5 July 1991*
> 1. Naked Gun 2½: The Smell of Fear
> 2. The Silence of the Lambs
> 3. The Pope Must Die
> 4. The Hairdresser's Husband
> 5. A Kiss Before Dying

THELMA AND LOUISE

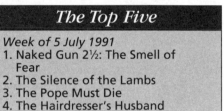

19 July 1991	1 week

Distributor:	UIP
Director:	Ridley Scott
Producer:	Ridley Scott, Mimi Polk
Screenplay:	Callie Khouri
Music:	Hans Zimmer

CAST
Susan Sarandon . . . . *Louise*
Geena Davis . . . . *Thelma*
Harvey Keitel . . . . *Hal*
Michael Madsen . . . . *Jimmy*
Christopher McDonald . . . . *Darryl*
Brad Pitt . . . . *J.D.*

Housewife Thelma is fed up with her chauvinistic husband Darryl and Louise is bored with her job as a waitress so they decide to take a break from

routine and go on a fishing trip together. They pile into Louise's T-Bird and hit the road, stopping along the way at a roadside club for a drink. Thelma attracts a man who becomes pushy and attempts to rape her in a car park. When Louise arrives on the scene, she pulls a gun and shoots him dead. Certain the police won't believe their story, they take to the road again and head for Mexico, getting themselves

> ### *The Top Five*
>
> *Week of 19 July 1991*
> 1. Thelma and Louise
> 2. Naked Gun 2½: The Smell of Fear
> 3. The Silence of the Lambs
> 4. Hudson Hawk
> 5. The Hairdresser's Husband

In Thelma and Louise *best friends Thelma (Geena Davis) and Louise (Susan Sarandon) take time out to get away from their everyday lives, but their planned short break turns into a journey of self discovery that ends in tragedy.*

into more and more trouble, and caring less and less, as they go along.

Actresses including Cher, Goldie Hawn, Julia Roberts and Michelle Pfeiffer were considered for the title roles.

Susan Sarandon made her film debut in a 1969 movie called *Joe*, directed by John G. Avildsen (*Rocky*, *Rocky V*). Her first number one movie was *The Witches of Eastwick* (1987).

Academy Awards: Best Original Screenplay (Callie Khouri)

Music: 'Part of Me Part of You' (Glenn Frey), 'Badlands', 'Tennessee Plates' (Charlie Sexton), 'The Ballad of Lucy Jordan' (Marianne Faithfull), 'Better Not Look Down' (B.B. King)

Video availability

ROBIN HOOD: PRINCE OF THIEVES

26 July 1991	2 weeks

Distributor:	Warner
Director:	Kevin Reynolds
Producer:	John Watson, Pen Densham, Richard B. Lewis
Screenplay:	Pen Densham, John Watson
Music:	Michael Kamen

CAST
Kevin Costner . . . . *Robin of Locksley*
Morgan Freeman . . . . *Azeem*
Mary Elizabeth Mastrantonio . . . . *Marian*
Christian Slater . . . . *Will Scarlett*
Alan Rickman . . . . . *Sheriff of Nottingham*
Geraldine McEwan . . . . *Mortianna*
Michael McShane . . . . *Friar Tuck*
Brian Blessed . . . . *Lord Locksley*

In 1194, Robin of Locksley escapes from a prison in Jerusalem with his colleague Azeem. The pair head for England, where Robin learns that his father has been murdered by the Sheriff of Nottingham and King John has taken over the leadership of the country from the absent King Richard. He takes up with Little John and his friends who, driven from their homes by the Sheriff and his men, are forced to live in Sherwood Forest. Renamed Robin Hood, he becomes their leader and teaches them how to fight as they prepare for an attack on Nottingham Castle. Maid Marian provides assistance and kindles more than a little romantic interest in Robin. The Sheriff has his own plans to marry Maid Marian and orders Robin to be killed while forcing Marian's hand in marriage. Luckily Robin Hood is at hand.

Sean Connery makes an unbilled cameo appearance as King Richard, having played Robin Hood himself,

In Robin Hood: Prince of Thieves, *the crazed Sheriff of Nottingham (Alan Rickman) crosses swords with Robin Hood (Kevin Costner) for the honour of Maid Marion (Mary Elizabeth Mastrantonio).*

opposite Audrey Hepburn, in the 1976 *Robin and Marian*. His involvement in *Robin Hood: Prince of Thieves* was kept a secret during filming and critics who saw previews were asked not to give it away when writing their reviews.

The film was Kevin Costner's second number one of the year in a very different role from his first, *Dances with Wolves*. Costner originally adopted an English accent for the movie, but once they began shooting, decided to abandon it.

Bryan Adams' hit song stayed at number one in the British charts for a record-breaking 16 weeks. In the USA it topped the charts for seven weeks. Peter Cetera and Julia Fordham had originally recorded the song with different lyrics.

Music: '(Everything I Do) I Do It For You' (Bryan Adams)

Video availability

The Top Five

Week of 26 July 1991
1. Robin Hood: Prince of Thieves
2. Thelma and Louise
3. Naked Gun 2½: The Smell of Fear
4. In Bed With Madonna
5. The Silence of the Lambs

BACKDRAFT

9 August 1991	2 weeks

Distributor:	UIP
Director:	Ron Howard
Producer:	Richard B. Lewis, Pen Densham, John Watson
Screenplay:	Gregory Widen
Music:	Hans Zimmer

CAST

Kurt Russell	Stephen McCaffrey/Elder McCaffrey
William Baldwin	Brian McCaffrey
Robert De Niro	Donald Rimgale
Donald Sutherland	Ronald Bartel
Jennifer Jason Leigh	Jennifer
Scott Glenn	John Adcox
Rebecca DeMornay	Helen

The McCaffrey brothers, Stephen and Brian, have spent much of their lives as rivals and continue to be so when they both join the Chicago Fire Department. They each deal in their own way with the memory of their father's death rescuing a child from a burning building. When they're not battling with each other they're battling blazes, a risky job made even more hazardous when it seems an arsonist is on the loose. Fire Department investigator Donald Rimgale is working as fast as he can to identify the pyromaniac, although Brian has his own ideas about the culprit.

Gregory Widen, who wrote the screenplay, was a former firefighter. The fire scenes were shot in a specially controlled set that was built for the movie at enormous expense. Until recently, the stage was a tourist attraction at the Universal Studios in Califor-

nia where scenes were re-created for spectators.

This was William Baldwin's first starring role, following his debut as a platoon soldier in *Born on the Fourth of July* (1990). He also appeared in *Internal Affairs* (1990) and *Flatliners* (1991).

Video availability

The Top Five

Week of 9 August 1991
1. Backdraft
2. Robin Hood: Prince of Thieves
3. Edward Scissorhands
4. The Rocketeer
5. Thelma and Louise

TERMINATOR 2: JUDGMENT DAY

23 August 1991	7 weeks

Distributor:	Guild
Director:	James Cameron
Producer:	James Cameron
Screenplay:	James Cameron, William Wisher
Music:	Brad Fiedel

CAST
Arnold Schwarzenegger . . . . . *Terminator*
Linda Hamilton . . . . *Sarah Connor*
Edward Furlong . . . . *John Connor*
Robert Patrick *T-1000*
Earl Boen . . . . *Dr Silberman*
Joe Morton . . . . *Miles Dyson*
S. Epatha Merkerson . . . . . . *Tarissa Dyson*
Castulo Guerra . . . . *Enrique Salceda*

In 1997 John Connor is a young boy living with foster parents. His mother, Sarah Connor, has been committed to an asylum. She escaped an assassination attempt by a cyborg sent back from the future (in *Terminator*) and knows that her son will grow up to be the leader of the human resistance to the android takeover of the world. She also knows that she and her son are in danger from more androids sent back from the future to kill them. The authorities just think she is insane and keep her under maximum security. Her worst fears are realized when a T-1000 android and a cyborg Terminator, both in human guise, appear looking for John. The Terminator this time round, however, has been sent to protect him. With stunning special effects, the two terminators battle it out for John's life.

Special effects genius Dennis Muren scored another Academy Award for his work on this film. No other living person holds more Oscars than Muren, with a

total of eight to his name for his efforts on films including *E.T.*, *The Abyss* and *Jurassic Park*.

Director James Cameron also directed and wrote the screenplay for *Aliens* (1986), and co-wrote the screenplay for *Rambo: First Blood Part 2* (1985), both of which were sequels although he didn't work on the originals.

The film had bad language and violence edited for British audiences.

The reported cost of the movie was in excess of $100 million, with an estimated $15 million going to Arnold Schwarzenegger.

Academy Awards: Best Make-up (Stan Winston and Jeff Dawn), Best Sound (Tom Johnson, Gary Rydstrom, Gary Summers and Lee Orloff), Best Sound Effects Editing (Gary Rydstrom and Gloria S. Borders), Best Visual Effects (Dennis Muren, Stan Winston, Gene Warren Jr and Robert Skotak)

Music: 'Bad to the Bone' (George Thorogood and the Destroyers), 'You Could Be Mine' (Guns N' Roses), 'Guitars, Cadillacs' (Dwight Yoakam)

Video availability

The Top Five

Week of 23 August 1991
1. Terminator 2: Judgment Day
2. Robin Hood: Prince of Thieves
3. Backdraft
4. Thelma and Louise
5. Truly Madly Deeply

THE COMMITMENTS

11 October 1991	3 weeks

Distributor:	Twentieth Century-Fox
Director:	Alan Parker
Producer:	Roger Randall-Cutler, Lynda Myles
Screenplay:	Dick Clement, Ian La Frenais, Roddy Doyle
Music:	G. Mark Roswell (Supervision) Paul Bushnell (Arrangements) John Hughes (Co-ordination)

CAST

Robert Arkins	*Jimmy Rabbitte*
Michael Aherne	*Steven Clifford*
Angeline Ball	*Imelda Quirke*
Maria Doyle	*Natalie Murphy*
Dave Finnegan	*Mickah Wallace*
Bronagh Gallagher	*Bernie*
Felim Gormley	*Dean Fay*
Andrew Strong	*Deco Cuffe*

Jimmy Rabbitte is an Irish musician with big-time dreams. He forms and manages a ten piece group of young hopefuls from Dublin who call themselves 'The Commitments'. Personality clashes among the band members make it difficult for Jimmy to keep the band together long enough to get some engagements. With their powerful renditions of 1960s soul classics, they do manage to develop a following and it seems success is well within reach, but temperaments take over and the group just can't keep it together.

Writers Dick Clement and Ian La Frenais wrote and created many hit TV comedy series, including *The Likely Lads*, *Porridge* and *Auf Wiedersehen Pet*.

More than 3000 hopeful Irish actors and musicians auditioned for parts in the movie. Almost all those cast were qualified musicians with little or no acting experience.

Music: 'Mustang Sally', 'Chain of Fools', 'Mr Pitiful', 'In The Midnight Hour', 'Take Me To The River', 'I Can't Stand The Rain'

Video availability

The Top Five

Week of 11 October 1991
1. The Commitments
2. Terminator 2: Judgment Day
3. Stepping Out
4. Robin Hood: Prince of Thieves
5. Meeting Venus

DEAD AGAIN

1 November 1991	1 week

Distributor:	Paramount
Director:	Kenneth Branagh
Producer:	Lindsay Doran, Charles H. Maguire
Screenplay:	Scott Frank
Music:	Patrick Doyle

CAST

Kenneth Branagh	*Mike Church/Roman Strauss*
Emma Thompson	*Grace/Margaret Strauss*
Andy Garcia	*Gary Baker*
Derek Jacobi	*Franklyn Madson*
Robin Williams	*Dr Cozy Carlisle*
Wayne Knight	*Piccolo Pete*
Hanna Schygulla	*Inga*

Doctor Cozy Carlisle, at the request of private detective Mike Church, tries to help Grace, a woman who has lost her memory and is troubled by vivid nightmares. By using hypnosis, the doctor takes Grace back to her past and discovers that in a previous life she was married to an accomplished pianist and was murdered with a pair of scissors, a crime for which her husband was sentenced to death. Grace becomes terrified that Mike was her murderer in his past life and that he will repeat his past deeds. Mike is convinced that she is wrong and sets out to prove that she was in fact murdered by someone else.

Branagh and Emma Thompson are husband and wife in real life.

You won't find Robin Williams' name on the credits of this film as producers were apparently worried moviegoers would expect a comedy if they saw Williams' name.

Video availability

The Top Five

Week of 1 November 1991
1. Dead Again
2. The Commitments
3. Boyz N The Hood
4. City Slickers
5. Robin Hood: Prince of Thieves

CITY SLICKERS

8 November 1991	1 week

Distributor: First Independent/Castle Rock
Director: Ron Underwood
Producer: Irby Smith
Screenplay: Lowell Ganz, Babaloo Mandel
Music: Marc Shaiman

CAST
Billy Crystal .... *Mitch Robbins*
Daniel Stern .... *Phil Berquist*
Bruno Kirby .... *Ed Furillo*
Patricia Wettig .... *Barbara Robbins*
Helen Slater .... *Bonnie Rayburn*
Jack Palance .... *Curly*
Noble Willingham .... *Clay Stone*
Tracey Walter .... *Cookie*

Mitch, Phil and Ed are three friends suffering from mid-life crisis and a host of individual problems. They decide to leave New York and go on a two-week commercially run cattle drive in the Wild West, in order to escape from life's everyday routine. They find themselves working as real cowboys under the guidance of trail boss Curly, driving a herd of cattle from one ranch to another. Beset by problems along the way, these city folk are forced to face up to the challenges of hard work and find that it does them a world of good, allowing them to resolve their inner conflicts and regain peace of mind.

Jack Palance picked up the Oscar for Best Supporting Actor, having had only one other nomination in his entire career, in 1953 for *Shane*. Keen to show what good shape he was in, Palance performed push ups in front of an astonished Academy audience.

The team returned for *City Slickers 2 - The Search for Curly's Gold*, in 1994, which flopped at the box office.

Academy Awards: Best Supporting Actor (Jack Palance)

Video availability

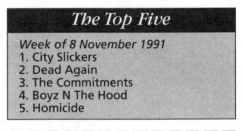

The Top Five

Week of 8 November 1991
1. City Slickers
2. Dead Again
3. The Commitments
4. Boyz N The Hood
5. Homicide

THE FISHER KING

15 November 1991	3 weeks

Distributor: Columbia Tri-Star
Director: Terry Gilliam
Producer: Debra Hill, Lynda Obst
Screenplay: Richard LaGravenese
Music: George Fenton

CAST
Robin Williams .... *Parry*
Jeff Bridges .... *Jack Lucas*
Amanda Plummer .... *Lydia*
Mercedes Ruehl .... *Anne Napolitano*
Michael Jeter .... *Homeless cabaret singer*

Selfish radio presenter Jack Lucas finds his life goes to pieces after a caller shoots several youngsters in a bar following a remark he makes on air. After a slide into alcoholism some years later, Lucas decides to commit suicide but is stopped by a street bum, Parry. The eccentric Parry is certain he is a knight and knows the whereabouts of the Holy Grail and convinces Lucas to help him in his search.

Robin Williams had previously worked with Gilliam in the 1989 *Adventures of Baron Munchausen* where he played the King of the Moon. His performance in *The Fisher King* earned him an Oscar nomination but he lost to Anthony Hopkins for *The Silence of the Lambs*.

Director Gilliam had tremendous difficulty filming a thousand extras waltzing in New York's Grand

Top Ten Films of 1991
1 Robin Hood: Prince of Thieves
2 Terminator 2: Judgment Day
3 The Silence of the Lambs
4 Three Men and a Little Lady
5 Home Alone
6 Dances with Wolves
7 Sleeping with the Enemy
8 Naked Gun 2½: The Smell of Fear
9 Kindergarten Cop
10 The Commitments

Central Station. The producers visited dancing schools across New York, but found very few students could waltz. They ended up with a choreographer and crew sitting on the station steps, teaching the extras as they went.

Academy Awards: Best Supporting Actress (Mercedes Ruehl)

Music: 'How About You' (Harry Nilsson), 'I'm Sorry' (Brenda Lee), 'The Power' (Chill Rob G)

The Top Five

Week of 15 November 1991
1. The Fisher King
2. Shattered
3. The Commitments
4. Dead Again
5. City Slickers

Video availability

HOT SHOTS!

6 December 1991	2 weeks

Distributor:	Twentieth Century-Fox
Director:	Jill Abrahams
Producer:	Bill Badalato
Screenplay:	Jim Abrahams
Music:	Sylvester LeVay

CAST
Charlie Sheen . . . . *Topper Harley*
Cary Elwes . . . . *Kent Gregory*
Valeria Golino . . . . *Ramada Thompson*
Lloyd Bridges . . . . *Admiral Benson*
Kevin Dunn . . . . *Lt Commander Block*
Jon Cryer . . . . *Jim (Wash Out) Pfaffenbach*
William O'Leary . . . . *Pete (Dead Meat) Thompson*

In this spoof action movie two hot-headed pilots, Kent and Topper, spend their lives either screaming abuse at each other over the radio as they fly their respective planes, or attempting to beat each other's brains out on the ground. Kent blames Topper's father, who was also a pilot, for the death of his own dad in a plane crash some years earlier.

The film contains scenes that parody a number of other movies, including *Top Gun*, *An Officer and a Gentleman*, *Gone with the Wind* and *Dances with Wolves*. A sequel followed in 1993, *Hot Shots: Part Deux!*

Efrem Zimbalist Jr, who shot to fame as Stu Bailey in the successful American TV series from the 1950s and 60s *77 Sunset Strip*, makes a cameo appearance as a villain.

Video availability

The Top Five

Week of 6 December 1991
1. Hot Shots!
2. The Fisher King
3. Shattered
4. Point Break
5. The Commitments

THE ADDAMS FAMILY

20 December 1991	4 weeks

Distributor:	Paramount
Director:	Barry Sonnenfeld
Producer:	Scot Rudin
Screenplay:	Caroline Thompson, Larry Wilson
Music:	Marc Shaiman

CAST
Anjelica Huston . . . . *Morticia Addams*
Raul Julia . . . . *Gomez Addams*
Christopher Lloyd . . . . *Uncle Fester*
Dan Hedaya . . . . *Tully Alford*
Elizabeth Wilson . . . . *Abigail Craven*
Judith Malina . . . . *Granny*
Carel Struycken . . . . *Lurch*

The creepy comic Addams family are joined by who they think is their long lost Uncle Fester. He looks like and sounds like Uncle Fester but is in fact an imposter, sent by the Addams's crooked lawyer to swindle them out of their small fortune hidden in the house. Gomez and Morticia are slow to suspect,

The Top Five

Week of 20 December 1991
1. The Addams Family
2. Hot Shots!
3. The Fisher King
4. Shattered
5. The Commitments

In The Addams Family *a long-lost family member arrives at the Addams mansion and is greeted by the morbid family headed by Morticia (Anjelica Huston) and Gomez (Raul Julia).*

but with the help of 'Thing' their household eventually returns to what they consider 'normality'.

The big-screen version of *The Addams Family* was adapted more from the Charles Addams original cartoons that appeared in *The New Yorker* than from the popular, but short-lived, ABC television series from the 1960s. It was the debut film for Barry Sonnenfeld.

Music: 'Playmates' (The Kipper Kids), 'Mamushka' (Raul Julia and Christopher Lloyd)

Video availability

DELICATESSEN

17 January 1992	1 week

Distributor:	Electric
Director:	Jean-Pierre Jeunet, Marc Caro
Producer:	Claudie Ossard
Screenplay:	Jean-Pierre Jeunet, Marc Caro, Gilles Adrien
Music:	Carlos D'Alessio

CAST
Dominique Pinon . . . . *Louison*
Marie-Laure Dougnac . . . . *Julie*
Jean-Claude Dreyfus . . . . *Butcher*
Rufus . . . . *Robert*
Ticky Holgado . . . . *Husband*
Anne-Marie Pisani . . . . *Wife*

In futuristic France there is a shortage of meat. The landlord of a block of derelict flats runs a butcher's shop on the ground floor. From somewhere the butcher procures meat for his tenants, usually after the disappearance of one of the many caretakers he takes on. Louison, a circus clown, arrives as the new caretaker and he and the butcher's short-sighted daughter, Julie, fall in love. As the butcher plans Louison's death and the making of sausages, the vegetarian underground movement make plans to save Louison and Julie.

The film was the debut for co-directors Jean-Pierre Jeunet and Marc Caro. Caro makes an appearance in the film as a cave dweller.

Video availability

The Top Five

Week of 17 January 1992
1. Delicatessen
2. Billy Bathgate
3. The Addams Family
4. Bill and Ted's Bogus Journey
5. Merci La Vie

FRANKIE AND JOHNNY

24 January 1992	1 week

Distributor:	Paramount
Director:	Garry Marshall
Producer:	Garry Marshall
Screenplay:	Terrence McNally
Music:	Marvin Hamlisch

CAST

Al Pacino .... Johnny
Michelle Pfeiffer .... Frankie
Hector Elizondo .... Nick
Nathan Lane.................... Tim
Kate Nelligan .... Cora
Jane Morris................... Nedda
Greg Lewis .... Tino

Recently released from prison for forgery, Johnny finds a job in a fast-food café. He is smitten by one of the waitresses, Frankie. She resists his advances and his charms and tries to keep her emotional distance, having been badly hurt before.

The film was based on Terrence McNally's play *Frankie and Johnny in the Clair De Lune*, which opened in New York in 1987, starring Kathy Bates. It was director Garry Marshall's third hit in a row, following on from *Beaches* (1989) and *Pretty Woman* (1990).

Music: 'Frankie and Johnny' (James Intveld), 'What A Fool Believes' (The Doobie Brothers), 'The Devil Made Me Do It' (Golden Earring), 'It Must Be Love' (Rickie Lee Jones), 'Until You Let Go' (Peter Beckett and Jeannette Clinger)

Video availability

The Top Five

Week of 24 January 1992
1. Frankie and Johnny
2. Freddy's Dead: The Final Nightmare
3. Delicatessen
4. Billy Bathgate
5. The Addams Family

JFK

31 January 1992	3 weeks

Distributor:	Warner
Director:	Oliver Stone
Producer:	A. Kitman Ho, Oliver Stone
Screenplay:	Oliver Stone, Zachary Sklar
Music:	John Williams

CAST

Kevin Costner .... Jim Garrison
Sissy Spacek.............. Liz Garrison
Joe Pesci .... David Ferrie
Tommy Lee Jones............ Clay Shaw
Gary Oldman .... Lee Harvey Oswald
Jay O. Sanders .... Lou Ivon
Michael Rooker .... Bill Broussard
Laurie Metcalf .... Susie Cox

Convinced that Lee Harvey Oswald was just one of a team involved in the killing, and probably didn't even fire the fatal shot, New Orleans District Attorney Jim Garrison becomes obsessed with finding out the truth about President Kennedy's assassination.

The screenplay for *JFK* is based on two books, *Crossfire: The Plot that Killed Kennedy* by Jim Marrs and *On the Trail of the Assassins* by Jim Garrison, who also makes an appearance in the film, playing the part of Earl Warren (of the Warren Report).

Joe Pesci began his career in show business as a singer, making records under the name of Joe Ritchie and later joining the one-time successful pop group Joey Dee and The Starliters as a guitarist. Jack Lemmon, Walter Matthau and John Candy made cameo appearances.

Academy Awards: Best Cinematography (Robert Richardson), Best Editing (Joe Hutshing and Peitro Scalia)

Video availability

The Top Five

Week of 31 January 1992
1. JFK
2. Frankie and Johnny
3. Blame It on the Bellboy
4. Delicatessen
5. Freddy's Dead: The Final Nightmare

STAR TREK VI: THE UNDISCOVERED COUNTRY

21 February 1992	1 week

Distributor:	UIP
Director:	Nicholas Meyer
Producer:	Ralph Winter, Steven-Charles Jaffe
Screenplay:	Nicholas Meyer, Denny Martin Flinn
Music:	Cliff Eidelman

CAST
William Shatner . . . . Kirk
Leonard Nimoy . . . . Spock
DeForest Kelley . . . . McCoy
James Doohan . . . . Scotty
Walter Koenig . . . . Chekov
Nichelle Nicholls . . . . Uhuru
George Takei . . . . Sulu
Kim Cattrall . . . . Lt Valeris

Captain Kirk and his team are sent, under protest, to escort the leader of the Klingons to earth for peace talks. But enemy agents are set on seeing the peace plans fail by assassinating the Klingon chief and making the crew of the *Enterprise* take the blame.

Nicholas Meyer made a return to the director's chair, having previously worked on *Star Trek II: The Wrath of Khan* (1982). *Star Trek III* and *Star Trek IV* were directed by Leonard Nimoy, and William Shatner had his turn with *Star Trek V*. He also directs one sequence in this sequel. *Star Trek VI* was believed to be the final chapter for Mr Spock and Captain Kirk, but *Star Trek VII (Star Trek Generations)* was in the pipeline.

Christian Slater makes a brief uncredited cameo appearance as a Corpsman, and Michael Dorn, who plays Lieutenant Worf in the TV series *Star Trek: The Next Generation*, makes an appearance as a Klingon lawyer.

Video availability

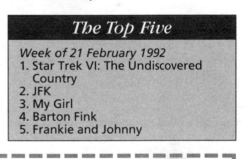

The Top Five
Week of 21 February 1992
1. Star Trek VI: The Undiscovered Country
2. JFK
3. My Girl
4. Barton Fink
5. Frankie and Johnny

FATHER OF THE BRIDE

28 February 1992	1 week

Distributor:	Touchstone
Director:	Charles Shyer
Producer:	Nancy Meyers, Carol Baum, Howard Rosenman
Screenplay:	Frances Goodrich, Albert Hackett, Nancy Meyers, Charles Shyer
Music:	Alan Silvestri

CAST
Steve Martin . . . . George Banks
Diane Keaton . . . . Nina Banks
Kimberly Williams . . . . Annie Banks
Kieran Culkin . . . . Matty Banks
George Newbern . . . . . . Bryan MacKenzie
Martin Short . . . . Franck Eggelhoffer
B.D. Wong . . . . Howard Weinstein
Peter Michael Goetz . . . . John MacKenzie

In this modern and almost unrecognizable remake of the 1950 original Steve Martin is George Banks, the head of a household that's turned upside down when his daughter Annie announces her plans to marry. While Annie and her mother try to ensure that everything is just perfect for the big day, George has apoplexy over the expense, the fuss, and the thought of losing his little girl.

Diane Keaton, who plays George Banks' wife, has had a successful acting career, including five number one films: all three of the *Godfather* films, *Reds* (1982) and *Manhattan Murder Mystery* (1994).

The Top Five
Week of 28 February 1992
1. The Father of the Bride
2. Star Trek VI: The Undiscovered Country
3. The Prince of Tides
4. JFK
5. Barton Fink

In Father of the Bride, *George Banks (Steve Martin) goes a little crazy when he learns that his daughter Annie (Kimberly Williams) has become engaged to Bryan MacKenzie (George Newbern).*

She has also tried her hand at directing. She directed the music video for Belinda Carlisle's first hit, 'Heaven is a Place on Earth', in 1987 and also an episode of the cult American TV series *Twin Peaks*.

Director Charles Shyer, who co-produced Goldie Hawn's film *Private Benjamin* (1981), is married to co-producer Nancy Meyers. In the early 1980s they formed their own production company.

Phoebe Cates, who starred in the *Gremlins* movies, was to play Annie but had to decline when she became pregnant.

Video availability

THE PRINCE OF TIDES

6 March 1992	1 week

Distributor:	Columbia
Director:	Barbra Streisand
Producer:	Barbra Streisand, Andrew Karsch
Screenplay:	Pat Conroy, Becky Johnston
Music:	James Newton Howard

CAST
Nick Nolte . . . . *Tom Wingo*
Barbra Streisand . . . . . . *Susan Lowenstein*
Blythe Danner . . . . *Sallie Wingo*
Kate Nelligan . . . . *Lila Wingo Newbury*
Jeroen Krabbé . . . . *Herbert Woodruff*
Melinda Dillon . . . . *Savannah Wingo*
George Carlin . . . . *Eddie Detreville*
Jason Gould . . . . *Bernard Woodruff*

Tom Wingo is facing a mid-life crisis with no job, his marriage (to Sallie) on the rocks, the begin-nings of a drink problem and a suicidal sister, Savannah. His sister's psychiatrist, Dr Susan Lowenstein, asks for his help in sorting out his sister's problems and before long he has fallen into her sympathetic arms.

Director Barbra Streisand became the third of only four women directors to date whose films have been Oscar nominated for Best Picture. The others are Randa Haines (*Children of a Lesser God*; 1986), Penny Marshall (*Awakenings*; 1990) and Jane

The Top Five

Week of 6 March 1992
1. The Prince of Tides
2. The Father of the Bride
3. The Last Boy Scout
4. Star Trek VI: The Undiscovered Country
5. Barton Fink

Campion (*The Piano*; 1993). *The Prince of Tides*, which was adapted from a novel by Pat Conroy, was Streisand's second self-directed movie, following *Yentl* (1984), which was a top five hit.

Jason Gould, who plays Barbra Streisand's son

Bernard, is in fact her real son. His father is actor Elliot Gould.

Music: 'For All We Know', 'Places That Belong To You' (Barbra Streisand)

Video availability

CAPE FEAR

13 March 1992	3 weeks

Distributor:	Universal
Director:	Martin Scorsese
Producer:	Barbara De Fina
Screenplay:	Wesley Strick
Music:	Bernard Herrmann

CAST
Robert De Niro . . . . *Max Cady*
Nick Nolte . . . . *Sam Bowden*
Jessica Lange . . . . *Leigh Bowden*
Juliette Lewis . . . . *Danielle Bowden*
Joe Don Baker . . . . *Claude Kersek*
Robert Mitchum . . . . *Lieutenant Elgart*
Gregory Peck . . . . *Lee Heller*
Martin Balsam . . . . *Judge*

In this remake of the 1962 classic Robert De Niro is Max Cady, a psychopath recently released from prison. Having gained a little knowledge of the law while inside, Cady is convinced that his old lawyer,

Sam Bowden, let him down. He stalks the Bowden family, particularly Sam's teenage daughter, Danielle, and finally unleashes a campaign of terror against them.

The original 1962 movie starred Gregory Peck and Robert Mitchum, both of whom make cameo appearances in Scorsese's film. Martin Balsam also appears in both. Musical director Elmer Bernstein adapted Bernard Herrmann's original 1962 score for the remake.

Video availability

The Top Five

Week of 13 March 1992
1. Cape Fear
2. The Prince of Tides
3. The Father of the Bride
4. Barton Fink
5. The Last Boy Scout

BUGSY

3 April 1992	2 weeks

Distributor:	Columbia TriStar
Director:	Barry Levinson
Producer:	Mark Johnson, Barry Levinson, Warren Beatty
Screenplay:	James Toback
Music:	Ennio Morricone

CAST
Warren Beatty . . . . *Bugsy Siegel*
Annette Bening . . . . *Virginia Hill*
Harvey Keitel . . . . *Mickey Cohen*
Ben Kingsley . . . . *Meyer Lansky*
Elliot Gould . . . . *Harry Greenberg*
Joe Mantegna . . . . *George Raft*
Bebe Neuwirth . . . . *Countess di Frasso*

Warren Beatty plays Bugsy in this biopic that chronicles the rise to notoriety of one of the 20th century's most famous gangsters. Sent to Los Angeles to take over the West Coast operations of

the Meyer Lansky gang, Bugsy Siegel sets out to fulfil his dream of opening a casino in the Nevada desert.

Beatty was nominated for an Oscar but lost out to Anthony Hopkins for his role in *The Silence of the Lambs*. Bebe Neuwirth, who plays Countess di Frasso, is probably best remembered as the neurotic psychologist Lilith Sternin-Crane in the American hit TV comedy series *Cheers*.

The movie is based on the book *We Only Kill Each Other: The Life and Bad Times of Bugsy Siegel* by Dean Jennings.

The Top Five

Week of 3 April 1992
1. Bugsy
2. Cape Fear
3. My Own Private Idaho
4. High Heels
5. Fried Green Tomatoes at the Whistle Stop Cafe

Music: 'Ac-Cent-Tchu-Ate The Positive' (Johnny Mercer), 'Candy' (Johnny Mercer), 'Come Rain or Shine' (Johnny Mercer), 'Fools Rush In (Where Angels Fear To Tread)' (Tommy Dorsey and His Orchestra), 'Long Ago and Far Away' (Jo Stafford), 'Why Don't You Do Right?' (Peggy Lee)

Video availability

HOOK

17 April 1992	2 weeks

Distributor:	Columbia TriStar
Director:	Steven Spielberg
Producer:	Kathleen Kennedy, Frank Marshall, Gerald R. Molen
Screenplay:	Jim V. Hart, Malia Scotch Marmo
Music:	John Williams

CAST

Dustin Hoffman . . . . *Captain Hook*
Robin Williams . . . *Peter Banning/Peter Pan*
Julia Roberts . . . . *Tinkerbell*
Bob Hoskins . . . . *Smee*
Maggie Smith . . . . *Granny Wendy*
Caroline Goodall . . . . *Moira*
Charlie Korsmo . . . . *Jack*
Amber Scott . . . . *Maggie*
Laurel Cronin . . . . *Liza*

Peter Banning, a busy company lawyer, takes his wife and children to London to visit Granny Wendy. The children are kidnapped by Captain Hook who rules, from his ship, a pirate town in Neverland. Banning is visited by Tinkerbell who insists that the only way he will get his young ones back is to go with her to visit Hook.

The film was only loosely based on the J.M. Barrie stories of Peter Pan. The co-writer of the screen story, Nick Castle, was originally in line to direct the film.

While filming *Hook*, Julia Roberts kept away from the press who were hounding her over her break-up with actor Kiefer Sutherland and her subsequent relationship with Jason Patric.

The many big names that appeared in the film included Phil Collins, Glenn Close and singer David Crosby.

The pirate ship *The Jolly Roger*, which was built specially for the movie, was 170 feet long, 35 feet wide and 70 feet high and cost over $1 million to

Kidnapped by Captain Hook (Dustin Hoffman), business lawyer Peter Banning (Robin Williams) is forced to rediscover his youth and travel back to Neverland to rescue his children in Hook.

construct. After completion of the film, the plan was to place the ship in a theme park, but because it wasn't strong enough to hold hundreds of visitors at a time it was finally broken down and destroyed.

Music: 'We Don't Wanna Grow Up', 'When You're Alone', 'Pick 'Em Up'

Video availability

The Top Five

Week of 17 April 1992
1. Hook
2. Final Analysis
3. Cape Fear
4. My Own Private Idaho
5. High Heels

THE HAND THAT ROCKS THE CRADLE

1 May 1992	2 weeks

Distributor:	Buena Vista
Director:	Curtis Hanson
Producer:	David Madden
Screenplay:	Amanda Silver
Music:	Graeme Revell

CAST
Annabella Sciorra . . . . *Claire Bartel*
Rebecca De Mornay . . . . . *Peyton Flanders*
Matt McCoy . . . . *Michael Bartel*
Ernie Hudson . . . . *Solomon*
Julianne Moore . . . . *Marlene*
Madeline Zima . . . . *Emma Bartel*
John de Lancie . . . . *Dr Mott*
Kevin Skousen . . . . *Marty*

Claire and Michael Bartel have a young daughter and another child on the way. They file charges against her gynaecologist for sexually abusing her. When other patients come forward with similar complaints, the doctor commits suicide, leaving his widow (Rebecca De Mornay) without a home, the worry of which causes her to miscarry. She seeks sinister revenge on the couple when she takes on a job as their nanny.

This was the first screenplay written by Amanda Silver, whose grandfather was the late Sidney Buchman. He wrote or co-wrote many screenplays, including those for *Here Comes Mr Jordan* (1941), starring Robert Montgomery and Claude Rains, *The Talk of the Town* (1942) with Cary Grant and Ronald Colman, *Jolson Sings Again* (1949) with Larry Parks, and *Cleopatra* (1963), starring Elizabeth Taylor and Richard Burton.

Annabella Sciorra was originally offered the part of the evil nanny, Peyton, and Rebecca De Mornay was to play Claire, but director Curtis Hanson felt the movie would work better if they swapped.

Video availability

The Top Five

Week of 1 May 1992
1. The Hand that Rocks the Cradle
2. Hook
3. Naked Lunch
4. Final Analysis
5. Ricochet

BASIC INSTINCT

15 May 1992	5 weeks*

Distributor:	Carolco/Guild
Director:	Paul Verhoeven
Producer:	Alan Marshall
Screenplay:	Joe Eszterhas
Music:	Jerry Goldsmith

CAST
Michael Douglas . . . *Detective Nick Curran*
Sharon Stone . . . . *Catherine Tramell*
George Dzundza . . . . *Gus*
Jeanne Tripplehorn . . . . . . *Dr Beth Garner*
Denis Arndt . . . . *Lt Walker*
Leilani Sarelle . . . . *Roxy*

Bruce A. Young . . . . *Andrews*
Chelcie Ross . . . . *Capt. Talcott*

San Francisco detective Nick Curran is under psychological review by the police shrink and ex-girlfriend, Dr Beth Garner, and is trying to lay off the drink and cigarettes. Like a bear with a sore head, he and his partner Gus head up an investigation into the murder of a man found with an ice pick in his chest after a bout of lovemaking. It emerges that the victim's girlfriend is the sexy authoress Catherine Tramell. She becomes their main suspect when it is revealed that one of her novels contains a similar murder. Curran may be trying to give up the booze and fags but not sex, and the temptation of Catherine gets the better of him.

In Basic Instinct *Detective Nick Curran (Michael Douglas) falls for his prime suspect, Catherine Tramell (Sharon Stone). She is the girlfriend of the murder victim who is discovered with an ice pick through his chest.*

Director Paul Verhoeven was born in Amsterdam and made a name for himself in the movie business in Holland. He later moved to Hollywood where he had great success with *Robocop* (1988) and *Total Recall* (1990), which also featured Sharon Stone.

Michael Douglas returns as a cop in San Francisco where he first made his name in the 1970s American TV series *The Streets of San Francisco*, playing Inspector Steve Keller alongside Karl Malden as Detective Lieutenant Mike Stone.

The Top Five

Week of 15 May 1992
1. Basic Instinct
2. The Hand that Rocks the Cradle
3. Grand Canyon
4. Howards End
5. Hook

Video availability

THE LAWNMOWER MAN

12 June 1992	1 week

Distributor:	First Independent
Director:	Brett Leonard
Producer:	Gimel Everett
Screenplay:	Brett Leonard, Gimel Everett
Music:	Dan Wyman

Dr Lawrence Angelo decides to try out one of his failed drug-therapy experiments, involving computer simulation, on a retarded gardener (Jeff Fahey) who spends much of his time mowing the lawn. The guinea pig finds his level of intellect improves and he decides to seek revenge on those who have treated him badly.

CAST
Jeff Fahey	Jobe Smith
Pierce Brosnan	Dr Lawrence Angelo
Jenny Wright	Marnie Burke
Mark Bringleson	Sebastian Timms
Geoffrey Lewis	Terry McKeen
Jeremy Slate	Father McKenn
Dean Norris	Director

The Top Five

Week of 12 June 1992
1. The Lawnmower Man
2. Basic Instinct
3. Wayne's World
4. Howards End
5. Medicine Man

The storyline of the film was loosely based on a short story by Stephen King whose name was removed from all publicity for this film after a lawsuit. The film was a very loose adaptation of a King story and he was unhappy that they were selling the film purely on his name.

The film was marketed as the first 'virtual reality' film, although the publicity department must have been unaware of the 1982 film *Tron*, starring Jeff Bridges.

Video availability

THE LOVER

26 June 1992	1 week

Distributor:	Guild
Director:	Jean-Jacques Annaud
Producer:	Claude Berri
Screenplay:	Gerard Brach, Jean-Jacques Annaud
Music:	Gabriel Yared

CAST
Jane March . . . . *the Young Girl*
Jeanne Moreau . . . . *voice of narrator*
Tony Leung . . . . *the Chinaman*
Frederique Meininger . . . . *the Mother*
Arnaud Giovaninette . . *the Elder Brother*
Melvil Poupaud . . . . *the Younger Brother*
Lisa Faulkner . . . . *Helene Lagonelle*

In Indochina during the 1920s a poor 15-year-old French girl attends the local school. She is spotted by a wealthy young Chinaman who invites her to exotic and expensive places. Seduced by him, she becomes his lover, incurring the wrath of his father and her family. However, his money manages to keep her mother quiet and the girl is happy to enjoy their erotic pleasures.

The film was based on a novel by Marguerite Duras.

Because of her sexual roles in this and other films, Jane March gained the tabloid nickname, 'the sinner from Pinner'. She went on to make *The Color of Night* with Bruce Willis.

Video availability

The Top Five
Week of 26 June 1992
1. The Lover
2. Basic Instinct
3. The Lawnmower Man
4. Howards End
5. Wayne's World

THE PLAYER

3 July 1992	2 weeks

Distributor:	Guild
Director:	Robert Altman
Producer:	David Brown, Michael Tolkin, Nick Wechsler
Screenplay:	Michael Tolkin
Music:	Thomas Newman

CAST
Tim Robbins . . . . *Griffin Mill*
Greta Scacchi . . . . . . *June Gudmundsdottir*
Fred Ward . . . . *Walter Stuckel*
Whoopi Goldberg . . . . . . *Detective Avery*
Peter Gallagher . . . . *Larry Levy*
Brion James . . . . *Joel Levison*
Cynthia Stevenson . . . . . . *Bonnie Sherow*
Vincent D'Onofrio . . . . *David Kahane*

Movie executive Griffin Mill is feeling the stress of the cut-throat industry. He keeps receiving postcards which state 'I'm going to kill you', which could be from any number of enemies. His stress causes him to lash out at a young man outside the cinema who subsequently dies. Guilt forces him to visit the victim's lover, Greta Scacchi, to whom he is himself attracted. Griffin will stop at nothing to keep from going to prison and hang on to the beautiful new woman in his life.

As the film was set in Hollywood a host of real movie stars appear in cameo roles, including Cher, Malcolm McDowell, Bruce Willis, Julia Roberts, Burt Reynolds, Rod Steiger, Jack Lemmon, James Coburn, Robert Wagner, Susan Sarandon (Mrs Tim Robbins), Nick Nolte, Andie MacDowell, Jeff Goldblum, Anjelica Huston, Peter Falk, Elliot Gould, Louise Fletcher and Richard E. Grant.

The Player was director Robert Altman's second number one movie; his first was *M*A*S*H* in 1970. In the 1950s and 60s Altman directed a number of episodes of the American TV series *Bonanza* and *Alfred Hitchcock Presents*.

Tim Robbins won the Best Actor prize at the 1992 Cannes Film Festival for his performance. Robbins' father was a member of the 1960s folk group 'The Highwaymen' who achieved a number one hit with 'Michael'.

Music: 'Snake and Drums of Kyoto' (Kurt Neumann), 'Tema Para Jobim' (Joyce and Milton Nascimento)

Video availability

BATMAN RETURNS

17 July 1992	3 weeks

Distributor:	Warner
Director:	Tim Burton
Producer:	Denise Di Novi, Tim Burton
Screenplay:	Daniel Waters
Music:	Danny Elfman

CAST
Michael Keaton .... *Batman/Bruce Wayne*
Danny DeVito... *Penguin/Oscar Cobblepot*
Michelle Pfeiffer .. *Catwoman/Selina Kyle*
Christopher Walken........ *Max Shreck*
Michael Gough................ *Alfred*
Michael Murphy.............. *Mayor*
Cristi Conaway............ *Ice Princess*

Gotham City is again under attack from the dastardly acts of The Penguin who has teamed up with Catwoman. The Penguin's wicked ways are the result of his abandonment by his father when still a baby. Nevertheless it is down to Batman to stop him.

Catwoman was originally going to be played by Annette Bening, who became pregnant before filming began, a condition the Catwoman costume would not easily hide.

Tim Burton, who directed the two *Batman* films, once worked at the Disney studios as an animator. His animation expertise is displayed to great effect in his later work *Tim Burton's The Nightmare Before Christmas* (1994). Prior to the *Batman* films, Tim Burton and Michael Keaton worked together on the 1988 film *Beetlejuice*.

Music: 'Face To Face' (Siouxsie and The Banshees)

Video availability

UNIVERSAL SOLDIER

7 August 1992	1 week

Distributor:	Guild
Director:	Ronald Emmerich
Producer:	Allen Shapiro, Craig Baumgarten, Joel B. Michaels
Screenplay:	Richard Rothstein
Music:	Christopher Franke

CAST
Jean-Claude Van Damme.......... *Luc*
Dolph Lundgren................ *Scott*
Ally Walker.................. *Veronica*
Ed O'Ross .... *Colonel Perry*
Jerry Orbach................ *Dr Gregor*
Leon Rippy .... *Woodward*

Luc and Scott are soldiers during the Vietnam War. In a fight the two kill each other but are revived more than twenty years later when they are turned into fighting machines. Although they have no memory, Luc begins to recall images of the past, mostly to do with the hell of the Vietnam War.

The film was originally developed as a vehicle for Sylvester Stallone, but the role went to younger action man Jean-Claude Van Damme. Belgian martial arts champion Van Damme was taken to karate classes by his father at the age of nine because he was small and always being picked on at school. His co-star, Dolph Lundgren, gained his first major role since his part as Ivan Drago in *Rocky IV* (1985). He

made his movie debut the same year with a minor role in the James Bond movie *A View To A Kill*, alongside his then girlfriend, Grace Jones.

Video availability

FAR AND AWAY

14 August 1992	1 week

Distributor:	Universal
Director:	Ron Howard
Producer:	Brian Grazer, Ron Howard
Screenplay:	Bob Dolman
Music:	John Williams

CAST
Tom Cruise . . . . *Joseph Donelly*
Nicole Kidman . . . . *Shannon Christie*
Thomas Gibson . . . . *Stephen*
Robert Prosky . . . . *Daniel Christie*
Barbara Babcock . . . . *Nora Christie*
Colm Meaney . . . . *Kelly*
Eileen Pollock . . . . *Molly Kay*
Michelle Johnson . . . . *Grace*

Joseph Donelly is a poor 19th-century Irish tenant farmer who falls for the daughter of a wealthy landowner, Shannon Christie. Unfortunately the Christie and the Donelly family are sworn enemies. When Shannon becomes separated from her family in their journey to America she teams up with Joseph. They pose as brother and sister as they scrimp and save, Joseph at one point becoming a

prizefighter. They need the money to make it to Oklahoma for the land rush.

Far and Away was the second movie Tom Cruise and real-life wife Nicole Kidman had teamed up. They married on Christmas Eve, 1990, shortly after completing *Days of Thunder*. When director Ron Howard signed Cruise and Kidman for the film, he claimed he had no idea that they were a couple, despite all the press coverage at the time.

At the age of two, director Ron Howard appeared with his parents in a stage production of *The Seven Year Itch*. In the 1970s he played the part of Richie Cunningham in the long-running American TV comedy series *Happy Days*.

Video availability

The Top Five
Week of 14 August 1992
1. Far and Away
2. Universal Soldier
3. The Player
4. Batman Returns
5. Night on Earth

LETHAL WEAPON 3

21 August 1992	1 week

Distributor:	Warner
Director:	Richard Donner
Producer:	Joel Silver, Richard Donner
Screenplay:	Jeffrey Boam, Robert Mark Kamen
Music:	Michael Kamen, Eric Clapton, David Sanborn

CAST
Mel Gibson . . . . *Martin Riggs*
Danny Glover . . . . *Roger Murtaugh*
Joe Pesci . . . . *Leo Getz*
Rene Russo . . . . *Lorna Cole*
Stuart Wilson . . . . *Jack Travis*
Steve Kahan . . . . *Captain Murphy*
Darlene Love . . . . *Trish Murtaugh*

Roger Murtaugh is counting the days until his retirement from the force, but his final days as a

policeman are far from peaceful. With partner Martin Riggs he discovers a bent cop (Stuart Wilson) selling confiscated guns to gangs of criminals. Their investigations bring them into contact with investigator Lorna Cole, a kick-boxing expert to whom Riggs takes a shine.

Lethal Weapon was Rene Russo's first number one movie. She also appears in *In the Line of Fire* (1993).

The Top Five
Week of 21 August 1992
1. Lethal Weapon 3
2. The Player
3. Far and Away
4. Universal Soldier
5. Night on Earth

Richard Donner, who directed all three *Lethal Weapon* films, worked in television before making his first movie in 1961, *X-15*, with Charles Bronson.

Darlene Love, who plays Trish Murtaugh, still performs in New York in a one-woman musical show based on her life story.

Joe Pesci revives his character of Leo Getz from *Lethal Weapon 2*, an estate agent turned government witness in a drug money case. In *Lethal Weapon 2* he was himself laundering cash in South Africa and was behaving like a madman.

Music: 'It's Probably Me' (Sting and Eric Clapton), 'Runaway Train' (Elton John and Eric Clapton)

Video availability

ALIEN 3

28 August 1992	3 weeks

Distributor:	Twentieth Century-Fox
Director:	David Fincher
Producer:	Gordon Carroll, David Giler, Walter Hill
Screenplay:	David Giler, Walter Hill, Larry Ferguson
Music:	Elliot Goldenthal

CAST

Sigourney Weaver . . . . *Ripley*
Charles S. Dutton . . . . *Dillon*
Charles Dance . . . . *Clemens*
Paul McGann . . . . *Golic*
Brian Glover . . . . *Andrews*
Ralph Brown . . . . *Aaron*
Danny Webb . . . . *Morse*

Ripley crash lands her craft on a planet that is dominated by a group of all-male serial killers who have found religion with the help of a man named Dillon. Only Clemens, the colony's doctor, befriends her. Unfortunately an alien egg was still on the shuttle and she finds herself stranded in space and about to embark on another nightmare experience.

Brian Glover, who plays the facility superintendent, was once a professional wrestler in England and was still fighting at the start of his movie career. Charles Dance worked as an actor in British television for many years, getting his first major break in the 1984 series *The Jewel in the Crown*. He made his movie debut with a small part in the 1981 James Bond movie *For Your Eyes Only*. Science fiction actor Lance Henriksen has appeared in all three *Alien* films as the android Bishop.

David Fincher, who had previously worked on many successful pop videos, made his movie debut as a director with *Alien 3*. There were plans for Vincent Ward, who wrote the original story, to direct the film.

Video availability

The Top Five

Week of 28 August 1992
1. Alien 3
2. Lethal Weapon 3
3. The Player
4. Far and Away
5. Waterland

Warrant Officer Ripley (Sigourney Weaver) becomes stranded on a remote planet inhabited by male prisoners in Alien 3. *Still pursued by the aliens, she and the prisoners have nothing but brain power to fight them.*

BOB ROBERTS

18 September 1992	1 week

Distributor: Polygram
Director: Tim Robbins
Producer: Forrest Murray
Screenplay: Tim Robbins
Music: David Robbins
   David Robbins, Tim Robbins
   (songs)

CAST
Tim Robbins . . . . *Bob Roberts*
Giancarlo Esposito . . . . *Bugs Raplin*
Ray Wise . . . . *Chet MacGregor*
Brian Murray . . . . *Terry Manchester*
Gore Vidal . . . . . . *Senator Brickley Paiste*
Rebecca Jenkins . . . . *Delores Perrigrew*
Harry J. Lennix . . . . *Franklin Dockett*
John Ottavino . . . . *Clark Anderson*

In this political satire Bob Roberts is running for political office. He is a successful singer-come-songwriter with a dubious past that involves drugs and the exploitation of the poor. Campaigning on a right-wing, Bible-bashing Republican ticket, he cynically manipulates both the people and the press.

The story of Bob Roberts began life as a sketch for *Saturday Night Live* in 1985.

As well as writing the songs and screenplay, Robbins made his directorial debut with this film. Fred Ward and Peter Gallagher, who both appear in *Bob Roberts*, also appeared with Robbins in *The Player*.

A number of stars made cameo appearances, including James Spader, Alan Rickman and Susan Sarandon.

Music: 'What Did The Teacher Tell You', 'This Land', 'Beautiful Girl', 'Complain', 'I Want To Live', 'This World turns', 'Wall Street Rap', 'Prevailing Tides', 'Drugs Stink', 'The Voting Song', 'We Are Marching', 'Times Are Changing Back', 'Retake America', 'I've Got To Know'

Video availability

The Top Five

Week of 18 September 1992
1. Bob Roberts
2. Housesitter
3. Alien 3
4. Lethal Weapon 3
5. The Player

UNFORGIVEN

25 September 1992	1 week

Distributor: Warner
Director: Clint Eastwood
Producer: Clint Eastwood
Screenplay: David Webb Peoples
Music: Lennie Niehaus

CAST
Clint Eastwood . . . . *Bill Munny*
Gene Hackman . . . . *Little Bill Daggett*
Morgan Freeman . . . . *Ned Logan*
Richard Harris . . . . *English Bob*
Jaimz Woolvett . . . . . . *The 'Schofield Kid'*
Saul Rubinek . . . . *W.W. Beauchamp*
Frances Fisher . . . . *Strawberry Alice*
Anna Thomson . . . . *Delilah Fitzgerald*

Bill Munny, a retired gunfighter, is persuaded by the 'Schofield Kid' to help him track down two cowboys who have disfigured a prostitute's face. There's a $1000 reward on offer, but Munny's more concerned with justice than the bounty and enlists the help of his old friend Ned Logan. Sadistic sheriff

Daggett has already kicked English Bob out of town for hunting the cowboys and he makes life difficult for Munny before justice prevails in a bloody shoot-out.

Unforgiven is one of only three Westerns to win the Best Picture Academy Award. The other two are *Cimarron* (1930) and *Dances with Wolves* (1990). Clint Eastwood dedicated the film to directors Sergio Leone, who died in 1989, and Don Siegel, who died in 1991. Leone directed Eastwood in the early Westerns *A Fistful of Dollars* (1964), *For a Few Dollars More* (1965) and *The Good, The Bad and The Ugly* (1966). Eastwood later worked with Siegel on vari-

The Top Five

Week of 25 September 1992
1. Unforgiven
2. A League of their Own
3. Bob Roberts
4. Housesitter
5. Alien 3

Retired gunslinger William Munny (Clint Eastwood) prepares to return to the fray in Unforgiven. *He is hired by local prostitutes to track down the villains responsible for disfiguring a woman's face.*

ous films, including *Coogan's Bluff* (1968), *Two Mules For Sister Sara* (1970), *Dirty Harry* (1971) and *Escape from Alcatraz* (1979).

Academy Awards: Best Film (Producer Clint Eastwood), Best Direction (Clint Eastwood), Best Supporting Actor (Gene Hackman), Best Editing (Joel Cox)

Video availability

PATRIOT GAMES

2 October 1992	3 weeks

Distributor:	Paramount
Director:	Phillip Noyce
Producer:	Mace Neufeld, Robert Rehme
Screenplay:	W. Peter Iliff, Donald Stewart
Music:	James Horner

CAST

Harrison Ford	Jack Ryan
Anne Archer	Cathy Ryan
Patrick Bergin	Kevin O'Donnell
Sean Bean	Sean Miller
Thora Birch	Sally Ryan
James Fox	Lord Holmes
Samuel L. Jackson	Robby
Polly Walker	Annette

Jack Ryan is a retired CIA analyst on a visit to London. He finds himself in the middle of an IRA terrorist attack on a high-ranking British official and manages to shoot dead one of the terrorists. The brother of the dead man (Sean Bean) pledges revenge for the killing and terrorizes Ryan and his family.

The film was based on a novel by Tom Clancy and a sequel to *The Hunt for Red October* (1990), in which Alec Baldwin played Jack Ryan. Baldwin turned down the part this time around because he wanted to appear in the Broadway revival of *A Streetcar Named Desire*. James Earl Jones returns to his role as Admiral James Greer, the part he played in *The Hunt for Red October*.

Video availability

The Top Five

Week of 2 October 1992
1. Patriot Games
2. Unforgiven
3. A League of their Own
4. Bob Roberts
5. Housesitter

BEAUTY AND THE BEAST

23 October 1992	1 week

Distributor:	Buena Vista
Director:	Gary Trousdale, Kirk Wise
Producer:	Don Hahn
Screenplay:	Linda Woolverton
Music:	Alan Menken

CAST (Voices)
Paige O'Hara .... Belle
Robby Benson .... Beast
Jerry Orbach................ Lumière
Angela Lansbury .... Mrs Potts
Richard White .... Gaston
David Ogden Stiers .. Cogsworth/Narrator
Jesse Corti .... LeFou

The Disney studio's 13th full-length cartoon movie was an interpretation of the classic story of Beauty and the Beast. The beautiful Belle is held prisoner in the Beast's castle, during which time the two fall in love.

Beauty and the Beast is the only animated film ever to be nominated for a Best Picture Academy Award. It took over three years to complete with 600 animators working on the project, producing over a million drawings. The film was originally planned as a non-musical cartoon, but after Disney's success in 1989 with *The Little Mermaid*, the studio had a change of heart.

The voice of Lumière (the candlestick) was created by actor Jerry Orbach, who appeared in an earlier 1992 film, *Universal Soldier*.

Academy Awards: Best Original Score (Alan Menken), Best Original Song – 'Beauty and the Beast' (Alan Menken, music; Howard Ashman, lyrics)

Music: 'Beauty and the Beast', 'Belle', 'Gaston', 'Be Our Guest', 'Something There', 'The Mob Song'

Video availability

The Top Five

Week of 23 October 1992
1. Beauty and the Beast
2. Strictly Ballroom
3. Patriot Games
4. White Men Can't Jump
5. Unforgiven

Celine Dion and Peabo Bryson created an international top ten hit for themselves with the title song from Walt Disney's movie version of the classic Beauty and the Beast.

1492: CONQUEST OF PARADISE

30 October 1992	1 week

Distributor: Paramount
Director: Ridley Scott
Producer: Ridley Scott, Alain Goldman
Screenplay: Roselyne Bosch
Music: Vangelis

CAST
Gérard Depardieu . . . . Columbus
Armand Assante . . . . Sanchez
Sigourney Weaver . . . . Queen Isabel
Loren Dean . . . . Older Fernando
Angela Molina . . . . Beatrix
Fernando Rey . . . . Marchena
Michael Wincott . . . . Moxica
Tcheky Karyo . . . . Pinzon

1492: Conquest of Paradise was one of three movies based on the life of Christopher Columbus that were released to mark the 500th anniversary of his discovery of America. Gérard Depardieu plays the explorer who, sickened by the Inquisition, spends much of his time with a group of monks. After twenty years of trying to raise funds for his mission, Columbus convinces Queen Isabel to grant him the necessary funds, and he sets forth on his voyage of discovery.

1492 was the most successful of the three Christopher Columbus movies released to celebrate the 500th anniversary of the exploits of the explorer. *Christopher Columbus: The Discovery* starred George Corraface, Tom Selleck and Rachel Ward. The 'Carry On' team made a comeback with their less than successful *Carry On Columbus*.

Screenwriter Roselyne Bosch made her movie-writing debut. She was formerly a French journalist.

Video availability

The Top Five

Week of 30 October 1992
1. 1492: Conquest of Paradise
2. Husbands and Wives
3. Strictly Ballroom
4. Beauty and the Beast
5. Patriot Games

STRICTLY BALLROOM

6 November 1992	1 week

Distributor: Rank
Director: Baz Luhrmann
Producer: Tristam Miall, Ted Albert
Screenplay: Baz Luhrmann, Craig Pearce
Music: David Hirshfelder

CAST
Paul Mercurio . . . . Scott Hastings
Tara Morice . . . . Fran
Bill Hunter . . . . Barry Fife
Barry Otto . . . . Doug Hastings
Pat Thompson . . . . Shirley Hastings
Gia Carides . . . . Liz Holt
Peter Whitford . . . . Les Kendall
John Hannan . . . . Ken Railings

Scott is a leading ballroom dancer in Australia but is bored with the strict regulations set by the Dance Federation and dares to create his own routines. His regular partner immediately dumps him, leaving him with nobody to dance with as the championships draw near. Shy bespectacled Fran, who has gone unnoticed by Scott in spite of her admiration for him, steps in at the right moment and after a crash course from him is transformed into a new person. Together they make the perfect partnership and dazzle spectators with their innovative and exciting dance routines.

The story of *Strictly Ballroom* originally began its life as an Australian stage play.

Music: 'Love Is In The Air' (John Paul Young), 'Perhaps Perhaps Perhaps' (Quizas Quizas Quizas) (Doris Day), 'Time After Time' (Mark Williams and Tara Morice)

Video availability

The Top Five

Week of 6 November 1992
1. Strictly Ballroom
2. Boomerang
3. Husbands and Wives
4. Beauty and the Beast
5. 1492: Conquest of Paradise

THE LAST OF THE MOHICANS

13 November 1992	1 week

Distributor: **Warner**
Director: **Michael Mann**
Producer: **Michael Mann, Hunt Lowry**
Screenplay: **Michael Mann, Christopher Crowe**
Music: **Trevor Jones, Randy Edelman**

CAST
Daniel Day-Lewis . . . . *Hawkeye*
Madeleine Stowe . . . . *Cora*
Russell Means . . . . *Chingachgook*
Eric Schweig . . . . *Uncas*
Jodhi May . . . . *Alice*
Steven Waddington . . . . *Heyward*
Wes Studi . . . . *Magua*

In the adaptation of James Fenimore Cooper's classic novel the British are fighting the Americans and the French are fighting the Indians in 1757. Colonial scout Hawkeye, with the help of Chingachgook and his son Uncas, who are the only remaining survivors of the Mohican tribe, escorts the daughters of a senior British officer, Cora and Alice, and Officer Heyward through hostile enemy lines. To complicate matters Hawkeye falls in love with Cora.

The screenplay was largely based on the 1936 film version of the story, which starred Randolph Scott in the leading role. In 1921 a silent version of the story was made by director Maurice Tourneur, starring Wallace Beery as Magua.

Daniel Day-Lewis, who plays Hawkeye, is the grandson of former poet laureate Cecil Day Lewis. In the early 1990s he suffered a nervous breakdown after playing Hamlet on stage, believing he saw his late father when the ghost appeared.

The Top Five

Week of 13 November 1992
1. The Last of the Mohicans
2. Strictly Ballroom
3. Unlawful Entry
4. The Crying Game
5. Husbands and Wives

Frontiersman Hawkeye (Daniel Day-Lewis) finds he is more at home with his adopted Mohican family than with the fighting French, English or Americans in The Last of the Mohicans.

Director Michael Mann wrote several episodes of the popular 1970s American television series *Starsky and Hutch* and *Police Story*. He also worked as executive producer on the 1980s series *Miami Vice*.

Academy Awards: Best Sound (Chris Jenkins, Doug Hemphill, Mark Smith and Simon Kaye)

Music: 'I Will Find You' (Clannad)

Video availability

PETER'S FRIENDS

20 November 1992	1 week

Distributor:	Renaissance Films
Director:	Kenneth Branagh
Producer:	Kenneth Branagh
Screenplay:	Rita Rudner, Martin Bergman
Music:	Garin Greenaway (director)

CAST

Kenneth Branagh	*Andrew*
Alphonsia Emmanuel	*Sarah*
Stephen Fry	*Peter*
Hugh Laurie	*Roger*
Phyllida Law	*Vera*
Alex Lowe	*Paul*
Rita Rudner	*Carol*
Imelda Staunton	*Mary*
Emma Thompson	*Maggie*

A group of old college friends are reunited for New Year at the country estate of the young aristocrat Peter. His friends bring all their emotional problems with them to the party. Andrew has fallen out with his bulimic American wife, Mary and Roger are still grieving over their dead child and Maggie, as always, is desperate for a man.

The complicated nature of the relationships between Peter's friends has some basis in truth. Most of the cast performed together as undergraduates in the Cambridge Footlights Review, Emma Thompson is married to Kenneth Branagh but used to be Hugh Laurie's partner and Phyllida Law is Emma Thompson's real mother.

Peter's Friends was Kenneth Branagh's third outing as a director, following on from *Henry V* (1989) and *Dead Again* (1991), both of which featured performances from Emma Thompson.

Hugh Laurie appeared as Lieutenant Colthurst St Barley and Stephen Fry as General Melchett in the British TV comedy series *Blackadder Goes Forth*. The comedy duo also worked together in the 1990s TV series *Jeeves and Wooster*.

Music: 'Everybody Wants To Rule The World' (Tears For Fears), 'My Baby Just Cares For Me' (Nina Simone), 'You're My Best Friend' (Queen), 'Girls Just Want To Have Fun' (Cyndi Lauper), 'Hungry Heart' (Bruce Springsteen), 'Don't Get Me Wrong' (The Pretenders), 'The King of Rock 'n' Roll' (Prefab Sprout), 'I Guess That's Why They Call It The Blues' (Elton John), 'What's Love Got To Do With It' (Tina Turner)

Video availability

The Top Five

Week of 20 November 1992
1. Peter's Friends
2. Sneakers
3. The Last of the Mohicans
4. Strictly Ballroom
5. Unlawful Entry

SISTER ACT

27 November 1992	2 weeks

Distributor:	Buena Vista
Director:	Emile Ardolino
Producer:	Teri Schwartz
Screenplay:	Joseph Howard
Music:	Marc Shaiman

CAST

Whoopi Goldberg	*Deloris*
Maggie Smith	*Mother Superior*
Kathy Najimy	*Mary Patrick*
Wendy Makkena	*Mary Robert*
Mary Wickes	*Mary Lazarus*

Top Ten Films of 1992

1 Basic Instinct
2 Hook
3 Lethal Weapon 3
4 Batman Returns
5 The Addams Family
6 Cape Fear
7 Beauty and the Beast
8 Wayne's World
9 My Girl
10 The Hand that Rocks the Cradle

Harvey Keitel . . . . *Vince LaRocca*
Bill Nunn . . . . *Eddie Souther*
Robert Miranda . . . . *Joey*
Richard Portnow . . . . *Willy*

Deloris is a Las Vegas nightclub singer threatened by her mobster boyfriend after she witnesses a murder. She is given refuge by the police in a convent in San Francisco, where she becomes the new choir leader and introduces the nuns to mayhem and rock and roll.

Whoopi Goldberg (real name Caryn Johnson) made her debut in the 1985 film *The Color Purple*, for which she received one of 11 Oscar nominations the movie clocked up. In the event Steven Spielberg's film didn't win a single Oscar. Whoopi Goldberg's part in *Sister Act* was originally planned for Bette Midler.

Veteran actress Mary Wickes, who played Mary Lazarus in *Sister Act*, has a movie career that spans

over fifty years. She has starred in dozens of successful films, including *The Man Who Came To Dinner* (1942), *White Christmas* (1954), *How To Murder Your Wife* (1965) and *Postcards From The Edge* (1990).

Music: 'My Guy ('My God'), 'Shout', 'I Will Follow Him' ('Chariot') (Deloris and The Sisters), 'Rescue Me' (Fontella Bass), 'Roll With Me Henry' (Etta James), 'Gravy' (Dee Dee Sharp), 'Just a Touch of Love (Everyday)' (C&C Music Factory)

Video availability

The Top Five

Week of 27 November 1992
1. Sister Act
2. Peter's Friends
3. Single White Female
4. Strictly Ballroom
5. The Last of the Mohicans

DEATH BECOMES HER

11 December 1992	1 week

Distributor:	Universal
Director:	Robert Zemeckis
Producer:	Robert Zemeckis, Steve Starkey

Screenplay:	Martin Donovan
Music:	Alan Silvestri

CAST
Meryl Streep . . . . *Madeline Ashton*
Bruce Willis . . . . *Ernest Menville*

Madeline Ashton (Meryl Streep) and Helen Sharp (Goldie Hawn) both take a potion for eternal life in Death Becomes Her. *However, they become rivals when they both set out to catch Dr Ernest Menville (Bruce Willis), the plastic surgeon who can maintain their youthful looks.*

Goldie Hawn . . . . *Helen Sharp*
Isabella Rossellini . . . . *Lisle*
Ian Ogilvy . . . . *Chagall*
Adam Storke . . . . *Dakota*

Helen Sharp is engaged to plastic surgeon Ernest Menville but he is wooed away by the charms of actress Madeline Ashton. In later years he meets Helen again and realizes his mistake in letting her go and the two plan to murder Madeline. The plan goes wrong as it emerges that the two women have both taken a formula for eternal life but need Ernest's scalpel skills to help keep their bodies looking young.

Robert Zemeckis, whose credits include *Back To The Future* parts I, II and III, *Who Framed Roger Rabbit* and *Romancing the Stone*, became one of the highest-grossing directors in Hollywood between 1982 and 1992.

Ian Ogilvy, who plays Chagall, another character with eternal life, first made his name on British

television as Simon Templar in the 1980s series *The Return of the Saint*.

Kevin Kline was the original choice for the role of Dr Ernest Menville, but he was unavailable.

The king of cameos, film director Sydney Pollack, makes an uncredited appearance as a Californian doctor.

Academy Awards: Best Visual Effects (Ken Ralston, Doug Chiang, Doug Smythe and Tom Woodruff)

Video availability

The Top Five

Week of 11 December 1992
1. Death Becomes Her
2. Sister Act
3. Peter's Friends
4. Blade Runner: The Director's Cut
5. Single White Female

HOME ALONE 2: LOST IN NEW YORK

18 December 1992	2 weeks

Distributor:	Twentieth Century-Fox
Director:	Chris Columbus
Producer:	John Hughes
Screenplay:	John Hughes
Music:	John Williams

CAST
Macaulay Culkin . . . . *Kevin*
Joe Pesci . . . . *Harry*
Daniel Stern . . . . *Marv*
Catherine O'Hara . . . . *Kate*
John Heard . . . . *Peter*
Devin Ratray . . . . *Buzz*
Tim Curry . . . . *Concierge*
Brenda Fricker . . . . *Pigeon Lady*

Once again Kevin and his family decide to take off for the holidays and visit Florida, but they get split up at the airport and Kevin boards the wrong plane, to New York. With not much more than his father's credit card, he books into a luxury hotel. The fun starts when the two bad guys from the original *Home Alone*, Marv and Harry, spot him.

In 1992 Joe Pesci starred in three number one

movies. He kicked off the year playing David Ferrie in *JFK* and repeated his *Lethal Weapon 2* role as Leo Getz in *Lethal Weapon 3*. He finished the year on top with *Home Alone 2*.

Brenda Fricker, who plays the pigeon lady, made her name in *Casualty*, the British television series which began in the 1980s. She went on to appear with Daniel Day-Lewis in *My Left Foot*, for which she won an Oscar for Best Supporting Actress.

Music: 'All Alone at Christmas' (Darlene Love), 'A Holly Jolly Christmas' (Alan Jackson), 'Somewhere In My Memory' (Bette Midler), 'Silver Bells' (Atlantic Starr), 'It's Beginning To Look A Lot Like Christmas' (Johnny Mathis)

Video availability

The Top Five

Week of 18 December 1992
1. Home Alone 2: Lost in New York
2. Death Becomes Her
3. Sister Act
4. Peter's Friends
5. Blade Runner: The Director's Cut

THE BODYGUARD

1 January 1993	1 week

Distributor:	Warner

Director:	Mick Jackson
Producer:	Lawrence Kasdan, Jim Wilson, Kevin Costner

| Screenplay: | Lawrence Kasdan |
| Music: | Alan Silvestri |

CAST

Kevin Costner	*Frank Farmer*
Whitney Houston	*Rachel Marron*
Gary Kemp	*Sy Spector*
Bill Cobbs	*Devaney*
Ralph Waite	*Herb Farmer*
Thomas Arana	*Portman*
Michele Lamar Richards	*Nicki*
Mike Starr	*Tony*

Someone is threatening the life of actress and singer Rachel Marron. It is thought that a member of her entourage is involved in the plot. Frank Farmer, who has a fear of becoming too attached to his clients, is hired as Rachel's bodyguard, but, despite his attempts to stay aloof, he falls in love with her.

Whitney Houston made her feature-film debut in *The Bodyguard*, which became the biggest-grossing film in Warner Brothers' history. The soundtrack album became Whitney's biggest-selling record to date with the single 'I Will Always Love You' topping the charts in the UK for 12 weeks. In the USA it became the longest running number one, remaining at the top for 14 weeks. Two songs, 'Run To You' and 'I Have Nothing', were Oscar nominated.

Music: 'I Will Always Love You'. 'I Have Nothing', 'I'm Every Woman', 'Queen of the Night, 'Jesus Loves Me' (Whitney Houston), 'Someday (I'm Coming Back)' (Lisa Stansfield), 'Even if My Heart Would Break' (Kenny G and Aaron Neville), '(What's So Funny 'Bout) Peace Love and Understanding' (Curtis Stigers), 'Trust In Me' (Joe Cocker featuring Sass Jordan)

Video availability

The Top Five

Week of 1 January 1993
1. The Bodyguard
2. Home Alone 2: Lost in New York
3. Peter's Friends
4. Sister Act
5. Death Becomes Her

A FEW GOOD MEN

8 January 1993	2 weeks*

Distributor:	Columbia TriStar
Director:	Rob Reiner
Producer:	David Brown, Rob Reiner, Andrew Scheinman
Screenplay:	Aaron Sorkin
Music:	Marc Shaiman

CAST

Tom Cruise	*Lt Daniel Kaffee*
Jack Nicholson	*Colonel Jessup*
Demi Moore	*Lt Commander Galloway*
Kevin Bacon	*Capt. Jack Ross*
Kiefer Sutherland ..	*Lt Jonathan Kendrick*
Kevin Pollak	*Lt Sam Weinberg*
James Marshall	*Pfc Downey*
J.T. Walsh ..	*Lt Colonel Matthew Markinson*

Daniel Kaffee is a young military lawyer living in the shadow of his brilliant lawyer father, and so prefers to play softball to practising law. When he is called to work on a case of a young marine accused of murder, he works out a deal with the prosecutor, Captain Jack Ross. In the process he locks horns with special counsel Lieutenant Commander Joanne Galloway, who believes there is more to the case than meets the eye and pushes him to investigate further. Together they meet Colonel Nathan Jessup, the only man that can shed any light on the truth and expose the real man behind the crime.

The personal lives of two members of the cast were publicized as much as the film when it was released. Demi Moore hit the headlines when she cancelled her wedding to Emilio Estevez and immediately married Bruce Willis. Kiefer Sutherland's engagement to Julia Roberts was called off just four days before their wedding day. Sutherland and Roberts co-starred in the 1990 film *Flatliners*. Kiefer is the son of actor Donald Sutherland and stage actress Shirley Douglas. This is his only number one, but his other credits include *Stand By Me* (1986), *The Lost Boys* (1987), *Bright Lights, Big City* (1988), *Young Guns* (1990) and *Young Guns II* (1990).

Music: 'Hound Dog' (Willie Mae Thornton), 'Timber, I'm Falling In Love' (Patty Loveless), 'Next Time You See Me' (Jimmy Cotton), 'All I Want To Do' (UB40)

Video availability

The Top Five

Week of 8 January 1993
1. A Few Good Men
2. The Bodyguard
3. Home Alone 2: Lost in New York
4. Tous Les Matins du Monde
5. Peter's Friends

RESERVOIR DOGS

15 January 1993	2 weeks

Distributor:	Rank
Director:	Quentin Tarantino
Producer:	Lawrence Bender
Screenplay:	Quentin Tarantino
Music:	Karyn Rachtman (supervisor)

CAST

Harvey Keitel . . . . *Mr White*
Tim Roth . . . . *Mr Orange*
Chris Penn . . . . *Nice Guy Eddie*
Steve Buscemi . . . . *Mr Pink*
Lawrence Tierney . . . . *Joe Cabot*
Michael Madsen . . . . *Mr Blonde*
Quentin Tarantino . . . . *Mr Brown*
Eddie Bunker . . . . *Mr Blue*

The members of a violent gang of criminals are named by the boss, Joe Cabot, by colours. Their jewel heist falls foul of the law and the recriminations amongst the gang begin.

Director Quentin Tarantino's three favourite films are Howard Hawks's *Rio Bravo*, Brian de Palma's *Blow Out* and Martin Scorsese's *Taxi Driver*.

Tarantino has also written two screenplays, *True Romance*, directed by Tony Scott, and *Natural Born Killers* for Oliver Stone, although he had his name removed from the credits of the latter. Harvey Keitel has appeared in Tarantino's other film, *Pulp Fiction* (1994). Keitel made his movie debut in the 1968 Martin Scorsese film *Who's That Knocking At My Door*. His other number ones are *The Border* (1982), *Thelma and Louise* (1991), *Bugsy* (1992), *Sister Act* (1992), and *The Piano* (1993).

The Top Five

Week of 15 January 1993
1. Reservoir Dogs
2. A Few Good Men
3. The Bodyguard
4. Tous les Matins Du Monde
5. Home Alone 2: Lost in New York

Quentin Tarantino's debut as screenwriter and director chronicles a robbery that goes badly wrong after the police have been tipped off.

Music: 'Little Green Bag' (George Baker Selection), 'Hooked On A Feeling' (Blue Swede), 'I Gotcha' (Joe Tex), 'Stuck In The Middle With You' (Stealers Wheel), 'Coconut' (Harry Nilsson)

BRAM STOKER'S DRACULA

5 February 1993   **4 weeks**

Distributor:	Columbia
Director:	Francis Ford Coppola
Producer:	Francis Ford Coppola, Fred Fuchs, Charles Mulvehill
Screenplay:	James V. Hart
Music:	Wojciech Kilar

CAST
Gary Oldman . . . . *Dracula*
Winona Ryder . . . . *Mina/Elisabeta*
Anthony Hopkins . . . . *Van Helsing*
Keanu Reeves . . . . *Jonathan Harker*
Richard E. Grant . . . . *Dr Jack Seward*
Cary Elwes . . . . . . *Lord Arthur Holmwood*
Bill Campbell . . . . *Quincey P. Morris*
Sadie Frost . . . . *Lucy Westenra*

Four centuries after the death of his lover, Elisabeta, Dracula meets the young lawyer Jonathan Harker. The lawyer has been sent to see the Count in Budapest after his colleague is committed to a lunatic asylum. Harker shows the Count a picture of his future wife, Mina, who looks identical to Elisabeta. Count Dracula insists Harker stays at his castle for an entire month. When Harker realizes he is being held prisoner, he escapes to a convent in Romania. The reincarnated Dracula now has the ability to appear in many different forms, and poses as Prince Vlad when he meets Mina, who is on her way to see her fiancé. As Prince Vlad, Dracula attempts to seduce Mina who initially resists. She relents when he offers her eternal life and sinks his fangs into her neck. But Mina is being used as a decoy by Professor Abraham Van Helsing, who has been on the trail of the vampire all his life.

At the age of 16 Keanu Reeves starred in a TV commercial for Coca Cola. He went on to success as the character Theodore Logan in the time-travel movies *Bill and Ted's Excellent Adventure* (1989) and *Bill and Ted's Bogus Journey* (1991). *Bram Stoker's Dracula* was his first number one movie, but he scored another one with *Speed* (1994). Singer Tom Waits makes an appearance as Renfield, a man who has a passion for eating insects.

In 1986 Gary Oldman appeared in his first major movie role as punk rock star Sid Vicious in *Sid and Nancy*. He made his debut in the 1981 film *Remembrance* made by Channel Four Television.

Academy Awards: Best Costume Design (Eiko Ishioka), Best Make-up (Greg Cannom, Michelle Burke and Matthew W. Mungle), Best Sound Effects Editing (Tom C. McCarthy and David E. Stone)

Music: 'Love Song for a Vampire' (Annie Lennox)

Video availability

The Top Five

Week of 5 February 1993
1. Bram Stoker's Dracula
2. The Bodyguard
3. A Few Good Men
4. Reservoir Dogs
5. Singles

UNDER SIEGE

5 March 1993   **1 week**

Distributor:	Warner
Director:	Andrew Davis
Producer:	Arnon Milchan, Steven Seagal, Steven Reuther
Screenplay:	J.F. Lawton
Music:	Gary Chang

CAST
Steven Seagal . . . . *Casey Ryback*
Tommy Lee Jones . . . . *William Strannix*
Gary Busey . . . . *Commander Krill*
Erika Eleniak . . . . *Jordan Tate*
Patrick O'Neal . . . . *Capt Adams*
Nick Mancuso . . . . *Tom Breaker*
Andy Romano . . . . *Admiral Bates*

A psychopathic terrorist (Tommy Lee Jones) manages to smuggle himself aboard the American battleship USS *Missouri* to steal the stock of nuclear weapons. But what he doesn't anticipate was Casey Ryback, recently demoted to ship's cook, and intent on sabotaging his plan.

Erika Eleniak, who played Jordan Tate, made a name for herself as the Rookie Shauni McClain in the popular TV series *Baywatch*. Gary Busey began in show business as a drummer with the pop group The Rubber Band. He later changed his name to Teddy Jack Eddy and played drums for Willie Nelson and Kris Kristofferson, among others.

Director Andrew Davis launched Steven Seagal's movie career in his 1988 film *Above The Law*. However, *Under Siege* was Seagal's only appearance at number one, although his other credits include *Above The Law* (1988), *Hard To Kill* (1989), *Marked For Death* (1990), *Out For Justice* (1990) and *Last To Surrender* (1992).

The Top Five

Week of 3 March 1993
1. Under Siege
2. Damage
3. Bram Stoker's Dracula
4. Honeymoon in Vegas
5. A River Runs Through It

Video availability

MALCOLM X

12 March 1993	1 week

Distributor:	Warner
Director:	Spike Lee
Producer:	Marvin Worth, Spike Lee
Screenplay:	Arnold Perl, Spike Lee
Music:	Terence Blanchard

CAST
Denzel Washington . . . . *Malcolm X*
Angela Bassett . . . . *Betty Shabazz*
Albert Hall . . . . *Baines*
Al Freeman Jr . . . . *Elijah Muhammad*

Delroy Lindo . . . . *West Indian Archie*
Spike Lee . . . . *Shorty*
Theresa Randle . . . . *Laura*
Kate Vernon . . . . *Sophia*

Spike Lee's biopic of Malcolm X chronicles the life of the Black activist from his time as a criminal in a zoot suit, peddling drugs, to his militant campaign for a separate Black homeland. His conversion to Islam and the cause of the Black man begins when he is in jail. With Muslim teacher Elijah Muhammad and wife Betty Shabazz, he becomes a charismatic leader. But his success creates enemies in the Black as well as the White communities.

Malcolm X (Denzel Washington) makes a visit to Mecca to investigate the roots of Islam in this biopic based on the autobiography of the militant black civil rights campaigner.

Malcolm X was based on the Alex Haley book *The Autobiography of Malcolm X*. Spike Lee's other films, *Do the Right Thing* (1989), *Mo' Better Blues* (1990) and *Jungle Fever* (1991), also deal with the Black American experience, but only *Malcolm X* was a number one.

Angela Bassett, who plays Malcolm X's wife, also played Tina Turner in *Tina: What's Love Got To Do With It?* (1993). She was Oscar nominated for this role, but lost to Holly Hunter in *The Piano*.

Music: 'Revolution' (Arrested Development), 'Roll 'em Pete' (Joe Turner), 'My Prayer' (The Ink Spots), 'Big Stuff' (Billie Holiday), 'Beans and Cornbread' (Louis Jordan), 'Azure' (Ella Fitzgerald), 'That Lucky Old Sun' (Ray Charles), 'Shot Gun' (Jnr Walker and the All Stars)

Video availability

The Top Five

Week of 12 March 1993
1. Malcolm X
2. Under Siege
3. Consenting Adults
4. Leon the Pig Farmer
5. Damage

SCENT OF A WOMAN

19 March 1993	2 weeks*

Distributor:	Universal
Director:	Martin Brest
Producer:	Martin Brest
Screenplay:	Bo Goldman
Music:	Thomas Newman

CAST
Al Pacino . . . . *Lt Colonel Frank Slade*
Chris O'Donnell . . . . *Charlie Simms*
James Rebhorn. . . . . *Mr Trask*
Gabrielle Anwar . . . . *Donna*
George Willis Jr . . . . *Philip S. Hoffman*
Richard Venture. . . . . *W.R. Slade*
Bradley Whitford . . . . *Randy*
Ron Eldard . . . . *Officer Gore*

Charlie Simms is a young college student in need of some extra money. He volunteers to take care of Lieutenant Colonel Frank Slade, and embittered near blind war veteran and former aide to Lyndon Johnson. The job turns out to be the adventure of a lifetime, with Slade taking them both off for a Thanksgiving weekend of luxury, fine wines, fine women and high-living in New York. But Slade plans to make this his last weekend and intends to kill himself.

Al Pacino finally won the elusive Best Actor Oscar for his sensitive portrayal of Frank Slade. It was his seventh nomination. The story is based on an Italian novel, *Il Buio E Il Miele* by Giovanni Arpino, which was filmed in Italy in 1974 by Dino Risi.

Director Martin Brest was commissioned to work on the computer-age movie *WarGames* (1983), but was dismissed before filming even began due to disagreements with the producers.

Academy Awards: Best Actor (Al Pacino)

Video availability

The Top Five

Week of 19 March 1993
1. Scent of a Woman
2. Malcolm X
3. Orlando
4. Under Siege
5. Toys

ORLANDO

26 March 1993	1 week

Distributor:	Electric
Director:	Sally Potter
Producer:	Christopher Sheppard
Screenplay:	Sally Potter
Music:	Bob Last

CAST
Tilda Swinton . . . . *Via Orlando*
Billy Zane . . . . *Shelmerdine*
Lothaire Bluteau . . . . *The Khan*
John Wood . . . . *Archduke Harry*
Charlotte Valandrey . . . . *Sasha*
Heathcote Williams . . . . *Nick/Publisher*
Quentin Crisp . . . . *Queen Elizabeth I*
Peter Eyre . . . . *Mr Pope*

This historical fantasy begins in 1600, when Via Orlando, as a young man, is taken under the wing of Queen Elizabeth I. Over the years the ageless Orlando falls in love with a beautiful Russian woman, becomes a British Ambassador, and curiously changes sex. As a woman, Orlando becomes pregnant after an encounter with a dashing American. After sweeping through nearly 400 years, we last see her living in present-day London.

The film was based on Virginia Woolf's 1928 bestselling novel. Most of the movie was filmed in St Petersburg and Uzbekistan in Asia. Quentin (*The Naked Civil Servant*) Crisp came out of his self-imposed exile as an Englishman in New York to appear as Queen Elizabeth I.

The director Sally Potter's only other notable film was the 1983 *Gold Diggers*, which starred Julie Christie and was made entirely by women. Potter

also co-wrote one of the songs in the film ('Coming') and provided backing vocals.

Music: 'Eliza is the Fairest Queen', 'Coming' (Jimmy Somerville)

Video availability

The Top Five

Week of 26 March 1993
1. Orlando
2. Scent of a Woman
3. Candyman
4. Hoffa
5. Malcolm X

THE DISTINGUISHED GENTLEMAN

2 April 1993	1 week

Distributor:	Buena Vista
Director:	Jonathan Lynn
Producer:	Leonard Goldberg, Michael Peyser
Screenplay:	Marty Kaplan
Music:	Randy Edelman

CAST
Eddie Murphy.. *Thomas Jefferson Johnson*
Lane Smith .... *Dick Dodge*
Sheryl Lee Ralph .... *Miss Loretta*
Joe Don Baker .... *Olaf Andersen*
Victoria Rowell .... *Celia Kirby*
Grant Shaud .... *Arthur Reinhardt*
Kevin McCarthy .... *Terry Corrigan*
Charles S. Dutton .... *Elijah Hawkins*

Jeff Johnson, a professional con man, descends on Washington and assumes the identity of a deceased congressman. He assumes, quite rightly, that the average person wouldn't know if their representative was still living anyway.

Director Jonathan Lynn was co-writer for the popular British 1970s TV comedy series *Doctor In The House* (in which he also appeared) and the 1980s *Yes Minister*. Screenwriter Marty Kaplan at one time wrote speeches for leading American politician Walter Mondale.

Music: 'The Thunderer', 'Happy Days Are Here Again', 'Soul Trilogy III', 'The Politics of Love'

Video availability

The Top Five

Week of 2 April 1993
1. The Distinguished Gentleman
2. Forever Young
3. Orlando
4. Scent of a Woman
5. Candyman

THE JUNGLE BOOK

16 April 1993	11 weeks*

(A re-release; see 1967)

The Top Five

Week of 16 April 1993
1. The Jungle Book
2. Scent of a Woman
3. Orlando
4. One False Move
5. The Distinguished Gentleman

ACCIDENTAL HERO

23 April 1993	1 week

Distributor: Columbia
Director: Stephen Frears
Producer: Laura Ziskin
Screenplay: David Peoples
Music: George Fenton

CAST

Dustin Hoffman . . . . *Bernie Laplante*
Geena Davis . . . . *Gale Gayley*
Andy Garcia . . . . *John Bubber*
Joan Cusack . . . . *Evelyn Laplante*
Kevin J. O'Connor . . . . *Chucky*
Maury Chaykin . . . . *Winston*
Stephen Tobolowsky . . . . *Wallace*
Christian Clemenson . . . . *Conklin*
Tom Arnold . . . . *Chick*

Bernie Laplante, a small-time villain, discovers by chance a crashed plane and saves all the passengers before disappearing. The media dub him 'The Angel of Flight 104' and a $1 million reward is offered to the hero. The media hunt for the hero is led by TV reporter Gale Gayley. The money is claimed by John Bubber who gave Bernie a lift as he left the scene of the accident.

Geena Davis turned down the role of Catherine Tramell in *Basic Instinct* (1992) on the grounds that the script was 'objectionable'. In 1994 she appeared in *Angie* in a role which was originally offered to Madonna. The pop singer turned it down due to work commitments but publicly announced that she did not think Geena Davis was right for the part.

Joan Cusack, who plays Bernie's estranged wife, was a regular contributor to the hit American TV series *Saturday Night Live* in 1985/6. For her performance in *Working Girl* (1988) she was Oscar nominated as Best Supporting Actress, but lost to Geena Davis for *The Accidental Tourist*.

Music: 'Heart of a Hero' (Luther Vandross), 'The Man I Love', 'Hoping That Someday You'd Care' (George and Ira Gershwin)

Video availability

The Top Five

Week of 23 April 1993
1. Accidental Hero
2. Body of Evidence
3. Orlando
4. One False Move
5. Scent of a Woman

Bernie Laplante, played by Dustin Hoffman in Accidental Hero, *inadvertently manages to rescue passengers aboard a crashed plane, only to have the glory stolen by John Bubber (Andy Garcia).*

SOMMERSBY

30 April 1993	2 weeks

Distributor:	Warner
Director:	John Amiel
Producer:	Arnon Milchan, Steven Reuther
Screenplay:	Nicholas Meyer, Sarah Kernochan
Music:	Danny Elfman

CAST

Richard Gere	Jack
Jodie Foster	Laurel
Lanny Flaherty	Buck
Wendell Wellman	Travis
Bill Pullman	Orin
Brett Kelley	Little Rob
William Windom	Reverend Powell
Clarice Taylor	Esther
Frankie Faison	Joseph

Landowner Jack Sommersby is presumed dead after the Civil War but suddenly turns up at his home. The tyrant husband that his wife Laurel remembers has changed into a sensitive and loving husband and a just landowner. He is intent on bringing prosperity back to his war-beaten estate and introduces his tenants to a profit-sharing scheme by getting them to grow tobacco. He also seeks revenge on members of a gang who stage attacks on his black workers. But Laurel's world is shattered when Jack is accused of being an imposter.

Sommersby was adapted from the well-known 1982 French film *La Retour de Martin Guerre* (The Return of Martin Guerre), which starred Gérard Depardieu.

English director John Amiel worked in British television, one of his biggest successes being the 1987 Dennis Potter series *The Singing Detective*.

Video availability

The Top Five

Week of 30 April 1993
1. Sommersby
2. Accidental Hero
3. Un Coeur en Hiver
4. Body of Evidence
5. Scent of a Woman

GROUNDHOG DAY

14 May 1993	1 week

Distributor:	Columbia
Director:	Harold Ramis
Producer:	Trevor Albert, Harold Ramis
Screenplay:	Danny Rubin, Harold Ramis
Music:	George Fenton

CAST

Bill Murray	Phil
Andie MacDowell	Rita
Chris Elliott	Larry
Stephen Tobolowsky	Ned
Brian Doyle-Murray	Buster
Marita Geraghty	Nancy
Angela Paton	Mrs Lancaster
Rick Ducommun	Gus
Rick Overton	Ralph

In this entertaining comedy Phil is a TV weatherman, covering a Groundhog Day festival in a small rural town. Phil's not really the country type and is less than happy when he and his producer, Rita, and cameraman, Larry, end up stuck in Punxsutawney when bad weather strikes. He's even more unhappy when he wakes up the next morning to find it's Groundhog Day – again. Phil's stuck in a time loop and no matter what he does, every morning when his alarm goes off at 6 a.m. he's repeating the same day, over and over. This does have its benefits; for example, he has plenty of second chances in his efforts to charm Rita. If his line doesn't work the first time, he just tries something else the next day until he gets it right.

Director Harold Ramis once worked as a porter in a hospital, and went on to become the jokes editor for *Playboy* Magazine. He previously directed Bill Murray in *Caddyshack* (1980). He worked again with Murray in *Ghostbusters* (1984), appearing in the film rather

The Top Five

Week of 14 May 1993
1. Groundhog Day
2. Sommersby
3. Alive
4. Un Coeur en Hiver
5. Accidental Hero

than directing it, as well as co-writing the screenplay with Dan Aykroyd.

Music: 'Weatherman' (Delbert McClinton), 'I Got You Babe' (Sonny and Cher), 'Pennsylvania Polka'

(Frankie Yankovic), 'Take Me Round Again' (Susie Stevens), 'You Don't Know Me' (Ray Charles), 'Almost Like Being In Love' (Nat King Cole)

Video availability

INDECENT PROPOSAL

21 May 1993	3 weeks

Distributor:	Paramount
Director:	Adrian Lyne
Producer:	Sherry Lansing
Screenplay:	Amy Holden Jones
Music:	John Barry

CAST
Robert Redford . . . . *John Gage*
Demi Moore . . . . *Diana Murphy*
Woody Harrelson . . . . *David Murphy*
Seymour Cassel . . . . *Mr Shackleford*
Oliver Platt . . . . *Jeremy*
Billy Bob Thornton . . . . *Day Tripper*
Rip Taylor . . . . *Mr Langford*
Billy Connolly . . . . *Auction Emcee*

Millionaire John Gage finds himself attracted to the lovely Diana Murphy, the wife of David. The couple are experiencing serious financial problems and when Gage offers a million dollars for one night with Diana they accept. But the decision leads to far more involved emotional problems.

Indecent Proposal, based on a novel by Jack Engelhard, was director Adrian Lyne's second number one movie. His first was *Fatal Attraction* (1988), for which he was Oscar nominated. His other credits include *Flashdance* (1983), *9½ Weeks* (1986) and *Jacob's Ladder* (1990).

Woody Harrelson became known to millions of TV viewers as Woody Boyd, the idiot bartender in the American comedy series *Cheers*.

Video availability

The Top Five

Week of 21 May 1993
1. Indecent Proposal
2. Groundhog Day
3. Sommersby
4. Un Coeur en Hiver
5. Alive

FALLING DOWN

11 June 1993	3 weeks

Distributor:	Warner
Director:	Joel Schumacher
Producer:	Arnold Kopelson, Timothy Harris, Herschel Weingrod
Screenplay:	Ebbe Roe Smith
Music:	James Newton Howard

CAST
Michael Douglas . . . . *D-Fens*
Robert Duvall . . . . *Prendergast*
Barbara Hershey . . . . *Beth*
Rachel Ticotin . . . . *Sandra*
Tuesday Weld . . . . *Mrs Prendergast*
Frederic Forrest . . . . . *Surplus Store Owner*
Lois Smith . . . . *D-Fens' mother*
Joey Hope Singer . . . . *Adele*

Former Los Angeles defence worker D-Fens is out of work, recently divorced and having a bad day. Trying to deliver a birthday present for his daughter Adele, he gets stuck in a heavy traffic jam on the freeway and blows a fuse. Determined to get to his ex-wife's (Barbara Hershey) house any way he can, he abandons the car and heads off on foot. Becoming crazed with the urban frustrations he encounters along the way, he leaves a trail of violence and mayhem behind him for LA cop Prendergast to follow.

In 1973, Barbara Hershey changed her name to Seagull after accidentally killing one of the birds. She reverted back to Hershey in 1975. Hershey made her movie debut in *With Six You Get Eggroll* (1968), starring Doris Day in her last major movie role.

The Top Five

Week of 11 June 1993
1. Falling Down
2. Indecent Proposal
3. Boxing Helena
4. Groundhog Day
5. Savage Nights

Robert Duvall, the cop on the trail of D-Fens, made his debut in *To Kill A Mockingbird* (1962), in which he played Cary Grant's next door neighbour. His other number one films include *The Godfather* (1972), *The Godfather Part II* (1975), *Network* (1977), *The Eagle Has Landed* (1977), *Apocalypse Now* (1980) and *The Paper* (1994).

Music: 'La Schmoove' (Fu-Schnickens), 'Estupida De Me' (Arabella), 'Murio Neustro Amor De Verano (Sin Por Que)' (Luisa Maria Guell)

Video availability

CLIFFHANGER

2 July 1993	3 weeks

Distributor:	Carolco
Director:	Renny Harlin
Producer:	Alan Marshall, Renny Harlin
Screenplay:	Michael France, Sylvester Stallone
Music:	Trevor Jones

CAST
Sylvester Stallone . . . . *Gabe Walker*
John Lithgow . . . . *Qualen*
Michael Rooker . . . . *Hal Tucker*
Janine Turner . . . . *Jessie Deighan*
Rex Linn . . . . *Travers*
Caroline Goodall . . . . *Dristel*
Leon . . . . *Kynette*
Craig Fairbrass . . . . *Delmar*

Gabe Walker and Hal Tucker are mountain rescue professionals. When a gang of hijackers crash in the mountains, Hal is sent to rescue them, believing them to be innocent travellers. When he goes missing Gabe heads up the perilous icy cliffs in blizzard conditions to find his friend. Both are captured by the gang and while Qualen is held hostage Gabe is forced to find the suitcases that were scattered over the mountains during the crash.

The film was estimated to have cost around $65 million to produce. A large expense was safe rigging for the actors, including Stallone, who had to hang off the side of a cliff for shots.

Video availability

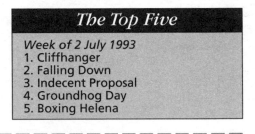

The Top Five

Week of 2 July 1993
1. Cliffhanger
2. Falling Down
3. Indecent Proposal
4. Groundhog Day
5. Boxing Helena

JURASSIC PARK

23 July 1993	6 weeks

Distributor:	Universal
Director:	Steven Spielberg
Producer:	Kathleen Kennedy, Gerald R. Molen
Screenplay:	Michael Crichton, David Koepp
Music:	John Williams

CAST
Sam Neill . . . . *Grant*
Laura Dern . . . . *Ellie*
Jeff Goldblum . . . . *Malcolm*
Richard Attenborough . . *John Hammond*
Bob Peck . . . . *Muldoon*
Martin Ferrero . . . . *Gennaro*
B.D. Wong . . . . *Wu*
Joseph Mazzello . . . . *Tim*
Ariana Richards . . . . *Lex*

A group of dinosaur experts arrive to inspect a new island theme park that is soon to be opened to the public by the obsessive billionaire John Hammond. He's been cloning dinosaurs from DNA deposits with great success. However, a power cut, caused by the tampering of a crooked computer genius, deactivates the electric fences that keep the dinosaurs at a safe distance. Hammond's guests – Grant, Ellie and Malcolm – along with his grandchildren Tim and Lex are caught in the middle of the park when the dinosaurs break loose.

Jurassic Park, based on Michael Crichton's best-selling novel, quickly became the most financially successful film ever, taking $52 million alone in it's first weekend in the USA. The British Censor insisted on a poster warning which read 'This film contains sequences which may be particularly disturbing to younger children or those of a sensitive disposition' before granting the PG certificate it needed to pull in the millions of children who made the film such a box office success.

Jurassic Park saw Richard Attenborough's return to acting after 14 years. His last appearance on

Palaeontologist Dr Alan Grant (Sam Neill) has a heart to heart with an enormous Tyrannosaurus Rex in Jurassic Park.

screen was in the spy film *The Human Factor*.

Academy Awards: Best Sound (Gary Summers, Gary Rydstrom, Shawn Murphy, Ron Judkins), Best Sound Effects Editing (Gary Rydstrom, Richard Hyms), Best Visual Effects (Dennis Muren, Stan Winston, Phil Tippett, Michael Lantieri)

Video availability

The Top Five

Week of 23 July 1993
1. Jurassic Park
2. Cliffhanger
3. Super Mario Bros
4. Mad Dog and Glory
5. Indecent Proposal

IN THE LINE OF FIRE

3 September 1993	2 weeks

Distributor: Columbia
Director: Wolfgang Petersen
Producer: Jeff Apple
Screenplay: Jeff Maguire
Music: Ennio Morricone

CAST
Clint Eastwood .... *Frank Horrigan*
John Malkovich .... *Mitch Leary*
René Russo .... *Lilly Raines*
Dylan McDermott .... *Al D'Andrea*
Gary Cole .... *Bill Watts*
Fred Dalton Thompson .... *Harry Sargent*
John Mahoney .... *Sam Campagna*
Jim Curley .... *President*

Veteran secret service agent Frank Horrigan is assigned to help protect the President's life, but is haunted by the belief that he failed in his duty to protect President Kennedy some twenty years earlier. It becomes a battle of wits when madman Mitch Leary makes known his intention to assassinate the current President just before the elections.

German-born director Wolfgang Petersen had a successful career in his homeland, making his first film in 1973. It wasn't until 1984 that he directed his first English-language movie, *The Never Ending Story*.

Ennio Morricone, who wrote the music, worked on several earlier Eastwood movies, including *A Fistful of Dollars* (1964), *The Good, The Bad and The Ugly* (1966) and *Two Mules for Sister Sara* (1970).

Music: 'I Only Have Eyes For You', 'These Foolish Things (Remind Me of You)', 'Willow Weep for Me', 'As Time Goes By', 'I Didn't Know What Time It Was'

Video availability

The Top Five

Week of 3 September 1993
1. In The Line of Fire
2. Much Ado About Nothing
3. Jurassic Park
4. Made In America
5. Hot Shots! Part Deux

THE FIRM

17 September 1993	2 weeks

Distributor: Paramount
Director: Sydney Pollack
Producer: Sydney Pollack, Scott Rudin,
    John Davis
Screenplay: David Rabe, Robert Towne
    and David Rayfiel
Music: Dave Grusin

CAST
Tom Cruise .... *Mitch McDeere*
Jeanne Tripplehorn ...... *Abby McDeere*
Gene Hackman .... *Avery Tolar*
Hal Holbrook .... *Oliver Lambert*
Terry Kinney .... *Lamar Quinn*
Wilford Brimley .... *William Devasher*
Ed Harris .... *Wayne Tarrance*
Holly Hunter .... *Tammy Hemphill*

Mitch McDeere is a young lawyer who is thrilled when he is accepted by an established law firm. But after two of the company's attorneys mysteriously die in a boating accident he discovers that the organization is run by the Mob. The only way to leave the firm is by dying of old age or by learning too much and being killed.

John Grisham, who wrote the original novel on which the film is based, was a professional lawyer before turning to writing. He is also the author of *Pelican Brief*, which became a film, starring Julia Roberts and Denzel Washington.

Despite his studious role, Cruise is in fact dyslexic and always carries a dictionary.

Music: 'Stars In The Water' (Jimmy Buffett), 'M-O-N-E-Y' (Lyle Lovett), 'Never Mind' (Nanci Griffith), 'Start It Up' (Robben Ford and The Blue Line)

Video availability

The Top Five

Week of 17 September 1993
1. The Firm
2. In The Line of Fire
3. Much Ado About Nothing
4. Jurassic Park
5. Sliver

THE FUGITIVE

1 October 1993	5 weeks

Distributor: **Warner**
Director: **Andrew Davis**
Producer: **Arnold Kopelson**
Screenplay: **Jeb Stuart, David Twohy**
Music: **James Newton Howard**

CAST
Harrison Ford . . . . *Dr Richard Kimble*
Tommy Lee Jones . . . . *Samuel Gerard*
Sela Ward . . . . *Helen Kimble*
Julianne Moore . . . . *Dr Anne Eastman*
Joe Pantoliano . . . . *Cosmo Renfro*
Andreas Katsulas . . . . *Sykes*
Jeroen Krabbé . . . . *Dr Charles Nichols*
L. Scott Caldwell . . . . *Poole*

Dr Richard Kimble is accused and convicted of his wife's murder. His claims that he saw a one-armed man running away from the scene of the crime is not believed. He escapes police custody on the way to prison and sets out to find the one-armed man, but becomes a fugitive hunted by Tommy Lee Jones.

The film was based on the popular American TV series from the 1960s, which starred David Janssen as Dr Richard Kimble and Barry Morse as Lieutenant Philip Gerard. Roy Huggins, who created the original TV series, worked on the movie as executive producer.

Director Andrew Davis and Tommy Lee Jones previously worked together on an earlier number one from this year, *Under Siege*. They also teamed up for the 1989 film *The Package*.

Academy Awards: Best Supporting Actor (Tommy Lee Jones)

Video availability

The Top Five

Week of 2 October 1993
1. The Fugitive
2. Sleepless In Seattle
3. The Firm
4. Tina: What's Love Got To Do With It?
5. Much Ado About Nothing

THE PIANO

5 November 1993	2 weeks

Distributor: **Entertainment**
Director: **Jane Campion**
Producer: **Jan Chapman**
Screenplay: **Jane Campion**
Music: **Michael Nyman**

CAST
Holly Hunter . . . . *Ada McGrath*
Harvey Keitel . . . . *George Baines*
Sam Neill . . . . *Stewart*
Anna Paquin . . . . *Fiona McGrath*
Kerry Walker . . . . *Aunt Morag*
Genevieve Lemon . . . . *Nessie*

Scotswoman Ada McGrath is to marry a man in New Zealand she has never met. Although she has her hearing, she cannot or will not speak, but manages to communicate through her daughter. Her prized possession is her piano, but her new husband (Sam Neill) gives it away. The new owner (Harvey Keitel) offers Ada the chance to buy back the piano by giving him lessons in love.

All three of the main actors in *The Piano* enjoyed particular success in 1993. Harvey Keitel also reached number one with *Reservoir Dogs*, Sam Neill played a central role in the success of top film *Jurassic Park*, and Holly Hunter appeared in the number one film *The Firm*.

Eleven-year-old Anna Paquin picked up an Oscar as Best Supporting Actress, much to her surprise. However, she was not the youngest actress to win an Academy Award. Tatum O'Neal was only ten when

Top Ten Films of 1993

1 Jurassic Park
2 The Bodyguard
3 Home Alone 2
4 The Fugitive
5 Indecent Proposal
6 Bram Stoker's Dracula
7 Cliffhanger
8 Sleepless In Seattle
9 A Few Good Men
10 The Jungle Book

Director Jane Campion's fourth feature film, The Piano, *tells the tale of Ada's (Holly Hunter) most treasured possession, her piano, which her new husband (Sam Neill) has no interest in rescuing from a New Zealand beach.*

she won for her performance in *Paper Moon* (1973). Shirley Temple was awarded an honorary Oscar in 1937, when she was five years old.

The Piano shared the Palm D'Or prize at the 1993 Cannes Film Festival with *Farewell My Concubine.*

Academy Awards: Best Actress (Holly Hunter), Best Supporting Actress (Anna Paquin), Best Original Screenplay (Jane Campion)

The Top Five

Week of 5 November 1993
1. The Piano
2. The Fugitive
3. Rising Sun
4. Sleepless In Seattle
5. True Romance

Video availability

DEMOLITION MAN

19 November 1993	1 week

Distributor:	Warner
Director:	Marco Brambilla
Producer:	Joel Silver, Michael Levy, Howard Kazanjian
Screenplay:	Daniel Waters, Robert Reneau, Peter M. Lenkov
Music:	Elliot Goldenthal

CAST
Sylvester Stallone . . . . *John Spartan*
Wesley Snipes . . . . *Simon Phoenix*
Sandra Bullock . . . . *Lenina Huxley*
Nigel Hawthorne . . . *Dr Raymond Cocteau*
Benjamin Bratt . . . . *Alfredo Garcia*
Bob Gunton . . . . *Chief George Earle*
Glenn Shadix . . . . *Associate Bob*

Denis Leary . . . . *Edgar Friendly*

Sergeant John Spartan, a no-nonsense cop, and Simon Phoenix, a crazy criminal, are both frozen in ice for 30 years. They awake from the thaw in a penitentiary in 21st-century San Angeles (the new name for LA). Phoenix escapes and begins a campaign of terror in the city which only Spartan can stop.

The Top Five

Week of 19 November 1993
1. Demolition Man
2. The Piano
3. The Remains of the Day
4. Dave
5. The Fugitive

Demolition Man was the directorial debut of Marco Brambilla who had previously worked on TV commercials. Wesley Snipes, who had appeared in Michael Jackson's 1987 pop video for 'Bad', had already made a name for himself in *Mo' Better Blues* (1990), *Jungle Fever* (1991) and *White Men Can't Jump* (1992). Co-producer Joel Silver had a small part as a movie director in the 1988 number one

Who Framed Roger Rabbit. It was also the first movie number one for actor Nigel Hawthorne (the boss of the futuristic city), better known for his role as Sir Humphrey in the British TV comedy series *Yes Minister*.

Video availability

ALADDIN

26 November 1993	7 weeks

Distributor:	Buena Vista
Director:	John Musker, Ron Clements
Producer:	John Musker, Ron Clements
Screenplay:	Ron Clements, John Musker, Ted Elliott, Terry Rossio
Music:	Alan Menken (original score) Howard Ashman, Alan Menken, Tim Rice (songs)

CAST (Voices)
Scott Weinger . . . . *Aladdin*
Robin Williams . . . . *Genie*
Linda Larkin . . . . *Princess Jasmine*
Jonathan Freeman . . . . *Jafar*
Frank Welker . . . . *Abu*
Randy Cartwright . . . . *Carpet*
Gilbert Gottfried . . . . *Jago*
Douglas Seale . . . . *Sultan*

Street urchin Aladdin helps Jafar, the adviser to the Sultan, to retrieve the magic lamp that has been lost in a desert cave. By chance he meets Princess Jasmine who has escaped from her palace to avoid a law that forces her to marry a prince. On a flying carpet he whisks them away to adventure and eventual safety.

Lyricist Howard Ashman, who worked closely with composer Alan Menken, tragically died during the making of this movie. Tim Rice was brought in to complete the project.

The face of Aladdin was based on the features of Tom Cruise.

Academy Awards: Best Original Score (Alan Menken), Best Original Song – 'A Whole New World' (Alan Menken, music; Tim Rice, lyrics)

Music: 'A Whole New World' (Peabo Bryson and Regina Belle), 'Arabian Nights' (Bruce Adler), 'One Jump Ahead' (Brad Kane), 'Friend Like Me', 'Prince Ali' (Robin Williams), 'A Whole New World' (Brad Kane and Lea Salonga)

Video availability

The Top Five

Week of 26 November 1993
1. Aladdin
2. The Piano
3. Demolition Man
4. The Remains of the Day
5. The Man Without a Face

MALICE

14 January 1994	2 weeks

Distributor:	Castle Rock
Director:	Harold Becker
Producer:	Rachel Pfeffer, Charles Mulvehill, Harold Becker
Screenplay:	Aaron Sorkin, Scott Frank
Music:	Jerry Goldsmith

CAST
Alec Baldwin . . . . *Jed*
Nicole Kidman . . . . *Tracy*
Bill Pullman . . . . *Andy*
Bebe Neuwirth . . . . *Dana*
George C. Scott . . . . *Dr Kessler*

Anne Bancroft . . . . *Ms Kennsinger*
Peter Gallagher . . . . *Dennis Riler*
Josef Sommer . . . . *Lester Adams*

In this suspense thriller surgeon Jed infiltrates the life of his old college chum Andy. He moves into

The Top Five

Week of 14 January 1994
1. Malice
2. Carlito's Way
3. Farewell My Concubine
4. A Perfect World
5. The Remains of the Day

his house, becomes involved with his wife (Kidman) and performs unnecessary surgery on her which leaves her unable to have children. The film's terror is heightened when a number of college students are attacked and raped, possibly by the college caretaker.

Nicole Kidman, who made her debut at the age of 14 in Australia, is married to Tom Cruise. Bebe Neuwirth played Lilith Sternin-Crane in the long-running American comedy series *Cheers*.

Video availability

MANHATTAN MURDER MYSTERY

28 January 1994	1 week

Distributor: Columbia TriStar
Director: Woody Allen
Producer: Robert Greenhut
Screenplay: Woody Allen, Marshall Brickman
Music: Various extracts

CAST
Alan Alda .... Ted
Woody Allen .... Larry Lipton
Anjelica Huston .... Marcia Fox
Diane Keaton .... Carol Lipton
Jerry Adler .... Paul House
Joy Behar .... Marilyn
Ron Rifkin..................... Sy
Lynn Cohen .... Lillian House
Melanie Norris .... Helen Moss

Woody Allen's comedy thriller is set, as ever, in Manhattan. Larry and Carol Lipton are the next-door neighbours of Paul and Lillian House, and when Lillian drops dead from a heart attack Carol is convinced she's been murdered. Noting the fact that Paul seems less than upset by his wife's death, she attempts to unravel what she is convinced is a conspiracy, dragging her reluctant husband with her. This gentle, light-hearted farce marked Woody Allen's return to comedy acting with one of his best partners, Diane Keaton.

Diane Keaton had previously appeared in a number of Woody Allen movies: *Play It Again Sam* (1972), *Sleeper* (1974), *Love and Death* (1975), *Annie Hall* (1977), *Manhattan* (1979) and *Radio Days* (1987). The screenplay for *Manhattan Murder Mystery* was by Marshall Brickman who had written one of

Woody's (and Diane's) biggest successes, *Annie Hall*.

Video availability

The Top Five

Week of 28 January 1994
1. Manhattan Murder Mystery
2. Farewell My Concubine
3. Tombstone
4. Carlito's Way
5. Malice

Top Male Actors 1969–94

Appearances in number one movies

Jack Nicholson	16
Harrison Ford	14
Clint Eastwood	11
Dustin Hoffman	11
Sylvester Stallone	10
Robert De Niro	10
Roger Moore	10
Sean Connery	9
Michael Douglas	9
Michael Caine	9
Alec Guinness	9
Arnold Schwarzenegger	9
Al Pacino	9
Tom Cruise	8
Danny DeVito	8
Gene Hackman	8
Robert Redford	8
Robert Duvall	7
Mel Gibson	7
Harvey Keitel	7
Ralph Richardson	7
Edward Fox	6
Richard Gere	6
James Earl Jones	6*
Eddie Murphy	6
Joe Pesci	6
Robin Williams	6**
Ned Beatty	5
Marlon Brando	5
Jeff Bridges	5
James Caan	5
Kevin Costner	5
Andy Garcia	5
Bob Hoskins	5
Bernard Lee	5
Paul Newman	5
Nick Nolte	5

* this figure does not include *The Lion King*
** this figure does not include *Aladdin*

MRS DOUBTFIRE

4 February 1994	3 weeks

Distributor:	Twentieth Century-Fox
Director:	Chris Columbus
Producer:	Marsha Garces Williams, Robin Williams, Mark Radcliffe
Screenplay:	Randi Mayem Singer, Leslie Dixon
Music:	Howard Shore

CAST
Robin Williams *Daniel Hillard/Mrs Doubtfire*
Sally Field . . . . *Miranda Hillard*
Pierce Brosnan . . . . *Stu*
Harvey Fierstein . . . . *Frank*
Polly Holliday . . . . *Gloria*
Lisa Jakub . . . . *Lydia Hillard*
Matthew Lawrence . . . . *Chris Hillard*
Mara Wilson . . . . *Natalie Hillard*

At the centre of this gentle bittersweet comedy is Daniel Hillard, a divorcé missing his three young children. In order to spend more time with his offspring, he applies for, and gets, the job as their nanny dressed as an elderly English lady. There are many laughs as he tries to keep his true identity secret from estranged wife Miranda and her new boyfriend Stu.

Mrs Doubtfire was two-time Oscar-winner Sally Field's first number one movie of 1994, the second was *Forrest Gump*. The film was also another smash hit for director Chris Columbus who made the two *Home Alone* movies.

Academy Awards: Best Make-up (Greg Cannom, Ve Neill, Yolanda Toussieng)

Video availability

The Top Five

Week of 4 February 1994
1. Mrs Doubtfire
2. The Age of Innocence
3. Manhattan Murder Mystery
4. Farewell My Concubine
5. Tombstone

Robin Williams masquerades as the extraordinary nanny Mrs Doubtfire *in order to spend more time with his children, having been thrown out of the family home by his wife.*

SCHINDLER'S LIST

25 February 1994	7 weeks*

Distributor: UIP
Director: Steven Spielberg
Producer: Steven Spielberg, Gerald R.
               Molen, Branko Lustig
Screenplay: Steven Zaillian
Music: John Williams

CAST
Liam Neeson. . . . . *Oskar Schindler*
Ben Kingsley . . . . *Itzhak Stern*
Ralph Fiennes. . . . . *Amon Goeth*
Caroline Goodall . . . . *Emilie Schindler*
Jonathan Sagalle . . . . . *Poldek Pfefferberg*
Embeth Davidtz . . . . *Helen Hirsch*
Malgoscha Gebel . . . . . *Victoria Klonowska*

The Czech businessman Oskar Schindler risks his life to protect and rescue more than 1000 Jewish workers at his factory during World War II. After taking over a confiscated enamelware plant in Krakow, Schindler makes his fortune with the unpaid skills of the Jewish workforce. His concern for his workers increases after he witnesses the Nazi atrocities against the Jews in the Krakow ghettos. He makes deals, offers bribes and does everything in his power to keep his workers out of the concentration camp.

Spielberg's black and white film, based on the true story of Oskar Schindler and Thomas Keneally's book about him, was filmed on location in Poland, using Schindler's actual factory, which still exists in Krakow.

John Williams won another Oscar for his original score. He has been nominated 18 times for that particular Academy Award and has won four so far. The others are for *Jaws* (1976), *Star Wars* (1978) and *E.T.* (1982).

Academy Awards: Best Picture (Producers Steven Spielberg, Gerald R. Molen and Branko Lustig), Best Direction (Steven Spielberg), Best Adapted Screenplay (Steven Zaillian), Best Cinematography (Janusz Kaminski), Best Editing (Michael Kahn), Best Original Score (John Williams), Best Art Direction (Allan Starski), Set Decoration (Ewa Braun)

Video availability

The Top Five

Week of 25 February 1994
1. Schindler's List
2. The Age of Innocence
3. Mrs Doubtfire
4. In the Name of the Father
5. The Three Musketeers

PHILADELPHIA

11 March 1994	3 weeks

Distributor: TriStar
Director: Jonathan Demme
Producer: Edward Saxon, Jonathan
               Demme
Screenplay: Ron Myswaner
Music: Howard Shore

CAST
Tom Hanks . . . . *Andrew Beckett*
Denzel Washington . . . . *Joe Miller*
Jason Robards . . . . *Charles Wheeler*
Mary Steenburgen . . . . *Belinda Conine*
Antonio Banderas . . . . *Miguel Alvarez*
Ron Vawter . . . . *Bob Seidman*
Robert Ridgely . . . . *Walter Kenton*
Charles Napier . . . . *Judge Garnett*

Bright Philadelphia lawyer (Hanks) is fired by his law firm when they discover he's HIV positive. He sues for wrongful dismissal with help from

lawyer Denzel Washington, and the case goes to court. His employers argue that they fired him for incompetence but Washington sets out to prove that he was discriminated against because of his illness.

Philadelphia was the first major Hollywood picture to tackle the prejudices surrounding Aids, and Hanks won Best Actor Oscar for his sensitive portrayal of a dying man.

Bruce Springsteen's video for the song 'Streets of Philadelphia' was also directed by Jonathan Demme

The Top Five

Week of 11 March 1994
1. Philadelphia
2. Schindler's List
3. The Pelican Brief
4. Short Cuts
5. Shadowlands

and was actually filmed on the streets of Philadelphia. It gave Bruce his biggest single success ever in the UK, reaching number two in the charts.

Academy Awards: Best Actor (Tom Hanks), Best Original Song – 'Streets of Philadelphia' (Bruce Springsteen, music and lyrics)

Music: 'Philadelphia' (Neil Young), 'Streets of Phila-

delphia' (Bruce Springsteen), 'Lovetown' (Peter Gabriel), 'Have You Ever Seen The Rain?' (The Spin Doctors), 'Please Send Me Someone To Love' (Sade), 'I Don't Wanna Talk About It' (Indigo Girls)

Video availability

ACE VENTURA: PET DETECTIVE

6 May 1994	1 week

Distributor:	Warner
Director:	Tom Shadyac
Producer:	James G. Robinson
Screenplay:	Jack Bernstein, Tom Shadyac and Jim Carrey
Music:	Ira Newborn

CAST
Jim Carrey .... *Ace Ventura*
Courteney Cox .... *Melissa*
Sean Young .... *Einhorn*
Tone Loc .... *Emilio*
Dan Marino .... *Dan Marino*
Noble Willingham .... *Riddle*
Troy Evans .... *Podacter*
Raynor Scheine .... *Woodstock*

Incompetent detective Ace Ventura tries to solve the mystery of the kidnapping of Snowflake, the dolphin who is the mascot of the Miami Dolphins Football team. Just before an important champion-

ship match the Dolphin's star player, Dan Marino, is also kidnapped and Ace, along with police chief Einhorn, has two kidnappings to solve.

Ace Ventura was Jim Carrey's first film. It was swiftly followed by *The Mask*, which also went to number one. Carrey had previously appeared in television's *In Living Colour*, in which he was the only white member of the cast. In the United States Jim Carrey clocked up another number one in 1994 with *Dumb and Dumber*.

Video availability

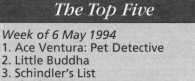

The Top Five

Week of 6 May 1994
1. Ace Ventura: Pet Detective
2. Little Buddha
3. Schindler's List
4. Shadowlands
5. Striking Distance

THE PAPER

13 May 1994	1 week

Distributor:	UIP
Director:	Ron Howard
Producer:	Brian Grazer, Frederick Zollo
Screenplay:	David Koepp and Stephen Koepp
Music:	Randy Newman

CAST
Michael Keaton .... *Henry Hackett*
Robert Duvall .... *Bernie White*
Glenn Close .... *Alicia Clark*
Marisa Tomei .... *Martha Hackett*
Randy Quaid .... *McDougal*
Jason Robards .... *Graham Keighley*
Jason Alexander ...... *Marion Sandusky*
Spalding Gray .... *Paul Bladden*

It's another hectic day in the life of tabloid newspaper *The New York Sun*. Journalist Henry Hackett

has a very pregnant wife, an exclusive on a fast-breaking story, an editor with a medical condition, colleagues with no scruples and most important of all an 8 o'clock deadline!

The Paper gave Glenn Close her first number one since her groundbreaking performance in *Fatal Attraction* (1987). She's been Oscar nominated five times, for *The World According To Garp* (1982),

The Top Five

Week of 13 May 1994
1. The Paper
2. My Father The Hero
3. What's Eating Gilbert Grape?
4. Little Buddha
5. Ace Ventura: Pet Detective

The Big Chill (1984), *The Natural* (1984), *Fatal Attraction* (1987) and *Dangerous Liaisons* (1988), but has yet to win. She spends half her time on the American stage, where she has appeared regularly on Broadway in shows like *Barnum*, *Death And* *The Maiden* and *Sunset Boulevard*. In Hollywood she made her motion picture debut in 1982 opposite Robin Williams in *The World According To Garp*.

Video availability

FOUR WEDDINGS AND A FUNERAL

20 May 1994	9 weeks

Distributor:	Polygram
Director:	Mike Newell
Producer:	Duncan Kenworthy
Screenplay:	Richard Curtis
Music:	Richard Rodney Bennett

CAST

Hugh Grant	Charles
Andie MacDowell	Carrie
Christin Scott Thomas	Fiona
Simon Callow	Gareth
James Fleet	Tom
John Hannah	Matthew
Charlotte Coleman	Scarlett
David Bower	David
Rowan Atkinson	Father Gerald

In this romantic comedy bachelor Charles attends a number of friends' weddings but never seems close to marriage himself. He's charming and witty but just can't make that commitment and the more weddings he attends the less likely it seems that he'll make it to the altar himself. However, when he meets the beautiful American Carrie he slowly but surely falls in love. He only realizes she's the girl for him after seeing her at four weddings and a funeral. By that point, however, he's stood in an English cathedral getting married himself – to someone else!

Four Weddings and a Funeral was the most successful British film ever. The film cost £4 million to make and grossed over £160 million. It was a huge

The Top Five

Week of 20 May 1994
1. Four Weddings and a Funeral
2. My Father the Hero
3. What's Eating Gilbert Grape?
4. The Paper
5. Little Buddha

In 1994 the most successful British movie to date, Four Weddings and a Funeral, *starring Hugh Grant and Andie MacDowell, failed to pick up any Oscars at the 1995 Academy Awards ceremony in Hollywood.*

hit in the USA before it opened in the UK, meaning the ads were able to read 'The number one box office hit in the US'. It was written by Richard Curtis, who wrote the TV comedy *Blackadder* for Rowan Atkinson and *The Tall Guy*, which starred Jeff Goldblum and Emma Thompson. The director Mike Newell's previous number one was *Dance with a Stranger* in 1985.

Music: 'Love Is All Around' (Wet Wet Wet), 'But Not for Me', 'Crocodile Rock'. 'Chapel of Love' (Elton John), 'La La La (Means I Love You)' (Swing Out Sister), 'You're The First My Last My Everything' (Barry White), 'I Will Survive' (Gloria Gaynor), 'It Should Have Been Me' (Gladys Knight and The Pips), 'Loving You Tonight' (Squeeze), 'Can't Smile Without You' (Lena Fiagbe)

Video availability

MAVERICK

22 July 1994	1 week

Distributor:	Warner
Director:	Richard Donner
Producer:	Bruce Davey, Richard Donner
Screenplay:	William Goldman
Music:	Randy Newman

CAST
Mel Gibson . . . . *Bret Maverick*
Jodie Foster . . . . *Annabelle Bransford*
James Garner . . . . *Zane Cooper*
Graham Greene . . . . *Joseph*
Alfred Molina . . . . *Angel*
James Coburn . . . . *Commodore*
Dub Taylor . . . . *Room Clerk*
Geoffrey Lewis . . . . *Matthew Wicker*

Bret Maverick is a smooth-talking gambler who tries to avoid trouble when travelling from town to town in the Wild West. He meets with the alluring Annabelle (Jodie Foster) who is also a con-artist. He decides to enter the poker championship set on board a steamship under the command of James Coburn.

James Garner had, of course, been the star of the long-running TV series *Maverick*, in which he played the title role. He was Oscar nominated for *Murphy's*

Romance in 1985 and played Jim Rockford in *The Rockford Files*, for which he won an Emmy Award.

Two-time Oscar-winner Jodie Foster said about *Maverick*, 'I wanted to do some comedy after a series of dramatic roles.'

Director Richard Donner worked with Mel Gibson on the three *Lethal Weapon* movies, all of which reached number one.

Music: 'Maverick' (Restless Heart), 'Renegades Rebels and Rogues' (Tracy Lawrence), 'A Good Run of Bad Luck' (Clint Black), 'Something Already Gone' (Carlene Carter), 'Ride Gambler Ride' (Randy Newman), 'You Don't Mess Around With Me' (Waylon Jennings), 'Amazing Grace' (The Maverick Choir)

Video availability

The Top Five

Week of 22 July 1994
1. Maverick
2. Four Weddings and a Funeral
3. Go Fish
4. Beverly Hill Cop III
5. The Beverly Hillbillies

THE FLINTSTONES

29 July 1994	2 weeks

Distributor:	UIP
Director:	Brian Levant
Producer:	Bruce Cohen
Screenplay:	Tom S. Parker and Jim Jennewein, Steven E. de Souza
Music:	David Newman

CAST
John Goodman . . . . *Fred Flintstone*
Elizabeth Perkins . . . . . . *Wilma Flintstone*

Rick Moranis . . . . *Barney Rubble*
Rosie O'Donnell . . . . *Betty Rubble*
Kyle MacLachlan . . . . *Cliff Vandercave*
Halle Berry . . . . *Miss Stone*
Elizabeth Taylor . . . . *Pearl Slaghoople*
Dann Florek . . . . *Mr Slate*

In this live-action trip to the town of Bedrock Fred and Wilma Flintstone fall out with their best friends, Barney and Betty Rubble, when Fred is promoted in his job at the Slate & Co. quarry by his unscrupulous boss. The modern Stone Age Family from 2,000,000 BC eventually realize that they've been duped and Fred sets about repairing the damage he's caused to his family and friends.

Joe Barbera and William Hanna, who created the original cartoon series, both have small cameo roles in the film. American late-night chat show host Jay Leno crops up again in a movie, this time as the host of *Bedrock's Most Wanted*, a Prehistoric TV show.

The poster credit for the film runs 'Steven Spielrock presents'.

Jim Henson's London-based Creature Shop supplied most of the creatures like the Dictabird and the Pigasaurus.

Elizabeth Taylor's role as Fred Flintstone's crazy mother-in-law was her first major film character since *The Mirror Crack'd* in 1980.

Music: '(Meet) The Flintstones', 'The Bedrock Twitch' (BC-52's), 'Walk The Dinosaur' (Was Not Was), 'Bedrock Anthem' ('Weird Al' Yankovic), 'Rock with the Caveman' (Big Audio Dynamite), 'Anarchy In The UK' (Green Jelly)

Video availability

The Top Five

Week of 29 July 1994
1. The Flintstones
2. Sirens
3. Maverick
4. Four Weddings and a Funeral
5. Love and Human Remains

SIRENS

12 August 1994	1 week

Distributor:	Buena Vista
Director:	John Duigan
Producer:	Sue Milliken
Screenplay:	John Duigan
Music:	Rachel Portman

CAST
Hugh Grant . . . . *Anthony Campion*
Tara Fitzgerald . . . . *Estella Campion*
Sam Neill . . . . *Norman Lindsay*
Elle MacPherson . . . . *Sheela*
Portia De Rossi . . . . *Giddy*
Kate Fischer . . . . *Pru*
Pamela Rabe . . . . *Rose Lindsay*
Ben Mendelsohn . . . . *Lewis*
John Polson . . . . *Tom*

An English clergyman, Anthony Campion, arrives in Australia in the early 1930s with his young bride Estella. Before he can take up his new job his Bishop asks him to stop at artist Norman Lindsay's house to try to persuade him to withdraw one of his risqué paintings from a forthcoming exhibition. While at Lindsay's house the Campions' marriage is put to the test as three young models (Sheela, Giddy and Pru) attempt to influence Estella away from her husband.

Sirens followed hot on the heels of Hugh Grant's other number one of 1994, *Four Weddings and a Funeral*. It was the first movie role for Australian supermodel Elle 'The Body' MacPherson.

The Top Five

Week of 12 August 1994
1. Sirens
2. The Flintstones
3. The Last Seduction
4. Four Weddings and a Funeral
5. Maverick

TRUE LIES

19 August 1994	2 weeks*

Distributor:	UIP
Director:	James Cameron
Producer:	James Cameron, Stephanie Austin
Screenplay:	James Cameron
Music:	Brad Fiedel

CAST
Arnold Schwarzenegger . . . . *Harry Tasker*
Jamie Lee Curtis . . . . *Helen Tasker*

Tom Arnold . . . . *Gib*
Bill Paxton . . . . *Simon*
Art Malik . . . . *Aziz*
Tia Carrere . . . . *Juno*
Eliza Dushku . . . . *Dana*
Grant Heslov . . . . *Faisil*
Charlton Heston . . . . *Spencer Trilby*

Special agent Harry Tasker leads a double life. His wife Helen thinks he sells computers but he's really an international spy with a top-secret government agency. When she eventually discovers his

Helen Tasker (Jamie Lee Curtis) is shocked to discover that Harry (Arnold Schwarzenegger), her husband of 15 years, is actually a secret agent in True Lies.

double life she joins him on his mission against a group of terrorists.

This spectacular action movie featured many mind-boggling stunts, particularly the sequences in the Florida Keys and the use of Harrier jump jets.

Director James Cameron previously worked with Schwarzenegger on the two *Terminator* movies.

Music: 'Sunshine of your Love' (Living Colour), 'Darkness Darkness' (Screaming Trees), 'Alone In The Dark' (John Hiatt), 'Entity' (Mother Tongue)

The Top Five

Week of 19 August 1994
1. True Lies
2. The Last Seduction
3. Sirens
4. Four Weddings and a Funeral
5. The Flintstones

Video availability

THE MASK

26 August 1994	2 weeks*

Distributor:	Entertainment
Director:	Charles Russell
Producer:	Bob Engelman
Screenplay:	Mike Werb
Music:	Bonnie Greenberg (supervisor)

CAST
Jim Carrey . . . . *Stanley Ipkiss*
Cameron Diaz . . . . *Tina Carlyle*
Peter Riegert . . . . *Lt Mitch Kellaway*
Peter Greene . . . . *Dorian Tyrel*
Amy Yasbeck . . . . *Peggy Brandt*
Richard Jeni . . . . *Charlie Schumacher*
Orestes Matacena . . . . *Niko*
Timothy Bagley . . . . *Irv*

Mild-mannered bank clerk Stanley Ipkiss turns into a superhero whenever he dons an ancient mask he found in a river. Transformed 'from zero to hero' he changes into a wisecracking indestructible crimefighter with super powers. Brilliant special effects (from George Lucas' Industrial Light and Magic) help Ipkiss become a whirling, all-dancing, all-charming prankster in this fun-filled action-comedy.

The Mask was Jim Carrey's second number one in 1994. The first was *Ace Ventura: Pet Detective*.

Carrey's make-up, by Greg Cannon, who won an Oscar for Francis Ford Coppola's *Dracula*, took four hours a day to apply.

Music: 'Durban Pete' (Jim Carrey), 'Bounce Around' (Tony Toni Tone), '(I Could Only) Whisper Your Name' (Harry Connick Jr), 'Let The Good Times Roll' (Fishbone), 'You Would Be My Baby' (Vanessa Williams)

Video availability

The Top Five

Week of 26 August 1994
1. The Mask
2. True Lies
3. The Last Seduction
4. Four Weddings and a Funeral
5. Sirens

WOLF

2 September 1994	1 week

Distributor:	Columbia
Director:	Mike Nichols
Producer:	Douglas Wick
Screenplay:	Jim Harrison, Wesley Strick
Music:	Ennio Morricone

CAST
Jack Nicholson . . . . *Will Randall*
Michelle Pfeiffer . . . . *Laura Alden*
James Spader . . . . *Stewart Swinton*
Kate Nelligan . . . . *Charlotte Randall*
Richard Jenkins . . . . *Detective Bridger*
Christopher Plummer . . . *Raymond Alden*
Eileen Atkins . . . . *Mary*
David Hyde Pierce . . . . *Roy*

When New York book editor Will Randall gets bitten by a wolf he finds his career and love-life revitalized. He undergoes changes to his personality, becomes involved with his boss's daughter (Pfeiffer) and sets about fending off the challenges to his position at work by setting up a rival company and taking their best authors with him.

Wolf featured the interesting pairing for two stars who had both appeared in *Batman* movies. Nicholson as the Joker in *Batman* and Pfeiffer as Catwoman in *Batman Returns*. The two had also worked together on *The Witches of Eastwick*.

This was the fourth pairing of Nicholson and director Nichols. They had also worked together on *Carnal Knowledge*, *The Fortune* and *Heartburn*.

The make-up artist Rick Baker had worked on the werewolf of *An American Werewolf in London*.

The Top Five

Week of 2 September 1994
1. Wolf
2. The Mask
3. True Lies
4. The Last Seduction
5. Four Weddings and a Funeral

CLEAR AND PRESENT DANGER

23 September 1994	2 weeks

Distributor:	Paramount
Director:	Phillip Noyce
Producer:	Mace Neufeld, Robert Rehme
Screenplay:	Donald Stewart, Steven Zaillian, John Milius
Music:	James Horner

CAST
Harrison Ford . . . . *Jack Ryan*
Willem Dafoe . . . . *Clark*
Anne Archer . . . . *Cathy Ryan*
Joaquim de Almeida . . . . *Felix Cortez*
Henry Czerny . . . . *Robert Ritter*
Harris Yulin . . . . *James Cutter*
Donald Moffat . . . . *President Bennett*
Miguel Sandoval . . . . . . *Ernesto Escobedo*
James Earl Jones . . . . *Admiral Greer*

Harrison Ford is again CIA agent Jack Ryan. This time he's promoted to Acting Deputy Director when his boss, Admiral Greer, becomes ill. Ryan goes to South America to bust a drug baron with the help of renegade agent Clark. Ryan discovers that the President of the United States has links with the Colombian drug barons and his life is in danger from many different sources. However, he cleans up the drug cartel and dramatically confronts the President with the evidence of his crimes.

The Top Five

Director Phillip Noyce had also made *Patriot Games* with Ford as Jack Ryan.

James Earl Jones made his film debut in Stanley Kubrick's *Dr Strangelove* in 1963. He reached number one again in 1994 as the voice of King Mafusa in *The Lion King*.

SPEED

7 October 1994	1 week

Distributor:	Twentieth Century-Fox
Director:	Jan De Bont
Producer:	Mark Gordon
Screenplay:	Graham Yost
Music:	Mark Mancina

CAST
Keanu Reeves . . . . *Jack Traven*
Dennis Hopper . . . . *Howard Payne*
Sandra Bullock . . . . *Annie*
Joe Morton . . . . *Capt. McMahon*
Jeff Daniels . . . . *Harry*
Alan Ruck . . . . *Stephens*

Sociopathic bomber Howard Payne (Hopper) has rigged a Los Angeles bus with a bomb primed to explode once the vehicle's speed goes under 50 mph. Reckless cop Jack Traven (Reeves) boards the crowded bus and attempts to disarm the bomb with the help of driver Annie. But the bus is running out of road, petrol and time.

One French reviewer worked out that it would have been far cheaper to pay the ransom demand than pay the price of the trail of destruction and mayhem, including the damage to the plane on the runway at the airport!

Speed was Dutch director Jan de Bont's first feature film. His previous cinematographer credits include *Die Hard*, *Lethal Weapon 3*, *The Hunt For Red October* and *Basic Instinct*.

Sandra Bullock appeared in an earlier number one, *Demolition Man*.

The Top Five

FORREST GUMP

14 October 1994	1 week

Distributor:	Paramount
Director:	Robert Zemeckis
Producer:	Wendy Finerman, Steve Tisch, Steve Starkey
Screenplay:	Eric Roth
Music:	Alan Silvestri

CAST
Tom Hanks . . . . *Forrest Gump*
Robin Wright . . . . *Jenny Curran*
Gary Sinise . . . . *Lt Dan Taylor*
Mykelti Williamson . . . . *Bubba Blue*
Sally Field . . . . *Mrs Gump*
Michael Conner Humphreys *Young Forrest*
Hanna R. Hall . . . . *Young Jenny*

Over 30 years the slow-witted Southern boy Forrest Gump inadvertently becomes a football star, a war hero, a millionaire shrimp-company owner and meets several US presidents. Forrest Gump has a low I.Q. but his mother wants the best for him. Encouraged by his childhood friend Jenny to 'run, run like the wind' whenever he encounters trouble, his path through the most momentous events of the second half of the 20th century becomes a real odyssey.

The Top Five

Tom Hanks first came to attention in the early 1980s TV situation comedy series *Bosom Buddies*. He played a New York office worker who, failing to find accommodation, dresses in drag in order to stay in a ladies only hostel. *Splash* (1984), in which he starred with Daryl Hannah, was his breakthrough movie.

Music: 'Hound Dog' (Elvis Presley), 'Respect' (Aretha Franklin), 'Rainy Day Women Numbers 12 and 35' (Bob Dylan), 'Sloop John B' (The Beach Boys), 'Mrs Robinson' (Simon and Garfunkel), 'Joy To The World' (Three Dog Night), 'California Dreamin'' (The Mamas and The Papas), 'Walk Right In' (The Rooftop Singers)

THE LION KING

21 October 1994	2 weeks

Distributor:	Buena Vista
Director:	Roger Allers, Rob Minkoff
Producer:	Don Hahn
Screenplay:	Irene Mecchi, Jonathan Roberts, Linda Woolverton
Music:	Tim Rice (lyrics) Elton John (music) Hans Zimmer (original score)

CAST (Voices)
Rowan Atkinson .... Zazu
Matthew Broderick .... Simba
Niketa Calame .... Young Nala
Jim Cummings .... Ed
Whoopi Goldberg .... Shenzi
Robert Guillaume .... Rafiki
Jeremy Irons................... Scar
James Earl Jones .... Mufasa

In this full-length Disney cartoon set in the African jungle the Lion King Mufasa is grooming his little cub Simba to take over as king. However, Uncle Scar, Mufasa's brother, has designs on the throne and plots to kill his young nephew. He leads Simba into forbidden territory, but Mufasa rescues his son and his friend and forbids his son from ever leaving their homeland again. Not to be deterred, Scar engineers another trip into danger, but this time Mufasa dies in the rescue of his son from a dangerous stampede. Scar convinces Simba that he's to blame

and sends the cub into exile where he's befriended by Pumbaa the flatulent warthog. Several years elapse before Simba, fully grown, returns home to claim his rightful inheritance.

The Lion King took 600 animators four years to make. They produced over a million drawings and the film consists of 1190 individual scenes and 1155 backgrounds. It became Disney's highest grossing film ever, taking $300 million in 1994 in the USA alone. It was also the first Disney film not to feature any humans, just animals.

Music: 'Circle of Life' (Carmen Twillie), 'I Just Can't Wait to be King' (Jason Weaver), 'Be Prepared' (Jeremy Irons, Jay Rifkin with Whoopi Goldberg), 'Hakuna Matata' (Nathan Lane, Ernie Shabella, Jason Weaver and Joseph Williams), 'Can You Feel the Love Tonight' (Joseph Williams, Sally Dworsky, Nathan Lane, Ernie Sabella and Kristle Edwards), 'Circle of Life', 'Can You Feel the Love Tonight', 'I Just Can't Wait to be King' (Elton John)

The Top Five

Week of 21 October 1994
1. The Lion King
2. Forrest Gump
3. Speed
4. The Adventures of Priscilla: Queen of the Desert
5. Clear and Present Danger

PULP FICTION

4 November 1994	4 weeks*

Distributor:	Buena Vista
Director:	Quentin Tarantino
Producer:	Lawrence Bender
Screenplay:	Quentin Tarantino
Music:	Karyn Rachtman (supervisor)

CAST
John Travolta .... Vincent Vega
Samuel L. Jackson .... Jules
Uma Thurman................... Mia
Harvey Keitel .... The Wolf
Tim Roth .... Pumpkin
Bruce Willis .... Butch
Amanda Plummer .... Honey Bunny
Maria de Madeiros........... Fabienne
Ving Rhames .... Marsellus Wallace
Eric Stoltz .... Lance

Tarantino's modern-day gangster movie follows three separate storylines, all inextricably linked. Pumpkin and Honey Bunny are plotting to hold up a diner. Vincent Vega and Jules have been despatched to bump off some petty crooks before Vincent takes his boss Marsellus's girlfriend Mia on a date. And boxer Butch (Bruce Willis) is on the run from Marsellus after he fails to take the dive he was ordered to. Added to this is The Wolf, whose job is to clean up the mess left by bloodthirsty criminals.

Pulp Fiction was Quentin Tarantino's second film as director and his second number one. His first was *Reservoir Dogs* (1993). Harvey Keitel also appeared in *Reservoir Dogs*.

Tarantino's film also put John Travolta back on top for the first time since *Look Who's Talking* (1990), which also starred the voice talents of his co-star here, Bruce Willis.

Music: 'Lonesome Town' (Ricky Nelson), 'Son of a

Preacher Man' (Dusty Springfield), 'Let's Stay Together' (Al Green), 'Flowers on the Wall' (The Statler Brothers), 'Girl, You'll Be A Woman Soon' (Urge Overkill), :If Love Is A Red Dress (Hang Me In Rags)' (Maria McKee), 'You Never Can Tell' (Chuck Berry)

The Top Five

Week of 4 November 1994
1. Pulp Fiction
2. The Lion King
3. Forrest Gump
4. Speed
5. The Adventures of Priscilla: Queen of the Desert

MARY SHELLEY'S FRANKENSTEIN

11 November 1994	2 weeks

Distributor:	Columbia TriStar
Director:	Kenneth Branagh
Producer:	Francis Ford Coppola, James V. Hart, John Veitch
Screenplay:	Steph Lady, Frank Darabont
Music:	Patrick Doyle

CAST
Robert De Niro Creature/sharp-featured man
Kenneth Branagh..... Victor Frankenstein
Tom Hulce.................... Henry
Helena Bonham Carter .... Elizabeth
Aidan Quinn.................. Walton
Ian Holm.............. Victor's Father
Richard Briers............. Grandfather
John Cleese .... Professor Waldman

Young scientist Victor Frankenstein hopes to create a living being in order to find a way to cheat death. Having witnessed his mother's death in childbirth, Victor leaves the family home in Geneva and the love of his life, his adopted sister Elizabeth,

to go to university in Angolstadt. He spends all his time in a laboratory learning from the sinister Professor Waldman about his experiments with man-made creations. Plundering limbs and other bodily parts from criminals in the morgue, Victor constructs a creature which duly comes to life to terrorize all those in its path.

Mary Shelley's Frankenstein was the third number one movie for Branagh as director and star. Others were *Dead Again* (1991) and *Peter's Friends* (1992), both of which co-starred Branagh's Oscar-winning wife, Emma Thompson.

The Top Five

Week of 11 November 1994
1. Mary Shelley's Frankenstein
2. Pulp Fiction
3. The Lion King
4. The Adventures of Priscilla: Queen of the Desert
5. Forrest Gump

JUNIOR

16 December 1994	2 weeks

Distributor:	Universal
Director:	Ivan Reitman
Producer:	Ivan Reitman
Screenplay:	Kevin Wade, Chris Conrad
Music:	James Newton Howard

CAST
Arnold Schwarzenegger Dr Alexander Hesse

Danny DeVito......... Dr Larry Arbogast
Emma Thompson .... Dr Diana Reddin
Frank Langella .... Noah Banes
Pamela Reed................. Angela
Judy Collins .... Naomi
James Eckhouse .... Dr Ned Sneller
Aida Turturro................ Louise

Doctors Hesse and Arbogast have been attempting to find a drug that will make pregnancy easier for women. Their laboratory is closed down when the Federal Drug Administration refuses to sanction their new drug and their workplace is taken over by British scientist Doctor Reddin. Dismayed that all their hard work is in vain Hesse agrees, after a lot of persuasion from Arbogast, to be a guinea-pig for the drug and becomes pregnant. With the help of Reddin, whose egg he's carrying, the pair thwart the authorities who have become suspicious, and soothe the aches and pains of the suffering father-to-be.

Junior was Ivan Reitman's third number one as both producer and director. The others were *Ghostbusters* (1984) and *Kindergarten Cop* (1991) also with Arnold Schwarzenegger. He also made *Twins* (1988) with his two stars Schwarzenegger and DeVito.

Emma Thompson returned to her comedy roots in *Junior*, having made *The Tall Guy* (1989) with Jeff Goldblum and her husband's *Peter's Friends* (1992).

Music: 'I've Got You Under My Skin' (Cassandra Wilson)

The Top Five

Week of 16 December 1994
1. Junior
2. Pulp Fiction
3. Miracle on 34th Street
4. Tim Burton's The Nightmare Before Christmas
5. Three Colours: Red

THE SPECIALIST

30 December 1994	1 weeks

Distributor:	Warner
Director:	Luis Llosa
Producer:	Jerry Weintraub
Screenplay:	Alexandra Seros
Music:	John Barry

CAST
Sylvester Stallone . . . . *Ray Quick*
Sharon Stone . . . . *May Munro*
James Woods . . . . *Ned Trent*
Rod Steiger . . . . *Joe Leon*
Eric Roberts . . . . *Tomas Leon*

At the centre of this action thriller set in Miami is former government explosives specialist Ray Quick. He takes on an assignment from May Munro, who wants to avenge her parents' deaths at the hands of a murderous syndicate of gangsters several years ago. Crime boss Joe Leon, who ordered the killings, and his son Tomas soon learn that someone is out for revenge. Although they hire Quick's former partner, Ned Trent, to investigate, they are soon powerless to prevent more bloodshed and retribution.

The Specialist was Stallone's tenth number one and Sharon Stone's third, after *Total Recall* (1990) and *Basic Instinct* (1992).

Rod Steiger last hit the top in a cameo role in Robert Altman's *The Player* (1992). James Woods' first appearance in a number one film was in *The Way We Were* in 1974 and he subsequently topped the chart in *Against all Odds* in 1984.

Music: 'Mental Picture' (Jon Secada), 'Turn The

Beat Around' (Gloria Estefan), 'Real', 'Love Is The Thing' (Donna Allen), 'All Because of You', 'Jambala' (Miami Sound Machine)

The Top Five

Week of 30 December 1994
1. The Specialist
2. Pulp Fiction
3. Junior
4. The Lion King
5. Forrest Gump

Top Twenty Films of 1994

1 Four Weddings and a Funeral
2 Mrs Doubtfire
3 The Flintstones
4 The Lion King
5 The Mask
6 Aladdin
7 Schindler's List
8 True Lies
9 Forrest Gump
10 Speed
11 Philadelphia
12 Cool Runnings
13 Wayne's World 2
14 Addams Family Values
15 Maverick
16 Beethoven's 2nd
17 Free Willy
18 Clear and Present Danger
19 Naked Gun 33⅓
20 Mary Shelley's Frankenstein

Number One Movies

1969

Date		Weeks at number one
11 Jul	The Most Dangerous Man in the World	1
18 Jul	Oliver!	1
25 Jul	Three Into Two Won't Go	1
01 Aug	Oliver!	4
29 Aug	The Wild Bunch	4
26 Sep	Battle of Britain	4
31 Oct	Virgin Soldiers	1
07 Nov	Battle of Britain	7
26 Dec	On Her Majesty's Secret Service	1

1970

Date		Weeks
02 Jan	On Her Majesty's Secret Service	5
06 Feb	Battle of Britain	2
20 Feb	Butch Cassidy and the Sundance Kid	1
27 Feb	Battle of Britain	1
06 Mar	Butch Cassidy and the Sundance Kid	2
20 Mar	Anne of the Thousand Days	6
01 May	Airport	6
12 Jun	Paint Your Wagon	1
19 Jun	M*A*S*H	4
17 Jul	Woodstock	1
24 Jul	Cromwell	8
18 Sep	Lawrence of Arabia	1
25 Sep	Kelly's Heroes	1
02 Oct	Lawrence of Arabia	1
09 Oct	Cromwell	1
16 Oct	Tora! Tora! Tora!	3
06 Nov	Waterloo	5
11 Dec	Scrooge	3

1971

Date		Weeks
01 Jan	Scrooge	3
22 Jan	Murphy's War	1
29 Jan	Song of Norway	5
05 Mar	The Music Lovers	1
12 Mar	Death In Venice	1
19 Mar	Love Story	13
18 Jun	Valdez Is Coming	1
25 Jun	Little Big Man	2
09 Jul	Sunday Bloody Sunday	2
23 Jul	Le Mans	1
30 Jul	The Devils	8
24 Sep	Carnal Knowledge	2
08 Oct	The Go-Between	3
29 Oct	Bedknobs and Broomsticks	4
27 Nov	Traffic	1
04 Dec	Straw Dogs	1
11 Dec	Nicholas and Alexandra	2
25 Dec	Fiddler on the Roof	1

1972

Date		Weeks
01 Jan	Nicholas and Alexandra	1
08 Jan	Diamonds are Forever	10
18 Mar	The French Connection	1
25 Mar	Diamonds are Forever	2
08 Apr	Mary, Queen of Scots	5
13 May	A Clockwork Orange	1
20 May	The Hospital	2
03 Jun	Frenzy	1
10 Jun	Cabaret	5
15 Jul	What's Up Doc?	2
29 Jul	Young Winston	5
02 Sep	The Godfather	13
02 Dec	Lady Caroline Lamb	3
23 Dec	Alice's Adventures In Wonderland	2

1973

06 Jan . . .	Alice's Adventures in Wonderland	1
13 Jan . . .	Lady Caroline Lamb	1
20 Jan . . .	The Valachi Papers	2
03 Feb . . .	The Getaway	5
10 Mar . .	Travels with My Aunt	2
24 Mar . .	Last Tango in Paris	8
19 May . .	Hitler–The Last Ten Days	1
26 May . .	Last Tango in Paris	2
09 Jun . . .	A Touch of Class	1
16 Jun . . .	Last Tango in Paris	1
23 Jun . . .	Day of the Jackal	3
14 Jul. . .	Live and Let Die	10
22 Sep . . .	Scorpio	4
20 Oct . . .	Don't Look Now	7
08 Dec . . .	Paper Moon	2
22 Dec . . .	Magnum Force	1
29 Dec . . .	Robin Hood	1

1974

05 Jan . . .	Robin Hood	1
12 Jan . . .	The Sting	1
19 Jan . . .	Enter The Dragon	2
02 Feb . . .	The Sting	2
16 Feb . . .	The Way We Were	1
23 Feb . . .	The Sting	2
09 Mar . .	The Way We Were	2
23 Mar . .	The Exorcist	9
25 May . .	Great Gatsby	8
20 Jul. . . .	The Exorcist	2
03 Aug . .	For Pete's Sake	2
17 Aug . .	Chinatown	4
14 Sep . . .	Gold	2
28 Sep . . .	Thunderbolt and Lightfoot	1
05 Oct . . .	Gold	1
12 Oct . . .	Emmanuelle	2
26 Oct . . .	The Odessa File	4
23 Nov. . .	Emmanuelle	1
30 Nov. . .	Murder on the Orient Express	1
07 Dec . . .	Earthquake	3
28 Dec . . .	The Man with the Golden Gun	1

1975

04 Jan . . .	The Man with the Golden Gun	5
08 Feb . . .	The Towering Inferno	7
29 Mar . .	Funny Lady	1
05 Apr . . .	Tommy	7
24 May . .	The Godfather Part II	5
28 Jun . . .	Tommy	5
02 Aug . .	French Connection II	1
09 Aug . .	Tommy	2
23 Aug . .	The Drowning Pool	1
30 Aug . .	The Eiger Sanction	2
13 Sep . . .	Rollerball	3
04 Oct . . .	Three Days of the Condor	4
01 Nov. . .	Jungle Book	3
22 Nov. . .	Lisztomania	2
06 Dec . . .	Lenny	2
20 Dec . . .	Barry Lyndon	2

1976

03 Jan . . .	Jaws	9
06 Mar . .	One Flew over the Cuckoo's Nest	7
24 Apr . . .	Shout at the Devil	1
01 May . .	One Flew over the Cuckoo's Nest	1
08 May . .	All the President's Men	10
17 Jul. . . .	The Missouri Breaks	2
31 Jul. . . .	Bugsy Malone	1
07 Aug . .	The Message	1
14 Aug . .	The Outlaw Josey Wales	2
28 Aug . .	Family Plot	1
04 Sep . . .	Murder By Death	2
18 Sep . . .	Drum	1
25 Sep . . .	The Omen	6
06 Nov. . .	Return of a Man Called Horse	1
13 Nov. . .	Emmanuelle 2	6
25 Dec . . .	The Pink Panther Strikes Again	1

1977

01 Jan . . .	The Pink Panther Strikes Again	5
05 Feb . . .	Silent Movie	1
12 Feb . . .	The Pink Panther Strikes Again	1
19 Feb . . .	Cross of Iron	1
26 Feb . . .	Network	1
05 Mar . .	The Last Tycoon	1
12 Mar . .	The Pink Panther Strikes Again	3
02 Apr . . .	A Star Is Born	1
09 Apr . . .	The Eagle Has Landed	1
16 Apr . . .	Airport '77	2
30 Apr . . .	Rocky	3
21 May . .	A Star Is Born	6
02 Jul. . . .	A Bridge Too Far	2
16 Jul. . . .	The Spy Who Loved Me	10
24 Sep . . .	Exorcist II: The Heretic	1
01 Oct . . .	New York, New York	2
15 Oct . . .	Valentino	2
29 Oct . . .	The Spy Who Loved Me	3
19 Nov. . .	Salon Kitty	2
03 Dec. . .	The Spy Who Loved Me	1
10 Dec. . .	Golden Rendezvous	2
24 Dec. . .	The Deep	2

1978

07 Jan . . .	Star Wars	11
25 Mar . .	Close Encounters of the Third Kind	15
08 Jul. . . .	Game of Death	1
15 Jul. . . .	Close Encounters of the Third Kind	1
22 Jul. . . .	Revenge of the Pink Panther	8
16 Sep . . .	Heaven Can Wait	1
23 Sep . . .	Grease	6
04 Nov. . .	Death on the Nile	6
16 Dec. . .	Force 10 from Navarone	1
23 Dec. . .	Superman	2

1979

06 Jan . . .	Superman	9
10 Mar . .	The Deer Hunter	3
31 Mar . .	California Suite	3
21 Apr . . .	Battlestar Galactica	1
28 Apr . . .	California Suite	2
12 May . .	The Deer Hunter	1
19 May . .	The Warriors	2
02 Jun . . .	Escape to Athena	1
09 Jun . . .	The Lady Vanishes	1
16 Jun . . .	The World is Full of Married Men	1
23 Jun . . .	Doctor Zhivago	1
30 Jun . . .	Players	1
07 Jul. . . .	Moonraker	10
15 Sep . . .	Alien	8
10 Nov. . .	Yanks	1
17 Nov. . .	Monty Python's Life of Brian	6
29 Dec. . .	Star Trek: The Motion Picture	1

1980

05 Jan . . .	Star Trek: The Motion Picture	1
12 Jan . . .	Apocalypse Now	1
19 Jan . . .	Monty Python's Life of Brian	2
02 Feb . . .	Escape from Alcatraz	2
16 Feb . . .	10	5
22 Mar . .	The Electric Horseman	1
29 Mar . .	Kramer vs Kramer	7
17 May . .	American Gigolo	2
31 May . .	The Empire Strikes Back	11
16 Aug . .	Airplane!	4
13 Sep . . .	McVicar	1
20 Sep . . .	Cruising	2
04 Oct . . .	Dressed to Kill	1
11 Oct . . .	The Shining	2
25 Oct . . .	The Elephant Man	2
08 Nov. . .	Caligula	6
20 Dec. . .	Flash Gordon	2

1981

03 Jan ...	Flash Gordon	4
31 Jan ...	The Exterminator	1
07 Feb ...	The Jazz Singer	3
28 Feb ...	Raging Bull	1
07 Mar ..	Private Benjamin	2
21 Mar ..	Ordinary People	2
04 Apr ...	Stir Crazy	1
11 Apr ...	Ordinary People	1
18 Apr ...	Superman II	4
16 May ..	The Postman Always Rings Twice	2
30 May ..	Tess.................	2
13 Jun ...	The Postman Always Rings Twice	2
27 Jun ...	Friday the 13th Part 2 ...	1
04 Jul....	For Your Eyes Only	10
12 Sep ...	Raiders of the Lost Ark ..	2
26 Sep ...	The Final Conflict	1
03 Oct ...	Raiders of the Lost Ark ..	2
17 Oct ...	History of the World Part 1	2
31 Oct ...	The French Lieutenant's Woman....	7
19 Dec ...	Gallipoli	1
26 Dec ...	Arthur	1

1982

02 Jan ...	Arthur	7
20 Feb ...	Death Wish 2	2
06 Mar ..	Reds	1
13 Mar ..	Mad Max 2...........	1
20 Mar ..	Reds	2
03 Apr ...	Evil under the Sun	2
17 Apr ...	Quest for Fire	2
01 May ..	The Border...........	1
08 May ..	Private Lessons	2
22 May ..	The Empire Strikes Back/Star Wars........	3
12 Jun ...	Missing	5
17 Jul....	Porky's	1
24 Jul....	Pink Floyd – The Wall ...	1
31 Jul....	Rocky III	1
07 Aug ..	Pink Floyd – The Wall ...	4
04 Sep ...	Conan the Barbarian....	1
11 Sep ...	Who Dares Wins	1
18 Sep ...	Blade Runner..........	1
25 Sep ...	Poltergeist	2
09 Oct ...	Cat People	1
16 Oct ...	The Entity	2
30 Oct ...	Tron	6
11 Dec ...	Gandhi	1
18 Dec ...	E.T. The Extra-Terrestrial	2

1983

01 Jan ...	E.T. The Extra-Terrestrial	4
29 Jan ...	Airplane II – The Sequel	1
05 Feb ...	Gandhi	2
19 Feb ...	An Officer and a Gentleman...........	1
26 Feb ...	Gandhi	8
23 Apr ...	Sophie's Choice	2
07 May ..	Tootsie	5
11 Jun ...	Return of the Jedi	5
16 Jul....	Octopussy	1
23 Jul....	Return of the Jedi	1
30 Jul....	Superman III	1
06 Aug ..	Octopussy	3
27 Aug ..	WarGames	5
01 Oct ...	Staying Alive	2
15 Oct ...	Zelig	2
29 Oct ...	The Jungle Book/ Mickey's Christmas Carol	7
17 Dec ...	Trading Places	1
24 Dec ...	Never Say Never Again ..	2

1984

07 Jan ...	Never Say Never Again .	2
21 Jan ...	Trading Places	1
28 Jan ...	Gorky Park	1
04 Feb ...	Sudden Impact	1
11 Feb ...	Scarface	3
03 Mar ..	To Be Or Not To Be	3
24 Mar ..	Terms of Endearment ..	4
21 Apr ...	Greystoke: The Legend of Tarzan	4
19 May ..	Against All Odds	3
09 Jun ...	Breakdance	1
16 Jun ...	Another Country	1
23 Jun ...	Indiana Jones and the Temple of Doom	9
25 Aug ..	Romancing the Stone ...	4
22 Sep ...	Paris, Texas	1
29 Sep ...	The Company of Wolves .	3
20 Oct ...	The Woman in Red	5

24 Nov . . . 1984 2	15 Dec . . . Ghostbusters 3	
08 Dec . . . Give My Regards to Broad Street 1		

1985

05 Jan . . . Ghostbusters 3	14 Sep . . . Desperately Seeking Susan 3
26 Jan . . . Water 1	05 Oct . . . Fletch 1
02 Feb . . . Beverly Hills Cop 5	12 Oct . . . Pale Rider 1
09 Mar . . Dance with a Stranger . 1	19 Oct . . . Life Force 1
16 Mar . . 2010 4	26 Oct . . . Mad Max Beyond Thunderdome 2
13 Apr . . . A Passage to India 5	
18 May . . The Cotton Club 2	09 Nov . . . The Emerald Forest 2
01 Jun . . . Witness 3	23 Nov . . . Prizzi's Honor 2
22 Jun . . . A View to a Kill 11	07 Dec . . . Santa Claus 1
07 Sep . . . Rambo: First Blood Part II 1	14 Dec . . . Back to the Future 3

1986

04 Jan . . . Back to the Future 2	26 Jul . . . . Hannah and Her Sisters . 2
18 Jan . . . A Chorus Line 2	09 Aug . . Cobra 1
01 Feb . . . Rocky IV 5	16 Aug . . Hannah and Her Sisters . 3
01 Mar . . Commando 2	06 Sep . . . Aliens 5
15 Mar . . Out of Africa 5	11 Oct . . . Top Gun 2
19 Apr . . . Absolute Beginners 2	25 Oct . . . Mona Lisa 1
03 May . . Out of Africa 1	01 Nov . . . The Mission 2
10 May . . The Jewel of the Nile . . 3	15 Nov . . . Ruthless People 2
31 May . . Down and Out in Beverly Hills 1	29 Nov . . . The Mission 1
	06 Dec . . . Top Gun 1
07 Jun . . . After Hours 1	13 Dec . . . Labyrinth 1
14 Jun . . . A Room with a View . . . 5	20 Dec . . . Crocodile Dundee 2
19 Jul . . . . Police Academy III: Back In Training 1	

1987

03 Jan . . . Crocodile Dundee 7	04 Jul . . . . The Secret of My Success 1
21 Feb . . . The Fly 3	11 Jul . . . . The Living Daylights 8
14 Mar . . The Color of Money . . . 3	05 Sep . . . Lethal Weapon 1
04 Apr . . . The Fourth Protocol . . . 1	12 Sep . . . The Living Daylights 1
11 Apr . . . Personal Services 1	19 Sep . . . Full Metal Jacket 1
18 Apr . . . The Voyage Home: Star Trek IV 2	26 Sep . . . The Untouchables 4
	24 Oct . . . Beverly Hills Cop II 1
02 May . . Platoon 6	31 Oct . . . The Witches of Eastwick . 5
13 Jun . . . The Morning After 3	05 Dec . . . Cry Freedom 4

1988

02 Jan . . . Cry Freedom 1	09 Apr . . . Three Men and a Baby . . 4
09 Jan . . . Predator 2	07 May . . . Wall Street 8
23 Jan . . . Fatal Attraction 3	02 Jul . . . . Crocodile Dundee II 5
13 Feb . . . Robocop 2	06 Aug . . . Coming to America 4
27 Feb . . . Fatal Attraction 1	03 Sep . . . Rambo III 1
05 Mar . . The Last Emperor 5	10 Sep . . . Coming to America 1

17 Sep . . .	Big Business	1
24 Sep . . .	Buster	2
08 Oct . . .	Good Morning Vietnam	2

22 Oct . . .	A Fish Called Wanda	7
10 Dec . . .	Who Framed Roger Rabbit	4

1989

07 Jan . . .	Who Framed Roger Rabbit	2
21 Jan . . .	Red Heat	1
28 Jan . . .	Cocktail	2
11 Feb . . .	Die Hard	1
18 Feb . . .	Naked Gun From the Files of Police Squad	3
11 Mar . .	Scandal	1
18 Mar . .	Rain Man	4
15 Apr . . .	Working Girl	3
06 May . .	My Stepmother is an Alien	1
13 May . .	Nightmare on Elm Street Part Four: The Dream Master	1

20 May . .	Mississippi Burning	4
17 Jun . . .	Beaches	1
24 Jun . . .	Licence to Kill	2
08 Jul	Indiana Jones and the Last Crusade	4
05 Aug . .	Licence to Kill	2
19 Aug . .	Batman	5
23 Sep . . .	Lethal Weapon 2	2
07 Oct . . .	Dead Poets Society	3
28 Oct . . .	Shirley Valentine	5
02 Dec . . .	Back to the Future Part II	3
23 Dec . . .	When Harry Met Sally . . .	2

1990

06 Jan . . .	When Harry Met Sally . .	4
03 Feb . . .	Black Rain	2
17 Feb . . .	Family Business	1
24 Feb . . .	Sea of love	2
10 Mar . .	Born on the Fourth of July	1
17 Mar . .	The War of the Roses . .	4
14 Apr . . .	Look Who's Talking . . .	2
28 Apr . . .	The Hunt for Red October	1
05 Mar . .	The Krays	2
19 May . .	Pretty Woman	8
14 Jul	Dick Tracy	1

21 Jul	Back to the Future Part III	1
28 Jul	Dick Tracy	1
04 Aug . .	Total Recall	3
25 Aug . .	Die Hard 2: Die Harder . .	3
15 Sep . . .	Memphis Belle	3
29 Sep . . .	Another 48 Hrs	1
06 Oct . . .	Presumed Innocent	1
13 Oct . . .	Ghost	8
08 Dec . . .	Teenage Mutant Ninja Turtles	1
15 Dec . . .	Home Alone	3

1991

03 Jan . . .	Home Alone	1
11 Jan . . .	Arachnophobia	1
18 Jan . . .	Cyrano de Bergerac	2
01 Feb . . .	Rocky V	1
08 Feb . . .	Kindergarten Cop	1
15 Feb . . .	Three Men and a Little Lady	3
08 Mar . .	Green Card	1
15 Mar . .	The Godfather: Part III .	1
22 Mar . .	Green Card	1
29 Mar . .	Dances with Wolves . . .	3
19 Apr . . .	Highlander II: The Quickening	1
26 Apr . . .	Sleeping with the Enemy	3
17 May . .	Misery	3

07 Jun . . .	Silence of the Lambs	4
05 Jul	Naked Gun 2½: The Smell of Fear	2
19 Jul	Thelma and Louise	1
26 Jul	Robin Hood: Prince of Thieves	2
09 Aug . .	Backdraft	2
23 Aug . .	Terminator 2: Judgment Day	7
11 Oct . . .	The Commitments	3
01 Nov . . .	Dead Again	1
08 Nov . . .	City Slickers	1
15 Nov . . .	The Fisher King	3
06 Dec . . .	Hot Shots!	2
20 Dec . . .	The Addams Family	2

1992

03 Jan	The Addams Family	2
17 Jan	Delicatessen	1
24 Jan	Frankie and Johnny	1
31 Jan	JFK	3
21 Feb	Star Trek VI: The Undiscovered Country	1
28 Feb	Father of the Bride	1
06 Mar	The Prince of Tides	1
13 Mar	Cape Fear	3
03 Apr	Bugsy	2
17 Apr	Hook	2
01 May	The Hand that Rocks the Cradle	2
15 May	Basic Instinct	4
12 Jun	The Lawnmower Man	1
19 Jun	Basic Instinct	1
26 Jun	The Lover	1
03 Jul	The Player	2
17 Jul	Batman Returns	3
07 Aug	Universal Soldier	1
14 Aug	Far and Away	1
21 Aug	Lethal Weapon 3	1
28 Aug	Alien 3	3
18 Sep	Bob Roberts	1
25 Sep	Unforgiven	1
02 Oct	Patriot Games	3
23 Oct	Beauty and the Beast	1
30 Oct	1492: Conquest of Paradise	1
06 Nov	Strictly Ballroom	1
13 Nov	Last of the Mohicans	1
20 Nov	Peter's Friends	1
27 Nov	Sister Act	2
11 Dec	Death Becomes Her	1
18 Dec	Home Alone 2: Lost in New York	2

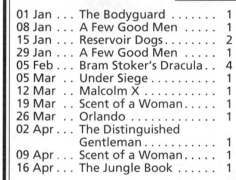

1993

01 Jan	The Bodyguard	1
08 Jan	A Few Good Men	1
15 Jan	Reservoir Dogs	2
29 Jan	A Few Good Men	1
05 Feb	Bram Stoker's Dracula	4
05 Mar	Under Siege	1
12 Mar	Malcolm X	1
19 Mar	Scent of a Woman	1
26 Mar	Orlando	1
02 Apr	The Distinguished Gentleman	1
09 Apr	Scent of a Woman	1
16 Apr	The Jungle Book	1
23 Apr	Accidental Hero	1
30 Apr	Sommersby	2
14 May	Groundhog Day	1
21 May	Indecent Proposal	3
11 Jun	Falling Down	3
02 Jul	Cliffhanger	3
23 Jul	Jurassic Park	6
03 Sep	In the Line of Fire	2
17 Sep	The Firm	2
01 Oct	The Fugitive	5
05 Nov	The Piano	2
19 Nov	Demolition Man	1
26 Nov	Aladdin	6

1994

07 Jan	Aladdin	1
14 Jan	Malice	2
28 Jan	Manhattan Murder Mystery	1
04 Feb	Mrs Doubtfire	3
25 Feb	Schindler's List	2
11 Mar	Philadelphia	3
01 Apr	Schindler's List	5
06 May	Ace Ventura: Pet Detective	1
13 May	The Paper	1
20 May	Four Weddings and a Funeral	9
22 Jul	Maverick	1
29 Jul	The Flintstones	2
12 Aug	Sirens	1
19 Aug	True Lies	1
26 Aug	The Mask	1
02 Sep	Wolf	1
09 Sep	The Mask	1
16 Sep	True Lies	1
23 Sep	Clear and Present Danger	2
07 Oct	Speed	1
14 Oct	Forrest Gump	1
21 Oct	The Lion King	2
04 Nov	Pulp Fiction	1
11 Nov	Mary Shelley's Frankenstein	2
25 Nov	Pulp Fiction	3
16 Dec	Junior	2
30 Dec	The Specialist	1

INDEX